History of Spartanburg County

Authentic Biographical Records, Social Events, and Civil War Stories of Spartanburg, South Carolina – 1783 to 1900

By J. B. O. Landrum

Author of Colonial and Revolutionary History of Upper South Carolina

Embracing an Account of Many Important Events, and Biographical Sketches of Statesmen, Divines and other Public Men, and the Names of Many Others worthy of Record in the History of their County

**PANTIANOS
CLASSICS**

Published by Pantianos Classics

ISBN-13: 978-1-78987-341-2

First published in 1900

Contents

To the Confederate heroes, both living and dead, and especially to those whose names are identified with Spartanburg County, nearly or quite all whose names are herein recorded, who for four years performed gallant and noble service in the armies of the Confederacy, whose marches and battles, wounds and suffering, willing sacrifice, patient endurance and steadfast devotion to principle has never been surpassed throughout the civilized world, this volume is consecrated to their lasting honor and memory by
The Author.

Preface

Three years ago the author published a volume entitled, "Colonial and Revolutionary History of Upper South Carolina," embracing for the most part the primitive and revolutionary history of the territory comprising the original county of Spartanburg, S.C., which narrative, so far as active hostilities were concerned, ends with the year 1781.

The present volume, comprising a history of the original county of Spartanburg proper, is intended to be a continuation of the first volume, and begins with the organization of said county in 1755. Of the events as occurring in the same between the years mentioned (1781-5) he has been unable to obtain information from any source.

The author, in presenting this volume to the public, has no apologies to make for whatever may appear to be his shortcomings in the humble but pleasant task which he has had before him. Written and compiled one hundred and fifteen years after the organization of his native county, he has labored under many trying difficulties to collect the material matter and data found recorded herein, most of which, in course of time, would have been lost in tradition. If his efforts along this line meet with the approval of a generous public, he will feel more than gratified.

Spartanburg County, now one of the most interesting and progressive in the State, has a history behind her worthy of preservation. In the advancement which she has already made in religious and educational institutions, in manufactures and agriculture, she has made a record inferior to none in the State. In the production of heroes, statesmen, divines, public men, and a long list of an honest, upright and industrious citizenship, she will compare favorably with other counties in the State.

It has been his intention, as much as possible, to revive the memories of those in his county, both living and dead, whose names are deserving of perpetuation, and particularly of the gallant soldiery furnished by Spartanburg County in the civil war between the States; to the rolls, or parts of rolls of the same, much time has been devoted and much space herein has been appropriated. Much valuable material, embracing sketches of many of the older family connections in Spartanburg County, which were carefully prepared by the author for publication, have been crowded out by reason of circumstances beyond his control and much to his regret.

If this volume should meet with favor, a future edition is contemplated, when, it is hoped, matter now omitted, with other material yet to be gathered, will be compiled and added.

For the many favors and courtesies which he has received in the preparation of this work, the author extends his grateful thanks.

J. B. O. L.
Campobello, S.C., Nov. 1, 1900.

Chapter One - Introductory

In a former volume, published by the writer, it is stated that by virtue of the treaty of Governor Glen with the Cherokee Indians in the year 1755, the greater portion of the up-country of South Carolina was ceded by these people to the whites. [1] In the subdivisions gained by this acquisition, the original territory of the county (called *district* prior to the adoption of the Constitution of 1868) of Spartanburg (a small portion of which now forms a part of Cherokee county) became a part of the old district of Ninety-six, which comprised the original counties of Edgefield, Abbeville, Newberry, Laurens, Union and Spartanburg, the district site of which was at the present old Star Fort, known in former times as Ninety-six, or Cambridge Court House.

The ending of the Revolutionary war with success to the American arms doubtless infused new life and energy into the people everywhere. The time had come for changes to be made to suit the existing conditions and circumstances.

In the year 1783 a convention was called by the people of South Carolina, which was the first to meet after the close of the Revolution. [2] In the same an ordinance was passed to divide the districts of Charlestown, Georgetown, Cheraw, Camden, *Ninety-six* Orangeburg and Beaufort into counties "of a convenient size, not more than forty-five miles square," and for each and all of these commissioners were appointed. Those appointed on the part of the district of Ninety-six were Andrew Pickens, Richard Anderson, Thomas Brandon, Levi Casey, Philmon Waters, Arthur Simpkins and Simon Burwick. Under this ordinance the counties of Edgefield, Abbeville and Newberry were laid out in 1783, leaving the remaining portion of the district of Ninety-six, composing the territory of the original counties of Spartanburg, Union and Laurens, as yet undivided, but changing the district site or courthouse from Cambridge to Pinckneyville, on Broad River.

By virtue of an act of the legislature of South Carolina, passed in 1785, the remainder of Ninety-six district, viz.: Laurens, Union and Spartanburg, was divided. In the same act, which is known in history as Judge Pendleton's "County Court Act," it was provided for a court to be held in each county once in three months by seven justices of the peace, to hold their commissions during: life or good behavior, and to be elected first by joint nomination before the Senate and House of Representatives, vacancies among them afterwards occurring to be filled by themselves. Any three of said justices were to constitute a quorum to transact any business coming before the county courts. By an act of March 10, 1786, the number of justices was increased two, and by an act of March 17, 1787, the number was increased to eleven.

In accordance with the provisions of the act referred to Spartanburg County was laid off. The following are the statutory words: "One other county bounded by Laurens county on the south, the Indian line on the west, the North Carolina line and Broad River to Tate's Ferry, thence along the road by John Ford's plantation on the Enoree, now including the same, and shall be called by the name of Spartanburgh."

The following is a copy from the statutes of our State, giving the original boundaries, etc., as already stated:

"Court Commission, Spartanburg County.

By His Excellency, Wm. Moultrie, Esq., [Seal.] Governor and Commander-in-Chief in and over the State aforesaid. Wm. Moultrie. To Baylis Earle, John Thomas, Jun'r, Henry White, John Ford, James Jorden, William Wood, Henry Machan Wood, Esquires. Know ye that in pursuance of an Act of the Legislature of this State passed the twenty-fourth day of March, in the year of our Lord one thousand seven hundred and eighty-five, entitled 'An Act for Establishing County Courts, and for Regulating the Proceedings therein, I do by these presents commission you the said Baylis Earle, John Thomas, Jun'r, Henry White, John Ford, James Jorden, William Wood and Henry Machan Wood to be Justices of the Peace in and for the County of Spartanburg, and you or any three of you, have full power and jurisdiction to hold the County Court in and for the said County by the aforesaid Act established, and you are to hear and determine all causes and other matters and controversies properly appertaining and referred by law to your jurisdiction.

This commission to continue in full force during good behavior.

Given under my hand and seal in the City of Charleston, this twenty-fourth of March, in the year of our Lord one thousand seven hundred and eighty-five, and in the sovereignty and independence of the United States of America, the ninth. By His Excellency's command.

John Vanderhorst,
Secretary."

On the old county court record book in clerk's office, we find the following entry:

"Court Certificate.

I do hereby certifie that Baylis Earle, John Thomas, Jr., Henry White, John Ford, William Wood and Henry Machan Wood, appointed justices to sit in the County Court of Spartanburg, this day took the oath prescribed by law, are therefore qualified to enter on the execution of these their respective offices. April 29th, 1785.

Henry Pendleton,
Judge."

On the same page in said book is also the following entry:

"James Jorden's certificate.

I do certify that James Jorden, Esquire, one of the Justices for the county of Spartanburg, hath taken the oath of allegiance agreeable to law before me, December 10th, 1785.

Aedenus Burke, Judge."

It will be noticed that in the statutory words of the act of the legislature of 1785, by which the original county of Spartanburg was laid out as a part of the old District of Ninety-six, the name *Spartanburgh* was adopted and incorporated into the act. The last syllable *burgh* was simply a suffix agreed upon and added to the old name *Spartan*. By common consent and modern usage the letter "h" has been dropped, leaving the word as we now have it, *Spartanburg*.

But an interesting inquiry is here raised as to how the name *Spartan* originated. We have stated in a former work, that in the beginning of the great Revolutionary struggle there were a number of people in the upper part of South Carolina who were not in sympathy with the Patriot cause. The largest number of these disaffected people were between the Broad and Saluda Rivers. At the beginning of hostilities with the government of Great Britain the Council of Safety in the year 1775 commissioned and appointed Hon. Wm. Henry Drayton and Rev. William Tennant [3] to visit the section referred to and explain to the inhabitants the nature of the disputes between the colonies and the mother country.

In a volume [4] which we have already published we have given an extended account of the visit of these gentlemen to the up-country of South Carolina during the same year of their appointment (1775). It was about August 1st when they entered on their mission, the first section visited being the Dutch Fork (now Lexington County) near the junction of the Broad and Saluda Rivers. They continued their journey to the up-country, stopping at different places to address the people, which they found more or less hostile to the American cause, until they reached the settlements on Upper Fair Forest, Lawson's Fork, and on the Tygers, all these being, for the most part, within the limits of the present county of Spartanburg. Here they found a patriotic sentiment prevailing among the people, who were fully alive to the questions at issue, and with some exceptions all proved true to the principles of freedom. We can produce no better evidence of this fact than to quote from Mr. Drayton's letter to the Council of Safety, written on Lawson's Fork (Wofford's Iron Works), August 21st, 1775. [5] Says Mr. Drayton: "I had this day a meeting with this frontier; many present were of the other party; but I have the pleasure to acquaint you that these became voluntary converts. Every person received satisfaction and departed with pleasure. I finished the day with a barbecued beef. I have so ordered matters here, that the whole frontier will be formed into volunteer companies, but as they are at present under Fletchall's command, they insist in being formed into *a regiment independent of him*. These people *are active and spirited*. They are *staunch* in our favor; are capable of forming a good barrier against the Indians, and of being a severe check upon Fletchall's people (upon whom they border) if they should think of quitting their habitations under the banners of Fletchall or his companions. For these reasons and to enable him to act with vigor, I shall take the liberty to supply them from Fort Charlotte with a small quantity of ammunition; for now they have not an ounce, when they shall be formed into regular companies. Several companies will be formed this day week." [6]

It will be seen by reference to Mr. Drayton's letter, that he refers to the people — the first settlers of the present county of Spartanburg, as *bordering* on Fletchall's people. To explain, at the outbreak of the Revolution, all the country between the Broad and Saluda Rivers in South Carolina was embraced in one regimental district under the command of Colonel Thomas Fletchall, at whose house Messrs. Drayton and Tennant visited on their way to the up-country, and who, during the entire period of the Revolution, proved hostile to the American cause. His residence was on Lower Fair Forest, and about six miles west of the present city of Union. Holding this important official position at this critical period in the history of South Carolina, we can readily understand the overpowering influence which he possessed in controlling the sentiments of his surroundings.

It will be seen by reference to this extract from Mr. Drayton's letter, that he ordered the whole frontier to be formed into volunteer companies, and that the people insisted on being formed into a regiment independent of Fletchall's command, a part of which they, at this time, composed. We notice further that by the 11th of the following month (September) this regiment was organized under the command of Colonel John Thomas. It was called the Spartan Regiment [7] (see Gibbs's Doc. History, 1764-1776, p. 176), and was organized at the house of Colonel Thomas. It was made up of material from scattering settlements in the up-country. Says Colonel Thomas in a letter to Mr. Drayton: "Your Honor must suppose it impossible to raise the whole regiment, as several have families, and no man would be left about the house if they should be called away. I shall make as large a draft as possible from every company, and, in short, do everything to the utmost of my power, and when encamped shall transmit to your Honor, as quick as possible, an account of my proceedings."

The Spartan Regiment was soon equipped and ready for action. Receiving their ammunition from Fort Charlotte on the Savannah River, by order of Mr. Drayton, it formed a part of Colonel Richardson's command in the famous "Snow Campaign," December, 1775, an account of which is given elsewhere.

Shortly after this campaign the Provincial Congress of South Carolina met in Charleston. It was deemed expedient to divide the great section of the country between the Broad and Saluda Rivers into three Congressional or election districts, which the record says was "for the convenience of Electors of Congress, as on account of the happy influence which it may have upon the peace and union of the inhabitants."

This resolution which divided this great section of country was passed on the 11th of February, 1776. (See map, p. 43, "Colonial and Revolutionary Hist. of South Carolina.") The first was called the *Lower* or *Dutch Fork*; the second, *Middle* or *Little River*, and the third, *Upper* or *Spartan* District. It will be observed that while the names as applied to the two first have only a local application, that as applied to the third was intended, unquestionably, to be *complimentary* to the section of the country to which it referred, and was doubtless suggested by the Hon. Wm. Henry Drayton, who was at that time president of the Provincial Congress, then convened, who desired to express his appreciation of the patriotic sentiments which he knew to prevail in said section visited by him during the previous year.

But the inquiry is here raised as to why the people of the up-country of South Carolina, inhabiting at that time the present region of Spartanburg, were more loyal and devoted to the Patriot cause than the people composing the settlements in the middle or lower part of said State (or colony as it was then called). The answer to this question is found in the pages of history.

Dr. Ramsey, in his "History of South Carolina" (see p. 118), informs us that the extreme up-country of South Carolina, was settled by emigrants who had advanced from north to south and in front of the eastern settlers. These settlements did not begin until after the ceding of said territory by the Cherokee Indians under the treaty of Governor Glen referred to. Dr. Ramsey further informs us that as far back as 1736, settlements from the seacoast had progressed westward only about eighty or ninety miles. In 1755 the population of the territory afterwards formed into the county of Spartanburg, including Colonel Clarke the first settler on the Pacolet, did not consist of more than eight or ten Scotch-Irish families from Pennsylvania, who, says Dr. Ramsey,, "settled on the forks of the Tygers." Between these settlers and the settlers which had advanced from the seacoast, a considerable tract of country had remained in the undisturbed possession of the aborigines. Soon, however, emigration began to pour in from Pennsylvania, Maryland, and Virginia, and other colonies, as well as from the old countries, and the country began to be rapidly settled up. Dr. Howe, in his "History of the Presbyterian Church of South Carolina," states that many families came directly from North Ireland and settled on the Tygers, Fair Forest, and on the Pacolets, intending as they did, to find a country - a *wilderness,* as it was then called - where they could enjoy, by the blessings of God, that ease and quiet to their consciences which was denied them in their native country. Many of the early settlers of the up-country were of English extraction and *dissenters* from the Established Church of the mother country. These were mostly immigrants from Virginia.

At the beginning of the Revolution, the two civilizations, — one having advanced from the north and the other from the seacoast — had barely met, as it were. This explains the force of the meaning of Mr. Drayton's letter when he speaks of the early settlers of upper Carolina as bordering on Fletchall's people.

They were, as we have already stated, of a different sentiment and mold from the people with whom Messrs. Drayton and Tennant had recently been intermingling. They understood and appreciated the great public questions

11

involved, having been educated into the great principles of freedom of speech, liberty of conscience and right of self-government. Living near the frontier line, they were, on the one hand, confronting the Indian tomahawk and scalping-knife, while on the other they had to contend against the insurgent or malignant forces who, says Colonel John Thomas, Sr., were forming "hellish schemes to frustrate the measures of the Continental Congress, and to use all those who" were "willing to stand by their measures in a most cruel manner."

They were indeed a Spartan people, and were willing to sacrifice their lives, if necessary, to meet all the difficulties which surrounded them. They had already, in previous wars with the Indians, undergone trials and sacrifices which justly entitled them to this honored name. Like the ancient Spartans of Greece, they were inured to hardship and sacrifices, and cherished the heroic virtues of courage, fortitude, patriotism, and public spirit. This same spirit, we are proud to say, has been imparted and infused into the generations that have come after them.

The present growth and progress in the county of Spartanburg in educational institutions, in agriculture, manufactures, and business enterprise generally, only reflect a brighter splendor upon the exalted virtues, lofty patriotism, and devotion to every principle of duty to God and country which characterized her first inhabitants, — the ancestry of a very large per cent, of her present thriving and industrious population.

Judge Henrys Pendleton, who administered the oaths of office to all the justices, except that of James Jorden, was an eminent jurist for his day and time. He was a judge in South Carolina under the new form of government at the beginning of the Revolution, and was in every sense a true patriot. He was a member of the first convention of South Carolina, which met after the Revolution to adopt the Federal Constitution. The vote stood for adoption 149 to 73. Among those who voted with the minority were Judges Pendleton and Burke. On the same side were also Generals Hamilton, Sumter and Butler, and also Colonel Taylor. Judge Pendleton was the author of the "County Court Act" already referred to, and was for a number of years a member of the State Legislature. It was while he was a member of this body that the question of calling the convention came up. It passed by a majority of one vote. The old District of Pendleton (now comprising the territory of Anderson, Pickens and Oconee) was named in his honor.

Judge Aedenus Burke, whose name is attached to the oath certificate of James Jorden, was an Irishman by birth, and came to South Carolina from one of the West India Islands. Like all of his countrymen he was a republican, espoused the American cause, and entered the army. In 1778 was elected a judge and also a member to Congress. After the Revolution, when the State adopted the Federal Constitution, he was elected United States Senator, and at a later period, he was one of the chancellors for South Carolina.

The late Governor Perry has published an interesting sketch of him, with some amusing reminiscences of life and character. He died an old bachelor, and in his will left an old lady in Charleston six hundred pounds sterling, and gave as a reason, by bestowing this legacy, that he had been courting her for ten years, and "before God he believed, if he had persevered, she would have had him."

It is said that while he was no temperate man, he prided himself on drinking good liquors. While holding court at some place there could be nothing found to drink except corn whisky. Of this he drank as he would have done of a bottle of wine, and got gloriously drunk. As he was being carried from the table some mischievous fellow slipped some silver spoons in his pocket. The next morning in dressing he discovered the spoons. Failing to account for them, he exclaimed: "Before God, I thought I was an honest man. I do not remember ever to have stolen anything when I was drunk. It must have been that vile stuff they call corn whisky which prompted me to steal these spoons."

Some time afterward a case of stealing was tried before him, in which it appeared that the offender was drunk when he committed the theft. His Honor inquired if any of the witnesses could tell him whether the prisoner had been drinking corn whisky. Being answered in the affirmative, he turned to the jury and said: "Before God, gentleman of the jury, you ought to acquit the prisoner. I know from my own experience that corn whisky does give a man the propensity to steal; and his reason being dethroned, he should not be held responsible for his larceny."

It is said that in going into court one morning, he mistook an old black silk dress of the landlady's for his judicial robe. As he ascended the judge's seat, he began to unfold the dress, and was for some time turning it about, trying in vain to get into it, to the great amusement of the bar and spectators. "Before God," he exclaimed "some devil has sewed it up in front."

Judge O'Neall, in his annals of Newberry, also gives a short sketch of Aedenus Burke. He was educated at St. Omens for the priesthood; he was a major in the American army, and elected a judge in South Carolina in April, '78. "He long filled with justice and mercy," says the writer, "this responsible office. During his administration he perpetrated many an Irish bull for his own amusement and the people around him."

Of the commissioners on the part of the District of Ninety-six to lay off said district into counties of sufficient size, says Judge O'Neall in his annals: "It is worthy of observation how the commissioners to lay off the district of Ninety-six were scattered. General Pickens, Richard Anderson and Judge Simpkins were south of the Sahida River; General Pickens in the county afterwards called Abbeville; Richard Anderson near the line between it and Edgefield; and Judge Simpkins in the latter, and near the present courthouse; Colonel Waters and General Casey were between Broad and Saluda Rivers, and in Newberry; Colonel Brandon north of Enoree, in the county afterwards called Union; and Simon Berwick in Spartanburg.

Simon Berwick, one of the commissioners referred to as being from Spartanburg County, was proprietor of *Berwick's Iron Works,* known also in history as *Wofford's Iron Works,* located on Lawson's Fork, a short distance above the present town of Glendale, which were destroyed by fire by the Tories under "Bloody Bill" Cunningham, November, 1781, about the close of the Revolution. He was a branch of the Elliot family in Charleston, and was one of the first representatives from Ninety-six District (before the Revolution) to the Legislature, (then called Burgesses). He was a brother of John Berwick, the signer of South Carolina old paper money issued by order of the Provincial Congress, 15th of November, 1775, one Bill which "entitled the Bearer to the sum of Ten Shillings currency," and another calling for "One Pound, Fifteen Shillings."

John Berwick was a man of great respectability and genius, originally a mechanic, carrying on an extensive and profitable business with his brother Simon. He married a Miss Ash, and left one child who married Thomas Legare, of John's Island, from which sprang a large family. Mr. Berwick was a member from Charleston to the South Carolina Legislature, and was warmly attached to the principles of the Revolution, and for this cause, when the British captured Charleston, May, 1780, he was exiled to St. Augustine, and detained there eleven months very unjustly.

It is stated in "Johnson's Traditions" that Simon Berwick was also a signer of this old paper currency. He was also an enterprising mechanic, and while returning from the seat of government (Charleston) soon after the close of the Revolution, he was foully murdered by two outlaws on the Congaree road when traveling up to where Columbia now stands. In his untimely death Spartanburg District suffered much loss; he was an active, enterprising man, being almost indispensable to the times in which he lived.

[1] See Colonial and Revolutionary History of Upper S.C., p. 23. The boundary line between the States North and South Carolina was not finally agreed upon until 1815. This was done by commissioners appointed on the part of the two States. (See Simms's History of S.C., Appendix.) Prior to the treaty of Governor Glen with the Cherokee Indians referred to, the dividing line, if agreed upon at all, was only made on the map of the original Carolinas. For this reason some deeds of execution or instruments of writing in upper South Carolina were improperly recorded at Raleigh, N.C. Among the same is a deed of conveyance from Wofford to Linsey for a tract of land whereon Clifton No. 2 is now located. This old paper is now to be found in the office of the clerk of the court at Spartanburg, having been transferred from Raleigh to that office as its proper place of custody.

[2] Among the delegates to this convention from the Spartanburg region was the Hon. James Jorden.

[3] In diary of Rev. Oliver Hart from A.D. 1740 to A.D. 1780 (see Year Book, 1896, City of Charleston, S.C. Review by Mayor Smythe), it appears that Mr. Drayton and Mr. Tennant were accompanied by Mr. Hart, although no reference is made to him in Drayton's Memoirs. Says Mr. Hart: "On Monday, July 31st, 1775, I set off for the Frontiers of this Province, being appointed by the Council of Safety to accompany Hon. William Henry Drayton and Rev. William Tennant

to try to reconcile the number of inhabitants who are disaffected to the Government. I was out until September ye 6th, following." Rev. Oliver Hart, a Baptist minister, was a great-granduncle of Rev. R. F. Whilden, O'Neall, S.C.

[4] See "Colonial and Revolutionary History of Upper S.C.," pp. 47 to 62.

[5] See Drayton's Memoirs.

[6] See Mr. Drayton's Letter — Gibbs's Documentary History of S.C., '64 to '76, p. 162.

[7] See sketch of Colonel John Thomas, Sr., in this volume.

Chapter Two - Continued Review of County Court Proceedings

Further investigation of the old County Court Record book reveals the fact that the first court ever held in Spartanburg County was at Nichols' Mill, which stood at or near Anderson's Mill on North Tyger River, near the residence of the late Captain David Anderson.

The following is the entry:

"June Court, 1785.

At a Court began to be holden at Nichols' Mill, on the third Monday in June, one thousand seven hundred and eighty-five, for the county of Spartanburg, in the State of South Carolina.

Present, Baylis Earle, John Thomas, Jun'r, Henry White, John Ford and Henry Machan Wood, Gentlemen Justices.

Court being opened John Thomas, Jun'r, being previously appointed clerk, the Court proceeded to the choice of a sheriff for said county. Thereupon casting up the votes, Mr. William Young was duly appointed to that office, and Josiah Buffington duly appointed coroner for said county.

Court adjourned until Court in course.

The minutes were signed by Baylis Earle, J."

This was the only court ever held at Nichols' Mill. By reference to the "County Court Act," it will be seen that the sessions of the courts were to be held every three months.

The next "Court in course," on the third Monday of September of the same year, was held on the plantation of Thomas Williamson. This is where the present city of Spartanburg is located.

The Court was opened by the Gentlemen Justices Baylis Earle, Henry White and John Ford.

William Young, who had been appointed sheriff, produced his commission under the hand of his Excellency the Governor; also presented a duly executed bond with approved sureties, and was sworn in. The sum for which he and his bondsmen were held was fifteen hundred pounds sterling money in gold or silver specie, at the rate of four shillings and eight pence to the dollar, and one pound one shilling and nine pence to the guinea, to be paid to the treasurer or his successor in office. The bond was necessarily heavy, as it was a part of the duties of the sheriff to collect the taxes as well as to discharge the functions of his office. It will be observed, further, by the wording of the bond of William Young, that the only possible money in the State at that time was English specie, as no constitution of the Federal Union had yet been adopted, and of course no Federal currency established. Even at this time there was no President or "United States of America," the constitution of the latter not having been adopted until April, 1787.

At this (December) Court, James Yancey, Esq., after taking the required oath, was admitted to plead, being the first attorney ever admitted to the practice in the courts at Spartanburg.

James Yancey lived in Laurens district, and was county court lawyer, and possibly county attorney. He represented Laurens county in the legislature of South Carolina in 1812. Removing to Charleston, he was afterwards a representative from the same county. He was the father of Benjamin C. Yancey, Sr., of Abbeville county, and grandfather of that distinguished statesman William L. Yancey from Alabama, and also Benjamin C. Yancey, Jr., who was United States minister to the Argentine Republic.

At this term of court the following persons were appointed to serve as constables for the period of one year, viz.: Richard Nally, Hancock Smith, Thomas Gordon, Henry Wolf and Robert Harper.

We also notice further, that on application, Thomas Wadsworth of Bilville, was granted license to retail spirituous liquors according to the rates prescribed by the Court, the clerk being ordered to issue said license, which was the first ever granted in Spartanburg for the sale of intoxicating liquors.

Soon after this, license was granted to George Gordon to keep a private house of entertainment on condition that he conform to the rules and rates prescribed by the court.

The following is the record as to rates, etc.:

"Ordered that the following rates be observed by all persons who shall have obtained license to keep private houses of entertainment:
To wit — Common cold dinner or supper, /6 (six pence). Hot'd or to do (ditto) neatly cook'd, 1/ (one shilling). Common breakfast, /8 do. of Green tea and loaf sugar, 1/ — Bohea do /9, ditto coffee or chocolate, /9 — Lodging in a clean bed, /4 — do for 2 in do, /3 each. Jamaca pr gallon, 12/— pr qt 3/6 (three shillings and six pence), pr pt 1/9— half do /9, gill /5—
West India rum pr gallon 6/ qt 2/ pt 1/ ½ do /6, gill /4—
North rum, pr Gal 5/ — qt 1/3, pt 1/8, half do /4. — **Taffia** pr qt 1/ and so in larger or smaller quantities. **Punch** made of Jamaca rum and loaf sugar, pr qt 1/4, and so in proportion for Larger or Smaller quantities.
West India rum in punch, pr 1/ and so in proportion North Ward **Rum** and **Taffia** in punch pr qt /8 and so in proportion. **Nantz Brandy,** pr Gallon 10/ pr qt 2/6, &c., &c. **Good Country Brandy** pr Gallon 5/ qt 1/3, pt /6, &c. Geneva pr Gallon 8/ qt 2/ pt 1/ — half do /6. **Whiskey,** pr Gallon 4/ qt 1/ pt/6 &c. Best Medera **Wine** pr bottle 4/8, draught 4/, &c. **Common** Wine, pr qt 3/ pr pt 1/6.

Port Wine, pr, bottle 3/6. **Sherry** and **Lisbon** pr qt 3/ **Bergundy** and **Champaign** pr bottle 4/. Other sweet wines, pr qt 2/. **English bottled Cyder** pr Bottle 2/. Home-made do pr qt. /6. — Stabling an Horse 24 Hours, with good and sufficient fodder or hay, 1/6. Corn /2 pr qt, Oats the same."

At this term of court it was ordered that the following persons be summoned to attend the next court to serve as grand jurors, to wit: Wm. Bensong, George Bruton, William Thomson, David Lewis, Charles James, John Head, William Lipscomb, James Oliphant, Capt. Wm. Smith, Charles Moore, Zadock Ford, Andrew Barry, William Poole (Tailor), John Carnick, Thomas Jackson, Edward Mitchison, Obediah Trimmier, Isreal Morris, Robert Goodlett, Sen'r, David McClain, Vachel Dilingham and Wm. Prince. According to the record, this is the first Grand Jury that was ever drawn in Spartanburg County.

The following persons were drawn as petit jurors for the March term: Isaic Bogan, Wm. Lynch, George Robuck, John Stone, John Tremia, James Hughs, James White, John Shands, John Leich, Thomas Williamson, Samuel Lancaster, David Golightly, Robt. McDowell, Thomas Wyatt, Fleming Smith, George Connel, John Nesbitt, Isham Foster, Bailey Anderson, John Butler, Thomas Davis, Henry Machan, Sam'l Culbertson, John Vice, John Banney, John Mapps, John Golightly, Wm. Croker, John Redmon and John Davis.

The following public roads were ordered to be opened, as shown by the record which we copy:

"Road ordered from John Head's Ford on Enoree to Isaic Crows; John Head, overseer, Mathew Couch, warner. From thence to John Patton's on So Tyger; overseer, George Bruton, Alex Alexander, warner. From thence to the narrow passage [1] above Nichols' Mill; overseer, John Barry, Moses Ward, warner. From thence to Lawson's Fork at Widow Bishop's; [2] overseer, Robert Jamison, warner, John Goodlett. From thence to So Pacolette to at Kilpatrick's old place; overseer, James McDowell, warner, William Branham. From thence to the State line by Hooper's Ford; overseer, James Hooper, warner, John Earle, Jun'r. From Blackstock's Ford on Tyger to opposite Widow Smith's at Davis old place; overseer, John Bearden, warner, David Pruit. From thence to Miller's old road; overseer, Albutes Bright, warner, Nathanial Davis. From thence to a branch on Sand road below Mrs. Prince's; overseer, Henry Wells, warner, William Underwood. From thence to the junction with Head's road; overseer Isham Foster, warner, Wm. Tinsley. From Tate's Ferry to opposite Wm. Hickman's plantation; overseer, Dan'l McClary, warner, John Fonderin. From thence to Byas' Mill; overseer, William Thomson, warner, Reuben Smith. From thence to Hammett's Ford on Pacolet; overseer, Malachi Jones, warner, William Wooten. From thence to the lower Iron Works; overseer, William Poole, I. M. (Iron Master), warner, Geo. Poole. From thence to the Shoal on Fair forest, above Mr. Joseph Buffington's; overseer, James Smith, warner, Fleming Smith. From thence to Dutchman's 'Creek at Widow Smith's; overseer, Capt. William Smith, warner, Thomas Thornton. Thence to Blackstock's road; the same and same.

Ordered that Major Ford and Samuel Farrow view the ground and conduct the road from Blackstock's Ford on Tyger to Musgrove's on Enoree; overseer, Sampson Bobo, warner, Edward Hooker.

Ordered that the clerk issue the orders to the several overseers.

Court adjourned until Court in Course.

The minutes were signed by

Baylis Earle, Henry White, John Ford, Esq'rs.

"December Court."

"At a County Court began and held for the county of Spartanburgh, at the plantation of Thomas Williamson, on the third Monday in December, 1785, Court met according to adjournment, at three o'clock, and at four o'clock adjourned until to-morrow morning at nine o'clock.

Tuesday, the 20th day of December, 1785, the Court met according to adjournment. Present: Baylis Earle, John Ford and Henry Machan Wood, Gentlemen Justices.

William Shaw, Esq., produced his commission to authorize to be admitted to practice as an attorney in this State. Ordered that he be entered on record and admitted to practice in this Court.

Jacob Brown, Esq., produced his license to plead and practice in the several courts in this State as an attorney. Ordered that the said Jacob Brown be admitted to practice in this Court.

Ordered that no attorney be admitted to practice in this Court in future unless licensed by the judges of the Supreme Court, according to law.

Daniel Brown, Esq., produced his commission to plead and practice as an attorney in this State. Ordered that he be entered on the records and be permitted to practice in this Court according.

Mr. Joseph Buffington produced a commission from His Excellency the Governor, authorizing to act as coroner for the county of Spartanburgh. He was qualified accordingly.

On motion, ordered that Thomas Williamson have license to retail spirituous liquors and keep a private house of entertainment on his applying to the clerk for the same and conforming to the rates prescribed by the Court.

Grand jurors drawn to serve this Court — Andrew Barry, John Barry, Charles Moore, Daniel McClary, William Poole, Israel Morris, Edward Mitchison, David Golightly, William Benson, William Lipscomb, Charles James, Robert Goodlett, Sr., and George Bruton.

The grand jury being drawn, empaneled and sworn by the county attorney, in behalf of the Court, delivered a charge unto them, and forthwith they withdrew.

Ordered that the court-house and public buildings be established and erected on the lands of Mr. John Wood, on the waters of Fair Forest, on a small hill near the said John Wood's dwelling house, [3] according to the first appointment.

Court adjourned until the third Monday in March next, at Mr. John Wood's, the place appointed.

The minutes were signed by Baylis Earle, John Ford, Henry Machan Wood."

[1] This is near and just below Nazareth Church.
[2] Adam Gramling place.
[3] According to the best information which the writer has obtained, the place referred to above was at or near the present Carver's mill, on Fair Forest creek and near the Southern railway crossing of said creek. It has been erroneously stated by some writers of local history in Spartanburg County, that the John Wood referred to was the same that was murdered by the Tories, under the leadership of "Bloody Bill" Cunningham, on Lawson's Fork, which occurred in November, 1781. The census list containing the names of heads of families in Spartanburg County for the year 1790, shows that there was a John Wood living in said county during that year, and as the record states, "on the waters of Fair Forest" (not on Lawson's Fork), we think there can be no mistake as to the locality where the county courts were at this time convened.

Chapter Three

In the preceding chapter it is stated, as shown by the public records of Spartanburg County, that "the court-house and public buildings be established on lands of Mr. John Wood, on the waters of Fair Forest, on a small hill near said John Wood's dwelling-house." We would further state that the county offices and public records were conveyed and kept there during the time, the courts were held there, and the question seemed to be settled for a time that this was to be the permanent location of the site for the court-house and public buildings for Spartanburg County. We quote further from the records as follows:
"March Court, 1786."
"At a County Court began to be holden at the plantation of John Wood, on the third Monday in March, 1786, present John Ford, James Jorden and Henry Machan Wood, Gentlemen Justices. The Court proceeded to draw a grand jury. They are as follows, to wit: Thomas Wadsworth, Joseph Wofford, William Tate, Iden Gowin, John McEhemy, John Timmons, John Nichols, Wm. Smith (capt.), George Salmon, William McDowell, Robert Nelson, William Poole, I. M., John Russel, William Foster, Henry Wells.

Charles Goodwin, Esq., admitted as an attorney to practice in this Court on his producing admission in the Court of Common Pleas, at our next Court.

Petit jurors for March Court — Richard Harrison, Robert Goodgion, William Simpson, Jesse Council, Christopher Casey, Alexander Vernon, John Smith, less., Roland Cornelius, James Wofford, John Ward, James White, Isaic Morgan, James Richey, Shands Golightly, James Keen and Joseph Venable.

Thomas Benson, appointed deputy sheriff, was duly sworn in open court.

Ordered that a road be opened from McDowell's Mill, on No Pacolette, to Spartanburg Court House. Overseer, Thomas Bennett; warner, John Conner.

Ordered by the Court that a road be laid out and opened from the main road at or near Major Farrow's, by Belville, to Capt. David McDowell's; thence the nearest and best way across the Forks of Pacolette to the State line into the road that leads by David Miller's, from Major Farrow's aforesaid to Lawsonfork, overseer, John Williams, warner, Christopher Long; from thence to Pacolette, overseer, David McDowell, warner, John Conen; from thence to North Pacolet, overseer, John Freeman, warner, John Carrol; from thence to State line aforesaid, overseer, John McKnight, warner, Robert McMillen.

Ordered, that a road be opened from William Jamison's to widow Bishop's, on Lawson's Fork, overseer, William Jamison, warner, Robert Henderson,

Court adjourned until to-morrow morning, nine o'clock. The minutes were signed by

John Ford, James Jorden, Henry Machan Wood.

The June term of court, 1786, was held at John Wood's place and was presided over by Baylis Earle, Henry White, James Jorden, John Ford and Thomas Wadsworth.

The following were the petit jurors for the term, viz.: Richard James, John White, Landon Farrow, Moses Timmons, Joseph Barnett, Rowland Johnson, Frances Nevil Wayland, Isaic Hendrix, Bay ley Taylor, Jeremiah Silmon, Peter Smith, William Smith and Abner Timmons.

"Charles Goodwin, Esq., produced his admission as atto."

The September Court, 1786, was held at John Wood's and was presided over by James Jorden, Thomas Wadsworth and Richard Harrison, esquires, with the following as grand jurors: Martin Armstrong, Thomas James, Josiah Culbertson, William Foster, Wm. Poole, William Lipscomb, John Gowin, George Bruton, Alexander Ray, Moses Casey, Thomas McKnight, David Lewis, Anthoney Coulter, Thomas Williamson, John Redman, Sam'l Lancaster, Wm. Tate, Alexander Vernon, Daniel McClain, Wm. Ford (upper), and Thomas Farrow.

The following were the petit jurors: Robert McDowell, Wm. Bird, David Lewis, Lawson Bobo, George Connel, Henry Moffatt, Wm. Crocker, Wm. Mellingham, Thomas Mellingham, Sam'l Jackson, Peter Elder, Jason Moore, Thomas Hannah, John Moore, Andrew Mellingham, John Golightly, Isham Yearby, John Alexander, James Jackson, Charles Smith, James Smith, Absolem Thomson and James Gilmore.

William Tenner Thomason was appointed at this term to serve the county as constable for one year.

The September term of court, 1786, convened at John Wood's third Monday of same month.

Thomas Peters Cams, Esq., produced his certificate of admission as an attorney and solicitor in the courts of law and equity in this State, which was enrolled on the records.

It was also ordered at this term that William Poole, Iron Master, have license to retail spirits and keep a public house of entertainment. The same privilege is also granted to Alexander Alexander.

But one more term of court was held at John Wood's place. This was convened at the regular term, third Monday in December, 1786, and was presided over by Thomas Wadsworth, Richard Harrison and Samuel Lancaster, esquires. The following is recorded:

"The determination of the governor and council respecting the court-house being produced and received, the court agreed to adjourn to-day and meet at Mr. Thomas Williamson's to-morrow, agreeable to said order, said order filed in clerk's office. Court then adjourned until tomorrow morning nine o'clock, to meet at Thomas Williamson's. Tuesday, 19th December, 1786, court met according to adjournment."

It would seem from the following clause in the minutes of the court proceedings that there was some determined opposition when the proposition was made to remove the county site from John Wood place to Thomas Williamson's plantation.

"Ordered, That the order respecting the Courthouse and other public buildings be reversed until the determination of the Legislature. Protested against, because it originated in an idea of carrying the Courthouse back; and because it is finally determined and cannot constitutionally be taken up again.

Richard Harrison.

Ordered, That the clerk's office be kept at Mr. Samuel Porter's plantation on Lawson's Fork, being the plantation whereon William McDowell lately lived, until otherwise ordered.

Ordered, That the Justices meet on the nineteenth day of January next, to agree on the plan of the public buildings, and on the twentieth of said January to let said buildings as commissioners, and that the clerk advertise the same as general as he can possibly. And that all absent members of the court be notified to appear on the above mentioned days at this place."

The Justices whose names are written met on the nineteenth day of January, 1787, agreeable to an order of court entered on record 23d December, A. D. 1786 (to wit): Baylis Earle, Richard Harrison, Sam'l Lancaster, and Obediah Tremmier, Esq's.

A memorandum of the dimensions of Spartanburg Court-house as agreed on the 19th of January, A. D. 1787:

Pursuant to the above order of court (to wit): 30 feet long by 20 feet wide, 12 feet pitch square roof, the timbers well-proportioned by the rules of architecture, in a good and sufficient manner. The shingles of heart pine nailed on with 6d. nails, 21 inches long, to show 7 inches. Weather-boards 6 inches wide of quartered plank to show 6 inches, and beaded, nailed with 6d. nails. Two doors of a common size, one on each side. Good casings and the doors plain. Six twelve-light windows, good casings and sashes, with glass 10 by 6 inches, two in the end of the court-room and one in each side, and two in each jury room. Six feet taken off the length for jury rooms by a partition of plank well confined, and that subdivided into rooms 10 feet by 8 by a light partition. The jury rooms elevated 4 feet above the floor of the court-room, and steps leading up into each. The justice's bench to be elevated 4 feet above the floor, done up with plain, smooth plank in a circular manner, and stairways leading up at each end. A jury bench on the floor within the circle and convenient boxes for the sheriff. A clerk's table and an attorney's bar at a convenient distance in front of the justice's bench. The eaves of the house boxed and corniced and the whole done in a workmanlike manner.

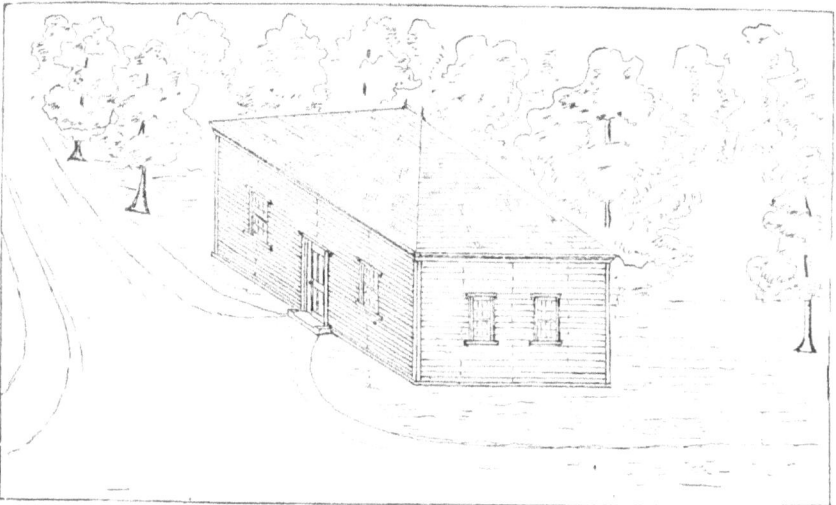

Spartanburg C. H.   Erected 1787

A GOAL

of 16 feet square, 10 inches squared oak logs, with a partition of square oak timber of the same size crossing the front at 6 feet distance from the door. The largest room divided by a partition of logs of the same size. Through each partition a door of 3 feet wide. Casings to the doors 10 inches by 4. Doors of a proportioned thickness such as are common to jails, and strengthened, by iron bars of a common size. A common -sized jail lock to each door. The two lower back rooms ceiled with good two-inch oak plank. One of the lower rooms in the ceiling to be laid off in checks of 4 inches distance and a spike of 4 inches long drove into each center section. The other back room ceiled with the same kind of plank, and checked at 12 inches distance and spiked in like manner. At the height of 7 feet a floor of the same kind of plank and sized timber, and spiked at four inches distance over the back room; that spiked in like manner, the floors of the other to be spiked as the wall, five feet from the upper floor to the plates whereon the roof is placed. The roof to be sheeted with inch plank and shingled with 21-inch shingles to show 7 inches. Steps from the front room up to the upper floor. Four windows to the goal of 10 inches square cased with iron bars of half an inch thickness, two bar grates crossing each other in each window. The foundation to be of logs of the same size of the walls, raised one foot from the ground, and the under part filled up with large stone.

The whole timbers to be let into each other. The partition to be dovetailed into the wall at each end. The upper floor to be let into them by shoulders, and the whole to be completed in a workmanlike manner.

Spartanburg Jail.   Erected 1787

THE PILLORY, WHIPPING-POST AND STOCKS

to be done in a uniform manner to the other buildings, such as is usual and will answer the purpose. The Goal, Stocks and Pillory to be finished in the present year, and the Court-house to be completed in the space of two years, to commence from the first day of this instant, January, 1787.

The sum of twenty-five pounds to be paid at the ensuing June court, and the balance to be paid in four equal payments at the expiration of each succeeding six months.

And should paper currency become a tender in law and a depreciation should ensue, the undertaker not to be injured in the payment.

23

Ordered, that the sheriff proceed to let the buildings to the lowest under-taker, and take bond with sufficient security for the faithful performance thereof.

Baylis Earle, Richard Harrison, Samuel Lancaster, Obediah Trimmier, Esq'rs.

Agreeable to the above order, the sheriff proceeded to let the buildings, but as the undertaker that attended had not time to make proper calculation of the costs, the letting said buildings are deferred until the first day of February next, at which time the sheriff is directed to let said buildings at the lowest terms offered, whether the Justices attend or not. And if the sheriff do not attend, the attending Justices or Justice is hereby authorized to do the same.

The Justices whose names are after written signed this order.

Bayus Earle, Richard Harrison, Obediah Trimmier, Sam'l Lancaster, Esq'rs.

The justices met agreeable to the above order on the first day of February, 1787, and let said building to Richard Harrison esquire, for the sum of two hundred and four pounds, who gave bond, as they required, which bond is ordered to be filed in the clerk's office. They then received as a donation from Thomas Williamson two acres of land for the use of the county, which they then proceeded to lay off, and ordered that said Thomas Williamson be required at the next court to convey the same in fee simple to the said court for the use of said county."

The contract being duly signed, the first public buildings for our country were erected. The court-house is said to have been erected within a few steps of the Morgan Monument, on Main street.

With regard to the permanent location of what is now the city of Spartan burg, which was once the plantation of Thomas Williamson, there is an ancient tradition, which we have always doubted, but which we give to the reader for what it is worth. It is said that the location of a suitable county-site was placed in the hands of a committee, who had been hunting all day without agreement. Having previously provided themselves with a jug of whisky, they selected a camp for the night at a little spring in the hollow in rear of the Spartan Inn. Having imbibed freely from the contents of the jug, they had a social jollification and declared that the court-house should be located there, and they discontinued further search for a better place.

Chapter Four - Spartanburg City - Beginning of Her Growth and Prosperity

In a former chapter of this work we have shown the circumstances under which the present progressive city of Spartanburg acquired its location which, as stated, was on the plantation of Thomas Williamson. This fact we obtain from examination into the proceedings of the first county courts held at said place, between the years 1785 and 1790. During the first quarter of a century of her existence we have no record whatever, and as there was not a newspaper published in the town earlier than 1843 or 1844, we have found it necessary to gather our information mainly by interviews with some of the older residents who formed a part of the population of the town during the period referred to. Among those with whom the writer sought an interview was General B. B. Foster, now deceased. In 1894 General Foster, then a citizen of Union county, S.C., stated to the writer that his recollection of the town of Spartanburg reached back for nearly three quarters of a century. [1] In speaking of the first buildings of prominence, he said that he remembered well the old Tolleson house, the leading hotel of the town where the Palmetto House was afterwards built (N. E. corner of Main and Church streets now known as Palmetto corner). Across the street from this stood the grocery store of James Alley (father of James and Henry). He also stated that in his early recollection, there were no houses between Alley's store and Kirby Hill on which stood the residence of Muse Tolleson, and between Tolleson's house and Fair Forest creek there was only one house. This was the house of Jammie Seay, — a soldier of the Revolution. The house stood off a short distance to the left of the road leading to the stream. On the road (now Main street) leading from the Palmetto corner towards White's mill on Lawson's Fork, there were but very few houses. Rudisail's shop stood where Cantrell's carriage establishment was located. The next house was Goldthaits, an old lawyer, which stood opposite the old Harris blacksmith shop, and long before the latter was built. Along Main street up and down about the old Walker House, on the site of which is the present residence of Colonel Joseph Walker, was a race-path, where on public days, horses would be run. From Goldthait's house until what is now Garrett's spring was reached there was not a house, but to the right of this, where Richard Thomson afterwards built, there was an old log house.

General F'oster further stated that from where the old court-house stood (corner of Main and Magnolia streets) to the residence of Elisha Bomar, which stood between the present court-house and graded school, there was not a single house, all the land between these points being thickly covered with chinkapin bushes and blackjack trees. Only one house stood between Mr. Bomar's residence and Chinkapin Creek. This was the Willis house, which was some distance from the Bomar residence.

After leaving Mr. Jesse Cleveland's residence, which stood near the spot where the Trimmier bookstore is now located, and the public house which was afterwards the residence of Colonel G. Cannon, there was not a house in that direction for a long ways.

Colonel Foster further stated that under the administration of Thomas Poole as sheriff, Mr. Jesse Cleveland bought all the lands between the present Palmetto (Dean's) livery-stable and Wofford College, including the place of Colonel J. H. Evins, for $1.37 per acre, and used the same as a cow-pasture. [2]

Among the old *Spartan* files, dated March 27th, 1856, under an article headed "Historic Views of Spartanburg, or Facts and Memories of Eighty Years," we find much interesting information as to the early settlement and growth of the town of Spartanburg. In this we find that the first settlers were Thomas Williamson, Wm. Wells, Thomas Edison, Alexander McKie, David Faust, Obadiah Watson, Muse Tolleson, James Brannon, Jesse Cleveland, B. Benson and H. Brown. The first named, Thomas Williamson, sold to Wm. Wells, who hailed from Mecklenburg county, N.C., his lands upon which the town was located.

"He (Wells) was the father of Jehu Wells, deceased, who was the ancestor of Mrs. Allen, wife of Woodard Allen and Mrs. Moss. Mr. Wells represented the district in the Legislature about 1800. [3] He afterwards sold his land, or part of it, to Wm. Thomson, and moved to the apex of the hill whereon L. B. Bishop and R. Bowden and others resided, known as the southern end of Hamburg. Thence he came on the north side of the ravine and erected a house near where the residence of Mrs. Cleveland stood. Thereafter he sold to Obadiah Watson, who was a hotel-keeper, and left Spartanburg in 1809. Muse Tolleson (half-brother of Alfred and J. B. Tolleson) married the 25th of May, 1809, and retailed goods in the house occupied by Watson, which he bought, and in a building that lately stood in front of the Palmetto House and afterwards owned by Colonel W. W. Harris. Alexander McKie was also a merchant, and lived a part of the time in an old house where Lee & Briggs had a grocery store. Messrs. Cleveland & Benson were merchants, and came to Spartanburg in 1808. They were both single, and boarded at the time with Thos. Ellison, who was a hotel-keeper and merchant. Mr. Ellison then resided in a building that stood at the lower end of Mrs. Cleveland's lot. He afterwards built the house now owned by Mr. Gentry, which at the time was regarded as very superior in taste and architecture to any building. in town. David Faust was a tailor, and lived in a neat little house afterwards owned by Peyton Turner, which is about where the opera-house stands. James Brannon (or Branon) was also a merchant, and sold goods in a house that stood where the late old courthouse was afterwards built, which is now the site of the Duncan building. The land was bought from him for the location of the court-house. Brannon moved to Spartanburg in 1808, and left in 1828. He resided on the Kirby Hill, which originally belonged to Wm. Poole, iron-master, the father of Thomas Poole, senator from Spartanburg, and Miss Jane Poole, well-remembered by the older citizens of the town. This hill was sold by Mr. Poole to Wm. Shaw, a stranger, originally from England. Mr. Henry Brown came to Spartanburg in 1809. The house he tenanted was partly in ruins (1856), and stood in the hollow adjacent to Mr. O. Burgess's residence. Mr. Brown was the grandfather of Alfred Brown. His house went to Spartanburg with him. It is said that it was fitted together near Mr. John Bomar's residence, three miles from the village, and rolled there. Where Mr.

John Maxwell now lives there stood a handsome house. It was occupied by J. D. Plunkett and Wm Hunt successively. They were both lawyers. Besides them there were John Earle, Isaac Smith, Major Wm. Trimmier and Major E. Roddy.

To 1820 there were no physicians in Spartanburg. In that year Dr. R. M. Young moved to that place and pursued his profession successfully for many years. In the same year Dr. Irby, of Laurens, commenced the practice of medicine with bright prospects, and Dr. Thomas also, who afterwards became a Methodist minister. All of these, in course of time, moved to other parts. Of the lawyers mentioned, only two were living in 1856. One of them (Mr. W. Hunt) had the honor of having been the legal preceptor of Hon. James Edward Henry."

It was not until 1839 that a church was organized in the town of Spartanburg. This was the present First Baptist Church. This was constituted February 23d, of said year, the late Rev. John G. Landrum being chosen its first pastor. The First Methodist Church was organized soon afterwards, the Rev. Thomas Hutchings being its first pastor. The Presbyterian Church, in said town was organized 5th Sunday in August, 1843, by the Rev. S. B. Lewis, but Rev. Z. L. Holmes was installed as the first pastor. The corner-stone of the church of Advent (Episcopal) was laid July 23d, 1850, and the erection of the present substantial rock building soon followed.

From all that can be gathered, it would appear that the town of Spartanburg as far as future progress was concerned, remained in a state of apathy for a long number of years. There were many causes for this, but the principal one, doubtless, was the rapid emigration from the district from time to time, to the countries of the great West. The U.S. census for Spartanburg District for 1840 shows a white population of 17,980; the same for 1850 shows 18,358. During this decade there was an increase of only 378 white inhabitants.

At the beginning of the year '50 the population of the town of Spartanburg had not reached more than one thousand, and not until about this time did there appear to be an increased and active energy on the part of the people to advance the business prosperity of the town. As an evidence of this, we quote from an editorial from Spartan files under date of November 20th, 1849, which reads as follows:

"Our town (Spartanburg) is improving more rapidly than formerly; homes are going up in almost every direction; building lots are being laid off by purchasers; and more than usual activity and interest are being manifested by our citizens in the way of private enterprise. During the past week property in real estate in this town has changed hands by way of sale and purchase to the amount of $7,000 and $10,000, and still there are large transactions in progress of negotiation. The purchasers generally are among our most enterprising citizens."

These facts as stated were significant of a rapidly growing prosperity due, no doubt, largely to a prospective railroad connection which was accomplished ten years later.

As proof of what has been stated above, we gather information from other sources.

Hon. Joseph W. Tucker, on assuming editorial control of the Spartan, January, 1851, in a salutatory address, after commenting on the prospective fortunes of his native district and those of the town in which he had the pleasure to reside, stated further as follows:

"We have in our district (county) a white population of about 20,000 persons; a comparatively large space of territory, say about 40 by 60 miles; an abundant and varied supply of unfailing water-power and other facilities for manufacturing purposes; inexhaustible quantities of iron and lime embedded in our soil; a climate for health such as is almost unknown in regions less favored by nature; numerous fountains of mineral water scattered over the whole territory, having almost every medicinal element in chemical union with nature's beverage; a population at once sober, industrious and order loving; a railroad in prospect, which we will never give up until we hear the noisy engine leading off our products to the great marts of commerce."

With regard to the future of the town of Spartanburg, the same eminent writer predicted in language as follows:

"Our town is steadily and rapidly increasing; and is exhibiting the unmistakable evidence of vital energy and prosperity. We shall soon have a college in the suburbs of our pleasant town; which will have its origin under the most favorable auspices; the Rev. Benjamin Wofford having bequeathed the sum of $100,000 for its establishment and endowment. This institution will attract to our quiet and healthy neighborhood its due share of wealth, intelligence and refinement of the State; and must induce the expenditure of large sums of money annually, proportionate to the increase and prosperity of the college. With all the advantages, natural and moral, what can prevent the District of Spartanburg from becoming prosperous, enlightened, independent and influential? Nothing but want of spirit — her inability to perceive her own vital interests."

We have quoted in part this editorial prophecy to show how true it has come to light with reference to the city of Spartanburg. The final completion of the Spartanburg and Union Railroad during the year 1859, for which much credit is due to Colonel John L. Young as president, and to Colonel Glenn D. Peake and Geo. W. Peake, superintendent and engineers, [4] proved to be a new era of prosperity that had dawned upon the district and town of Spartanburg, notwithstanding the four years of bloody war which soon followed, causing for a. time a suspension of all business industry.

The war being over and peace again reigning over the country, notwithstanding there were yet many drawbacks, a renewed life and energy was imparted to the rapidly increasing population of the town of Spartanburg, which in a few years gave a sufficient number of inhabitants as to entitle her to become incorporated as a city. Since then so rapid has been the upbuilding, progress and industry of the city in every line of advancement and industry that we are unable to follow further in detail. With the rapid development of the South since the civil war, the city of Spartanburg has kept pace with a majority of other rival cities with equal advantages and surroundings, and with the foothold already gained it can scarcely be conceived what will be her future importance, greatness and magnitude.

New Jail at Spartanburg. (Erected 1895.)

In 1870 Spartanburg had 1,050 inhabitants; in 1880, 3,258; in 1890, 5,550, and it is believed that the coming U.S. census for 1900 will show a population of more than 14,000 inhabitants.

The educational institutions, churches, manufacturing establishments and particularly the cotton mills, within the corporate limits of the city of Spartanburg will receive proper notice in this work under other headings. Suffice it to say that as a city, Spartanburg is scarcely excelled as a distributing point for the Piedmont belt, of South Carolina, having already railroads in five different directions, viz.: Charlotte, [5] Columbia, Augusta, Atlanta and Asheville, and is the metropolis of the most prosperous county in the state, producing corn, cotton, tobacco, grapes and the grasses, and abounding in the minerals gold, lead, copper, iron and limestone.

Within the limits of Spartanburg city is the largest cotton mill in the South, having 35,000 spindles under one roof, and within the circle of a twelve-mile radius are nine cotton mills (not including the Lolo mill at Valley Falls in course of construction) aggregating over 141,000 spindles and employing nearly 50,000 operators. The city has gas, electric lights, electric motor cars under way to connect with the adjacent villages and towns, waterworks and a complete system of sewerage; hotels with modern style accommodations; has an abundant supply of excellent water; graded and macadamized streets; has some fifteen churches representing the various denominations, and besides the colleges Wofford and Converse, has the! Wofford fitting school and eight graded schools, thus affording excellent educational advantages. There are also five leading newspapers in Spartanburg. *The Spar-*

tan Herald, Headlight, Free Lance, and *Evening Telegram,* all doing a good work in advancing the best interests of the country. In addition Spartanburg has three banks with capital of not less than, $300,000 with equal amounts of deposits, a free public library, an opera-house and a handsome city hall; has within her limits every class of progressive enterprise and business industry, including two ice plants and bottling works, grist, flour and planing mills, door, sash and blind factories, etc.

Besides these, both the city and county can boast of a large and handsome court-house, with all modern conveniences and with offices well fitted up for the convenience, comfort and accommodation of all the county officials, and further, there is near by a large and commodious jail of recent construction and after the latest and most modern style of improvement, thus affording security and safety to criminals and ample protection against assaults from the outside.

New Courthouse at Spartanburg. (Erected 1895.)

The municipal government of Spartanburg is fully alive to the climatic, health and natural advantages of the city, possessing as it does an altitude of 1,020 feet above the level of the sea, which insures at all times a delightful climate and the great blessing of health. Truly it may be said that Spartanburg, founded on the original plantation of Thomas Williamson in 1787, is a growing city, and its immediate future is full of promise. In coming years the city is destined to become one of the chief inland cities of the southeast.

[1] He was then seventy-seven years of age.
[2] While in conversation with General Foster, he recalled some pleasant recollections of Jesse Cleveland, who at that time was *the merchant* of Spartanburg. General F. had seen him mount his old flea-bitten gray (a horse upon which he hunted deer) and start to Baltimore to buy goods. His teams would start several days ahead of him. Among the teams which he employed to haul goods was that of "Old Wagoner," James Ballenger, an honest, genial, whole-souled farmer, residing on the waters of North Tyger (now the plantation of Mrs. Margaret Oeland). Mr. Ballenger at that time kept the finest team of horses in the up-country, and spent much of his time in hauling goods to Spartanburg and other places from Charleston, Augusta and Baltimore. General F. remembered that when a boy, at his father's old place (the present residence of Mrs. E. H. Bobo, near Cedar Spring), that the approach of Mr. Ballenger's team was always announced by the ringing of the bells, which was then a great attraction to him.

Referring to the residence of Mrs. Bobo as being the old homestead residence of his father, Anthony Foster, General Foster stated that this was the first brick-house built in Spartanburg County; that he, with others, rode the horses that

30

made the mortar to mold the brick that were used in building that stately old mansion.

[3] 1790 to 1800. See Record of Senators and Representatives.

[4] A notable event in the town of Spartanburg was the great railroad barbecue which took place near the old S. & U. R. R. depot, on Friday, November 25th, 1859. It was indeed a day of rejoicing in Spartanburg, the day on which the first trains arrived which marked the completion of railroad connection with Union, Columbia, Charleston and other places. For ten years the completion of the road had been an object of cherished hope now realized. The barbecue was attended by countless thousands of women, men and children. By common consent it was a holiday for the colored people, who turned out en masse. The writer was present on that occasion, and cannot express the pride, exultation and enthusiasm manifested on the arrival of the "iron horse." It was nearly one o'clock before the first train arrived from Union. The people waited wearily, but their flagging spirits were revived when nearly four miles away the piercing notes of the steam whistle were heard reverberating ever the hills. Soon the crowded train and laboring engine approached, shrieking her summons to the living masses lining the road to clear the track. Such a shout of welcome was never before witnessed in Spartanburg, which was followed by the enlivening music of the brass band. A rush was made for the stand, where a reception was tendered Colonel Young and other officials of the road, and which was followed by an appropriate response by him. Hon. Bail Edney, of North Carolina, was principal orator of the day. Then followed the devouring of the barbecued beef and loaves of bread which had been provided in sufficient plentifulness to feed the multitude. At night a ball was tendered Colonel Young and other officials of the road at the Palmetto House, which ended the program of the day.

[5] The first telegram message ever received at the office at Spartanburg was on the completion of the line from Charlotte to that place and was as follows: —

"Received from Charlotte, N.C., Sept. 14th, 1873; addressed to Intendant of Spartanburg.

"The 'Hornets of old Mecklenburg' congratulate the 'Sons of Cowpens' upon your first communication over the telegraph wire of the enterprising Southern & Atlantic Telegraph Co. W. F. Davidson, Mayor.

Chapter Five - A General Review of the Progress of Education in Spartanburg County from Its Organization (1785) to the Present Time

For more than a half century from the beginning of the history of Spartanburg County proper the educational facilities, as provided by law, were very poor as to the masses of the people, and the number of schools limited.

We have made inquiries for information and statistics at the office of the Superintendent of Education in Columbia as to the number and character of schools taught in Spartanburg County in the early period of her history, but could gain no information whatever, and the only matter touching upon the same which we have found is recorded in Sims's History of South Carolina (see Appendix), which contains a report of returns of the State census for 1839. This report shows *that for Spartanburg County there were taught during said year only nine schools with an attendance of one hundred and fifty scholars and an expenditure of $1,500.* It will be observed that this report is made fifty-four years from the date of the organization of the county.

For some valuable information, obtained other than the sources referred to, we are indebted to Major William Hoy for a series of interesting articles contributed to the county press, covering a period of many years, giving some information as to the first schools and school-teachers in the early history of Spartanburg County.

In referring to the early school-teachers, Major Hoy says: "In making inquiry for the first school-teachers in the county, I find that the first three that there is any tradition of were *Rev. W. C. David Judge Smith and Mr. Blundell. The first two rose to national fame, Davis in Theology.* He would compare favorably with Edwards of New England, and Chalmers of Scotland. I have heard one of the daughters say, that he taught on the Tyger while he was pastor of Nazareth Church. It is known that there was a classical school at Rock Spring, on Charles Moore's land, several years before 1800."

It is further stated that Davis was the teacher of this school, and that among the pupils were Postmaster-General Barry, under Jackson's administration, and afterwards Envoy Extraordinary to Spain.

It is also stated that Dr. Andrew B. Moore was prepared for college at this school and that his preparation was excellent.

Davis, while recognized as an eminent minister of the Presbyterian Church of South Carolina, yet entertained peculiar views on some theological *questions, of which he had a considerable following,* and which caused for a time a division in his church, for the particulars of which the reader is referred to "Howe's History of the Presbyterian Church of South Carolina."

Judge William Smith, [1] another school-teacher mentioned by Major Hoy, had a national reputation, as already stated. A sketch of him is presented in "O'Neall's Bench and Bar," and also by Governor Perry, in his "Sketches of Public Men," etc. The place where he taught school in Spartanburg County is not given, but it is stated that among his pupils was Richard Thomson, father of H. H. Thomson. While it is said that Mr. Thomson possessed a good business education, it is further stated that the school of Judge Smith is the only one he ever attended.

While Judge Smith, it is said, possessed excellent learning, yet the statements are conflicting as to where he received his education. One is that he was educated in Virginia, while Judge O'Neall states that he was a schoolmate of Andrew Jackson's which, if true, was probably in the Waxhaw settlement, in Lancaster county, S.C., where the latter was born.

It is further stated of Judge Smith that in early life he was very poor. He married early, and is described as traveling the circuit on foot when he commenced the practice of law. His first case was "The State v. Elchander," in which he appeared as attorney. Elchander, it seems, put up all the money he had in gambling; lost it and then put up his horse, which he also lost. Afterwards he secured, by some unlawful means, his horse, and was charged with clergyable felony, which at that time was a hanging crime. He was tried and acquitted through the efforts of Smith, which soon placed him in the front rank as a lawyer. Afterwards he became a judge, and later a United States senator. At the age of seventy-eight he was tendered by President Van Buren a seat on the bench of the United States Supreme Court, which he very properly declined.

At the time of his death, which was about the year 1838, he was the owner of 800 slaves in Alabama and Tennessee. It is further stated that Elchander became a prominent man and a member to Congress from the State of Ohio, and while in Congress met his old friend Judge Smith, and amply remunerated him for his timely services.

"Davis, Smith and Blundell," says Major Hoy, "taught in this county considerably over one hundred years ago. Blundell taught several schools in this county and Greenville since the year 1800. One noticeable school that he taught was on Tyger River, where Commodore Berry now lives. One of his scholars was Nesbitt (Wilson), who went to Congress. Four of the Evinses, and several others of his scholars, went to the Legislature. One school was taught by him in the bend of the Enoree, near Anderson's Bridge, on the Greenville side, and had about an equal number of students from each county. This school was very remarkable, as I have never heard of a male member of that school but what made his mark in the world, which made some parts of their lives unusually useful. Five of the Kilgores, on the Greenville side, became graduates. In the Dean family, on the Spartanburg side, that family produced at least five superior business men. This school produced a man that was surveyor-general and secretary of state. All have passed the dark valley long since."

The writer, in his effort to seek information as to the early schools taught in Spartanburg County, and particularly as to the Minerva School, mentioned in Ramsey's "History of South Carolina," and of the Academies, Rocky Spring, Poplar Springs and Pine Grove, is indebted to Colonel Thomas J, Moore, of Moore, S.C., for the following interesting letter, which we herein subjoin:

Moore, S.C., March 15th, 1899.

Dr. J. B. O. Landrum., Campobello, S.C.

Dear Sir: — As regards the matter of early education in the Tyger River section of Spartanburg County, about which you inquired, I beg leave to say that it is involved in a great deal of uncertainty. Scarcely any records have been preserved, so that now it is a question of local tradition and speculation. That some attention was paid to higher education, even from the very beginning, in fact, from the earliest settlement, and before the county was formed as it now exists, is to be inferred from the number of educated men who went forth from this section to adorn the different walks of life. It is not to be supposed that all the early settlers were uneducated men. the fact is, some of them were well educated, for instance the Jordans, and probably old Alexander Vernon, who settled near Wellford; Charles Moore and Andrew Barry, who settled near here, and Andrew Thomson, of the Walnut Grove section. The tradition is that Charles Moore was a graduate of Trinity College, Dublin, Ireland, or of Oxford, England. At any rate, he is described, in a deed of land on file in North Carolina, as a *"school-teacher."* Dr. Howe, in his "History of the Presbyterian Church in South Carolina," says that Andrew Barrv received a liberal English education before he came to this country. I have in my library a Greek Testament with this inscription, in a beautiful hand, "Andrew Thomson, Ejus Liber, Anno Domini 1772," thus showing his acquaintance with two classic languages. In the back of the same book is inscribed, "Lawson Thomson, A.D. 1791," and "Andrew W. Thomson, A.D. 1809," thus showing for many years they studied the Scriptures of the New Testament in the original language. It has already been said that there must have been schools of a high order at a very early date, which fact is inferred from the number of young men who were sent away to distant colleges; amongst the number I may mention, in this connection, only two — Wm. Taylor Barry, who went to Kentucky and filled many high positions, including the Postmaster-Generalship under President Andrew Jackson, and Dr. Andrew Barry Moore, [2] who graduated in Dickinson College, Carlisle, Pa., in 1795, and afterwards took his degree of M.D. at some medical college and settled near here, where he lived and died, celebrated as an eminent physician.

Dr. David Ramsay in his "History of South Carolina," in writing on educational matters in Spartanburg District as it then was, mentions "the Minerva School of a high order of about twenty scholars," and "a flourishing school at Rocky Springs." The Minerva school location has always been a sort of mystery to me, but I have no doubt now that it was in the bounds of Nazareth Church and was presided over or fostered by the pastors of that church, who were always men of fine education. My old grandmother [3] once pointed out to me the site of an old school, which I take to have been the Minerva School. The exact location is on the right of the Saluda Gap road as you go north, about midway between Mr. Rowland Gresham's and his mother's residences.

Dr. Howe, before alluded to, further says that James Gilleland, Jr., who stood high as a linguist, taught a grammar school in Spartanburg District before the beginning of this century, to which school went Dr. John McIlhenny and Dr. Samuel B. Wilson, Professor of Theology in Union Seminary, Prince Edward county, Va., both eminent divines. This was in 1798 to 1801. This was probably the Minerva School.

At this time, in fact in 1794, Rev. James Templeton became the supply of Nazareth Church, in which capacity he served eight years, devoting much attention to educational matters. As head, he organized the Philanthropic Society with the view of advancing and perpetuating an academy of high order, which society was incorporated by the Legislature of South Carolina in 1797. I have seen the list of incorporators, but do not have it by me now. I think, however, the Jordans of Wellford, General Thomas Moore of this section, and Wm. Smith of the Glenn Springs section, were the principal ones. This society furnished teachers to destitute neighborhoods, doubtless from the Minerva and Rocky Spring schools. The Minerva School must have flourished for a good many years, for Colonel Thomas P. Brockman, of Greenville county, who was born in 1799, went to school there, boarding with old Aunt Polly Crawford, relict of John Crawford. At the time he went there, there were a number of young men boarding at the same place. I will add that James Gilleland, Jr., was not a preacher when he was first in charge of the school, but afterwards studied theology and ministered to Nazareth, where he had some conscientious scruples on the subject of African slavery, which he held to be wrong in principle. He was enjoined by Presbytery in 1806 to be silent in the pulpit on this question. Unable to still his conscience he moved to a free State.

Rocky Spring school, of which Dr. Ramsay spoke, was located one half mile north of the railroad station of Moore, on the left of the Saluda Gap road going north, opposite the present residence of Mr. W. J. Otts. It was patronized by the Moores, Barrys, Crooks and Means, the last two families living on the south side of South Tyger River in the vicinity of Switzer. That it was a fine school I have no doubt. I have seen many an old copy-book, arithmetic and geography in manuscript, generally in elegant chirography, which I would prize highly now if I had them, but I am sorry to say that I was foolish enough in my younger days to allow them to be destroyed along with much other valuable matter. The names of the teachers even have been lost to tradition, except a noted one named Thirlkill, of very early date, and Jonathan Haddon and H. D. W. Alexander, who was the last one, about 1846 or 1847, when the school became extinct.

The location of Poplar Springs school is well known. Poplar Springs was the site of a Presbyterian camp ground about 1800 to 1802. The water-supply being deficient, they moved to Samuel Pearson's big spring, for the same reason that John was baptizing at Aenon — because there was "much water" (udata polla) there. When the school was established there, we do not know at this day. We can only go back to 1816, for in that year, Maj. Wm. Hoy and the late Capt. David Anderson went there in their sixth year. About the year 1833 or 1834, the Rev. John L. Kennedy, a Presbyterian minister, commenced a school which he taught for several years, four or five at least. Under him the school attained some celebrity. It was he who afterwards went to Anderson county and spent his life in founding and conducting the famous Thalian Academy, more familiarly known as "Slabtown," where most of the Tyger River boys were sent for preparation for life or college. He was succeeded by James K. Dickson, who taught several years. He was succeeded by B. F. Winslow from Vermont in 1841, who wrote a most beautiful hand, and in the language of one of his pupils "was the most accomplished teacher that ever graced the academy." The succession after this was George M. Broyles, of Tennessee, Rev. Z. L. Holmes and Henry M. Anderson, after which the school became extinct.

During the time of the Poplar Springs school there must have been some years when it was vacant. This was probably before the school of Rev. J. L. Kennedy in 1833 or 1834. About this time Tyger James Anderson, a patron of Poplar Springs, patronized a school at Flint Hill taught by the Rev. John Boggs. Flint Hill is one half mile north of the Rocky Spring school, before noted, in the fork of the roads just below Mrs. J. J. Wood's residence.

The Rev. John Boggs was of very small stature, but with great learning. He had a large family of daughters and boarded a number of boys. The joke is still preserved that he had some long family prayers, and on one occasion, after the 'Amen' was said, only he and one other arose from their knees, the other being the late Dr. John C. Anderson of Alabama. When the learned divine saw the situation he said, "John, I reckon you had better wake them up," which he proceeded to do.

After all these schools had run their courses, a large and flourishing school was established at Pine Grove, about one mile north of the Rocky Spring location before noted, opposite to and a little below the residence of Capt. C. A. Barry. It was established in 1848, most probably, and was intended mostly for girls, as there were quite a number in the neighborhood. I remember to have gone there in 1849, and with three more little boys constituted the male department.

Miss Hamilton, of Anderson county, taught in 1848, and Miss Mary Juhan in 1849, under both of whom instrumental music on the piano was taught. The school these years was filled with girls from the families of Evins, Millers, Strobels, Moores, Fielders, &c. After this it was a mixed school. Mr. Z. D. Cottrell taught there in 1850 and 1851, David Jones, 1852 and 1853. In 1854 it was vacant. In 1855 Mr. Dick Kennedy, son of the old Poplar Springs teacher, taught a fine, large school, principally in the classics. In 1856 Mr. H. P. Barry taught there, after which the school became extinct. But the interest of the founders of the Minerva School, Rocky Spring Poplar Springs, Flint Hill and Pine Grove seemed to be transferred to their descendants, for they became, immediately upon the extinction of Pine Grove Academy, the founders of schools of a still higher order, the Reidville Male and Female High Schools, the former intended to prepare boys for college and life-work, the latter to graduate and confer degrees upon girls. In 1859, under the leadership of the Rev. R. H. Reid, these schools were founded, having been chartered, with a board of trustees numbering thirty members, two-thirds of whom were to be Presbyterians. Since then the board of trustees consists of fifteen members, divided into three classes of five each, one class going out of office every year.

In 1858 the male school building having been completed was opened as a mixed school, under the Rev. Thos. E. Davis, who taught it two years.

The other buildings having been completed, the female school was opened with a full corps of teachers in 1859. Since then both schools have been flourishing, doing great good in educating the minds and hearts of a very large number of boys and girls. Some of my sweetest recollections cluster around these schools, for two years of my life were spent in them. The venerable R. H. Reid, the founder, is still, after a lapse of forty-two years, president of the board of trustees.

Trusting that what I have said may be of use to you in the preparation of your book, I remain,

Yours truly,
Thomas J. Moore.

Colonel Moore in his letter refers to the organization of the Philanthropic Society at Nazareth Church in 1797, the Rev. James Templeton being the pastor of said church at the time and the prime mover of the steps taken leading to the organization of the society.

The following is an extract from the first page of the minutes of the first meeting, which is as follows:

April 24th, 1797.

CONSTITUTION OF THE PHILANTHROPIC SOCIETY

The following gentlemen, now members of the Spartanburg Philanthropic Society, met according to a previous appointment at Nazareth meeting-house, viz.: J. Jorden, Esq., Major I. Foster, Col. T. Moore, Mr. Samuel Nesbitt, the Rev. James Templeton, Mr. G. Benson and Mr. Samuel Miller. They agreed to form themselves into a society and signed the paper which contains their constitution, and is as follows:

We, the subscribers, inhabitants of Spartanburg County, in the State of South Carolina, taking into our most serious consideration how we may best contribute to the public and general interests of our country, and knowing how a much more general diffusion of knowledge and sound literature amongst our fellow-citizens might, with the smiles of a kind and gracious providence, contribute to this purpose, especially how much it might affect the civil, political and religious interests of the rising generation, we do, therefore, voluntarily and unanimously agree to form ourselves into a society for the benevolent and patriotic purposes of patronizing and promoting the interests of learning in our county in particular, and throughout the State in general, as far as it may be reasonably and conveniently in our power, or as far as our influence may extend:

Jas. Jorden,	Peter Gray,	Gab Benson,
Isham Foster,	Jas. Templeton,	Sam'l Miller,
Sam'l Nesbitt,	Thos. Moore,	Isham Harrison,

Sam'l Farrow,	Wm, Farrow,	Daniel White,
Berryman Shumate,	John Harrison, Wm.	Jas. Smith,
John Nesbitt,	Thos. Williamson,	Thomas James,
Wm. Wells,	Thos. Patton,	John Barnett,
Wm. Smith,	John Sloane,	Aaron Smith,
John Collins,	W. Lancaster,	W. Golightly,
A. B. Moore,	Hugh Means,	Wm. Ross Smith,
Ab'm Nott,	Wm. Williamson,	Thos. Hanna,
D. Golightly,	Arch'd Taylor,	Moses Casey, Jr.,
Burrell Bobo,	John Thomas, Jr.,	William Palmer,
Christopher Johnson,	D. Johnson,	Wm. Kingsborough,
Osborne West,	Willis Willeford,	R. S. Saunders,
Benj. Peak,	John O'Neill,	A. Casey,
Thomas Johnson,	Samuel Morrow,	Wm. Wilbanks.

The writer is indebted to Major A. H. Kirby for a manuscript memoranda relating to the early schools taught in the village of Spartanburg. In 1837 Major Kirby [4] became a resident of what is now the city of Spartanburg when a boy of only eight summers, and at that time the old Male Academy (which was located near the old Spartanburg union depot) was in operation. It was a substantial brick building, which stood for many years after the school was discontinued.

At the time Major Kirby came to Spartanburg this school was being taught by Jonathan Hadden, who was a fair type of the old schoolmaster of those days. He was strict in discipline and always opened the school with a short prayer. He was an elder in the old Nazareth (Presbyterian) Church, and resided about half way between the court-house of Spartanburg and said church (boarding in the village and returning home every Friday afternoon).

At an earlier period in his life, perhaps about 1825, Jonathan Hadden taught a school in the vicinity of Wellford, of which the maternal guardian of the writer, was a pupil. In his childhood days he has often heard her speak of him as among her early instructors and of some amusing incidents in connection with the school. Mr. Hadden would not only open his school with prayer, but at that day and time, when Sunday-school education and training was deficient, he would at its close in the afternoon catechize his scholars on the Scriptures. His pupils were not always as well posted as he would have washed for. On one occasion, in answer to the question, "Who was the wisest man?" a little boy answered with a loud and clear voice, "Old Solomon Thompson, sir!" [5] It has been stated by another, however, that these offhand shoots from the little urchins under his charge were by no means indicative of the standard of scriptural knowledge in the school, and the good man impressed man)lessons of inspired truth upon his pupils, which yielded rich fruit in after years.

Previous to 1837 Major Kirby learned that E. C. Leitner and, perhaps, other teachers, had run the Male Academy at Spartanburg successfully, drawing pupils from some of the lower districts.

Major Kirby further states, that at the year referred to (1837) there was also a female school in Spartanburg village, known as the *Spartanburg Female Seminary,* which was located on Main street, on the lot now occupied by Captain Petty and Mrs. Jennings, which was in a fairly flourishing condition. It was taught by the Rev. James Boggs of the Presbyterian Church, assisted by his wife and daughters. They also kept up a Sunday-school during the spring and summer months, as there were then no organized Sunday-schools in the churches.

About 1839, there seems to have been an advanced movement in the matter of schools in the town of Spartanburg, both for males and females. An effort was made to secure the services of an accomplished teacher for the Female Seminary, which resulted in the choice of Miss Phebe Paine, who landed in Spartanburg during said year as a "Yankee school-teacher." She was a native of one of the New England States, and her reputation as an educator was claimed to be equal to any in the United States, and by reason of this fact she was offered situations where money and patronage exceeded that of Spartanburg, notwithstanding the Female Seminary then, while under her care, was liberally patronized, and she had under her charge some of the very best young ladies, both in the town and country, and about as many as could be boarded in the town.

Miss Paine, when she came to Spartanburg, brought with her two sisters and a niece. Miss Webb, from Carlisle, Pa., who assisted in the various departments of the school, which was kept up for several years. She also brought with her at this, or some subsequent time, Miss George Anna Moore, a music teacher, and also a pupil and assistant, Miss Mary Owen, who afterwards became Mrs. Mary Owen Dean. All of these ladies possessed rare accomplishments and intelligence, and did their full share to advance the educational interest, both in the town and country at that time.

After Miss Paine had taught in Spartanburg for a number of years she accepted a situation at Cokesbury, S.C., where she also taught with success. In late years, upon the completion of the Spartanburg Female College, she returned to Spartanburg and was employed as one of the teachers of that institution. After teaching for several years she returned North. Her reputation as a female teacher still increased, and her latter days, it is said, were more brilliant than the first. She lived to the advanced age of ninety years, and among the chronicles of the illustrious dead, for the year that she died, all over the world her name was given prominence as a noted instructor of youth.

Among the lady teachers referred to as coming to Spartanburg with Miss Paine, we will state that during the forties Miss George Anna Moore married to Mr. A. J. Vernon, Miss Webb to Dr. R. M. Daniel, and Miss Mary Owen to Hon. Hosea J. Dean.

After the retirement of Miss Paine as principal of the Female Seminary at Spartanburg, the school was successfully taught for several years by Miss Louisa Hamilton and Miss Rosa Wallace, of Anderson, S.C., and also by Miss Foster (afterwards Mrs. D. C. Judd), Miss Hood, Miss Harlow and others. The last named was also employed by the Drs. Curtis in the Limestone Female High School for several years.

In 1849 the Female Seminary at Spartanburg was presided over by Rev. Z. L. Holmes, assisted by Mr. C. F. Judd; and in 1850 an advertisement appears in the *Spartan* files announcing the employment of Miss Tupper, of the Troy (N.Y.) Female Seminary, who had been sent out by Miss Willard, of that celebrated institution, to establish one of a similar character in the South. She was assisted by Miss Temple, a lady well known for her musical attainments and critical knowledge of the French language.

Returning again to the Spartanburg Male Academy, we will state that about the time Miss Paine took charge of the Female Seminary there, Rev. Erastus Rowley and Milton Rowdey (both from the North) were secured as teachers for that school, and under their management quite a number of boys and young men were drawn to the school from the lower districts, among them the Keitts, Housers, Dantzlers, Wannamakers and others. There was also Matt Wallace and others from Union District, for it was then considered a classical school, preparing young men for college.

After the withdrawal of the Rowleys from said school, the same was taught successfully and successively by Elias Hall, Major John A. Leland, Z. D. Cottrell, William Irwin, Rev. Clough S. Beard and others, all of whom were first-rate teachers.

Among the early schools taught in Spartanburg County was one opened up at Mt. Zion (near Welford) by Rev. John G. Landrum, in 1836. Mr. Landrum had taught successfully schools at Wilbanks schoolhouse in Union county and at Clayford Academy, on the waters of Lawson's Fork (near the present residence of Mr. Calvin Foster), and at Rock Spring, on the waters of North Tyger River (near the Isaic Morgan homestead residence), prior to the opening of the school at Mt. Zion. His biographer states that "he opened a school at Mount Zion, into which he gathered the boys and girls of the neighborhood, and it was not long before his reputation as a teacher had extended beyond his immediate locality, and pupils came from other communities to avail themselves of the benefits of his instruction." At one time in this school he was assisted by Mr. Memory N. Chapman, who possessed a finished education for that day, and enjoyed the reputation of being one of the finest penmen in the State. Afterwards he represented Spartanburg County in the State Legislature for several years.

Mr. Landrum's biographer further states: "He (Landrum) continued in charge of the school at Mount Zion for a period of ten or twelve years. His school at this place became very popular, and was attended by many who afterwards occupied eminent positions in life. His house was open to boarders, as were the houses of the neighborhood, and on the school-roll were the names of the Chapmans, Wingos, Highs, Fosters, Turners, Bomars, Ballengers and others." [6]

Among the early pioneer school-teachers in Spartanburg County was Christopher Golightly, who taught back in the thirties. He was also a land surveyor, and in the capacity of teacher or surveyor he was rather above the average man of his day. Although possessing by nature some eccentricities, he was, notwithstanding, a man of intelligence, force of character and sterling integrity. He was the father of eight sons, three of whom were known personally to the writer, viz.: William, Richard and Patillo. All of these taught in different portions of the upper part of Spartanburg district in the forties and perhaps in the early part of the fifties. Possessing as they did many of the peculiar characteristics that belonged to their father, they were nevertheless teachers of more than ordinary intelligence and ability, and were not only well versed in the English branches but taught Latin and the higher mathematics. William, the oldest son (father of Mr. J. Calvin Golightly, on South Pacolet), was instructed in the schoolroom by his father until he was eighteen years old. He then went to the town of Union, S.C., to a boarding-school, and learned Latin, Greek and Algebra; but Latin was his favorite throughout his life. His instructor at this school was Wm. E. Clowney, who afterwards became a representative in Congress of the Congressional District of which Spartanburg formed a part.

William Golightly also taught music and was at times associated with William Walker (A. S. H.), Henry White and Isaac Neighbors; he married when a young man a Miss Vaughn, seventh daughter of ___ Vaughn, who was also a school-teacher in the early history of Spartanburg District. He came from Virginia to South Carolina soon after the close of the Revolution peddling on cotton cards, and married a Miss Leach, who belonged to a family representing the early settlers around old Fort Prince.

Christopher Golightly, the progenitor of the Golightlys referred to, married a Miss Harrison, daughter of Richard Harrison, one of the first county court judges for Spartanburg County and whose name is mentioned elsewhere. The late James Moss and Andrew Barry were his brothers-in-law, having also married daughters of Mr. Harrison.

As early as 1845 or '46 a good school was taught at Ridgefield Academy, a schoolhouse near Hill's old factory, at that time, one of the best school buildings in the county. The first school taught there was by Professor John W. Wofford (brother of Dr. Jos. L. Wofford, Cherokee Springs), who was a graduate of Athens College, Georgia. He taught two years and then became a candidate for the legislature to represent Spartanburg County, on the side of prohibition, at that time an unpopular issue, and was defeated, but received a very handsome vote. He then emigrated to Mississippi and filled some important offices. While in charge of the Ridgefield Academy, very liberal inducements were offered to pupils outside the neighborhood to patronize the school. At the house of Mr. Joseph Wofford students were boarded at the low rate of $4 per month, washing and lights included. It was a very large school; the teacher was employed and pay assured by Thomas Young, Samuel Tucker and Joseph Wofford. Among the pupils who attended this school was Major John Bankston Davis of Campobello, S.C., who was a man of general reading and intelligence and possessed a scientific education, particularly in the higher mathematics, and had a first-class reputation as a land surveyor and civil engineer.

As early perhaps as 1825, a teacher of some prominence, whose name was James Hutchinson, taught successfully at an academy in the vicinity of Cross Anchor, the school building standing near the present New Hope (Baptist) church. Among the pupils who attended this school was the late Hon. Simpson Bobo, Colonel O. E. Edwards, and the children of Col. Thomas Farrow, who lived near by. The accidental burning of the schoolhouse put an end to the further progress of the school. [7]

Major Wm. Hoy, in his articles to the county press, states that Henry Patillo Barry taught long in the section of the present town of Switzer, and that among his pupils were several members of the Switzer family, Mr. Miles Gentry, Dr. Ward and others. He also states that among the girl pupils was Miss Lula Tucker, who has long had the reputation of being among the best educators in the State of Florida, and is still engaged in that profession.

Near Trinity Church, in the vicinity of Cross Anchor, was taught, in the years gone by, a flourishing school. This was called the Pear Field schoolhouse, and among the teachers who taught there were Chana Stone and Simpson Burnett, and among the chief patrons was Mr. Johnny Rhodes.

Mr. Hezekiah Ducker, who lives within a few miles of Cross Anchor, at the advanced age of seventy-eight years, was a successful school-teacher in Spartanburg County back in the forties. In 1847 or 1848 he taught at Davis Academy, on Cane creek, near the home of "stone-cutter" John Davis. He, Davis, owned a quarry on Cane creek, and was noted for his fine millstones.

Among the pupils who attended the school of Mr. Ducker during the year referred to, was Captain John W. Wofford, of Hendersonville, N.C. It might be further said of Mr. Ducker in this connection, that he was a gallant Confederate soldier, though advanced in years, and was among the first volunteers of Company "D," 3d S.C. Regiment of Volunteers.

Of the schools in the vicinity of Woodruff we can gather but little information. In 1851 the Bethel Academy was presided over by Dr. John Dean, and in 1853 by Mr. M. D. Kennedy, assisted by Mr. W. F. Pearson,, and later by Mr. E. F. Davis, author of a "Universal" schoolbook. Hon. Edwin H. Bobo, of Spartanburg, who was a graduate of Oxford College, Georgia, also taught there for a few years prior to the civil war.

Mr. Henry G. Gaffney, now aged about ninety years, has recalled some pleasant recollections in connection with his schoolboy days in the vicinity of Gaffney. Under date of July 25th, 1896, Mr. Gaffney states through the county press as follows:

"I can give a good many dots from my own knowledge as to Fendal Robertson, the one-legged schoolteacher, and from other reliable sources. He taught school from my boyhood; for several years at the schoolhouse about one mile up the old Georgia road and about 200 yards west from the Pole Bridge branch in the woods near James Cooper's old place...If I was able to get out there I could point out the spot where the old bull-pen, as it was called, was located, where we all played ball under different names, viz.: town-ball, cat, etc. The girls also played with us and caught the ball in their aprons. I could give several names and where they lived, but would make it very lengthy."

As early as 1825 Wm. W Hasting began a school which lasted about fifteen years near Van Patten's Shoals on Enoree. In the course of said time he pre-pared students for higher institutions of learning, and, it is said, taught as many as fifteen students that afterwards graduated in medicine, and among these were three Drs. Westmoreland. He was a good scribe, wrote with a quill pen; had twelve children and gave all of them a fair education.

The writer recalls some pleasant memories in connection with his school-boy days at old Fort Prince Academy, and among the teachers there by whom he was instructed was Dr. Oliver G. Chapman, afterwards a promi-nent physician in Hunt county, Texas; Mr. Calvin Foster, who resides near Campton, S.C.; Mrs. M. A. Wood, of Rusk county, Texas, who was a first honor graduate, before the civil war, at the Holstein Conference M. E. College, lo-cated at Asheville, N.C., and Mr. Leland Jackson, of Jackson Hill, S.C., who subsequently removed to the West.

The writer also attended a school at Beech Springs (near Howell's Mill), taught by Mr. Oliver P. Richardson, who might be styled as a typical repre-sentative of the "old field" school-teacher of his day. He taught the English and mathematics only, with considerable ability. He was, however, an excel-lent citizen and progressive farmer, a civil magistrate holding the scales of justice equally between all, and was for several years judge-advocate of the 36th Regiment South Carolina militia on the staffs of Colonels Snoddy and Vandyke. He married Miss Hester Wingo, and removed to Texas before the civil war; and by this marriage he had one son to graduate at the Military Academy at West Point.

At New Prospect Academy flourishing schools were taught during the years '58, '59 and '60. In '58 by the Rev. T. J. Earle, a graduate of Mercer Uni-versity, Georgia, assisted by Mr. Wm. H. Ray, a graduate of the South Caroli-na Military Academy at Charleston, Mr. Earle afterwards opened up a flour-ishing seminary for both sexes at Gowensville, S.C., which was liberally pat-ronized at home and from abroad and which remained in a prosperous con-dition for a number of years after the close of the war. In 1859, the school at New Prospect was presided over by Mr. L. Perrin Foster, a graduate of South Carolina College, assisted by Miss Angle Edwards, who was a graduate of the Moravian college at Salem, N.C. In 1860 the same school was taught by Mr. Thomas Lee, son of the celebrated teacher, Colonel Stephen Lee, of Ashe-ville, N.C., assisted by Mr. Samuel Lancaster, a popular teacher in the neigh-borhood. During the years '59 and '60 the writer attended these schools for a period of ten months each year, which ended his days as a pupil in the schoolroom. The great civil war coming up, both Mr. Foster and Mr. Lee volunteered in the service of their country. The former was a lieutenant of Company K, 3d Regiment South Carolina Volunteers, and was killed at the battle of Fredericksburg, The latter (Thos. Lee), was at first color corporal of the 5th Regiment South Carolina Volunteers and later a corporal of Company D, Palmetto Sharp Shooters, commanded by Captain Alfred H. Foster, and died of disease at Charlottesville, Va., September 16th, 1861. Two braver or more patriotic spirits never entered the service of their country or sacrificed their lives in its defense, than Perrin Foster and Thomas. Lee. Their memories will always be cherished by the writer, who held both in highest esteem as his instructors in the schoolroom and who afterwards suffered with them great hardships in the years of the bloody war which followed.

In 1842 or '43 Colonel Stephen Lee, father of Thomas Lee, just mentioned, started a select school for young men at the homestead residence of Dr. Alfred Moore, which subsequently became the town of Welford, S.C. We have been unable to gather much information in reference to this school, but its curriculum was high, the object being to prepare young men for college. Col. Lee afterwards removed to Asheville, N.C., where he conducted a school of the same character for many years. During the civil war he was colonel of the 16th Regiment N.C. Volunteers.

In 1842 a male academy was opened at Glenn's Spring for the benefit of the resident families. The most prominent of these were Mr. John C. Zimmerman, Dr. David Peake, Dr. Maurice A. Moore, Mr. R. A. Gates, and the Winsmiths and Smiths who lived near by. The school was first taught by Mr. John Eison, a prominent educator in his day. Young men from all parts of the State went to this academy to be prepared for the South Carolina College. Afterward Rev. Clough Beard, a Methodist minister, had charge of the school for a number of years until his death in the sixties.

In addition to the schools already mentioned in the town of Spartanburg, there were still other good schools taught there before the war. One of these was the Odd Fellows' school, which was opened up in the old Baptist church lot back of where the new court-house now stands and near the new jail. This was taught for a year or so by Major David R. Duncan, who, after his graduation in the Randolph Macon College in Virginia, came to Spartanburg, his father then being a professor in the Wofford College.

About the year 1854, or 1855, a good school was taught at Fingerville for a number of years, and among those who taught successfully there, were Captain Samuel C. Means and Esquires Elias Johnson and Samuel Lancaster, and among the patrons were the late Colonel Gabriel Cannon, Mr. Jos. Finger, the McMillens, McDowells, Whites, Fosters and other progressive families on the Pacolets.

The St. John's College, for young ladies, was opened about 1854 or '55 at Spartanburg, under the management of the Episcopal Church at that place.

This was at a later period changed into a high school for boys, with a military feature, under the tutorship of Captain J. E. Black.

Wofford College

In December, 1850, Rev. Benjamin Wofford died, leaving one hundred thousand dollars for the establishment and endowment of a college for literary and scientific education, to be located in Spartanburg District, to be under the control and management of the Conference of the Methodist Episcopal Church of South Carolina. The town of Spartanburg secured the location of this college by donating the land whereon the elegant building was afterwards erected.

The college, known as Wofford College, was named in honor of its founder. The following gentlemen comprised the first Board of Trustees, viz.:

Rev. H. A. C. Walker, President; Revs. W. A. Gamewell, T. R. Walsh, W. A. McSwain, C. Betts, C. S. Walker, J. R. Pickett, Esquires Simpson Bobo, J. Wofford Tucker, Harvey Wofford, George W. Williams, Robert Bryce and Dr. J. H. Dogan.

In 1854 the buildings of the Wofford College were completed and in October of the same year the college was opened with the following able faculty:

Rev. W. M. Wightman, D.D., President; Professor of Mental and Moral Science; David Duncan, A.M., Professor of Ancient Languages; Rev. Whiteford Smith, D.D., Professor of English Literature; James H. Carlisle, A.M., Professor of Mathematics; Warren Dupre, A.M., Professor of Natural Science; R. W. Boyd, A.B., Principal of Primary Department.

After the resignation of Dr. Wightman, about 1858, Rev. A. M. Shipp was made President, who served for several years, when he was transferred to Vanderbilt University, Nashville, Tenn.

James H. Carlisle, LL.D., was then elected President of the college, and has been ever since ably presiding in that capacity.

Wofford College, at this writing, is in a flourishing condition, with a faculty of eminence and distinguished ability, and with first-class modern equipments, and ranks among the first in the South.

James H. Carlisle, A.M., LL.D., President of Wofford College, Spartanburg, S.C., was born in Winnsboro, Fairfield County, S.C., May 4th, 1825. He is a son of Dr. William Carlisle, a native of the north of Ireland, who was born in 1795, came to America in 1818 and located at Winnsboro, S.C. He was a physician by profession and practiced in South Carolina for thirty years, dying in 1866. He was twice married, his first wife being Mary Ann Buchannon, also a native of Ireland, who died in 1858, leaving six children — four sons and two daughters — the subject of this sketch being the second son. He was reared partly at Winnsboro and partly at Camden, S.C. In 1844 he graduated from the South Carolina College and began the vocation of a teacher, which he has since followed. For nine years he was an instructor in a classical school in Columbia. Upon the opening of the Wofford College, in 1854, he was elected professor of mathematics. In July of the same year he removed to Spartanburg and has ever since been a member of the faculty of Wofford College, embracing a period of forty-four years. Since 1875 he has been its President, his immediate predecessor in office being Rev. A. M. Shipp, D.D.

Dr. Carlisle is one of the few surviving members of the State Convention which met in Charleston and passed the ordinance of secession, December 20th, 1860. He was also elected a representative from Spartanburg to the State Legislature in 1864. This was doubtless against his wishes or inclinations, but it was at a time in the history of South Carolina when men of sound judgment and eminent ability were needed in her legislative halls.

James H. Carlisle, LL.D.

Dr. Carlisle was married December 12th, 1848, to Miss Margaret Jane, daughter of Robert Bryce, a merchant of Columbia, S.C. She died in 1891. They had three children, two of whom are living.

Dr. Carlisle is one of the best educators in the Southern States, and has lectured quite extensively. He is the author of "The Young Astronomer" and editor of a volume in the Chautauqua course containing the lives of Thomas Arnold and Roger Ascham. He is an honored and distinguished member of the Methodist Church South, and has been a member of several of its conferences.

Among the citizens of Spartanburg who have won distinction and by their humble walk in life have met popular approval, respect and admiration, none are more prominent than Dr. Carlisle. He is deeply interested in the Sunday-school work and in the moral and intellectual development of the rising generations of our country. In reviewing his great and lofty character three distinctive traits appear to be prominent, viz.: largeness of heart, nobility of soul and brilliancy of intellect.

Spartanburg Female College

While the Wofford College building was in course of construction the ministers and some of the laymen of the South Carolina Conference began to agitate the question of building a female college, and Spartanburg, by a liberal subscription of money and lands, secured the location and very soon after Wofford College was opened, the Spartanburg Female College was opened also and successfully operated. The first professors and teachers of that institution were:

J. Wofford Tucker, President; Rev. Charles Taylor and Miss Phoebe Paine, professors, and other assistants besides the music teachers.

After the resignation of Mr. Tucker, Rev. Charles; Taylor was elected President, who served about one year and was succeeded by Rev. Joseph Cross, D.D. The latter was succeeded by Professor Wm. K. Blake about the year 1858 or '59, who presided over the institution with eminent ability until towards the close of the period embraced in the civil war, and then the institution was closed for several years. During the time that President Blake had charge of the institution preceding the war he was assisted by Professor Charles Petty, and during the war and perhaps a short time before by Professor Falk of Virginia.

After the war, about 1870, the college revived under the management of Rev. S. B. Jones, D.D., and Rev. S. Lander, D.D. The latter withdrew, however, in a few months and Dr. Jones remained at the head of the institution for several years, when, on being chosen President of the Columbia Female College, it was deemed advisable to close up the Female College at Spartanburg, which was done. This ended its career. The property falling into the hands of Rev. R. C. Oliver, was opened as an orphanage and kept open as such for a time, but for want of a liberal patronage, or for some other cause, it was closed. Later the same buildings were converted into the Fitting School for the Wofford College, but the adjacent location of the factory buildings made them no longer desirable for educational purposes and the Wofford Fitting School was. transferred to another locality.

[1] The person here alluded to is not the Judge William Smith of Spartanburg County (father of Dr. John Winsmith), a sketch of whom will appear at another place.
[2] Father of Colonel T. J. Moore.
[3] Mrs. Margaret Montgomery, wife of John Montgomery, Esq.
[4] Major Kirby received the honorary title of Major from the fact that he commanded for four years the Lower Battalion, 36th Regiment South Carolina militia, from 1856 to 1860.
[5] See Griffith's "Life of Landrum," p. 139.
[6] See Griffith's "Life of Landrum," pp. 65 and 143.
[7] The writer obtains this information from Mrs. Levi Stone, living near Cross Anchor, now eighty-seven years old.

Chapter Six - A General Review of the Progress of Education in Spartanburg County Continued

The Limestone Springs Female High School was founded in 1846 by Rev. Thomas Curtis, D.D., and his son, Rev. Wm. Curtis, D.D. (See sketches elsewhere in this work.) The substantial and elegant brick building in which said institution was begun was built by a joint stock company, mostly low-country gentlemen, for hotel purposes, the famous Limestone Spring near by being an attraction, with the Race Paths at the Gaffney place, one mile distant, where the finest horses the country afforded were groomed, exercised and run, and these, together with the close proximity to the mountain region, offered special inducements to establish a popular resort for the summer season; but a financial failure of the company caused the property to be advertised for sale, which was purchased in the fall of 1845 by the Drs. Curtis. Here was established for the education of females an institution which acquired a wide reputation and liberal patronage, which soon made it one of the most popular schools in the South. The number of pupils amounted sometimes to nearly three hundred, and the roll showed them as representing almost every State in the South. The co-principals brought to this institution the most distinguished talent that could be obtained, and all of the higher branches of literature were taught, including music and the fine arts. In short, the tone of education was set high, care being taken to cultivate the mind to points of refinement and elegance, which was successfully done at this institution, and which was operated for about fifteen years, when the untimely death of the senior principal and the civil war between the States, which came up a few years later, put an end to its existence for a time. Several years after the war in the same building a school was begun (1874) under the auspices of others, but not with any marked success until the opening of what was afterwards known as the *Cooper-Limestone Institute,* which had its origin under the following circumstances:

The attention of the Hon. Peter Cooper, of New York, being called to the healthful locality and attractive features around Limestone Springs, he bought the property, including the buildings and two hundred and sixty acres of land. It was his purpose to so model and fashion and beautify that it might become his pleasant and attractive winter resort from the severity of temperature of more northern latitudes. Some members of his family strenuously objected to its use as originally intended by Mr. Cooper, and hence he donated the property to the Spartanburg Baptist Association. From Griffith's "Life of J. G. Landrum," page 221, we gather the following:

"At a meeting of the Association in 1879, information was received through Major Thomas Bomar, to the effect that Hon. Peter Cooper, of New York, had intimated a willingness to donate the celebrated Limestone Springs property...to some religious or benevolent corporation to be used by them for educational purposes. Mr. Landrum was appointed chairman of a committee to confer with Mr. Cooper, and the final result was that Mr. Cooper donated the property, valued at $22,000, to the Spartanburg Baptist Association, with the provision that it is to be used for purposes of education. The Association was then incorporated by an act of the legislature, a board of trustees was elected with J. G. Landrum as president, and in the fall of 1881 the famous Limestone Springs Female High School was reopened under the name of 'The Cooper-Limestone Institute for Young Ladies.'

48

"Mr. Landrum worked indefatigably for this enterprise, and gave it the best energies of his declining years. He was through life an earnest advocate of education...The Cooper-Limestone Institute was the pet of his old age."

The Cooper-Limestone Institute was opened, as stated, in the fall of 1881, under the management of Professors H. P. Griffith and R. O. Sams, co-principals, and was successfully operated by them for a number of years. Subsequently Professor Sams retired from the Institute, leaving Professor Griffith in charge, which he conducted with marked success, notwithstanding many drawbacks, for ten years or more. Under his management the school was liberally patronized and its alumnae are found in the faculties of many schools and colleges of South Carolina and other States.

Upon the death of Rev. J. G. Landrum in January, 1882, Major John Earle Bomar was elected President of the Board of Trustees, who served faithfully and with efficiency for a number of years, when he was succeeded by Captain John H. Montgomery (in 1888), whose management and liberal expenditure of his private as well as other funds collected have placed the institution on safe footing. Besides his last gift of $10,000 in moneys and assumption of bonded indebtedness, he gave at one time $1,000 and $300 to the library of said institution.

At the meeting of the Spartanburg Baptist Association in 1897 a visiting committee to visit Cooper-Limestone Institute and investigate its condition and needs reported at the meeting of the Association a year later that some permanent arrangement must be made as to repairs and for supplying the building with water, etc. The Association thereupon resolved that the sum of not less than $10,000 be raised for Cooper-Limestone Institute by the Association by January 1st, 1899. The name of the institution was changed from Cooper-Limestone Institute to *Limestone College*.

The committee further reported, voicing its own true wishes and expressing the sentiment of the Association, that it would prefer to have the college called Montgomery College, in honor of its generous supporter. Captain John H. Montgomery, but solely in deference to his feelings and judgment suggested the name Limestone College.

It was further provided in said resolutions that said committee be fully authorized and empowered to take all necessary steps in conjunction with the proper officers of the Association of the Cooper-Limestone Institute as might be required by law to effect a transfer of the institution to a board of fifteen trustees, to be held by them in trust for the Baptists of the State. Eight members of the first board to be elected by the Association, and when elected to be empowered to select seven other members of the board from prominent and influential Baptists of the State, said board to be a self-perpetuating body, etc.

Under this new arrangement the trustees during the present year (1899) have spent $20,000 on equipment, making it one of the most superbly furnished colleges in the State. The Art Department is fitted up in a stylish and fascinating manner; a large historical library is being provided, and the trustees have determined to establish a department of history, to be known as the Winnie Davis School of History, in which, without neglecting other branches of the subject, particular attention will be paid to history of the Southern States.

At the head of the institution is Lee Davis Lodge, an A.M. and Ph.D. of Columbian University, assisted by Professor H. P. Griffith, an able and popular instructor, together with other competent teachers in all its departments, and which as a whole compose a strong and experienced faculty.

We would further add, that the location of Limestone College is one of the most beautiful and romantic in the South, which will always command for it a generous support and liberal patronage.

Converse College

The marvelous growth of the city of Spartanburg up to the beginning of 1889 pointed clearly to the fact that the educational advantages were not amply sufficient to meet the requirements of the rising generations in that city, and a number of her more progressive citizens, appreciating this fact, called a meeting in March of the same year.

The object of said meeting was to inaugurate a movement for the building up of a high grade female school to be located in the city of Spartanburg. Among those who were present at this first meeting were D. E. Converse, Geo. Cofield, C. H. Carlisle, Jos. Walker, Bishop Duncan, D. R. Duncan, H. E. Heinisch, Rev. B. F. Wilson, Rev. W. T. Devieux, Rev. A. Coke Smith, Dr. Geo. R. Dean and W. E. Burnett. Steps were at once taken looking to the formation of a joint stock company for such a college to start with 1,000 shares, at $25 per share. A committee, consisting of D. E. Converse, W. B. Burnett, Jos. Walker, John B, Cleveland and Rev. A. C Smith, was appointed to solicit subscriptions. In the course of a few weeks the requisite amount was raised, the beautiful grounds which embraced St. John's College were purchased, and the college was organized under the following Board of Directors: D. E. Converse, Hon. D. R. Duncan, Dr. C. E. Fleming, Col. Joseph Walker, W. S. Manning, Captain J. H. Montgomery, Hon. J. B. Cleveland, N. F. Walker and W. E. Burnett. Mr. Converse was made President and Mr. Manning Secretary and Treasurer of said board.

Rev. B. F. Wilson, A.B., was chosen as President of an able faculty; the building of Saint John's College was repaired and remodeled and the first session of Converse College (named in honor of Mr. D. E. Converse) began Wednesday, October 1st, 1890, under favorable circumstances and with a liberal patronage.

In the course of one or two years, however, the main college building was destroyed by fire, but other buildings were provided and the school only suspended its exercises for a few days. The same public spirit which gave rise to the first movement to erect a college building caused another, a handsomer and more commodious building to be constructed.

The institution, which was chartered by the State of South Carolina in 1889, was incorporated by enactment of the General Assembly of South Carolina in 1896, under the name and style of "Converse College." The following gentlemen are named in said Act: D. Edgar Converse, John B. Cleveland, Joseph Walker, John H. Montgomery, David R. Duncan, Newton F. Walker, William S. Manning, Wilber E. Burnett, Albert H. Twitchell, John Earle Bomar, H. Arthur Ligon and Benjamin F, Wilson.

Converse College has at the present writing (1899) been in operation for nearly ten years, and has continued to grow in patronage and influence from year to year. During the past year the attendance amounted to 452 students from 22 different States, and many applicants were refused for want of room space. The college is well equipped in every sense, and in connection with the buildings is a handsome Conservatory of Music and Concert Hall at a cost of $14,000, and an auditorium which accommodates 2,000 people. The college has purchased and completed its own electric light plant at a cost of $5,000, and an elegant dormitory and gymnasium building, constructed of brick and granite, is in course of erection, which will soon be completed, at a cost of about $12,000. The college plant now represents something like $200,000; of this amount the citizens of Spartanburg contributed about $40,000 and Mr. Converse the balance. This does not, however, include the amount bequeathed to the college under the last will and testament of Mr. Converse, which will amount to at least $100,000 more. The original contributors number about 150 of the citizens of Spartanburg.

Rev. B. F. Wilson.

Should the college grow in influence and property within the next ten years as it has done in the past, it will have sufficient equipment to become a university and will continue to rank, as it does now, as one of the foremost institutions of learning in the South.

REV. BENJAMIN F. WILSON, President of Converse College, of Spartanburg, was born in Sumter County, S.C., March 20th, 1862. He is a son of Captain Benjamin F. Wilson, of Sumter County, S.C., one of the largest cotton planters in said county. The subject of this sketch was reared on his father's farm until he arrived at the age of seventeen years, receiving the benefit of the common schools of his neighborhood. In the fall of 1880, when eighteen years of age, he entered Davidson College, of North Carolina, from which he graduated in 1884 as a Bachelor of Arts. So well did he advance during these years that he received medals both in his junior and senior years, the former

51

of which was awarded to him as the best representative of the two literary societies of said college, and the latter as the best representative in his own society proper. He was elected the valedictorian of his class during the senior year by the literary society of which he was a member. Having decided to become a minister of the gospel, he entered, in the fall of 1884, the Theological Seminary at Columbia, S.C., in which he spent one year. In the fall of 1885 he entered Princeton Theological Seminary, at Princeton, N.J., from which he graduated in the summer of 1887. During his first year there he took the second scholarship prize in Greek, and during his last year he took the first scholarship prize in Hebrew. In the summer of 1887 he became pastor of the Presbyterian church in Spartanburg. In 1888 he spent the summer in the University of Berlin, Germany, pursuing philosophical and philological studies. For the commencement in '89 he was elected by his *alma mater* alumnus orator, and during the same year was elected pastor of the First Presbyterian Church, Richmond, Ky., and also, at the same time, to the chair of Christian Apologetics of the Central University of Richmond, Ky., both of which he declined. In the winter of 1889 he was elected president of the Converse College, which position he now holds, having presided over the institution with distinguished ability, as has been shown by its continued upgrowth, equipment and prosperity from year to year. Mr. Wilson is a member of the Sigma Alpha Epsilon fraternity. He is yet young and talented; and the achievements which he has already attained by his connection with Converse College are such as to foreshadow for him a continued useful and brilliant career.

He was joined in marriage, July 30th, 1890, to Mrs. Sallie Foster, widow of J. Adolphus Foster, and daughter of J. C. Farrer, a resident of Union county. By this marriage he has several children.

DEXTER EDGAR CONVERSE, the founder of Converse College, was born in Vermont

Dexter E. Converse

in 1828, and died at his home in Spartanburg October 5th, 1899. His father was Orlin Converse, also a native of the same State. His grandfather was Paine Converse, a farmer of Massachusetts, and direct descendant of Edward Converse, who came from England to America with Governor Winthrop in 1620. His mother was Louisa Twitchell, a native of Massachusetts, and daughter of Peter Twitchell. She died in 1888.

D. Edgar Converse, when but three years old, was deprived by death of a father's care, and was placed in the care of an uncle in Canada, where he was reared and educated. This uncle was, like his father, a woolen manufacturer,

and it was from him that the subject of this sketch received his first lessons in this line of business, which he conducted to the end of his life with marvelous success. In 1850, after reaching his years of maturity, he went to Cohoes, N.Y., where he was employed in a cotton mill for five years, and thus obtained a good knowledge of that business in all its branches.

In 1855 he came South, and, after a brief connection with a cotton mill at Lincolnton, N.C., he removed to the present county of Spartanburg, and was employed in a cotton mill at Bivingsville, now known as Glendale, of which he soon acquired a proprietary interest, and at the time of his death owned a controlling interest in the stock. At the beginning of the war he enlisted as a private in Company I, 13th Regiment, S.C.V. His captain was D. R. Duncan. There was, however, such need of accomplished manufacturers that the Confederate government detailed him to return -home and conduct the business of cotton manufacturing, requiring of his company one-third of the product of their mill, which was carried out in good faith.

After the close of the war the old factory building at Bivingsville was removed and a fine new establishment was built, the business of which grew steadily as the ravages of war disappeared. The name of Bivingsville was changed to Glendale, and Mr. Converse was made president of the new mills. In 1880, in connection with business associates, he purchased the water privilege and site of the old South Carolina Iron Works on Pacolet River, Spartanburg County, and here three new mills have been erected, known as Clifton Nos. 1, 2 and 3. The total capacity of these, with Glendale Mills, at this writing (1899), amounts to 3,768 looms and 118,072 spindles. Of the Clifton Manufacturing Company Mr. Converse was president and business manager from its organization to the time of his death. He was a director in various other cotton mills and in several of the banks at Spartanburg. He was a trustee of the South Carolina Institute for the deaf, dumb and blind, at Cedar Spring, and, as already stated, the founder of Converse College for the education of young women, which will always rank among the foremost institutions of our country and which has added imperishable honor to his name and character. This institution was the pride of his heart, and will endure for all time as a monument to his memory as lasting as can be carved from stone. By his last will and testament he bequeathed one third of his magnificent estate, amounting to some $600,000, to Converse College, and just before his death made known in writing his purpose in founding said college, which reads as follows:

"It is my opinion that the well-being of any country depends upon the culture of the women, and I have done what I could to found a college that would provide for women thorough and liberal culture, so that for them the highest motives may become clear purposes and fixed habits of life; and I desire that the instruction and influence of Converse College be always such that the students may be enabled to see clearly, to decide wisely and act justly; and that they may learn to love God and humanity and be faithful to truth and duty, so that their influence may be characterized by purity and power.

"It is also my desire and hope that Converse College may always be truly religious but never denominational. I believe that religion is essential to all that is purest and best in life here and hereafter. I wish the college to be really, but liberally and tolerantly, Christian; for I believe that the revelation of God in Christ is for salvation, and I commend and commit the college to the love and guidance of God and to the care, sympathy and fidelity of my fellow men."

In character Mr. Converse was benevolent and liberal in his contributions to all worthy objects which came before him. He was temperate, pure and upright, with lofty ideas for the elevation of humanity; but his excellent traits of character can be better summed up in the address of Dr. Jas. H. Carlisle on the occasion of his funeral obsequies, who spoke the following words:

"Perhaps my acquaintance with our deceased friend dates further back than that of almost any one else who speaks to-day. More than forty years ago I used to meet him at the religious occasions which he loved to encourage among his people, near his home. During the great war I saw him in his office, where needy women, the wives and widows of soldiers, had learned to go for help. He was old enough to bear his share in the burdens and dangers of the war. He was not too old to adjust himself to new and strange conditions when peace returned. While some of our citizens were eloquently abusing his native section and others were sitting down in sullen despair, he threw himself with all his energies into needed and honorable work, to help in rebuilding the shattered fortunes of our people. He depended for his success only on skill, prudence, patience and integrity. We suppose it never occurred to him that money might be sought in gambling speculations. He must have been endued to an unusual degree with the rare qualities to gain wealth honorably, and the still rarer qualities to use it wisely and unselfishly. A few years ago, in this growing city, a critical opportunity occurred to take a signal step forward in the most important fields of education. The place, the time, called for the man. Thrown in early life upon the care of a widowed mother, his own fine character a tribute of her worth, and having been privileged, in her case, to 'rock the cradle of reposing age,' our friend was well prepared to put a high estimate on female influence and character. Quietly, without pretense of show, he came forward and met the grand occasion grandly. A man of few words, of unusual modesty, whose 'virtues were rather felt than seen,' it almost seemed easier for him to sign a large check for the college than to take his place on the platform on Commencement day and receive the congratulations of his friends. He took all the precautions that the education imparted to young women here should be safe, moral and religious. Perhaps no surer means could be taken by any man to embalm his money and give it earthly continuance.

"The orphan stranger came among us without means. He has given to his adopted State an offering such as very few of her own sons, with ancestral wealth, have laid upon her altar."

The wife of Mr. Converse was Miss Helen A. Twitchell, of Cohoes, N.Y., who survives him, with one daughter, the issue of said marriage.

History of the South Carolina Institution for the Education of the Deaf and the Blind

Cedar Spring, situated four miles south of Spartanburg, is a place of historic and educational interest. It was near here that two memorable engagements took place during the Revolution — one on the 12th day of July, 1780, and the other on the 7th day of August of the same year. The first of these was fought near the Cedar Spring (known in the annals of Revolutionary history as *Green Spring*), and the other mainly at the old Thomson place, near Glendale (R. R.) Station, known in history as the second battle of Cedar Spring, or Wofford's Iron Works. In another volume we have given an extended account of both of these battles. [1] To the mind of the present generation it at once suggests the home of the South Carolina Institution for the Deaf and the Blind. However, it must not be forgotten that the educational interest of the place dates back further than the establishment of the above mentioned institution.

In 1824 the Word Academy was erected in the grove near the spring. This school was well attended. Rev. Porter, a Presbyterian minister, was the first teacher, the school being what was then termed a "Latin school." Colonel E. C. Leitner, George Packer, a Mr. Dye, Roland Burdette, Mr. Sims, James Smith and Mrs. Betsy McClintock were some of Rev. Porter's successors. Col. H. H. Thomson, Madison Thomson, Joel Foster, Barhani B. Foster, Mike Whetstone, Charles White, Calvin White, Javan Barnett, David Zimmerman, Colonel Joseph Walker, and many other well-known men of that day attended this academy.

About the same date that the above named academy was established, a number of summer residents erected a school building southwest of the present building of the School for the Deaf and Blind, and secured the services of Mr. Scarborough to open there an academy for girls. Both of these schools were among the best in Spartanburg District at that date.

In 1849, Rev. N. P. Walker, having become interested in the education of the deaf, bought the hotel building near the spring, and there established a private school for the deaf. On the 22d of January of that year he had a class of five deaf children in his school for speaking and hearing children. The names of these were John M. Hughston, E. Melton Hughston, E. Jane Hughston, Irene A. Cooper and Harvey W. Bennett, all of whom were residents of Spartanburg district.

Before the opening of this school Mr. Walker had attended for a few months a school at the Cave Spring (Georgia) School for the Deaf, in which he had prepared himself for this special work. It was not long until this school had the cordial patronage of the State, and finally, in 1857, became a State institution. The State erected, in 1857-59, the present (1900) buildings.

The founder of the South Carolina Institution for the Deaf and the Blind, and also his son, his successor, deserve more than passing recognition and casual mention.

REV. NEWTON PINCKNEY WALKER was born in Spartanburg County, S.C., November 29th, 1816, He, like others who have achieved success, was born poor, and was beset in his boyhood days by all the drawbacks inseparable from his adverse surroundings. There were struggles, to be made, there were peculiar difficulties in the way of his success that he had to overcome; but the faithful love and labor in the great

Rev. N. P. Walker

cause for afflicted humanity has had its reward, for to-day the Institution for the Deaf and Blind stands as a monumental record of his triumph. His wife had some deaf relatives, and becoming interested in these, he determined to make an effort to do something for the amelioration of their condition. Hence he visited, as already stated, the then little school for the deaf, located at Cave Spring, Ga., in a log cabin, to familiarize himself with the methods of instructing the deaf, to enable him to perform a great work which was before him. But few men in so short a time have accomplished a more humane and a more Christian work.

Mr. Richard C. Springs, of York County, S.C., a graduate of the New York School for the Deaf, was employed by Mr. Walker as his first assistant teacher. In 1855 he secured the services of Professor James S. Henderson, a graduate of the Tennessee School for the Blind, and opened a department for the blind with Professor Henderson as Principal. Professor J. M. Hughston, who was one of the first graduates of this school, was for many years prominently associated with the school.

Rev. N. P. Walker, the founder of the school, died in 1861. His son. Prof. Newton F. Walker, succeeded his father in the management of the institution. Among the many beautiful tributes to the noble work of this father and son may be read the account given in the *Century,* by the Rev. A. W. Moore, which we quote below:

"Rev. N. P. Walker was preeminently a self-made man, a pioneer in the education of the deaf, a close student, clear but advanced in his religious views, and a true philanthropist. In his Annual Report of the institution at the time it was being changed from an individual enterprise to a State school, he says: 'This day, with a soul swelled in thankfulness to Heaven's

God, I point you, my countrymen, to this institution as an offering of my life to the State which gave me birth.'

"Professor Newton F. Walker, eldest son of Rev. N. P. Walker, is the present superintendent of the South Carolina Institution for the education of the deaf and "blind. Having filled in succession every office in said institution, from clerk in the office to that of superintendent, he is eminently qualified for the work, as is evidenced by his successful management of the school in all its details.

"This school might well be termed the Walker School, being founded by the present superintendent and principally under the management of the subject of this sketch since the death of its founder. Few schools of its kind have encountered so many and so great difficulties, but Professor Walker has by his good sense and judgment overcome them, and to-day may be congratulated in that he presents his State an institution of which she may well be proud. As his "father left him as a legacy to the educational interests of the deaf and blind of South Carolina, so he has fitted two sons for the same work, and promises in them to leave a legacy to the educational interests of the deaf of the United States.

Prof. N. F. Walker.

"PROFESSOR HORACE EPPES WALKER, the eldest son of Professor N. F Walker, after graduating from the South Carolina University with the degree of A. B., in 1887, accepted an offer to become a teacher in the Missouri School for the Deaf, and by close application to his work, has risen to the head of his profession as a teacher of the highest class in that institution.

"PROFESSOR ALBERT H. WALKER, the second son of Professor N. F. Walker, since his graduation from the South Carolina University, with the degree of A.B., in 1889, has been teaching in the Texas School for the Deaf (Austin), and bids fair to make his mark in his chosen profession."

The South Carolina Institution for the Deaf and the Blind has become the pride of the State, receiving yearly by the legislature an appropriation, which is done in a spirit of most cheerful benefaction. "The thorough work that is being done by the institution from year to year in opening sources of enjoyment to the deaf and blind, and in preparing numbers of these unfortunates for useful and happy lives, is appreciated by the people everywhere. The gifted. God-fearing founder builded more wisely than he dreamed."

The public school system and the facilities provided for public school education have all the while been on the increase since the system was first organized in 1870.

According to the last annual report (1898) of Mr. B. B. Chapman, County Superintendent of Education for Spartanburg County (exclusive of that portion of said county cut off into Cherokee county), we find the following statement:

Valuation of taxable property...$10,206,399 00
The valuation for present year in office of county auditor shows
....11,013,841 00
Enrollment of pupils — white...9,535
Enrollment of pupils — colored..5,172
    Total..14,707
Number of teachers employed — white...173
Number of teachers employed — colored..72
    Total..245
Number of schoolhouses...104
Number of school districts..60
Amount of public school funds, 3 mills and polls............................$45,200 00
Length of school session...5 months

The more prominent public schools [2] of the county are: The Spartanburg City Graded Schools, Reidville Female College and Male High School, Wofford Graded School, Fair Forest, Clifton, Pacolet Mills, Pacolet, Inman, Landrumj Campobello, Welford Graded, Cross Anchor, New Prospect, Boiling Springs, Cowpens, Philadelphia, Glenn Springs, Disputanta, Rural, Academy, Duncan, Holly Springs, Oakland, Hampton, Enoree, Bellevue, Center Point, Rich Hill, Glendale, Whitney, Cavins, Liberty, Carlisle and Woodruff.

The Gaffney High School has been in successful operation for twenty years or more, under Professors Wm. S. McArthur, R. M. Sams and others. The academy at the same place, taught by Professors Dargan, Surratt and others, has also had the reputation of being a good school.

The Legislature of South Carolina has from time to time amended the school law by eliminating objectionable features and inserting others adapted to the needs of the people.

There is now a public school within easy reach of every family in Spartanburg County, with a constantly increasing number of commodious schoolhouses of modern build, and supplied with modern and improved school apparatus.

The standard of common school education has been greatly raised; a higher standard is required of teachers, until now many of the public schools give the pupils not only a practical business education, but prepare them for the freshman class in college.

The average length of session for the whole county is about five months, and quite a number of schools are supplementing by local tax and run nine months in the year.

The public school has become a popular institution and indispensable in the educating of the masses of the people. Mr. Chapman was first elected School Commissioner for Spartanburg County in 1876. In 1877 his first annual report shows that there were enrolled in the schools of the county

6,543 pupils. The report for 1898 shows a gain of 8,264 over said report. The report for the present year (1900) will exceed that by at least 1,000, making a grand total of about 16,000 children enrolled in the public schools.

The annual report of taxable property for school purposes for 1898 shows an increase over the report for 1897 of over $5,000,000. With the continued increase of taxable property, with the rapid upbuilding and growth of our educational institutions, and the general interest which is now being manifested in the cause of education, we are scarcely able to grasp what is destined to be the future greatness and importance of Spartanburg County.

[1] See "Colonial and Revolutionary History of Upper South Carolina," pp. 110 and 135.
[2] The present graded school building on Magnolia Street is the first building erected specifically for graded school purposes in the State outside of Charleston.

Chapter Seven - A General Review of the Progress of the Christian Religion in Spartanburg County, During the 19th Century

In searching the pages of history as to the spread of the Christian religion in Spartanburg County during the 19th century, the first revival occurring, which we find recorded, as attracting special interest was within the bounds of the Nazareth (Presbyterian) Church, which was held under the auspices of the Second Presbytery of South Carolina. The precise place of this meeting is said to have been at Poplar Springs, and it made its remarkable appearance Friday, July 2d, 1802. It is stated that while the District of Spartanburg contained at that time no less than twelve thousand souls, there were at the meeting of this Presbytery some four or five thousand people, mainly from the districts of Union, York, Laurens and Greenville, but there were also members attending from the districts of Pendleton, Abbeville, Chester and Newberry, and some from the counties of Greene, Jackson, Elbert and Franklin, in the State of Georgia.

This great meeting and revival was attended and participated in by not only Presbyterians, but by Baptists and Methodists as well, and was conducted on the old camp-meeting style, and the camp was pitched in a beautiful grove on one of the branches of the Tyger River, "and being" says a writer, "in a vale, which lay between two hills, gently inclining towards each other and very suitably adapted for this purpose."

This interesting occasion was attended by thirteen Presbyterian preachers, viz.: Messrs. Simpson, Cummins, Davis, Cunningham, Wilson, Waddel, Williamson, Brown, Kenedy, Gilleland Sr., McElhaney, Dixon, Gilleland Jr., and quite a number of Methodists and Baptists.

The most interesting account of this great revival of religion in our county, we find contained in a letter written by Ebenezer H. Cummins, dated "Abbeville, S.C., July 7th, 1802" (nearly 98 years ago), which the reader will find in full by referring to Howe's History of the Presbyterian Church of South Carolina, Vol. 11.

Says this writer:

"I have just returned from Nazareth, where I have seen and heard things which no tongue can tell, no pen can paint, no language can describe, or of which no man can have a just conception until he has seen, heard and felt." After describing the services of the first day, which was taken up in encampment until 2 o'clock, the writer goes on to further say, that "the evening was spent in singing and prayer alternately. About sundown the people were dismissed to their respective tents. By this time the countenances of all began to be shaded by the clouds of solemnity and to assume a very serious aspect. At 10 o'clock two young men were lying speechless, motionless and sometimes to all appearance, except in the mere act of breathing, dead. Before day five others were down. These I did not see. The whole night was employed in reading and commenting upon the Word of God; and also in singing, praying and exhorting; scarcely had the light of the morning sun dawned upon the people ere they were engaged in what we call family worship, the adjacent tents collecting in groups here and there all around the whole line. The (central) place of worship was early repaired to, by a numerous throng. Divine service commenced at eight, by one of the Methodist brethren, whom I do not recollect. He was followed by the Rev. Wm. Shackelford, of the Baptist profession. Singing, praying and exhorting, by the Presbyterian clergymen continued until two o'clock, when .an intermission of some minutes was granted that the people might refresh themselves with water, etc. By this time the audience became so numerous that it was impossible for all to crowd near enough to hear our speaker, although the ground rising above the stage, theatrically, afforded aid to the voice. Hence the assembly divided, and afterwards preaching was performed at two stages." It would consume too much time and space to recount here, as described, all scenes that transpired at this great revival meeting and the great power, force and effect of the preaching to the vast multitude assembled, the grace imparted, and the great spiritual good resulting therefrom.

The same writer, in closing his account of this great meeting, states further, as follows:

"I cannot but say that the parting was one of the most moving and affecting scenes which presented itself throughout the whole. Families, who had never seen each other until they met on the ground, would pour forth in tears of sympathy like streams of waters; many friendships were formed and many attachments contracted which, although the persons may never meet again, shall never be dissolved. Not one quarter of an hour before I mounted my horse to come away, I saw one of the most beautiful sights which ever mortal beheld. It would not only have afforded pleasure to the plainest observer, but the profoundest philosopher would have found it food for imagination. The case to which I allude was the exercise of Miss Dean, [1] one of the three sisters who fell near the close of the work. Her reflections presented mostly objects of pleasure to her view. But sometimes, for the space of a minute, she would lose them, the consequence of which was painful distress. By the very features of her face I could see the afflictive sensations approached as plain as I ever saw the sun's light obscured by the overpassing clouds. In her happy moments she awakened in my recollection Milton's lovely picture of Eve when in a state of innocence."

Says the same writer, further:

"Another extraordinary case occurred at the very moment of departure. Two young men disputing, one for, the other against, the work, referred their contest to a clergyman of respectability, who happened to be passing that way. He immediately took hold of the hand of the unbeliever, and thus addressed him: 'If you were in your heart's desire to wait on the means of grace, God would show you the truth. You may expect mercy to visit you; but remember, my hand for it, it will cost you something; a stroke would now come at a successless hour.' Scarcely had the words dropped from his lips, when a man on the ground pleading for an interest in the Kingdom of Heaven, and begging pardon of God for dishonoring him and the cause of religion through unbelief. I understood the man to be a pious man and his hesitations of a religious and conscientious kind. The other men who had been in the crowd, where many had been lying under the operations of the work, attempted to run off. One, leaving his hat in haste, ran about twenty or thirty paces and fell on his face. His shrieks declared the terrors of anguish under which he labored. The other ran a different course about fifty yards and fell."

Says the same writer, further:

"The number of those stricken could not be ascertained, but I believe it to be much greater than any one would conceive. On Sabbath night, about twelve or one o'clock, I stood alone on a spot whence I could see and hear all over the camp, and found that the work was not confined to one, two or three places, but overspread the whole field, and in some large crowds the ground appeared almost covered. In the course of one single prayer, of duration of about ten minutes, twelve persons fell to the ground, the majority of whom declared, in terms audible and explicit, that they never prayed before."

How long the annual camp-meeting continued under the auspices of the Second Presbytery of South Carolina, we are not advised; but as the Presbytery met from year to year in other sections within its bounds, it is reasonable to suppose, from the good results already attained, that they were continued for many years.

In Logan's "History of the Broad River" and "King's Mountain" Associations, and in Griffith's "Life of Landrum," we have accounts of a great revival of religion in 1831, Says the latter writer:

"In August, 1831, the Saluda Association convened with the Brushy Creek church, eight miles from Greenville C.H., and during the meeting there began a revival of religion, which for extent and duration has hardly a parallel in the history of revivals.

"Several circumstances connected with the beginning of this revival are worthy of notice. One was the death of Rev, Lewis Rector, which took place a short time before the commencement. Lewis Rector was a man far ahead of the age in which he lived. It is said that he had the hillsides of his farm ditched thirty years before hillside ditching became generally known and practiced in his part of the country. He was a man of powerful intellect and unquestionable piety. He had preached in the section of country lying along the base of the Blue Ridge and extending as far south as the counties of Laurens, Newberry and Union, with all the powers of his great mind and with all the fervor of his warm, devoted heart, ever since about the year 1800; but to those who judged by the immediate fruits, his preaching had seemed almost in vain, yet the good old man, strong still in the faith, looked out into the unexplored future, and just before he died, cried out as if filled with a spirit of prophecy: 'A great revival of religion is near at hand. I have labored and prayed for it, but I shall not live to see it.' As Moses from the top of Pisgah looked over upon the sweet fields of Canaan, so, from the last mount of earthly affliction, Lewis Rector caught a sight of the coming harvest.

"Another circumstance connected with the beginning of this revival, was a strange phenomenon in nature. The rays of the sun were dimmed by a dark spot on his disk, visible to the natural eye, and men who were not alarmed felt humbled, as under the finger of God, when they saw the pale, sombre hue that rested on the whole face of creation. The preachers, who were at that time meeting at Brushy Creek, eager to lay hold of every means adapted to the awakening and humbling of sinners, made happy and forcible allusions to the surrounding scene. Several preachers were there from Georgia, who had recently been in a great revival at home, and all things being seemingly ready, the work began. Landrum was then a young man and a stranger. But he was appointed to preach, and he did preach with a power that astonished his hearers, and caused the most hardened sinners to tremble. The meeting closed on the fourth day, but the revival extended to other parts of the country and continued with little or no abatement for three years. During these years men and women rode on horseback fifteen, twenty, and frequently as far as twenty-five miles, to hear the gospel preached; the preachers went from house to house, preached from stands in the woods, and often when these rude accommodations were wanting, stood under the spreading oak by the roadside and 'reasoned of righteousness, temperance and judgment to come.' It is difficult now to state the precise result of this revival. Within an area of twenty-five miles square, thirteen new churches were formed, while the old ones were filled to overflowing. It is safe to estimate that during the whole period there were added to these churches between two and three thousand souls. Nor was the great work confined to the ignorant and excitable; the best material in the country was gathered into the folds of the church and a new era dawned upon the Baptists of Upper Carolina."

Says the same writer further (see Griffith's "Life of Landrum," page 79):

"In the year 1831 Landrum and others began to preach in the town of Spartanburg. Spartanburg now (1882) numbers between five and six thousand inhabitants and boasts of its complement of churches, schools and colleges, but at that time there were but three Baptists out of a population of a thousand or fifteen hundred, in the whole town. One account says there was but one professor of religion, and that lady was upwards of seventy years of age. [2] But Mr. James Harris and wife, who still survive, were members of the Baptist Church at that time, and there were probably a few others of other denominations scattered over the town. But there was not a single house of worship and no church organization of any kind. If there were more than the number stated, pledged to the service of Jesus Christ, they were hidden away in the multitude not to be known by their fruits. How the people spent their Sabbaths with no 'Church-going bell' to summon them to worship; what were the influences brought to bear upon the young; what was the character of the amusements and employments of a thousand people in the absence of Sunday-schools, benevolent societies and all religious influences, we are left only to imagine.

"But the influence of the revival started at Brushy Creek soon began to be felt, not definitely at first, but vaguely and mysteriously. The manifestations were allied to those of presentiment — that unaccountable feeling, which sometimes weighs heavily upon the heart and which, men say, heralds the approach of mighty events. An observer would have been struck at first with an air of restlessness, worn by those he met; he would have seen that restlessness then settle into a deep solemnity, pervading the entire community, and he would have sought in vain for the cause of any outward circumstances or condition. It was the troubling of the waters of the pool of Bethesda by the angel of God.

"When Landrum first began to visit the town he preached from the judge's stand in the Court House; afterward he stood under the branches of a great oak near by and preached to large congregations, so uncomfortably situated that nothing but the intense interest of the occasions could have held them together. So thrilling were the scenes that transpired here, that the spot became enshrined in the hearts of the people, and some were known to shed tears when they visited it many years after the scenes by which it was hallowed had passed away. Samuel Gibson and Thomas Ray, of the Baptist, Michael Dickson, of the Presbyterian, and Charles Smith of the Methodist Church, all took part in these meetings under the oak, and their labors laid the foundations of the present Baptist, Methodist and Presbyterian churches of Spartanburg.

"At one time, too, during the year 1832, Rev. John Watts, of the Methodist Church, and Rev. John G. Landrum, held a joint meeting in the Court House at which meeting twenty-two persons united with the Baptists, and a considerable number with the Methodists. The preachers would alternately give opportunities for converts to unite with the denominations of their choice and all worked together in perfect harmony."

The Rev. John Watts was living in Greenville County (1882), near Sandy Flat. During this year the writer received a letter from his daughter, Miss Sallie Watts. In referring to her father, who was then bowed down with age and infirmities, she wrote: "Even the state of the revival in Spartanburg has escaped my father's memory. However, the fact exists clearly in his mind that the Rev. John G. Landrum joined Rev. Armstrong, Rev. Dr. Lewis and himself on the second or third day of the meeting and labored with zeal and power, both on the stand and around the altar."

Many of the converts at the meetings just mentioned went to Mount Zion and Bethlehem, about seven miles from town, and became members of those churches. Among those who connected themselves with the former, were Maj. Hosea J. Dean and Dr. Robert Young.

In our researches we gather further information of the preaching and revival meetings referred to. Under the head of "Kentucky Correspondence" to the *Spartan,* by Rev. Joseph Cottrell, we find the following paragraph:

"I have been to church since writing the above, and now, before dinner call, I'll pen a little mention of names of preachers, who, in Spartanburg, ministered Ho us boys' effectively. Bond English, Gamewell, J. W. Wheeler, Durant, Walker (father of Charlie), and Clough Beard were the Methodists; Holmes, the Presbyterian; Landrum and the Drs. Curtis from Limestone Springs, Baptists. These were the preachers who held sway by the mystic wand of spirit and vocation over the youth of the town."

Among the material which we have preserved, to form a part of the contents of this volume, is an old letter written by Samuel F. Hill' to Miss Elizabeth Wright, dated "Carrolton, Pickens county, Ala., August 21st, 1874." After Miss Wright had been dead about a dozen years, the letter referred to was found among her papers and published in the *Spartan.* Mr. Hill writes as follows:

"My Dear Old Friend and Sister:

"Many a day has passed since last I saw you, and many a change has occurred. The older citizens have nearly all passed away, and many of the young. Little did I think when I gave you the parting hand, at Mr. Joseph Michals', that you would ever recover; neither did Dr. Vernon, with whom I visited you, but God in his great wisdom has spared you thirty-four years longer, no doubt, for a wise and good purpose.

"Thousands upon thousands of times have I thought of the little church as it started, and our little prayer-meeting as it was in 1838, when there were but yourself and I to pray, and the great principal attendants were Mrs. Gault and some of her family and Mrs. Rowland and some of hers, the whole company comprising about eight or ten persons. Yet these prayer-meetings were meetings of great interest. The next year the Bros. Rowley came and we had the first great ingathering. Bros. Bobo, Henry, D. W. Moore, and many others joined the church. How oft have I referred to that good meeting with pleasant reflection, and never had I stronger faith than at that meeting.

"I have never forgotten the kind visit you made me when I first went to Spartanburg a boy; when you, learning that I was a member of the church, hunted me up at Mr. Brem's and gave me kind advice. A member of the church of any name was hard to find, there being at that time (1834) only six Baptists, three

Methodists and one Presbyterian in the place. I was told that if I stayed there twelvemonths I would be wrecked and, for fear, I made no associates for over twelve months, and there being no church and but little preaching my Sabbaths were Sabbaths of solitude, but not alone, for in my solitary hours I had frequent visits from the Great Head of the church, and I was permitted to hold sweet communion with my Heavenly Father. I have had frequent occasion to refer to that year as one of the happiest I ever spent, and I attributed, it to my closer walk with God, my frequent communion with Him who always blesses in all our associations with Him.

"I would like to see the church of which I was the first class leader, and talk" with one of its first members. What a change has taken place since then. I look back at that meeting of 1839, and I think of old Brother Hutchings, John Watts, Samuel Armstrong, Joseph Moore and others of the Methodist church, and John G. Landrum, Dr. Lewis and others of the Baptist church, and the great interest manifested, the many tender emotions manifested by almost every one, and my heart swells with gratitude to God. I can see in my imagination Sister Moore, who was the first convert, clapping her hands, and then calling for her husband. It is but yesterday in my imagination.

"And that long love-feast, when so many told the dealings of God with their hearts.

"There are many interesting recollections connected with that good meeting. I shall never forget my Sabbath-school pupil, John Walker, who professed at that meeting and died the next year.

"I hope to hear from you, if you can possibly write, and if we never meet on earth, that we will meet in the Haven of rest. Give my kindest regards to any of the old citizens who may be still living in the place.

"I am your friend and brother,

"Samuel F. Hill."

The late David W. Moore, the party referred to in the above, once related to the writer the circumstances of this revival meeting, of its spirituality, and the deep conviction of sin which overcame him. He was at the time engaged in the saloon business (possibly in connection with the grocery business, as was the case in many instances at that time) in a frame building which stood almost opposite the carriage manufacturing establishment of Fowler & Robinson and very near where the *Herald* office was located. He stated that he was so thoroughly convinced of the sin and, the sinfulness of the business in which he was engaged, that he determined at once to put an end to the same. In the building referred to, he showed the writer a window through which he one night emptied the entire contents of spirituous liquors in his establishment, saving, only some wine; to be used for sacramental purposes,, fearing lest, when the morning came, he would be over-persuaded by his old customers for the morning dram, as he expressed it.

Mr. Moore, having been converted to the principles of the Christian religion, ever afterwards remained true and faithful, and the subject of religion was always his happiest theme.

The great revivals in the Methodist Church at Spartanburg referred to, in which Mr. Moore and others were converted to the Christian religion, were largely due to "bread which had been cast upon the waters" by a few pioneer ministers of this faith and order who traveled through the present county of Spartanburg a few years before. It will be remembered that the organization of Methodism occurred in Baltimore during the year 1784 — only one year before said county was laid out and organized — and then spread over the Southern States reaching South Carolina and Georgia in 1785; and it was some time during that year or the year following that Bishop Asbury passed through Upper South Carolina, and doubtless through Spartanburg District to Salisbury, N.C. In Shipp's "History of Methodism," it is stated that John Turwell and Henry Willis were sent to South Carolina to form the circuits in the lower and upper portions of said State, and were assisted in so doing by James Foster, especially in forming the Broad River circuit in 1786, which included Spartanburg District (now county). Stephen Johnson also traveled that circuit in that year with Mr. Foster. In 1787 Richard Ivey, John Mason and Thos. Davis were on the circuit, including Spartanburg, and were men of solid parts and of earnest piety who never thought of growing rich by the Gospel — their sole purpose being to grow rich in grace and in saving souls to Christ, thus promoting and advancing the principles of their Church and society.

"In the year 1752 there was born in Pennsylvania a daughter to Quaker parents, who, moving to Spartanburg District with that child, wrought a great influence for good in that community and ultimately for the whole district. Being brought up under the example and religious influence of that noted and worthy people, the Quakers, and educated in the best schools of that day, she was prepared to receive the Gospel from the mouths of John Mason and Thomas Davis in 1787, whom she regarded as the proper exponents of the teachings of that Gospel and of her own opinions. They believed that Gospel taught a sound conversion, 'justification by faith,' and she never rested until she attained that true and great position. Shipp's History of Methodism says: 'She traveled for fifteen years the way to Zion alone, her husband and children not giving heed to the teachings of the Gospel and the divine impressions that the Good Spirit always makes, in connection with that Gospel.' In the year 1802, however, they were awakened and converted and brought into the Methodist Church, under the preaching of Lewis Meyers and George Dougherty. That good woman was Martha Lewellyn, the wife of Joseph Wofford, and the mother of Rev. Benjamin Wofford, the liberal founder of Wofford College, in the growing city of his native district of Spartanburg, S.C. That good woman after living to a ripe old age in prayer and usefulness, went to Heaven on the 24th of March, 1826, leaving a gracious influence behind her. She being dead still speaks through her children and grand and great-grandchildren, to her Church and people of her native county. Wofford College, the gift of her noble son, the Rev. Benjamin Wofford, is like, in its gracious influence of a proper religious education, its own stream, the beautiful and fertile Pacolet rising in the mountains not far away and growing larger as it rolls on and making every hill and valley to rejoice that it touches in its onward course to the eternal beyond." [3] The Wofford family has exerted and still exerts a good influence upon their native county.

"There are others — preachers and laymen of the Methodist Church — within the bounds of Spartanburg District that took up the work and carried it on in their own way and with its irresistible doctrines until, with the help of other denominations, who are likely to take the present large and progressive county of Spartanburg for Christ in a saving, personal and experimental religion. Some of the names of the ministers on the rolls of the past and worthy of perpetuation are the Mullinaxes, [4] the Gramlings (Andrew and John), Postells, Capers, Wheeler, Hutchings, Samuel Armstrong. David Drummond, Donelly, Potter, Rev. Henry Wood (who gave rise to the name *Wood's Chapel*) John Watts, Ben Wofford, and others not so prominent whose names we cannot now gather. The laymen, besides the Woffords, Tuckers, Simpson Bobo, Tucks, John Bishop, Adam Gramling, Mack Tinsley, Waters, Fingers, Fosters, Jas. H. Carlisle, and a great host who still live, are pressing on the victories of the Cross in their children — and children's children. In later days Barnett, Dr. Whiteford Smith, James F. Smith, Wightman, Shipp, Gamewell, Herbert, the Moods, Walkers (Charles and Alexander), the Boyds, J. M. Carlisle, and a great many others — some of whom have gone to receive their reward and others on the way."

The names of the churches over which these preachers ministered and to which these leading laymen belonged in the past are Shiloh, Foster's Meeting House, the two Antiochs, Spartanburg, Tabernacle, Chapel, Liberty, and Cannon's, where is now, and has been for nearly eighty years, the famous camp-meeting ground, the promoter of much of the spread of Methodism and vital piety. Besides these, we would also mention Fingerville, Lebanon, Rocky Mount, Hebron, Walnut Grove, Zoar and Bivingsville. The campmeetings besides Cannon's were at Shiloh, Bird Mountain (near Landrum), one near Lebanon Church, one near Pacolet, and one near Fingerville. All these reflected an influence for great good, but none exist now except Cannon's, and but few in the State, mostly in the low country.

The great Scotch preacher, Dr. Chalmers, said of Methodism, "It is Christianity in earnest"; and it deserves to prevail, with all true religion, as it always will in Spartanburg County.

In the beginning of the nineteenth century we estimate that there were about five hundred persons professing the Christian religion in the original county of Spartanburg. The following brief statistics will show about the present status of the different denominations in said county:

Whites

Baptist — *Broad River Association.*
Official report 1899.
Cedar Spring 208, Bethesda 63, Zion Hill 121, Cowpens 143, Pacolet (No. 2) 78, Glendale 164, Clifton 310, Converse 77, Brown's Chapel 156, Shiloh 69, Cooley Spring 84, State Line 126, Buck Creek 187, Piedmont 232, Arrowwood 333, Mountain View 40. 2,391
Approximate increase since Aug. 26, 1899 200
Cherokee county (Spartanburg portion of same):
Goucher's Creek 230, Corinth 206, First Gaffney 325, Second Gaffney 240, Limestone 70, Providence 277, Macedonia 240, Grassy Pond 200, New Pleasant 122, Beaverdam 66, Cherokee Creek 131 - 2,107-4,698

Spartanburg Association
Statistical report August 27, 1899, exclusive of Tryon (N.C.) Church 7,111
Approximated increase since said date — 200-7,311
Total 12,009
Methodist —
Exclusive of Cherokee county 4,650
(Reported by Rev. W. P. Meadows, P.E., under date May 31, 1899.)
Probable increase since said date 150

Cherokee County
Gaffney No. 1: 225
Gaffney No 2: 200
Grassy Pond: 40-5,265
Presbyterian —
Report of 89th Session of Enoree Presbytery, April 4th and 6th, 1899:
Nazareth 76, North Pacolet 12, Spartanburg 354, Mt. Calvary 107, Antioch 61, Woodruff 67, Glenn's Spring 63, Welford 39, Center Point 68, Pacolet 26, Clifton 40, Oakland 11, Tucapau 43, Becca 13, Spartan Mill 100, Whitney 16, Mountain Shoals 42, Trough Shoals 45--1,173
Gaffney Church added 50
Approximated increase since April, '99 -50-1,283
Episcopal —
Spartanburg 150, Gaffney 20, Glenn's Spring 30; total 200
A. R. Presbyterian —
Woodruff 42, Welford 24; total 66
Roman Catholic —
Spartanburg 165, Gaffney 8; total 173

Colored

Baptist —
Spartanburg County Association, official report September 8, 1898 — total 155

Approximated increase since said date 100

Tyger River Association, official report August 17, 1899 — total 1,524

Approximate increase since said date 76 - 2,285

Methodist — Approximated entire membership in original county of Spartanburg — total 1,500

Presbyterian — Approximated 250

Recapitulation

White —

    Baptist 12,009

    Methodist 5,265

    Presbyterian 1283

    Episcopal 200

    A. R. Presbyterian.._ 66

    Roman Catholic 173 — 18,996

Colored —

    Baptist _ 2,285

    Methodist.. 1,500

    Presbyterian. 250 — 4,035

      Grand total — 23,031

Deduct supposed number at beginning of 19th century, 500

Approximated increase during 19th century, 22,531

Note. — During the first half of the nineteenth century the emigration from Spartanburg County to other States largely exceeded the immigration and almost the increase of population during the same time, but these conditions have been reversed during the latter half of said century.

[1] This lady afterwards became the wife of "Sheriff Sam" Miller, and the mother of General Joel W. and Dr. Pinckney Miller, both well-known and popular citizens of Spartanburg County.

[2] The person referred to here was Mrs. Rebecca Earle, wife of Col. John Earle, and grandmother of the late Hon. John Earle Bomar. She was married twice; her first husband being Col. John Wood, who was murdered by "Bloody Bill" Cunningham and his band, for an account of which the reader is referred to the "Colonial and Revolutionary History of Upper South Carolina," published by the writer.

[3] The writer is indebted to Rev. James F. Smith, Spartanburg, S.C., for information transmitted herein relating to the introduction and spread of Methodism in Spartanburg County.

[4] At the old Foster's meeting-house place, near Fair Forest, S.C., is to be found the grave of Rev. John Mullinax. The following is the inscription on his tomb:

"Sacred to the memory of Rev. John Mullinax, who was born July 25th, 1769, and died July 14th, 1836, aged 66 years, 11 months and 10 days.

"For the last 33 years of his life he was a devoted herald of the Cross in the Methodist Episcopal Church, and died in the hope of a joyful Resurrection. 'Blessed are the dead which die in the Lord from henceforth; yea, saith the Spirit, that they may rest from their labors; and their works do follow them,'

"The gracious Savior smiles and says well done.
Enter my rest, my faithful servant thou;
The strife is o'er, thou hast the victory won.
No sin nor sorrow can disturb thee now."

His wife lies buried beside him. She was a sister of Rev. Benjamin Wofford, founder of Wofford College. The following is the inscription on her tomb: "In memory of Rebecca Mullinax, born August 4th, 1774. Died in great peace July 26th, 1858. Having lived over 50 years in the communion of the M. E. Church. Her record is on high."

Chapter Eight - A General Review of the Progress of Temperance in Spartanburg County from Time to Time

From the record before us, we notice that the first temperance society organized in South Carolina was on the call of a meeting of sundry citizens of Columbia on the 17th of July, 1829. Several gentlemen of prominence addressed the meeting, pointing out the evils of intemperance and the measures which had been adopted in different parts of the Union to check its alarming ravages.

Two committees were appointed at this meeting, one consisting of three members to draft a constitution for a temperance society, and another consisting of seven members to report as to the influence of intemperance on the health, the morals and prosperity of the country.

We notice that a second meeting of this society was held on the 8th of October of the same year (1829), at which the committees previously appointed made their reports. (See Report Permanent Temperance Documents, Vol. I, page 10.) A third meeting of the same society was held on the 12th of the same month, at which permanent officers were elected, Colonel Thomas Taylor being chosen President.

From the documents before us, we find no further record of the proceedings of this society outside of the published reports of the committees referred to. How long it remained organized for work in the good cause in which it was engaged we are unable to determine, but it may have served a "stepping stone," as it were, to the organization of other temperance societies in the several districts comprising our State.

From Griffith's "Life of Landrum" we find record of the first movement looking to the formation of a temperance society in Spartanburg district. Says this writer:

"The first public advocates of the temperance cause in Spartanburg were Hon. Simpson Bobo, Major H. J. Dean and Dr. Young, father of General P. M. B. Young of Georgia. The first named of these is still living (1883), full of days and honors; the other two have long since passed away.

"It was about the year 1830, when these three men, whose souls were stirred by the ravages that intemperance was making upon society, and whose hearts were sickened by the scenes of debauchery to be witnessed, especially on public days, at Spartanburg, came together, determined to do something toward stemming the mighty torrent and abating the awful scourge. After a consultation, they concluded to call a public meeting in the court-house, without making known the object for which such meeting was to be held. Accordingly notices of such meeting were posted on the street corners and on the highways, and when the day arrived a considerable crowd assembled in the court-house, eager to know what was to be done. By a pre-concerted arrangement, a certain prominent citizen, known to be a constant dram-drinker, was called to the chair. The object of the meeting was then stated by one of the trio to be the organization of a temperance society, and while the speaker had the floor he made a strong speech against the evils everywhere apparent, and called upon all good citizens to unite in one effort for their abatement. Then, like those who were struck dumb by the announcement, 'he that is without sin should cast the first stone,' the audience began to disperse. They went out one by one, chairman and all, until only four men were left to organize the society, the three already named and one other. But the movers in the cause were not discouraged. They completed the organization — held the ground already gained, though it seemed hardly worth holding — and vowed they would wage unceasing war against the gigantic evil that was nursing crime and preying upon the vitals of society. They boldly raised the temperance banner in Spartanburg and called upon the people of the county to rally beneath its folds. The first to respond to the call were Major John Stroble, Dr. John W. Lewis and Rev. John G. Landrum. By these additions the little band was doubled in number, and greatly strengthened in intellectual and moral power. The crusade began in earnest."

The society as thus organized was known as the *Spartanburg Village Temperance Society*.

Soon after the death of Rev. J. G. Landrum (January, 1882) the writer received a letter from the late Hon. Simpson Bobo, in which, among other things, he stated as follows:

"Very early in life, in 1830, I think, he (John G. Landrum) joined the first temperance society ever formed in the county, and was to his death a noble and consistent worker in the temperance cause, going far and near to advance it and to break up the drinking habits of the people. To show the magnitude of the efforts of him and his colaborers in the temperance cause, in 1843 there were nearly three thousand persons in the county pledged to total abstinence. When Mr. Landrum first came among us dram-drinking was common with members of the church, so much so that it was a matter of constant reproach to the church. Treating with whisky at elections by candidates was almost universal. A candidate refusing to do so could not be elected to office. He and his colaborers never ceased to oppose this degrading practice until it was entirely broken up, at least before the public, and no one could be elected to office who was known to indulge in it." (See copy of original letter of Mr. Bobo, Griffith's "Life of J. G. Landrum," p. 72.)

We find further from the documents before us that the first State Temperance Society of South Carolina was organized at a meeting of delegates appointed to attend a convention in Columbia on the third and fourth days of July, 1838, who met on the evening of the third at the Lecture Room of the Baptist church, in that city. Hon. Chan Johnson was called to the chair and G. T. Snowden was appointed secretary. This convention was composed of about thirty members from the districts of Laurens, Newberry, Darlington, Marlborough, Lexington, Abbeville and Richland. The Hon. Job Johnson was elected permanent President, G. T. Snowden Secretary, and Robert Bryce Treasurer — the last named gentleman at that time a resident of Columbia, but in later years a resident of the city of Spartanburg and proprietor of a book -store, where he died about the year 1876, honored and respected by all as a sincere advocate and worker in the cause of religion and temperance.

At this convention, which organized as stated, The State Temperance Society of South Carolina, a constitution was framed and adopted. The committee which prepared the same, reported the following:

"The promotion of the temperance cause is intimately connected with the permanence of our free institutions, with domestic comfort, with the happiness of the human family and with the interests of the Redeemer's Kingdom. It devolves, therefore, on those who would be the benefactors of mankind, to aid in spreading its benign influences over their own country and the world, by the exertion of kind and moral influence and united public principle."

The first annual meeting of the State Temperance Society met in the Lecture Room of the Baptist church, at Columbia, on Wednesday night, 28th of November, 1838. There were present at this meeting about sixteen members, representing societies from the districts of Laurens, Newberry, Darlington, Lexington, Richland, Williamsburgh, Kershaw, Charleston and Anderson.

Reports and communications from auxiliary societies and others requesting to become auxiliary, addressed to the Corresponding Secretary, were read, and among the latter were three from temperance societies organized in the district of Spartanburg, named as follows: *Young Men's Society of Spartanburg, Nazareth Temperance Society* and *Jefferson Temperance Society.*

The second annual meeting of the South Carolina State Temperance Society met in the Lecture Room of the Presbyterian church, at Columbia, on Thursday, 5th of December, 1839. There were present about nineteen members from several of the districts in the State, among whom was the Hon. Hosea J, Dean, representing the *Spartanburg Village Temperance Society.*

The third annual meeting of the South Carolina Temperance Society met at the Lecture Room of the Presbyterian church, in Columbia, on Thursday, December 3d, 1840, only ten members being present, and among them was the Hon. Hosea J. Dean, who again represented the *Spartanburg Village Temperance Society*, and who was also elected at the same time one of the Vice-Presidents of said society.

The fourth annual meeting of the South Carolina State Temperance Society met at the Baptist Lecture Room in Columbia, on Wednesday, November 24, 1841, which was presided over by the Hon. John Belton O'Neall. Only fourteen members are reported as being present from the different organizations in the State, of which there was no representation from the District of Spartanburg.

The first State Temperance Convention of South Carolina was held at Greenville August 8, 1842, which was in pursuance of a call made by the President of the State Temperance Society. The delegates appointed by the different temperance societies throughout the State assembled at the Methodist Church at 10 o'clock A. M., and after prayer by the Rev. C. C. Pinckney, the Hon. John Belton O'Neall, President of the State Temperance Society, took the chair and appointed J. M. Roberts and E. J. Arthur secretaries of the convention.

The President, after organizing the convention, delivered an eloquent address highly appropriate to the occasion, in which he congratulated the members of the convention upon the favorable circumstances under which they had been permitted to assemble, and the indications with which they were furnished of the success and the prospects of ultimate triumph in the noble enterprise in which they were engaged.

There were present at this convention one hundred and eighty-four delegates from the following districts, viz.: Charleston, Richland, Abbeville, Greenville, Spartanburg, Laurens, Union, Lexington, Chesterfield, Marlborough, Barnwell, Colleton, Edgefield, Pendleton, York, Newberry, Orangeburg, Fairfield, Lancaster, Darlington, Marion and Chester, besides the *Henderson County (N.C.) Temperance Society*, two delegates present, and the *Clayton Total Abstinence Society* of Georgia, one delegate present.

Of the delegates composing this convention, the following was the representation from the District of Spartanburg, viz.:

Spartanburg Village Temperance Society, J. Bomar, Jr., Simpson Bobo and H. J, Dean.

Spartanburg Village Washington Society, A. J. Muir, P. Jordan, J. A. Leland, William B. Seay, G. W. Bomar and Frederick Harley.

Young Men's Temperance Society of Spartanburg District, Thomas O. P. Vernan, J. W. Miller, H. J. Moore, W. W. Anderson, H. M. Anderson, John W. Hoy, James K. Dickson, R. M. Dickson and Samuel Nesbitt.

Bivingsville Total Abstinence Society, James Bivings and John Simpson.

Nazareth Temperance Society, A, G. Campbell and William M. Gowen.

Antioch Temperance Society of Spartanburg District, H. P. Woodruff.

Important resolutions were introduced and passed, among which was one endorsing the Temperance Advocate, the official organ of the State Society, another to prepare an address to the people of the State on the subject of temperance, and another endorsing the formation of a temperance society in the South Carolina College, in order to insure its usefulness.

The following resolutions were passed by the convention declaratory of its principles, viz.:

"1st. That our object is not to force, but to persuade men to be sober.

"2d. That we disclaim, utterly, all sectarian or political combinations and all dependence upon or intention to seek legislative aid in the reformation in which we are engaged."

The published reports by the several committees, as well as the address of the President, are able and interesting, and we regret that we have not space to reproduce them in this brief outline of the proceedings of the convention.

Among other facts contained in the statistical report, it was stated there were about *ninety* temperance societies in the State, of which *fifty* had adopted the total abstinence pledge, *twenty* the Washington pledge, and *twenty* the partial pledge. The number of members belonging to different societies of the State were reported to be *eleven thousand one hundred and sixty-nine,* of whom about *three thousand three hundred* were ladies.

The fifth annual meeting of the State Temperance Society was held in the South Carolina Hall, in Columbia on Wednesday, the 30th November, 1842, the President, Hon. J. B. O'Neall, in the chair. One hundred and forty-one members were present, representing twenty-six districts in the State. The *Spartanburg Washingtonian* Society was represented by Col. E. C. Leitner, John A. Leland and Wm. K. Barkley. Among the proceedings of this society, it was set forth that the *only* object of temperance societies was to improve and direct public opinion, by disseminating such information as will exhibit strongly the great evils flowing from the use of intoxicating drinks, and resolutions were passed earnestly recommending to the district societies that they abstain entirely from all interference with the district police. That such was a subject which the Legislature had wisely entrusted to competent boards of commissioners, etc. Another resolution was passed to the effect that the subject of the license law was one with which temperance societies had nothing to do, except by so improving public opinion as to make the keeping of a drinking-house or the patronizing the same disreputable; and further, a resolution was passed declaring that there exists no connection between the church and temperance societies, and that any attempt to connect the cause of religion with the cause of temperance will be injurious to both.

The second meeting of the State temperance convention was held at Spartanburg court-house on Wednesday, the 2d of August, 1843. This was in accordance with a call made by the president of the State Temperance Society. At ten o'clock on the date referred to, the delegates assembled in the Methodist Church, where, after prayer by the Rev. D. McNeill Turner, the Hon.

John Belton O'Neall, President of the State Temperance Society, took the chair and appointed John S. James and C. J. Elford secretaries of the convention.

The convention was composed of three hundred and twenty-four delegates from South Carolina, and three from North Carolina, making three hundred and twenty-seven in all. Those from South Carolina represented the Districts of Abbeville, Anderson, Charleston, Chester, Chesterfield, Edgefield, Fairfield, Greenville, Kershaw, Lancaster, Laurens, Lexington, Marlborough, Newberry, Orangeburg, Pickens, Richland, Spartanburg, Union, Williamsburgh, and York; and from North Carolina, the *Henderson County Temperance Society* was represented by Gen. B. Edney and James M. Edney and the *Davidson College T. A. Society,* by W. T. Caston.

It may be observed here that this was probably the largest representative body from the various Districts in the State that had ever assembled in the present city of Spartanburg.

Of the various society organizations in the District of Spartanburg, the following were represented in this convention, viz.:

Spartanburg District Temperance Association, Z. C. Cottrel, Wm. B. Seay, Rev. Elias Rogers.

Spartanburg Village Washington Society, Simpson Bobo, J. Bomar, Jr., Rev. Z. L. Holms, Col. E. C. Leitner, A. H. Lancaster, Maj. J. T. Kirby, Dr. J. J. Vernon.

Lawson's Fork Washington Society, Rev. A. Gramling.

Shiloh Washington Society, Reuben Gramling, Adam Gramling,

New Prospect Washington Society, H. Dodd, J. Ezell,. and Rev. P. H. Folker.

Mount Zion Total Abstinence Society, John Chapman, G. Foster, Moses Foster, Rev. H. Hawkins, Rev. J. G. Landrum and B. F. Montgomery.

Boiling Spring Total Abstinence Society, Wm. McBerry, A, Nolen and Lewis J. Patterson.

Trinity Washington Society, James Watson.

Chapel Washington Society, Coleman C. Layton.

Foster's Meeting House Total Abstinence Society, A. G. Brannon and Alfred Shores.

New Hope Washington Society, Lewis Camp and Chesterfield McKinney.

Young Men's Temperance Society of Spartanburg District, D. M. Brice, J. K. Dickson, R. M. Dickson, J. S. Collins, W. W. Anderson, J. W. Miller and T. O. P. Vernon.

Washington Bethlehem Society, Andrew J. Daniel, Aaron Smith and Jehu Wells.

Republican Washington Society, Philip Bruton, J. M. Crook, Jared Drummond, S. M. Drnmmond, D. B. Clayton, R. W. Foster, F. Ward, and J. D. Westmoreland.

Bivingsville Total Abstinence Society, Dr. James Bivings, James D. Bivings, G. B. Brem, Newton Haynes, Wm. Anderson and Birdsong Tollison.

Washington Society of Maberryville, Jefferson Bishop, W. Dodd and D. F. Maberry.

Nazareth Temperance Society, John Stroble, Jr., John Wingo, Samuel Miller, Stephen Lee, S. N. Evins, Thomas B. Collins and John Fielder.

Tuck's School House Temperance Society, Rev. A. Gramling, J. G. Harris, Wm. Tuck.

Zion Temperance Society, Reuben Bryant, Stephen Kirby, and A. W. T. McBride.

Ridgefield Washingtonian Society, Jos. W. Tucker, Col. Harvey Wofford, John Wesley Wofford, Benj. Wofford, and Thomas Young.

Holly Spring Temperance Society, Thomas Ballenger, Ramson Tinsley and Thomas Tucker.

South Pacolet Total Abstinence Society, William Golightly, John Gramling, Andrew P. Gramling and William Stewart.

Mount Pleasant Temperance Society, Wm. L. Hilliard.

After the organization, it is stated, the convention moved in procession, headed by its officers to a beautiful grove near the Walker House [1] where a stand and seats were provided for its accommodation.

It is further stated that "on arriving at the grove, the convention was called to order and addressed by the President, in his peculiarly eloquent and energetic style. He congratulated the friends of temperance on the success of the cause during the past year, and on the increasing interest felt in its behalf throughout the State, manifested in the vast assemblage before him."

Among the resolutions introduced and passed was one to the effect that the success of the past year called for increasing gratitude to God who had so signally blessed the cause of the temperance advocates, and that the same demanded renewed and more vigorous action for the present and coming year. It is further stated that the temperance choir of Spartanburg sang a beautiful and appropriate ode; *air* "Scots wha hae."

The Spartanburg convention remained in session for three successive days, and for a full account of its interesting proceedings, consisting mainly of resolutions, the appointing of committees, reports and appropriate addresses, the reader is referred to "Permanent Temperance Documents," Vol. 1.

The convention, before its adjournment, passed resolutions of thanks to the citizens of Spartanburg Village and its vicinity for the kindness and hospitality which had been extended to its members and to the Spartanburg Village Washington Society for their kindness in preparing a stand and seats for the use of the convention.

The convention also resolved that the thanks of the same be tendered to the President, 'the Hon. J. B. O'Neall, for the able and pleasant manner with which he had presided over their deliberations, and to the Secretaries also for the able and faithful discharge of the arduous duties which devolved upon them.

An ode was sung to the air of "Auld Lang Syne," and after prayer by Rev. D. Humphries, the convention, on motion of Col. J. L. Orr, adjourned until the

Wednesday after the fourth Monday in November following, then to meet in Columbia.

These different organizations of temperance societies served a noble purpose in their day, but like all organizations of a similar character, they *had their day* and in fact at the outbreak of the war between the States, there were few or none in existence in the State of South Carolina.

Some time after the close of said war there were many organizations of the society known as the Good Templars in Spartanburg County and other localities, but these, too, had comparatively a brief existence, and there are none at present in working order known to the writer.

The great work in the temperance cause in Spartanburg County appears to have been transferred to the temperance workers among the Christian women in said county who are interested in staying or arresting the torrent of intemperance yet prevailing as one of the great evils of our land.

The writer is indebted to the Recording Secretary of "Christian Temperance Workers of Spartanburg, S.C.," for the following information (December, 1899): "In one of Miss Francis Willard's tours of the United States, she stopped in Spartanburg, March, 1881. The women met in the room in Central Methodist churchyard, which room had been previously the home of 'Aunt' Betsy Wright, the first Methodist in the town of Spartanburg.

"Miss Willard organized a society of thirty-three members, making Mrs. W. K. Blake President, and Mrs. Mulligan Secretary. There were many plans of work suggested and committees were appointed to carry out the plans, viz.: Scattering temperance tracts in post offices, depots and other public places, visiting the jail, securing space in town papers for temperance extracts, asking ministers of the gospel to preach on temperance, visiting the county parish two or three times a year and carrying a treat in the way of dinner and presents. A Sunday-school was soon organized and a committee appointed to write to the members of the Legislature to vote for temperance measures and further the cause, also to pass a law that scientific temperance and hygiene be taught in public schools. The latter law was passed in 1874. A work among the children outside of Sunday-schools was begun by forming societies called Bands of Hope.

"As years passed on this society increased to 100 and about $100 per year was expended in carrying on the work. Dr. Ben Wofford donated to the society a small plot of land in the upper part of the city. A committee collected a sufficient sum to put up a chapel. A. Sunday-school numbering about sixty scholars has been conducted by Miss Eliza Mulligan and other women every Sunday afternoon since its organization, teaching, temperance truths."

The members of this society worked in harmony and with satisfaction till 1898, when, at the annual State meeting, for sufficient reasons, delegates proposed organization of a Woman's Christian Temperance Union No. 2. A meeting was appointed to organize and elect State officers. The National W. C. T. U. sent a delegate to inform the society that it could not have two organizations in the State. The society therefore withdrew and organized a

State society, calling themselves the *Christian Temperance Workers of South Carolina*. Under this new name they are continuing the same plans of work. Mrs. Carrie Wofford, widow of Dr. Ben Wofford, organized a W. C. T. U. under the auspices of the national organization. There is a wide field of work for both the two societies in the constantly growing city of Spartanburg. Great good has already been accomplished as shown by the annual report of the Christian Temperance Workers. Let us hope that the good work already under way by these societies, with the cooperation of others, may continue from year to year until by their reflecting influence on the rising generations, the long-prevailing, sin-cursed evil of intemperance may be not only stayed, but forever rooted out as one of the destroyers of the human race.

[1] The present residence of Col. Jos Walker is on the original site of the Walker House.

Chapter Nine - A General Review of Political Events, Elections, Appointments, Etc., in Spartanburg District, from the Year 1830 to the Year 1860, Inclusive

In the absence of a newspaper in the district of Spartanburg during the first half century of her existence, it is impossible at this time, except by the perusal of the pages of history in general to appreciate what must have been the political agitations on public issues before the people, during the mentioned period, and to take up a general consideration of all the great political questions, State or National, which have from time to time come before the people of South Carolina, is a matter which is not contemplated in this volume, being solely, as already stated in the outset, a history intending to embrace in a large degree the important events as occurring within the county of Spartanburg.

The first great political agitation affecting the whole people of South Carolina and other Southern States, began with what is known as the Nullification movement, in 1824, which was the result of an imposition of a tariff on certain indispensable articles of import, thereby discriminating in favor of similar articles of manufacture in the New England States. The Southern States at that time being exclusively agricultural, the people of these States felt that such legislation by the National Congress was an outrageous proceeding and hence the stubborn resistance that followed.

It is said that during this year (1824) the anti-tariff feeling was very strong all over the State of South Carolina. There was also about this time a strong feeling against internal improvements springing up all over the State. These two measures, says Governor Perry, first destroyed the National feeling in South Carolina,, which, prior to this, had been one of the strongest Federal States in the Union.

After the passage of the tariff in 1824, there were numerous meetings held in different parts of South Carolina protesting against its injustice and inexpediency.

In 1828, upon the recommendation of the President, John Quincy Adams, a Tariff Act was passed in Congress which was bitterly opposed by the South Carolina delegation. The latter, however, determined, on their return home, after the adjournment of Congress, to call public meetings of their constituents and stir them up in opposition to the act, which was done all over the State.

In the Legislature of South Carolina, which met in 1828, the tariff was discussed for two weeks. This was the beginning of the formation of future factional parties upon which depended the future action of the State. All were opposed to the tariff, but they differed very widely as to the mode of redress. Governor Perry states that from 1828 to the fall of 1830 there was a gradual formation of parties in South Carolina for and against Nullification; that in the winter of 1829 and 1830 Governor Hayne announced the doctrine of Nullification and called it the "Carolina Doctrine," which gave great popularity to the doctrine during the ensuing spring and summer.

In the summer of 1830 the propriety of calling a State convention in South Carolina was discussed by the candidates for the Legislature all over the State. On this question parties were formed for and against, which turned the elections in every district. "Nothing," says Governor Perry, "was advocated beyond the expediency of calling a convention, the question of Nullification being kept in the background." Whatever action the State was to take was dependent on the proposed convention, through which the people were to decide what course of action should be adopted to resist the encroachment of the tariff in South Carolina. This, it is said, was the most prudent and politic course to be pursued by the advocates of Nullification, and it was in this way, it was claimed by Governor Perry, who strongly opposed the measure, that the State was carried for a Convention and, ultimately, Nullification. Says Governor Perry, further:

"Those who opposed a Convention were denounced as Federalists, Aristocrats and Tariff men, who were afraid to trust the people. There were a good many who were strongly opposed to Nullification, and yet went for a Convention on the ground that the people ought to decide for themselves on so grave and momentous a question. There were others, however, who, although decided in their opposition to the Tariff, did not go for a State Convention. They could not see how it was possible for a Convention to remedy an evil unless it was by resorting to Nullification, dis-Union and civil war. They regarded the Convention as Nullification in disguise and that Nullification was nothing less than destruction of the National Government. They were unwilling to break up the Union to get rid of the tariff. This class of persons assumed the name of 'Union Men,' and the others that of 'States' Rights or Free Trade.'"

From one of Major William Hoy's articles to the *Spartan*, it appears that the political sentiment in Spartanburg District on the question of Nullification was controlled largely by the visit of Judge Smith to the district in the fall of 1831, when he made his great Union speech. In the same he charged Mr. Calhoun with being the originator of the tariff of 1816 and other measures of consolidation, all against the interests of the South. He stated that all of the South Carolina delegation voted for the measure except General Thomas Moore of Spartanburg, and in support of this he brought up an array of documents and newspaper charges to prove it. His contention was that there was no need of a separate State action on the tariff, and said it was a measure upon which public opinion was reaching and laid great stress upon an article prepared by Mr. Lee, of Boston, against protective tariffs, and said that this was the ablest exposition of the subject that had been written. He brought up Verplank, the Chairman of the Committee on Ways and Means, in the lower house of Congress, as a strong opponent to the protective principle, and declared further that Verplank was the ablest debater in either house of Congress, notwithstanding Clay, Webster, Forsyth and others were in the two houses. It is said that it took Judge Smith five hours to deliver this speech, and that it was afterwards published in book form by a newspaper in Charleston called *The Irishman,* and sold for twenty-five cents a copy.

In Spartanburg District where the two factions were formed and well divided, the result of the fall election in 1832 proved the Union men to be largely in the majority. In referring to the prevailing sentiment in the district at that time. Major Hoy in one of his communications to the *Spartan* states as follows:

"The celebration of the Fourth of July at Spartanburg in 1832 was partly political, from the fact that there was going to be an effort made to raise a strong Nullification party in the county (district). Thomas Moore, a talented young lawyer, early in the year published an able address to the voters of the county, urging them to join the Nullification party. His address was signed 'A Descendant of the Cowpens.' It was not concealed who was the author of the appeal, and it was well known that his father was a general in the war of 1812. The address strongly hinted that the county needed missionary work. He stated that there was not a single post-office north of the court-house. Another cause that gave uneasiness to those that were inclined to be Union men was that Colonel Zachary Edwards, up to that time the most popular man in the county, was going to join the States' Rights party, as they called themselves.

"A meeting of the leaders of the Union party was convened, and the result was the whole county formed into a celebration at Spartanburg on the Fourth of July. Joshua Richards, [1] a Baptist preacher and a soldier of the Revolution, was president of the meeting; J. M. Crook, a young member of the bar, orator of the day; James E. Henry was to read Washington's Farewell Address in place of the Declaration of Independence; Berryman Hicks, chaplain; Lieutenant-Colonel Evans, marshal of the day; William Trimmier, chairman of the committee of arrangements. It is due to his memory to say that he made a good one. At sunrise on the 4th a salute was fired which was heard all over the county. The people began early to collect on the public square. At 11 o'clock the line was formed, the longest that was ever seen in the place except the Hampton meeting in 1876. It was put in motion by the marshal, headed by the president of the day and several Revolutionary soldiers, Collins, Caldwell, Dodd and Seay are remembered. When the center of the procession was about opposite the Palmetto House a call was made to know the length of the line. The call, though apparently very simple, caused one of the most ludicrous events of the day. It appeared to start from the center and was communicated to the ends of the line, causing much laughter and merriment. There were two persons who attempted to see the ends; one was John (Jack) S. Collins, well-remembered as a very tall man. He tiptoed and reported that he could see no ends either way. The other effort was made by a perfect dwarf. Of course he had nothing to report and received a severe rebuke from a free-spoken old gentleman, who thought he had a spattering of wit and scripture, but perhaps more whisky than either. He called him Zaccheus who climbed the tree and attempted to do what Collins had failed in. He remarked that if any man could reach the North star by tiptoeing a little, Collins was the man. The procession reached the stand. Chairman Trimmier, of the committee of arrangements, showed his gallantry by seeing that every lady was provided for. He then addressed the president of the meeting, regretting that they had no Joshua to command the sun to stand still until they got through with their arrangements.

"After prayer, Major Henry advanced to the front and made an explanation why Washington's Address was to be read in place of the Declaration of Independence. The orator of the day then came forward and made an address that was highly spoken of by his audience.

"In those times what was called regular toasts were read. The citizens were called on for their sentiments. I remember a few of them. There was a brilliant comet and the Asiatic cholera had reached this continent, and an elderly gentleman by the name of Spencer said that this sentiment occurred to him on hearing the salute fired in the morning: 'Black is the heart that would from his country depart.'

"By Major Trimmier: 'Cholera to nullification and then a complete nullification to the cholera and the comet tail to both.'

"By S. Bobo: 'The advocates of the new-fangled doctrine of nullification may find this sentiment in Jefferson's second inaugural: Absolute acquiescence to the will of the majority is the vital principle of a republic from which there is no appeal but by force.'

"By Colonel Zachary Edwards: 'Those virtuously contending for the Union, may they ever wear the laurels achieved by their ancestors.'

"Colonel Edwards appeared that day in his brilliant uniform, in which he, in addition to his being a very handsome man, made a fine appearance; but the report having gone out that he leaned to the nullification side, caused him not being asked to act as marshal of the day. He was, without doubt, the greatest militia officer in the State. He ever acted after that day with the Nullifiers.

"The election in the fall resulted in a large majority for the Union candidates. The Union nominee received about 1,800 votes. Colonel Moore, leading his ticket, received about 800 votes and his colleagues about 700 each."

81

After the fall elections in 1832 were over, the result showed that two-thirds of both houses in the Legislature were in favor of calling a State convention. Governor Hayne immediately convened the Legislature,, which called forthwith a convention of the State which embraced the. leading men of the State of both parties. Among those elected to represent Spartanburg District in that convention were Judges J. B. O'Neall, J. S. Richardson and Alfred Huger, none of these residing in said district being ardent Union men, but the people of Spartanburg composing that faction wisely selected them as able standard-bearers to represent their principles. The other three delegates elected on the same ticket with these gentlemen were John S. Rowland,. James Crook and John P. Evins.

In reference to the election by the people of Spartanburg District of Hon. Alfred Huger of Charleston, one of the delegates referred to, Judge Simonton once related to the writer a pleasant little incident complimentary to Spartanburg, and not remembering the particulars, he wrote him and received the following reply:

"Flat Rock, No. Car.,
20th Sept., 1890.

"'*Dr. J. B. O. Landrum, Landrum, S.C.:*

"Dear Doctor: — Yours of 18th inst. came by last mail. The incident to which you refer was this: During the Convention of 1865, in a debate under the operation of the five-minutes' rule, the Hon. Alfred Huger had the floor. When he had been speaking for five minutes Judge Wardlaw, the President of the Convention, dropped the gavel, and so notified him that his time had expired. A member of the Convention rose and moved that the rule be suspended as to Mr. Huger, and Judge Wardlaw put the question, 'The gentleman from Spartanburg moves that the rule be suspended and the gentleman be permitted to proceed.' This was carried, and Mr. Huger resumed his speech thus: 'The gentleman from Spartanburg! the gentleman from Spartanburg! None of you are old enough to remember, and I will never be old enough to forget, that Spartanburg honored me, a stranger, with a seat in the Convention of 1832 as one of her delegates.'

"Mr. Huger was postmaster at Charleston from 1830 to 1861, and was quite an old man in 1865.

"Yours truly,
"Charles H. Simonton."

In the Nullification Convention of 1832 Judge Huger was quite a prominent member, and was one of the ablest counselors in caucus among the Union men of that Convention. In the first caucus he made a speech against the delegates taking their seats in the Convention. He said: "If we take our seats in the Convention we shall be the means of keeping the Nullification party together. We shall hear things that will call for blood." He said it would be impossible to sit there and listen to the speeches of the delegates on the opposite side without resenting what was said. "If they talk as I suppose they will, blood must be shed! It cannot be avoided." It was believed in the caucus that a test-oath of allegiance to the State would be required of the

Union members, which would be inconsistent with their allegiance to the Federal Government.

When, however, the Convention met, it was, indeed, a most dignified body, containing most of the great men of both parties in South Carolina. They were fine-looking gentlemen, and showed great respect for each other throughout the entire sitting of that body.

It is well known to every reader of our State history that the ordinance of Nullification was passed at this Convention. It was drawn by Chancellor Harper, and provided for a dissolution of the Union. The tariff laws were declared null and void, and judges and juries were to be sworn to say so whenever the question came before them. The Legislature was authorized to make all laws for carrying the ordinance into effect.

Immediately after the adjournment of the Convention the Legislature assembled and appropriated money for the purchase of arms, and authorized the raising of an army of twenty thousand volunteers to enforce the enactment of the Nullification ordinance, which in its reading declared that no customs should be collected in South Carolina after the first day of February, 1833.

Soon after this, President Jackson, in a proclamation,, declared the proceedings of the State Convention of South Carolina treasonable, and that, as the Chief Executive of the Government of the United States, he would enforce absolute obedience to its laws. Forces were at once sent to Castle Pinckney and Sullivan's Island. These forts were at once put in a proper state of defence. General Scott was sent to take command of the United States forces. The sloop *Natchez* was stationed in the port of Charleston, and it was evident that unless there was very soon some pacifying measures adopted a bloody conflict was inevitable. Virginia deputed a commission to South Carolina, with the request that the Nullification ordinance be not enforced until the next regular session of Congress. The Nullifiers called a meeting of their party in Charleston and suspended the operation of the ordinance. In the following spring a compromise of the tariff question was effected at Washington between Mr. Clay and Mr. Calhoun. The protection of domestic manufactures was provided for, and a gradual reduction of the tariff was to take place for the period of ten years until it reached the low point demanded by Mr. Calhoun, United States Senator and the exponent of the principles of Nullification in South Carolina.

Immediately after this, the State Convention of South Carolina was convened and rescinded the ordinance of Nullification.

With the subsidence of the Tariff agitation in South Carolina, other National issues, in the course of time, sprung up. The systematic agitation of slavery came up as early as 1835, by a party called *Abolitionists,* which, it was claimed, instead of striking at an express and specific provision of the Constitution, aimed directly to destroy the relation between the two races in the South, their avowed intention being to bring about a state of things which would force the abolition of slavery. As the years advanced, the party grew stronger at the North; so much so, that in 1849 the Southern delegates in Congress issued an address to their constituents which, among other things, set forth the fact that societies and newspapers were everywhere established, debating clubs opened, lecturers employed, pamphlets and other publications disseminated, pictures and jDetitions to Congress resorted to, regardless of truth and decency; that both the object and means were aggressive and dangerous to the rights of the South; that slavery was a domestic institution and belonged to the States, each for itself to decide whether it shall be established or not, etc.; that in the sacrifices and efforts of all the States to maintain the National Government the South had contributed more than her share of volunteers and money.

In the same address it was recommended that meetings be held in the congressional districts of the Southern States in order to give the people an opportunity to express themselves on this subject, signifying their approbation of their representatives in Congress and, like their Revolutionary ancestors, pledge "their lives, their fortunes, and their sacred honor" to defend their constitutional rights. In response to this request, public meetings were held all over the Southern States, and among the first meetings held in South Carolina was at Spartanburg court-house, March 6th, 1849. The number of citizens present was unusually large, it being court week.

Dr. John Winsmith, by a unanimous vote, was called to preside over the deliberations of the meeting, and Z. T. Cottrell and G. W. H. Legg were requested to act as secretaries.

Dr. Winsmith, assuming the chair, stated that the meeting had assembled for the purpose of taking under consideration the address of the Southern Delegates in Congress, and delivered an extended address, and among other things stated that when the State of Missouri was admitted into the Union in 1816 under a compromise known as the *Missouri Compromise,* by which the South was required to make important concessions for the sake of the Union, it was hoped that she would be permitted to repose in the enjoyment of her rights. He urged that not only the slave interest, but every other interest in our country was involved. He stated that the question must be met at once, and he hoped all were fully prepared to meet it as became freemen of Carolina and of Spartanburg District.

Hon. J. Edward Henry offered a resolution that a committee of twenty-one be appointed by the chair to report a preamble and resolutions for the meeting responsive to the address of the Southern Delegates in Congress, which was adopted, and under the same Mr. Henry was made chairman. Very soon a lengthy preamble and resolutions were reported by the committee, which set forth a cordial approval of the action of the Southern Delegates; that no evil whatever could befall us more intolerable than submission to the grievances, injustice and degradation which had been induced and with which the country was threatened, and that the citizens of Spartanburg District were prepared to unite with others in arresting further progress of such injustice, oppression, etc.

The chair appointed the following committee of vigilance, viz.: Col. H. H. Thomson, Maj. H. J. Dean, S. Bobo, Esq., Dr. W. C. Bennett, Hon. G. Cannon, Capt. Robert Jackson, Gen. J. W. Miller, Col. S. N. Evins, Jonas Brewton, Esq., Dr. C. P. Woodruff, Mr. James Nesbitt, Z. D. Bragg, Esq., Messrs. J. Davis, C. P. Smith, J. C. Zimmerman, Thomas Littlejohn, Dr. S. Otterson, Capt. A. Bonner and Henry Dodd, Esq.

The preamble and resolutions were adopted by a rising vote.

Upon the assembling of the Legislature of South Carolina, November 27th, 1849, the message of Governor Whitemarsh B. Seabrook was received and read. Under the head of the subject, *Federal Relations,* he transmitted certain resolutions of the States of Virginia, North Carolina, Georgia, Florida and Missouri, on the restriction of slavery in the Territories of the United States. Governor Seabrook in commenting on these, said that the opinion of South Carolina on the grave matter at issue had been repeatedly expressed, that, at its last session, the Legislature of South Carolina, unanimously declared that the time for discussion by the slave-holding States had passed, and that the General Assembly, representing the feelings of the State, was prepared to co-operate with her sister States in resisting the application of the Wilmot Proviso [2] to the territory acquired from Mexico at any and every hazard. Governor Seabrook, also in said message, called attention to the fact, that at a convention held in Columbia the May previous, composed of delegates of the Committees of Safety, it was, among other things, resolved that, in the passage of the Wilmot Proviso, or an equivalent measure, the Governor be requested to convene the Legislature, if not already in session, "to consider the mode and measure of redress."

The Governor in said message endorsed the project of a Southern convention and hailed with satisfaction the proposition of Mississippi, for a convention of the people of the Southern States, the permanent object being the preservation of the Union, in conformity with the principles of the Constitution of the United States, and if that could not be attained, then to let it be resolved to protect and defend, at all hazards, the sovereignty and independence of the members which compose it, and if the latter alternative should, by dire necessity, be forced upon the South, then, at once, commit its cause and destiny to God.

The attitudes of Alabama, Georgia and other Southern States were similar to South Carolina, the great principle being laid down, that, whenever the Congress of the United States attempted to exercise control over the territory which had been acquired by treaty with Mexico, so far as the question of domestic servitude was concerned, they had by said act violated the. Constitution and *dissolved* the union of the States.

The Georgia resolutions declared that the Government of the United States was one of limited powers, and could not rightfully exercise any authority except authorized by the Constitution, and that said Constitution granted no power to Congress to prohibit the introduction of slavery into any territory belonging to the United States.

It was upon this momentous question that, by concerted agreement between all the Southern States, a convention was called to meet at Nashville, Tenn., in June, 1850, to be composed of two delegates from each of the congressional districts in all the Southern States.

For what was then called the Pinckneyville Congressional District, composed of the districts of Spartanburg, Union, York, and Chester, the names of a number of prominent gentlemen were suggested through the press as suitable persons to represent said Congressional district in the Nashville convention, and among those mentioned in Spartanburg District were. Dr. C. P. "Woodruff of Woodruff, and Col. E. C. Leitner.

The convention to nominate delegates to attend the Nashville convention to represent the Pinckneyville District met at Union, May 6th, 1850, and selected .Hon. David Johnson and Col. B. F. Beatie.

Dr. Samuel Otterson, of Limestone Springs, and J. A. Bradley, of Chester District, were chosen as alternates.

Hon. David Johnson, on account of ill health, failing to attend the said convention, his place was filled in that body by Dr. Otterson, who, on his return home, delivered an address before the citizens of Spartanburg of considerable length (see *Spartan* files, Oct. 17th, 1850), in which, among other things, he stated that, as a member of the Southern convention at Nashville, he would always treasure it as one of the greatest honors ever conferred upon him; that he received from the citizens of that city the most respectful attention.

An address, called the "Southern Address," was issued by the convention to the people of Maryland, Virginia, North Carolina, South Carolina, Georgia, Florida, Alabama, Tennessee, Kentucky, Mississippi, Louisiana, Texas, Missouri and Delaware, which contained some information as to the results and counsels of the convention. (See *Spartan* files, June 24th and July 4th, 1850.) The address stated that it was no ordinary occasion which had brought the convention together. The Constitution and the Union it created, so long dear in the hearts of the people, were to be preserved and our liberties and our institutions maintained.

In December, 1850, the Legislature of South Carolina passed a bill which provided for the election of delegates on the second Monday in October of the following year to elect delegates to a Southern Congress, to meet in Montgomery, Alabama, in January, 1852, provided other sister Southern States, or any of them, would then and there meet. Also, a bill providing for an election, by the people, of delegates to a State convention, said election to be held on the second Monday of February of the following year, and the convention to meet by a call of the governor whenever he deemed it proper, after the meeting of said Southern Congress, provided, that if not sooner convened, the next legislature should, by a majority vote, fix the time for the meeting of said convention.

It is said that in the passage of this bill providing for the election of delegates to a State convention, there was unanimity of feeling. All rejoiced at the happy issue of the discussion, and in accordance with its provisions, providing for the election of delegates, February 2, 1851, to the said convention, the following gentlemen were elected and are herein named, as they were highest on the list of votes polled, viz.:

James G. Landrum,
James Farrow,
John Winsmith,
Peter M. Wallace,
Robert C. Poole,
James J. Vernon.

At the election of delegates second Monday in October, 1851, to represent the Pinckneyville Congressional District in the Southern Congress, to meet at Montgomery, Ala., January, 1852, the following was the result of the vote in Spartanburg District, each gentleman receiving the number of votes opposite his name, viz.:

Thomas N. Dawkins......1,448
Samuel Rainy.................1,426
Peter M. Wallace............1,176
Thos. O. P.Vernon...........1,186

The two first named (Dawkins and Rainy) represented the Southern Rights Cooperative ticket; *i.e.*, they were opposed to separate State action in regard to secession, but were in favor of a great *Southern Party* banded together by the ties of affection and interest.

The two last named (Wallace and Vernon) believed in asserting the *sovereignty of South Carolina* by separate State action; that nothing but the bold and fearless action of the State could save the South and preserve the liberty, safety and prosperity of our country.

In searching the pages of history, we have been unable to gather any information as to the action of the Southern Congress, which met according to appointment in Montgomery, Ala., in January, 1852, but we believe it adjourned without taking any definite action whatever, the main reason being the want of a general cooperation among the sister Southern States.

Upon the call of the Governor of South Carolina, the delegates which had been elected in February, 1851, met in Columbia, S.C., in April, 1852.

It was composed of three factions, viz.: *Secessionists,* in favor of separate State action, *Cooperationists,* favoring secession along with other sister Southern States, and *Union men.* Prominent among the latter faction was Hon. B. F. Perry, of Greenville, and Judge Alfred H. Huger, of Charleston, both of whom had figured prominently in the Nullification Convention of 1832, as we have already stated in the preceding pages of our account of the proceedings of that convention.

When the convention met a committee of twenty-one was appointed to consider the legality of the Legislature authorizing the calling of said body together. Said committee was composed of twelve Cooperationists, eight Secessionists and one Union man. The work of the convention was practically through this committee, in which harmony and good feeling, it is said, existed. There was no disposition more than to assert *the right of secession.*

Judge Huger made a speech before the committee in which he said that the present Federal Government, as formed by the Constitution, was the most perfect system of government in the world, or ever had been, and that he was opposed to cooperation because it was unconstitutional for States to cooperate or to enter into any compact or agreement.

There was a question raised before the committee as to the right of the convention to alter the State Constitution, and, strange to say. Chancellor Wardlaw, Judges Whitner and Evins and a majority of the committee voted that the sovereign power of South Carolina had no right to alter or change their Constitution. Certainly it had this right, if it had the power to throw off the Federal Government.

As to the final action of the committee, it reported to the convention an ordinance declaring the constitutional right of a State to secede from the Union.

Dr. Bellenger offered an amendment to the report of the committee, giving the Legislature the right to secede by a vote of two-thirds of that body, which was tabled.

The ordinance, as reported by the committee, being ratified, the convention adjourned *sine die.*

By virtue of an act of Congress passed in the year 1846, which enacted that "the Electors of President and Vice-President shall be appointed on Tuesday next after the first Monday in the month of November of the year in which they are to be appointed," and the annual meeting of the Legislature of South Carolina, by a constitutional provision, not taking place until the fourth Monday of November of each year, the governor, Hon. Wm. H. Gist, called that body together in extraordinary session, early in November, 1860, stating in the message to the same, that under ordinary circumstances the duty of that body would soon be discharged by the election of electors representing the choice of the people of the State, but in view of the threatening aspect of affairs and the strong probability of the election to the presidency of a sectional candidate by a party committed to the support of measures which, if carried out, would inevitably destroy our equality in the Union and ultimately reduce the Southern States to mere provinces of a consolidated despotism to be governed by a fixed majority in Congress, hostile to our institutions and fatally bent upon our ruin, he (the governor), respectfully suggested that the Legislature remain in session and take such action as would prepare the State for any emergency that would arise.

The Governor further stated that an expression of the people should be obtained on a question involving such momentous consequences, and earnestly recommended, in the event of the election of Abraham Lincoln to the presidency, that a convention of the people of the State be immediately called to consider and determine the "mode and measure of redress."

Governor Gist, in said message, further declared that his own opinions of what the convention should do were of little moment; but believing that the time had arrived when every one, however humble he might be, should express his opinions in unmistakable language,, he was constrained to say that the only alternative left, in his judgment, was the secession of South Carolina from the Federal Union; that the indications from many of the Southern States justified the conclusion that the secession of South Carolina would be immediately followed, if not adopted simultaneously by them, and ultimately the entire South; that the long-desired cooperation of other States having similar institutions for which the State had been waiting, seemed to be near at hand, and if we were true to ourselves would soon be realized; that the State had already declared with great unanimity that she had a right peacefully to secede, and no power on earth could rightfully prevent it.

The governor further declared that, if in the exercise of arbitrary power and forgetful of the lessons of history, the Government of the United States should attempt coercion, it would be our solemn duty to meet force by force, and whatever might be the decision of the convention representing the sovereignty of the State — and amenable to no earthly tribunal — should, during the remainder of his administration be carried out to the letter, regardless of any hazards that might surround its execution.

Governor Gist also, in his message, recommended a thorough reorganization of the militia, so as to place the whole military force of the State in a position to be used at the shortest notice and with the greatest efficiency; that every man in the State between the ages of eighteen and forty-five should be well armed with the most effective weapons of modern warfare, and all the available means of the State used for that purpose. In addition to this, the governor recommended that the services of ten thousand volunteers be immediately accepted; that they be organized and drilled by officers chosen by themselves in readiness to be called on, upon the shortest notice.

"With this preparation for defence," said the governor, "and with all the hallowed memories of past achievements, and with our love for liberty and hatred for tyranny, and with the knowledge that we are contending for our homes and firesides, we confidently appeal to the Disposer of all human events and safely trust our cause to His keeping."

It is unnecessary to relate the excitement, the enthusiasm and the hearty response with which this message was approved by the people of South Carolina. In a few days, even the quota of volunteers asked for by the governor, were already organized and ready to march forth, even before the Legislature had time to take action on the recommendations contained in the message. That body within a few days passed unanimously a joint resolution providing for the call of a convention, the delegates to the same to be elected on the 6th of December, and the convention to be convened on the 17th of the same month.

The other recommendations set forth in the message of Governor Gist were fully carried out by the Legislature. A bill was immediately enacted for the organization and equipment of an army in the State, supported by a heavy appropriation to maintain the same.

The scenes of those days are yet fresh in the memory of the writer, who was among the first to respond to the call for volunteer troops. The people awaited the action of the Legislature with intense interest and excitement after the reception, reading and publication of the message of Governor Gist. The Hon. Gabriel Cannon, at that time the senator representing the District of Spartanburg, issued an address to the people of said district, in which he clearly set forth the recent action of the Legislature, and urged upon his constituents the necessity of making a prudent selection of delegates to the approaching State convention; that they should look around for such men as they were willing to trust with their destinies; to let them be wise and prudent men who would act cautiously but firmly; that the occasion demanded and the times called for harmony and union amongst ourselves, and that we should consider well and act like men.

Other prominent political leaders in the State were also out, through the press, with a full expression of their views and sentiments on the critical situation of affairs, and among this number was Hon. Thomas N. Dawkins of Union, who had been for years the recognized leader of the faction known as *Cooperationists,* which, as we have already stated, carried Spartanburg District by a considerable majority in the election of delegates in October, '51, to the Southern Congress at Montgomery, Alabama.

Judge Dawkins, in responding to a call made on him at the Walker House in Spartanburg, November 15th, '60, spoke eloquently of the wrongs which the South had suffered in the Union, and said that the Constitution had been violated to such an extent by our enemies of the Northern States, that we could no longer remain in a government with them consistently with our honor and with due regard to our cherished institutions.

The Hon. Simpson Bobo, in a meeting of the citizens of the town of Spartanburg, stated that he had at last fallen into strange company; that he had always been a Union man; that, in 1832 he belonged to that party in opposition to Nullification, because he did not believe the State had a right to remain in the Union and nullify its laws; that in 1852 he was a Union man and a Cooperationist, as he did not at that time think the aggressions of the General Government sufficient to warrant extreme measures, but since the Republican party had got the rule and control of the Free States and had sent their senators and members of Congress to the capitol, and there proclaiming eternal war on the South, avowing "a higher law" than the *Constitution* or even the Bible — that there was an "irrepressible conflict" declared by their leaders, between the labor of the sections which could never be overcome "which the churches," said Mr. Bobo, "instead of preaching *salvation,* have made the institutions of the South the subject of their denunciations in every pulpit in the Free States; that the infamous raid of John Brown was eulogized by them and their church-bells were tolled throughout their land in sympathy for the wretch — for his dark and wicked offenses." Said Mr. Bobo further, "They have sent their minions abroad in the South, with weapons of death in one hand and the lighted torch in the other, exciting insurrection in the country, thereby working our ruin throughout the land."

Said Mr. Bobo in his closing remarks: "In view of all this, I feel that the crisis is upon us, and as painful as it is to utter the word, I must say that this *Union must be dissolved.*"

Governor Francis W. Pickens, on assuming the executive chair of South Carolina, December, 1860, stated in his Inaugural Address, that South Carolina had no other alternative left but to interpose her sovereignty as an independent State, to protect the rights and ancient privileges of her people; that the State was one of the parties to the Federal compact of Union; that we had agreed to this as a State, under peculiar circumstances when we were surrounded with great external pressure for purposes of the national protection and to advance the interests and general welfare of the States equally and alike, and that when it ceased to do this, it was no longer a perpetual union; that it would be an absurdity to suppose it was a perpetual union for our ruin. That the Constitution was a compact between co-States and not with the Federal Government; that on questions vital and involving the peace and safety of parties to the compact, from the very nature of the instrument, each State must judge of the mode and measure of protection necessary for her peace and the preservation of her local and domestic institutions, and that South Carolina should, therefore, decide for herself, as she had a right to do — to resume her original powers of government as an independent State.

We cannot here go further — thirty-eight years after the scenes we have described were enacted — to relate all the particulars of the stirring events as they occurred in rapid succession, in the District of Spartanburg, as they came under the immediate observation of the writer. Liberty poles were raised in different sections of the district, upon which were hoisted a red flag with the emblem of the palmetto tree on one side and the *Lone Star* on the other, amid the shouting of the multitude, the pealing of guns and the rattle of the drum. Public meetings were held, patriotic speeches were made, spirited resolutions were passed, and their proceedings sent abroad for publication.

The most noted mass-meeting, however, held in the district during this exciting period was on a general call for a meeting at Spartanburg, on Saturday, November 24th, 1860. The writer was present at this meeting, and, although the day was cold and bleak, there was present a large and enthusiastic number of citizens from every section of the district. All over this dense crowd, which had assembled in front of the Palmetto House (the capacity of the court-house being too small to accommodate the meeting), were seen, with unmistakable meaning, the blue rosettes or cockades pinned on the hats of the *Minute Men* — a society which had already organized and were ready to respond to the very first call for their services. Over this meeting Mr. S. Bobo, Chairman of Committee of Arrangements, announced the following officers had been chosen to preside, viz.:

President, Rev. John G. Landrum; Vice-Presidents, Samuel N. Evins, John Davis, J. W. Miller, James Nesbitt, Samuel Morgan, John Stroble, O. P. Earle, John B. Davis, Rev. Clough S. Beard, Rev. Wm. Curtis, LL.D., Dr. Wm. Nott, Andrew Bonner, Edward E. Parker, N. P. Walker, Dr. Maurice A. Moore, O. E. Edwards, A. B. Woodruff, Harvey Wofford, Jared Drummond, James Anderson, Rev. R. H. Reid, Dr. James Bivings, Henry Dodd, Wm. Ballenger, A. C. Bomar, Dr. Ibra Cannon, Samuel Jackson, J. H. Ezell, Sum Sumner, Rev. A. M. Shipp, D.D., B. F. Bates, E. P. Smith, Dr. B. F. Kilgore, Rev. H. H. Durant, Dr. J. Winsmith, Joel Foster, John D. Wright, John M. Crook, John B. Cleveland, Joseph Foster, Henry Gaffney and Woodard Allen.

The President, on taking the chair, made a few brief remarks, and stated the object of the meeting.

After prayer by the Rev. Whiteford Smith, D.D., the Hon. James Chesnut, Jr., late United States senator from South Carolina, was introduced amidst the wildest enthusiasm and cheering, who stated that he had only the day previous addressed a number of the patriotic citizens of Carolina, sixty miles away; and that his love for South Carolina would not permit him to remain quiet and silent when so many from the "Old Iron District" of South Carolina desired to hear him; and through the rain, the dark, wet night, and the chilling blasts he had come at their invitation, and was now ready to state to them our wrongs and grievances — which he did in such a plain and practical manner that all who heard him felt the force of his remarks and the importance of the occasion.

Hon. A. G. Magrath, recently judge of the United States District Court for South Carolina, was present by invitation and introduced. He had laid aside his judicial robes so soon as the first blast from the North rune the intelligence in his ears that we were no longer free; and in a most eloquent and effective manner he told his audience a tale true, but which many of them had never heard before.

Suitable resolutions to the occasion were introduced and passed, and the entire day was consumed in listening to the speeches of a number of gentlemen who were called out, and who expressed their views, all of them favoring immediate separate State action.

At night there was a torchlight procession of the Minute Men.

On the 6th of December, 1860, the election in Spartanburg District for delegates to the State convention was held. Each of the following named gentlemen were elected, receiving at the polls the number of votes opposite their respective names:

John G. Landrum — 1,326
B. B. Foster — 1,257
Benj. F. Kilgore — 1,254

Jas. H. Carlisle — 1,217
Simpson Bobo — 1,165
William Curtis — 1,006

On the 17th of December, 1860, the Convention of South Carolina — known in history as the *Secession Convention* — according to the time fixed by legislative enactment, met in Columbia and organized, but immediately adjourned to meet in Charleston, where, on the 20th of the same month, passed the following ordinance:

State of South Carolina.

We, the people of South Carolina, in Convention assembled, do declare and ordain that the ordinance adopted by us in Convention, on the 2nd day of May, 1788, whereby the Constitution of the United States was ratified, and also all Acts and parts of Acts of the General Assembly of this State ratifying amendments of said Constitution, are hereby repealed, and that the Union now subsisting between South Carolina and other States under the name of the United States of America, is hereby dissolved.

(Signed)   D, F. Jamison,
President.

(And members of entire Convention.)
Attest: B. F. Arthur, Clerk.

It is unnecessary to go further to review the great events recorded in the pages of American history, resulting from the passage of this famous ordinance by a convention of the people of South Carolina assembled for that purpose. They are still fresh in the memories of the survivors of that period, and it has been an oft-repeated story to the generations that have come after them. Whatever was the wisdom or justice of this action of the State of South Carolina, under all the trying and pressing circumstances which surrounded her, remains to be recorded by the impartial historian yet unborn. We are willing to leave the matter in his hands with no fears as to a full vindication of the South in her alleged wrongs, and with full justice to the memories, valor and patriotism of the brave defenders of a "Lost Cause."

[1] See sketch of Joshua Richards at another place in this volume.
[2] "The probability that the war with Mexico would result in the acquisition of extensive territory in the southwest early led to the reagitation of the slavery question. In 1846 David Wilmot, of Pennsylvania, introduced into Congress a proposition, called by him the *Wilmot Proviso,* that slavery should be prohibited in all territory that might be acquired by treaty. This proviso failed to receive the sanction of Congress, and the question being thrown before the country for discussion a party holding the views of Mr. Wilmot was organized. They took the name of *Free-soilers,* and in June, 1848, nominated Martin Van Buren, as their candidate for the presidency. The Democrats nominated Gen. Lewis Cass, of Michigan; the Whigs, Gen. Taylor, whose brilliant victories in Mexico made him the favorite of the Nation. Taylor was elected, and with him Millard Fillmore, of New York, as Vice-President." See Quackenbos's History, page 444.

Chapter Ten - Review of the Progress of Manufactures in Spartanburg County during the Nineteenth Century

Iron Industry

In "Ramsey's History of South Carolina" (Appendix, p. 307), we learn that the first iron ore works in South Carolina were erected within the borders of the present county of Spartanburg in 1773. These have been called in the pages of history *Buffington's Iron Works, Wofford's Iron Works,* and *Berwick's Iron Works,* but, from what we have been able to gather, they were one and the same, possibly a joint stock company. Of Buffington we know nothing except that the land grants in that immediate vicinity show him to have been one of the first settlers there. Of William Wofford, who was also one of the proprietors, we have given a sketch elsewhere in connection with the Wofford family. It would appear, however, that he had disposed of his interest in these works, either before the beginning or during the Revolution, for, in 1780, we learn from Draper's "King's Mountain" that he was living in the upper Catawba Valley, N.C., where he had erected a small fort, which the over-mountain men passed on the route to King's Mountain, just preceding the battle there. Of Simon Berwick, the last proprietor of Wofford's Iron Works, we have a notice in an another place in this work. (See Chapter I.)

Wofford's Iron Works, a name that has been made famous in the pages of our Revolutionary history, by reason of the battle that was fought nearby, were located on the left bank of the stream, Lawson's Fork, about a half mile above the present manufacturing village of Glendale. This was perhaps the most noted point within the territory of the present county of Spartanburg before and during the Revolution. It was here that Mr. Drayton and Mr. Tenant, commissioners sent out by the Council of Safety in 1775, to explain to the people the nature of the dispute between the colonies and the mother country, repaired for a time; and it was from this point that Mr. Drayton wrote to the Council of Safety, informing them of the patriotism of the people comprising the early settlements of the up-country, stating, among other things, that they were active and spirited, and that he was taking steps at once to organize a regiment; which resulted in a short time in the organization of the famous Spartan regiment commanded by Colonel John Thomas, Sr. It was also to this place that Sumter and his gallant followers retreated after the battle of Blackstocks. Colonel Sumter, having been seriously wounded in said battle, was here placed on a litter between two horses and carried to a more secure region in the mountains, where he remained until after his recovery, when he again took the field.

In another volume [1] we have given some account of the raid of the notorious "Bloody Bill" Cunningham to the up-country of South Carolina in November, 1781. One of his most infamous acts of open incendiarism was the destruction by fire of this valuable property, which, doubtless, by reason of the death of Mr. Berwick, a few years later, were never rebuilt.

Besides Wofford's Iron Works, there were other works located in the up-country, perhaps less extensive and important. It is said that in the Southern colonies iron-making became an important industry even before the beginning of the eighteenth century, and it has been a well-established fact that the early settlers of what is now Spartanburg County understood something of the manufacture of iron, and when the Revolution broke out there were several forges in the up-country of South Carolina, and one of these was Poole's Iron Works, which were located somewhere on Pacolet River. Colonel John L. Black, son of one of the pioneer iron-makers of South Carolina, in a letter to Mr. Richard H. Edmonds, editor of the *Manufacturer's Record,* in speaking of the early days of iron manufacturing in upper South Carolina, says:

"Small quantities of iron were made in Catalan forges along the Piedmont slope in the Carolinas prior to and during the Revolutionary War. The limonite ores...were used, and small quantities of iron were made...

"During the Revolutionary war William Hill, father of the late General D. H. Hill of the Confederate army, operated a forge and a small blast-furnace on Allison's Creek,...and made iron from these very pure ores. Lord Cornwallis, in his advance from upper South Carolina to Charlotte, burned Hill's works, and destroyed some small iron guns Mr. Hill had cast to aid the colonial rebellion. Vestiges of this furnace are still to be seen, and a fragment of an iron cannon taken lately from Allison Creek can now be seen in Yorkville, S.C.

"A small blast-furnace was erected on King's Creek, seven miles southwest of Blacksburg, by one Stroup, in 1822; also a Catalan forge. In 1824 Stroup left King's Creek and moved seven miles to the present site of the Cherokee Cotton Factory, and began to build iron works on Broad River. This move was to get alongside the gray ores of Blacksburg, S.C. In 1826 a company known as E. Graham & Co., composed of James A. Black, Emon Graham, Jacob Deal and P. R. Brice, all of Columbia, S.C., and David Johnson, of Union county, bought the Stroup interest and proceeded to build an iron works. E. Graham & Co.'s interests were merged into an incorporated company — the King's Mountain Iron Co. — with $100,000 capital, a portion of which was invested in slaves as operatives and mechanics.

"In 1827 the King's Mountain Iron Co. erected a blast-furnace. This was replaced by a large furnace on the same site in 1837, and was designed for a hot-blast, but only cold blasts were ever applied. The present Cherokee cotton mill occupies the same site. In 1832 E. Graham & Co. built a rolling-mill in Union county, two miles below their furnace. In 1830 they cast guns — six and nine pounders — for the State of South Carolina, and quantities of round shot; also grape and canister. In 1837 the King's Mountain Iron Co. built a second blast-furnace on King's Creek, four miles southeast of the town of Blacksburg. In the same year the Magnetic Iron Co., capital $250,000, of which 60 per cent, was invested in slaves, was incorporated and built at Cherokee Ford, on Broad River, one mile above King's Mountain Iron Works and near the present town of

Blacksburg, four furnaces, rolling-mill, nail-factory, etc. This company graded and operated a tramway five miles long, to bring in ores, limestone, charcoal and supplies. This was operated in 1838, and the old grade, in a good state of preservation, may now be seen, from Cherokee Ford to Gaffney City.

"In 1837 a furnace was erected by the South Carolina Manufacturing Company, near the old Cowpens battle-ground in Spartanburg County. Wilson Nesbitt, afterwards member of Congress, Wm. C. Clark and others formed a part of said company. Mr. W. Hollis was for many years the superintendent of these works. So also was the Hon. Gabriel Cannon in the early years of his manhood. This company also built and operated a mill to roll iron, and a nail factory (called the Rolling Mill), at Hurricane Shoals on the Pacolet River, now the site of the Clifton Cotton Mills (No. 1)."...

The South Carolina Manufacturing Company owned more than twenty-five thousand acres of land lying between the rivers Pacolet and Broad, and a tramway was constructed leading out to the ore-beds on these lands, which the writer has often seen. The late Hon. Simpson Bobo owned considerable stock, and in some way had charge of the business management of this company, which was successfully operated until the close of the war, when the emancipation of the slaves, and the Confederate securities in which the company had largely invested, interrupted this and all other companies and put an end to the iron industry in upper South Carolina.

Colonel Black further states that during the late civil war between the States the rolling-mill at Hurricane Shoals was operated to its fullest capacity, casting bolts, shot and shell. No large guns were cast. [2]

As early as 1820, Michael Miller, a native of Pennsylvania, who left behind him a numerous posterity, of which the writer is a great-grandson, owned and operated an iron forge on Middle Tyger River, near the present location of the Gross Oil Mill. It remained in operation for a number of years. The old ore-pits are yet to be seen in the vicinity of Welford. Mr. Jas. S. Ballenger, residing near that place, informs the writer that his father, Mr. William Ballenger, wagoned ore to this furnace back in the twenties.

Cotton Factories [3]

From the best information as to the beginning of the manufacture of cotton in Spartanburg County, the writer is indebted to Mr. Wm. A. Hill, Enoree, S.C., who, in a letter under date of February 28, 1899, states that he has, for some years, been collecting such authentic information as could be obtained in reference to Hill's factory, the place of his birth. Mr. Hill states it is a matter of history that in the years 1815 and 1816 there were great colonies emigrating from "The New England States" into "The Southern States," principally cotton manufacturers, who dotted our Southern States with small yarn-mills.

With this colony came Mr. Hill's grandfather, Mr. Leonard Hill, together with other relatives. They came to Charleston, S.C., hired conveyances, and

started to explore what was then a wild and romantic country. They jour-
neyed through the lower and middle belt, which brought them into the
Piedmont section of South Carolina. They arrived on the banks of the main
Tyger, with her rapid-flowing stream and magnificent shoals, and here they
put down stakes, and decided to try their success at manufacturing cotton
into thread. But little cotton was then grown in the up-country of South Carolina, but the plant had been found — a most magnificent plant, too, as it
proved to be. It was here that Leonard Hill, George Hill, Wm. B. Shelden and
John Clark, all parties from near Providence, Rhode Island, decided to go no
further, but to cast their lot with the good people of the "Old Iron District."
The remainder of the party consisted of William Bates and John Weaver. [4]
William Bates pursued his journey into Rutherford county, N.C., where he
erected a building and began the spinning of cotton into yarn, while John
Weaver drove down stakes and began the same business on the banks of
Beaverdam, near O'Neall, S.C. The present ruins of the old factory building,
an illustration of which we present herein, was erected in 1820. [5]

Ruins of Weaver's Old Factory Building, erected in 1820.

Mr. Hill further states that some five miles below Hill's factory, on the
same stream, another colony of New Englanders drove down stakes and
began improvements, preparatory to the erection of a cotton mill. The place
referred to is now known as "Burnt Factory," and, from the best information
that can be gathered, these mills were being erected at the same time, but
which began the spinning of yarn thread first cannot now be ascertained,
but both probably began in the same year.

In a few years after this William Bates returned to South Carolina and took charge of a cotton mill which had been erected by local capitalists in Greenville district, afterwards known as "Batesville," which property he greatly improved.

Leonard Hill, George Hill, William B. Shelden and John Clark, all being master mechanics and manufacturers, went to work in earnest preparatory to erecting the mill, afterwards known as Hill's Factory, Leonard Hill being chosen as foreman or business manager. All the machinery had to be conveyed by wagons from Charleston through a scant settled country when public highways were much neglected. In 1816 or 1817 a small mill was started up, containing about 700 spindles, and people, far and near, went to see "the cotton factory." Mr. Hill states that he has often heard his grandmother speak of the astonishment exhibited even by the best-informed citizens of that day and time.

From an old chain of titles Mr. Hill gathers the following facts, viz.:

"In 1820 William Shelden retired from the firm, selling out his interest to the company. In 1825 George Hill retired, selling out his interest. He returned to his native State, Rhode Island. In 1830 John Clark, of the firm of Hill & Clark, sold his interest to Leonard Hill, who now became the sole owner, and who conducted the business until his death, in 1840. Between the years 1816 and 1830 the building at Hill's Factory was twice consumed by fire, upon which there was not a dollar of insurance. After the death of Leonard Hill the property fell into the hands of his four oldest sons, James, Albert, Whipple, and Leonard. In 1845 or '46 Whipple and Leonard retired, selling out their interest to James and Albert, who operated it until 1866, selling out the machinery to Nesbitt & Wright."

Mr. Hill further states, that on the north side of Tyger River, at Hill's Factory, now owned by the Enoree Manufacturing Co., can be traced an old canal said to be once used to convey water to an old iron works which Mr. Hill has heard called "The Wofford Iron Works"; but as to this name there may be some mistake, as there had been another iron works of the same name on Lawson's Fork, of which mention has been already made. This supposed name for the iron works referred to doubtless grew out of the fact that the old chain of titles to the Hills and others shows that "Beard Shoals" was once owned by a family of Woffords, and that seven small islands were at one time conveyed by title to the Cotton Mill Co. at Hill's Factory by one Wofford.

The present generation of people can never appreciate what our pioneer manufacturers had to contend with in the introduction of machinery into the up-country of South Carolina, and at a time, too, when there was but little cotton produced and no cotton-gins in operation to prepare it for the machinery, and no transportation but on wagons, the nearest market being Charleston, some 250 miles distant, traversing a thinly settled country and over natural cut roads, with little or no attention as to the convenience of the traveling public. Such is a part of history that belongs to the past.

Not long after the Hills and others began the business of manufacturing cotton into yarn, the Rev. Thomas Hutchings came to what is now called Pelham and erected a cotton factory, which was in operation as early as 1822. Mr. Hutchings continued to operate this factory until some time near 1830, when he sold out to Philip Lester, who, after a short time, took into partnership Josiah Kilgore, who had plenty of capital, and they made it a success.

Major Hoy has heard Mr. Kilgore say that it took $20,000 a year to buy cotton. Said amount would pay for about five hundred bales, which number is now spun at Pelham in five days. To turn this $20,000 dollars paid out for cotton back into cash was a matter of importance, and to make a success of the business the thread was transported by wagons to Western North Carolina, East Tennessee, and a great quantity to the lower portion of South Carolina. A quantity of cotton thread was bartered in East Tennessee for flax thread, which was sold to the shoemakers, but a large amount of it was woven in the country looms, the factory paying a skein of cotton thread for weaving a yard of flax cloth, which had a ready sale.

Pelham, known in former times as Lester's Factory, is located only about sixty yards from the present line between the counties of Greenville and Spartanburg.

When Mr. Hutchings sold his factory on Enoree, he built another on a large creek, a short distance from what is now Batesville, which was in operation in 1833. He afterwards sold it and was running another on South Tyger River in 1837, at what was formerly called Cedar Hill but now Arlington. In this factory the late Simpson Bobo, James McMaken and David W. Moore were largely interested, having furnished most of the money that built the factory. A lawsuit in equity sprang up between the parties, which resulted in Mr. Hutchings losing his case, and the factory in some way fell into Mr. Moore's hands. It was subsequently purchased and operated for some years by Dr. Peter M. Wallace. Afterwards it was owned and operated by Mr. Lewis Green and others, and is now owned and operated by Miller, Walker and others.

From information gained from Mr. D. E. Converse, who came to "Bivingsville" February, 1855, we learn that the factory at that place started about 1830. Dr. James Bivings was the moving spirit, and conducted the business for some years, but eventually had some disagreement with the stockholders which resulted in litigation. Dr. Bivings came from Lincolnton, N.C., bringing with him a full set of competent workmen, such as stone-masons, carpenters, machinists, etc. The factory building was in those days quite an imposing affair, and the arrangement of the machinery was well planned, all made in Patterson, N.J. One feature was power, which consisted of an overshot wheel of 26 feet diameter and 12 feet breast, while now the same power is obtained by an 18-inch diameter turbine.

Dr. Bivings, after leaving Bivingsville, started a small spinning-mill on the Chincapin Branch, where the Spartanburg water-works are now located, and not having power enough, supplemented by hitching mules to a long sweep attached to a revolving wheel. This was a primitive way, but only shows what advancements have been made in this line of business.

Dr. James Bivings, after he failed to make a success of his cotton mill on Chincapin Branch, with his son, James D. Bivings, erected a cotton factory on Middle Tyger, which was successfully operated. This he called *Crawfordsville,* named in honor of Hon. John Crawford, who lived near by. The same factory is now called Fairmont, owned and managed by Mr. Guy Harris and others.

After the withdrawal of Dr. James Bivings from Bivingsville, the property was owned and operated by Mr. J. H. Leitner and others, but prior to and up to the beginning of the war between the States, Mr. John Bomar, Jr. (sometimes called "Big John," to distinguish him from others of the same name), was principal owner and manager.

After the war the property was rebuilt by Messrs. John Bomar, Jr., John C. Zimmerman, and D. E. Converse, under the firm name of Bomar, Converse & Zimmerman, but after the death of Mr. Bomar in the latter part of 1868, Mr. D. E. Converse, always the leading spirit, became, with Mr. A. H. Twichell, his brother-inlaw, the manager and principal owner of this valuable property.

About 1880 the name *Bivingsville* was changed to **Glendale,** which latter name the factory and town bears at present.

In the beginning of the factory at Bivingsville it operated 1,200 spindles and 24 looms, while the same factory, remodeled, now called D. E. Converse & Co., has 17,280 spindles and 518 looms.

Fingerville cotton factory takes its name from Joseph Finger, who came to the District of Spartanburg from Lincoln county, N.C., in 1839, and in 1849, in partnership with Gabriel Cannon, who was at that time engaged in merchandizing at New Prospect, began the erection of a cotton factory. The factory is located on North Pacolet River, near the old homestead residence of Mr. Finger. The first investment in buildings, machinery, etc., was about $5,000, and the original number of spindles was about 400. Within the past ten years (the original factory building and machinery having been destroyed by fire) a new company has been organized, with Mr. J. Belton Liles as president, with an investment of capital amounting to $50,000. New and elegant buildings have been erected, and the number of spindles at present amounts to 10,000.

The factory at Valley Falls, Lawson Fork, was originally built by Mr. James McMakin, of Spartanburg, but was subsequently owned and operated by Messrs. Henry White and William Finger. The decease of these gentlemen caused the property to fall into other hands, when, about 1891 or '92, it was demolished by a stroke of lightning, being at this time the property of Mr. F. H. Cash. A new company, however, has been organized at this place and the mills rebuilt, with Mr. T. R. Trimmer at the head, with a capital stock, spindles, etc., as shown in table below.

The following table will show the amount of capital invested, spindles and looms in Spartanburg County, including the Gaffney Manufacturing Co., Cherokee Manufacturing Co., now in Cherokee county, which formerly comprised a part of the original county of Spartanburg:

	CAPITAL.	SPINDLES.	LOOMS.
Arkwright	$ 200,000	22,000	700
Arlington	36,000	3,500	36
Beaumont	60,000	3,100	——
Clifton—1, 2 and 3	1,000,000	100,800	3,250
Cowpens	60,000	7,072	250
Enoree	400,000	30,720	820
Fingerville	50,000	10,000	——
Fairmont	50,000	6,000	168
Pacolet—1, 2 and 3	700,000	57,000	2,190
Pelham	150,000	11,000	——
Spartan Mills 1 and 2	1,000,000	74,000	2,458
D. E. Converse Co.	300,000	17,280	518
Tucapau	269,200	16,656	468
Victor—1 and 2	360,000	25,000	648
Whitney—1 and 2	350,000	19,472	648
Island Creek (Private)	25,000	1,040	——
Valley Falls	100,000	6,000	300
CHEROKEE COUNTY.	$ 5,110,200	410,640	12,454
Gaffney M'f'g Co	800,000	67,000	1,400
Cherokee M'f'g Co	200,000	10,000	600
	$ 6,110,200	487,000	14,454

Eighteen corporations; 1 firm; 26 cotton mills; $6,110,200 capital; 487,640 spindles; 14,454 looms; 300,000 bales of cotton consumed annually.

[1] See "Colonial and Revolutionary History of Upper South Carolina," p. 341.

[2] Colonel Black, in his letter, assigns as a reason why no cannon were cast at these works, that Yorkville, S.C., twenty miles, was the nearest railway point. This is a mistake: the railroad from Columbia to Spartanburg, six miles distant from Hurricane Shoals, was completed before the civil war, and in full operation during said war.

[3] Since chapter relating to progress of city of Spartanburg was written, in which it was stated that one of the cotton mills in Spartanburg contained the largest number of spindles and looms under one roof, the writer is informed that this is a mistake; that this is now claimed for some other mills in South Carolina which have been built since said article was written.

[4] Major William Hoy, in a communication to the *Spartan*, under date of December 25th, 1895, states that Major James Edward Henry came with the Hills to Spartanburg County about 1817 or 1818, and was for some time engaged with them in spinning cotton on Tyger River, but that he quit the business, and was a lawyer in full practice as early as 1822.

[5] Major Win. Hoy, in his writings, states that Weaver was for some time the proprietor of the cotton mills afterwards known as "Burnt Factory" (the same

having been destroyed by fire and never rebuilt), and became engaged in a law-suit with one McDowell, of Charleston, S.C. McDowell died, and his executor carried on the suit and gained it. Weaver afterwards erected a cotton factory on Beaverdam Creek, as above stated.

Chapter Eleven - General Elijah Clarke

According to the pages of history, Elijah Clarke was the first settler in the territory afterwards embraced in the county of Spartanburg (see Ramsey's *History of South Carolina,* page 118). Spartanburg County has every reason to be proud of and revere his memory, not only as her "Daniel Boone," but for other acts of heroism performed on her soil, which we shall mention further on in this narrative devoted to him.

Elijah Clarke was born in North Carolina, but the precise place or date of his birth, we have been unable to gather. By the treaty of Governor James Glen with the Cherokee Indians in 1755, the particulars of which, we have published in another volume, [1] very nearly half of the present territory of South Carolina was ceded by them, which comprised the original counties of Edgefield, Abbeville, Laurens, Newberry, Union, Spartanburg, York, Chester, Fairfield and Richland. This new and beautiful country being thus thrown open to settlement, there was an immigration of settlers into all of these counties, mostly from Virginia, but many from North Carolina, Maryland and Pennsylvania, as well also as an advance of civilization from the seacoast. The settlements in many of the sections thrown open were more rapid than in the up-country lying next to the Cherokee Indian Nation, which at that time the present counties of Greenville, Anderson, Pickens and Oconee formed a part. Mills, in his statistics, says that "this section of the country was settled between 1750 and 1760, but from its exterior and exposed situation, it did not much increase in population until 1776."

According to Dr. Howe's "History of the Presbyterian Church of South Carolina," the settlements on the rivers, north, middle and south, Tyger did not take place earlier than 1755, which was the year of Governor Glen's treaty. These were mostly Scotch-Irish and embraced, for the most part, the present familiar family names of Moore, Barry, Jordan, Nesbitt, Vernon, Collins, Nichols, Caldwell, Anderson, Snoddy, Miller, Pearson and others.

Colonel Elijah Clarke, who afterwards became noted as a soldier of the Revolution and an officer of distinction, settled on Pacolet River at no great distance from the present manufacturing town of Clifton, about the year referred to (1755). In the course of time he was followed by other families, but at the end of said year there were not more than a dozen families residing within the present limits of Spartanburg County.

For about nine or ten years Elijah Clarke remained on Pacolet River, spending most of his time, doubtless, in building houses, opening roads, clearing lands, and preparing a future home for himself and family, but the tardy progress of civilization and the many disadvantages by which he was surrounded, caused him, no doubt, to seek another and a more inviting country for his future habitation, and he removed from South Carolina to Georgia in the year 1774, settling in Wilkes county. His first appearance in the history of Georgia dates with 1776, as captain of a company entrusted with the care of some wagons loaded with provisions for the army. Whilst crossing a small stream he was attacked by a body of Indians which he put to flight, and thus he won his first reputation as a soldier and inspired the confidence of the people as a trustworthy leader in those perilous times. In Howe's expedition against East Florida he rendered important service, but we have not time to go into the particulars of this.

In the battle of Kettle Creek his fame was increased. (See account of this battle — "White's Historical Collections of Georgia," page 684.) After this battle many of the citizens of Georgia who had gone to South Carolina for safety returned with their families and property to Wilkes county, but shortly afterwards were much alarmed by the approach of a body of Indians, and to Colonel Clarke was committed the highly responsible duty of remaining on the frontier to guard the forts. This was a trying period, as the enemy had devastated the fairest portion of Georgia. Colonel Clark's house was pillaged and burnt and his, family ordered to leave the State, but these indignities only inspired him the more. He recruited his regiment for more active service and entered the field with the avowed determination to conquer or die in defence of a cause which he believed to be right and just.

In the battle of Long Cane Colonel Clarke was severely wounded and carried off the field. After his recovery he again entered the field of active service, but was shortly afterwards attacked with smallpox, which lasted him but a brief period.

After the fall of Savannah and Charleston the territory of Georgia, like that of South Carolina, was completely overrun by the enemy, and it became necessary for Colonel Clarke and his command to retreat to more secure regions. While yet remaining in Georgia, he and his command had to secrete themselves in the woods and be fed by friends. When his command reassembled, however, its numbers had increased, and it was the desire of all that Colonel Clarke should lead them to North Carolina. The command set out at once along the eastern slope of the Blue Ridge Mountains. On the way Colonel Clarke was joined by the command of Captain Joseph McCall, consisting of about twenty men, and later he was joined by Colonel John Jones's command, which was from Burke county, Ga., and which had preceded him only a short time before. This junction with Colonel Jones's command was near Cherokee Ford on Broad River, where Colonel Charles McDowell was encamped, and in command of all the forces there, but for want of confidence in his activity, Colonel Clarke, with his united commands, pushed on and joined Colonel Sumter on or near the Catawba. These different commands having come together under brave partisan leaders, it was impossible for active military operations to remain idle very long, while the plunderings and maraudings of the British and Tories were increasing every-where.

The next event of importance in which Colonel Clarke participated was in the capture of Fort Thickety or Anderson, under the command of Captain Patrick Moore, an account of which we have related in the volume already referred to. [2] It was from Thickety Fort that Moore and his Tory associates would sally forth to plunder Whig families in the surrounding country, leaving women and children often without clothing, shoes, bread, meat and salt, and many are the incidents on record of these acts of lawlessness and robbery, which we have not time or space to recall here; but the inroads of this noted character and his followers, reaching the ears of Sumter, this officer directed Colonel Clarke and his Georgians to gather such persons in his camp as resided in that region and who desired to aid in its protection against the outrages of the Tories. It is said that among the first who volunteered to perform this service was Captain William Smith (afterwards one of the early judges for Spartanburg County, who will receive further notice) and his company. Arriving at Cherokee Ford, they met Colonel McDowell just as he was, with Colonels Shelby, Andrew Hampton and Major Robinson of Sevier's Regiment, organizing a force of six hundred men to surprise and capture Thickety Fort, not many miles away. [3] They took up their line of march about sunset on the evening of the 25th of July, 1780, and surrounded and captured the fort the next morning at daybreak.

In the month of August, 1780, immediately following the capture of Fort Thickety, two important engagements with the enemy occurred within the limits of the present county of Spartanburg, in which Colonel Clarke and his command were active participants. One of these was the second battle of Cedar Spring or Wofford's Iron Works, fought on the 8th, and the other the battle of Musgrove's Mill, fought on the 18th of said month. In the volume already referred to, in which we have attempted to chronicle the important events as occurring in said county during the Revolutionary period, we have dwelt at length, and have devoted much time and space in our narrative of these battles, which we cannot again reproduce in this volume, but which, though insignificant as they may appear with some of the battles of a more modern date, went very far, in the judgment of the writer, in serving as stepping-stones, as it were, in deciding the destiny of this great American Republic. They occurred at a time when it was believed by many that South Carolina was already subjugated by the British government, and when many had already laid down their arms and sought British protection, and but for such gallant spirits and daring leaders as Clarke, Shelby, Williams, and others, it is very difficult to determine what might have been the final result. These little engagements gave an important *prestige* to the strength of the American arms, and of the valor, patriotism and determination of her soldiers. In the history of the Revolution, these engagements occurred during a very critical period. For instance, the disastrous defeat of General Gates at Camden (August 16th, 1780), occurred but two days before the battle of

Musgrove's Mill, and the repulse of the enemy at the latter place gave new life and courage to the Whigs everywhere and caused many to rejoin the ranks, and once more to take up arms in defence of a just and righteous cause.

After the battle of Musgrove's Mill, Colonel Clarke, with his command, retreated with the forces of Colonels Shelby and Williams to Gilberttown (near Rutherfordton, N.C.), where a reunion was made with the remainder of McDowell's forces, considerably reduced in numbers, whom they had left at Cherokee Ford before the beginning of the; Musgrove's expedition. Here the various commands separated with the understanding that, after the overmountain men returned to their homes, an army was to be raised from both sides of the mountains sufficient in numbers to cope with Furguson, who seemed at this time to be overpowering in strength and numbers. The Musgrove's prisoners were turned over to Colonel Clarke, who, after continuing some distance on the route in the direction of Charlotte, now concluded to return to Georgia by the mountain trails. The prisoners were turned over to Colonel Williams, who, with Captain Hammond, conducted them safely to Hillsboro, N.C.; but it yet remained for Colonel Clarke to render gallant service to his county, which was in connection with the siege of Augusta in the following year.

After the fall of Fort Granby only two important British posts remained commanding the upper part of South Carolina, viz.: Augusta and Ninety-six. The defences immediately around Augusta consisted of two forts, Cornwallis and Grierson. The former was commanded by Colonel Brown and the latter by Colonel Grierson. Lower down the Savannah River a few miles was Fort Gilpin (or *Galpin, Galphen,* called by some writers).

Pickens, who had recently been created a brigadier, was ordered by General Greene to collect and enlist in his commands the Whig elements in upper Carolina, concentrate before Augusta, looking to the reduction of that post, and to cut off all communication between Augusta and Ninety-six. Lieutenant-Colonel Lee with his legion was also ordered, after the fall of Granby, to join Pickens at Augusta. The distance between these places was about one hundred miles. Lee's Legion had recently been recruited by the addition of Colonel Eaton's command of two hundred North Carolina militia.

And now as to the part performed by Colonel Clarke. Says Johnson:

"Among those who hastened into action upon the approach of the American army (into South Carolina) was Colonel Clarke of Georgia. His followers immediately gathered around him, and he found himself at the head of a party sufficient to invest Augusta, as soon as Pickens was able to hold in check the garrison at Ninety-six."

Clarke's approach to Augusta was sudden and unexpected. It was the custom of the British authorities to send annually presents to the Cherokee Indians. Several boats loaded with these presents were on their way up the Savannah River. Clarke heard of these, and before they could make good their retreat he waylaid them. The stream, though deep, is narrow, and Clarke's riflemen among the trees along the banks would soon have swept the deck of any boat not provided against attack. Unable to ascend or descend, these boats took shelter under Fort Gilpin; and Colonel Clarke was carefully guarding this invaluable prize when he was joined some days afterward by Lee.

Immediately upon Lee's arrival he was complimented with the task of capturing Fort Gilpin. This was on the 21st of May, 1781. Lee captured the post by stratagem, as it were. Appearing before it with a small force, the garrison marched out to engage it, when Captain Rudolph, of Lee's Legion, who was concealed near by with a larger force, rushed into the fort and captured it. All those outside were taken prisoners.

By the fall of this fort there were captured one hundred and twenty-six prisoners of all descriptions, including seventy commissioned officers and privates in the regular service, besides the boats on the stream with their loaded cargoes. The American casualties were small — only twelve wounded. The capture of these boats was a valuable acquisition to the American cause. They were loaded with a quantity of clothing, blankets, small arms, rum, salt, and other useful and much-needed articles of which the American army had long been deprived. There was also a good supply of ammunition and some articles of military equipment.

Notwithstanding the command of General Pickens, representing the States of South Carolina and Georgia (the latter embracing Colonel Clarke's command), were in a naked and destitute condition, yet the distribution of these articles exhibited the characters of Pickens and Greene transferred into a light that was honorable to both. Pickens, with modesty, begged of General Greene, that his men be allowed to share, in their destitute condition, a part of the booty captured. Greene, in reply, authorized him to divide the same according to his sense of justice and the good of the service. Pickens set aside the military stores for public service, and loaded thirteen wagons with rum, salt, sugar, medicines, etc., for the main army. He divided the clothing into three equal parts, assigning one lot to Georgia, another to South Carolina, and the third to the Continental troops. The fowling-pieces were distributed among the militia on condition that they would remain in the army for specific service.

In the capture of Fort Gilpin two forts still remained in the hands of the British, viz.: Grierson and Cornwallis. In the capture of these, which occurred soon after the fall of Gilpin, Colonel Clarke took an active part; but for the particulars of their capture the reader is referred to the first volume of our work; [4] time would fail us to go into a more extended account of the siege and capture of Augusta, to which great credit was due Colonel Clarke for having gallantly confined the British garrison to their works for weeks before the arrival of Lee.

Colonel Clarke remained in the service until the final cessation of active hostilities, which ended at Yorktown, in October of the same year. In the course of his brilliant career he was commissioned a brigadier-general, and before his death a major-general; the former commission doubtless in recognition of his gallant services in connection with the fall of forts Gilpin, Grierson and Cornwallis.

After the close of the Revolution General Clarke rendered some public service in the State of Georgia, but that which gave him greatest achievement was at Jack's Creek in 1787, against the Indians, in which he defeated the Creeks. He died upon the dawning of the nineteenth century, which was about 1801, leaving a name behind him worthy of preservation and perpetuation by the generations that survive him.

Mrs. Hannah Clarke, relict of Major-General Elijah Clarke, died August 26th, 1829, aged ninety years, having outlived her husband twenty-eight years. She attended her husband through many interesting periods of the American Revolution, and had often experienced some of the distressing vicissitudes of the war, having had her house burned as stated and all of its contents destroyed during the absence of her husband by a plundering set of British and Tories who ravaged that part of the country in which she then resided, and had to seek shelter as best she could with a family of children. She was afterwards robbed of the horse on which she was riding to meet her husband near the North Carolina line. During a part of the campaigns of General Clarke she accompanied him, and on one occasion in attempting to remove from a place of danger, near which an engagement was soon expected, her horse was shot from under her, while two children were on his back with her. She was at the siege of Augusta, and was present when Brown capitulated, and many of the prisoners there, and at other times, taken by her husband, experienced her benevolence and hospitality. She lived to behold and rejoice over the happiness of her country, which she had frequently seen desolated by cruelty and bloodshed. Her remains were interred at Woodburn, Ga., near the last resting-place of her husband.

Having attained a good old age "she entered," says her biographer, *"into a rest that remaineth for the people of God."*

[1] See "Colonial and Revolutionary History of Upper South Carolina," p. 21.
[2] See "Colonial and Revolutionary History of Upper South Carolina," p. 128.
[3] The site of Thickety Fort is within a few steps of the present residence of Mr. Ben. Bonner on Thickety creek.
[4] See "Colonial and Revolutionary History of Upper South Carolina," pp. 319-323.

Chapter Twelve - Colonel John Thomas, Sr.

In presenting to the reader the name of this patriot of the Revolution, we desire to say in the outset that full justice to his memory, and valuable services to his country in one of its most critical periods, has never been done by the historians of the past, and we believe the impartial reader will so decide after following us through this narrative, which is but a brief outline of his character and of the prominent part he took at the beginning of hostilities between the colonies and the mother country.

From the best information that can be gained, John Thomas, Sr., was born in Wales, but was reared in Chester county, Pennsylvania. Of his early education and training we know but little; but from his marriage to a a lady of high culture and from the reading of his manuscript letters, still in existence, it is to be presumed that he possessed advantages and opportunities equal to other youths of his day and time.

John Thomas married in 1740 to Miss Jane Black, who was a native of Chester county, Pennsylvania, and the sister of the Rev. John Black of Carlisle, the first president of Dickinson College. An interesting sketch of the life of Jane Thomas is presented in Mrs. Ellet's "Women of the Revolution" (Vol. 1, p. 250), to which the reader is referred for an extended account of her character and heroic service to her country.

Some ten or fifteen years after this marriage, Mr. Thomas, with his family, removed to South Carolina. His residence for some time was on Fishing Creek, in Chester district. About the year 1762 he removed to the territory now embraced in the county of Spartanburg. His homestead residence, which can yet be pointed out, was in the vicinity of Rich Hill.

We would here state, by way of digression, that by reason of the treaty of Gov. Glen with the Cherokee Indians in 1755, the particulars of which we have given in another volume, [1] the upper portion of South Carolina, embracing the counties of Edgefield, Abbeville, Laurens, Newberry, Union, Spartanburg, York, Chester, Fairfield, and Richland, were thrown open to settlement. As we have shown in the volume referred to the settlements in what is now Spartanburg County did not begin earlier than 1755, and it will be seen that John Thomas, in removing to said region (1762), was only a few years behind the advance settlers.

The particulars of the breaking out of the Revolution we have given elsewhere, and have not time or space to go over the ground again; but we will say that prior to 1775 all the country between the Broad and Saluda rivers belonged to one regimental district, commanded by Col. Thomas Fletchall, whose home was on Fair Forest, in the present county of Union. These regimental commanders swayed a wide influence in controlling the political sentiment of their surroundings, and as Thomas Fletchall proved to be a *Tory* of the worst type to the patriot cause, it can be easily imagined the extent of the unwholesome influence which he spread over the region of the country which he commanded. The Council of Safety at Charleston resolved that an association was necessary, to be composed of all those who sided with the patriot cause, or the cause of the colony against the mother country. There was left now no alternative but a mean submission or a manly resistance. The question before the people was, "Shall we live slaves or die freemen?" The instrument, or *Articles of the Association* were first signed by

Henry Laurens, president, and members of the Provincial Congress, and then copies of the same were afterwards transmitted to the inhabitants of the State (or *Province*, as it was then called) through the different regimental commanders of the several military districts. The Provincial militia of South Carolina, in the early part of 1775, consisted of twelve regiments. The copy of the instrument of the association which was transmitted through Colonel Fletchall was not by him submitted to the inhabitants of his district, but in lieu of this, through the assistance of his confères, he drew up another instrument of writing to be submitted to the people, which he claimed was suited to their wishes and the conditions which surrounded them, and which was generally signed by the people from the Broad to Savannah rivers. It may be truly said here that the up-country of South Carolina was in a peculiar and distracted condition. Lord William Campbell, of England, who had arrived about this time, holding under the authority of Great Britain a commission as governor of South Carolina, was unremitting in his efforts to persuade the uninformed of the back-settlers that the power of Great Britain could never be effectually resisted by the American colonies; that the whole dispute was about a trifling tax on tea, which they were not in the habit of using, and the matter was of little or no interest to them. Through his well-paid emissaries he insisted that *the gentlemen* of the seacoast, in order to obtain their tea free, were willing to involve the people of the whole of the back country in a quarrel that would deprive them of salt and other imported necessaries, and that the expenses of an insignificant tax on tea was nothing compared to the expenses of a war with the mother country, and that the instrument which had been prepared by the association for their signatures was intended only to dragoon them into submission. These harangues naturally aroused in the bosoms of many a spirit of resistance and independence, and they openly declared their unwillingness to concur in the measures recommended by the Provincial Congress.

The conduct of Fletchall and the distracted condition of the minds of the people in the up-country gave great uneasiness to the Council of Safety. An effort was made to induce Fletchall to join the common cause or to make known his sentiments on the situation of affairs. He was written to by the Council of Safety on the 14th day of June, 1775. In his reply, on the 24th of the same month, he claimed that many reports had been maliciously circulated against him, which he could prove to be false; he expressed great concern that he was looked upon as an enemy to his country, and thought the government had greater cause to complain of some who were less suspected than himself. Upon the main subject upon which Fletchall had been approached by the Council of Safety, he declared that he would not take up arms against his king until it became his duty to do so and he was convinced of the propriety of the measure.

The Council of Safety, feeling the necessity of a full explanation to the people of South Carolina of the nature of the controversy between the colonies and the mother country, sent to the country between the Broad and

Saluda rivers the Hon. William Henry Drayton and Rev. William Tennant. The mission of these gentlemen was to pacify the inhabitants and to bring them into cooperation with the Council of Safety and General Committee, which had been appointed by the Provincial Congress. They set out on their journey in August; but as we have already, in the first chapter of this work, related the general particulars of the visit of these gentlemen to the up-country, we think repetition here unnecessary. [2]

Not long after the departure of Mr. Drayton and Mr. Tennant a regiment was organized, made up of inhabitants comprising the sections of what was afterwards the counties of Union and Spartanburg. A leader to command the newly formed regiment had to be selected, which resulted in the choice of *John Thomas, Sr.,* the subject of this narrative. Colonel Thomas had been for many years a magistrate and captain of militia, but had resigned both of these positions. He had now arrived at an age beyond the average of the ordinary soldier, but he was a man of wide-spread influence and popularity, and was the man to inspire the people and overawe the evil influences that were being promulgated by Fletchall and his associates.

The regiment as organized was called The Spartan Regiment, which name was doubtless conferred by Mr. Drayton, intending the same as a compliment, and comparing the material that composed it to the Greek *Spartans.* The number of men who comprised it we are unable now to determine, but as the up-country of South Carolina was yet sparsely settled, we suppose it was small, containing, perhaps, not more than two or three hundred.

It was only a few months until the Spartan Regiment commanded by Colonel Thomas was called into active service. In December of the same year (1775) occurred the famous *snow campaign,* a full account of which we have presented in another volume. [3]

The troops in this campaign were commanded by Colonel Richard Richardson, an officer of distinguished ability, and who, with his command, performed on this occasion important and signal service to his country and to the common cause by putting a stop to the late alarming and dangerous insurrections which the enemies to the American cause had excited in the interior part of the colony of South Carolina.

The Provincial Congress of South Carolina met in February, 1776, soon after the expedition of Colonel Richardson. After the accounts of the campaign were audited and arranged, that body voted thanks to Colonel Richardson and to the officers and men under his command for the signal and patriotic service rendered to their country under the most trying circumstances and conditions. It was at this session of the Provincial Congress that this body resolved, "as well for the convenience of electors of members of Congress, as on account of the happy influence which it may have upon the peace and union of the inhabitants," to divide the district heretofore spoken of as under Colonel Fletchall's command (embracing the country between the Broad and Saluda rivers) into three election districts or regimental divisions. The Lower or Dutch Fork, comprehending one, the country below Little River another, and the Upper or Spartan District the third. [4]

By this new formation of regimental districts. Colonel John Thomas became commander of the territory comprising the Upper or Spartan District, which comprised the original county of Spartanburg and almost all of the present county of Union.

During these trying times, when the country was beset by Toryism on the one side and the Nation of Cherokee Indians on the other, ready at any time to swoop down upon the white settlements with tomahawk or scalping-knife, we can readily appreciate the duties and responsibilities resting upon Colonel John Thomas in his effort to preserve the peace and good order of his district.

From the sketch of Mrs. Jane Thomas, already referred to, we learn that Colonel John Thomas furnished his quota of men from his regiment to repel the invasion and massacres of the Cherokee Indians in 1776, [5] and shared the privations and dangers connected with the expedition under General Andrew Williamson into the heart of the Indian Nation, in the autumn of that year.

We have scarcely time here to refer to the Indian outrages of 1776. It was at the very beginning of hostilities that these people, under tempting bribes from British emissaries or agents, were instigated to commit their outrages and massacres upon the innocent of the frontier settlements. But for these they might otherwise have remained quiet. As an argument to induce them to side with Great Britain, they were told of her great power in armies, fleets, resources, etc. Principal among those who figured among them at this time was John Stuart, superintendent, and Alexander Cameron, deputy superintendent of the Cherokee Nation. These were acting under the authority and direction of Lord William Campbell, governor, who clothed them with royal authority. It is said that Cameron, under the influence of Stuart, was a bad and dangerous man. He held a meeting in the early part of 1776 with the Cherokee warriors, about four hundred in number, in which he exhorted them that the people of America had used the king very ill, and had killed a considerable number of his army; that the king was to send out more soldiers to suppress them; that they (the Indians) ought not to turn against their father, the king, but that *they should join the army* against the people of America; that firearms and ammunition would be furnished them, and, in short, he did everything in his power to induce the Indians to join the king's forces against the organized forces in upper South Carolina, of which Colonel Thomas's regiment formed a part.

At the conclusion of his remarks the Indians turned their backs upon him and discharged their arms. The whole assembly set up the war-whoop, which was a signal that they approved of his discourse. (See Drayton's Memoirs, Vol. 1, p. 414.)

It was not long after this until the Cherokees began their invasions and massacres upon the defenceless white settlements along the borders of upper South Carolina. Some of these we have recorded in another volume, including the "Hampton Massacre" and the "Hannon Massacre"; but their barbarities to a great extent have faded in tradition. Prompt and decisive measures had to be resorted to quell these people, which was successfully done by the expedition of General Williamson, already referred to, assisted by Colonel Griffith Rutherford and his command from North Carolina. The combined forces consisted of about two thousand. After several serious encounters the Indians were finally put to flight. Williamson's command continued the work of devastation, destroying the Indian towns and their growing crops in the beautiful valleys. The poor deluded Indians soon sued for peace, and a treaty was made with them by which they ceded all of their lands southeast of the mountains of Unacaya. By this treaty the present counties of Greenville, Anderson, and Pickens (the last two named once forming old Pendleton District) were gained and added to the territory of South Carolina. That portion which the Indians reserved to themselves embraces for the most part the present county of Oconee, [6] which was purchased from them not long after the close of the Revolution.

Peace having been again declared with the Cherokees the commands of Williams and Rutherford returned to their respective States, and Colonel John Thomas again assumed command of the upper or Spartan District. A long line of frontier was entrusted to him. With diligence, fidelity and zeal he performed this duty for several years and retained his command until the fall of Charleston, which was in May, 1780. [7] South Carolina was now practically at the mercy of the British soldiery and the Tory element of the colony. The British believed that the colony was thoroughly conquered. Subsequent events, however, proved that they had conquered the territory only and not the people. The proud spirits of the Whigs of upper South Carolina determined not to submit without making a manly resistance. Cornwallis, who had received the surrender of Lincoln at Charleston, determined, to follow up the success already attained and to press the conquest into the neighboring province of North Carolina, and also into Georgia. To accomplish this end three expeditions were formed and sent out. The first was towards the river Savannah, in Georgia. The second was placed under the command of Colonel Tarleton, who was ordered to scour the country between the Cooper and Santee rivers. In this expedition Tarleton encountered a body of Whigs under the command of Colonel Buford, who had been marching to the succor of General Lincoln in Charleston, but having heard of his surrender, were now retreating by forced marches. He fell upon them and the carnage was dreadful. He butchered many who offered to surrender. This horrible massacre gave a bloody turn to the war, and the Americans everywhere ever afterwards remembered this engagement with horror, and from that time it became a proverbial mode of expressing the cruelties of a barbarous enemy to call them *Tarleton's Quarter*. The third expedition was that of Colonel Patrick Ferguson, who was sent to the District of Ninety-six, and whose wicked career after seventeen months ended at King's Mountain.

As soon as the news of the surrender of Lincoln at Charleston reached the up-country of South Carolina, measures were concerted between the commanders of the scattered Whig forces, Colonels Brandon, Thomas and Lyles, for the concentration of their forces with the view of resisting the invasions from the low country. Their plans were frustrated by the devices of Colonel Fletchall, who had remained at his home since his release from imprisonment a few years before. Having discovered their intentions, he gave notice to Ferguson's forces, who had recently marched into the vicinity of his home, and to a body of Tory cavalry thirty miles away. These were brought together and surprised the force collected by Brandon at the point designated as the rendezvous before the others had time to arrive. The country was now seemingly overawed and subdued, and almost every Whig between the Broad and Saluda rivers was compelled to abandon the country or accept British protection. By the latter course they hoped to secure permission to remain at home unmolested with their families. Colonel Thomas, then advanced in life, with Andrew Williamson, Isaac Huger, Andrew Pickens, Isaac Hayne and others took protection, while others preferred to remain in open partisan warfare, among whom were Francis Marion, Thomas Sumter, the Hamptons, Williams and others. But in the supposition of those who had taken British protection, that they were to remain at home unmolested, they were lamentably mistaken. They could not quietly remain at home and witness the scenes of plunder, robbery and murder which surrounded them, without lifting their voices in protest. The Tories who had espoused the Royal cause were men of no moral or political principle, their greatest ambition being plunder and robbery. It was the policy of Cornwallis to compel submission by the severest measures. The bloody slaughter of Buford's command by Tarleton, just narrated, was but a foretaste of what those who ventured resistance might expect. This course was pursued with unscrupulous cruelty, and the unfortunate patriots were made to feel the vengeance of an exasperated tyranny. Cornwallis, through his emissaries, Ferguson and others, hoped "thus eventually," says a writer, "to crush and extinguish the spirit still struggling and flashing forth, like hidden fire among the people whom the arm of power had for a season brought under subjection."

But the oppressor, though he might overawe for a time, could not subdue the spirit of a gallant and outraged people. The proud spirits of John Thomas, Sr., Andrew Pickens and others resolved to again take the field. They fought through the remainder of the war, says Johnson, "with halters around their necks." Some were made to pay the penalty of this bold resolve, and there is no brighter example on record than the execution of Colonel Isaac Hayne of Charleston.

Colonel Thomas having determined to cast aside the pretended protection, was taking steps to organize a regiment in the Fair Forest region when he was arrested and sent to prison at Ninety-six. From thence he was conveyed to Charleston, where he remained in durance till the end of the war. The regiment referred to was called the *Fair Forest* regiment, and was com-

manded by Colonel John Thomas, Jr. (son of John Thomas, Sr.), and was encamped at Cedar Spring when the first engagement there took place.

After the close of the war Colonel Thomas returned to his home on Fair
Forest, but soon afterwards removed to Greenville District, where he and
his wife resided until their death.

Colonel and Mrs. Thomas had nine children, and their sons and sons-in-
law were active in the American service. John, the eldest son, rose during
the war from the rank of captain till he succeeded his father to the colonelcy
of the regiment, called by Draper the *Fair Forest* regiment, and by the biographer of Mrs. Jane Thomas, in Mrs. Ellet's works *Spartan* regiment. [8]
Robert, another son, was killed in Roebuck's defeat, mentioned elsewhere.
Abram, who was wounded at Ninety-six, and taken prisoner, died in the enemy's hands. William, a youth who assisted in defending his home, the circumstance of which we will mention later, took part in other actions. Martha, one of the daughters, married Josiah Culbertson, a noted scout, who will
receive further attention. Ann, another daughter, married Joseph McJunkin,
a soldier of the Revolution, whose gallant services will be recorded later.
Jane, the third daughter, married to Captain Joseph McCool, and Letitia, another daughter, was the wife of Major James Lusk. The last two mentioned
were efficient patriots, but the scenes of their exploits and the valuable service they rendered their country are remembered now in tradition only,
except the sketch in connection with Mrs. Jane Thomas in Mrs. Ellet's works.
It is unfortunate now that history is silent of so many that deserve the gratitude of their country. It appears that every member of this family had a personal interest in the cause of their country.

It is related in the pages of history that Mrs. Thomas, wife of Colonel
Thomas, was not only distinguished for her indomitable perseverance and
ardent spirit of patriotism, but also for her eminent piety, discretion and
industry. She is described as rather below the ordinary stature, with brown
eyes and hair, rounded and pleasing features, fair complexion, and counte-
nance sprightly and expressive. The daughters also exhibited the same love-
liness of character and beauty of person, which they inherited from their
mother. Mrs. Culbertson is represented as being a woman of great beauty;
and her sister Ann is said to have been little inferior to her in personal appearance. More will be said of Mrs. Jane Thomas in in another place.

We have already stated that Colonel Thomas removed to Greenville District soon after the close of the Revolution. Few of his descendants now remain in the section of country where he and his family resided, being now
scattered over the regions of the great West.

Let it be the pride of the coming generations to preserve and perpetuate
the name of John Thomas, Sr. At the outbreak of the great Revolution he appears to have been the right man in the right place to assume a leadership to
counteract the dangerous and unwholesome influences which had been
spread by others in authority who had preceded him; and the responsibility
for the preservation and perpetuation of his memory, his lofty patriotism,

his bold leadership and gallant deeds belong to the people of Spartanburg and the generations that come after.

[1] See "Colonial and Revolutionary History of Upper South Carolina," p. 21.
[2] For a more extended account of the visit of Messrs. Drayton and Tennant to the up-country the reader is referred to "Colonial and Revolutionary History of South Carolina," pp. 44-62.
[3] See "Colonial and Revolutionary History of Upper South Carolina," page 71.
[4] See map showing this division, "Colonial and Revolutionary History of Upper South Carolina," p. 43.
[5] For a more extended account of this expedition, see "Colonial and Revolutionary History of Upper South Carolina," pp. 84 to 99.
[6] See map frontispiece Ramsey's History South Carolina.
[7] See account of particulars of this surrender "Colonial and Revolutionary History of Upper South Carolina," pp. 100 to 104.
[8] This was undoubtedly a new regiment organized in 1881. It had been six years (1775) since the original Spartan regiment had been organized.

Chapter Thirteen - The Moore Family

Charles Moore Sr. & Mary Moore

Charles Moore was born in 1727, and died in 1805. Mary, his wife, was born in 1733, and died in 1805.

They emigrated from the north of Ireland to Pennsylvania, from which State they came to Spartanburg County, S.C., between the years 1760 and 1764, being amongst the very first settlers. They belonged to the Scotch-Irish race, and, from the best information now possible to obtain, it is thought that the ancestors of Charles Moore went down into Ireland from Scotland with the Duke of Hamilton, to whom large landed possessions were given by the English sovereign from the confiscated estates of Irish noblemen. Foote, in his "Sketches of North Carolina," says that "along with Hamilton went the Moores, Maxwells, Rosses and Baileys, whose names hold good to this day." It is supposed that the Moores were related to the Hamiltons, and that either Charles Moore's mother, or his wife's mother, was a Hamilton.

Charles Moore took up a grant of land in 1763 on Tyger River, ten miles south of the city of Spartanburg, upon which he lived and died, together with his wife, and upon which both lie buried, having nice marble tombstones to their memories. He is described in a deed of land on file in North Carolina as a school-teacher, and the tradition is that he was a graduate of Trinity College, Dublin, Ireland, or of Oxford, England. What important part he took in the war of the Revolution is not now known, further than that his son Thomas and the husbands of his daughters all acted prominent parts on the side of the colonies, as will appear later on.

His will is on file in the Spartanburg court-house, from which it appears he had ten children, named in the following order, viz.:

1. Margaret, married to Captain Andrew Barry. 2., __ married John Lawson. 3. Rosa, married Richard Barry. 4., __ married Robert Hanna. 5., __ married Mathew Patton. 6., __ married Mathew Patton. 7. Thomas, known as General Moore. 8. Elizabeth, married Rev. R. M. Cunningham, D.D. 9. Andrew Barry Moore. 10. Charles, Jr.

First Child — Margaret, who married Captain Andrew Barry, a sketch of whom see in another place, was born in 1752, and died in 1823, aged 71 years. She lies buried in the Moore cemetery on Tyger River, where her father originally settled. It was she who planted the seed chat gave rise to the name of the place, viz.. Walnut Grove. She outlived her husband, and left a will which is on file in the Spartanburg court-house. She was an important character during the Revolution, and tradition says was the "Kate Barry" of history, "The Heroine of Cowpens." She was noted as a scout, and was once flogged by the Tories to make her tell the whereabouts of her husband and his company. Her children will be named under the head of Andrew Barry.

Second Child — Whose name is not known, but who married John Lawson, left no descendants in Spartanburg. She is supposed to have been the wife of Colonel John Lawson, who died in Twiggs comity, Georgia in 1816, after a long life, spent as a soldier in the Revolution and in public capacities afterwards. (See histories of Georgia by White, McCall and others.)

Third Child — Rosa married Richard Barry, of whom a sketch will be given in another place. She outlived her husband, and went west with some of her children, where she died. She was noted for her piety, and tradition records that she was a ministering angel in the sick chamber and by the dying bedside. Her prayers in the hours of trial and bereavement made indelible impressions. The children are named under the head of Richard Barry.

Fourth Child — Married Robert Hanna, who lived and died in York county, S.C., having many descendants, Robert Hanna [1] was a noted soldier, and it is said acted as scout for General Thos. Sumter before the battle of Blackstocks, and that, concealed in a tree, he counted the enemy as they marched against Sumter, and reported the number before the battle.

Fifth and Sixth Children — Married Mathew Patton, a noted continental soldier. If these two daughters had any children it is not now known positively, though Mathew Patton had one son named William, who is supposed to have been by one of his Moore wives, and who married Sally Means, a sister of the late Jas. K. Means, with whom he moved to Crab Orchard, Tenn. Mathew Patton married a third wife, of Tory blood, who mistreated him in his old age.

Seventh Child — General Thomas Moore, who died July 11th, 1822, in his 63d year. He was quite a young man in the Revolution, but played a conspicuous part. He lies buried in the Moore burial ground. He served several years in Congress, and was a major-general in the war of 1812 to 1815. He was twice married, the first time to Patsey Price, the second time to Mary Reagan.

By his first wife, Patsey Price, who died 1808, aged 43 years, he had the following children, viz.: John, died in the South Carolina College. Hamilton, went West. Polly (Mary S.), married Dr. Eber Smith, born 1788, died 1813. Betsey, married Colonel S. N. Evins. Violet, married J. H. Barry of York, S.C. Peggy, married Roddy. Rachel, married Means of Memphis, Tenn. Patsey, married Benson of Alabama.

By the second wife, Mary Reagan, he had the following children, viz.: Barry Moore, Thomas J. Moore, Ann and Amanda. Barry Moore went West. Thomas J. graduated at Athens College, Ga., studied law, married Miss Irwin of Charlotte, N.C., but soon died, leaving a posthumous son, the late Dr. T. J. Moore, of Richmond, Va. He was one of the most brilliant men Spartanburg County ever produced. Ann Moore married at 13 years of age a man named Crump, afterwards to Dr. Harrison, and again to Mr. Martin, of Mississippi. Amanda Moore married first Henderson, and second Dr. Effinger, of Portland, Oregon. She had only one child, Emma.

The only representatives of the family of General Thomas Moore now in this county are the families of Dr. Alfred Moore, who married Martha, the daughter of Colonel S. N. Evins, and his wife Betsey, and of Colonel John H. Evins, son of Colonel S. N. Evins.

Eighth Child — Elizabeth, after marrying Dr. R. M. Cunningham, soon died, leaving no issue. For a sketch of Dr. C. see "Sprague's Annals of the American Pulpit."

Ninth Child — was Dr. Andrew Barry Moore, born February 11th, 1771, and died January 23d, 1848, aged 76 years, 11 months and 12 days. He lies buried in the Moore burial ground on Tyger River. He graduated in 1795 at Dickinson College, Carlisle, Penn., and afterwards studied medicine, in which he attained eminence. It was not uncommon for him to have in his home several young men studying medicine at the same time.

He was twice married. First to Anna A. Maxwell, of Pendleton, S.C., who died February 9th, 1831, in her 43d year. By her he had no children to live. His second wife was Nancy Miller Montgomery, who was born November 13th, 1804, and died March 14th, 1862. She married a second time Colonel S. N. Evins, December 20th, 1860, leaving no children by this last marriage. Her children by Dr. A. B. Moore are:

1st. Margaret Anna, born December 17th, 1834, who was married to Captain Samuel C. Means, December 20th, 1856, and died May 18th, 1879, leaving no issue, having had an only son, Andrew James, who was accidentally killed, March 1st, 1875, in his 16th year.

2d. Mary Elizabeth, born May 31st, 1836, died September 3d, 1836.

3d. Andrew Charles, born March 11th, 1838, and was killed in the second battle of Manassas, August 30th, 1862. He married Mary J. Foster, of Alabama, on December 11th, 1860, but left no children. He graduated in the South Carolina College in 1858, and in law at the University of Virginia in

1860, in both instances with distinguished honor. He was noted for his beauty of person, strength of mind, and noble qualities of heart. He died universally lamented. "Whom the gods love die young," was applied to him. His remains were brought home from Virginia and deposited in Nazareth church cemetery, over which has been erected a beautiful and costly monument, commemorative of his life as a soldier of the Southern Confederacy.

4th. Thomas J. Moore, born April 29th, 1843; married Mary Elizabeth Anderson, February 27th, 1866. His children are:

1. Andrew Charles (see sketch of).

2. James Anderson, born November 18th, 1868; died January 29th, 1869.

3. Thomas Brockman, born November 28th, 1869; died July 3d, 1871.

4. Annie Mary, born November 16th, 1871; died at Charlotte Female Institute June 13th, 1889.

Andrew Charles Moore, Sr.

5. Paul Vernon, born April 2d, 1874; graduated in South Carolina College 1894.

6. Harriet Means, born February 5th, 1877; graduated in Converse College 1897.

7. Henrietta Sue, born October 7th, 1879; Junior Converse College 1899.

8. Nancy Montgomery, born November 19th, 1882; preparing for Converse College.

This Thomas J. Moore is the sole representative of the Charles Moore family by the name of Moore in South Carolina. He was educated at the South Carolina College, leaving there in April, 1862, permanently (having twice in 1861 been called out at Fort Sumter, when the first gun was fired, and when Port Royal fell), in his senior year, to enter the Confederate army, in which he served as a private for the balance of the war, excepting he was

Colonel Thomas J. Moore

made color ensign of the regiment, and carried the colors in the last battles. He joined first Co. E, 18th S.C. Regt., but afterwards was a member of Co. A, Holcombe Legion. He was captured at the Five Forks battle, after passing the winter in the trenches at Petersburg, Va., April 1st, 1865, and was carried to prison on Johnson's Island, in Lake Erie, from which he was released June 16th, 1865, the war being over. He was never wounded or sick in a hospital.

Since then he has been engaged in planting operations, living at and owning the original ancestral home. Not long after the close of the civil war, he was appointed a colonel in the State militia, from which he obtained his title. He has always been progressive as a farmer, and during the year 1899 he planted rice extensively on his low grounds, and has demonstrated the fact beyond a question of doubt that this article of product can be successfully grown in the up-country of South 'Carolina. He was a member of the South Carolina House of Representatives in 1872 to 1874, and State senator from 1880 to 1884. He served seventeen years as chairman of the State Board of

Mrs. Mary E. Moore, Wife of Colonel Thomas J. Moore.

Commissioners of the State Institution for the education of the deaf and dumb and the blind, and has been again elected by the legislature a member of said board. He was also for a number of years a member of the State Board of Agriculture, and in 1894 and '95 was president of the State Agricultural and Mechanical Society, and for many years a member of the executive committee thereof.

In religion he is a Presbyterian, the church of his fathers, being an elder therein, and for many years an active Sunday-school superintendent.

Andrew Charles Moore, Jr.

Son of Colonel T. J. and Mary E. Moore — named in honor of his uncle of the same name whom we have already noticed — was born at Fredonia, the old family homestead in Spartanburg County, December 27, 1866. He was graduated at the South Carolina College, with honors, in 1887.

Andrew Charles Moore Jr. Son of Col. T. J. Moore.

He adopted teaching as his profession, and did his first work in filling the unexpired term (three months) of the superintendent of the graded school of Spartanburg. From this place he went to Camden, S.C., where he organized the graded school of that town. After three years there he was elected to a position in the graded schools of Birmingham, Alabama, as principal of the high school. After eight years' successful labor there, he resigned, to the regret of the trustees and pupils, to pursue his studies in the University of Chicago, which he entered in 1898. After one year he was awarded a fellowship in that institution over many competitors. His chosen department is botany, along with which he is taking the French and German languages. His college course was the full classical, by which he became acquainted with Latin and Greek, and with which he became more conversant in the schoolroom. Besides his eminent abilities mentally, he is of the highest Christian character and exceedingly popular, and loved and admired by all with whom he conies in contact. He will soon obtain his title of Ph.D. The high position which he has already attained not only affords pleasure to his family and friends, but reflects honor on his native county and State.

The tenth and last child of Charles Moore, Sr., was Charles Moore, Jr., who married Jane Barry of York County, S.C., and moved to Perry County, Ala., dying there in 1836, aged 62 years and 8 months.

His children are: 1. William Moore. 2. Andrew Barry Moore, judge and governor of Alabama in 1860. 3. Charles Hamilton Moore. 4. Alfred. 5. Mary, married to James Evins. 6. Juliet, married to Dr. Robert Foster. 7. Adaline, died young and unmarried, and, 8, Betsy, who also died young and unmarried.

All these were born in Spartanburg County, but went in early life to Alabama. The most of them live in the town of Marion, Perry County, or near there.

Charles Moore, Jr., lies buried in the graveyard of Fairview Church, Perry County, Alabama. "He was noted for hospitality and patriotism, and was revered for probity and punctuality, and highly esteemed for general knowledge and quick discrimination." His wife was born May 20th, 1783, and died 20th December, 1857.

1. His first son William had children, viz.: 1. Charles Hamilton. 2. Andrew. 3. Rhoda Jane, married to Dr. Jas. A. Moore. 4. James A. 5. Samuel. 6. Mittie, married to Mr. Wyatt.

2. His second son, Andrew B., died April 5th, 1873. He was governor of Alabama in 1860, when the State seceded, and had children by his wife, Mary Goree, viz.: Martha J., married to Powhattan Lockett; Annie, married Albert Lockett; Andrew Barry, married Mary Smith.

3. His third son, Charles Hamilton, married Mary Billingslea, and had children, viz.: Dr. James A., Andrew Barry, Cornelia Josephine, and Thomas.

4. His fourth son, Alfred, married Miss Hanna, and had children, viz.: William J. and Emma.

1. His first daughter, Mary, married James Gilleland Evans, with children, viz.: Charles Alexander, Thad. A., Thomas J., James S., Julia (Graham), Robert Hamilton, Andrew, Lucius Septimus, and Jane Anna.

2. His second daughter, Juliet, married Dr. R. Foster, with children: Mary J., first married to A. C. Moore and then to Dr. Wm. R. Barron, by whom she has two daughters, Julia and Bessie; Eliza, married Leonard H. Seawell; Mattie, married Caius F. Fennel; Robena, married Lucius S. Evins; Lutie, married David W. Pitts; and Robert, married to Emma Lavinia Barron.

[1] See "Colonial and Revolutionary History of Upper South Carolina," p. 253.

Chapter Fourteen - The Barry Family

This family was originally from Ireland, but first settled in Pennsylvania, coming from there to South Carolina about 1760 to 1764. Tradition says that the family in Pennsylvania consisted of five sons and five daughters. Three sons came to Spartanburg with Charles Moore, viz., Andrew, Richard, and John, while one son — James, probably — settled in York county, S.C. When the family first landed in Pennsylvania is not known, nor how long they remained there. They were originally from Scotland.

The three brothers, Andrew, Richard and John, all settled on Tyger River, near Charles Moore's.

Captain Andrew Barry married Margaret Moore, daughter of Charles Moore. Dr. Howe, in his "History of the Presbyterian Church in South Carolina," says he was born in Pennsylvania in 1832, and received before he came here a liberal English education. He is in error as to the date of his birth, for his tombstone in the Moore cemetery shows he died on June 17th, 1811, aged 65 years, which would have made him born in 1746. Dr. Howe describes him as six feet one inch high, and of powerful muscular strength, and that he married in 1767 or 1768. He was a magistrate under George II., and continued to exercise the office until the Revolution. He held the office of captain from the same power. He was captain of a company during the Revolution, and was at Musgrove's and Cowpens, and probably in several skirmishes, as at Cedar Springs and elsewhere. He was one of the first elders elected by Nazareth Presbyterian Church, in which capacity he served till death.

The children of Andrew Barry and his wife, Margaret Moore, are:

1. John Barry, who married a Miss Watson of York County, S.C. 2. Charles Barry. 3. Andrew Barry, who lived and died in Spartanburg County. 4. Hughey, who married Malinda Kilgore and went to Mississippi. 5. Richard, who married Margaret Kilgore and went to Mississippi. 6. Polly, who married Thomson Lawson. 7. Violet, who married James Hanna of York County, S.C. 8. Peggy, who married David Thomas, son of Colonel Jno. Thomas, Sr. 9.

Katy, who married Jesse Crook. 10. Alice, who married De Forest Allgood of Laurens county, S.C.

All these moved westward except Katy, who married Jesse Crook, and Andrew Barry, known as "Major Barry," who located near the home of his father, one mile north of Moore, S.C., on Tyger River, dying there December 18th, 1860, aged 73 years, 3 months and 23 days. He married Sarah P. Harrison, who was born January 21st, 1791, and died November 30th, 1843. They were married 19th September, 1815.

Their children are: 1. Margaret Ann, born August 11, 1818, and married Major Wm. Hoy 1839. 2. Richard Albert, born 1821; died 1841, unmarried. 3. Emily Augusta, born 1824; died 1898; married J. Wofford Tucker 1844. 4. Henry Patillo, born 1826; died 1898; married Mary Jane Evans 1847. 5. Charles A., born 1828; married Anna Maria Sudduth July 28, 1859.

The first child, Mrs. Hoy, died in 1840, leaving one son, Albert A., who, serving the Confederacy as a soldier, sealed the cause with his life.

The third child, Emily A. Tucker, died in Sanford, Florida, her husband having preceded her a short time. Their children were: (1) Louisa, born 1845, now Mrs. Phillips, with no children; (2) Samuel, born 1847, who married a Miss Gwin of Mobile, Alabama, but died early leaving four children — Gwin (now dead), Wofford, Emmie, and Samuel, all of Sanford, Florida; (3) Howard, born 1848, unmarried.

Henry Patillo Barry's wife was of Chesterfield county. South Carolina, where her kindred now reside. They moved about 1857 or 1858 to Dardanelle, Arkansas, and had several children, viz.: Thomas Jefferson 1848, Andrew Evans 1850, Robert Edward 1853, Henry Patillo 1856 (died 1856), Kolb 1857, William — He married a second time, and died in 1898.

Charles A. Barry, son of Major Andrew Barry, was the representative of the family left in Spartanburg till 1900, His children are:

1. Sallie Maria, died 15th January, 1866, aged 4 years 3 months and 20 days. 2. Emily Carolina, born 11th July, 1863. 3. Virginia Major, born 21st March, 1866. 4. Richard Hugh, born June 10th, 1868. 5. Annie Selina, born February 23d, 1874; died May 30th, 1875.

(2) Emily Carolina married Charles Hill of Greenville, S.C., June 21st, 1888, where she now resides, with children, as follows: Charles, Barry, Sarah Joyce, William (died in infancy), and Jesse Brockman.

(3) Virginia Major married June 21st, 1888, to Jesse K. Brockman, now living in Birmingham, Ala., with children as follows, viz.: Mary Barry, Virginia, and Jesse K.

Emily Carolina and Virginia Major were married at the same time and by the same ceremony under their father's roof.

(4) Richard Hugh married Henrietta Buist Anderson, who died in early life, leaving one child, John Charles, born 28th August, 1892. He lives with his father, Charles A., two miles north of Moore, in Spartanburg County.

Charles A. Barry, who was the head of the family, now residing in Spartanburg County, played an important part both in Church and State. Bereft of a mother's care in early life, he grew up a wayward youth, leading a wild life till marriage, when, touched by God's grace, he became a Christian, under many adverse circumstances, connecting himself with the Nazareth Presbyterian Church, in which he soon became an elder, as was his father and grandfather before him. He often represented his church in Presbytery, and was twice Presbytery's representative in the General Assembly. He was an elder of Center Point Church, being one of its founders. He died January, 1900.

In State affairs, he was a soldier in the Spartan Rifle Company while they were State troops, going to Charleston when Fort Sumter fell. Afterwards he was a member of the 22d Regiment, S.C.V., the Charleston Battalion, and of Company E, 18th Regiment S.C.V., from which last he was discharged. Later he was a member of Co. A, Holcombe Legion, in which he served as a private till the close of the war, surrendering at Appomattox. He served on the County Board of Equalization for sixteen years, and was chairman the most of the time. He was county commissioner for twelve years, and most of the time chairman of the board.

Hon. Charles A. Barry.

He served three terms in the Legislature, and was a part of the time chairman of the Ways and Means Committee. During the third term, on account of failing health, he resigned. He was a member of the State convention which framed the present constitution. Almost blind and worn out, he laid down the burdens of life.

Richard Barry, brother of Andrew and John, was born in 1751; died July 29th, 1816, aged 65 years. Coming here with Charles Moore, he married his daughter Rosa, who survived him and went west with some of her children, where she died. He is buried in the Moore cemetery. What part he took in the Revolution is not known. He stuttered in conversation, but it is related that in his public prayers, in which he was fluent, he never did so.

His children by Rosa Moore are: Richard Barry, familiarly known as "Devil Dick"; Katy, married a Sloan and lived about Rome, Ga.; Polly, married Colonel Isaac Smith. There may have been other children.

From Colonel Isaac Smith, who was a prominent man in his day, descended some families about Gaffney, S.C. The late Colonel Sam Smith was his son.

Of John Barry, brother of Andrew and Richard, nothing is now known here, as he left no descendants in this county, further than that he lived in the fork of the Middle and North Tyger Rivers. His son, William Taylor Barry, was given a college education, and became a statesman from Kentucky, serving as President Andrew Jackson's postmaster -general, besides filling other high positions.

Chapter Fifteen - The Smith Family

Descendants of the Elder Ralph Smith.

In Revolutionary times there resided several branches of the great Smith family within the limits of the original county of Spartanburg, from which have sprung a long and respectable line of posterity. Among the first settlers within the territorial limits of Spartanburg County was Ralph Smith, [1] son of William Smith, of Wrightstown, Pennsylvania.

Ralph Smith emigrated from Bucks County, Penn., to South Carolina in 1765, and was a prominent citizen in his day. At the outbreak of the Revolution, he was a justice of the peace, and though well advanced in years, he threw up his commission and served in the army. When he removed to South Carolina he brought with him three sons and a daughter. The names of the sons were William, Samuel and Aaron; all these became distinguished soldiers during the Revolution.

William, the eldest, was born in Bucks County, Penn., September 20th, 1751. Of his early life but little can now be ascertained. From the responsible and elevated positions which he filled, he must have received the very best educational advantages that could be offered in his day. His military career began when he was twenty-four years old. He served in the snow campaign in the winter of 1775, as a member of the Spartan regiment under the command of Colonel Thomas, Sr., and in the next year (1776) in Williamson's expedition against the Cherokees.

In 1777 William Smith was made a captain of the militia and was stationed for a time in Wood's Fort, near Beaver Dam Creek, between Middle and South Tyger rivers. This old fort was constructed near the border line of the Cherokee Indian Nation (the present line between the counties of Greenville and Spartanburg), as a protection to the white settlers living in vicinity of the border line, against unexpected outbreaks and invasions by the Indians.

In the Revolutionary sketch by Samuel Smith, brother of William Smith, republished in the Spartan, June 28th 1899, it is stated that Benjamin Roebuck was First Lieutenant in the company of Captain William Smith, and that Lieutenant Roebuck was not advanced by promotion until after the fall of Charleston, May, 1780.

In December, 1778, Captain Wm. Smith was ordered to Georgia with his company, serving under General Lincoln, and participated in the battle of Stono, June, 1779.

After the surrender of General Lincoln at Charleston, the territory of South Carolina was completely overrun by the British and Tories, and by many the province was considered as completely subjugated to British authority. Many of the brave spirits of the Revolution sought and accepted British protection. Many of these, and among the number General Andrew Pickens, took the field again and fought bravely to the end of the war. Many, however, like Marion, Sumter, the Hamptons, and others preferred to remain in the field and continue the struggle. Among the latter class were William, Samuel and Aaron Smith, who were uncompromising patriots and true to the American cause.

During the year 1780 Captain William Smith participated in the capture of Fort Thickety and in the battles of Wofford's Iron Works, Musgrove's Mill and Blackstocks. It appears that after Sumter recovered from his wound received at Blackstocks, Captain Wm. Smith became attached to his command and was promoted to the office of major. He was at Guilford Court-house, the siege of Granby, the skirmish at Quincy Bridge, the affair at Juniper, and the capture of some British vessels at Watboo Landing under Colonel Wade Hampton, whose command formed a part of Sumter's forces. He continued in the service of his country until the end of the war. [2]

Soon after the organization of Spartanburg County in 1785, by virtue of what was known as Judge Pendleton's "County Court Act," William Smith was chosen as one of the county court judges for Spartanburg. He served in this capacity until 1797, when he was elected to the Congress of the United States and served several terms in that body. Joseph M. Rodgers says of him: "He was leader of the House, a solid man of some eloquence, but he lacked the magnetism of true leadership. Had he remained longer in Congress he would have become a leading figure in American politics." He died June 22, 1837, in the eighty-sixth year of his age.

The official records in Columbia, S.C., show William Smith to have been State senator, representing the upper or Spartan District from 1788 to '92. This election district embraced all of the territory of the original county of Spartanburg, and the larger portion of the county of Union (see map "Colonial and Revolutionary History of Upper South Carolina," p. 43). He was also senator representing Spartanburg District proper from 1792 to 1800, and from 1812 to 1816, having served his constituents as State senator for a period of sixteen years. Few men served the public longer or more faithfully than Judge Smith. He married in early life to Miss Mourning, daughter of Mrs. Lettice Bearden, who was a sister of General Richard Winn of Fairfield District. By this marriage fourteen children were born, eight sons and six daughters. The names of the sons were Isaac, Eber, John Winn, Elihu, Eliphas, Ralph, William and Aaron. The names of the daughters were Lettice, Marsey, Polly, Jane and two daughters unmarried. Several of the sons became prominent in State politics. Colonel Isaac Smith, the eldest son, was State senator, representing Spartanburg District from 1818 to '26, a period of eight years, and was a representative from the same district in the House from 1828 to '30. He married a Miss Barry, and by said marriage four sons and four daughters were born. The youngest son, Elihu, was a soldier in the civil war and is still living.

Dr. Eber Smith, second son, was a prominent physician in his day, and was elected a representative from Spartanburg District to the State legislature for three times consecutively, which embraced the years 1818, '20 and '22. He married a daughter of General Thomas Moore, by which marriage one son was born — Mr. Aaron Smith, on Dutchman's Creek, who died in 1880, leaving a wife and eight children, five sons and three daughters.

Dr. Smith married a second time to Miss Ashford, of Fairfield District. They had one son, George, who died of yellow fever in Charleston in 1858.

Dr. John Winsmith, [3] third son, was a prominent physician and a man of extensive reading. He possessed a broad intellect, and figured for a number of years in the politics of his native country. He represented Spartanburg District in the State legislature from 1856 to '58, and from 1860 to '62.

After the close of the war between the States, he served one or two terms in the State legislature, and was also elected one term to the State senate. He was also one of the delegates to the State Convention of 1852 from Spartanburg District. In character he was devoted to his friends, but bitter to his political enemies; but during his life he contributed to many objects of charity, and was kind and benevolent in disposition.

Hon. E. P. Smith.

From his extensive library he made a valuable contribution of books, both historical and biographical, to the Kennedy Library of Spartanburg, which if destroyed, could not be replaced.

Dr. Winsmith was the father of J. Christopher Winsmith, a graduate of the Citadel Academy in Charleston, S.C., a gallant soldier of the Confederate army, and Captain of Co. H, 1st Regt., S.C.V., commanded by Colonel Haygood. Dr. Winsmith was also the father of Mrs. Baxter Moore, of Charlotte, N.C., these being his only children. He married Miss Catharine Faber.

Major Elihu Penquite Smith, another son of Judge William Smith, was a prominent and influential citizen and politician in his day, possessing the same distinctive characteristics that belonged to his distinguished father. He was a polished gentleman, a true patriot and represented his native district (Spartanburg) in the State legislature for eight years, from 1842 to '50, as shown by the official records. He married Miss Christina Faber, by which marriage he had nine children, six sons and three daughters.

The eldest, Dr. Wm. F. Smith, of Glenn's Spring, is a prominent citizen and physician, well-known to the people of Spartanburg. He is well educated and a finished gentleman. He was in Europe when the war between the States began, but came home immediately and volunteered. He was for a time a member of the cavalry company known as the Brooks Troop from Greenville, but being a physician, he felt that he could serve his country better as an army surgeon, which position he held when the war closed. Since then he has practiced his profession in and around Glenn's Spring with success.

The second son, Eliphas, was a successful farmer. He entered the army at the commencement of the war and remained in service until its close. He then resumed planting, and continued this business until his death in 1888.

The third son, Ralph, was in the South Carolina College when the war began, and, like thousands of noble young men of that period, left the schoolroom and enlisted in the service of his country. He was wounded in one of the battles around Richmond, and died from effects of same shortly afterwards.

The fourth son, Eber C., was also in the South Carolina College at the outbreak of the war, but quitted the schoolroom and entered the army, and remained until the close of the war. He is farming successfully near Glenn's Spring.

Dr. Wm. F. Smith, Ex-Confederate Surgeon.

The fifth son, Elihu, was quite a boy when the war began, but during the war he entered the army, and towards its close he was captured and carried to prison at Elmira, New York, where he died of disease.

The sixth son, Miner, resides near Glenn's Spring, and is engaged in planting.

The eldest daughter, Miss Kate, married to Major J. W. Minter of Lanrens.

The second daughter, Miss Minnie, has been and is still a successful teacher near Glenn's Spring.

The third daughter, Miss Bessie,' married Mr. Frasier of Abbeville County.

Judge Eliphas Smith, fifth son of Judge Wm. Smith, removed to Alabama when quite young, and was a prominent citizen in that State, and became a captain in the Mexican war. He married Miss Elizabeth, daughter of General Washington Earle. They had two daughters — Miss Lizzie, who married Dr. Durham of Fairfield, and Miss Cassie, who 'married-Captain John Sondley of Newberry county, S.C. He married a second time to a lady in Jacksonville, Ala., from which a daughter was born, Miss Jane, who married Eliphas Smith, now deceased. She survives her husband, and is a successful teacher.

Captain Ralph Smith, sixth son of Judge Smith, was also a prominent citizen in his day, though never in public life. He was a merchant and farmer, and married Miss Susan Turner of Clarke County, Ga. They had four children, one son and three daughters.

The son, Captain William James Smith, was prominently known to the people of Spartanburg County as an honest, intelligent and patriotic citizen, always taking an interest in everything looking to the welfare of his country. He was a typical Southern man, courtly in appearance, with large, penetrating eyes, which gave him the sobriquet of "Big-eyed Bill," only to distinguish him from others of the same name.

He was the first captain of Company A, Holcombe Legion, being selected as the most suitable person to lead that company of gallant young men to the army, but being well advanced in years at the time, he resigned his commission after serving a year or more. This was on account of ill health, being unable to withstand the fatigues of active camp life; but after returning home and recruiting his health he continued to serve his country as best he could until the close of the war. After this, to the time of his death, he continued in his farming operations

Capt. Wm. J. Smith.

on his plantation near Roebuck, S.C., where his family now reside. He was a prominent member of the Grange organization until this was superseded by the Alliance movement. He was also for a number of years the chairman of the Democratic Club of his township and an efficient member of the County Democratic Executive Committee, and tendered important service here in the management of political affairs in Spartanburg County when the State was under despotic rule.

Early in the fifties Captain Smith was married to Miss Mary R. Austin, a lady of intelligence and refinement, who survives him. She was a daughter of Dr. Thomas Austin, of Greenville District, S.C., a soldier of the war of 1812, and granddaughter of Colonel Wm. Austin, a Revolutionary soldier, and also a granddaughter, on the maternal side, of Mrs. Jane James, a sketch of whom appears at another place in this volume. By this marriage eight children were born — three sons and five daughters. Of these only five are living. Clifford, the eldest, is a planter in Marengo county, Ala. He married a niece of Rev. J. L. M. Curry, D.D., well-known in the South. He was a minister to Spain under Cleveland's first administration. One daughter, Miss Emma, married Mr. G. F. Bobo, near Roebuck, well-known to the people of Spartanburg as a progressive farmer. Another daughter, Miss Ella, married Mr. W. B. McDaniel, of Greenville, where they now live. The youngest son, Ralph, resides in Demopolis, Ala., and is engaged in planting. He married Miss Evelyn Hatch of that place. One daughter, Mourning, is single, and lives with her mother.

Of the daughters of Captain Ralph Smith, Miss Mourning, the eldest, married Josiah Smith of Abbeville, S.C., who died a few years after this marriage. She then married Mr. Miner Gracey of Newberry County. He lived ten years after their marriage. Three years after his death she married General W. P.

Bocock, of Appomattox county, Va., who was an eminent lawyer and attorney-general of the State of Virginia at the time of their marriage. She died in 1886 and her husband shortly afterwards. The second daughter, Miss Jane, married General L. W. Lawler, of Talladega County, Ala., a prominent man in that State, where he filled various positions of importance. He was appointed one of the commissioners to settle the debt of Alabama after the close of the war, in which he displayed great financial ability. He was also a prominent member of the Baptist church, and died in 1892. His widow survives him as the only living child of Captain Ralph Smith. Two accomplished daughters were the issue of this marriage. One, Mrs. Richardson, who died in 1887, leaving a daughter, and another, Mrs. General Whiting, of Mobile, who has two sons and two daughters. The third daughter of Captain Ralph Smith, Miss Elizabeth, married Mr. S. N. Steele, of Newberry, S.C., a successful merchant. They removed to Marengo county, Ala., where he died in 1886, leaving two daughters, Mrs. Dr. Turk and Mrs. Wm. Spencer.

Colonel William Smith, another son of Judge Wm. Smith, removed to Fairfield District, many years before the civil war between the States and engaged in planting. He married a Miss Ashford, of Fairfield District, S.C. They had a large family, but most of them died young. One son, Mr. Joel Smith, served in the Confederate army; was wounded and died not long after the close of the war from the effects of the same. Aaron, the youngest son, died before he reached the age of manhood.

Among the daughters of William Smith, Lettice, the eldest, married to William Jenkins of Chester District, S.C., and subsequently removed to Talladega, Ala.

Of the other daughters mentioned, Marsey married to Thomas Rabb of Fairfield District, Polly to Mr. Goel Brewton of Spartanburg District, and Jane to Mr. William Bogan of Union county.

It is said that during the war the family of William Smith were greatly persecuted by the Tories. They went to his house, destroyed his property and threatened his life. A Tory went to his house one day and told his wife that he and some other Tories, who were neighbors, had resolved to kill Captain Billy as soon as they laid eyes on him. Not long after his departure the captain rode up, and learning of the intention of the Tories, went immediately to the house of the Tory giving the information for the purpose of killing him. When the door was opened the Tory was not to be seen, but noticing that a plank in the floor had recently been moved, he prized it up with his gun and there lay the cowardly wretch, who begged most piteously for his life. "Go," said the captain, "but beware of making any more threats."

On one occasion Captain William Smith ventured home to see his wife. A Mr. West, who was a neighbor and a member of his company, accompanied him. Mr. West and he parted and were to remain a few hours .at their homes and then meet to return to their command. The wife of Captain Smith prepared a hurried meal, and as he was in the act of sitting down to the table, he heard a firing in the direction of West's house. He immediately left, and

129

when he came to the place of meeting, which was near where Philadelphia Church now stands, he was horrified to see the dead body of West suspended from a hickory tree. The fact has been related to the writer that Captain Ralph Smith (son of William) said his father had often shown him the tree, when they would be deer-hunting, where his friend West was placed after they had killed him before his wife's eyes.

Another time William Smith was going home alone, and hearing some persons talking, he concealed himself in some bushes near the road. The moon was shining brightly, and he recognized them as they passed. One of them remarked: "What a glorious night to kill Bill Smith!" Although he was treated badly by them, after the war he befriended them. He would say to their persecutors: "Come, men, the war is over; let them alone." Many Tories would have been driven from their homes had not his peaceful counsel prevailed. In after years when old age was growing upon him he would call his grandsons around him and tell them to always go to the elections and vote early for good and true men, and preserve the liberty which he fought seven years to give them.

Samuel Smith, second son of Ralph, the ancestor of this branch of the Smith family, and brother of Judge William Smith, was a resident of Spartanburg District, and also a gallant soldier of the Revolution. From a fragment of a Revolutionary sketch published in the *Carolina Spartan* under date of June 28th, 1899, containing recollections of Samuel Smith, we gather much valuable information as to his career in the army, and particularly as to the battle of Cowpens. He performed, however, gallant service against the Tories after the retreat of Morgan's army from the Cowpens, he being detained at the latter place on account of his wounded brother. In his sketch he states: "After the battle of Cowpens we stayed a few days in this neighborhood. We got word of a company of Tories coming up; we rallied what force we could to meet them. Captain Shelby, from the mountains, came along and joined us. There were other captains, Carey of Newberry, Elder and Berry from up Tyger. The command was given to Shelby, and we went after the Tories. The Tories had taken up for the night at a house near Enoree, where Odle lived. Shelby gave them a fire which the Tories returned, but we retired, as they were in the house. Elder was shot and a rain came up and our scout went to another house; when our party came back the Tories had gone.

"When Roebuck came back from North Carolina, I was with him in several excursions in search of squads of Tories. After one of our excursions Roebuck, with Captain Mat Patton, went to stay at a neighbor's house to get some clothing which was in preparation for him but not ready; so he had to stay through the day and at night some Tories came and took him and Patton. I was taken the same night and, perhaps, a dozen others in different places. This was the 10th of March, 1781. We were taken to Little River to a Tory station and tried for our lives. Captain Patton, Charles Bruce and two of the Elders were condemned to be hung. The rest of us were taken to Ninety-six, where we remained until the day before Greene laid siege to the place. A number of us were paroled and started home. We turned back at the Saluda River. Major McJunkin was of this number. I had the smallpox while in the jail at Ninety-six. We came near perishing to death while there. The reason we turned back was that Colonel Brandon told us it was not safe to venture and that he would come back with us. After this I kept scouting about after the mischievous Tories till the war was ended. I was not able to do regular service on account of losing the skin from the soles of my feet with the smallpox."

In a manuscript letter before us of this branch of the Smith family, it is stated that Ralph Smith, the elder, was taken prisoner with his young son Samuel, and incarcerated at Ninety-six, where they were nearly starved to death. They chewed bits of leather to appease their hunger, and their finger- and toe-nails dropped off in that loathsome prison.

In the sketch of the recollections of Samuel Smith, already referred to, he does not allude to his father, Ralph Smith, in this connection, but says he "was taken the same night" that Roebuck and Patton were taken, and, "perhaps, a dozen others in different places," and further states that they "came near perishing to death while there." Aaron Smith, third son of Ralph Smith, Sr., was also a gallant soldier of the Revolution, and was among the gallant heroes slain at the battle of Cowpens, receiving there a mortal wound, which caused his death in a few days. In referring to that battle, says Samuel Smith, in the sketch already quoted from: "I heard one gun fire before the general fire; after this the British infantry commenced a general fire. We presently retired behind the line commanded by Pickens. Brother Aaron was wounded there about the time we began to give back. I remained with him till the next day, when we carried him over Broad River where he died."

Let the name and memory of Aaron Smith live and be perpetuated in connection with that brilliant achievement for American liberty. It has been truthfully said that had there been no victory at Cowpens, there would have been no surrender at Yorktown.

[1] In a revolutionary sketch published in *Spartan* June 28th, 1899, Samuel Smith, son of Ralph, states that his father was raised among the Quakers in New Jersey, but that he did not follow them; that he moved to Pennsylvania before he (Samuel) was born.

[2] In searching among the records in the office of Secretary of State, Columbia, S.C., January, 1900, the writer ran across the roll of Captain Wm. Smith's company while a member of Sumter's command. This, the writer was informed, had been picked from the rubbish of a vacant room only a few months before. The following names appear on said roll: Captain Wm. Smith, Lieutenant Berry Jeffers, George Autly, Richard Bearden, Wm. Bearden, Nathan Bird, Jesse Chandler, Wm. Caldwell, James Dawkins, Samuel Day, Charles Elliot, James Flinn, James Gaston, Thomas Griffis, Robert Glasco, John Harris, Wm. Herrie, George Hughes, Wm. Houldich, George Jeffries, Jonathan Jones, Samuel Lancaster, Robert Lusk,

John Morton, James Neal, Benj'n Neighbors, Henry Petitte, John Rest, Rob't Scott, John Steele, Wm. Swords, Nathan Smith, James Strother, Zopher Smith, Wm. Seigler, Abraham Lowery, Joseph Walliston, Archison White and Wm. Young.

[3] By special enactment of the Legislature of South Carolina, the name John Winn Smith was changed to John Winsmith.

Chapter Sixteen - The Wofford Family

Among the very first settlers of the territory of Spartanburg County were the families of Wofford which name has become illustrious in the annals of the history of said county, and deserves more than passing notice.

From the information which we have gathered, it appears that five brothers of this name came from Maryland, and most of them settled in the vicinity of Hill's Factory, on Tyger River. The ancestry of these descended from the North of England, and their names were respectively William, Joseph, James, John and Benjamin. The tradition in the family is that two brothers from the North of England came to America and settled in Pennsylvania near the Maryland line, and that one of these brothers was the father of these five brothers.

William, the elder, was born near Rock Creek, in then Prince George, now Montgomery County, about twelve miles above Washington City, October 25, 1728. Of his early life but little can be ascertained; but he most likely served among the Maryland troops in the French and Indian war, raging on the frontiers of that and neighboring colonies, in his younger days, and somewhere it seems he obtained the title of *colonel,* as he was called.

Colonel William Wofford, being a man of enterprise, early migrated, as already stated, to the region embraced in the present county of Spartanburg, and erected on Lawson Fork the noted iron works bearing his name, and which became noted in the pages of Revolutionary history by reason of the battle which was fought near by and which were destroyed by the raid of the noted "Bloody Bill" Cunningham, November, 1781. [1] He was one of the leading patriots of that region and served as lieutenant-colonel on Williamson's Cherokee campaign of 1776 (for which he drew a pension).

Early in 1779 he was in service in pursuit of the fugitive Tory party under Colonel John Moore, when fleeing from North Carolina to Georgia, and in the spring and summer of that year he served in Georgia and South Carolina under General Lincoln, and doubtless shared in the battle of Stono.

It appears that after this campaign Colonel William Wofford disposed of his interest in the iron works to Simon Berwick and retired to the Upper Catawba in the Turkey Creek Cove, purchasing a tract of 900 acres with improvements, and on this tract he erected a fort, [2] for his own and his neighbors' protection against the Indians. This was on the line of march of the over-mountain men to King's Mountain, and Draper, in his "King's

Mountain and its Heroes," refers to Colonel Wofford in words complimentary to his character,

Wm. C. Wofford, son of Colonel Wm. Wofford, was a member of the Georgia Legislature for over twenty years, was several times Speaker of the House, and for a period. President of the Senate. He was a man of strong mind; his advantages of early education were poor, but in later years he acquired considerable knowledge and experience.

The Wofford Iron Works referred to were known by other names. In Johnson's Traditions they are called *Berwick's* and in Ramsey's History of South Carolina, *Buffington's Iron Works*.

After the war of the Revolution was over Colonel William Wofford removed to Habersham County, Ga., where he gave much attention to surveying lands. He was an influential citizen of that State, and left a numerous posterity, among whom is General Wm. T. Wofford, of the Confederate Army, an officer of distinguished ability. He died at the age of ninety-five years, and it is said, was able to read without spectacles to the end of his life.

Joseph Wofford, another brother, is mentioned in history as captain of a company in the famous "snow campaign" which formed a part of the famous Spartan regiment under the command of Colonel John Thomas, Sr. He mustered before the war at a place called the "Walnut Trees," just beyond James's Creek, near a spring, and near Reuman Newman's place. He was with the troops in Charleston, in command of a company before the fall of that city, and fell back to Ninety-six.

We find no further record of Joseph Wofford as a Revolutionary soldier, but there is no doubt but that he did valiant service until the end of the struggle. Certain it is that he remained a devoted Whig; was always true to the patriot cause and was influential among the leaders of that cause. Tradition informs us that he was a target for the Tories, whose animus for *Captain Joe,* as he was called, was very bitter and hostile, which continued for several years after the war. Some very tragic, interesting and exciting episodes, are related to this day, which occurred between him and certain Tory leaders of that time who were noted for their many acts of violence, murder and burnings perpetrated against the Whigs and their property. His services to his country during these trying times were, therefore, valuable, not so much as a soldier in the ranks, but against the maraudings of these unscrupulous adherents to the Royal cause, whose frequent forays were often made upon unprotected settlements. For this reason, while not in active service, he was known as an outlyer, for fear of being assassinated by the Tories. Assembled oftentimes with his compeers in squads, in out-of-the-way places, with well understood and recognized signals to come together on the approach of danger, he was the recognized leader against these plundering excursions of the British and Tories; hence the bitter animosity displayed against him, which caused his log-cabin to be closely watched. It is related that it was the ingenious and womanly tact of his devoted wife that saved his neck from the halter when arrested by a band of Tories while at home, which was the same night she gave birth to *Benjamin,* the founder of the Wofford College.

Joseph Wofford was a noted hunter and fisherman in his day, when game and fish abounded in plentifulness, and there are many interesting traditions lingering among his posterity relative to his old hunting grounds, his fishing holes on the Tyger, and his superior marksmanship.

James, another brother, lived during the Revolution near the Frank Wofford place on the road between Spartanburgand Woodruff. He was small and a very infirm man. His wife was a Miss Hoopuck, a Scotch-Irish lady, whom he married in Maryland. He was a staunch Whig, and his descendants are nearly all Baptists. He was buried on his homestead, at his request, under a large oak that he himself had planted, which stood until 1890, when it was destroyed by a thoughtless tenant. He was an ardent supporter of the infant colony, outspoken in behalf of the American cause, and the animosity of the Tories was very great towards him. Oft-times he was in great danger of losing his life. He was a surveyor, and owned at one time 9,000 acres of land in his region. He had eight children, four boys and four girls. Their descendants are very numerous, many of them going west at different periods, and some of the staunchest citizens around Woodruff are to be found among them. Many of the valiant defenders of the "Lost Cause" are to be found among them, some of whom laid down their lives and lie buried in the soil of the "Old Dominion," while under Lee, Jackson and Longstreet.

Of John Wofford, another of the five brothers, we have but little information; but from the best that can be obtained, he was an enlisted soldier in the Revolution; certain it is that he was on the Whig side during that great struggle for American liberty. He was the father of eleven children, viz.: John, James, Isaac, William, Hiram, Precilla, Dorcas, Lienor, Clary, Sarah, and Syntha. Many of the descendants of these live in Spartanburg County, many in Georgia and in other States out west, some of whom have distinguished themselves in war and in peace. Among these was L. J. Wofford, chief of artillery under General S. D. Lee in the western army.

As to the fifth brother, Benjamin, while we have no information that he took up arms on either side during the Revolutionary war, yet, like many good men in the early part of 1775, his sympathies were with the king. On one occasion he was arrested as a suspect with Colonel Fletchall and others, and was released through the influence of his brother Joseph.

There are many extenuating circumstances why many of the early and best settlers of the up-country of South Carolina adhered to the cause of the king in the beginning of the Revolution, They lived in remote sections of the country where the British oppression complained of was barely known, where the circulation of current news and literature was unknown, and it was almost impossible to obtain any reliable information. Many good men were led off from the path of patriotic duty under these circumstances, and especially under the overpowering influence of Colonel Fletchall, who held the commission of *colonel* under royal authority, and whose regimental district, at the outbreak of hostilities, covered all the country between the Broad and Saluda rivers. Fletchall was all the time in constant communication with Governor Campbell and other loyalist leaders, and kept his people well informed on the existing troubles from his standpoint; but as soon as the true inwardness of the situation was well understood, some of them became ardent supporters of the American cause, and it is to be hoped that Ben Wofford was one of these, and that the pledges he made while his brother Joe was importuning for his release from custody were afterwards faithfully kept.

The children of Captain Joseph Wofford, one of the five brothers already mentioned, and Martha Lewellyn, his wife, were Martha, Benjamin, Joseph, Jeremiah, Rebecca, and Nancy. Only three, Joseph, Nancy and Martha, died leaving children. Joseph, the elder, married Jane Huckabee. He chose early in life the avocation of a farmer, and lived and died near where his father had settled before the Revolution, in the bend of Tyger River above Beard's Shoals. His educational advantages were limited. He was a very successful farmer, and raised a large family of children; was one of the pillars of the Methodist Tabernacle Church, near by, and whose mother was one of the principal founders. He was loved, honored and respected by his neighbors, and one of the leading citizens in that part of the country. He was a magistrate, and for a long period one of the Commissioners of the Poor for Spartanburg District. His children were Harvey, Benjamin, John, Westley, Jerry, Joseph Lewellyn, Rebecca, Sallie, Nancy, Pattie, and Jane.

Harvey Wofford, the eldest, married Nellie White, an estimable, good woman, and settled across the river from the old homestead, near Hebron Church. He was a plain, practical, hard-sense farmer. His term in school consisted of only' three months, yet by dint of perseverance around the pine-knot fire at night, studying and reading every chance moment he could get, at the age of twenty-one he had a fair English education, and was able to teach, which he did for a year or so, in a neighborhood school. He never sought preferment of any kind, being retiring in his disposition. The office of major in the militia was thrust upon him *nolens volens,* and the office of magistrate was held by him nearly all the years of his mature life. He was especially noted for his official capacity as a magistrate and surveyor, as well as in his private capacity, throughout the lower part of the county; as an "arbiter" his services in this respect were almost constantly in demand, and many a quarrel, feud, dispute or misunderstanding was amicably settled without appeal to the courts. No one doubted his word, and all had implicit confidence in his judgment as to what ought to be done in all matters of controversy or dispute. He was a steward in the Hebron M. E. Church for over forty years of his life. Also the active executor of the estate of Rev. Benjamin Wofford, the founder of the Wofford College, and a trustee of the same to the close of his life. Given to hospitality, the rich and poor alike were always welcome to his table. He was a well-rounded, modest citizen, but, more than all, was estimated in the community in which he lived for his strong Christian character, whose life was a benediction to all.

His eldest son, Sergeant Wm. B. Wofford, was killed at the battle of Fredericksburg, Virginia, being shot down with the foremost men on top of Mayre's heights.

Jerry Wofford, brother of Harvey, married Rachel Shands, a lovable good woman, and he, like his elder brother, lived the plain, practical life of a farmer, on the river Tyger near the old homestead, loved and respected by his neighbors and a large number of friends throughout the county.

Rebecca married C. C. Layton, well known in the Cross Anchor section, and among her children were Dr. J. T. Layton, who died in the city of Spartanburg in 1894.

Sallie married John Lanford, of Lanford Station, Laurens County, S.C. She was the mother of Captain Benj. W. Lanford, who at one period of the war was commander of Company G, 3d South Carolina Regiment Volunteers, and for one term sheriff of Laurens County.

Nancy married Willis Layton of Walnut Grove. Among her children was the Hon. A. Baxter Layton, a member of the lower house of the South Carolina Legislature in 1896 and '97. Also, during the civil war, a lieutenant in Company K, 3d Regiment S.C.V.

Pattie married Wm. Burnett, a well-known citizen in the county of Spartanburg.

Jane married Isaac Epton of Cherokee Springs, a good citizen.

The descendants of these families are very numerous in the county of Spartanburg.

Martha, daughter of Captain Joseph Wofford, married Moses White, who, about the year 1839, moved to Mississippi, whose descendants there are very numerous. Her son, Captain John W. White, born in Spartanburg District, a talented and prominent man, was killed while leading his company of Mississippians at the bloody battle of Chickamauga, in Georgia.

Nancy, the only other daughter that died leaving children, married John Tucker, a young Revolutionary soldier from Maryland. Of them were born six children, all of whom went west except Samuel and Nancy. The latter married Emanuel Allen, an estimable and worthy citizen in the lower part of the county. They were the parents of Drs. Wade and Garland Allen, both noble young men, who gave up their lives in the service of their beloved Southland. The former, Dr. Wade, was a brilliant young man, and an officer in Company D, 3d Regiment S.C.V., and heroically distinguished himself at the battle of Knoxville, Tenn., under Longstreet, where he fell.

Samuel W. Tucker married a daughter of James Howard, a soldier of the Revolution, named Laodicea, His education was limited, but being endowed with a strong, vigorous intellect, excellent judgment, strong determination, and by a liberal use of the pine knots, became one of the most prominent citizens of the section of the country in which he lived; was devoted to his church (Methodist), and was honest and fair in all his dealings. His sons were Joseph W., John A., and F. Marion.

Joseph Wofford Tucker, the eldest, was educated at Cokesbury, South Carolina; studied law and began practice in the town of Spartanburg, and was for several years associated with Dr. Peter M. Wallace in the editorial management of the *Carolina Spartan*. He also, for several terms, represented the district of Spartanburg in the State Legislature, and was the first president of the Spartanburg Female College. He resigned this position and removed to St. Louis, Mo., where he resumed the practice of law; became a judge; was editor of the Missouri *State Journal*, and so pronounced an advocate of States' rights the paper was suppressed by Federal bayonets.

During the civil war between the States he accompanied the army of General Sterling Price southward from St. Louis, and published regularly a paper called "The Army Argus." He soon entered the special secret service of the Confederate States, in which he remained to the close of the war. A reward for his arrest was offered. He went to Bermuda and remained for several years. When the amnesty proclamation was proclaimed he returned to his native land and settled in Florida, and remained there to the close of his life. He was a lay delegate to the great Ecumenical Conference held in London. He was a man of varied and extensive information, a ripe scholar, a gifted writer, a Christian gentleman, and a born leader among men. He married to Miss Emily Barry of Spartanburg District.

Hon. J. Wofford Tuck

John A. Tucker went to Georgia, practiced law and was elected to a judgeship.

Francis Marion Tucker was a physician of ability, and at the breaking out of the war he raised a company of volunteers, composed of the best material the country afforded, and fell at the second battle of Manassas while gallantly leading his men in charge, loved and mourned by his comrades. He married to Miss Addie Nesbitt on Enoree.

The daughters of Samuel Tucker were: Louisa D., who married James Madison Lanham; Nancy, who married J. W. Durham; and Annie W., who married Capt. John McCravy. They all reared quite a number of children, and among them Hon. S. W. T. Lanham, now of Texas, who, while yet a beardless boy, joined Company K, 3d Regiment S.C.V., under Longstreet in Tennessee, and distinguished himself as a private on a number of battlefields from then to the close of the war. After the war he married Miss Sallie Meng of Pacolet, S.C., moved to Texas in a two-horse wagon, taught school and read law, was admitted to the bar, elected solicitor of his circuit, and entered politics, and for seven terms he has represented one of the largest districts in the State in the Congress of the United States, and only a few years ago was a prominent candidate for governor, and missed the nomination by only a few votes. His many friends believe that he will yet preside over the destinies of one of the greatest States in the West, and occupy the Executive Mansion.

A younger brother, Dr. J. Marion Lanham, is one of the most popular citizens in the county of Spartanburg, and also one of its leading physicians, being yet comparatively young, active and progressive in his profession.

Another also, is Samuel Tucker McCravy, Esq., one of the leading members of the bar at Spartanburg, and one of the progressive, influential members of the city council, and efficient secretary of the Wofford Memorial Association, which meets annually at Tabernacle church. His great-grandfather was Archibald McCravy, a stalwart, sturdy, fearless soldier of the American Revolution. He was in Captain John Nelson's company

Captain F. M. Tucker

in the Fourth Regiment in the line of the State of North Carolina, commanded by Colonel Polk, who, we have stated in another volume, figured prominently in the famous "snow campaign," in the winter of 1775.

Those who can justly claim Captain Joseph Wofford and his wife Martha Llewellyn as their common ancestors, run into the thousands, and are intermingled with hundreds of families in Spartanburg County.

From the Confederate rolls, which we publish in another place in this volume, showing the number — as we have been enabled to secure — of troops furnished by Spartanburg District to the armies of the Confederacy, it will be seen that there were about thirty of the Wofford family that donned the gray, scattered among the forces on the seacoast, in Virginia, and in the West, not one of whom, so far as known, was not true to the flag of his country, and while only a few of them rose to higher positions, yet they all possessed and exhibited a high degree of bravery well worth the cause which they espoused.

Dr. Benjamin Wofford

Besides those already mentioned reaching a degree of prominence in the Wofford family, including the Tucker branch of the same already mentioned, are the late Dr. Benjamin Wofford of Spartanburg, Dr. Joseph Llewellyn Wofford at Cherokee Springs, Hon. John W. Wofford at Hendersonville, N.C., and Rev. Benjamin Wofford, founder of Wofford College.

DR. BENJAMIN WOFFORD

a son of Joseph Wofford, born on Tyger River, attended the Methodist High School at Cokesbury, S.C., studied medicine under Dr. C. P. Woodruff at Woodruffs, S.C., and received his diploma from the medical college at Augusta, Ga. He married Miss Julia Woodruff, a lovely, industrious, frugal woman. He lived and practiced his chosen profession near the old homestead for twenty-three years. As a physician, he was as faithful in attendance upon the poor as he was to the wealthiest slave-owner in his large, extensive practice. After the death of his first wife he married Miss Corrie Farrow, who survives him. He was fond of children and they all loved him. He served as captain of a company of reserves during the latter part of the war, and did some service at Charleston, S.C. After the war he removed to the town of Spartanburg and for a few years engaged in merchandizing. He was then elected to the office of probate judge for two terms, one term as county auditor, and two terms as school commissioner. He was one of the executors of his uncle's estate (the Rev. Benjamin Wofford), and for quite a number of years was a trustee of the college his uncle had founded. Very few people had more good staunch friends in the "old iron district" than he had. He was the first president of the Wofford Memorial Association. He was a total abstainer and a life-long advocate of temperance. In his private life, in his extended official capacity, in his church relationship, many bear witness to his uprightness, and his sterling integrity of character. He outlived his two sons, Charles Pinkney Wofford and John Young Wofford. The former was a graduate of Vanderbilt University, Nashville, Tenn., and at his death was superintendent of the Central Methodist Sunday-school at Spartanburg, and was a young, rising, prominent lawyer at the Spartanburg bar.

John T. Wofford attended the school at Ridgefield and some others in the Hebron neighborhood and prepared himself at Marietta, in Greenville County, to enter the West Point military school, having received the appointment thereto from Hon. J. D. Ashmore, then member of Congress from his district. He remained there for nearly two years, when his native State passed the ordinance of secession. He then sent in his resignation. About this time some Northern cadet, in his presence, said something unsavory about South Carolina and Cadet Wofford resented it and a very severe personal altercation followed. On his return at the organization of Co. K, 3d

Dr. Jos. L. Wofford.

S.C. Regt., S.C.V., he was elected first lieutenant and served until the expiration of the first twelve months' term of enlistment. He then came home, assisted in organizing another company, was again elected a lieutenant in 13th S.C. Regt., and died at Jordan Springs, in Virginia. His superior officers speak highly of his efficiency and his calm, cool bravery in time of action. He was a studious, brilliant young man, and stood high in his class at the military academy at West Point.

DR. JOS. L. WOFFORD.

Joseph Llewellyn Wofford, whose picture we present herein, and whose familiar face is well known to the people of Spartanburg, is a son of Joseph Wofford, who married Jane Huckabee, as stated in a preceding page, and was born January 17th, 1833, and received in the schools of his county a good education; after which he read medicine and graduated at Augusta, Ga., in 1853. Returning to his native county he located in the practice of his profession at Cherokee Springs, at which place he still resides.

When South Carolina called for volunteers at the beginning of the war between the States, he entered the service in Captain Joseph Walker's company (Spartan Rifles), which was attached to the 5th Regiment, S.C.V., commanded by Colonel Micah Jenkins, and was for some time, at the beginning of hostilities, stationed on Sullivan's Island, S.C.

When the regiment enlisted regularly in the Confederate service, he returned home and raised a company which formed a part of the 13th Regt., S.C.V., commanded by Colonel Oliver E. Edwards, and went to Virginia, where it performed gallant service on different battlefields. Dr, Wofford rose by promotion and was commissioned as major of the 13th Regt., but was wounded in the battle at Fredericksburg, which incapacitated him from further service in the army. He represented his native county as a Democrat in the State legislature of 1871 and '72.

Hon. John W. Wofford

He is still practicing his profession at Cherokee Springs.

HON. JOHN WESLEY WOFFORD

John W. Wofford, the third son of Harvey Wofford, was born at the old homestead in the Wofford settlement; attended the common neighborhood schools, and at the breaking out of the war was attending school at Antioch, near Glenn's Spring, taught by Professor P. J. Oeland; was preparing for college at the breaking out of the war between the States. He entered the service at the first call for troops and remained a private in Co. K, 3d Regt., S.C.V., until the battle of Gettysburg, soon thereafter receiving a commission as lieutenant in said company, and after the recovery from a wound received at the battle of Chickamauga he assumed the command of the company from that time to the close of the war, being in command of the infantry and rear-guard that brought up the rear from Bentonville, on one of the main roads of retreat from the last battle of the war.

Soon after the war he married Miss Margaret Ann Nesbitt, daughter of Mr. Madison Nesbitt, and went to farming; was his father's successor in the office of magistrate in the neighborhood; was a delegate (straightout) in the Democratic State Convention that nominated Wade Hampton for governor in 1876. Soon thereafter he was nominated and participated actively in the campaign which followed, and which led to the overthrow of carpetbag misrule in South Carolina; was elected and became a member of the historic Wallace House; was again elected to the lower house for two more years in 1880 and '81, and to the State Senate for two years to fill the unexpired term of the Hon. Edwin H. Bobo, after which he retired from politics, but frequently being elected to represent the county in State conventions, and devoted his time thereafter to his farm and the building up and improvement of his county in agricultural matters. He was, while he held his residence in Spartanburg County, a member of the State Agricultural Society, and an officer in the State Grange, and for a number of years master of the county grange, and was the first known advocate in the county for terracing lands.

He is progressive and practical in his ideas. Although a Methodist by profession and a useful member in his church, yet he is broad-minded and public-spirited in all his views. He takes a special interest in preserving the history of his country, the memory of his Revolutionary ancestry, and the memories of the heroes of the great civil war. He also takes a special interest in collecting and preserving the battle-flags of the Confederacy, and other interesting relics, in the relic-room at Spartanburg.

REV. BENJAMIN WOFFORD

Within a few steps of the residence of Mr. Levi Allen, and only a short distance from Chapel (M. E.) Church, in the present county of Spartanburg, repose the mortal remains of Benjamin Wofford beside those of Anna Wofford, his wife.

The memory of no man deserves to be more fondly cherished in the pages of history than that of Benjamin Wofford, the founder of the Wofford College at Spartanburg — one of the foremost institutions of learning in the South,

Benjamin Wofford was the first Methodist to give $100,000 to education, and whose gift, it is said, has never been duplicated by any one man in the Southern Methodist Church.

Benjamin Wofford, son of Joseph Wofford, a soldier of the Revolution whose memory and patriotic service to his country we have already noticed, was born (1780) during the stormy period of the Revolution, near the south bank of Tyger River, within the limits of Spartanburg County. He commenced his life of usefulness with the beginning and growth of this great American Republic. He was born of pious parentage, who, doubtless, early impressed upon his mind the principles of honesty, integrity, frugality, and the truths of the Christian religion. He received only such advantages of education as could be afforded in his day and time, to which he added by close and constant research into the things which always tend to adorn and elevate the human character. Being called to preach the gospel, he was a minister of the Methodist Episcopal Church for nearly a half century. It is said that he possessed a strong and active mind, imbued with plain republican principles, and always stood firm in his ardor for the rights and honor of his native State. He lived, the larger portion of his life, at his old homestead place, near Chapel Church (the present residence of Mr. Allen), where his remains were interred, as stated, but died in the town of Spartanburg, S.C., December, 1850. It is recorded of him that, first and last, thousands shared his generous hospitality. In his last will and testament it was found that he had made one of the most magnificent bequests ever made in South Carolina. This was for the purpose of establishing and endowing a college for literary, classical and scientific education, to be located in his native District, Spartanburg, and to be under the control and management of the Conference of the Methodist Episcopal Church of South Carolina. In other words, it was found that, for the benefit of the young generations surviving him and for generations yet unborn, he had, in order to advance religion and science, bestowed the garnered fruits of a long and busy life. It has been asserted that one of the causes which led him to offer this princely gift to his church was largely due to the influence of a good, intelligent mother who died in 1826, with a well-read volume of Clarke's Commentary on her lap; and it has also been stated that his excellent wife, Anna Todd, who died in 1835, suggested his impulse to do something for the further promotion of education. Certain it is this noble bequest will always prove a sufficient memorial of his affection and devotion to the church of which he was a faithful member and minister.

The following is the inscription on his tombstone:

"Entombed beneath are the mortal remains of the Rev. Benjamin Wofford, son of Joseph and Martha Wofford, who was born the 19th day of October, A.D. 1780, and departed this life, in the full triumphs of the Christian faith, the 2d day of December, A.D. 1850, aged 70 years, 1 month and 13 days.

"For 48 years he was a member of the Methodist Episcopal Church; for 46 years a minister of the Gospel. He gave to the country and the church an institution for the benefit of which countless thousands yet unborn may have reason to be thankful and reverence the donor's name. Peace to his ashes."

[1] See "Colonial and Revolutionary History of South Carolina," p. 356.
[2] The following is a copy of a furlough granted by Colonel Wm. Wofford, the original of which is now in possession of Mrs. Nevil Holcombe, at Hobbysville, S.C.:

"Fort Charles, June 16, 1782.

"The bearer, James Brown, declares he had a promise from the colonel that after two weeks' duty at their station he should have leave of absence. Therefore he has leave of absence.

"Signed   W. Wofford."

The following is copied by General W. T. Wofford from a blank leaf in Boyer's French Dictionary in his possession, written by Colonel Wofford:

"Wm. Wofford was born in the province, now State of Maryland, near Rock Creek, about 12 miles above the federal city, on the 25th day of Oct. 1728, then Prince Georges County, now in the ninety-third year of his age. Wrote without spectacles the 30th day of July, 1820."

Chapter Seventeen - The Hampton Family

The ancestor of the Hampton family in South Carolina was Anthony Hampton, who, with his wife and daughter, his sons, Preston, Wade, [1] Edward, Henry and Richard, and his son-in-law, James Harrison, emigrated in the year 1774 from Virginia to the extreme western border of South Carolina, settling in the territory afterwards embraced in Spartanburg County. The place of his settlement was at what was afterwards known as the Asa Cunningham place, about one mile northeast of South Tyger River, [2] which is within a few hundred yards of the dividing line between the counties of Greenville and Spartanburg, but was at that time the dividing line between the old district of Ninety-six and the Cherokee Indian Nation.

While the lower and middle portions of the territory in South Carolina, acquired by the treaty of Governor Glen in 1756, were being generally settled up, the emigrants from the colonies north were slow to venture to make settlement in the western portion of this valuable acquisition of territory which was obtained by treaty, as stated. The reason being that it bordered along the frontier line of the Indian Nation, in close proximity to the Cherokee villages and at no great distance across said line. We notice that Anthony Hampton did not make his settlement until almost on the verge of the outbreak of the Revolution.

Of the early history of Anthony Hampton we can gather but little. He was a man, unquestionably, of the highest respectability, and the tradition of the neighborhood is that he was a flax-breaker by trade, and well up to his business in that line. Major William Hoy, in his writings states that he itinerated amongst the Irish people and dressed their flax, and that they regarded him as one of their most useful citizens. His importance and usefulness in this line can be better appreciated when it is remembered that at that time cotton was not produced in the country, and, with the exception of the imported flax spinning-wheel, machinery only of the rudest construction was used for the manufacture of flax from which the necessary clothing was made.

It may be truly said of Anthony Hampton that he was one of the entering wedges, as it were, of the opening up of a civilization along the borders of Western Carolina. He, with his sons and son-in-law, in their manhood, and a few others of like patriotic spirit, with the determination to confront the Indian tomahawk and scalping-knife, and to brave all the dangers which surrounded them, settled upon the border line where, heretofore, others had not dared to venture settlement. Living as they did, on the very out-skirts of civilization in South Carolina, they fully realized the dangers to which they were all the time exposed, and as a means of protection to their families and defence against unexpected outbreaks by the Indians, Wood's Fort on Beaverdam Creek, in the immediate neighborhood of Anthony Hampton, was built.

The near approach of hostilities between the colonies and the mother country admonished these pioneer settlers of the increased dangers to which they were about to be exposed. They believed that whenever war was openly declared the Indian, under tempting bribes, would in all probability side with Great Britain, in which event they would be exposed to impending danger. An effort was made to enlist them on the side of the patriots, or else make such terms with them as would cause them to remain neutral in their attitude toward their neighboring white settlers.

To effect this object, Edward and Preston, [3] sons of Anthony Hampton, were sent by the people of the frontier settlements who resided within the present limits of Spartanburg County, to invite the nation to "a talk" at any convenient town they might propose, and to see if they could not be made to comprehend the cause of differences growing between the colonies and the mother country.

Edward and Preston Hampton, upon their arrival in the Indian country, found Cameron, deputy superintendent among the Cherokees under royal authority, and other emissaries already at work among them. Cameron made prisoners of the Hamptons, and gave their horses, guns and a case of pistols and holsters to the Indians. By some means they managed to escape with their lives, and returning home they reported to the people of the set-tlements the result of their mission. The people grew alarmed for their safe-ty, and sought protection in the old forts that were already constructed, and in others, perhaps, that were being hurriedly constructed. Through the machinations of the British emissaries, the Indians commenced their ma-rauding expeditions in 1776 in western North Carolina and along the fron-tier settlements of South Carolina. In another volume [4] we have given an extended account of these Indian invasions and massacres, hence we cannot again, in this brief narrative, recount them.

After the murder of the Hite family on Enoree River (see Johnson's Tradi-tions, p. 458), the Indians visited the home of Anthony Hampton, in the month of July, 1776, the location of which has already been described. As they approached the house they recognized the face of Preston Hampton, whom, as we have already stated, had recently, with his brother Edward,

returned from the Indian towns and had given warning of the intended rising of the Indians. Some of the children of Mr. Hampton were sent to give
warning to their neighbors. Mr. and Mrs. Harrison were at the time absent
for a short distance. Old Mr. Hampton, it is said, met the Indians cordially.
He gave the chief a friendly grasp of the hand, but had not more than done
this, when he saw his son Preston fall from the fire of a gun. The same hand
which he himself had grasped a moment before sent a tomahawk through
his skull. In the same way his wife was killed. An infant son of Mr. and Mrs.
Harrison was dashed against the wall of the house, which was spattered
with its blood and brains. The Indians then set fire to the house of Mr.
Hampton. Mrs. Harrison, on coming up and seeing her father's house in
flames, [5] came very near rushing in the midst of the savages; her husband,
anticipating what the trouble was, held her back until the savages were
gone. Edward Hampton was at this time at the house of Baylis Earle, his father-in-law, on North Pacolet, and Henry and Wade, the other sons of Mr.
Hampton, were also absent, and thus preserved to avenge this atrocious
deed.

Of the members who escaped this terrible massacre in the Hampton family, we would specially refer to Henry, Richard, Edward and Wade, the surviving sons of Anthony Hampton.

On account of the Indian depredations occurring at different points along
the borders of the outer settlements, it became necessary for the constituted
authorities to take active and decisive steps to protect the people, and it was
not long after the massacre in the Hampton family before General Williamson's expedition, which consisted of about twelve hundred men, was
marched against the Cherokees. In this famous expedition, Captain Henry
Hampton commanded a company, and behaved nobly in Williamson's second engagement with the Cherokees. He ordered his company to fire by
platoons and then fall on the ground and reload, while the rest advanced in
their smoke. He thus led them to the charge, advancing in the smoke, and
then firing, and reloading on their backs. When he came near enough he ordered his command to charge with the fixed bayonet, and the Indians fled.
He himself captured an Indian wearing the coat of his brother Preston, who
had no doubt been murdered by this man when they destroyed his father's
family. [6]

Edward Hampton was also engaged in the battle referred to with the
Cherokee Indians, and when the latter were closely pursued, they began
first to kill their own prisoners and then their own aged and wounded
friends. Following close on the Indian trail, Edward Hampton came close to
the body of a white woman, recently murdered by them and left shockingly
exposed. He alighted, in the hurry of the moment, covered the body with his
own shirt (the only one he had), drew it under a bush, and resumed the pursuit.

Of the career of Edward Hampton we only get faint glimpses here and
there in the pages of history. In that trying period in South Carolina during

the Revolution we find that he was true and devoted to the American cause. At the battle of Earle's Ford, [7] which occurred on the 15th of July, 1780, he acted a conspicuous part, and among the slain at this engagement was his son Noah, whose remains were interred in an old burial ground nearby which can still be pointed out.

Noah Hampton was killed alongside of a companion whose name was Andrew Dunn. Young Hampton, when aroused from his sleep, was asked his name. He replied "Hampton." The very name enraged the Tories, who cursed him for a rebel and ran a bayonet through him. Young Dunn met with the same fate. [8]

The officers in charge of this expedition against the Whig forces on North Pacolet, were Major Dunlap, with seventy dragoons, and Colonel Ambrose Mills, with a party of loyalists. They had been detached by Colonel Innes, in command of the British and loyalists stationed at Fort Prince (on the waters of North Tyger, about eighteen miles from Earles Ford) to surprise and attack what was believed to be a small force under Colonel Jones of Georgia, who had been making some bold dashes against his enemy at Gowen's Fort and other places. On reaching Earles Ford, on the west side in night time, Dunlap supposed he was only confronted by Jones's command, on the opposite side of the stream, being unapprised of the arrival of Colonel McDowell's command. He therefore decided to attack it; but discovering his mistake as to the numbers in front of him, he made a hasty retreat across the river, where, with his command, he remained for the balance of the night.

Says Draper: "Before sunrise the ensuing morning, fifty-two of the most active men...mounted on the best horses in camp were ordered to pursue the retreating enemy." This command was placed under Colonel Edward Hampton. Had the forces of the enemy retreated immediately it would have been impossible for Colonel Hampton's command to have overtaken them before reaching Innes's camp at Fort Prince. The account of Draper says that Colonel Hampton, "after a rapid pursuit of two hours, overtook the enemy fifteen miles away; and making a sudden and unexpected attack completely routed them, killing eight of them at the first fire. This attack, according to the traditions which the writer gathered years ago, was on what is known as the old Blackstock road, near Shiloh church and about one and one-half miles south of the town of Inman. The fight with the enemy continued along this road until Fort Prince was reached, and several men fell at different places along the road.

The pursuit of Colonel Hampton's forces was continued to a point within three hundred yards of the fort, where three hundred men were posted. Hampton did not pursue them any further as his forces were too weak to attack his enemy within the confines of Fort Prince; but his bold dash sent consternation into their ranks. They were evidently struck with the same terror that Dunlap's forces were, who had been stampeded by Hampton's men five miles away.

Dunlap doubtless thought that McDowell's whole command was upon him, and beat a hasty retreat from Fort Prince, leaving his dead along the roadside unburied. The following is the entry in the diary of Allare, an English officer, for Sunday the 16th of August: "Dunlap with the men under his command marched down to Stephen White's plantation where the American volunteers and militia lay."

It will thus be seen that this daring expedition of Colonel Edward Hampton drove back for a time the British and Tory forces to the happy relief of the Whigs of the surrounding country, and by 2 o'clock in the same afternoon Colonel Hampton, with a heart burdened with grief, in the death of a brave and devoted son the night previous, had returned to McDowell's camp with thirty-five good horses, dragoon equipage, and a considerable portion of the enemy's baggage as trophies of the victory, and all this, too, without the loss of a single man. Draper says that this was a "bold and successful venture, worthy of the heroic leader and his intrepid followers."

But Edward Hampton, in the sad decrees of fate, was to permitted to enjoy the precious Liberty which, for five years, he had fought for under the most trying circumstances, enduring hardships and self-sacrifices to accomplish, and which was now about to be realized. Even after the surrender of Cornwallis at Yorktown, when the people were rejoicing that the struggle for American freedom was at an end, the unexpected raid of "Bloody Bill" Cunningham occurred in the up-country of South Carolina, [9] and one of the victims of his rage was Colonel Edward Hampton.

Colonel Hampton had been to the settlement on the Congaree where his family connections lived. He was returning to the house of his father-in-law, Baylis Earle, on the North Pacolet. The Tories, perchance, got wind of his passing near them and pursued him. Colonel Hampton, after having traveled all night, stopped at a house for breakfast. Very soon after he entered the building it was surrounded by the Tories. He snatched his pistols from the table, thinking to defend himself, but it was no use. He fired his pistols in the air. The Tories shot him down. [10]

A truer patriot than Edward Hampton never lived. Like many of the heroes that perished in the Revolution, he sleeps in a forgotten grave, but his memory still lives and will ever remain imperishable in the annals of our country's history.

Colonels Henry, Richard and Wade acted with conspicuous gallantry to the end of the Revolution. The record of their gallant deeds may be found in different places in the pages of history, but more especially in that part which relates to the closing scenes of Greene's operations in South Carolina and of Sumter's movements also, the particulars of which the reader is referred to Johnson's "Life of Greene." (See Vol. II., pages 133 to 177.)

Wade Hampton, one of the brothers referred to, was the father of Colonel Wade Hampton, his only surviving son, and grandfather of the present Lieutenant-General Wade Hampton of the Confederate army, than whom there is no living Carolinian more loved and respected for his lofty patriotism and distinguished services to his country both in time of peace and war. The name of Wade Hampton has been distinguished for three generations for patriotic services, talents, influence and wealth in South Carolina. The elder Wade Hampton held only the commission of colonel during the Revolution. He was a dashing cavalry officer and distinguished himself in several engagements with the enemy.

While Greene was retreating before the British army in North Carolina, after Morgan's victory at Cowpens (January 17, 1781), great efforts were made to excite the militia in the enemy's rear, in order to alarm Cornwallis for the safety of his posts, which he had left behind him. General Sumter, although far from being recovered from his wound received at the battle of Blackstocks (November 20, 1780), resolved to take the field. At that time many of his officers and bravest men were in captivity after the unfortunate affair at Fishing Creek, and some of the former, having been paroled, were scattered over the country on their plantations. Of these Colonel Wade Hampton was one. A confidential emissary was sent by General Sumter into the country through which he intended very soon to march his command, to prepare the Whigs for his reception, and to collect whatever intelligence necessary to direct his movements. Some treachery, however, betrayed this intended movement to the enemy, and apprehensive of trusting Sumter's officers at large, an order was issued for seizing them and conveying them to Charleston. Of these Colonel Wade Hampton was one. A party of twelve men were transporting him to a prison ship, but did not confine his hands or feet. When the party stopped at a house for refreshments, he was made to stand in one corner of a room; the firearms were leaned in the opposite corner, diagonally, and the guard sat down between them, in the middle of the room. Hampton shuffled a little from his corner, sometimes to the right and then to the left. At last, by one of those extraordinary efforts, which characterized the actions of men of that day, he made a spring, seized the arms, and made the guard his prisoners. He then paroled them, secured the captured arms, mounted himself and made good his escape. [11]

Colonel Wade Hampton, now finding himself released from his parole, soon made his way good to join Sumter at the head of a little band of gallant followers. Sumter, having recruited his command, made expeditions against Forts Granby and Watson, and gaining a stock of intelligence as to the positions and strength of the enemy, he immediately transmitted the same to General Greene by Colonel Wade Hampton.

In Johnson's "Life of Greene," Vol. II., page 52, we find the following paragraph:

"The day after the battle of Guilford, Colonel Hampton arrived in the American camp, and the view presented of the state of the British posts, by one whose intelligence could be so thoroughly depended upon, afforded General Greene the best grounds on which to decide upon his future measures. The project of penetrating into the country was revived, and in order to give it unerring effect, a letter was addressed to Gov. Jefferson to order a detachment of 1,500 men to advance to Salisbury as a support to the army in its intended movement to Camden."

Soon after this the armies of Generals Greene and Cornwallis were back to back, and the successes or reverses which attended each are well known to every reader of the history of the American Revolution.

After the close of the Revolutionary war Colonel Wade Hampton represented one of the districts in South Carolina in the National Congress as soon as the Federal Government was organized. But he soon abandoned political life and devoted his great energies and talents to planting.

He made large investments in Louisiana soon after the purchase of that territory by the United States from the French Government, which increased in value and made him a princely estate.

In the war of 1812 Colonel Wade Hampton, by reason of his distinguished services in the Revolution, was appointed a major-general in the United States army and commanded on the frontiers of Canada. He was in every sense a very remarkable man and lived to a great old age. Having been among the first to espouse the patriot cause in the territory afterwards embraced in the original county of Spartanburg, it should ever be the pleasure and pride of the people of said county to preserve and perpetuate his memory in the annals of her history.

Colonel Wade Hampton, only surviving son of General Wade Hampton the elder, and father of the present General Wade Hampton, was, like his father, a man of distinguished ability. He was a volunteer aid of General Andrew Jackson in the celebrated battle of New Orleans, which ended so gloriously to the American arms. He was for a number of years State senator from the county of Richland.

James Harrison, Esq., who married the daughter of Anthony Hampton and sister of General Wade Hampton of Revolutionary fame, and who with his wife so narrowly escaped the massacre in the Hampton family referred to, settled in Greenville District after the close of the Revolution. From him descended a highly respectable posterity. He had seven sons, one of whom was John Hampton Harrison, who represented Greenville for several years in the State Legislature. One of his daughters married Samuel Earle. (See Sketch of Earle Family.)

Governor Perry, in his writings, states that there were several other sons of Anthony Hampton who survived the Revolution and lived in the middle part of South Carolina, but none of them accumulated fortunes. In our account of the Hampton massacre, just related, it is stated that some of the children of Mr. Hampton were sent to give warning to their neighbors. These having escaped the massacre were doubtless the same referred to by Governor Perry.

[1] In the account of the Hampton family in Howe's "History of the Presbyterian Church of South Carolina" the name *Wade Hampton* is omitted, leaving the matter in doubt as to whether he emigrated with his father to South Carolina. This

doubt is removed in reading the account of the Hampton Massacre, in Johnson's Traditions of South Carolina. (See p. 443.)

[2] For a more accurate description of the place where the Hampton's lived, were murdered and buried, see Professor Morrison's letter, July 27th, 1891, in "Colonial and Revolutionary History of Upper South Carolina," p. 87.

[3] Howe's History states Edward and Preston, but in Johnson's "Traditions and Reminiscences," p. 443, it is stated that it was Edward, Richard and Henry that were sent on the mission to the Cherokees.

[4] See "Colonial and Revolutionary History of Upper South Carolina," p. 84 to 89.

[5] The particulars of the murders in the Hampton family and the burning of Mr. Hampton's house were obtained principally from Howe's History of the Presbyterian Church of South Carolina. From the Revolutionary sketch of Samuel Smith (see Spartan, June 28, 1899), there seems to be some doubt about the Hampton house being burned. In said sketch Mr. Smith states that he has seen the house where the Hamptons lived, and the bullet holes shot by the Indians when Preston Hampton was killed.

[6] See "Traditions and Reminiscences of the American Revolution," p. 443.

[7] For an account of the battle of Earle's Ford, see "Colonial and Revolutionary History of Upper South Carolina," pp. 118-123.

[8] The particulars of the killing of young Hampton and Dunn were furnished by MS. communications to Hon. Lyman C. Draper, author of "Kings Mountain and her Heroes," by Adam and James J. Hampton, grandsons of Colonel Edward Hampton.

[9] For an extended account of the raids of the "Bloody Bills" Cunningham and Bates see "Colonial and Revolutionary History of Upper South Carolina," pp. 341 to 364.

[10] In the Revolutionary sketch of Samuel Smith, published in Spartan, June 28, '99, it is stated that Edward Hampton was killed by the Tories at the house of John Blassingame, who lived on Middle Tyger.

[11] See Johnson's "Life of Greene," Vol. II., p. 31, and also Johnson's "Traditions," p. 444, for accounts of the escape of Colonel Wade Hampton.

Chapter Eighteen - The Anderson Family

William Anderson was a Scotch-Irishman, who settled in Pennsylvania, and had a mill on Connechocheauge Creek. He emigrated from there to the Waxhaws, S.C., and thence to Charleston, S.C., and thence to Spartanburg county, S.C., settling on the Tygersin 1763. His daughter, Sarah Anderson, remained in Charleston, and subsequently became the matron of the Orphan House, and on the occasion of the visit of General Washington to that city, entertained him at her table as her guest. She married Wm. Breaken, and had one son, William, In her old age and infirmity, she became an inmate of the home of her nephew "Tyger Jim" Anderson, and as long as she lived, she always looked back with pride,, when it was her pleasure to entertain General Washington. After the surrender of General Lincoln in Charleston, May, 1780, the British took possession of her house.

William Anderson was a staunch Whig and patriot during the Revolution, and as such incurred the displeasure of the Tories. He was a very old man at the time, and unable to participate in active warfare. Soon after the close of the Revolution, he was murdered (1783) by a band of Tories, painted and disguised as Indians. They took him out of the house, and split his head with a tomahawk and scalped him. He was living at the time with his son David Anderson, whose house they burnt, and whose wife made her escape to the house of Mr. Crawford five or six miles distant, with nothing on but her night-clothes, wading two Tygers, South and Middle, after binding up the wounds of James Silliman, a lad of about thirteen years of age, whom they had in their employ, who had been scalped and stabbed in two or three places, and had been thrown upon a brush-heap. He recovered and lived to a good old age.

William Anderson was buried in the Snoddy bottoms wrapped in a cow's hide. His remains were afterwards removed to a burial ground near James Chamblin's, by "Tyger Jim" Anderson, who put neat tombstones to his memory and that of his wife.

The wife of Wm. Anderson was a Miss Denny, and by this marriage he had five children, three sons and two daughters: 1. David, the ancestor of the Tyger River Anderson families; 2. John, the ancestor of the Anderson families in York county, S.C.; 3. Denny, the ancestor of the Anderson families on Enoree River; 4. Sallie, who married a Breaken, and, 5, Rebecca, who never married.

Major David Anderson, the eldest son of William Anderson, was born August 25th, 1741. He owned nearly all the lands around where Major F. L. Anderson now lives, and his remains were interred in the family graveyard on the Monday Chamblin place. He received a liberal English education, probably in Pennsylvania, before the removal of his father to South Carolina. He married Miriam (Maria) Mason, an English lady in the city of Charleston, in the year 1772. Her father, Major Mason, [1] emigrated to the Province of Carolina a few years before the marriage of his daughter, and settled near the Island Ford on Saluda River, in the present county of Edgefield.

Major Anderson was engaged for some years before the Revolution surveying public lands for the Colonial government. When the war commenced, fearing lest his house might be burned by the Tories or Indians, he prepared a nice buckskin sack and sewed up his plats, surveys and claims against the government, and suspended them in the hollow of a tree in the woods, where he thought they would be secure. At the close of the war he went to hunt for his buckskin, when to his great surprise and mortification, he found skin and papers cut and torn into innumerable fragments lying at the foot of the tree, having been devoured by the flying squirrels. Thus was the labor of years lost. The government afterwards offered him thirty or forty negroes to reimburse him for his services, which he refused to accept. He preferred the gold eagles — which he never received.

Before the war he held a commission from the King of England as magistrate. Espousing the Whig cause he acted a conspicuous part during the Revolution, participating in the siege of Ninety-six, the battle of Eutaw Spring, and other engagements. In another volume, we have mentioned him in connection with the battle of the Cane-brakes, and also as a member of Captain John Barry's company, which marched in pursuit of "Bloody Bill" Cunningham after his murderous raid to the upcountry of South Carolina, November, 1781, an account of which we have noticed in another volume. [2]

By the marriage between Major David and Miriam (Mason) Anderson the following children were born, viz.:

1. William Anderson, who married Patsey Greer, who resided near Greers, S.C. He first settled on Tyger River, but afterwards removed to Stone Mountain, Ga. His children were (1) David and (2) Robert Anderson of Cherokee county, Ga., each marrying and having families, there; (3) Samuel Anderson, who was in the Florida war,, died near Stone Mountain, Ga., leaving a family; [3] (4) Mary,, who married, to whom unknown, leaving two children,, a son and daughter; (5) Maria, who married Isaac Woodruff, leaving a family; (6) Sallie, who never married; (7) Katy, who married an Elam, and (8) Henrietta, who married a Hambrick, both of the two latter leaving families,

James Mason Anderson, known as "Tyger Jim," who married Polly Miller, daughter of Michael Miller, and who will receive further notice in this narrative.

3. Sallie, who married Samuel Jamison, and who, having no children, in her will left $1,000 as a donation; to Nazareth Church.

4. Henrietta, who married James Chamblin, called "Monday" Chamblin, and lived one mile east of "Tyger Jim" Anderson, on the road to Spartanburg. His descendants will be noticed in another place.

James M. (Tyger Jim) and Polly (Miller) Anderson, had the following children, viz.:

1. Captain David Anderson, who married Harriet Brockman, daughter of Colonel Thomas P. Brockman, of Greenville District, S.C.; 2. Henrietta, who married Rev. Wm. Harris, a Presbyterian minister in Abbeville District, S.C.; 3. Dr. John Crawford Anderson, a graduate of Jefferson College, Philadelphia, Pa.., who married first a Miss Ale Alpine, of Greene county, Ala., and a second time to a Miss McLemore, of the same State. By the first marriage referred to is a son, John C. Anderson, at present the youngest judge on the bench in Alabama, and several daughters. By the second marriage two daughters were born, one of whom is the present wife of Charles A. Moore, of Pacolet, S.C., she being his only descendant in Spartanburg County. Dr. Anderson, after his graduation in Philadelphia, was tendered a position in the hospital there. He died in Eutaw, Ala.

4. Wm. Washington Anderson (son of "Tyger Jim") married Jane Cauble, of Greenville, S.C., and died at Bellbuckle, Tenn.

5. Henry Miller Anderson, who never married, graduated in Franklin College, Athens, Ga. (now the State University), and died three months after graduation.

6. Michael Miller Anderson married Margaret Cresswell of Anderson County, S.C., and moved to Georgia, near Adairsville, where he lived the remainder of his life and raised a highly respectable family.

7. James Alexander Anderson married Rebecca McLemore, of Greene county, Ala., half-sister of the wife of his brother. Dr. John C. Anderson. He died, leaving two daughters.

8. Major Franklin Leland Anderson, another son of "Tyger Jim," will receive further notice in this article.

9. Mason Gilliland Anderson married Sarah Gillam, of Abbeville county, daughter of Genera.1 James Gillam, who was a first cousin of John C. Calhoun, his mother being a Caldwell, sister of Calhoun's mother. He had four children, three daughters and a son. One daughter is the present wife of Major John A. Lee, at Spartanburg.

Mason G. Anderson was a graduate of the South Carolina College of the class of '54. He read law with Tucker & Farrow at Spartanburg and after being admitted to the bar, his father offered him advantages to quit the profession and go to farming, which he did. He removed first to Mississippi, thence to Florida, where he died.

10. Nancy M. Anderson, third child of "Tyger Jim," married Thomas Cunningham, of Anderson, S.C., leaving two children, viz.: John, now living in Mississippi, and Nancy, who died in infancy.

The children of Captain David and Harriet (Brockman) Anderson are as follows:

1. General John C. Anderson, who married Emma Buist, daughter of Rev. E. T. Buist, D.D., of Greenville S.C., and died in 1892 or '93. General Anderson was a man of more than ordinary intelligence and force of character. He was a graduate of the South Carolina Military Academy, served for a time during the war as adjutant of the 13th South Carolina Regiment, and after the war was promoted to a brigadier-generalship in the State troops. He was elected to the legislature of South Carolina from his native county in 1878, and served two years. In 1884 or '85, he was appointed by President Cleveland postmaster at Spartanburg, which position he held for five years. He then removed ta his home, near Moore, S.C., where he lived the remainder of his days, devoting his attention to his farm, orchard and vineyard, in all of which he was successful. He was cut down in the prime of his life. He was in. every sense of the word a patriotic, progressive and public-spirited citizen. His widow and several children survive him.

2. Mary E., wife of Col. Thos. J. Moore (see sketch Moore family).

3. Henrietta A., wife of C. Eber Smith, of Glenn's Spring. They have eight children.

4. Jas. H. Anderson, married Sallie Watson, of York county S.C. — eight children.

5. Thos, B. Anderson, married Ella Trippe, of Americus, Ga. — five children.

6. Hattie M., married Geo. B. Anderson, of Enoree; lives at Rock Hill, S.C. — seven children.

7. Emma P., married Dr. John C. Oeland, of Spartanburg — died, leaving one daughter, Margaret.

James Mason Anderson, "Tyger Jim," whose descendants we have already noticed, was a prominent citizen and a successful farmer and business man in his day. He was a man of fine judgment, indomitable perseverance and originality in nature. He was as much a wagoner as a farmer and accumulated a fine estate of lands and other property on Ben's Creek and South Tyger. During the war of 1812 he drove his wagon to Baltimore, Md., and stopped the same on the public square in Washington, and walked into the capitol where he recognized an old friend, Elchendor, then a member of Congress from Ohio.

We have already stated that at the time of the murder of William Anderson (1783), the house of his son Maj. David Anderson was burnt. The latter improvised a wagon shed to live in until he could erect another dwelling. It was under this wagon shed that "Tyger Jim" was born ___ 1784. The shed blew down the night he was moved to the new house.

John Anderson, son of William Anderson, the original settler and brother of Major David and Denny Anderson, removed to York County, S.C. He had five children, viz.: William, who never married; John, who married a lady unknown to writer; Sallie, who was married to a Starr; Elizabeth, who married a Steele, and one daughter who never married.

John Anderson, his son, had two children, viz.: 1. Rev. J. Monroe Anderson, professor in Davidson College, and, 2, Mary. The former married a Miss Neil, and had children as follows: Rev. Neil Anderson, Montgomery, Ala.; Lois, Barnwell, in California; Mary, unmarried; Sue, married Rev. Paul Winn; and Lizzie, married Major John A. Lee, of Spartanburg (second wife). 2. The daughter (Mary) married Dr. David Watson, of York County. They had five children, viz.: Sallie, who married Jas. H. Anderson, of Spartanburg County (before noticed), and David Watson, married and living in California, no children; Dr. John A. Watson, Asheville, N.C.; Emma, married Thos, Neill, now in Texas; and Lizzie, who died unmarried.

Denny Anderson, third son of the original William Anderson, settled on Enoree River. He was a Revolutionary soldier, married and had children as follows:

1. John Anderson, Esq., who married Nancy Alexander of Fairview, Greenville County, S.C. He was a surveyor and magistrate, and one of the prominent men of his day, and was an elder in the Antioch Presbyterian church.

2. Denny Anderson, who married a Miss McCravy, located on Ben's Creek and left a numerous and highly respectable family in the vicinity of Reidville,

S.C. Among his daughters, was the wife of Thos. P. Gaston, Esq.; wife of Andrew Collins, still living, and wife of James Darby.

3. Elbert Anderson, who married a Miss Bryson of Laurens County. Among the children by said marriage is Rev. Elbert Anderson, a minister in the Associate Reformed Presbyterian church, his present charge being in Rockbridge County, Va.

4. Rebecca, who married Hiram Bennett.

5. Betsey, who married Wm. Leonard of Reidville, S.C.

6. Elizabeth, who married Thomas Leonard, a prominent member of the Methodist church. William and Thomas Leonard and Hiram Bennett raised highly respectable families.

7. Henry Anderson, who married and died early.

8. Samuel A., who married a Miss Nesbitt of Fairview, S.C.

9. James Anderson (Enoree Jim), who married first Peggy Dorah, and second, Jane Mills. He was a successful farmer, a progressive and highly respected citizen, and had children as follows, viz., all by the first wife:

1. John Anderson, married a daughter of Congressman A. S. Wallace, removed to Texas, and raised a highly respectable family,

2. Samuel Anderson, who contracted consumption before the close of the civil war and died.

3. Dr. David R. Anderson of Greenville County, S.C., a prominent physician and highly respected citizen. He is an exemplary member and elder of Fairview (Presbyterian) church. Two of his sons-in-law, W. H. Burwell and Thomas B. Craig, are prominent ministers of the Gospel in the Presbyterian church. Another son-in-law, Selden Kenedy, is also a prominent and useful member of the Associate Reformed Church. His only son, James Anderson, married Lucy Wilson, a sister of Rev. B. F. Wilson of Converse College.

4. Professor James Anderson, graduate of South Carolina College, 1860; has been president of several female colleges — first at Laurens, S.C., afterwards at Huntsville, Ala.; he married a Miss Dudley. He has filled several distinguished positions, and has quite a reputation as an educator.

5. George Byrd Anderson, married a daughter of Captain David Anderson, to whom reference has been made.

6. Maggie, an only daughter, married Wm. Boyd, one of the most highly respected citizens of Laurens County, S.C.

Among the daughters of the original William Anderson is Sallie Breaken, already mentioned, and Rebecca, who never married. Both of these sisters lived on Ben's Creek, not far from its confluence with South Tyger. Sallie was married to Breaken in Charleston, whilst her father lived there, and the one son (William), referred to, went to Missouri, about whom nothing is known at this time.

Henrietta, daughter of Major David Anderson, married James Chamblin, called "Monday," and lived one mile east of Tyger James Anderson on the road to Spartanburg. They had children, viz.:

1. David Chamblin, married four times, first to Miss Pearson, second to Miss Jane Corry, third to Miss Cynthia Darwin, and fourth to Mrs. Eliza Hunter.

2. Samuel Chamblin, who married a Miss Boggs of Pickens County, S.C., and went there to live, leaving a large family.

3. William Chamblin, who married Lucinda Drummond, lived opposite the Monday Chamblin place; removed thence to Pontotoc County, Miss.

4. James Chamblin, who married Caroline Hill and went to Belton, Texas.

5. Henrietta Chamblin, who married James Meadows of Laurens County, S.C., and went to Texas.

6. Maria Chamblin, who married a Hawkins, who died early leaving a widow and children, viz.: Wyatt, Nannie and Sallie, all of whom went to Texas.

Sally Chamblin, who married Samuel Miller at Flint Hill, near Moore, S.C., and had children, viz.:

W. Thomas Miller, lived and died unmarried at the old homestead. Dr. Pinckney Miller, married Belle Young, and went to Mississippi, where he died. Samuel Wyatt Miller, married Miss Elliott Drummond, and went to Texas. Dr. David Miller, married in Texas. Charles Miller, married Mrs. Elliot Miller, and lives in Texas. Henrietta married Henley N. Mattox, and went to Texas. Permelia, married Dr. Sam Knight, Fountain Inn, Greenville county, S.C., and Fannie, married Major Thomas Anderson of Anderson county, S.C., who, soon dying, left her a widow; she returned to the old family homestead, where she now resides.

Maj. F. L. Anderson.

Major Franklin Leland Anderson

Among the oldest of the surviving members of the Anderson connection in Spartanburg County is Maj. Frank L. Anderson, one of the sons mentioned of James M. (Tyger Jim) and Polly (Miller) Anderson, who was born January 30th, 1830, at his father's old homestead place on the waters of Ben's Creek and South Tyger, where he at present resides, which has been the home of - four generations in his family.

Maj. Anderson received his first school instructions in the Poplar Spring Academy. His teachers were Jas. K. Dickson, Geo. McDuffie Broyles, and others. Afterwards he attended the University of Virginia at Charlottesville, where he completed a good classical education. After this, he gained much practical information by travel and observation.

For some years before the outbreak of the civil war "between the States, he was elected and commissioned by the governor of South Carolina, as captain of the Cashville Beat company, which formed a part of the old Thirty-sixth Regiment South Carolina militia. Subsequently he was elected and commissioned as major of the lower battalion of said regiment. He served seven years as an officer in the State militia, which under the laws of the State at that time, exempted him from further service in the same.

A few months before the beginning of the civil war, he enlisted in the Spartan Rifles (Captain Jos. Walker), one of the first companies organized for the service, and was made a sergeant in said company. He left his native county with the first troops for the war, and served during the first year of the same in the 5th regiment South Carolina Volunteers (Col. Micah Jenkins). Upon the reorganization of the troops in Virginia in '62, he became a member of Company A, Holcomb Legion (Col. P. F. Stephens). With the exception of two or three days, he kept his health during the entire war, was in every battle and skirmish in which his regiment was engaged, and escaped without injury. While the siege at Petersburg was in progress, during the latter part of the war during a fight he planned a traverse on the picket line in front of the crater, where orders had been given to reverse the enemy's picket line and push it further back. This saved the lives of many of his company from an enfilading fire of the enemy, while other companies, not having the benefit of a traverse, suffered heavily, many being killed. The picket line at this time and place was under the command of Capt. A. B. Woodruff, who always stood to his post and discharged his duty under the most trying dangers and circumstances surrounding him. In early life, Major Anderson connected himself with the Nazareth (Presbyterian) church — the mother church of his ancestry — and was some time after ordained an elder in the same, which office he still retains. He has always been a prominent member of this branch of the Christian church, and from first to last, has led an exemplary Christian life. He has often been a delegate to the Presbyteries and Synods, and has been twice a delegate to the General Assembly, the highest court of the church.

Upon the reorganization of Antioch church (near Cashville, S.C.), which was removed to Reidville, S.C., he connected himself with that church, and was in fact its founder under the new organization, which is now in a flourishing condition. He is a man of large benevolence, a liberal contributor to all the objects of his church, and has contributed to the churches of other denominations in the country surrounding him. He takes a lively interest in everything concerning the welfare of his neighborhood and country. With Col. T. J. Moore, he educated a young minister, who is now making his mark as a minister of the gospel in the Presbyterian Church.

Major Anderson, although now about sixty-nine years of age, is still in the full vigor of health, maintaining the splendid physique, height and dignified bearing which belonged to a hardy and robust ancestry. He may be classed among the leading agriculturists of Spartanburg County, having always been successful in his chosen line of occupation. He has always lived above want, is a bountiful provider and is hospitable and entertaining in his home. He has never aspired to public office or political honors, but has always lived the life of a law-abiding, progressive and industrious citizen, commanding the respect and esteem of all.

In 1859, Major Anderson married Miss Susan N. Norris, daughter of Capt. Wm. Norris, of Union, S.C., who died in 1863, leaving two children, Frank Nuckles Anderson and William Norris Anderson, both now residents of the State of Tennessee. He married a second time Miss Ada Eppes, of Sussex county, Va., by which marriage he has the following children: Victor, Robert Reid, Ben Mason, Tom Moore, Walter Carey, James Leland, John Marshall and Henrietta Maria.

[1] In Drayton's Memoirs, the name of Major Mason is spelled *Mayson*. For an account of the gallant part he performed in the Siege of Williamson's fort at Ninety-six, see "Colonial and Revolutionary History of Upper South Carolina," pp. 57 to 68.
[2] See "Colonial and Revolutionary History of Upper South Carolina," pp. 101 and 357.
[3] One son by this marriage was Wm. Harrison Woodruff. (See sketch.)

Chapter Nineteen - The Earle Family

Among the earliest settlers on North Pacolet were the brothers, Baylis and John Earle. The former settled about one-half mile south of the North Carolina colony line at what was afterwards known as Earlesville, two miles northeast of Landrum, S.C. The latter permanently settled about two miles north of said colony line, higher up the river in the present county of Polk, N.C., whereon his grandson, Mr. Lafayette Prince, now resides. Here he erected a fort in revolutionary times, known as Earle's fort.

After the treaty of Governor Glen with the Cherokee Indians in 1755, the upper portion of South Carolina, up to the Indian boundary line, was thrown open to settlement. This line, separating the territory of South Carolina proper and the Cherokee Indian Nation, was the present dividing line between the counties of Greenville and Spartanburg, and the present line between the counties of Anderson and Laurens. It is true that while the lower portion of this newly acquired territory was rapidly settled up by emigrants from Pennsylvania (mostly Scotch-Irish), Maryland, Virginia and other colonies, yet there were but few who dared to venture settlement along the border line, where they would be constantly exposed to the invasions and massacres of the Indians, but among those who did venture to open up a civilization on North Pacolet were Baylis and John Earle. At the time of their emigration from old Virginia to the Carolinas, which was in the early seventies of the eighteenth century, the great cane-brakes on North Pacolet were the favorite hunting-grounds of the Indians, and the latter were jealous of the approach of civilization in that section. It was during this trying period that the early settlers of that region sheltered themselves in the old Block House fort (where the line between Greenville and Spartanburg joins the North Carolina line), Earle's fort, and other places of refuge.

Baylis Earle, one of the brothers referred to, was born in Virginia (Westmoreland county), August 8th, 1734, O. S. He was the son of Samuel Earle and Anna (daughter of Thomas and Elizabeth Sorrel); grandson of Samuel and' Phyllis Earle; great-grandson of Samuel and Bridget Earle; great-great-grandson of John and Mary Earle, who, supposed royalists in the great rebellion just consummated in the death of King Charles I., emigrated with three children, Samuel, John and Mary, from the southwest of England in 1649, first to St. Mary's, Md. (seventeenth year of the founding of the colony), and afterwards, in 1652, to Northumberland county, Va. (forty-fifth year of the founding of the colony). Between 1652 and 1660, the year of his death, John Earle received for the transportation of the thirty-four persons into the colony patents, besides the earlier ones revoked, aggregating seventeen hundred acres of land, located on Earle's creek, Jescomico Neck and Potomac in the latter located county of Westmoreland, which, exclusive of others subsequently granted by the Lords Proprietors of the Northern Neck to his immediate successors, descended in a single male representative for one hundred years to Samuel, the elder brother of Baylis Earle. His father, Samuel Earle, born in Westmoreland county 1692, educated at William and Mary College, was a planter, attorney-at-law, member of the house of burgesses from Frederick 1746, justice, colleague of Lord Fairfax 1749 to '52, collector of tobacco 1748, high sheriff, church warden 1751, and major of George William Fairfax's colonial regiment. He married, as already stated, Anna Sorrel, Richmond County, 1726, she being his first wife, and had issue: Samuel, *Baylis, John,* Rachel, and Hannah. He married a second time to Elizabeth (daughter of Randolph and Jeannette) Holbrook, of Prince William, and had issue: Esaias, Samuel, Zioh, and Lettie. He died near the present Front Royal, Va., at a place called Earle's Ferry, on the Shenandoah River.

John Earle, brother of Baylis, born June 5th, 1737, soon after his first marriage emigrated to South Carolina, and settled the "old place," Earlesville, on the west bank of North Pacolet, and made a crop there in 1773, before his brother Baylis came; then moving beyond the colony line, on the east side of North Pacolet, selling the place already described as Earle's Fort.

Baylis, when he came, entered into the home and improvements made by his brother, where the balance of his long life was spent.

John Earle was a staunch patriot during the Revolution, and served as a militia captain a portion of the time, repelling the Tory and Indian invasion in his section. He was doubtless in the expedition of Major Howard against "Big Warrior" and his gang at the battle of Round Mountain, which occurred soon after the "Hannon Massacre," on North Pacolet, in 1776. (See "Colonial and Revolutionary History of Upper South Carolina," page 353.)

John Earle, some time during the revolution, obtained the title of *colonel.* He was married twice. A second time to Mrs. Rebecca (Berry) Wood, relict of John Wood, who was foully murdered by "Bloody Bill" Cunningham and his band of Tories, in November, 1781, an account of which we have given in the volume referred to. By the marriage between Colonel John Earle and Mrs. Rebecca Wood several children were born, among whom we would mention Mrs. Lydia Prince, wife of Wm. Prince, who lived and died at the old John Earle homestead on North Pacolet, and Mrs. Amaryllis Bomar of Spartanburg, relict of Elisha Bomar and mother of Major John Earle Bomar, and Mrs. T. O. P. Vernon.

In referring to the old family Bible of Baylis Earle, it is recorded that he "married Mary Prince April 16th, 1757, aged 13 years nearly." She was born December 1744, being a daughter of John Prince, a neighbor family in Virginia, who was a descendant of Edmund Prince, Gentleman, to whom, for the transportation of persons into the colony was issued, on the 4th of October, 1639, a patent for 500 acres of land "in the countie of Charles citie."

The issue of the marriage between Baylis and Mary (Prince) Earle were fourteen children, of whom eight were sons and six daughters, as follows:

1. Sallie, born January 4th, 1759, in Virginia. In South Carolina, after migration, she married Edward Hampton (second wife), whose son Noah, by his first wife, was killed at the battle of Earle's Ford, and who himself was foully murdered by the Tories about the close of the Revolution. (See Hampton family.)

Sallie Hampton, after her husband's death, married Charles Littleton. Her issue by the first marriage were two daughters, Anna and Elizabeth, of whose after-life we can learn nothing. By the second marriage was born one son, Marcus Littleton.

2. Samuel Earle, first son, who will receive further notice.

3. Jack Earle, who died in Virginia at the age of five years.

4. Anna (called Nancy), born December 24th, 1764, married Ephraim Reese; had issue: Daniel, Hampton,. Samuel, Joseph, Ephraim, Sarah and Rhoda.

5. John Earle, born September 18th, 1766, married Nancy Holland Burns (called Earle), and had issue: Samuel, Esaias, Benjamin, Harriet, Messiniah and Elizabeth. The last named married Dr. John M. Johnson of Paducah, Ky., and with him refugeed to Atlanta, in 1863, where he died soon afterwards. John Earle moved from South Carolina to Pontotoc, Mississippi, thence to Southwest Kentucky.

6. Baylis Earle, born September 11th, 1768, married Mrs. Hewlett, formerly Miss Moseley, and had issue: Thomas, Baylis, Elizabeth, and one or two more, names not known. Baylis Earle is said, by the author of "Myra Cunningham, Tale of 1780," to have dressed as a lady and liberated Captain Harry Wood from the hand of the Tories. (See Magnolia, August, 1844.)

7. Damaris Earle, born January, 1771, died March 8th, 1804, married Benjamin Dillingham, and had issue: John, Rachel, Reese, Providence and Amanda.

8. Rhoda Earle, born May 25th, 1773 (the last born in Virginia), married Benjamin Clark, and had issue: Sallie, Mahala, and the next also named Mahala, then Amanda and Baylis.

9. Miriam Earle, born November 4th, 1775, in South Carolina; married January 28th, 1796, to William Gowen, a Revolutionary soldier, known as Major Buck Gowen (see "'Colonial and Revolutionary History of Upper South Carolina," pages 361-2), had issue: Mahala, Matilda, John and Letitia.

10. Thomas Prince Earle, born September 16th, 1778; married Mary Stallerd, and had one daughter, Elizabeth.

11. Edward Hampton Earle, born October 15th, 1780; married Susan Davis, and had issue: Ann, Richard,, William, John, Berkley,, Thomas and Josephine.

12. Theron Karle, born March 13th, 1783, who will receive further notice.

13. Aspasia Earle, born February 21st, 1785; married Mary Montegue, and had issue: Charlotte and Henry M. The former married John Dodd, had one daughter, Ann, who married Richard Bowdoine; the latter married Sophia Rowland, and had issue: William E., Emma, Mary, John and Miriam.

14. Providence Earle, born July 10th, 1788; married John Lucas, and had issue: Cora, Adelia, Messiniah, Benjamin, Nancy and Elizabeth.

These all married in South Carolina, and eight of them, viz., John, Baylis, Thomas P., Edward H., Anna,, Damaris, Rhoda and Providence, removed to Kentucky, the balance remaining in South Carolina for a time. Sallie died on North Pacolet. Theron died at his father's old place. Aspasia first settled on the north bank of North Pacolet, one mile from his father's old place, in the present county of Polk, N.C., and in March, 1846, removed to Floyd County, Ga., and settled on Oostanaula River.

Baylis Earle was a staunch Whig during the Revolution, though he was too far advanced in years to take the field as a soldier. In a MS. letter to a friend under date September 11th, 1814, he states that on "the Sunday next before Colonel Ferguson's defeat at King's Mountain, a large party of British and Tories came to his dwelling and plundered at their pleasure, killed a steer and destroyed a large quantity of oats, say four or five hundred dozen. It was near his homestead that the battle of Earle's Ford took place, an account of which we have given in another volume. [1]

After the close of the Revolution and upon the organization of the county (afterwards called district) of Spartanburg (1785), Baylis Earle was appointed by the governor as one of the county court judges for Spartanburg, which office he served with ability and fidelity to the people of said county for several years. His commission as such hangs neatly framed in the Kenedy Laboratory at Spartanburg, issued from the Executive Department at Columbia by Governor Charles Pinckney, on February 13th, 1791, to continue during good behavior, "to be a judge of the County Court in and for the County Court of Spartanburg," etc.

Baylis Earle was one of the founders of Wolf Creek (Baptist) Church (at Landrum, S.C.), organized in 1803. He was the first clerk of said church. The old church book, with his record of the proceedings, neatly and legibly written, is still to be seen among the archives of the church, now almost a century old.

Baylis Earle lost his wife, who had long been his faithful companion, in 1807, but survived himself until January 6th, 1825, dying in his 91st year. It is said that he retained to a remarkable degree to the last his strength, faculties and suavity, and was perfectly resigned to his approaching end.

HON. SAMUEL EARLE, eldest son of Baylis and Mary (Prince) Earle, was born in Frederick County, Va., November 28, 1760. In 1774 he followed his father's migration to South Carolina, settling with him at the old homestead on North Pacolet in what was then Ninety-six District.

On the 20th May, 1777, when in his 17th year, he received through the unsolicited interest of Major Andrew Pickens a commission which he took up on the 11th of June following, of ensign of the 5th S.C. Regiment of the Continental Line. He was promoted two grades, second and first lieutenant at the battle of Stono, June 20th, 1779, and was paroled on the terms of capitulation by General Lincoln, of Charleston, June 11th, 1780. About October of the same year he again took up arms, acting independently, but under authority of his Continental commission. He acted as a volunteer with different officers or with different corps: with Sumter at Blackstocks, November 20th, 1780, and declined a captaincy with him in 1781; was at Bush River with Colonel Roebuck, and was in the famous retreat into Virginia with General Greene, after Morgan's victory at Cowpens; was at the siege of Ninety-six with Lee's Legion, and Hammond's Cavalry, June, 1781. He was acting on the staff of General Pickens, when, during the Cherokee expedition in 1782, he was detached to raise a troop of cavalry, South Carolina Rangers, and operated against the "authors," one of whom he engaged in a single mortal combat, and when his pistol failed to fire was rescued from instant death by the timely arrival and interposition of his lieutenant, Henry Machan Wood, afterwards one of the first county court judges for Spartanburg. He served to the end of the war, his corps being probably the last in arms in the upper part of South Carolina.

After the close of the Revolution, as Deputy Provost Marshal, he served the first writ ever made returnable to Old Cambridge or Ninety-six. As deputy to John (afterwards general) Martin of Edgefield, the first high sheriff for Ninety-six District, Judge Heyward holding court under an arbor, and General Thomas Pinckney being the only attorney present, Samuel Earle levied on a mill on Bush River in Newberry — the first civil process served in the upper part of the State after the war.

Governor Perry in his "Reminiscences of Public Men," gives an interesting sketch of Samuel Earle. He was elected a member of the State convention which framed, the Constitution, and he was also a member of the State convention which adopted the Constitution of the United States. He was afterwards elected a member of the 4th Congress, from 1795 to '97, for the districts of Greenville, Pendleton, Laurens, Abbeville and Spartanburg as the successor of General Andrew Pickens, who was the first member to represent said congressional district under the Federal Constitution. He was a Federalist, and supported Washington's administration and favored Jay's treaty. He removed to Pendleton about 1809; was elected sheriff of that district by the legislature and served in that office for four years. He was appointed one of the commissioners, on the part of South Carolina, to settle the boundary line between the latter State and Georgia — this being about the last public service rendered by him to his country.

He married March 12th, 1793, to Harriet, daughter of James and Elizabeth (Hampton) Harrison. Issue: Baylis John, Andrew Pickens, James Harrison, Elizabeth Hampton, Edward Preston, Morgan Priestly, Mary Prince (Maxwell), Damaris Miriam (Mays), Sarah Mariah (Lewis), Harriet (Earle), Elias Theron, Samuel Maxcy, and Edward Hampton.

Mr. Earle was a pious member of the Baptist church, and all through life was a man of high and pure character, his honor, integrity or patriotism never having been questioned throughout his long life.

HON. THERON EARLE, son of Baylis and Mary (Prince) Earle, was born at Earlesville, the old homestead place of his father, March 13th, 1783, where he ever afterwards lived and died. He was a man of more than ordinary intelligence, honest, upright, and progressive as a farmer. He was a representative in the State legislature from Spartanburg District from 1832 to '36. In politics he was a *Protectionist*. Major Hoy, in his writings, states that he issued a sensible circular advocating protection for home manufacturing; that he admired the logic of Hayne and McDuffie and commenced his circular by wishing their ability to help him do his subject justice.

He served for several years as adjutant of the old 36th Regiment, South Carolina Militia, and made an efficient officer. We hear no more of him in public life.

He married Hannah, daughter of Michael Miller, an estimable lady, and had children: Samuel Earle, who died at the age of twelve or thirteen years; Dr. Michael Baylis Earle, an eminent physician, who lived and died in Greenville, S.C., married Harriet, daughter of John Maxwell of Pendleton, S.C.; Oliver P. Earle, who will receive further notice; John Chevis Earle, who died young; Elizabeth Earle, who married General Joel W. Miller; Nancy Miller Earle, who married Rev. John G. Landrum (second wife); Rev. Thomas J. Earle, an earnest, able and humble (Baptist) minister of the Gospel for more than a quarter of a century, whose works "follow him," who married Miss Jane Kenedy of Georgia; Crawford Earle, a promising young man who died in Greenville, S.C., and James Earle, who died aged four or five years. Theron Earle died November 3d, 1841. His widow survived him for nearly twenty-five years.

HON. OLIVER PERRY EARLE, son of Theron and Hannah (Miller) Earle, was born September 25th, 1816, at the old homestead (Earlesville) of his father and grandfather, where, in after years, he became the proprietor of this valuable estate, which he held up to the time of his death, which took place November 4th, 1894. He was raised on his father's farm, but was educated in the very best common schools of his day, and acquired a good, practical, business education, which was manifest throughout his life.

But few men have ever lived in his community or county who measured up to his pure and upright standard of citizenship. He was a man of the purest motives, and unsullied honor and integrity. He was well known in a wide locality as a thriving, progressive and successful planter, and in financial judgment and business forethought he had but few superiors. In a word, he ranked among the solid men of his county. He was rather reserved in deportment, prudent in the expression of his opinions, and modest almost to a fault.

Hon. O. P. Earle

In 1856, at the earnest solicitation of many friends, he entered the race and was elected to the State legislature as one of the representatives from Spartanburg District, his colleagues being J. W. Miller, O. E. Edwards, J. Winsmith and James Farrow. On all public questions that came before the House of Representatives, while he was a member of the same, it was accorded to him that he showed excellent judgment in the recording of his vote, as he well understood and appreciated the best interests of his constituents.

In 1858 he married Miss Catharine, daughter of Hon. Tolliver Davis of Rutherford County, N.C., who still survives him. Some time after his marriage he connected himself with the Wolf Creek Baptist church, and was made a deacon of the same, which office he filled to the day of his death, with a conscientious discharge of duty to his Saviour and brethren.

By his marriage with Miss Davis he had children as follows: Tolliver D., married Miss Hallie Lee; Hannah, married George Harrison; Sarah Catharine, died in infancy; Nancy Elizabeth, married Rev. Paul Bomar; Eliza Harriet, married Joseph Lee; Mary Miller, married Dr. R. G. Christopher, and Baylis Theron, merchant at Spartanburg.

[1] See "Colonial and Revolutionary History of Upper South Carolina," p. 118.

Chapter Twenty - Smith Family

Descendants of James, John and Charles Smith

Just before the Revolutionary war five brothers came from Bull Run, Va., and settled in the vicinity of Glenn's Spring, in Spartanburg County, viz.: James, Fleming, Thomas, John and Charles. Their father came from Wales, and their mother, a Miss Fleming, from France. Of these brothers, Thomas was never married, hence he has no descendants; of Fleming we can learn nothing; James had two sons — John and Enoch. Enoch went to Alabama and John, his brother, settled in Union county, S.C. He was by occupation a farmer, and his homestead residence was about five miles below the court-house of said county on the Spartanburg & Union Railroad. He had two sons — Franklin and Thomas W. Franklin died during the war unmarried. Thom-as W. was a Baptist minister of considerable note and ability, and served acceptably for a number of years churches in Union and Spartanburg coun-ties. He was educated at the Furman University, at Greenville, S.C. He died in 1883, leaving behind him an interesting family who still reside at the old homestead place of his father.

John, one of the original five brothers mentioned, had one son, Thomas, who went to Georgia; two daughters, one was a cripple and never married, the other, Susanna, married Thomas Finch, and became the mother of James, Benjamin, Simpson and Enoch Finch, from whom have sprung numerous descendants of respectability, many of whom yet reside in the present coun-ty of Spartanburg.

Charles, the youngest of the five Smith brothers referred to, from whom a large portion of the Smith family now living in Spartanburg County de-scended, married a Miss Rhodes about 1760. He was a soldier of the Revolu-tion, but owing to a defective eyesight, he was assigned to duty in the com-missary department. He was a man of eminent piety, having early embraced the Christian religion. He was made a deacon in Philadelphia (Baptist) church in 1805. From the death of Rev. Christopher Johnson, August, 1809, to the close of 1820, the church had no regular pastor, and for several years but little preaching. Charles Smith was the mainstay of the church through adversity as well as prosperity. He enjoyed the confidence of his brethren, for when there was no minister present, he was made moderator and con-ducted the services. He died in 1824. He had six sons: Elijah, Sanford, Wil-liam, Daniel, Moses and Aaron; and six daughters: Martha, who married Hugh White and lived in the community of Philadelphia church; Abigail, who married Joseph Golightly and went west; Elizabeth, who married Robert Page; Rachel, who married James Page; Ann, who married William Page; three sisters marrying three brothers, and Mary, who married George Sloan.

Concerning the sons of Charles Smith, Aaron went to Missouri; Moses was drowned while a young man, unmarried; Daniel married Elizabeth Trail; they lived in the Philadelphia community. The children of Isaac T. Smith are the only descendants of this Daniel Smith living in Spartanburg County.

William married Sallie Trail. They had three children; only one remained in Spartanburg; she married Giles Bearden, near Friendship church on Dutchman's Creek.

Sanford married Mary Morrow, daughter of the old Revolutionary soldier. They had three sons: Samuel M., David M. and Robert R. Robert R. was a me-chanic — had a regular shop where he made wagons, buggies, carriages, etc. His work was well done. There were six daughters: two of them went to Alabama, one to Arkansas, one to Illinois, and two married to their cousins — sons of Elijah.

William and Sanford had the first and only gun factory anywhere in the southern portion of Spartanburg County. They manufactured rifles, made the barrel, bored and stocked them, and they were of what was known as the old time flint and steel, which were much used in their day. Their works, which were begun in the early part of the 19th century, were on Reedy Fork of Dutchman, one and a half miles southwest of Philadelphia church. A part of the old rock dam is yet to be seen there.

Elijah Smith was made a deacon at the organization of Philadelphia church in July, 1803. For near two years he was the only deacon of said church. He served his church faithfully in that capacity until his death in 1834. He married Diana Ham, sister of Squire James Ham. They had twelve children. Three died while young. There were three daughters who married and lived in the same neighborhood of the six sons, which was in the vicinity of Philadelphia church.

Moses went to Georgia about 1835; William S. was a mechanic, followed making and repairing wagons, buggies, carriages, etc., and his work was substantially done. He was an active worker in the Philadelphia church, a deacon in the same for nearly fifty years, and truly a good man.

Enoch H, was a farmer, had a grist and sawmill, cotton-gin and thresher, all run by water, one mile west of Philadelphia church, and half a mile above the old gun factory referred to, on the same stream. He was an excellent citizen, a Christian gentleman, and the clerk of Philadelphia church for twenty-five years. Among his sons were Dr. Robert M., Elias and Albert Smith, the two latter living and residing in the same community. They are honest, intelligent and progressive farmers. They married two sisters: Elias to Miss Wallace, and Albert to Miss Lizzie Pool, now deceased, both educated, refined and intelligent ladies and graduates of the female college at Asheville, N.C., before the war. Elias has followed teaching a portion of his life.

Dr. Robert M. Smith, son of Enoch and Nancy Smith, was born October 19th, 1833. His boyhood was spent on his father's plantation. He received a good education in literature, and in 1856 began the study of medicine under Dr. G. H. King, at Walnut Grove, S.C. He graduated in medicine with distinction from the Atlanta Medical College in 1858, and for several years following had an extensive and lucrative practice.

At the outbreak of the civil war he enlisted in Company K, 3d Regiment, S.C.V., and was elected as one of its lieutenants. He remained with the company until serious illness compelled him to resign. After recovery he joined Captain Westfield's company, which formed a part of the 2d Regiment, S.C. Cavalry. In the battle on John's Island, S.C., in 1864, he was wounded in the right arm, which necessitated amputation at the shoulder-joint.

After the war he became a prominent politician in Spartanburg, and was seldom defeated in his political aspirations. For fourteen years he was a prominent member of the House of Representatives and in the Senate. He was a good stump orator, an able debater, and a strong advocate of home rule against "carpetbag government," which principle resulted in the election of Wade Hampton in 1876.

In 1862 Dr. Smith married to Adeline Skinner, of Walnut Grove, S.C. To them were born eight children, four sons and four daughters, two of which are deceased. Those living are Annie Eugenia (Mrs. Dr. S. T. D. Lancaster), Carrie Pauline (Mrs. I. P. Mahoney), Mary Virginia (Airs. J. F. Alexander), Nannie (Mrs. Henri Bernhardt), Charles O'Conner, and Earle Hix.

David H. Smith, son of Elijah, was a blacksmith and woodworkman. He made wagons and other vehicles. His work would stand the test, and always found ready sale. He and his son, E. E. Smith, had a plow patented just before the civil war.

Noah H. Smith, another brother, was a farmer. He was a man of exemplary character, and reared a large family of children, who have proven themselves worthy citizens. Two of his sons, John B. and Lecil, gave their lives in their country's defense. Two sons, W. J. and E. B. Smith, reside in the county, while the others are either dead or have gone west.

Col. Dan'l H. Smith

Colonel Daniel H. was the youngest child of Elijah Smith. He was a farmer by occupation, and married Miss Jane Lanford, a granddaughter of James Lanford, a soldier of the Revolution, who in an early day settled in Spartanburg County below Woodruff. Her father was John Lanford.

Colonel Smith was clerk of Philadelphia (Baptist) church for twenty-five years, a deacon for over fifty, and a Sunday-school superintendent for about fifteen years. Soon after he attained to military age he became a commissioned officer in one of the companies of the old 45th S.C. Militia, and served as such for seven consecutive years. Then he was elected colonel of said regiment. At a later period he was brought out and reelected colonel of the same regiment without any desire or effort on his part, being already muster free.

But when the war broke out and the services of every available man were needed, though well advanced in years, he did not hesitate to volunteer his services to his country. He was orderly sergeant in Dr. Ben Wofford's company in the winter of 1862-3 at Charleston, and was captain of Company A, 1st Battalion of S.C. Reserves from August, 1864, to the end of the war.

The following is an extract of a tribute paid his memory after his death by his third lieutenant:

"No one who knew Captain Smith will doubt his high Christian character. I knew him thirty-five years, and I knew him best at a time in the history of his life when men's souls were tried — in the army. Under all circumstances he bore out the same character that he built up at home...He was a strict disciplinarian — always the same on picket, on the march, on the battle-line or in camp. The same unswerving Christian officer and soldier."

Colonel Daniel Smith had four children, two sons and two daughters. One of the sons. Rev. William Pinckney Smith, is well known to the people of Spartanburg as an able, humble and earnest minister of the gospel of the Baptist faith. He is well educated for this specific work, and has been, at this writing (1900), in the ministry for about twenty-one years, and has served churches both in the counties of Union and Spartanburg, and is now in the twentieth year of his pastorate at Sulphur Springs.

He married Miss O 'Shields, who died in 1898, leaving four children. Of these Furman was educated at the Furman University; Lamar is a graduate of Wofford College; Elmore is in business and Falls in school.

The other son, Marshall G. Smith, who died in 1890, was a model and progressive young man and did much for the community in which he lived.

Of the daughters of Colonel Smith, Miss Ella is unmarried. The other daughter is the wife of Mr. John W. Stribling of Spartanburg. They have five children. Willie is a graduate of the Citadel Academy at Charleston, Miss Alice of Converse College, Hickman of Wofford College, and two daughters at present students in Converse College.

The men of this branch of the Smith family have been mostly farmers and mechanics. Some of the family, especially among the females, have followed teaching. As a whole they have formed a part of the best class of citizenship in Spartanburg County, and both in times of peace and in war they have always been patriotic and true to their country's welfare. In the civil war between the States no less than nine of the grandsons of Elijah Smith gave up their lives in their country's defence. Let the descendants of the families mentioned herein be proud to emulate the example of a noble ancestry.

Chapter Twenty-One - The Foster Family

Descendants of William Foster and Thomas James.

William Foster (or Major Billie, as he was called) moved from Amelia county, Va., to South Carolina in 1791 and settled a mile or so east of Mount Zion church (near Fort Prince) in Spartanburg District. The plantation on which he settled has never departed from the Foster family; it is now owned by Mr. Ed. Foster.

He acquired the title major by reason of the fact that he held that title in the American army during the Revolutionary war. He married before the close of the Revolution to Mrs. Mary Ann James, relict of Thomas James, who fills a soldier's grave on the battle-field of Stono, S.C., fought in 1779. Her maiden name was Jones, a sister of Harrison Jones, who lost a leg at the battle of Guilford Court-house, N.C. She had one son, John James, by her first husband, and James, Elijah, Moses, Garland and Calvin by the second husband. She had three daughters, viz.: Annie Young, Maiden Smith and Sallie Chapman (wife of Beverly Chapman). These have long since passed "over the river."

James Foster was the only one of the sons that acquired a superior English education, and was for many years the best teacher of the section of country in which he lived; he was proverbial as the best arithmetician of the county. He studied the classics one year under Mr. Gilliland, in which time he read Virgil, Ovid and other authors; but he never taught them, as there was but little demand in those days for higher education.

James Foster taught school in Abbeville County, on the Saluda River, for the period of three years, and at the breaking out of the war of 1812 he volunteered and went to Charleston, where he remained until the close of the war. After this he married Ann Turner in the year 1814 and settled on the waters of Pacolet River, where he died in 1863, in the 77th year of his age. By his marriage with Ann Turner he raised a family of seven children, viz.: Jane H,, wife of ___ Turner; Hannah M., wife of Rev. Bryant Bonner; Thomas Foster, Wm. M, Foster (Major), James T. Foster, Jones W. Foster, and Mary H., wife of W. J. McDowell, Esq. Five of these still live.

Rev. Wm. Moultrie Foster, one of the sons above mentioned (familiarly known as Major Bill), is a native of Spartanburg County. He was born July 28th, 1825. His father being an educated man and an excellent instructor in the schoolroom, he obtained a fair English and classical education, and was himself a successful teacher for a number of years.

Being a young man of bright promise and more than ordinary intelligence, his name was announced by his friends in 1858 as a candidate for the legislature to represent his native district. Being a captivating speaker and well posted on all the issues of the day, his popularity soon spread abroad and he was elected along with other popular candidates of that period. His colleagues were O. E. Edwards, B. F. Kilgore, J. W. Miller and Jas. Farrow. He was again elected in 1860 and '62, which terms covered almost the entire period of the civil war.

But in a few months after the outbreak of the civil war between the States he raised a company of young men for the Confederate service and was chosen as its captain. This company became Company C, 9th Regt., S.C.V., commanded by Colonel J. D. Blanding. At the reorganization of the South Carolina troops in Virginia Captain Foster was elected major of the 5th Regt., S.C.V., which office he held until the end of the war.

After he had reached the age of fifty years an overruling Providence opened the eyes of his understanding. He began to work for the Master from the day of his conversion, and connected himself with the Baptist church at Cherokee Springs. Having impressions to preach he was soon afterwards ordained to the Gospel ministry, and has to the present time been a faithful worker in the Master's cause.

In the year 1887 he was chosen to take charge of the People's High School at West's Springs, Union county, S.C., and later he was elected school commissioner for said county, and served with efficiency for two years.

Returning to his native county he was again honored with a seat in the State legislature in 1890, and served in this capacity for one or two terms. He has now retired from public life, being well advanced in years, though well preserved. He is now devoting much of his time to writing and publishing, through the county press, poetry in verse, which in course of time will be collected and compiled and which will reflect additional credit to his excellent character and intellectual abilities which he has so well sustained throughout his entire life.

Besides James Foster (son of Major Billie), whose character we have already reviewed, the other brothers to whom we have referred, viz.: Jones, Elijah, Moses, Garland and Calvin, also claim our attention.

Of these Elijah removed to Tennessee. Calvin, a very promising young man, died in the city of Philadelphia, where he was attending medical lectures. Jones and Moses (called Pacolet Moses) resided on the Pacolets. Wm. H. Foster, on South Pacolet, and Mrs. Polly Younger, at New Prospect, are the surviving children of Jones Foster. Among the children of Moses Foster were William H. Sr., John and Mrs. Hunter. Garland Foster resided on the plantation where his father settled, which is, as stated, the present home of Mr. Ed. Foster. He married Miss Moss, by whom he raised a large and respectable family of sons and daughters, all of whom have either died or emigrated to Texas, except Mr. Calvin Foster, near Campton, S.C., Mrs. J. W. Simpson of Pendleton, S.C., and Mrs. Mary Foster, who married James Foster.

These brothers were all good and substantial citizens, "whose word was their bond." Garland Foster was for a long number of years a deacon of Mount Zion church, and was exemplary in his walk as a Christian throughout his life.

John James, only son of Mrs. Mary Ann Jones by her first marriage, and stepson of Major Billie Foster, was born in Appomattox County, Va. He came with his father to South Carolina when a boy only ten years old. When he reached his majority he returned to Virginia and farmed on his lands there, but eventually sold his possessions there and returned to South Carolina and settled near his mother. He was a prosperous and successful farmer and accumulated property. He married Miss Jane Anderson Turner, a niece of Major Billie Foster, who was born in Clarke County, Ga. Her parents were Virginians. The bride was only seventeen years old at the time of the marriage, and the husband only lived two weeks afterwards.

As a result of this marriage a daughter, Mary Turner James, was born November 28th, 1805, a bright and beautiful girl, who subsequently became the wife of Dr. Thomas Austin, a highly respected citizen of Greenville District, S.C., a physician of eminence in his day and a soldier of the war of 1812. The present surviving children of Dr. Austin, including Hon. Thomas

W. Austin of Greenville, and sister, Mrs. Mary R. Smith and family, near Roebuck,. S.C., are the only descendants of John and Jane A. James.

The writer, in his boyhood, lived a near neighbor and enjoyed a pleasant acquaintance with Mrs. James. He was oftentimes the recipient of her kind hospitality, and had an opportunity to become acquainted with her excellent traits of character. Bereft of her husband in two weeks after her marriage, and only at the age of seventeen years, with the great battle of life before her, she proved herself to be equal to the emergency. Owning at the time a valuable negro property, she possessed an indomitable will, was excellent in management, possessing, as she did, splendid judgment. Being of a superior mind, she was fond of reading, and had a remarkable memory. She was kind and hospitable in her home, and enjoyed having young people visit her. She was good to the poor and devoted to the church and loved to have the ministers of the Gospel visit her. At the time of her death she was a member of Mount Zion church, and sleeps in the cemetery nearby. She died at the age of seventy-three years.

Chapter Twenty-Two - The Foster Family

Descendants of Robert, Richard and William Foster.

Robert Foster emigrated from Amelia County, Va., in 1783, and settled on the waters of Tyger River within the present territory of Spartanburg County. His wife was Miss Sallie James. He had seven sons, viz.: Thomas, Robert, William, John, James, Ransom and Moses.

Thomas and Robert were residents of Greenville County, and died in that county.

William lived and died near Bethlehem church in Spartanburg County. He married Miss Exie Wingo. James married Patience Benson, daughter of Wm. Benson, whose wife was Eleanor Key. He lived near the historic Fort Prince, and he and his wife are buried nearby. Mr. Benson died away from home on one of his market trips.

Ransom was a soldier in the war of 1812. He married a Miss Tanner.

Moses died in Spartanburg County and his family removed to Alabama. He and Ransom were twins.

Among the children of Thomas Foster mentioned was Jesse Foster, father of Major A. J. and Jesse Foster. The former served as major of the Lower Battalion, 36th Regiment, S. C. M., before the war, and later, during said war, as captain of Co. B, 22d Regiment, S.C.V.

Among the children of William and Exie (Wingo) was Colonel Robert W. Foster, who resided near Holly Spring, who was a man of more than ordinary intelligence and information, and who from 1848 to '50 was a representative from Spartanburg District in the State legislature, and was also for several years colonel of the 36th Regiment, S.C. M.

Among the children of James Foster was Eleanor, [1] who married Andy Foster and removed to Georgia, where he died in 1897; Jane, who married Zachariah Wingo and removed to Georgia, settling on the Chattahoochee River, Forsyth county, where he died; Eliza, who married Albert Cunningham; Abner B., who married Oney, a daughter of "Mill Creek" Billy Foster; Mary, who married Thomas A. Rogers, — both lived and died in Pickens county, S.C.; Robert J., who married Polly A. Bowdan; James J., who married Mary, daughter of Garland Foster, and was killed near Petersburg, March 29th, 1865; Theresa, who married George F. Steading, killed in the army; and Moses, who married Mrs. Brewton, who was Miss Sarah Alexander. [2]

The last named. Captain Moses Foster, is well and popularly known to the people of Spartanburg County. He was born January, 1833, and was raised on his father's farm near Bethlehem church. He was educated in the schools of his neighborhood taught by Thomas Scruggs, Wm. Cooper, Elias Stephens, Hampton Posey and others. He connected himself with Bethlehem church early in life, and has been a deacon of said church since 1866; is a useful man in his church and community both by precept and example. He has very often been a delegate from his church to the associations to which it has belonged, and is an earnest advocate and contributor to all the benevolent objects which come before it.

Capt. Moses Foster.

Before the civil war between the States he was commissioned by the Governor of South Carolina a captain of the militia (May's old field), the company which he commanded being a part of the 36th Regiment, S.C. M. He served seven years as a commissioned officer, which, under the law, made him muster free, but at the outbreak of said war (or even a few months before) he volunteered in the Spartan Rifles (Captain Joseph Walker), which was one of the first companies to leave Spartanburg for the army. While serving in Virginia he was transferred (1862) to Co. D, Palmetto Sharpshooters, commanded by Captain A. H. Foster. In both of these companies he held the position of sergeant. He was in nearly all the battles in which his company was engaged. Was always at his post except when prevented by sickness, and was at the surrender at Appomattox Court-house.

After this he returned to his farm, where he has lived for sixty years or more. He has never aspired to public office, but, by reason of his fitness for the position, was nominated and elected by the Democrats of Spartanburg County as coroner for said county, which position he held for four years.

By his marriage, referred to, he has three children: James Alexander, married Miss Emma, daughter of Virgil Rogers; John G. Landrum, single, and Mary Patience, single — a graduate of Limestone College.

172

Richard Foster, a first cousin of Robert Foster, emigrated from Virginia to Spartanburg District and settled in the Bethlehem neighborhood about the time that Robert came. He was married four times. Among his children were Spencer B. Foster, who was a deacon and prominent member of Bethlehem church. He was also captain of a militia company before the civil war, and was for a time the captain of the old Tyger band which belonged to the 36th Regiment, S.C. M., his favorite instrument being the clarionet, which the writer, in his boyhood, delighted to hear him play. He was the father of Richard and Martin Foster; the former losing an arm at the battle of Frazier's Farm, Virginia,

William Foster, "Mill Creek Billy," first cousin to the first two, also from Amelia county, Va., lived on Fair Forest Creek. He had nine children, viz.: Moses, who married Polly Hurt; Ransom, who married a daughter of Robert Foster in Greenville county (uncle of Captain Moses Foster); John; Jinsey, who married Jesse Wingo, father of Wm. J, Wingo, a well-known merchant who died in Spartanburg in 1895 or '96; Maiden, who married Paschal Wingo, father of Rev. I. W. Wingo; Delilah, who married Burrel Wingo, father of Robert Wingo and grandfather of Hon, John O. Wingo, Greenville county, S.C., and Stewart Wingo, merchant at Spartanburg; Oney, who married Abner B. Foster; Annie, who married Isham Hurt; and Malinda, who married Asa Cunningham.

The entire families of the Foster connection in Spartanburg County have always been distinguished for their piety and high order of law-abiding citizenship. Nowhere have any people ever been found more patriotic, true and loyal to their country's best interests than the worthy sons which belonged to these families. No brighter example can be produced as an evidence of this fact than the case of Joseph Foster, son of Moses and Polly (Hurt) Foster. In one of the battles in Virginia, during the civil war, he was shot through the head with a Minie ball. The ball ranging below the brain entered near the eyeball and made its exit behind one ear. His recovery was one of the most remarkable occurrences in the history of surgery. From this dreadful wound he recovered in a few months and reentered the service in Virginia, and had not been there long when he was cut in two by a cannon ball in an engagement on Blackwater. He was a member of the company of Captain A. H. Foster, Palmetto Sharpshooters. James J. Foster, whose death we have already mentioned, was killed but a few days before the surrender at Appomattox. George Steading, brother-in-law of Captain Moses Foster, was killed below Richmond in front of Fort Harrison. There were several others of these families killed and a considerable number wounded during the civil war. The last one that could shoulder a musket marched boldly to the front to defend his country's rights in her hour of greatest peril.

[1] This was the first lady ever baptized by Rev. John G. Landrum. At this time he was pastor of Bethlehem (Baptist) church. On the same occasion he baptized

David Bray, Sr., and Malinda Foster, who afterward became Mrs. Asa Cunningham.

[2] The whole nine of these children were baptized ·by Rev. J. G. Landrum, at Bethlehem church.

Chapter Twenty-Three - The Snoddy Family

The families of Snoddy in Spartanburg County, and those of the same name who have emigrated from said county to other States, are descendants of John and Jane Snoddy, who emigrated from Ireland, Antrim county, in 1773. They first landed in Charleston, S.C., but continued their journey to the up-country, and made settlement on Jimmies Creek, about midway between Welford and Nazareth church, in the present county of Spartanburg. According to the best information we can gather, John and Jane Snoddy had two sons, John and Isaac, both of whom will receive further notice in this article.

The remains of John and Jane Snoddy, whose maiden name was Cowen, lie buried in the cemetery of Nazareth church. The husband died in 1806, aged 76 years, and the wife in 1816, aged 96 years. Besides the two sons mentioned, it has been stated that an older brother served in the Revolution, but of this fact we can gather no definite information.

Near the close of the Revolution (November, 1781) John, one of the sons mentioned, was murdered by the Tories under "Bloody Bill" Cunningham, at Poole's Iron Works, an account of which we have given in another volume. [1] He had been an active partisan in the service of his country, and as such was an object of hatred by the Tories. The maiden name of his wife was Elizabeth Riddle, but was known as "Aunt Betsy," and was remarkable for her energy and business judgment. After the sad death of her husband she would saddle her horse and oversee two plantations, and on Sundays drive twelve miles to Nazareth church, being a regular attendant of the same. Her children were small when her husband was murdered. She had five sons and three daughters, viz.:

Captain John Snoddy, whose homestead residence was four miles southwest of the city of Spartanburg, and who married Polly Daniel, daughter of Richard Daniel.

Isaac, second son, who married Elizabeth (Betsy) Vernon, daughter of James Vernon. By this marriage there were two children: James A. Snoddy, who met his death soon after the close of the civil war, and Mrs. Margaret Oeland, relict of Dr. John C. Oeland (see sketch), who resides at Spartanburg. Mrs. Snoddy married a second time to Richard Ballenger, by which marriage a son, Oscar P. Ballenger, near Welford, S.C., was born.

Two sons of John Snoddy, Andrew and Dr. Samuel, removed in early life to Alabama. The latter died while attending medical lectures at Lexington, Ky. Dr. Joseph Thompson, who will receive notice elsewhere, was attending lectures at the same time and place, and brought home with him his servant Aaron, and Buck, his favorite saddle horse.

Alexander, the youngest son of John Snoddy, married Mary Moore, daughter of Michael Moore of Rutherford county, N.C., and sister of Dr. A. L. Moore of Welford, S.C. Her mother's maiden name was Winnie Love, of Haywood county, a highly respected family. Alexander Snoddy died soon after his marriage, the only issue being Mrs. Edward L. Miller of Tuccapau, S.C. Mrs. Snoddy, her mother, subsequently became the wife of Dr. Pinckney Miller of Spartanburg County, a prominent physician and a highly respected citizen.

Of the daughters of John Snoddy referred to, Annie married David Brewton, Polly married Jones Brewton, and Peggy married Rev. Warren Drummond.

Isaac Snoddy, the other son mentioned of John and Jane Snoddy, was born in North Ireland, Antrim County, 1770, and was brought to America by his parents when only three years old. As already stated, John and his family landed in Charleston, and little Isaac was carried on the back of Samuel Miller from the ship to the landing.

Samuel Miller was a half uncle of Isaac Snoddy, and lived with the latter the remainder of his life. He never married, and died at the age of 104 years.

It is related that the Tories had orders to put to death every male child in the neighborhood in which John Snoddy lived. The tradition is that Isaac Snoddy was hidden in the wheat-field nearby in the daytime, and cautioned by his mother not to shake the straw lest he might be discovered, and at night he was concealed about the house. The wheat-field where Isaac lay concealed was pointed out to Mr. Crawford S. Thompson by Colonel S. M. Snoddy about one year before the latter died.

On his father's farm, the location of which has already been described, Isaac Snoddy received a good English education in such schools as the country then afforded. He taught several years before his marriage. In 1802, being then 32 years of age, he married Jane Crawford, third child of Patrick Crawford, [2] 23 years of age. For two years following he and his wife lived with his parents on the very spot where Dr. Samuel T. Snoddy lived and died. After the birth of their first child they began housekeeping for themselves. They built a house of logs, each facing from 12 to 18 inches, on the old Greenville and Spartanburg stage-coach road, near the spot where stands the present residence of James R. Snoddy. In this house, with some additions subsequently made, Isaac Snoddy and his wife died. In the same, for many years, was kept a post-office called New Hope. This was back in the twenties when letter postage was twenty-five cents, and there were no stamps or envelopes. Letters at that time were folded and sealed with wafers sold for that purpose. His house was also a famous stopping-place for the stage-coach, where horses were exchanged. "When the mellow notes of the stage-driver's horn were heard it indicated the number of passengers on board. Then there was a busy scene in the kitchen and stable-yard — the busy housewife preparing meals for the tired and hungry travelers, and the negroes getting fresh horses ready for the lumbering stage-coach. This was a famous stopping-place for emigrants on their way from Virginia and North Carolina to the southwest; also, the Creek and Catawba Indians, in passing back and forth, would stop here to rest."

As a citizen Isaac Snoddy "was patriotic, peaceable, hospitable, truthful, and kind to the poor, a liberal supporter of the church, but not a member and rarely attended. To his log-rollings, corn-shuckings and wedding feasts of his children all his neighbors, even the poorest, were invited. He often said if his poor neighbors were good enough to come to his log-rollings they were good enough to come to his wedding feasts... He was a kind husband, father and grandfather."

From a sketch by Dr. H. R. Black at the union of the descendants of Patrick Crawford at Nazareth church 18— we copy the following paragraph:

"The following descendants (of Isaac Snoddy) are mentioned in order of their births: John Snoddy, Jr., was born January 28th, 1803, married Theresa R. Daniel, December 12th, 1833, by Rev. John G. Landrum; the second time, Ellender P. Pearson, July 9th, 1845, by Rev. Z. L. Hohnes, and died February 14th, 1846. Margaret was born August 23d, 1804, married Joseph Thompson October 4th, 1827; died May 12th, 1882. Elizabeth was born April 11th, 1807, and married Joseph Nesbitt, September 8th, 1833, by Rev. Michael Dickson; died May 24th, 1867. Patrick Crawford, born January 16th, 1809, unmarried, acted as assistant surgeon in the U.S. troops on the frontiers about 1829. He died January 31st, 1830, about one month before his time for graduation in Lexington, Ky. Infant son 1810. Mary was born January 28th, 1812, married John H. Hoy, February 23d, 1837, by Rev. J. G. Landrum. Jane was born January 24th, 1814, and married Martin O. Miller, February 28th, 1839, by Dr. E. J. Buist, and died January 21st, 1885. Samuel M. was born December 12th, 1815, and married Rosa Benson October 5th, 1853, by Rev. R. H. Reed; died 1898. Ann was born January 16th, 1818, and married S. N. Drummond October 5th, 1843, by Rev. Pedan; second marriage, N. B. Davis, November 8th, 1859, by Rev. Simpson Drummond; died January 27th, 1869. Nancy V., born December 27th, 1820, married Andrew J. Daniel, April 5th, 1838, by Rev. J. G. Landrum; died February 9th, 1895."

Isaac Snoddy died January 28th, 1842. His widow, Jane Snoddy survived her husband twenty-two years and died on the 20th day of January, 1864, in the eighty-fifth year of her age. She was born on the Crawford place about one mile from Nazareth church, on the 27th day of February, 1779. She was a kind and devoted wife, and after the death of her husband managed well the business of a large farm, and divided every year the profits of the same among her children.

COLONEL SAMUEL MILLER SNODDY, son of Isaac and Jane Snoddy, was born December 12th, 1815, and was named in honor of Samuel Miller, his great half-uncle, to whom we have already referred. He was raised on his father's farm and received a fair English education in the best schools of his neighborhood. He chose farming for his occupation, and after he grew up to manhood purchased a valuable farm on Jorden's "Creek, waters of North

Tyger, about three miles northeast of Welford, S.C., where he resided the remainder of his life. From the time that he settled this place until he was about thirty-eight years of age, he lived the life of a bachelor in a community then more sparsely settled than at present, and during this time amused himself largely in fishing and hunting. Wild deer were then plentiful in the section of country between him and the mountains, and with a trained pack of hounds, which he kept all the time, and with his favorite hunting companions, "Tyger" Moses Foster and Samuel Johnson, he kept his table supplied with the choicest venison. He was a good shot and possessed a vigorous and robust constitution. In 1849 or '50 he was elected captain of the beat company at Gowen's old muster ground, and later major of the upper battalion, 36th Regt., S.C. M., and finally to the colonelcy of said regiment. To the last two mentioned positions he was elected without opposition, and his military career as an officer over the militia covered a period of about seven years.

Col. S. M. Snoddy, in uniform as Colonel of 36th Regiment, S.C. Militia.

As commander of the 36th Regiment Colonel Snoddy stood high. He seemed to appreciate fully the impending danger which threatened the country and the importance of maintaining good military discipline. The 36th Regiment mustered about 1,500 strong of men between the ages of 18 and 45 years, covering a military district of more than, half the present county of Spartanburg. As a further evidence of what we have stated in reference to Colonel Snoddy as commander of the 36th Regiment, we quote from the *Spartan* files, August 21st, 1856:

"On Wednesday the review of the 36th Regiment took place. The early day gave promise of enjoyment, and we estimated the number upon the field at Bomar's at about 3,000 persons of all ages and sexes. We were pleased to see so many ladies present to heighten the charms of the occasion.

"When the line had been formed and preparations for review completed by Col. Snoddy, Adjutant Webber was dispatched to apprise the commander-in-chief of the fact. At the head of his staff he immediately appeared at the camp colors, and was saluted by a discharge of artillery. The formality of military salute over, the regiment was put in motion, and executed the card of manoeuvres previously arranged for the day in a manner highly creditable to the officers and men. The regiment was then addressed by the Governor (Adams). He complimented them for their discipline and prompt and cheerful discharge of duty, saying, that while he could not award them the distinction of the best drilled regiment, he could say they were second to none he had reviewed on his present tour of duty; and while not wishing to make invidious distinctions where all were praiseworthy, he felt impelled to bestow special commendation upon the artillery, which he thought equal to any uniformed company in the State."

Not many years after the resignation of Colonel Snoddy as colonel of the 36th Regiment, the civil war between the States came on, and although he was too far advanced in years for active service in the field, yet he did not fail to respond to his country's call when men of his age were called for. He enlisted, and was captain of a company in the Battalion of State Reserves commanded by Major Joel Ballenger. [3] He discharged his duty faithfully as an officer and soldier, and bore with patience the fatigues and hardships incidental to camp life.

After the war was over Colonel Snoddy returned home, accepting the situation and adapting himself to the conditions which surrounded him as best he could. He bestowed his attention on his farm, garden, etc. He was especially devoted to the culture of select flowering plants and trees, and his home was beautiful and attractive. He felt a pride in his ancestry, and in 1897, in a field near George Bennett's between Reidville and Cashville, S.C. — the scene of the accidental killing of Patrick Crawford by Thomas Moore — he erected at his own expense a slab or stone to the memory of the former, placing his initials thereon.

Colonel Snoddy kept himself well posted on all the current news of the day. He was an honest and upright citizen and a progressive farmer. He was a good neighbor, hospitable in his home, was a kind husband and affectionate father. His remains repose among his ancestors at Nazareth cemetery. By his marriage (1853) with Miss Rosa Benson, he had children as follows: — James R. Snoddy, who married Mary, daughter of Elias Richardson; Nannie, who married David M. Coan; and Mary, who married Dr. H. R. Black.

The Caldwell Family

Killing of Patrick Crawford.

Among the oldest of the present familiar family names in Spartanburg County is the Caldwell family, nearly all of whom descended from John and Mary Caldwell, who emigrated from North Ireland to the present territory of Spartanburg County about 1766 or '67, and formed a part of the early Scotch-Irish settlement on the Tygers.

John Caldwell secured the King's grant to a tract of land within a mile of Nazareth Church which is still in the possession of some of the regular line of his posterity. The maiden name of his wife was Mary Young. When they came to America they brought with them one son, William Caldwell, who was born near Belfast, in the county of Antrim, about the year 1760.

At the breaking out of the Revolutionary war William Caldwell was about sixteen or seventeen years old and took an active part on the side of liberty. He served in that struggle in various ways, first as a scout and then as a private soldier. At different times he was a member of the companies of Captains John Collins and John Barry, which, in 1780, formed a part of the Spartan or Fair-forest Regiment under the command of Colonel John Thomas, Jr. He was in two regular engagements, Blackstocks and Cowpens. In the latter battle, one of his comrades recognizing a brother in the British ranks, standing behind a tree, said: "Don't shoot that man, for he is my brother."

When the enemy had been defeated and nearly all of Tarleton's army captured, Wm. Caldwell got leave of absence and was the first to carry the glorious news of the battle at Cowpens back to his neighbors at home. At Nicholl's Ford, on North Tyger, near the present Anderson's Mill, he met Mrs. Kate Barry (Margaret Catharine) wife of Captain Andrew Barry, swimming the river. The first thing she heard after crossing the river was one of the Nicholls girls running to meet her and shouting, "Glorious news, Peggy Barry, we whipped the British yesterday, and I have seen the man (Wm. Caldwell) that shook hands with Andrew Barry after the battle was over." Mrs. Barry had heard the firing of cannons the day before and had left three or four children at home, and had ridden out to hear the tidings of the battle. Wm. Caldwell assured her that her husband was safe, and would soon be home.

After the war was over and American Independence was gained, William Caldwell settled down and went to farming. He was a good neighbor and citizen. On February 20th, 1792, he married Margaret, second child and oldest daughter of Patrick Crawford, whose sad fate has been handed down to the present generations by tradition only. Patrick Crawford, through mistake, was killed during the latter part of the Revolution by his best friend, Thomas Moore, in an engagement near Cashville, in Spartanburg County. They were both members of Captain Andrew Barry's company. The company was to rendezvous at the two roads above Cashville for the purpose of following up a noted Tory scouting party. Two parties of said company came in contact, each believing the other the enemy they were seeking. Patrick Crawford was at the head of one of the Whig scouts and was killed before the mistake was discovered. Thomas Moore took deliberate aim and killed him in the fight, which continued until Captain Barry's noted dog trotted between the combatants, and seeing old Hunter, as the dog was called, they at once realized their mistake and ceased firing. It is said that Mr. Crawford's name was never mentioned afterward in Thomas Moore's presence without bringing tears to his eyes (see sketch of General Thomas Moore, page 191).

William Caldwell, when he married to Margaret Crawford, was about thirty-two, while his bride was only about fifteen years of age. The latter was a lifelong member of Nazareth Church, and as good a woman as any sleeping in the cemetery nearby.

By the marriage between William Caldwell and Margaret Crawford eleven children were born, four sons and seven daughters, and all were raised. The boys grew up and became good and useful citizens. Two of them, John C. and James, filled the office of magistrate for many years, to the credit and satisfaction of the people of Spartanburg District. They both, living in different sections of the district, did a great deal of business, especially James, as he moved to and lived in the upper part of the district, on South Pacolet, near Gowensville, a section in which there was no other magistrate.

Patrick Crawford Caldwell, one of the four sons referred to, was a blacksmith of good repute and an excellent citizen. William Harvey Caldwell, another son, was also highly esteemed as a citizen.

All the daughters of William Caldwell grew to womanhood, and all married, making good wives, good mothers, and useful women. They, it is said, were all noted for their domestic refinement and cleanliness — one of the chief Christian virtues. Their names were Polly Miller, Jane McCarley, Katie Young Hadden, Elizabeth Hadden, Ann Anderson, Margaret Gaston, and Eleanor Wright.

From these daughters, together with the four sons mentioned, the number of descendants, both living and dead, will amount to between five and six hundred. Of the daughters mentioned, Elizabeth Hadden lived to the age of about ninety-five years. With the exception of Ann Anderson, burial place unknown, and Elizabeth Wright, buried at Woodruff, S.C., the remains of almost the entire Caldwell family repose in the cemetery of Nazareth.

It is said that Wm. Caldwell had an inveterate hatred for the Tories. It is further said that among the victims of the noted raid of "Bloody Bill" Cunningham and his command to the up-country in November, 1780, were John Caldwell, brother of William, hacked to pieces, and John Snoddy, besides others. (See "Colonial and Revolutionary History of Upper South Carolina," pp, 341-364.)

On the tombstone of William Caldwell are the following lines placed there at his own request:

"Remember me as you pass by,
  As you are now, so once was I.
  As I am now, so you must be.
  Prepare for death and follow me."

[1] See "Colonial and Revolutionary History of Upper South Carolina," p. 356.
[2] Under the heading, "The Caldwell Family," we have given the particulars of the killing of Patrick Crawford, to which the reader is referred.
[3] For the particulars of the service, hardships, etc., performed by Major Ballenger's Battalion, the reader is referred to the sketch of Captain J. F. Sloan, in this volume.

Chapter Twenty-Four - Hon. James Jorden

In the early history of Spartanburg County no one figured more prominently than James Jorden, who was among the first settlers on the Tygers.
On his paternal side it is said that he was Scotch, and on his maternal side
Irish. He was doubtless well nurtured and trained by his parents, receiving
the best education that could be obtained at his day and time. His birthplace
was probably in the State of Pennsylvania, as most of the Scotch-Irish settlers on the Tygers came from that country.

In the annals of the documentary history of the important events which
occurred within the territory embraced in the original county of Spartanburg, which we gather in fragments here and there, the first record we find
of any public service rendered by James Jorden was when he was commissary of old Fort Prince during the year 1776. As an evidence of this fact, his
old record book, while serving in this capacity, was found eighty-two years
afterwards, and copies of entries made therein are at present to be found in
Spartan files under date of October 7th, 1858.

The book referred to is described as being two by four inches in size,
much mutilated, and containing about thirty or forty pages. From the appearance of the copies made from the original entries, a splendid system of
bookkeeping is displayed, well worthy of modern imitation.

The site of Old Fort Prince is seven miles west of Spartanburg, one mile
below Mount Zion Church, and very near the old historic Blackstock road. It
was built by the early settlers, says Draper, about twelve years before the
beginning of the Revolution, as a defence against the outbreak and massacres of the Indians on the borders during the war between France and Great
Britain, some particulars of which we have given in another volume. [1] It
was called from the Princes, who lived nearby. Among the earliest settlers
living in the vicinity of Fort Prince were the families Vernons, Jordens, Timmons, Reas or Rays, Millers, Dodds, Collins, Lawrences, Bishops, Goodletts,
Jamisons, and others. These came to this section before the Revolution, and
some of their descendants still hover around the home of their ancestors.

It was during the Indian outrages of 1776, instigated by Indian emissaries
or agents, an account of which we have published elsewhere, [2] that the
early settlers in the vicinities of Fort Prince, Poole's Fort near Wofford's Iron
Works (now Glendale), Nicholl's Fort at "Narrow Pass" near the residence of
the late Captain David Anderson, Blockhouse near Landrum, Thickety and
other forts gathered and erected forts to defend themselves from an impending danger. During these trying ordeals it was necessary that a proper
person be selected to purchase supplies for the maintenance of these people, and the person selected for this responsible duty at Fort Prince was
James Jorden.

At the period when the entries referred to were made, James Jorden was
an old bachelor, and lived at the house of Robert Goodlett, about one mile

from the fort, which was sufficiently near for him to attend to his duties as commissary of the fort.

Some time during or after the Revolution James Jorden married to Mrs. Margaret Miller, whose name appears in the old commissary book. In another volume [3] we have given an account of the killing of Mr. John Miller, which occurred during the Indian outrages of 1776, at or near Barry's Bridge. The writer is in possession of a MS. letter from Mr. Lawrence D. Miller, Jacksonville, Ala., under date of July 7th, 1890, which states that at the time this murder took place, Mrs. Margaret Miller, wife of John Miller (to whom James Jorden afterwards married), and her son Samuel were, with other neighbors, in Fort Nicholls for protection, which was about one mile distant. The son Samuel referred to was known in late years as *Sheriff* Sam Miller, whose name and character are well known to many of the older citizens of Spartanburg County.

It would appear from the letter of Mr. Miller referred to and the old account book of James Jorden, that Mrs. Margaret Miller was the inmate, at different times, of the two forts during the years 1776-77. It was some time during these years that James Jorden, then an old bachelor, became enamored by her charms and made her the wife of his bosom. By this union three children were born, viz.: Elizabeth, John and Margaret. The latter became the wife of James Vernon, son of Alexander, whose name also appears in the MS. accounts of James Jorden.

We are unable at this time to state fully the part that James Jorden took in the great Revolutionary struggle for independence, but can say without fear of contradiction that it was a prominent one, and that he greatly aided in the work of disenthrallment from British tyranny. It may be truly said of him that he was a prominent and distinguished man for his day and generation, not only for his advocacy of letters, but as an administrator of law, having received the commission of judge of the first courts held in Spartanburg County, as shown elsewhere. He was also a member from Spartanburg County of the first Constitutional Convention of South Carolina held after the close of the Revolution; and he, with the entire delegation from his county, voted for a form of government that pertained more to a monarchy than a republic, the latter being an *experiment* rather than a reality. But, despite the immaturity of public opinion which prevailed at that time, he, in this, as in all other public acts of his life, consulted not the public sentiment of his day, but boldly and independently pursued the leadings of his own judgment.

As shown elsewhere, James Jorden was a representative to the State Legislature from 1788 to '90, and senator from the same county from 1800 to '02. His death occurred in 1802.

During the time that he was a member of the Legislature of South Carolina, owing to his high appreciation of the advantages of education, he voted for the first appropriation for the establishment of the South Carolina College.

It has been said of him, that, despite the many virtues that shone resplendent in his private character, the Hon. James Jorden was not influential alone from private worth, but in his day stood preeminently forth as an orator. He was not only remarkable for his flow of language, but also for the chasteness of his style, the development of his argumentative power, and the earnestness, grace and elegance of his manner. Such is the testimony handed down by those who heard him in debate as well as on the rostrum.

We are unable to obtain the date of birth of James Jorden, but we would fix it not far from 1725. His wife, Margaret, whose first husband, John Miller, was killed by the Tories, as already stated, was born April 1st, 1740. Her son Samuel Miller (Sheriff Sam), by first husband, was born June 11th, 1768. The children of James and Margaret Jorden, being three, were born following dates: Elizabeth, September 8th, 1778; John, July 11th, 1780; and Margaret (wife of James Vernon), October 13th, 1782.

The Vernon Family

Among the early settlers on the Tygers in the present county of Spartanburg was Alexander Vernon, from whom has sprung a long and respectable line of posterity. He was born in Scotland January 24th, 1732, and emigrated to America when about twenty-one years of age, finally, in 1755, settling on North Tyger River at the present homestead residence of James J. Vernon. It was during this year (1755) that this section of country was thrown open to settlement by virtue of the treaty of Governor Glen with the Cherokee Indians. His wife was Margaret Chesnee, born also in Scotland. He brought with him evidences of high respectability and Christian character, both for himself and wife. On the 29th of May, 1755, he obtained a letter from the minister (Sam Brown) of his church in the parish of Tarry town, stating that he had lived in said parish "from his infancy in an innocent and inoffensive manner in all respects"; that he had "ever been free of any public scandal or church censure," and was "justly entitled to the privileges of any Christian society or congregation where Providence" should "order his lot," the same being signed not only by his minister, but by Will Hannah and other elders. Another letter of a similar character, dated May 17th, 1760, was obtained for his wife Margaret Chesnee, and one for his brother James Vernon. The tradition in the family is, that five years after he left his native parish in Scotland he returned and married Margaret Chesnee. His old family Bible is yet in a state of preservation, being in the hands of the family of Judge T. O. P. Vernon. He died at the age of 55 years, and his remains were interred in the cemetery at Nazareth Church. His will was recorded at Ninety-six C. H.

Alexander and Margaret (Chesnee) Vernon had children as follows: John Vernon, born 1758; Nancy Vernon, born 1761, married Michael Miller; Margaret Vernon, born 1763, married David Jorden; James Vernon, born 1765, married Margaret, daughter of James Jorden; Mary Vernon, born 1767, married John Crawford.

Michael and Nancy (Vernon) Miller had children as follows: John V. Miller, born 1761; Margaret (Peggy) Miller, born 1786, married John Montgomery (see Montgomery family); Mary (Polly) Miller, born 1788, married James M. Anderson ("Tyger Jim," see Anderson family); Hannah Miller, born 1793, married Theron Earle (see Earle family); Elizabeth (Betsy) Miller, born 1791, married David Dantzler; Henry Miller, born 1795; James V. Miller, born 1797, married Mariah Hannon; Alexander Miller, born 1800, married Silvina Whetstone; Clarinda Miller, born 1803, married David Whetstone; and Catharine (Katy) Miller, born 1806, married Willis Benson.

The children of James and Margaret (Jorden) Vernon were as follows: Alexander Vernon, born 1799, married Ann Gray; Nancy Vernon, born 1802; Mary (Polly) Vernon, born 1804, married John Bomar, Jr. (see Bomar family); Jas. J. Vernon, born 1806, married Ann Oeland (see sketch); John G. Vernon, born 1808, married Miss Gault; Elizabeth (Betsy) Vernon, born 1810, married first Isaac Snoddy (see Snoddy family), and second Richard Ballenger; Andrew J. Vernon, first, born 1815; Andrew J. Vernon, second, born 1816, married Georgiana Moore; Thomas O. P. Vernon, born 1818, married Harriet Bomar (see sketch of Judge T. O. P. Vernon)'; and Henry Franklin Vernon, born 1822, married Letitia Blackwell.

Alexander Miller, son of Michael and Silvina (Whetstone) Miller, had children as follows: William Henry Miller, James M. Miller, Andrew B. Miller, Nancy and Mary Jane Miller.

David and Clarinda (Miller) Whetstone had children as follows: Asbury Whetstone, Jas. A. Whetstone, Michael Whetstone (married Charity Lites), Dantzler Whetstone, Nancy W. Whetstone (married Dr. Samuel Means), Mary Whetstone (married L. Weeks), Elizabeth and Laura Whetstone.

Willis and Catharine (Miller) Benson had children as follows: Nancy (married Peter Joe Oeland), Henry, Margaret, Fannie, and Samuel Benson.

John and Polly (Vernon) Bomar had children as follows: Elizabeth (Betty), married Dr. R. E. Cleveland (see sketch); Margaret, married Major Thos. H. Bomar; Louesa, married Major John Earle Bomar (see sketch).

David and Betsey (Miller) Dantzler had children as follows: Barbary, married Major John Stroble; Louis, married Eliza Shuler; Cedie, married John Poole; Margaret, married Rev. Andrew Pedan; and Mary, married Henry Rush.

James and Mariah (Hannon) Miller had children as follows: Caroline, Elizabeth, Catharine Jane, Eliza, James, Michael and Henrietta Miller (now Mrs. Colonel Witt of Arkansas).

Isaac and Betsey (Vernon) Snoddy had children as follows: Margaret, married Dr. John C. Oeland (see sketch of Dr. J. C. Oeland), and James Snoddy. By marriage between Richard and Betsey (Snoddy) Ballenger, one son was born, Oscar, who married Miss Staggs.

JAMES JORDEN VERNON, M.D., son of James and Margaret (Jorden) Vernon, was born -on North Tyger at the old homestead of his father (now the residence of his son, Mr. James J. Vernon) near Welford, S.C., March 2d,

1807, and died in Spartanburg, S.C., September 18th, 1864, aged fifty-seven years.

Receiving a good English education and some fitness in the classics, Dr. Vernon began the study of medicine at the age of seventeen in the office of Dr. Robert M. Young, then a prominent physician in the town of Spartanburg, and graduated at the University of Pennsylvania in 1828.

Returning home from Philadelphia he practiced medicine at his father's homestead (which subsequently became his property) for two years, and then removed to Spartanburg, where he built up an extensive practice and earned an enviable reputation in medicine, being a noted diagnostician. He had a wide scope of labor which reached to neighboring towns into North Carolina, a distance from Spartanburg upwards of over thirty miles. During his professional life he had a number of young men in his office preparing for a medical

Dr. J. J. Vernon.

course, and among them we would mention the names of Dr. Booker, Dr. R. E. Cleveland, Dr. John Anderson, Dr. O. G. Chapman (Texas), and Dr. John C. Oeland.

Dr. Vernon married to Miss Ann Eliza Oeland January 25th, 1844, danghter of John and Catharine Oeland, who resided at Forest Hill (on Fair Forest) in Spartanburg District, S.C. By this marriage two sons and three daughters were born, viz.: J. J. Vernon, Dr. John O. Vernon, Mary, Hattie and Lizzie. After his marriage Dr. Vernon returned to his plantation on North Tyger, where he resided and continued in the practice of his profession until within a few years prior to the outbreak of the civil war, when he removed to Spartanburg, where he resided until the day of his death.

In personal appearance he was tall, well-proportioned, and always had a cheerful face; he was always kind and genial in disposition and administered not only as a physician, but as a neighbor to the wants and comforts of others. He was a consistent member of the Presbyterian Church, and a generous contributor to all of its objects.

He was elected by the people of Spartanburg District to the Convention of South Carolina in 1852, and served during the session of that body which met in Columbia. His colleagues were Rev. J. G. Landrum, Colonel James Farrow, Colonel R. C. Poole, Dr. John Winsmith and Dr. Peter M. Wallace.

His remains lie buried in the cemetery of Nazareth Church. Let his memory be preserved as a man who made the world better by his having lived in it.

JUDGE THOMAS O. P. VERNON. Among the native born sons of the "Old Iron District" who have figured in a past day in her history, none are deserving of more special notice than Judge T. O. P. Vernon, the subject of this sketch.

He was the son of James and Margaret (Jorden) Vernon, born 1818, on North Tyger at the old homestead place of his father, which was settled by his grandfather Alexander Vernon, and which still remains in the Vernon family. Here he was principally brought up, and when about nineteen years of age he entered the University of Georgia (Athens), from which institution he was graduated. Returning home he read law, was admitted to the bar, and his brilliant talents were soon recognized by the people of his native county. He was specially distinguished for his eloquence as an orator,

Judge T. O. P. Vernon.

his influence as a journalist, his ability as an attorney, and his firmness and impartiality as a jurist.

He had not been long at the bar before the legislature elected him commissioner in equity for Spartanburg District, and he was also for many years associate editor of the *Carolina Spartan,* and in this capacity always wielded his pen for whatever he considered the best interests of his country. As already stated, he excelled in brilliant oratory, and "every celebration of the battle of Cowpens, every Fourth of July celebration, every public reception of distinguished visitors, in fact, every occasion calling for the orator or ready speaker within reach, claimed his name as the most prominent on the list." In 1858 he was forced out against his will as a candidate for Congress, and although unsuccessful in the congressional district, he carried his native district by an overwhelming majority. He served as judge of the inferior (district) court in Spartanburg, soon after the civil war, under the reconstruction measures devised under the administration of President Johnson. Afterwards he was elected judge of the circuit court, and during the time that he served as such won the approval and admiration of his countrymen, which should always be remembered and preserved in the pages of history.

"It was in the fall of 1870, the day after the election in Laurens, where, during the sitting of his (Judge Vernon's) court, the celebrated Laurens riot, the first serious revolt in the State against radical oppression, broke out and involved the surrounding country. Regardless of the presentment of the grand jury, prepared under the direction of the court, a command of six hundred troops under General Corbin, were sent to Laurens to arrest some of her best citizens, who were carried to Columbia and imprisoned.

"After several weeks imprisonment, with the constant threat of lynching or assassination hanging over them, and after many ineffectual efforts on the part of their counsel to secure bail from other judges, and a direct refusal to allow them to be brought to Spartanburg to appear before Judge Vernon, he determined to go to Columbia to hear their cases. Finding it impossible by bribe or threats to influence his action, the legislature, then in session, determined to impeach him before he could act. The prisoners were in the court-room and the judge in his seat hearing argument on the writ of *habeas corpus* when the messenger from the House rushed in and handed the judge the resolutions of impeachment, thinking that would suspend further actions. It was then that his true nature asserted itself, as he threw aside the resolutions with the indignant remark that it did not prevent him from exercising the functions of his office, and that he would proceed with the cases and release the gentlemen on bond and allow them to return to their homes. He knew that this step would cost him his position, but, to use the phrase of a distinguished spectator, 'he died with the great writ of *habeas corpus* in his hands,' and the people of the State, particularly those of Laurens, will always remember it."

It is needless to say that while this bold and decided action of Judge Vernon, which required continuous sitting on the bench thirty-six hours, did cost him his official head, yet time soon vindicated his action, and the political prosecutions against the prisoners released were dropped or *nol-prossed.*

Judge Vernon, in retiring from the bench, was highly complimented by a formal address from the members of the Abbeville bar and by the press over the entire State. He died in the 57th year of his age. Appropriate resolutions were passed upon his death in 1877 by the Spartanburg bar.

Judge Vernon, as already stated, married Miss Harriet, daughter of Elisha Bomar, Esq., and sister of Major John Earle Bomar, a congenial and devoted wife, who survived him for some ten or fifteen years. By this marriage the following children were born: John E. Vernon, Paul B. Vernon, Frank P. Vernon, Thomas W. Vernon, James Edward Vernon and Misses Ellen L. and Lillie E. Vernon.

[1] See "Colonial and Revolutionary History of Upper South Carolina," p. 28.
[2] See "Colonial and Revolutionary History of Upper South Carolina," pp. 84 to 99.
[3] See "Colonial and Revolutionary History of Upper South Carolina," p. 90.

Chapter Twenty-Five - The Montgomery Family

In our researches into the "Genealogical History of" the Family of Montgomery," including the Montgomery pedigree compiled by Thomas Harrison Montgomery of Philadelphia, and published in 1863, we find that the families referred to in said volume descended from distinguished ancestry. The earliest records we have of the family place its origin in the north of France in the ninth century. Its history leads up to the present through an unbroken succession of ten centuries in length, as shown by accompanying chart to said volume, the first known of the name being Roger de Montgomerie, who was "Count of Montgomerie before the coming of Rolle" in 912.

Throughout the entire succession of generations in this family we find the familiar names of Alexander, William, Hugh, James, John and Robert, and among the females Mary, Elizabeth and Margaret.

During the period mentioned a number of these occupied the distinguished positions of earls, lords, and baronets in England, Wales, Scotland and Ireland. Some of the descendants of these were distinguished soldiers of the Revolution and in the War of 1812 with Great Britain. Among this number we would mention General Richard Montgomery, whose name in Revolutionary annals is specially identified with the siege of Quebec,, where he lost his life, December, 1775, and Brigadier-General John Montgomery, of New Hampshire, who,, during the war of 1812, defended the harbor of Portsmouth against the attacks of the British.

The original ancestor of the Montgomery family that made settlement in the present county of Spartanburg was John Montgomery, Scotch-Irish, who emigrated from north of Ireland to Pennsylvania before the Revolution, and subsequently to Spartanburg in 1785, and settled on North Tyger River, near Snoddy's Bridge. He married in Pennsylvania to Rosa Roddy, and by this marriage had seven children, as follows:

Alexander, who married Miss Samons; John, [1] who married Margaret Miller; James, who married a Miss Walker; Robert, who never married; Hugh, who married a Miss Reynolds; Margaret, who married Edward (Neddy) Clemont; and Mary, who married James Morton.

Of the sons mentioned, Alexander had thirteen children, and among these we gather the names of Alfred, Anoldus, Robert, Mathias, Edward, Elias, John and Minerva. The last named married Curtis Bradley.

James Montgomery had two sons, viz.: John W. and Robert.

Hugh Montgomery had eight children, viz.: John, James, Thomas, Walker, David, Elias, Mary and Elizabeth. Of these, Mary married ___ Gross, and Elizabeth married Shadrach Barton.

John Montgomery, Esq., one of the sons mentioned, was a man of considerable prominence and influence in his day, being above the average in intelligence and general information. He was a progressive farmer and carried on the business of blacksmithing and woodwork. He was a manufacturer of wagons at a time in the history of Spartanburg District when imported wagons were unknown. By honest industry he accumulated a handsome property. He was a good provider, hospitable in his home, and a progressive citizen. He was for many years a magistrate, appointed by enactment of the General Assembly of South Carolina, and was an efficient officer in this capacity. He was a soldier of the war of 1812, being orderly sergeant in the company of Captain James Brannon, which was known as the Old Artillery Company, and which paraded for a half century or more at Timmon's Old Field prior to the outbreak of the civil war.

His death occurred in 1847 or '48. As already stated, he married Margaret Miller, daughter of Michael Miller, who was a very remarkable woman for her day and generation. She was born near the close of the Revolutionary war, September 16th, 1786, and died in 1882, in the 96th year of her age. For eighty years or more she had been a consistent and faithful member of the Presbyterian Church at Nazareth. Her life was marked by her love of the Bible and her intelligent comprehension of its contents. As her physical constitution was of the iron type, so her mental faculties were strong and vigorous. She studied the Bible attentively, carefully and prayerfully all through life, and committed to memory large portions of it, and also many of Newton's hymns. The treasures which she gathered in early youth proved to be a great comfort to her in old age. All through her long life duty was to her a word full of meaning. Living remote from her church (Nazareth), she and John Smith, a neighbor and a useful and acceptable elder in the same, organized and conducted a Sunday-school near her dwelling, which was sustained for thirty years. Old and weary of the world, she passed away as gently as the wave dies along the shore when the storm is over.

The children of John and Margaret (Miller) Montgomery were thirteen in number, viz.: Nancy Miller, married Dr. Andrew B. Moore first, and Colonel Samuel N. Evans second; Rosa Roddy, married John Chapman, Jr., Esq.; Mary (Polly), married William Cunningham, Esq.; Benjamin Franklin, married Miss Harriet, daughter of James Moss; Elizabeth, married Rev. John G. Landrum; John Crawford, died in childhood; Michael Miller, married Miss Martha Corry of Union District, S.C.; Chevis C., married Miss Mary McCarrell of Greenville District, S.C.; Hannah Amanda, married Colonel S. N. Evins (second wife); Catharine, married Edward Ballenger; Thomas Earle, married Miss Sarah Ballenger; Prater Scott, married Miss Catharine (Kate) Goudelock of Union District, S.C.; and Margaret, married William Moore of Morganton, N.C.

Of these only three are living at this writing (1900): B. F. Montgomery, Rusk county, Texas; Mrs. Hannah Evins, Welford, S.C., and Mrs. Margaret Moore at Spartanburg. One of the sons, Prater S. Montgomery, contracted disease during the civil war from which he died at its close, leaving a wife and three children, viz.: James, John, and Mary (Mrs. Daniel, now deceased).

Of the grandsons of John and Margaret Montgomery five gave up their lives on field of battle in the civil war between the States, viz.: Andrew Charles Moore (18th Regt., S.C.V.), son of Dr. A. B. and Nancy Moore, killed second Manassas; Warren Davis Chapman (Richmond Battalion), son of John and Rosa R. Chapman, wounded below Richmond and died a few days afterward; Captain Michael M. Cunningham (6th Regt., S.C.V.), son of William and Mary Cunningham, killed in Virginia; Robert Scott Montgomery (Texas Regiment), son of B. F. and Harriet Montgomery, killed at Franklin, Tenn.; and John Oscar Montgomery (18th S.C. Regiment), son of Michael M. and Martha Montgomery, killed at second Manassas.

B. F. and Harriet (Moss) Montgomery had twelve children, viz.: John Henry, James M., Nancy Elizabeth, Robert Scott, Benjamin Landrum, Emily Margaret, Francis B., Mary Crawford, William C., Anna Caroline, Sarah Cornelius and Joseph Oscar. At this writing (1899) only four of these are living, viz.: John H., Benjamin L. (Hillville, near Enoree, S.C.), Elizabeth McCravy and Anna Rogers, the two latter residing in Texas.

CAPTAIN JOHN HENRY MONTGOMERY, eldest of the twelve children referred to of Benj. F. and Harriet (Moss) Montgomery, was born fourteen miles west of the city of Spartanburg, December 8th, 1833. He was brought up on his father's farm, receiving the best education that could be afforded in the common schools of his neighborhood. One of his instructors was Richard Golightly, whom we have mentioned at another place in this volume. Not possessing what might be called a strong constitution, he was, at the age of nineteen years, placed in the country store of James Nesbitt, in the southern portion of the present county of Spartanburg. He held this position for a year, for which he was paid $5 per month and board. During this year, without questioning the propriety, he performed all the requirements of his employer. He worked around the house and barn, and though hired as a clerk, his first work was to drive a four-horse team loaded with flour to the iron works at the present site of Clifton, S.C., a distance of thirty miles, loading back with iron and nails.

Capt. John H. Montgomery

From Mr. Nesbitt's store he went to Columbia and worked as a clerk for four months in the store of Robert Brice, which was during the winter of 1853-'54. The next spring he entered into a partnership with his brother-in-law, Dr. E. R. W. McCrary, in the mercantile business at Hobbyville, S.C., which was but a few miles from the store of his old employer.

In the fall of 1855 the parents of Mr. Montgomery, his four brothers and six sisters, together with his brother-in-law and partner, removed to Texas, leaving him the sole member of the family remaining in South Carolina. With a limited capital he continued in the mercantile business at Hobbyville for three years or more, meeting all the obligations which had been contracted by the firm in good faith, but under trying difficulties.

In 1857 he married to Miss Susan A. Holcombe, daughter of David Holcombe, a native of Union county, S.C., who settled in Spartanburg in 1845. In 1858 he moved his stock of merchandise to a store owned by his father-in-law two miles distant, where he continued in the business of a merchant in connection with a small tannery until the outbreak of the civil war. In December, 1861, he volunteered his services to his country and was enrolled as a private in Co. E, 18th Regt., S.C.V. Upon the organization 01 said regiment, however, he was appointed regimental commissary with the rank of captain. This office, under new army regulations, was abolished in 1863, and Captain Montgomery was made an assistant commissary of the brigade, which office was also abolished in 1864, and he was then made an assistant division commissary, continuing as such until the close of the war, surrendering with General Lee at Appomattox, April, 1865.

Returning home after the war, he began life anew as it were. Besides owning a small farm, upon which he had depended for the support of his family during the war, he had a small stock of leather, the accumulation of his small tannery, which was the only property he possessed.

In 1866 he began the use of commercial fertilizers upon his farm, and soon demonstrated to his neighbors the importance of stimulating plant growth. He at once engaged in the sale of fertilizers to his neighbors and surrounding country, which was the dawning of a new era of prosperity in his business career. He had all the while successfully conducted the business of his tannery, and in 1870 resumed his merchandizing at the same place.

His sale of commercial fertilizers had assumed such proportions as to make it necessary to give up farming, and later, all other branches of business. In 1874 he removed to Spartanburg and turned his attention exclusively to fertilizers, associating himself with Colonel Joseph Walker and Dr. C. E. Fleming, under the name of Walker, Fleming & Co.

In 1881 this firm purchased a water-power on Pacolet River, known as Trough Shoals, and in 1882 commenced the erection of the Pacolet Manufacturing Company, which was completed the following year. The company was incorporated in 1881, with Captain Montgomery as its president and treasurer, which position he still holds. In 1887 the capacity of this mill was 26,224 spindles and 840 looms, but it was again enlarged in 1894, making it the third mill of the company, containing in the aggregate 57,000 spindles and 22,000 looms. Its annual consumption of cotton is about 30,000 bales, and its capital about $500,000.

In 1889 Captain Montgomery was made the president and treasurer of the Spartan mills. For information as to the capacity of these mills the reader is referred to our review on the progress of manufacturing in Spartanburg at another place in this volume. Captain Montgomery is a stockholder and director in the Whitney mill, the Lockhart mill and Morgan Iron works, and also a stockholder in the Clifton mills.

Aside from his business relations to the companies referred to, he is in every sense of the word a model gentleman, fully alive to every enterprise and business industry looking to the development and upbuilding of his country. Notwithstanding he has been successful in his business investments, and has accumulated a handsome fortune, he has been liberal with his means and a generous contributor to every worthy object of charity with which he has been confronted.

He has been for nearly a half century a consistent member of the Baptist church, which he has most always represented in the annual meetings of the association. In his church he is among the foremost in the support of his pastor, and of all the claims of missions and charity coming before it.

In another place in this volume we have endeavored to state the circumstances under which the Hon. Peter Cooper of New York donated the valuable property comprising the institution building and surrounding grounds at Limestone Springs to the Spartanburg Baptist Association, the history of the progress of which we have recorded. In 1888 Captain Montgomery succeeded to the presidency of the board of trustees of the Cooper Limestone Institute, now known as Limestone College, and its marked success from year to year has been mainly due to his indomitable energy, excellent judgment and contributions from his private means, which have already amounted to some $15,000 or more. He still presides at the head of an able board of trustees of this college, which, by reason of the work of remodeling and its modern equipment, will, for all time to come, add additional honors to his name and character. In all these generous gifts, however (at one time the sum of $500 for the library of the college), he has had no reference whatever to the perpetuation of his name or memory. He has simply done what he felt to be *a duty* in the distribution of the means with which he has been so abundantly blessed by his own perseverance and the assistance of a kind Providence.

In the ordinary walks of life he is the same humble and unassuming citizen that he was when a country boy on his father's farm at the age of eighteen years. The humblest operative in his employ can approach him with as much freedom as the wealthy capitalist with whom, in a business way, he is much associated.

Captain Montgomery, by his marriage with Miss Holcombe, had eight children, only three of whom are now living, viz.: Victor M., Walter S., and Benjamin W. Those who have died were: David F., Mary, John, Katie Lois and an infant unnamed.

A true patriot and philanthropist, Captain Montgomery still stands before the people of Spartanburg as one of her best, most influential and progressive citizens.

The Crook and Nicholas Families

The ancestor of the Crook families in Spartanburg County was James Crook, who came from Virginia, and was numbered among the early settlers on the Tygers. He had six sons, but we have been enabled to gather the names of only two, viz.: James and Jesse.

James Crook, the first mentioned name of the sons, was a man of considerable prominence in his day. He lived on South Tyger, and built the house in which James M. Switzer now lives. He was a member of the Nullification Convention on the Union side, from Spartanburg District in 1832. He also served for two terms from the same district in the State legislature from 1826 to '28, and from 1828 to '30. After this he removed to Alabama, where his descendants are numerous and prominent, among whom we would mention James Crook, at present one of the railroad commissioners for that State.

The other brother mentioned, Jesse Crook, married Katy Barry, the daughter of Captain Andrew Barry. Katy was the little girl who was tied by the leg to the bedpost by her mother during the Revolution, whilst she went and gave notice of the raid of marauding Tories.

She died November 1, 1844. They lived on South Tyger River, near the present railroad station of Switzer, S.C. Their children were:

1st. Dr. Andrew Barry Crook, a noted physician of Greenville, S.C., who died in 1862, and whose wife was a Miss Hoke of Lincolnton, N.C., by whom he left one child, Sallie, married to Wm. Lester, who had only one child, Nannie, married to Dr. Black of Greenville, S.C. Dr. Crook married second wife, Catharine Smith of Asheville, N.C., by whom he had two children, viz.: Harriet and Jesse.

2d. Margaret Barry, married Wyllis Dickey and went to Texas, and left numerous children.

3d. Martha, married Newport Bragg, went to Alabama, thence to Arkansas. Newport Bragg was killed in a sawmill disaster; he left a family of which one W. L. Bragg was one of Alabama's most distinguished sons, having served in the State in many capacities, and finally was United States railroad commissioner.

4th. James Crook, studied law, went to Alabama; married a Miss Saunders; no children; returned to Spartanburg after the civil war, and died a few years thereafter.

5th. Violet L. C., married Frank Woodruff; went to Alabama and died childless.

6th. Williams W. C., married a French lady from Charleston, named Bonneau; went to Alabama and had a large family of children.

7th. Catharine Malissa, married George Nicholls.

8th. Colonel John Moore Crook, born November 10th, 1816; married Miss Lou Brewton, November 25, 1867, who died July 25th, 1885. The children by this marriage are Jesse E., died 1890; Janie E., Catherine E., John M., Andrew Barry and Mary Louisa.

Major George Nicholls married "Katie" Crook, as she was known by her friends, January 12th, 1843; she was born April 4th, 1817, and died October 24th, 1854. George Nicholls was sheriff of Spartanburg four years. He died August 10th, 1849. Their children are: 1st, John Moore Nicholls, who will receive further notice; 2d, Andrew Barry Crook, born January 14th, 1845; 3d, Benj. Franklin, born November 3d, 1847; and 4th, George Williams, born December 5th, 1849.

JOHN M. NICHOLLS was born December 4th, 1843. Being deprived of the care of his widowed mother when about twelve years of age, he spent, for the most part, the remaining years of his life, until he had reached the age of eighteen, with his uncle. Colonel John M. Crook, whom we have already noticed.

When about eighteen years old he enlisted in Co. H, 1st. S.C.V., of which he was a sergeant, and participated, after becoming a member of said regiment, in all the battles and skirmishes in which it was engaged.

During the period of his service he performed an act of distinguished valor, which has given him renown. His praises have been sung for a daring deed in crossing the breastworks in front of Spotsylvania under heavy fire to give a dying Federal soldier some water. In *The Diocese,* February, 1898, we find the following account, by a comrade, of this heroic act:

John M. Nicholls

"It was a hot July day in 1864...Our men had hurriedly dug rifle pits to protect themselves from the sharpshooters, and dead and dying Federals were lying up to the very edge of those pits. In one of the pits was an ungainly, raw, red-headed boy (John M. Nicholls); he was a retiring lad, green as grass, but a reliable fighter; we never paid much attention to him, one way or the other. The wounded had been lying for hours, unattended before the pits, and the sun was getting hotter and hotter, they were suffering horribly from pain and thirst. Not fifteen feet away, outside the rifle pit, lay a mortally wounded officer, who was our enemy. As the heat grew more intolerable, this officer's cries for water increased; he was evidently dying hard, and his appeals were of the most piteous nature. The red-headed boy found it hard to bear them. He had just joined the regiment, and was not yet callous to suffering. At last, with tears flooding his grimy face, he cried out, 'I can't stand it longer, boys; I am going to take that poor fellow my canteen.' For answer to this foolhardy speech, one of us stuck a cap on a ramrod and hoisted it above the pit; instantly it was pierced with a dozen bullets; to venture outside a step was the maddest suicide, and all the while we could hear the officer's moans: 'Water, water; just one drop, for God-sake, somebody! only one drop!' The tender-hearted boy could stand the appeal no longer. Once, twice, three times, in spite of our utmost remonstrance, he tried unsuccessfully to clear the pit. At last he gave a desperate leap over the embankment, and once on the other side, he threw himself flat on the ground and crawled toward his dying foe; he could not get close to him because of the terrible fire; but he broke a sumac bush, tied to the stick his precious canteen and landed it in the sufferer's trembling hands. You never heard such gratitude in your life — perhaps there was never any like it before. The officer was for tying his gold watch on the stick and sending it back, as a slight return for the disinterested act; but this the boy would not allow. He only smiled happily and returned as he had gone — crawling amid a hailstorm of bullets. When he reached the edge of the pit he called out to his comrades to clear the way for him, and with a mighty leap he was among us once more."

After the close of the civil war John M. Nicholls returned to his native county and engaged for a time in farming. He was for eight years sheriff of Spartanburg County, which office he held to the satisfaction of the people. He married Mrs. Ella Bobo, widow of Captain Alex Copeland and daughter of Hon. Simpson Bobo, May, 1891, and has one child, Catharine, born May, 1892.

Andrew Barry Crook Nicholls, M.D., married Mary Ellen, daughter of Rev. John and Georgia A (Foster) Collier, in 1871, in Tuscaloosa County, Alabama, by whom he has five children.

He was a member of the 1st Regt., S.C.V., to which he joined in 1863, and served as color guard; was wounded in hip in 1864, and surrendered at Appomattox April, 1865. After peace he was a farmer; then went to school at Greenville, S.C., under Captain Patrick; studied medicine with Dr. A. D. Hoke; graduated in medicine in 1869, from Philadelphia University; went to Alabama, Talladega County, then to Tuscaloosa City, where he has a large practice, and was president of the Tuscaloosa Medical Society.

Benjamin Franklin Nicholls married Elizabeth Louise, daughter of Dr. Joseph and Anna Pauline Klapp of Philadelphia, Pa., 1875, and died February 15th, 1895, leaving several children.

He studied medicine and settled in Philadelphia, Pa., where he gained credit as a medical man, having filled several positions in hospitals and colleges and societies. He was fast rising to the top, when an untimely death cut short his career. He was a soldier of the Southern Confederacy.

George W. Nicholls, Esq., married Mary Lavinia, daughter of Rev. Samuel Jones, D.D., on May 29th, 1884. He is a prominent lawyer in Spartanburg, and served Spartanburg County for ten years as probate judge. He lives in the city of Spartanburg. He has five children.

These four sons of Major George Nicholls are especially worthy of high commendation, for they are emphatically *self-made* men, having lost both parents in early life, and being left to the care of a bachelor uncle. They raised themselves from childhood to high stations in society, church and state.

[1] Grandfather of the author of the present work.

Chapter Twenty-Six - The Dean Family

In the list containing the names of heads of families in Spartanburg County, as shown by the original census returns of first census, taken in 1790, which we publish in this volume, we find but one name of the Dean family, being that of Joel Dean, Sr., from whom all the families of this name in said county have descended.

Joel Dean, born February 16th, 1755, emigrated from Virginia to North Carolina, and from there to South Carolina, settling on Enoree River in the territory afterwards embraced in Spartanburg County. He was a progressive farmer for his day and time and a highly respected citizen. He died February 5th, 1842, being 87 years of age. His wife was Mary Brockman, who was born January 7th, 1759, and died October 28th, 1825, in the 67th year of her age. They were married September 5th, 1775, and to them were born twelve children, viz.:

John, born September 26th, 1776; Amelia, born December 18th, 1778; Casandra, born March 19th, 1781; Frances, born March 23d, 1783; Charles, born May 5th, 1785; Anna, born July 18th, 1787; Lucy, born October 2d, 1789; Thomas, born October 31st, 1791; Henry, born February 11th, 1794; Joel, Jr., born April 26th, 1796; Alfred, born September 19th, 1798; and Alvin, born February 11th, 1801.

Of these sons, John Dean, Esq., the eldest, was the father of Major Hosea J. Dean, who will receive further notice. One of the daughters, Casandra, married Sheriff Sam Miller, who was the father of Dr. J. Pinckney and General Joel W. Miller. [1]

Alfred Dean, one of the sons mentioned, was born in Spartanburg County. He resided at or near the old homestead place of his father; was an honest and industrious farmer, and a member of the Baptist Church at Abner's Creek. He died at the age of 77 years. His wife was Jane Bobo, daughter of Absolem Bobo, who lived on Two-mile Creek, waters of Enoree. She was a daughter of a son of Allen Musgrove, who was the father of Mary Musgrove, the renowned heroine of Mr. Kennedy's novel, "Horseshoe Robinson." The children by this marriage were:

(1) Nancy, who married Thomas Sims, leaving one daughter, who married Dr. McKown of Gainesville, Ga.

(2) Jane Elizabeth and (3) Edward, both died of scarlet fever at the ages of 9 and 11.

(4) Dr. Thomas Perry Dean, who died at the age of 27 years. Read medicine with his uncle, Dr. Alvin Dean, of Cobb county, Ga., and graduated at the Charleston (S. C.) Medical College. Married Mary, daughter of Joseph Davis, on South Pacolet (sister of Major John Bankston Davis), leaving one daughter, Lula, who is the wife of Rev. I. W. Wingo. Pie was a member of the Presbyterian Church, and his life, when cut off, was one of promise and usefulness.

(5) Frances C., who married Major William Hoy, who died of smallpox, leaving three children.

(6) Alvin Henry, oldest living son, a sketch of whom we present below.

(7) George Bobo, who will also receive further notice.

CAPTAIN ALVIN H. DEAN, one of the sons mentioned of Alfred and Jane (Bobo) Dean, was born in Spartanburg County in 1837. He was educated in the schools of his neighborhood, and attended the Davidson College, N.C., when General D. H. Hill was one of its faculty.

Soon after the outbreak of the civil war between the States he raised a company of cavalry for the service, which subsequently became Company E, 2d Regiment, S.C. Cavalry. The first officers of this company besides Captain Dean were Dr. Wm. H. Coan, 1st lieutenant; Crawford S. Thompson, 2d lieutenant; and John G. Wham, junior 2d lieutenant. The first mentioned of the lieutenants (Dr. Coan) failed in health, but Lieutenants Thompson and Wham were in the service of their country till the end of the war.

This company, uniting with three others in the State, formed the cavalry battalion of Major W K. Easley, who was succeeded by Major Frank Hampton. During the seven days battles around Richmond, this battalion, doing service around Charleston, was ordered to Virginia. Upon going into camps near Richmond, it united with the cavalry of the Hampton Legion and two other cavalry companies, and organized the 2d S.C. Regiment of Cavalry, Colonel M. C. Butler commanding, which formed a part of the brigade of cavalry under General Wade Hampton, Division of J. E. B. Stuart.

Captain Alvin H. Dean

Company E, 2d S.C. Cavalry, commanded by Captain Dean, participated in the closing scenes of seven days battles, Second Manassas, and all the engagements of the Maryland campaign, including Sharpsburg. The regiment participated also in the memorable cavalry combats of Culpepper Courthouse, Brandy Station and Stevensburg, Va.

In November, 1862, Captain Dean, on account of ill health, resigned, and was succeeded to the captaincy of Company E by his brother, First Lieutenant Geo. B. Dean. In 1864 the 2d S.C. Regiment of Cavalry was ordered back to South Carolina, where it encountered the enemy on James and Johns Islands. After the return of the regiment to South Carolina, Captain Dean, having recruited his health, was offered the position of major in the State troops, but having been re-elected a commissioned officer in his same old company, he accepted the latter position, which was an evidence of the high esteem in which he was held by the soldiers whom he at first had the honor to command. He continued to serve until the end of the war, participating in the battles of Fort Fisher, Anderson, Bentonville and other engagements.

Returning home after the war, Captain Dean has engaged for the most part in farming. He is at present Colonel of Spartanburg Regiment of United Confederate Veterans, and is also a representative in the State Legislature from his native county.

In 1860 he married Eugenia A. Miller, daughter of James A. Miller, whose wife's maiden name was Winnie Love, of Haywood County, N.C. She married first to a Mr. Moore (father of Dr. Alfred Moore of Welford, S.C.). Captain and Mrs. Dean have five living children, viz.: James M., Kate A., Alvin H., A. Boyce, and Anna Belle. Of these sons, Alvin H. Dean is present senator from Greenville County.

CAPTAIN GEORGE BOBO DEAN, present sheriff of Spartanburg County, was born October 20th, 1839. He was educated in the common schools of his neighborhood and attended for a time Erskine College before the outbreak of

Capt. Geo. B. Dean.

the civil war. He suffered from a severe attack of pneumonia, and before he had sufficiently recovered he enlisted as a private in the Spartan Rifles and went to Sullivan's Island in April, 1861. After six weeks' service he returned home to recruit his health. In a few months afterwards his brother. Captain Alvin H. Dean, raising a company of cavalry, he enlisted in the same as a private. The company volunteered at first for State service only, and upon the reorganization for Confederate service he was elected first lieutenant.

In November, 1862, his brother resigning on account of ill health, he was made captain of the company, which position he held until the close of the war. This company was known as Company E, 2d S.C. Cavalry, commanded respectively by Colonels M. C. Butler and T. J. Lipscomb. The writer served the three last years of the war as a member of this company, and can testify to the faithful and arduous service rendered his country by Captain Dean and the men belonging to his command. In the great battle of Gettysburg, July, '63, Captain Dean had his horse shot from under him, and at the battle of Brandy Station, August 1st of the same year, he was seriously wounded.

After the war Captain Dean resumed farming on the old homestead place of his grandfather, near Cashville, S.C. This he continued until 1874, when he removed to the Price (brick house) place on Tyger River. In 1881 he purchased land and made improvements near Spartanburg. Captain Dean while engaged in farming had the reputation of being among the foremost and most progressive in his county.

In 1890 he was elected to the State Legislature, receiving over four thousand votes, the highest total vote cast. In 1892 he was elected sheriff of Spartanburg County, and re-elected to the same position in 1896, which position he still holds, and it is needless to say that he has proven himself to be an able and efficient officer.

In 1864 Captain Dean married to Louisa, daughter of Madison Alexander. They have had six children: J. Madison, Geo. Thomas (deceased), Annie (wife of J. B. Liles), Edward, Alfred and Lewis.

HON. HOSEA J. DEAN - In reviewing the lives of the public men of Spartanburg who figured prominently before the people during the middle of the 19th century, there are none deserving of more special interest than Major Hosea J. Dean, the subject of this sketch, who was born July 11th, 1806. His father, John Dean, Esq., was the son of Joel Dean, a soldier of the Revolution, and, as already stated, among the early settlers of Spartanburg District. His mother, Mary Farrow, was the eldest daughter of Captain Thomas Farrow, a Revolutionary soldier belonging

Hon. Hosea J. Dean

to the Continental line. She, it is said, was a lady remarkable for her beauty of person as for her noble qualities of mind and heart.

Major Dean, called *Major* from the fact that he at one time m his life held the office of brigade-major, was the only son of a family of thirteen children. The careful training of a pious parentage and the influence of a family of devoted sisters did much in the formation of his character, and made him, while yet a boy, remarkable for a certain dignified manliness of deportment which belonged to him throughout his entire life. These were combined with the most delicate and assiduous care for his mother and sisters, which he always manifested.

Among the most prominent traits in his character were self-reliance, fortitude and truth. "But while the cultivation of the heart and the growth of every good and noble quality were most carefully fostered by his judicious parents, they were unable to give him the benefits of scholastic education. His labor was absolutely essential to the support of a family of thirteen children; cheerfully and ungrudgingly he bestowed it, though his heart longed and sighed for knowledge!"

Through his great uncle, Samuel Farrow, a member of Congress from the Pinckney Congressional District, he received an appointment to West Point, but was prevented from accepting on account of an unexpected financial embarrassment of his father. He received his best instruction in the schoolroom from James Bostick, who once taught school in his father's neighborhood. This gentleman had been a merchant in London, but failing in business came to America and supported himself by teaching. The boy, listening attentively to his instructions, soon gained an education, including a knowledge of Greek, Latin and the higher mathematics, which, in after years, served him in the important positions which he filled. At the age of about twenty-one he entered the law office of Colonel Patillo Farrow, at Laurens Court-house, S.C., where he devoted himself assiduously to the study of law, which for a time impaired his health. He was successful, however, and in May, 1828, was admitted to the practice, and at once entered into co-partnership with Colonel Farrow, his preceptor, at Laurens Court-house. Eighteen months after this he returned to his native district and settled at Spartanburg Court-house, August, 1829, hoping by this change to improve the condition of his health. It was not long after this removal that, by constant and vigilant application to study and prompt and faithful attention to the business confided to him, he gained the good opinion, respect and confidence of all who knew him. He entered for a time into partnership with Henry C. Young, Esq., of Laurens; but being elected by the State Legislature Commissioner of Equity for Spartanburg district, his partnership with Colonel Young was dissolved. He entered upon the duties of the office of Commissioner of Equity, was a model officer, equal to any in the State. This office he continued to hold, being reelected from time to time, until 1844, when he resigned and associated himself in the practice of law with James Edward Henry, and devoted himself to the duties of his profession until the death of the latter, which occurred in 1850, after which he continued alone in the practice of his profession with eminent ability until within one or two years of the time of his death, which took place at White Sulphur Springs, Va., August 3d, 1855, in the fiftieth year of his age. Notwithstanding his health had for a time been recuperated, yet in the last years of his life heart disease manifested itself, to which he was forced to succumb.

Major Dean was elected from Spartanburg District to a seat in the State Legislature in 1850, and again in 1852, and during this time showed himself to be an able and discreet politician and a popular and useful member. He served with eminent ability as a member of the Committee on Claims, and shortly after the commencement of his second term the office of Clerk of House of Representatives became vacant. He was put in nomination by his friends and was elected by a handsome majority. He immediately resigned his seat as a member of this body and entered upon the duties of his office, which for a number of years he filled with honor to himself and the State.

In our review of the progress of temperance during the nineteenth century, at another place in this volume, we have shown that Major Dean was among the first advocates for this cause in Spartanburg District. He "raised the temperance flag and headed the forlorn hope in the cause of reform." He was a prominent member of the order known as "Sons of Temperance," and was nearly always a delegate to the meetings and annual conventions of this body.

In 1830 Major Dean lost his pious mother, who, during her dying hours, so deeply impressed him with the truths of the Christian religion that he determined to seek the same. "For days and months and weeks he sought in secret until he found that 'which passeth all understanding,'" There being at this time no organization in the town of Spartanburg of the church of his choice, he, in 1832, united with the Baptist Church of Mount Zion, of which Rev. John G. Landrum was pastor. Subsequently he participated in the organization of the Baptist Church at Spartanburg, of which he was made a deacon. The Sabbath-school of this church was "the object of his special care and attention," and the success of the present large and flourishing church, now known as the First Baptist Church of Spartanburg, was largely due to his wise counsel and liberal support. His pastor always found in him a fast friend and liberal supporter, and for a quarter of a century his house was always open to all good ministers of the gospel who called to partake of the open hospitality extended by him and his devoted wife.

In 1834 Major Dean married Elizabeth Ellen, second daughter of Colonel John Mills, of Rutherford, N.C., a lady universally loved and respected, who died in 1838, leaving one son, John Mills Dean, who will receive further notice.

On the 9th of August, 1840, he again married to Mary, only daughter of Edward Owen of Washington City, a lady of talents and education.

By this marriage there were six children, viz.: Edward J., who will receive further notice; Elizabeth, who became the wife of Dr. C. E. Fleming; Mills, who will also receive further notice; St. Lawrence; Hosea J., a resident in the city of Spartanburg, occupying the homestead residence of his parents, and Alice.

Major Dean was not only a lawyer of eminent legal attainments, but, as a citizen, was enterprising and public-spirited. Whatever promised to be the greatest good to the greatest number always found him liberal with his purse and prompt with his influence. His brilliant career was one of honor and usefulness, and in his death Spartanburg mourned the death of one of her most valued citizens. His memory still lives.

COLONEL JOHN MILLS DEAN, Son of Hosea and Elizabeth (Mills) Dean, was born at Spartanburg C. H., S.C., August 25th, 1835, descended through both parents from English ancestry. At the age of twenty-one he graduated at the South Carolina Military Academy. Choosing civil engineering as his profession, he spent the winter of 1855-56 as a member of the engineering corps on the New York and Erie Railroad, perfecting himself in practical work.

Inheriting a number of slaves, he adopted a planter's life, and settled in Van Buren County, Arkansas.

"At the first call for volunteers by the governor of Arkansas, he raised a company and went to Little Rock, where, in organizing, he was commissioned lieutenant-colonel of the 7th (Ark.) Regiment Infantry. The regiment at once went into active service in the Trans-Mississippi Department...Taking part in all the important movements of General Hardee's command during 1861, and in the spring of 1862 we find the 7th Arkansas Regiment lying on their arms near Shiloh, April 5th, 1862. General Albert Sidney Johnston had concentrated his forces to give battle to the advancing Federal army under General Grant. Fighting began early Sunday morning the 6th, and the battle raged literally from sunrise to sunset...The battle of Shiloh was one of the bloodiest in the annals of this continent, and was the first great field-fight of the war. It was the death-grapple of the Western men of the Western continent...Between two fields a quarter of a mile apart, on a slight ridge of land covered by oaks and patches of brush, lies the historic spot that was made rich by the blood of hundreds of human beings. Passing through the woods and connecting these fields was an old unused road, washed down in places by the rains of scores of years; it served the Federals as a miniature breastwork, and is known in their reports as 'The old washed-out road.'...Here...was posted a strong force of as hardy troops as ever fought, almost perfectly protected by the conformation of the ground, by logs and other hastily prepared defences... Brigade after brigade was led against it. But valor was of no avail. Four times the position was charged. Four times the assault was unavailing. After hours of this slaughter, the enemy's left was turned and they were driven from the field and finally captured, two thousand surrendering at once.

"From six in the morning until late in the afternoon Colonel Dean's command was in the thickest of the fight. Leading an assault across 'The Sunken Road,' he fell about 5 p.m. Shot in the neck by a sharpshooter, he died instantly. One of his comrades wrote: 'The men faltered a little as they reached the road. So the colonel ran in front, cheering them on, waving his sword, and as he gave the command. Fire! fell with his face to the foe.' General Hardee, in speaking to the mother of Colonel Dean, said: 'Madam, your son was a brave man. I sometimes thought in action he was almost foolhardy, but he was a brave soldier and knew no fear, only inspiration under fire. His promotion had been approved at headquarters, and the papers reached me after his death.'" [2]

Colonel Dean died unmarried in his twenty-seventh year. A true Spartan hero — "a better soldier," said General Hardee, "never lived, a braver man never died."

CAPTAIN EDWARD JEFFERSON DEAN, second son of Major H. J. Dean, was born in Spartanburg January, 1842. Was attending St. James College in Maryland when a call was made by the governor of South Carolina for volunteers. He returned home at once and joined one of the first companies raised, Company K (Spartan Rifles), Fifth Regiment, South Carolina Volunteers, which left for Charleston April 13th, 1861, and after the fall of Fort Sumter went to Virginia. He was for one and a half years a corporal in Company K, when he obtained a transfer to the Twenty-second Regiment, South Carolina Volunteers, and was elected captain of Company C of said regiment, which occupied the trenches at Petersburg at the time of the fearful mine explosion July 30, 1864. Colonel David G. Fleming, of the Twenty-second, was in command of the line that morning and he, with his adjutant and orderly, were buried under the mountain of earth. To this day they have never been found. Company C was dug out one by one by the enemy and made prisoners. Captain Dean, with other officers, was imprisoned at Fort Delaware, in the mouth of the Delaware River. Here for eleven months he was confined in miserable open quarters, exposed to the blazing sun of summer and the bitter cold of winter, and limited in the supply of water, food and coal. When released after the surrender of General Lee Captain Dean's health was a wreck. He settled on a plantation in Calhoun County, Ala., hoping to regain his health and strength, but after several years of suffering, he laid down a life sacrificed for his country. He died in 1883 and is buried at Talladega, Ala., in the churchyard of the Baptist church, of which he was a deacon. He was a gentleman of fine appearance, measuring six feet and five inches, erect and dignified; was of a genial, generous temperament, attracting to himself strong friends wherever he lived.

MILLS DEAN, ESQ., third son of Major H. J. and Mary (Owen) Dean, was born in Spartanburg, S.C., April 3d, 1847, and died in Washington, D.C., April 3d, 1897.

While a student in Wofford College he volunteered in his seventeenth year and enlisted in Company C, Twenty-second Regiment, South Carolina Volunteers. While on the front lines in Petersburg in 1864, digging trenches, cutting trees and throwing up embankments in the burning sun, the health of the slender college boy failed, and he was brought home to die by his faithful servant. After long weeks and months of illness he returned to his regiment and served with it until the surrender at Appomattox.

Mills Dean, Esq.

In 1866 he entered the law office of Fairthorne & Rand, in Philadelphia, where he remained several years as student and clerk. The writer, while attending his second course of medical lectures in that city in the winter of 1867-68, was intimately associated with him and can testify to the excellent and congenial traits in his character. He also shared his hospitable roof in Washington City in 1893, while seeking a government appointment which he secured, and learned to appreciate more his amiable and lovable qualities, his kindness of heart and noble traits of character, which he exemplified as long as he lived.

Soon after he finished his law course in Philadelphia he settled in Washington City and continued in the practice of law up to the time of his death. At his death many poor and distressed people in Washington came to take a last look at him, saying, "I have lost my best friend," He never said no! when help was needed. The order of the Sons of the Confederacy attended his funeral in a body. He was one of the original members of this organization in Washington, and also the Sons of the Revolution. He was a man whom his friends loved.

Mr. Dean married Miss Annie Fearon, of Philadelphia, who still survives him. He left four children: Mary Owen, Mildred, Mills, and Paul.

THE WOODRUFF FAMILY

Thomas Woodruff, son of Joseph and Annie (Linsey) Woodruff, came to Spartanburg District from the Yadkin Valley, N.C., after the Revolution. He married Mary Patillo Harrison, a daughter of Dr. Richard Harrison, one of the early county court judges for Spartanburg. His children were Harrison Patillo, Charles Pinckney, Richard, James Monroe, Andrew Barry, Martha Mariah, Julia Ann, and two children died in infancy.

Of these children, Harrison P. Woodruff married Sarah McHugh; Dr. Charles P. Woodruff married Eliza Julia Ann Todd; Rev. Richard Woodruff married Elizabeth J. Foster; James M. Woodruff married a Miss Lockhart; Captain A. B. Woodruff married Maria Louisa Todd, sister to the wife of Dr. Woodruff; Martha Maria Woodruff married Stephen Griffith, father of Professor H. P. Griffith of Limestone College, and Julia Ann married Dr. Benjamin Wofford.

These families have always occupied positions of the highest respectability and have ranked among the foremost in the communities in which they lived. The present town of Woodruff, S.C., takes its name from Thomas Woodruff, the first settler at that place, and has become one of the most flourishing inland towns in upper South Carolina and has a bright future before it.

Among the prominent citizens and physicians of this town was Dr. Charles P. Woodruff, well known to many of the older citizens of Spartanburg County. He was born at Woodruff February 8th, 1808, and died April 27th, 1887, in his eightieth year. He graduated at the Medical College, Cincinnati, Ohio, 1831. He had an extensive scope of practice, and was a man of more than ordinary intelligence and influence among the people of his neighborhood. He was a member of the Bethel Baptist church and led a consistent Christian life.

Rev. Richard Woodruff was ordained a minister of the gospel in early life and devoted the remainder of his life to the advancement of the Saviour's kingdom. He supplied during his ministry, covering a period of about fifty years, a number of churches in Spartanburg County, and expounded the word with zeal and correctness. During the civil war he served in defense of his country and acted for a time as chaplain of the Fifth Regiment, South Carolina Volunteers.

Throughout his entire ministerial career he retained many peculiarities of an eventful life. He was a man of warm heart and deep, earnest piety, and says another: "But for constitutional eccentricities of disposition would have been a widely useful man." His grandmother, the wife of Dr. Richard Harrison, became a widow and subsequently married Captain Thomas Farrow, a soldier of the Revolution. His wife was a sister to Dr. Iry Foster, an eminent physician who removed from Spartanburg district to Alabama, many years before the outbreak of the civil war, and who participated in the Florida war and was wounded.

CAPTAIN ANDREW BARRY WOODRUFF was born at Woodruff, S.C., February 25th, 1825. His educational advantages were limited. One of his instructors was Wm. Jones, who taught about one mile east of Woodruff. He also attended for a time the school of his sister Martha, and then that of her future husband, Stephen Griffith. His parents, considering him too delicate to go to school or work on the farm, secured a situation for him in a store as clerk, of which his brother. Dr. Woodruff, was a partner. He remained with this firm for several years, during which time he married Miss Maria Todd, a lady of intelligence and refinement, who was a daughter of Dr. John and Mrs. Eliza J. Todd, of Laurens County, S.C.

In 1842 he connected himself with Bethel (Baptist) Church and was some years afterwards ordained as one of its deacons

Capt. A. B. Woodruff

and has held every office in the church, being clerk of the same for thirty-two years. He has been nearly always a delegate from his church to the Old Tyger River and Spartanburg Associations, and was for a long number of years the clerk of these bodies, having succeeded C. J. Elford as clerk of the Tyger River immediately after the close of the civil war. He was also for several years assistant clerk of the State (S.C.) Baptist Convention. He was postmaster and a magistrate at Woodruff before the civil war. These offices would have exempted him from any service in the army, perhaps, during the entire war; but in January, 1862, he enlisted in Company E, Holcombe Legion, and upon the reorganization of said company in May of the same year he was elected its captain and held this office to the end of the war. During this time he was in twelve different engagements, according to his estimate, and wounded at the Second Manassas battle. At the battle of Five Forks, Va., his company formed a part of a detachment under General W. H. Wallace, which was overwhelmed by a Federal flank movement and was captured. He, with other Confederate officers, was taken to Johnson's Island, in Lake Erie. He states that this was a great grief to him, as he loved the battle and was willing at any time to risk the danger of losing his life.

In the absence of the field-officers of the Holcombe Legion, he was for a considerable time in command of that regiment, and by General Bushrod Johnson, who commanded the division to which the Holcombe Legion belonged, he was tendered the position of major of his regiment, but for honorable reasons he declined it. Major Zeigler, who held the commission of major of the Holcombe Legion, had been captured and was held as a hostage by the enemy, being in close confinement. He and Captain Woodruff were close friends, and the latter, out of a tender sympathy for his suffering and painful suspense, refused to be promoted over him.

Captain Woodruff, after his return home from imprisonment, accepted the situation and went to work in earnest to bring about a peaceful restoration of the chaotic conditions which confronted him. Under the then existing dominant party controlling the affairs of the State of South Carolina he was elected as a Democrat to the State Legislature in 1865 and in 1868. While a member of this body he introduced a bill, which passed, forbidding the sale of intoxicating liquors, either with or without license, within three miles of churches and schoolhouses outside of municipalities, which law has never been changed. He was again elected to the State Legislature in 1874 and served for one term. He held also, for a number of years after the close of the civil war, the position of trial justice with efficiency and to the satisfaction of the people.

Captain Woodruff, however, has rendered inestimable service to his church and denomination, not only in the conventions and associations, but also as a trustee of Cooper Limestone Institute and Furman University.

For a long number of years he presided as superintendent over a large Sunday-school in his church, and was at one time secretary of the State Sunday-school Convention. Says another of him: "Wherever in our county and State there is good to be done and sacrifice of time and money to be made, there we may expect to find A. B. Woodruff. Quiet, self-sacrificing, patient, hopeful, earnest, he toils on, sustained by a lofty faith and cheered by the approval of an enlightened conscience."

[1] John Miller, father of Sheriff Sam Miller, it will be remembered, was killed by the Indians and Tories during the Revolution. His wife, Margaret Miller, subsequently became the wife of James Jorden.

[2] That part of this sketch of Colonel Dean under quotation marks is copied from Thomas's "History of the South Carolina Military Academy."

Chapter Twenty-Seven - The Bomar Family

The first information we have of the Bomar family goes back to their residence in Halifax County, Va., whither they had come about the year 1778 in their migrations from Essex County, Va. The tradition in the family is that there were three brothers who came from England, whose names were William, John and Thomas. All of these died in the last decade of the eighteenth century (except Thomas, who died in 1802).

Those of the family who came to South Carolina from Virginia after the Revolution are all descended from William and John. The descendants of Thomas Bomar, the youngest of the three brothers referred to, are all in Tennessee, Kentucky and in the far West, as far as they are known. The tradition is positive that the latter, John Bomar, and some of his sons, were soldiers of the Revolution. The "Writings of Rev. Thomas Bomar" show that all were Whigs.

Some time in the latter part of the eighteenth century Armstead Bomar, son of John, settled in Spartanburg district, on South Pacolet, about two miles southwest of New Prospect. Subsequently he moved to Georgia, where some of his descendants still live. Reuben Bomar, another son of John, evidently lived for a short time in Spartanburg district, for he left a large tract of unimproved land, which was sold and divided among his descendants. His brother, Edward Bomar, settled on North Tyger River, near the town of Fair Forest. About the same time his cousins, Thomas and John Bomar, settled near him, and his brother Elisha settled in the village of Spartanburg, with lands on Fair Forest creek and Lawson Fork. The present families of Bomar in Spartanburg County are all descendants of Edward, Thomas and Elisha, except a few of the lineal descendants of Armstead Bomar, which still remain.

Thomas Bomar became a minister of the gospel. A brief biography of him was written by Wilson N. Hunt, Esq., published in 1827, which gives the date of his birth April 13th, 1770, in Essex County, Va. In 1778 his parents moved to Halifax County. He was educated in the best schools to be found in his day and time. His father, William Bomar, was an Episcopalian in his religious profession, and one whose exemplary course of conduct was highly characteristic of genuine piety.

Thomas Bomar was of delicate health, and his afflictions at last brought him to Christ. He was baptized by Rev. Thomas Dobson, united with Hunting Creek Baptist church and ordained a minister in 1803, at the annual session of Ronoake (Va.) Association. The next year he migrated to Spartanburg district, S.C. His first charges were Bethlehem and Mount Zion churches, the latter being an "arm" (the old name for mission) of Bethlehem, Subsequently he became pastor of New Prospect church and the citizens of Spartanburg village received a liberal share of his exertions. His life was actively given to the cause of Christ and was attended with great results. He was an ardent missionary in speech, and was for a time president of the Spartanburg Auxiliary Bible Society. At one time he filled the office of tax-collector in Spartanburg district. He died suddenly at the house of John S. Rowland, near Boiling Spring, June 13th, 1830. His body lies buried in the cemetery of Bethlehem church, his first pastoral charge. The vacancy in his ministerial work caused by his death was filled by Rev. J. G. Landrum. He married in October, 1797, Miss Elizabeth C. High, and left a family of twelve children, most of whom migrated to the West. Among those that remained was one son whose name is inseparably connected with Spartanburg County; this was General Alexander C. Bomar. He is remembered as the sheriff of said county, which office he held for several years. He was also brigadier-general of the Ninth Brigade South Carolina Militia, and was an efficient officer and active member of Mount Zion church. He was a man of more than ordinary intelligence, firmness and decision of character; was useful to his neighborhood and possessed all the traits of character that go to make up a good man and gentleman. He was married twice, his first wife being Miss Norman, of Cross Keys, Union county, by whom he had three children, the eldest son, Norman, having lost his life during the civil war. His second marriage was to Miss Emily Chapman, by whom he also had several children.

Edward Bomar, already mentioned, was born in Virginia 1769 and emigrated from that State to Spartanburg district [1] in 1796, with his wife, *née* Mary Wood, and three children, Catharine, Patience and John. He settled, as we have already stated, on North Tyger River, near the town of Fair Forest. Here, in his quiet and hospitable home, near his beloved church, Mount Zion, he spent a long and useful life, and his remains lie buried in the family graveyard on his estate. His life was uneventful; he bore no part in county politics, held no office so far as can be learned, but

> "Along the cool, sequestered vale of life
> He kept the even tenor of his way."

He is affectionately remembered not only by his descendants, but by others who knew him and still live, and his memory is held in high esteem because of his pure character, exemplary piety and good works.

The following are the names and dates of the birth of his children: Catherine, born October 31st, 1791; Patience, October 17th, 1793; John, February 15th, 1795; Elizabeth, April 6th, 1799; William, August 5th, 1801; Mary, July 16th, 1804; George W., May 7th, 1807, and Booker, April 26th, 1810. His descendants number about one thousand, nine-tenths of whom are Baptists.

JOHN BOMAR, JR., son of Edward and Mary (Wood) Bomar, was born in Halifax county, Va., February 15th, 1796, and while an infant was carried by his father to Spartanburg district, where he grew up to manhood and spent all his life, with the exception of a few years in early life when he resided in Kentucky and taught school, and the further exception of a short sojourn in Charleston, S.C., whether he had gone after his marriage to embark in the mercantile business. He married Mary Crawford Vernon, daughter of James Vernon, and to this happy marriage and to the loving sympathy of his wife was due much of the success of his earlier years. She, the wife of his youth, died at the early age of thirty-seven, leaving him with a family of three girls: Elizabeth, who became the wife of Dr. R. E. Cleveland; Margaret, who became the wife of Major Thomas Bomar; and Louisa, who became the wife of

Major John Earle Bomar. Subsequently he married Mrs. Sarah Blassingame *née* Sloan, with whom he lived until his death, in 1868. Two children were born of this union. Belle V., now Mrs. Trimmier of Georgia, and Thomas Converse, who accidentally killed himself when but sixteen years of age.

Perhaps but few men who ever lived in Spartanburg County were more useful than the subject of this sketch. In early life he embraced Christianity and was an active and useful member of Mt. Zion church. He was also one of the prominent temperance workers in the county, and was one of the first men to discontinue the old-time practice of keeping wines and liquors for the hospitable entertainment of his friends. In the earlier years of his life he was a farmer, merchant, builder, and for a time an innkeeper, and even then in a small way a manufacturer, for he was never without a flour and grist-mill, or both, and a tan-yard. His purchase of Bivingsville (now Glendale) cotton factory as bankrupt property

John Bomar, Jr.

was one of his business ventures. Success in this enterprise would have been difficult, if not impossible even with his associates in the business, had it not been for this power of knowing men. His hope lay in getting some one with practical expert knowledge to "run" the factory. This was found in the person of D. E. Converse (see sketch), whose business management and reputation as a manufacturer will always follow him.

In a notice which appeared in the Spartan soon after his death, it is truthfully stated that "he possessed in the highest degree the confidence and respect of all who knew him...He was chosen ordinary of the district for several years, the responsible duties of which he discharged to the utmost public satisfaction."

In the organization of the Tyger River (Baptist) Association he bore an active part, being one of a committee of four (Rev. John G. Landrum, Dr. John W. Lewis and Dr. Robt. M. Young being the other three members) who brought about its organization.

His body was buried in his beloved town, Spartanburg, and his tomb bears this appropriate inscription: "Diligent in business, fervent in spirit, serving the Lord."

ELISHA BOMAR, ESQ., was the son of William Bomar and his wife Elizabeth Hurt, the fifth son and one of seven children. Rev. Thomas Bomar, whom we have mentioned, being a full brother. One other of his brothers, John, died in Spartanburg district, and another, William, in Georgia. His father having died in 1790, it was early in life when Elisha Bomar moved to Spartanburg district. He was nearly all of his life a resident of Spartanburg village, where early in his married life he built the house which stood for many years on the site of the present court-house grounds.

On the 11th of March, 1823, he was married by Rev. Wm. Rector, to Amaryllis Earle, daughter of Colonel John Earle, on North Pacolet (Polk County, N.C.), on the present Prince homestead. His father was a soldier of the Revolution, a captain of the Rangers, and her mother, *née* Rebecca Berry, was, by her first husband, the wife of John Wood, who was killed by the Tories under "Bloody Bill" Cunningham during his infamous raid to the Spartanburg region November, 1781.

Elisha Bomar was for over twenty years clerk of court for Spartanburg district, and died suddenly, March 27th, 1836, while still in office, as he was preparing to attend Bethlehem church, of which he was an active member. A public meeting was held by the citizens of Spartanburg to express their appreciation of the deceased and their sorrow at his sudden death and sympathy for the bereaved family.

The members of the Spartanburg bar and other members of the court and community generally, Judge O'Neall presiding, held a meeting which, after expressing lament in the loss of a valuable friend, resolved that the public had "lost an able, impartial and industrious officer, and the members of the bar and other officers of the court a liberal, high-minded and faithful associate."

Elisha Bomar took the liveliest interest in the educational efforts of his day, and was one of the founders and promoters of the high schools in Spartanburg, one for the boys and another for the girls, which flourished in other days; besides, part of his estate was donated by his widow to found the Spartanburg Female College.

By his marriage with Miss Earle he raised two children, Harriet and John Earle. The former became the wife of Judge T. O. P. Vernon (see sketch).

HON. JOHN EARLE BOMAR, son of Elisha and Amaryllis (Earle) Bomar, was born July 29th, 1827. His father having died when he was a lad, he was carefully educated and trained by his mother. In Spartanburg he was taught by Erastus and Milton Rowley. Afterwards he attended the Citadel Academy

Hon. John Earle Bomar.

at Charleston, but withdrew in a short time on account of the lax discipline which prevailed and which led to the reorganization of the Citadel within a few years after his departure. Then for a time he attended Erskine College at Due West, S.C., where he made a good record, but left for some cause shortly before his graduation.

In 1855-56 he was editor and one of the proprietors of the *Carolina Spartan*, in connection with Major Wm. H. Trimmier. "No one," wrote one of his successors, "of the many who had editorial control of that paper, ever wielded a more graceful pen."

It was while a young editor that he became interested in military life. In this he rose to the rank of brigade major and thus obtained his title of major, by which he was ever afterwards called.

In 1857 he was elected ordinary of Spartanburg district, to which he was elected by successive elections until after the close of the civil war.

In 1862 he reorganized the Morgan Rifles in Spartanburg, which, as captain, he led to the army and which was known as Company C, Holcombe Legion. He served faithfully in this capacity for several months, participating in several engagements on the seacoast. His health, however, breaking down, he obtained honorable discharge. About the same time he was reelected ordinary.

In 1869 he began the practice of law in co-partnership with Colonel John H. Evins, under the firm name of Evins & Bomar; subsequently, upon the entrance of S. J. Simpson, the firm was known as Evins, Bomar & Simpson, and upon the death of Colonel Evins in 1884, as Bomar & Simpson, till the death of Major Bomar, February 3d, 1899. At the time of his death he was *the Nestor* of the Spartanburg bar.

"He seldom appeared before a jury or judge in an argument, not because he did not understand the case in point, but he was modest and retiring in manners and always put it upon his partner to do the talking."

During the time he practiced law he was also for several terms county commissioner, being chairman of the board. He also served one term in the Legislature (1874-76) during that terrible period which preceded the revolution of 1876. While he never sought this position, yet he held various positions of honor and trust. Under the constitution of 1866 he was elected by the Legislature and commissioned by Governor Orr district judge, but declined to serve. He was for many years trustee of the schools which preceded the graded school system, vice-president of the Board of Trustees of Converse College, a trustee (for many years chairman of the Board) of Cooper Limestone Institute, and treasurer of Kennedy Library, in which he took the liveliest interest. He was a master mason, but for some years before his death, not an active member. For many years he was deacon of Spartanburg Baptist Church and served for two or three years as moderator of Spartanburg Baptist Association.

Touching his death, appropriate resolutions were passed by Boards of Trustees of Kennedy Library and Converse College and by the Spartanburg bar, which the latter set forth among other things the following: "In Major Bomar the elements of character were so blended as to make his influence an estimable moral force in the community. A gentleman of the old school, he kept fully abreast of the movements of the times, remaining actively in the practice of his profession to the last. His career was a striking example of energy and activity, without that inordinate greed for gain which is so marked an evil of the times. Major Bomar was positive in his convictions, yet kind in his judgments; a Christian of such ample mould as to be admired by all denominations. While his public services to the religious and charitable organizations are a part of the history of Spartanburg, he exemplified yet more,

"'That best portion of a good man's life,
The little nameless, unrecorded acts of kindness and love.'"

It was while as yet a young editor that he married his distant cousin, Louisa N. Bomar, [2] daughter of John Bomar, Jr. The blessing of heaven rested upon this union, for she was one of the loveliest of women. By this marrriage the following children survive: Rev. E. E. Bomar, D.D.; Elisha Bomar, Rev. Paul Bomar, John Bomar, Horace Bomar, Mamie, wife of Beverly Montgomery; Louise, wife of Dr. J. H. Montgomery, and Amaryllis, single.

[1] The counties in our State were called *districts* before the outbreak of the civil war between the States.
[2] His grandfather William and her great-grandfather John were brothers.

Chapter Twenty-Eight - The Wilkins Family

The ancestor of the Wilkins families in Spartanburg and Union counties, South Carolina, and in Rutherford County, North Carolina, was William Wilkins, a native of Virginia, who was among the early settlers in the territory afterwards embraced in the original county of Spartanburg. He came before the outbreak of the Revolution, and the place of his settlement was in the vicinity of Goucher Creek, one of the tributaries of Thickety Creek. The tradition that we gather with reference to him is that he was a most estimable citizen, and raised a large and highly respectable family, as we will further show.

The wife of Wm. Wilkins was Elizabeth (called Betsey) Terrell, who descended from a distinguished ancestry as shown by reference to a compiled genealogy of the family in both England and France by General W. H. Terrell of Indiana. Elizabeth Wilkins came from the Terrell family in Culpepper County, Va. They were gentlemen and held large grants of land from the King. In the privy council of Charles I. was Sir Timothy Terrell, gentleman, the father of Robert Terrell (born 1696), who was the father of Edmond Terrell to whom he (Robert) Terrell willed large tracts of land in Culpepper County. Edmond left seven or nine children, of whom Mrs. Wilkins is believed to be one, as she was a member of the Culpepper branch of this family.

William and Elizabeth Wilkins had born unto them sixteen children as shown by the family record as follows:

Mary, born November 11th, 1769, married Thomas Gillenwater; Elizabeth, born August 11th, 1771, married Wm. Cantrell; Milly, born March 5th, 1773, married Davis Goudelock; Terrell, born February 21st, 1775, married Sallie Hardin; Robert (Robin) born December 5th, 1776, married Sallie Littlejohn; Jane, born August 14th, 1778, married Wm. Austell; Sallie, born July 28th, 1780, married J. L. Davis; William, born July 28th, 1782, married first Patsey Jackson, and second time to Frankie Foster; Nancy, born March 17th, 1784, married Joshua Draper; Moses and Aaron (twins) born November 21st, 1785, Moses married Sallie Lipscomb, and Aaron married Elinor Jeffries; Kesiah, born November 20th, 1787, married Stephen Tolleson; John, born June 1st, 1789, married Polly Lipscomb; George, born July 13th, 1791, married Elizabeth Martin; Ruth, born February 26th, 1794, and Rachel, born January 26th, 1797.

WILLIAM WILKINS, in reviewing the characters of the individual members of the Wilkins family none are more deserving of special notice than William Wilkins, who died at his home at Greenville, S.C., in 1897, aged about 65 or 70 years. He was called "New York William" to distinguish him from others of the same name. He was the son of John and Polly Wilkins, and was raised on his father's farm on Goucher Creek in Spartanburg County, receiving such advantages of education as could be afforded in the common schools of his neighborhood.

Soon after reaching the age of manhood, when only about twenty years of age, he left his parental roof and sought and secured a position in a wholesale mercantile house in Charleston, S.C., where he remained a few

William Wilkins

years and then went to New York City, where he secured a better position in the same line of business, and was doing a good business when the civil war between the States broke out. His love and devotion for his native State, however, was stronger than worldly gain, and when South Carolina called for her sons to defend her proud name and sovereignty, he immediately surrendered his lucrative job and returned home and entered the Confederate service. He volunteered in 1861 in Co. A (Johnson Rifles, Union, S.C), 5th Regt., S.C.V., and during this year participated in all the hardships of this regiment and was engaged in the first Manassas battle.

Upon the reorganization of the armies in Virginia in 1862 he reenlisted in the same company, which formed a part of the Palmetto Sharpshooters, and was made its orderly sergeant. In a few days thereafter he was wounded at Seven Pines, which incapacitated him from further active service. He was put on light duty and remained with his company and regiment until the end of the war.

After the war he returned to New York City, where he remained for some years, during which time he associated himself with A. H, Foster at Union, S.C., in the mercantile business under the name of Foster & Wilkins, and in Greenville, S.C., with J. T. Williams and A. H. Foster under the name of Wilkins, Williams & Co., afterwards Wilkins, Poe & Co., in which firms he was active and successful.

Some time after the war Mr. Wilkins married to Miss Hattie Cleveland of Greenville, S.C., daughter of Harvey Cleveland, who still survives him. After his marriage he took up his residence in Greenville, where he remained the balance of his life.

William Wilkins was far above the average business man of his day. He showed what could be accomplished by ambition, pluck, energy and close application to business. Notwithstanding he had learned in early life lessons of thrift and economy, yet he was liberal, public-spirited, and was at all times patriotic and true to the welfare and best interests of his country. His character for honesty and fair dealing was very high, and as such, he will be long remembered.

CAPTAIN WILLIAM TERRELL WILKINS, son of Colonel William and Martha (Jackson) Wilkins, was born in Spartanburg County, September 28th, 1818, and died while on a visit to his sons in Texas, May, 1896. He was reared on his father's farm on North Pacolet River within two or three miles of New Prospect, where he received the very best education that could be afforded in the schools of his neighborhood. He also attended for a time the Spartanburg Male Academy. Before he reached the age of eighteen years, however, he married Miss Adaline Duncan, and not many years after this he embarked in the mercantile business near New Prospect, which he successfully conducted in connection with his farm on

Capt. Wm. T. Wilkins.

South Pacolet River until the beginning of the civil war between the States.

At the outbreak of the civil war he went forth to serve his country at the sacrifice of every pecuniary interest. During the first year of the same (1861) he was connected with the 5th Regiment, S.C.V., as an independent volunteer, and the writer, who belonged to the same regiment, can testify to the valuable service he rendered.

As the years of the bloody conflict went on there was an increased demand for every available man to enlist in the service. Captain Wilkins, although well advanced in years (being then 44 years of age), took it upon himself to raise a company of cavalry, which he did, in 1862, and which was known as the *Spartan Rangers*. This company, though independent of any regimental organization, did gallant and efficient service, both in North and South Carolina, during the last two years of the war.

Returning home after the war he had to begin anew to retrieve his lost fortune. In time of peace he had made sales on time of his valuable stock of merchandise, which, but for the war, he would have collected, and saved much of the financial embarrassment which he suffered; but the devastation and ravages of the war had ruined, for the time, the country, and the fortunes of many men who were good for their obligations at its beginning were now wrecked or destroyed. Captain Wilkins, however, did not sulk under the conditions which surrounded him, but with a renewed energy he put forth every effort to meet his honest obligations and to make a comfortable support for himself and family.

It is due to his memory to say that he was an honest, upright, and conscientious citizen. During the many years of his mercantile life he had a wide field of custom, was noted for his fair dealing, and had the entire confidence of the people with whom he dealt in a business way.

In early life he embraced the Christian religion, and was a steadfast member and deacon of New Prospect Church, and was very often its representative in the Associations and other religious bodies. Especially did he take an interest and a part in the Sunday-school work, and was for a number of years the President of the Campobello Township (interdenominational) Sunday-school Convention, which met annually.

In the winter of 1859 he lost his devoted wife, by whom he had twelve children, nine sons and three daughters. The life of one son (Robert) was sacrificed on the altar of his country during the civil war. Of his twelve children about one-half are deceased. The others are living, we believe, in the State of Texas, including W. D. Wilkins, a prominent merchant at Honey Grove, in that State.

The Wood Family

In our efforts to gain some information concerning the Wood family we find among the same a prevailing tradition that two brothers emigrated from Virginia to South Carolina before the Revolution, and during that struggle for American independence both entered the service of their country.

At the close of the Revolution they separated; one returned to Virginia and the other removed to Tennessee, The one who returned to Virginia, however, came back to South Carolina, settling in the eastern portion of the present county of Spartanburg. It is supposed that he married in Virginia, and it is not known how many children he had, but William Wood was one of his sons who lived on Pacolet, near Easterwood Shoals. He was a prominent and highly respectable citizen in his day and time, and married Miss Nancy, daughter of the elder William Lipscomb. By this marriage he had seven children as follows: Lucinda, who married Wm. Littlejohn (known as Wm.

215

Kink); James, who married Harriet E. Wilkins; N. Lipscomb, who married Mary Austell; David, who married in Alabama; Caroline, who married Daniel Draper; John, who married Agnes Lipscomb; and Thomas,, who married Addie Lipscomb.

The children of John Wood, one of the sons mentioned, are as follows: Sallie, who married Smith Lipscomb (son of Edward Lipscomb, Sr.); Moses, who married J. Elma, daughter of G. T. Meng, Union county. S.C.; Adolphus N., who married Millie Draper; Atlanta, who married W. F. Bryant, Pacolet, S.C.; Lou H., who married R. R. Brown, Cowpens, S.C., and Miss Terisa E., single Of the sons mentioned above, Moses Wood, now a resident of Gaffney, S.C., claims special notice. Being a native born of Spartanburg County, he has always enjoyed a position of respectability, influence and popularity.

Lieut. Moses Wood

He was a gallant officer in the Confederate army, being among the first to enlist in the service in his native county. He was first lieutenant of Co. F, 15th Regt., S.C.V., and served with said command until the end of the war. At the surrender at Greensboro, N.C., he was in command of his company and had been for several months.

It is only necessary to refer to the roll of said company with accompanying remarks, as to casualties published elsewhere in this volume, to appreciate the splendid record it made during the four years of a bloody war, and on said roll there is not to be found the name of a braver spirit than that of Moses Wood — its last commander. He was wounded at the battle of the Wilderness, May, 1864.

By his marriage with Miss Meng, as already stated, he has eight living children, as follows: Lula B., who married to Dr. R. R. Brown at Pacolet; Julia E., who married W. Oscar Lipscomb, Gaffney, S.C.; Beona, who married W. F. Brown, Gaffney, S.C., and unmarried children, Nellie H., Lawrence S., James K., Louisa and Emma Elizabeth.

The Lipscomb Family

Among the first settlers in the original county of Spartanburg was William Lipscomb, the ancestor of nearly all the families of this name who have ever resided in said county.

It is stated that just after the close of the Revolution he was moving with his family from Louisa County, Va., to Georgia, and that on the way his wagon broke down near Thickety Creek. While awaiting repairs he concluded to look around over the country, and was so well pleased that he decided to make settlement in that immediate vicinity. He made entry of a large scope of lands on Little Thickety and Goucher creeks, which has been in the family ever since. He was born in Virginia, March 28th, 1731, and died March 13th, 1810, aged 79 years. He had five sons and two daughters, viz.: Smith (known as Judge L.)? John, David, William, Nathan, Nancy and Polly.

Of these sons Smith Lipscomb, the eldest, had four sons and two daughters, viz.: William (Billy Pete) who married a Miss Lockart, daughter of an old settler; Jammie, who married a Miss Ferguson; Wyatt, who married Rebecca Lockart, sister of William's wife; David, who married a Miss Macomson; Betsey, who married Hiram Lockart (brother of the wives of William and Wyatt), and Nancy, who married Spencer Morgan, a Baptist preacher.

Of these sons, William (or Billy Pete) had eight children, as follows: Agnes, who married John H. Wood; Josaphine (now deceased) who married Crawford Miller; Christina P., who married John J. Lipscomb; Alexander, who married a Miss Jane Finley (daughter of Daniel Finley, Esq.); Moses, who died during the war unmarried; Smith, who married Miss Sarah Goudelock; Jimmie, unknown; Hiram, who married Miss Janie Holmes; and Wyatt, who married Miss Mildred Streetman of Texas.

John Lipscomb, one of the sons of the elder William Lipscomb, had four sons and four daughters, viz.: John, William, Smith, Edward, Betsey, Agnes, Polly and Nancy, Of the four sons, Edward Lipscomb, Esq., had eleven children, as follows: Nazareth, who married Rev. M. C. Barnett; Elizabeth, who married Willis Smith; Sarah, who married A. N. Poole; Clara, who married K. C. Watkins; Evelina, who married Willis Smith (second wife); Narcissa, who married Captain A. B. Bryant (killed in the army); Elias, who married Artemia Golightly; William L. (Billy Cap), who married Nancy Elizabeth, daughter of Wyatt Lipscomb; Smith Lipscomb, father of R. S. Lipscomb, who married Sallie Wood, and who died in Virginia during the civil war; John J., who married Christina Lipscomb, and Nathan, who married Mary, daughter of Russell Wilkins. Of the four daughters of John (son of William Lipscomb, the elder) mentioned, Betsy married Frank Littlejohn; Agnes married Thomas Littlejohn first and afterwards to Drury Wood (cousins); Polly married John Wilkins, and Nancy married Dr. Nance.

Of the daughters of the elder William Lipscomb mentioned, Nancy married William Wood and Polly married Thomas Littlejohn.

William Lipscomb, son of John and grandson of William Lipscomb the elder, had five sons and three daughters, viz.: John W., Martin, Smith, William R., Edward, Julia Ann, Nancy W., and Agatha B.

Of the sons mentioned, William R. Lipscomb of Limestone Springs (now Gaffney) is a highly respected citizen, well known in both the original counties of Spartanburg and Union. He was born March 2nd, 1828, and at this writing is seventy-one years of age. He embraced Christianity at the age of eleven years, and has always been an exemplary member of the Baptist Church. He has always been a generous contributor to the cause of religion and education. During the war he was a true defender of the "Lost Cause," and since then he has followed the avocation of a farmer.

He has been married three times — first, to Miss Nancy Austell; second, to Mrs. Elmina Jeffries; and, third, to Miss Susan Lafar. By the last marriage he has four sons.

Edward (Pompey Ned) Lipscomb is also well known in the section of the country in which he lives as an honest, upright and well-to-do farmer.

Of the daughters of William (son of John) Lipscomb mentioned, Julia Ann married James M. Surratt, Nancy W. married Luther Poole, and Agatha B. married Holman R. Smith.

It may be truly said of the entire Lipscomb family that they are and always have been a highly respectable and law-abiding generation of people. They have always been true, loyal and patriotic, both in times of peace and in war; and in the civil war between the States every available man of this large family connection shouldered his musket and defended a cause which they believed (and was) right and just. Some of them sacrificed their lives in defense of their country, both in the hospital and on the field of battle.

Among the battle-scarred veterans of the families of this name referred to, we would mention William R. (Billy Cap) Lipscomb, whose jaw was lacerated by an explosion of a shell on the battle-field.

In this connection we would again refer to Captain Alfred B. Bryant, who married Miss Narcissa, daughter of Edward Lipscomb, Esq. He was a brave and heroic officer in the Confederate army. He entered the service as lieutenant of Company B, Holcombe Legion, and succeeded Captain Sloan (the latter resigning on account of ill health) to the captaincy of said company January, 1863, which he commanded until within about three weeks before the surrender at Appomattox. He was killed near Fort Steadman, Va., March 25th, 1865.

W. S. Lipscomb

WILLIAM SMITH LIPSCOMB - In our efforts to preserve the history and perpetuate the memories of the worthy sons belonging to the Lipscomb families, there are none more worthy of our special attention than William Smith Lipscomb, eldest son of Wyatt and Rebecca (Lockart) Lipscomb, who was born November 21st, 1834, and died December 10th, 1898, being in the sixty-fourth year of his age.

He was reared on his father's farm on Thickety Creek, in the present county of Cherokee, and only a few miles from Gaffney, S.C., where he died.

Being a son of an honorable and respectable parentage, he had instilled into him in early life all the principles which go to make up a true man, gentleman and patriot, which he was. But, aside from this, he possessed and maintained throughout his entire life a moral character that was pure and beyond reproach. He was strictly temperate, never having during his life tasted a drop of alcoholic liquors.

In January, 1862, he entered the service of the Confederate States as a member of Captain Felix Walker's company, 18th Regiment, S.C.V., and was wounded seriously at the battle of Clay's farm, in Virginia, in 1864; and once during his career as a soldier, when in the heat of battle, the color-bearer of his regiment having been shot down, he seized the fallen colors and bore them on to victory.

Lieut. Smith Lipscomb

After the war, for a quarter of a century or more, he maintained the reputation of a first-class hotel man, in which business he was engaged at the time of his death.

He had been a member of the Baptist Church for about fifteen years, and was always ready, in an humble way, to contribute, when called upon, to all the objects of charity and benevolence.

In 1860 he married Miss Albertine Goudelock, of Union, fifth daughter of John W. Goudelock, Esq., by whom he had eight children, six of whom are living.

LIEUT. SMITH LIPSCOMB, son of William (Billy Pete) and Sarah (Lockart) Lipscomb, was born February 26th, 1840, near the present town of Thickety, S.C. He was educated in the common schools of his neighborhood, and attended the classical school of J. Banks Lyle at Limestone Springs.

At the outbreak of the civil war between the States he volunteered for the service in Company F, 18th Regiment, S.C.V. (Colonel Gadbury), commanded respectively by Captains Felix J. Walker and Goodman Jeffries. Of this company Smith Lipscomb was senior 2d lieutenant, having been promoted to this position from junior 2d lieutenant. Throughout the entire war of four years in which he served, he was noted for his gallantry and faithfulness, in every sense of the word, to his country's cause.

After his return home from the army in 1865 he married Sallie Goudelock, daughter of John W. Goudelock, of Union county, S.C., a congenial and devoted companion, and removed to the State of Texas, where he has since resided. His home is at Bonham, Fannin County, which he has served with efficiency for many years, both in the office of sheriff and tax-collector. He has now returned to private life, but is numbered among the honest, upright and progressive citizens of his adopted State, and has always conducted himself in such a way as to reflect credit on his mother State.

By his marriage with Miss Goudelock he has raised an orderly and interesting family of children, one son, Wade Hampton, having served in Cuba in the recent war with Spain.

219

Chapter Twenty-Nine - The Ballenger Family

From the best information obtainable, two brothers, Edward and James Ballenger, migrated to the present county of Spartanburg before the outbreak of the Revolution. During that struggle for American Liberty they sided with the patriots, were noted Whigs and objects of hatred by the Tory element, so much so that one of these brothers came very near being murdered by "Bloody Bill" Cunningham and his following during his notorious raid to the up-country of South Carolina in November, 1781. [1]

In the "Genealogy of the Lewis Family of America," by Wm. Terrell Lewis, page 205, it is stated that Edward (Neddie) Ballenger was a Revolutionary soldier and did good service for his country. He was wounded at the siege of Augusta, was in the battle of Cowpens and many others. He is described as being six feet in stature, was kind and hospitable to his friends, brave and fearless, in battle and uncompromising with the Tories. He married Pleasant, a daughter of David and Elizabeth (Lockart) Lewis. They had seven children, viz.: Margaret; James, married Mahala Foster; Pressley, married Nancy Dodd; Larkin, married Elizabeth, daughter of John (Jackey) Wood; Rebecca Lavina mar Tied Henry Cothran; Edward J.; and Elizabeth, married Wm. White. [2]

James Ballenger, brother of Edward, married Dorcas Dodson in Virginia, and had sons, John, James (Wagoner Jimmie), William, Edward (Neddie), Elijah, and daughters, Frances (Frankee), Margaret (Peggy) and Tabitha. Of these sons, John married Alsie Leachman and had children as follows: Joshua, James, Cornier, John, William and two daughters, Sarah and Alice. Joshua, the eldest, married Mary Davis; James married Margaret (Peggy) Turner; John married Rachel Garrett, and William Tabitha Garrett (sisters); Sarah married Benj. Farmer; and Alice married Thomson Davis.

The children of Joshua and Mary (Davis) Ballenger were eight in number, viz.: Elizabeth, Tinsley, Elijah, Margaret, James, Alberry, David and John. Of these, Elizabeth, aged 86, Tinsley, aged 84, Elijah, aged 80, Margaret, aged 76, and John, aged 66, are all living and residing in Greenville county, S.C. The children of James C. and Margaret (Turner) Ballenger were, Jinsey, who married John Wheeler; Turner, who never married; Dillingham, who married Saphrona Ponder; Margaret Ann, who married Adolphus Turner; and Peyton, who will receive further notice.

James (Wagoner Jimmie), second son of James Ballenger, born June 11th, 1780, married twice: first to Judith Foster, and had five children as follows: Richard, who married Mrs. Elizabeth (Betsey) Snoddy (relict of Isaac Snoddy); William, who married first Mary Goodlett, and afterwards to Virginia Owens; Joel, who married Mary Murph; Edward (Neddie), who married Catharine Montgomery; Thomas, who married first Mary Wingo, and second Mary Landrum; and Sarah, who married Nathaniel Dodd. Mrs. J. P. Jackson, of Independence, Mo., is a surviving heir of Nathaniel Dodd. His second marriage was to Susan Davis — no children.

William Ballenger, third son of the elder James Ballenger, married first a Miss Wilson, and second to Polly Wingo. The latter surviving, married a second time to Reuben Gramling. By the first marriage there were two sons and one daughter, viz.: Edward (Blacksmith Neddie), Madison and Phateme. The latter married first to Wm. Gentry, and second to Zera Alverson. She had one son by each marriage, viz.: Wm. Gentry of Georgia, and Rev. Edward Alverson.

Edward and Elijah, the other sons of the elder James Ballenger, migrated to Missouri, where they died. Of the daughters, Frankie married Isaac Bishop, [3] Peggie married David Lewis and Tabitha married a Foster.

The entire families of Ballenger have always been honest, upright and true to their country, both in times of peace and in war. Among those who fell in the civil war between the States were four sons of John (son of Joshua) Ballenger, viz.: Jasper, Lewis, Hamilton and John; Dillingham, son of James C. Ballenger; one son of Benjamin and Sallie (Ballenger) Farmer, and one son (Thomas) of Thomson and Halie (Ballenger) Davis. To this list might be appropriately added the name of J. Smiley Wheeler, son of Capt. John Wheeler and grandson of James C. Ballenger who was a lieutenant in Company B, 22d Regiment, S.C.V., and who was killed in battle at Jackson, Miss.

CAPTAIN PEYTON BALLENGER, son of James C. and Margaret (Turner) Ballenger, was born near Holly Spring, S.C., De-

Captain Peyton Ballenger

cember 9th, 1831. He was raised on his father's farm, was educated in the common schools of his neighborhood, and has been all his life a progressive citizen and successful farmer.

He entered the Confederate service as a lieutenant in Company B, 22d Regiment, S.C.V., was in several of the battles in which said regiment was engaged, and was in command of his company for fifteen months. Subsequently he resigned and entered the cavalry branch of the service. He was captured December 1st, '64, at Stony Creek, Va., and was carried to Point Lookout, where he was kept until the 23d of June, '65, when he was released. He then returned to his home.

Before the outbreak of the civil war Captain Ballenger served as a captain in the South Carolina militia for seven years.

He connected himself with the Baptist Church in early life and has been a deacon in the same for a number of years. No man stands higher in the community in which he lives than Captain

Peyton Ballenger. He is a popular citizen and a natural born gentleman.

Some time in the fifties he married Carrie, daughter of Colonel Spartan Goodlett of Greenville District, S.C., with whom he lived about twelve years, when she died, leaving six children, viz.: Maggie, who married K. G. Wingo; Carrie, who married P. H. Wheeler; Lula, who married John O. Wingo; Jas. Smiley, who married Alice Ballenger; Mary Emily, single, and Spartan Goodlett, dead.

He married a second time to Emily, daughter of Jason Wall. By the latter marriage one child is born, Ethel, aged twelve years.

CAPTAIN ADAM WASHINGTON BALLENGER, son of Edward B. and Cassia Ann (Hempley) Ballenger, was born near the present town of Inman, S.C., January 17th, 1844. He was raised on his father's farm, and soon after the beginning of hostilities of the civil war between the States he enlisted in Company C, 13th Regiment, S.C.V., and was a sergeant in said company until some

Lieut. A. W. Ballenger.

time in 1863, when, by order of General R. E. Lee, he was promoted for distinguished gallantry on the battle-field. At the second battle of Cold Harbor, in a charge against the enemy when the latter were thrown into confusion and were in the act of retreating, young Ballenger, separating himself from his command and alone, rushed forward and mounted one of the guns of the enemy's artillery. This bold daring caused the driver of the horses conveying the piece to jump off on the tongue between the horses and make his escape out at the end of the tongue. Ballenger immediately, in order to secure the capture of the gun, jumped off the piece, cut loose the traces and unfastened the off-horse, which he mounted. In returning to his command he met his captain (J. W. Carlisle), who informed him that his brother Joseph was wounded and had been left in the rear. Ballenger then went in quest of his brother. But in the meanwhile a party of the enemy had whipped around one wing of the Confederate forces, but finding they were liable to be cut off retreated, but carried Joseph Ballenger away with them, who was imprisoned at Point Lookout, and soon died. Lieutenant Ballenger never saw his brother again after he left him before the beginning of the charge.

This gallant conduct on the part of young Ballenger had been witnessed by General McGowen, who sent for him in a day or two afterwards to report to his headquarters. Young Ballenger obeyed orders and reported, having no idea for what purpose he was wanted. On arriving at the headquarters of General McGowen, he was congratulated by the general, who informed him that he had recommended that he be commissioned a first lieutenant. Receiving his commission, he was assigned to Company H of the 13th Regiment, but in a few months thereafter he was appointed to one of the companies of Dunlop's Battalion of Lee's Sharpshooters, three companies of which were made up out of McGowen's Brigade. Here he remained in command of the first company of this organization, rendering distinguished service, until the 27th of March, 1865, when he was severely wounded in the arm and hip on the picket line in front of Petersburg. He was conveyed to Richmond, and was there when the surrender at Appomattox took place a few days afterwards. While in the Jackson Hospital at Richmond still suffering from his wounds, he was taken with typhoid fever, from which he came very near losing his life. During this time he was visited and administered to by three daughters of General R. E. Lee, a daughter of General Ewell, and Miss Rosa Lee Powers. After some four months of suffering he recovered sufficiently to return home. He was ordered to the State capitol building to take the oath of allegiance. Not relishing this, however, he slipped away, bringing with him his army sword, and after walking several miles out of the city he boarded the train, and after many trying difficulties reached his home in safety.

In 1866 Lieutenant Ballenger married Miss Emma Victoria Wingo. They have had fourteen children, twelve of whom are living, viz.: Melton, married Miss Mattie Morgan; Joel M.; Mamie, married

Lieut. Jas. S. Ballenger.

John Poole, Esq.; Minnie, married Rev. W. F. Sorrels (deceased); Alfred, married Miss Bessie Hurt; Horace, married Miss Swain; Carl, (Trace, Clarence, Leila, Fred, and Joyce.

LIEUT. JAMES SPARTAN BALLENGER. Among those who served their country with conspicuous gallantry during the civil war between the States was Lieutenant James S. Ballenger, son of "William and Mary (Goodlett) Ballenger, who was born December 13th, 1835. He was raised, for the most part, on his father's farm, near Wellford, S.C., and was educated in the schools of his neighborhood.

At the outbreak of the civil war he enlisted in the service of his native State, and was a sergeant in the Morgan Light Infantry, which was mustered into the service April 13th, 1861, as a part of the 5th Regiment, S.C.V. Six weeks later, however, this company reorganized on Sullivan's Island, S.C., for the Confederate service, electing Alfred H. Foster, captain; John M. Benson, first lieutenant; and Robert A. Snoddy and Jas, S. Ballenger, senior and junior second lieutenants. The company was known as F, 5th Regiment, S.C.V. At the end of twelve months' enlistment the company again reorganized in Virginia, re-electing A. H. Foster captain. Lieutenant Benson was promoted in another service. Lieutenant Snoddy was made first lieutenant, and James S. and Richard D. Ballenger, senior and junior second lieutenants. The company, known afterwards as Company D, formed a part of Colonel Jenkins's regiment of Palmetto Sharpshooters. In 1863 Lieutenant Snoddy died of wounds at Campbell's Station, Tenn., and James S. Ballenger rose by

223

promotion to first lieutenant of his company, which position he held to the end of the war. He was never wounded, but participated in nearly or quite all the battles in which his regiment was engaged. Limited space will not allow here a detailed account of the heroic service he rendered his country in her time of greatest peril.

Returning home from the army he settled down, and has lived the quiet life of a farmer, never having aspired to political life. He is, however, an honest, upright and progressive citizen and exemplary deacon of the Baptist Church.

In 1863 he married Mary Amaryllis, daughter of Rev. J. G. Landrum. They have four living children, viz.: Minnie (Mrs. Hester), Carrie (Mrs. Smiley Ballenger), Broadus, and Lida (Mrs. John Jones).

Lieut. R. D. Ballenger

LIEUTENANT RICHARD D. BALLENGER, son of William and Mary Ballenger and brother of James S. Ballenger, was numbered among the long and countless list of gallant heroes that gave up their lives in defense of the "Lost Cause." He was born in 1837, and had reached the best years of his manhood when he enlisted in the service of his country, being among the very first to volunteer. He was elected second lieutenant of Company D, Palmetto Sharpshooters, upon the reorganization of the Southern army in Virginia in 1862, and participated in all the battles in which his regiment was engaged, including the great battle of the Wilderness, where he was mortally wounded May 6th, 1864.

He died from his wounds at Orange Court-house a few days afterwards. No braver spirit ever offered up his life to his country. Let not his memory be forgotten in the annals of his country's history.

SILAS BENSON was born in Greenville District, S.C., in the year 1800, his parents being among the early settlers of that district. He was educated in the best schools that could be afforded in his day and time, but possessed by nature an ingenious turn of mind, and was by occupation a machinist and millwright. He was a model citizen, honest, industrious and progressive, and well-informed on all the current topics of the day.

He married Nancy Miller, daughter of John Miller, and granddaughter of Michael Miller, a woman of domestic accomplishments and exemplary piety; both she and her husband were consistent members of the Baptist Church.

Not many years after this marriage Mr. Benson removed to Spartanburg District settling on North Tyger River, about three miles east of Wellford, where he erected a merchant flouring-mill, and in connection therewith he conducted the business of sawmilling and wool-carding. The latter proved a great convenience to the surrounding country during the civil war, and especially to many of the soldiers in the army, who were dependent for clothing and blankets made at home.

By the marriage of Silas and Nancy (Miller) Benson a family of the highest respectability was reared, the eldest of whom was Rosa, who married Colonel S. M. Snoddy (see sketch); the second, Narcissa, who never married; the third. Captain W. A. Benson, who will receive further notice; the fourth, Frances, who married Wm. G. High; the fifth, Harriet, who married a Mr. Roe of Greenville county, S.C.; the sixth, Captain John M. Benson of Wellford, S.C., who married Miss Fannie Bernard of Richmond, Va.; the seventh, Nancy Marinda, who married Wm. B. Bennett, a lieutenant in Co. G, 10th Arkansas Volunteers, during the civil war, who was wounded at the battle of Shiloh, necessitating the amputation of a part of one foot; the eighth, Margaret, who married Isaac Nesbitt; the ninth, Robert, who died in boyhood; the tenth, Antoinette, who married Dr. De Bard; and the eleventh, Henrietta, who married Wm. Bomar.

CAPTAIN WILLIS ALEXANDER BENSON, referred to as the son of Silas and Nancy Benson, was born May 24th, 1831. He was brought up on his father's homestead and attended the schools of his neighborhood. He was very industrious in his business habits, and possessing an active mind and a vigorous constitution, he bid fair to have a long and useful life before him. Some time in the fifties he united in marriage with Martha, eldest daughter of William and Mary (Goodlett) Ballenger. By this marriage three children were born, viz.: Mary, present wife of James D. Norman, master in equity, Spartanburg, S.C.; Alexander Benson of Greers, S.C., and John Benson of Wellford, S.C. Soon after the outbreak of the civil war between

Capt. W. A. Benson

the States Captain Benson volunteered in Co. B, 22d Regiment, S.C.V. This company, of which John Wheeler was its first captain, was made up, for the most part, of material from Spartanburg District, with a few volunteers from Greenville District. Captain Benson in course of time was elected as one of its lieutenants, and upon the resignation or discharge of Captain Robert G. Fleming, who was severely wounded in a fight between Richmond and Petersburg, May 22d, 1864, he became captain of his company, which position he held at the time of his death, which occurred in the trenches near Petersburg, June 18th, 1864, caused by the explosion of a shell from the enemy's batteries in his front.

His immediate successor in office was Captain Geo. B. Lake (see sketch), who, with thirty-three men in said company, was covered up in the crater caused by mine explosion near the same place the following month (July 30th), from which Captain Lake and two other men were dug out alive.

The writer was born and reared within one and a fourth miles of the home of Captain Benson. He attended the same school with him, and is perfectly familiar with the excellent traits that belonged to his character. A purer patriot or a more gallant hero never drew his sword in defence of his country than Willis Alexander Benson, whom his descendants and the generations that are to come after him should remember with pride.

[1] See "Colonial and Revolutionary History of Upper S.C." Maj. Bomar's letter, pp. 355-4.
[2] Father of Mrs. Thos. W. Richardson, Inman, S.C.
[3] This was the Isaac Bishop who, in 1776, was stolen by the Indians after his father had been murdered by them near Shiloh church. (See Colonial and Revolutionary History of Upper S.C., p. 91.)

Chapter Thirty - The Bowden Family

The original ancestor of the Bowden family in Spartanburg District was Benjamin Bowden, who was a native of Virginia and one of the early settlers. He was born in 1770. His wife was Nancy Roach, born 1771. They had six sons and no daughters. The names of the sons were Reuben, William, George, John, James and Benjamin. All of these sons moved West except Reuben, the eldest, who was well known to the older citizens of Spartanburg County.

Reuben Bowden was born in Virginia, October 10th, 1798, and married August 21st, 1823, to Nancy Linder, daughter of the elder Lee Linder, who was born October 27th, 1809. He was always prominent in his neighborhood, filling such offices as magistrate, officer of the militia, deacon in the Baptist Church, etc. Later he was elected four continuous terms to the office of ordinary for the Spartanburg District, and made a most efficient and accommodating official, saving many lawyers' fees to those having business in that office. It is said that not one of his decisions during all those years was reversed by the higher courts. On account of declining health he resigned during his fourth term as ordinary, and removed to his plantation on South Pacolet near Gowersville, where he died in 1866.

He had six children, as follows: John Ramsey, a captain in the Confederate army, who married Miss Lucy Elliot of York District, S. S.; Mary Ann, who married Robert J. Foster; Charity L., who married Thomas Lipscomb, a gallant soldier in the Confederate army, killed Second Manassas; James Maybin, who married Miss Virginia Nolly; Romulus L., who married Miss Mary Fleck of Greenville, S.C.; Wm. Jeffries, who never married; and Cleopatra Telulah, who married Tho S.C. Davis, now resident of Atlanta, Ga.

CAPTAIN ROMULUS LEE BOWDEN, of Spartanburg, S.C., son of Reuben and Nancy (Lin-der) Bowden, was born near that city February 27th, 1834.

His mother was, as previously stated, the daughter of Lee and Mary (Templeton) Linder, his descent on both sides being English.

Captain Bowden, until he reached the age of sixteen, was reared on his father's farm in Spartanburg County, and at that age he became a clerk in a store at Spartanburg, which was but the beginning of a long and successful business career. In 1855 he went to Martin's Depot, Laurens county, S.C., where he was employed as a clerk in a mercantile establishment until 1858, when he became a partner in the firm, and continued in the business of general merchandizing until August, 1861, when he entered as a volunteer from Laurens County, S.C., joining Company A, 13th Regiment, S.C.V., as a first lieutenant. Upon the organization of said regiment P. L. Calhoun, the captain of Company A, was elected lieutenant-colonel of the regiment, and Lieutenant Bowden succeeded him to the captaincy of the company, and commanded the same until disability resulting from wounds compelled his retirement, in the summer of 1864. He commanded his company in the battles of Mechanicsville, Gaines Mill (First Cold Harbor), Frazier's Farm, Malvern Hill, Second Manassas, Chancellorsville, and Gettysburg. At Second Manassas he was wounded in the left leg, and at Gettysburg he was twice wounded, being shot in the left arm and left hand. For fifteen years after the war he carried a bullet in his left arm, and the loss of the index-finger of his left hand is evidence of one of the wounds he received at Gettysburg. As already stated, it was by reason of these wounds that he was placed on the retired list in 1864.

At Chancellorsville Captain Bowden was complimented by Colonel E. O. Edwards, the gallant commander of the 13th Regiment. It was on that terrible night when General *Stonewall* Jackson was killed. His corps had been on a forced march all day to flank Hooker's army and attack his right and rear. It was natural that some should straggle. During a halt after dark Colonel Edwards passed down the line inquiring of company commanders as to any absent officers. On reaching Company A, and being informed that all were present, he replied, "Yes, and always are." Colonel Edwards himself received his death-wound on the following day.

On returning home Captain Bowden resumed his former occupation, and in 1867 began the mercantile business at Gowensville, S.C., where he remained until 1873, when he removed to Spartanburg, where he has since been engaged in the dry-goods business. He is a reliable merchant in every respect. He gives his personal attention to his business, and his elegant storeroom on Main street is one of the attractions of the city, and will compare favorably in point of size and beauty of arrangement with many others in cities larger than Spartanburg.

Captain Bowden not only looks well to his private business, but is a progressive and public-spirited citizen in every sense of the word. He has been three times alderman of his city, is director of a building and loan association, and a pillar of Spartanburg's financial strength.

In times of peace he has come up to the standard of an upright citizenship, and in time of war, we may say, that a more devoted patriot never drew his sword in defense of the rights of his cherished State.

By his marriage with Miss Mary Fleck he has five children, as follows:

J. Malcolm Bowden, 1st Lieutenant Company K, 2d Regiment, S.C.V., served in Cuba in the recent war with Spain; Maggie F., wife of G. W. Hodges; Melvin E., Otis M., Mary R., and Agnes.

The McDowell Family

The families of McDowells were Scotch-Irish, and were Covenanters and Presbyterians. They first emigrated from North Ireland to Pennsylvania, and from thence to North and South Carolina. Of this numerous family connection there were two brothers, Silas and Robert. Silas McDowell made settlement in North Carolina, while his brother, Robert McDowell, came further south and settled on South Pacolet, in the present county of Spartanburg, which was before the outbreak of the Revolution. He had two sons, Robert and James, and five daughters: Elizabeth, who married a Mr. Jeffries on Thickety Creek in Union county, S.C.; Sarah, who married Robert Love on Broad River, in the same county; Nancy, who married a Harper and moved to Tennessee; Jane, who married Captain Hugh McMillen; and Mary, who married John Clark, father of Oliver, David, Benjamin, Robert, Foster, James and Mrs. Polly Kelso, wife of Henry Kelso.

Robert McDowell, the eldest, who was a soldier in the Continental Line, served to the end of the war, and was at the surrender of Cornwallis at Yorktown. His father, the elder Robert, was too old to take up arms when the Revolution began.

James McDowell, the other brother, served with the partisans, the Whig soldiers, during the Revolution, under the command of Captain Barry, who joined Morgan's army the day before that battle and participated in that battle. He married a Miss McMillen, and had nine children — eight boys and one girl: David, Robert, James, Andrew, Hugh, William F., John Y., Calvin and Jane. David married a daughter of Wm. Chapman; Robert married a Miss Williams; James married a Miss Ferguson of York County; Andrew married Miss Harriet Liles of Polk County, N.C.; Hugh married a daughter of Wm. Chapman; Wm. F. married a Miss Ramsey; John Y. married Miss Polly Ramsey (sister); and Calvin married a Miss Ballenger.

William Chapman, the father-in-law of David and Hugh McDowell, was one of the first settlers on the Pacolets. His wife was a Miss Jones; they emigrated from Virginia, and had fifteen children — twelve girls and three boys. The names of the boys were John (called Jackey), William and James.

Four of Wm. Chapman's daughters married to Copelands, two to McDowells (David and Hugh, as stated), one to Lemuel C. Clements, one to Perry Clement, one to a Bullington of Tennessee, one to a Nicholls, one to Jackson Green, and one to Rice Ramsey.

David McDowell had nine children — three boys and six girls; James had eight children — two boys and six girls; Andrew had nine children — four boys and five girls; Hugh had twelve children — seven boys and five girls; William F. had nine children — six boys and three girls; John Y. had five children — one boy and four girls; and Calvin had four children — three girls and one boy.

Of the seven sons of Hugh McDowell, two died at the ages of about eleven and thirteen. The other five: James, Marcus, Martin Van Buren (called Vanney), William J. (called Dene), and Hugh J. (called Hugy), deserve special notice.

James, the eldest, a member of Co. I, 5th Regiment, S.C.V., was wounded at the battle of Frazier's Farm, in 1862, and died of same at Richmond a short time afterwards.

Marcus, second lieutenant of same company, died in his tent near Richmond, Va., in 1863, of disease contracted in camps.

Martin Van Buren was killed at the battle of Seven Pines in 1862.

Wm. J., now residing on South Pacolet, was also second lieutenant in Co. I, 5th S.C. Regiment, and was wounded in the arm by the explosion of a shell at Sharpsburg, which necessitated amputation. He still lives within a few miles of his father's old homestead place, and is well known in his section as an honest, intelligent and progressive farmer. For quite a number of years since the war he has filled the office of trial justice. He is a member of the Baptist Church, and as a citizen is highly esteemed by all.

Hugh A. McDowell volunteered in the Confederate service at the outset in 1861, and was the only one of the brothers referred to that escaped unhurt.

William F. McDowell (known as fifer Billy) had three sons, James, Rice and John, to volunteer in the Confederate army at the very beginning of the struggle. Rice, a member of the 5th S.C. Regiment, died of fever in the camps at Germantown, Va., in 1861. He was buried nearby in the honors of war, which the writer witnessed, being a member of the same company and regiment at the time.

It may be truly said of the entire McDowell connection on the Pacolets, that they are, and have always been, an honest, industrious, and law-abiding class of citizens, never aspiring for public office, but always ready to defend their State when called upon.

Of the older brothers mentioned, William McDowell was a deacon of New Prospect (Baptist) church for many years, and Calvin McDowell was major of the second battalion 36th Regiment, S.C. militia, which office he held for several years before the outbreak of the civil war.

CAPTAIN JOSEPH H. MCDOWELL, only son of Major Calvin McDowell, was a gallant officer in the Confederate army and deserves more than a passing notice. He was born September 26th, 1839, being at this writing (1899) sixty years of age. He was brought up on his father's farm on South Pacolet River, in Spartanburg County, and was educated in the schools of the neighborhood, his last attendance being at the New Prospect Academy in 1858, taught by Rev. T. J. Earle.

At the outbreak of the civil war between the States he enlisted in the service, having previously served while in his teens as an officer in the State militia. He was a member of Captain Seay's company, 5th Regiment, S.C.V., and in August, 1861, was elected a lieutenant in the same, which position he held until the following December, when he resigned by reason of a severe illness. He rejoined his company, however, a short time before the seven days battle around Richmond, and was in all the battles in which his regiment participated. He continued to serve as a private in his company until July, '62, when he was again elected a second lieutenant.

Capt. Joseph H. McDowell

In the second battle of Manassas and in the Maryland campaign, which soon followed, including the battle of Sharpsburg, in which he was engaged, he had command of his company, the other officers being absent by reason of sickness. He performed distinguished services during the last two years of the war, being assigned to the special command of the skirmishers of the brigade (Bratton's), to which his regiment belonged. At Deep Bottom, Va., August 16th, '62, he was wounded in the arm and shoulder.

During the Tennessee campaign, in which Longstreet's corps was detached, he was wounded again, at Loudon, Tenn. He had charge of the skirmish line under the command of Lieutenant-Colonel Logan, who, although young, was a brave and chivalrous officer. Colonel Logan ordered Lieutenant McDowell to charge the Federal line, which he did, and was shot down within twenty-five yards of their rear-guard or skirmish line. He was conveyed to the hospital in Atlanta, where he remained three months. When he had sufficiently recovered, however, he rejoined his regiment in '64, and participated in the Virginia campaigns which followed. Early in '65, by reason of the resignation of Captain Choice, he was promoted to the captaincy of his company, and was at the surrender at Appomattox.

The fact has been stated to the writer that Captain McDowell discharged his duty in such a way as to meet with the highest appreciation of his supe-

rior officers, and especially with Colonel Coward, his regimental commander.

After the close of the civil war Captain McDowell married Miss Martha Dodd, by whom he raised a family. For some fifteen or twenty years he continued to reside in his native county, but subsequently removed with his family to Clifford, Texas, where he at present resides.

Chapter Thirty-One - The Wingo Family

The Wingos are very numerous. Their ancestors came either from Cumberland or Halifax counties, Va. John Wingo, a Revolutionary soldier, came to Spartanburg County just after the close of the Revolutionary War and settled about two miles east of Mount Zion Church, where John W. Wingo now lives. His wife was Polly Seay, also of Revolutionary stock, whom he married in Virginia and brought with him. He was a citizen of the highest respectability and a man of exemplary piety.

He had twelve children, as follows: Annie, who married Burnel High; Mayson (daughter), who married Moses Foster (Pacolet Moses); Polly, who married Swepson High; Exie, who married William Foster; Oney, who married a Parkerson; Elenor, who married Wm. (Billy) Moore; Hester, who married a Young on South Pacolet; Jinsey, who married a West and went to Georgia; Ransom, who married Polly Dodd; Coleman, who married Katy Bomar; Alberry, who married a Lewis; Elias, who married Jane Finch.

Ransom, one of these sons, raised ten children, as follows: James, who married Herbert Hawkins; Alexander (sheriff), who married Catharine Bivings; Oliver, who married a Chana in Alabama; Elizabeth (Betsy), who married Elias Richardson; John, who never married, and died in California; William, who died a young man while studying medicine; Thomas, who never married, and also died in California; Jane (still living), who married Simpson Wingo; Mary (Polly), who married Calvin Wingo; and Nancy, who married James A. Fowler.

William (Billy) Wingo was a first cousin of John Wingo, the ancestor of the families just mentioned. He also came to the same neighborhood in Spartanburg County after the Revolution. He was married twice, and had three children by first marriage. One of these was the first wife of Reuben Gramling. The other two were Thomas and John Wingo — the latter sometimes called *Johnnie Crust* or *Blinkey Johnnie* to distinguish him from others of the same name. Thomas removed to Missouri some time in the forties, and was married four times. His brother, John (*Crust*) Wingo, married Cintha Wood (whose mother was a Seay, sister of wife of the first mentioned, John Wingo). He was a substantial, honest, and upright citizen, and had children as follows: Hamilton, who married Caroline Hawkins; Calvin, who married Polly Wingo; Polly, who married Manning Ross and went to Texas; Simpson, who married Jane Wingo; Franklin, who married Lizzie Royston; Maiden, who never married; Wiley, who married Theresa Cunningham; Jackson, who married Margaret McMaken; Lewis Landrum, who married Mary Berry; Memory, who married Mary Pennington; and Nancy, who married Robert Reynolds. Of the eight sons mentioned, all entered the Confederate army; all served their country faithfully during its existence, and all survived to return to their homes after its close.

Zachariah Wingo, Abner Wingo, and the first John Wingo mentioned were brothers. They also came from Virginia to Spartanburg District after the close of the Revolution, Zachariah settling on Jorden's Creek waters of North Tyger, whose wife was Sallie Fosset, whom he married in Virginia before his emigration from that State. By this marriage he had eight children, as follows: Betsey, who married Patton Tinsley; Anna, who married Peter Haskins; Dolly, who married David Tinsley; Burrel, who married Delilah Foster; Zachariah, who married Jane Foster; Anderson, who married Maiden High; Wilson, who married Mary Chapman; and Paschal, who married Maiden Foster.

Abner Wingo married Elizabeth Seay, and had nine children, and among those whose names we are enabled to gather were two sons: Willis and John. The former was a Methodist minister for a great number of years and died "with the harness on" a few years since in Texas. He was the father of Mr. Thomas W. Wingo, a well-known and highly respected citizen residing at Duncans, S.C.

John Wingo, known as "Fifer John," married Margaret Thompson and had nine children, viz.: Allen, who married a Miss Brice and went to Georgia; James, who also married a Miss Brice and went to Alabama; John, who never married and died out West; Lewis, who married Miss Edwards and went to Illinois, where he died; Mahala, who married David Bettis; Polly, who married Henry Wood, and who died in Tennessee; Betsey, who was a cripple and never married, and Rebecca who married Simpson Lowe, near Fair Forest, S.C. She has recently died.

Rev. I. W. Wingo

John or "Fifer John" Wingo was born in Spartanburg County, and died about the year 1895, in the ninety-first year of his age. He was a quiet law-abiding citizen, a soldier of the war of 1812, and an exemplary member of Nazareth (Presbyterian) church, where in the cemetery his remains repose.

REV. ISHAM WOODRUFF WINGO - Among the prominent representative members of this large family connection we would mention Rev. I. W. Wingo, well known to all the people of Spartanburg County, both as an educator of her young and as a minister of the gospel. He is a son of Paschal and Maiden (Foster) Wingo, and was born in Spartanburg County, May 22d, 1850.

After attending the common schools of his neighborhood, he entered the Gowensville Seminary under Rev. T. J. Earle, where he remained three years. Afterwards he entered the Furman University at Greenville, S.C., where, after a course of three years, he was graduated. He then entered the Southern Baptist Theological Seminary while it was still located at Greenville, where he attended for several years and from which he was graduated.

His first pastoral work was at Pendleton, S.C., where he served from the latter part of 1877 to '81, serving, meanwhile, the church at Walhalla one year and also other churches in the surrounding country. He then went to Camden, S.C., and served the Baptist Church fifteen months, when he was called to the Baptist Church at Gaffney, S.C., where he remained nine years, leaving there in 1892. While at Gaffney, he served the Baptist church at Limestone Springs part of his time, and taught mathematics in the Cooper Limestone Institute located at the latter place. From Gaffney he went to Ridge Spring, S.C., where he remained three years, during which time he was engaged in pastoral and ministerial work. In 1894 he removed to Campobello, S.C., when he opened up the present High School, which ranks among the best schools of our country, and which has had much to do with the upbuilding and business prosperity in that thriving town.

Oak Knob Hotel, Mineral Spring, near Campobello, S.C.

Mr. Wingo has rendered the country valuable service in developing and bringing to the notice of the public the valuable medicinal properties of the Chalybeate Sulphur Spring of Campobello, which had been known for fifty

233

years or more to a few citizens. The constituent elements of the water from this spring, as analyzed, are carbonates and sulphates of lime, iron, soda and magnesia, a little sulphate of potash, silica, lithia, and carbonic acid gas. The spring is surrounded with a substantial brick wall and building overhead, and a handsome and well-equipped hotel has been erected nearby, all due to the indomitable energy and perseverance of Mr. Wingo. Numerous testimonials can be produced as to the value and health-giving properties of this spring, which in the future is destined to take its place as among the most popular summer resorts in the up-country of South Carolina. Mr. Wingo is rendering not only important service as an educator, but is also laboring earnestly and zealously as a minister of the gospel. He is at present pastor of Wellford, Friendship and other churches, and is doing a good work in the Master's vineyard.

In 1878 or '79 he married Miss Lula Dean, a graduate of the Spartanburg Female College. She is the only daughter of Dr. Thomas P. and Mrs. Mary (Davis) Dean. By this marriage he has had six children, viz.: Mary Dean (deceased), Anna Lula, Joseph Paschal, Ruth Earle, Isham Dean, and William Wallace.

GEORGE WASHINGTON WINGO. Among those deserving of special notice of the Wingo family connection is George Washington Wingo, son of Burrel and Delilah (Foster) Wingo, who was born July 5th, 1838,

Sergt. Geo. Washington Wingo

and died of consumptive disease, contracted in the army, February, 1870. He was raised on his father's farm and attended the schools of his neighborhood, some of which the writer also attended. He was much associated with him in his schoolboy days, and can testify to the genial and excellent traits of character with which by nature he was happily endowed.

He was a sergeant in Company C, 13th Regiment, S.C.V., commanded by Captain John W. Carlisle. In this battle-scarred company, which has left an unimpeachable record behind it, he was among the foremost as a true and valiant soldier, ready at all times to discharge every duty which confronted him. He was in quite all the battles in which his company was engaged, and never was known to shirk the post of danger or responsibility. Some months before the close of the war he was captured and imprisoned, where he was held until its close. Returning home it was found that he had contracted a consumptive disease, from which he never recovered.

Some time before or during the war he married Mary, daughter of Edward Ballenger. By this marriage two children survive, viz.: Rhoda, wife of Dr. Wm. H. Chapman, near Brannon, S.C., a prominent and influential citizen and physician in Spartanburg County; and Stewart Wingo, well known as a progressive business man, and resident of Spartanburg city.

Chapter Thirty-Two - The Turner Family

James Turner, Sr., migrated from Virginia with his father to South Carolina before the Revolution, when he was only twelve years of age. He was the only child of his mother, whose maiden name was Hannah Middleton. He had reached the age of manhood when the Revolution broke out, and was in the service of his country.

His father (whose first name we have been unable to obtain) settled on Pacolet River near Coulter's Ford, and raised by a second wife three sons and three daughters, viz.: Henry, Richard, Samuel, Phebe (Mrs. Solomon Abbott), Sallie (Mrs. Ephraim Potter), and Betty (Mrs. Wm. Garrett).

James Turner, Sr., married Margaret Heydon, and had nine children, viz.: Edward, William, Samuel, Middleton, James, Mary, Ann (Mrs. James Foster), Elizabeth and Tamer. His home was on Pacolet River, near Coulter's Ford, where his father settled. It was here during the bloody scenes of the Revolution that he crept into his log cabin one night to get a good rest, but dreamed during the night that "there was danger about." So he got up and secreted himself in a plum nursery nearby, and soon a Tory appeared with his gun, when James commenced pelting him with rocks, and ran him off through a cow-mire.

At another time he was taken prisoner by a band of Tories, who were preparing to kill him at once; but as fortune would have it, one of the Tories said, "The first man that hurts Jimmie Turner I will kill him." Turner had done this Tory a kindness heretofore, and so his life was saved.

James Turner, Sr., was a brother-in-law to *Horse Shoe* Robinson, the hero of Mr. Kenedy's famous novel of the same name, both of whom were scouts during the Revolution and a terror to the Tories,

Some time after the close of the Revolution James Turner, accompanied by his little son Samuel, visited Horse Shoe Robinson, who resided in what was then Pendleton District, S.C. It is stated that they sat up all night discussing their ups and downs, but that Mrs. Robinson made them lie down while she was preparing breakfast. James Turner, Sr., was a pious and consecrated Christian, and for many years a deacon of Buck Creek (Baptist) Church.

Samuel Turner, son of James Turner, Sr., to whom we have referred, was a popular, well-to-do and highly respected citizen, whose homestead (near Mount Zion Church) embraced the historic site of old Fort Prince. Here he spent the greater portion of his life. The writer lived near him till he grew to manhood, and was much associated with him. He was a good and intelligent citizen, an obliging neighbor, kind in disposition, scrupulously neat in person, and in deportment as polite as a Frenchman. He married Mahala, daughter of John Chapman, Sr., and had eleven children, as follows:

(1) Lenora, married William Rush first, and second John D. Cannon; (2) Adolphus and (3) Ann, both dying young; (4) Augustus John, a distinguished professor of music. Was for many years connected with the State institution,

Deaf, Dumb and Blind, Staunton, Va. Was captain and instructor of the famous Stonewall band, which ranked among the first in the Confederate army. (5) Memory Horatio, who migrated to Georgia and married Addie Parsons in that State; (6) Randolph, an intelligent, industrious and progressive citizen and farmer, who married Eleanor, eldest daughter of Paschal Wingo, both now deceased; (7) George Washington, well known to the people of Spartanburg County as an upright and patriotic citizen and Christian gentleman, fully alive to every enterprise looking to the upbuilding of his country, devoting much of his time to the garden, orchard, and vineyard, who married Maiden Wood, daughter of Richard Moss, both living and being in good health, this (1900) being the fiftieth anniversary year of their marriage; (8) Abigail, who married John Landrum, eldest son of Paschal Wingo, and removed to Texas; (9) Abner Benson, who migrated to Texas, and married Elizabeth, daughter of Thomas Ballenger; (10) Claudius Calhoun, an intelligent and highly respected citizen, well known in his native county, who married Nancy Catharine (now deceased), daughter of John Chapman, Jr., Esq. He was engaged in journalism before the outbreak of the civil war, and at the beginning of the same enlisted in Company F, 5th Regiment, S.C.V., and upon the reorganization of said company in 1862 was elected a lieutenant in Company I (Captain W. D. Camp), which position he held until the end of the war. Was, upon the reorganization of the State militia, after close of war, elected major. Was a representative in the State Legislature from 1868 to 1870, and was a trial justice for a number of years. He is now a resident of Spartanburg city, being engaged in the real estate business. (11) Cassius Lewis (youngest child of Samuel Turner), died in childhood.

The High Family

Among the early families that settled in the vicinity of old Fort Prince immediately after the close of the Revolution were the Highs, Wingos, Chapmans, Bomars,. Woods, Pollards, Bushes and others. These families all emigrated from Virginia. They and their ancestors belonged to that class, before the Revolution in Virginia, known as *Dissenters* from the Established Church of England. Coming from the "Old Dominion," they were thoroughly indoctrinated into the ideas of Thomas Jefferson, that the government of the United States was a government "of the people, for the people, and by the people." Being opposed to the Established Church, they were all *Baptists* in principle, and were among the founders of old Mount Zion Church, organized in 1810. The government of the Baptist Church being advisory only, one church organization being entirely independent of another, these good people, in embracing the principles of this faith, still held to the ideas of Jefferson, that the government of the Baptist churches was "a government of the Baptists, for the Baptists, and by the Baptists." They were opposed to any form of *centralized* government, either civil or religious.

The oldest ancestor among the High family that we can learn of was William High, who was the father of five children, viz.: Burnel, Swepson, Paschal Benjamin, David, and Elizabeth C. (called Betsy). Of these Paschal Benjamin and David removed to the great West, and have left a numerous posterity behind them; Betsey married Reuben Gramling, an industrious and progressive farmer, blacksmith and wood-workman, who settled on South Pacolet. and who, as a citizen, occupied a position of the highest respectability. He had two sons, the late Henry H. Gramling of Gramling Station, on the Asheville and Spartanburg Railroad, and David Gramling in the neighborhood of Macedonia church, Spartanburg County. Both of these brothers were well known to the people of Spartanburg County, and they left behind them a posterity of the highest respectability. Elizabeth C. married Rev. Thomas Bomar, who is noticed in connection with the Bomar family in this volume.

The children of Burnel High were William Giles, James Madison, Polly, Rebecca, Maiden, Madora, Francis, and Hester. Of these Polly married to Thomas Roe, who removed to Texas, Rebecca to Jennings, Maiden to Anderson Wingo, Madora to Captain Wm. Caldwell, Frances to Henry Turner, and Hester to Turner Cantrel. Of these William Giles High was most intimately known to the writer, who will always cherish a pleasant recollection of his memory. He married first Mrs. Thursy Oliver, who at the time of her death (1860) had been a member of Mount Zion church for near twenty years, and was in all respects a lady and true Christian. For his second wife he married Miss Francis Benson, daughter of Silas Benson, who still survives him, and who is a lady of domestic refinement, occupying a position of the highest respectability in the neighborhood in which she lives.

Wm. G. High was a typical representative of that old Virginia type of hospitality which he by nature inherited. He was an honest and industrious and well-to-do farmer and a magnificent entertainer at home. He was a good provider, and nothing afforded him so much pleasure as to have his friends around him, and especially the pastor of his church, [1] to whom he was devoted.

The children of Swepson High were Thomas P., married to Sarah Ann Caldwell; Benjamin, married first to Margaret Caldwell, and second to Amanda Brice; James Van Buren, married to Malinda Wingo, daughter of Burrel Wingo; Franklin, never married; Mary, married John Strange.

Of the children of Madison High, brother of William G., there are numerous descendants in the county, which have every reason to be proud of a respectable ancestry, who have always been faithful to every principle of duty and right as law-abiding citizens.

The sons mentioned of Swepson High are: Thomas Benjamin, Van Buren and Franklin, who were all brave soldiers in the civil war between the States, true in every sense of the word to the cause which they espoused, being among the last to yield, and have always sustained an enviable reputation as peaceable, honest and patriotic citizens of Spartanburg County.

Chapman Family

Among the early settlers in Spartanburg County was John Chapman, Sr., who settled on the waters of North Tyger about one-half mile west of the historic Fort Prince. He was born in Amelia County, Va., from which State he migrated to South Carolina. He is still remembered by many who yet survive the period of the latter years of his life, among whom is the writer, who can testify to his excellent character as a citizen. He was industrious and progressive as a farmer, kind and gentle in his manners, and a devout member and deacon of the Baptist Church. Living near Mount Zion (Baptist) Church, of which he was numbered among its founders, he donated the land on which said church is located, in all about ten acres.

He was twice married. His first wife was a Miss Dodson, by which marriage he had two children, viz.: Edmond, who married a Miss Wood, daughter of John Wood (sister of Captain Coleman Wood); and Elizabeth (Betsey), who married Moses Richardson. He married a second time to Mary (Polly) Seay, sister to Mrs. John Wingo, Mrs. John Wood, and Mrs. Wm. Pollard, by which marriage he had children as follows:

1st. Beverly Randolph Chapman, who married Sallie Foster, and had thirteen children, viz.: Wm. Pinckney, John Calvin, Garland (died in the army), Memory N., Dr. Oliver Goldsmith, Virgil Randolph Jackson, Granville Washington, Mary (Mrs. Wilson Wingo), Emily (Mrs. General A. C. Bomar), Jane (Mrs. Andrew Holtzonser), Louisa (Mrs. Clough H. Mabry), Ann (Mrs. Henry H. Turner), and Bettie (Mrs. Miles Floyd).

2d. John Chapman, Jr., Esq., married Rose R. Montgomery, and had children as follows: Warren Davis, died of wounds received during the war. He volunteered at the beginning of the war between the States, and was commissioned a lieutenant. He was a surveyor by occupation, and was possessed of brilliant literary talents. He was cut off in the prime of his manhood. Marcus Brutus, a gentleman, Christian, patriot and soldier, whose health was broken down in the service of his country. John Newton, Chevis Montgomery (residing in California), Margaret Ann (Mrs. John Wood, Texas), Memory Petigrew (died in childhood), Nancy Catherine (deceased, Mrs. C. C. Turner), Octavia Olivia, single, and Perry Earle, who resides at the old homestead place of his father (near Mount Zion), and who is well known as an industrious, honest, upright and progressive citizen. He married Miss Mattie, daughter of Randolph Turner, Esq. John Chapman, Jr., Esq., was a man who commanded the respect and esteem of the people of Spartanburg District. He was for many years a magistrate, and administered the law with firmness and impartiality. He was a progressive business man, and for many years a deacon in the Baptist Church.

3d. Mahala Johnson Chapman, married Samuel Turner. (See Turner family.)

4th. Memory Noble Chapman, a prominent and influential citizen in his day, and a member of the State legislature for a number of years.

5th. Mary (Polly), married Fortunatus Legg, Esq.

6th. Ann, married Mathew Evans.

7th. Lorenzo Dow, who never married, was a man of the strictest honor, integrity, truthfulness and Christian character.

Richardson Family

Moses Richardson migrated from Virginia to Spartanburg District, South Carolina, about the year 1820. He married Elizabeth (Betsey), daughter of John Chapman, Sr., and settled on the old Blackstock road on the plantation now owned by Mr. Henry Wingo. He was an honest and industrious farmer. He and his wife were exemplary members of the Baptist church at Mount Zion.

By his marriage with Elizabeth Chapman he had children as follows: John, who married Harriet Copeland; Mathew, who married Fannie Ramsey; Pinckney, who married Emily, daughter of Garland Foster; Elias, who married Elizabeth, daughter of Ransom Wingo; and Oliver Perry, who married Hester, daughter of Paschal Wingo.

These sons were all moral, intelligent, upright and highly respected citizens, standing well before the people. Under the head of our review of the progress of education in Spartanburg County during the nineteenth century, we have noticed O. P. Richardson as a popular school-teacher in his day. After his marriage with Miss Wingo he removed to Hunt County, Texas, where he died.

Among his children surviving is one son, Willis Preston Richardson, who has risen to considerable prominence. He competed successfully for a vacancy at West Point, where he graduated after a four-years course, standing near the head of his class. Since that time he has remained in the United States army, except four years, during which time he was appointed tutor at West Point. He is now captain of a company in the Klondike doing valiant service for the government.

Elias and Elizabeth (Wingo) Richardson had children as follows: Wm. Henry Harrison, married Miss Anna O. Wingo, daughter of Paschal Wingo; Thomas Wilds, married Miss Hallie E. White, daughter of William White; Benjamin Franklin, died in the army during the war; Louisa Josephine, married Samuel W. Keller, both deceased; Emily Elizabeth, married Henry Wingo; Mary, married James R. Snoddy. Wm. H. H. Richardson, the only surviving son of above mentioned sons, is a resident of Gaffney, S.C., and is one of the enterprising and influential citizens of that city.

THOMAS WILDS RICHARDSON, second son of Elias and Elizabeth Richardson, to whom we have already referred, was born near Campton, S.C., March 3d, 1843. He was raised on his father's farm, and attended the schools of his neighborhood.

Soon after the outbreak of the civil war between the States he volunteered in Co. D, Palmetto Sharpshooters, commanded by Captain A. H. Foster, and was wounded at the battle of Seven Pines. Recovering from the same he continued in the service of his country, participating in all the battles in which his regiment was engaged until near the close of the war, when he was captured near Petersburg. He was imprisoned at Point Lookout, where he was kept until July some four months, after the war had ended.

Returning home after his release from imprisonment he adapted himself to the new conditions which surrounded him. The time had arrived when almost every young man in the country had to set himself to work to make an honest living for himself, and to this end Thomas W. Richardson proved himself equal to the emergency. He united in marriage with Miss Hattie White, and proved himself to be one of the most progressive and industrious farmers in the community in which he lived. He kept himself well posted on the current events of the day and was especially

Thos. W. Richardson

fond of literature devoted to progressive agriculture. He was an intelligent thinker, always entertaining advanced ideas. So much so, that he was sometimes considered eccentric, but no one stood higher in the estimation of his fellow citizens as an honest and upright citizen. He never sought office promotion, but in times of peace as well as in war, he proved himself to be a man of the sternest patriotism and integrity, leaving a character behind him well worthy of imitation. He had for many years been a member of the Baptist Church. He died in 1898. By his marriage with Miss White, who survives him, he had one child. Alma Estelle, wife of Dr. J. R. Gibson, who resides at Inman, S.C.

[1] The late Rev. John G. Landrum, who occupied the pastorate of Mount Zion, with an interval, for thirty-six years, beginning with the year 1832.

Chapter Thirty-Three - The Collins Family

Descendants of Thomas Collins Sr.

Among the early settlers on the Tygers was Thomas Collins, Sr., who emigrated from York, England, to York, Pennsylvania, and from thence to the territory embraced in the present county of Spartanburg, and took up a large survey near Nazareth church on Tyger River, covering lands where W. Ellis Collins now lives. He married before he left England. He had four sons and two daughters, viz.: John, Richard, Joseph, William, Jane (Mrs. William Austin) [1], and Nancy. (Mrs. Alexander Thomson).

The eldest son John was probably born before he left England. He had grown up to manhood when the Revolutionary war broke out, and rose to the rank of captain in that war, and was distinguished for his gallantry. He participated in nearly all the battles fought in South Carolina, and was in the battle of Cowpens January 17, 1781. [2] He married Miss Elizabeth Brown, of Newberry, S.C. Their children were Mrs. Sallie Swansey, Thomas B. Collins (father of wife of Rev. A. A. James), John S. Collins, who was known as "Bachelor Jack," and who was put to death by some unknown party; Alexander Collins, who died when sixteen years of age; and Mrs. Martha Westmoreland, wife of Sterling Westmoreland. Richard and William Collins, second and third sons, went to Kentucky after the Revolution before it was admitted as a State. Some of their descendants are quite prominent there.

Joseph Collins, the fourth son, was born before the Revolution, but was not old enough at its outbreak to enter the army. He was, however, a true patriot and a citizen of the highest respectability. He married Elizabeth Fleming, by whom he had nine children as follows: Mary W., who married Samuel Kelso; Martha (Patsey), married Samuel Jackson; Thomas (father of James A. Collins, Boiling Springs, S.C.), married Mariah Foster; Ann Fleming, married Mathew T, Hudson of Greenville district, S.C.; Rebecca Wells, married Westley Gilreath; Andrew Fleming, married Amanda L. Anderson; William Austin, married Margaret P. Jackson, daughter of Foster Jackson on North Pacolet; Joseph Alexander, married Nancy Conner of Georgia; and Nancy Thompson, married Colonel Gabriel Cannon (first wife).

The Thompson Family

is among the oldest of the early settlers in upper Carolina. It is said that this family, being Scotch-Irish, first made settlement in Pennsylvania, coming to South Carolina before the outbreak of the Revolution. The ancestor of this branch of the family is traced back to Joseph Thompson. He made settlement in the forks of the T3-gers (near Wellford, S.C.), known as the old Thompson place on the old Cowpens furnace road, leading from the latter place to Greenville, S.C. He had two sons, Alexander and John. Alexander, born 1768, after the death of his father, continued to reside at the old homestead place of his father. His wife was Nancy, the daughter of Thomas Collins, and sister of Captain John Collins, a Revolutionary soldier. Alexander Thompson died at the age of seventy-five. His wife, born same year (1768), lived to the age of ninety-one years, and could recite many events of the Revolution.

Alexander and Nancy Thompson had three sons and three daughters: 1. Joseph Thompson, who married Margaret Snoddy, daughter of Isaac Snoddy. They had two children, Mrs. Nancy Jane Jackson of Wellford, S.C., relict of Captain Robert Jackson (mother of Mrs. Wm, S. Morrison and Joseph Jackson), and Crawford S. Thompson, a highly respected citizen of Haywood County, N.C., who married Miss Lizzie, eldest daughter of Samuel Morgan of

Spartanburg district.

2. John Thompson, married a Miss Hamilton of old Pendleton; no children.

3. Madison Lewis Thompson, married a daughter of Captain John Snoddy, who lived only six months. He died a few years afterward at Macon, Ga.

4. Rosa Thompson, who married John Thompson, her cousin. The latter dying soon afterward without issue, she married to Wm. G. Smith (called "Mutton Ham Billy" to distinguish him from others of the same name). They left two daughters: Mary, who married Dr. Lee Smith, and Fannie, who died single.

5. Jane Thompson, who married Elias Fleming; no children.

John Thompson, the other son of Joseph and brother of Alexander (commonly called Aleck), settled in Fairview Township, Greenville county, S.C., and had three sons: 1. Alexander Thompson, who married first an Alexander and raised a large family, and second to a Pedan, and raised several more children.

2. Dr. Joseph Thompson, who practiced medicine in Greenville County for a while, and then removed to a country cross-roads town in Georgia, then called Marthasville, but which afterwards became the great city of Atlanta. He was one of the prime movers of the Kimball House. He has two daughters in Atlanta, viz.: Mrs. Richard Peters and Mrs. Black.

3. John Thompson, already referred to as marrying Rosa, the daughter of his uncle Alexander Thompson.

The Thompsons belonged to an honest, hardy class of pioneer yeomanry in the early settlement of the territory now embraced in the present county of Spartanburg.

Mr. Crawford S. Thompson, Haywood county, N.C., now the only one left to perpetuate this family name, writes: "Joseph Thompson, my great-grandfather, was a blacksmith; Alexander Thompson, my grandfather, was a blacksmith, and Joseph Thompson, my father, was a blacksmith — all celebrated for their horse-shoeing. My great-grandfather brought his anvil from the old country with him. My father had it when he died. I suppose it could be seen yet. Had two horns to it. The sign of the old blacksmith shop can be seen yet at the old Thompson place, in the fork of the road, near the two creeks."

The White Family

Daniel White lived on South Pacolet. He was a revolutionary soldier and a citizen of good standing in the community in which he lived. His oldest son, Berry White, married a Miss Booker of Spartanburg and emigrated to Georgia, and represented his county in the legislature of that State for several years. He was a gallant captain in the Confederate army.

Henry White, Esq., another son of Daniel White, married Margaret, daughter of Major John Graves McClure, and had eight children, viz.: One daughter, who married Robert McMillen; Elvira, who married Will. Chapman, father of

B. B. Chapman; Francis M., who married Rebecca Copeland, sister of Captain Alex. Copeland, and removed to Idaho; Jane, who married Wm. Finger; John, who married Mary Younger; Major Henry, who married Margaret Finger; Pinckney, who married Miss Martha Robbs, and removed to Georgia; and Peggy, who married John Younger and removed West.

The McMillen Family

Captain Hugh McMillen was the father of the brothers, Robert, David and Love McMillen on North Pacolet, who resided in the vicinity of Fingerville, S.C. He was also the father of two daughters: Elizabeth ___ and Mary Ann.

Robert McMillen married Susan Bomar, daughter of Armstead Bomar, who removed to Campbell County, Ga. Love McMillen married a Miss Hannon, and David McMillen married Jane Clement, a granddaughter of the elder James McDowell.

Of the daughters mentioned, Elizabeth married William McClure, son of Major John Graves McClure, a soldier of the Revolution. The son William referred to removed to Campbell County, Ga., and was one of the pioneer settlers of that county immediately after the removal of the Cherokee Indians, which was about the year 1836. He was a prominent and influential citizen of that county, and left behind him a respectable posterity. One of his daughters, Jane, married Judge Reuben Beavers, who was ordinary of Campbell County for forty years, and another daughter married James G. Sturdivant, who was judge of the inferior court for Chattooga County, Ga., for a number of years. All of the family were prominent in official positions and other pursuits. His grandson, John C. Camp, represented Campbell County in the legislature of Georgia for a number of years.

The second daughter of Captain Hugh McMillen married Charles McClure, father of David, Rudisail, Marion, John, Jackson, Madison, and wives of Captain John Camp of Georgia, Crawford and Frank Alverson.

The youngest daughter, Mary Ann, of Captain Hugh McMillen married Philip C. Rudisail, who removed from Spartanburg district to Georgia a few years before the outbreak of the civil war. He had five children, among whom was Dr. R. Y. Rudisail who deserves more than passing notice.

Dr. Robert Young Rudisail was born and reared on his father's farm on North Pacolet, near Fingerville, S.C. The date of his birth is August 8th, 1832. He went to school to the Golightlys, William and Patillo, was a diligent student, and under the rigid system and training (to use his own words) of these teachers he acquired a good English and classical education. He read medicine with Dr. W. P. Compton, and after two courses in the South Carolina Medical College graduated in 1855, and soon after removed to Georgia, settling at Summerville, in Chattooga county, where he at once entered into the practice of his profession.

At the outbreak of the civil war he volunteered in the Confederate army and was commissioned as a surgeon. Served as such to the end of the war, and was at the surrender of General Johnson at Greensboro, N.C. He was elected to the State legislature from his county in 1874 and served two years. Was reelected to the same body in 1895, and in the reelections that followed, has served to the present year (1900).

He married soon after his removal to Georgia to Miss Eliza E. Knox, who is now dead, but who was a graduate of the Synodical Female College, Talladega County. Ala. His only daughter, Madora E., is the present wife of Judge Wm. M. Henry of the Rome judicial circuit. His eldest son, Charles C. L. Rudisail, is a physician of prominence in Georgia. He married Miss Eliza Rowland, granddaughter of John S. Rowland, formerly a citizen of Spartanburg district.

Dr. R. Y. Rudisail is a prominent member of the Presbyterian Church and a Royal Arch Mason.

The families of McMillen on the Pacolets and in Spartanburg County have always maintained positions of the highest respectability, and should take a pride in preserving the memories of a worthy ancestry.

The Lanford Family

The ancestor of the Lanford family in Spartanburg County was James Lanford, who was a native of Virginia and a soldier of the Revolution. He enlisted first in the continental ranks and afterwards in the navy. His wife was a Miss Lowery, who died before the close of the Revolution. Immediately after the Revolutionary war he settled in North Carolina, but subsequently removed to the present county of Spartanburg and settled on Jammie's Creek, near Cavin's Old Field. He leased lands and erected a mill on said creek. After his lease was out he removed to Two Mile Creek, near Antioch church, where he erected a cotton-gin and lived the remainder of his life. He was buried on his premises nearby. With his bounty money, which he obtained from the government, he bought all the lands now owned by the Leonards, near Sharon (Methodist) church. He had three sons: John, William and Lewis. John was born on the day of Gates's defeat at Camden, S.C. (August 16th, 1780) — a tradition that has come down through the family. William Lanford married Jane Leatherwood and had eleven children, viz.: Lowery, who married Permelia Dean; Zachary, who married Zillie Posey; James, who married Rachel Page; William, who moved to Alabama, married Betsey Hobby, first wife, and Jane Leatherwood, second wife; Roddy, who married Rebecca Calvert; David, who married Catharine Lee in Alabama; Elias, who married Jane Hobby; Frances, who married James Leatherwood; Priscilla, who married Danial Page; Mary, who married Martin Parsins; and Jane, who married Pattillo Hanna.

Lewis Lanford married to a lady unknown to the writer and raised a respectable family.

The entire Lanford family connection, which the writer has been unable to gather in full, have always maintained positions of the highest respectability. They are specially noted for their piety, uprightness and honesty, and have always been true to their country's interest, both in times of peace and in war.

The Drummond Family

The ancestor of the Drummond families in Spartanburg County was Ephrim Drummond, who married Polly Johnson. Both removed from Virginia to South Carolina in 1789, he from Lunenburg and she from another burg only a few miles away, and settled in the vicinity of the present town of Woodruff, S.C. Both he and his wife were of Scotch-Irish descent. The wife was a relative of General Joseph E. Johnston, who was also a native of Virginia. Ephrim Drummond, coming from a family that was full of pluck and energy, made his start in business by raising tobacco and rolling it to Charleston in hogsheads. He was successful in raising corn, and his place was often called Egypt.

He served for a time in the Revolutionary war when only fifteen or sixteen years of age. He had twelve children, as follows: Jared, who married Sweeney Parks; Warren, who married first Margaret Snoddy, second Nancy Howell, and third Julia Hammond; Ephrim, who married first Nancy Cox, and second Katy Castleberry; Simpson, who married Malinda Brewton; Freeman, who married first Nancy Clifton, and second a Miss Barton, daughter of Rev. Jesse Barton; Harrison, who married Rebecca Martin; daughters — Mabel, who married Isaac Wofford; Betsey, who married John Wofford; Rebecca, who married Matthew Allen; Delilah, who married Simeon Brewton; Polly, who married Jesse Wofford; and Martha, who married Franklin Martin of Laurens county.

Jared Drummond had thirteen children, as follows: Adaline, who married James Brandenburg of Orangeburg, S.C.; Mary, who married John Miller and removed to Mississippi; Nancy, who married John Switzer; Lucinda, who married Wm. Chamblin; Elvira, who married A. W. Parks; Jane, who married Wm. Parks; Ella, who married first to Samuel Wyatt Miller and moved to Texas, and afterwards married his brother Charles Miller; Martha, who married Albert Deal; Emma, who married E. H. Bobo, Esq.; Corrie, who married Geo. W. Lester; Lizzie, who married a Mr. Austin; William L., who was drowned at school when seventeen or eighteen years old; and James, who married first, Lizzie Allen, and second Drucilla, daughter of Major Melmouth Young of Laurens county, S.C.

Rev. Warren Drummond had six children, as follows: Major Samuel N., who married Ann Snoddy; Harvey, who married Mary M. Switzer; Warren, who was killed during the civil war, and Alexander, who never married. By second wife. Pierce Howell, who married Nora Arnold. By third wife, Susan, who married B. M. Parsons.

Ephrim Drummond had eight children, as follows: Hosea, who married Elizabeth Castleberry; Freeman, who married Elizabeth Trammell; and

Rowland, who married Polly Phillips. By second marriage, Barham, who married first Josephine Darby, and second Nancy Poole of Laurens county, S.C.; Mabel, who married first George Reeful, and second W. P. Bragg; Polly Ann, who married first Jesse Cole, and second C. C. Waddel; Nevina, who married Hugh Workman; and Elvira, who married J. N. Brown.

Rev. Simpson Drummond had seven children, as follows: Dr. Madison Wiley, who married first Sallie Allen, and second Annie Gertrude Shell; Mahala Catharine, who married J. B. Gray; Fannie, who married James Woodruff; Jane, who married S. V. Brockman; Cebern Simpson, who married Margaret Alexander; Ira L., who married Lucy M. Parks; and Mary Adaline, who married L. C. Wofford.

Among the sons mentioned there were two who were noted as ministers of the Gospel, viz.: Warren and Simpson. Rev. Warren Drummond is still remembered by the older citizens of Spartanburg County as a zealous, earnest expounder of the Word, and served for a time Bethel and other churches as pastor. "He was an independent thinker and preacher, formed his own conclusions, and preached independently what he believed to be the truth. He was successful as a revival preacher, warming up very often to a height of impassioned eloquence that would captivate and sway a crowd as some mighty influence."

Rev. Simpson Drummond was an acceptable minister of the gospel. He was a man of the deepest humility and wielded an influence over the churches which he ably served the best years of his long life. He was modest and retiring, but delighted to hold up the banner of the cross and enlist souls to Jesus. He, like his elder brother Warren, died at a good old age in the full triumph of the Christian faith.

Jared, Ephraim and Harrison Drummond were well known as progressive farmers and citizens of the highest respectability in Spartanburg district, and a respectable and intelligent posterity follows them.

Dr. Madison W. Drummond, son of Rev. Simpson Drummond, is now the oldest surviving member of the Drummond family in Spartanburg County. He was born January 19th, 1834, and has always resided at Woodruff, or in that immediate vicinity. Receiving a good education he read and graduated in medicine a few years before the beginning of the war between the States, and at the outbreak of said war he enlisted as a private, but men of his chosen profession being in demand, he was commissioned as a surgeon in the Confederate army, which position he held until the end of the war, discharging his duty towards all who come under his care and treatment with faithfulness and fidelity to the "Lost Cause." Since the war he has more or less been in constant practice of his profession. He is a useful member of Bethel (Baptist) church, and an honest, upright citizen.

By his marriage with Miss Sallie Allen he had four children: Minnie and Mittie, twins; Minnie married W. W. Walker, Glendale; Mittie married J. E. Ward, Chattanooga, Tenn.; Edwin, who lives in Alabama; and Sarah, who married J. M. Sharp. By his second marriage with Miss Annie G. Shell he has six children, all minors, viz.: Henry Simpson, Charles Manly, James Boyce, Willie Laurens, John Broaddus, and Florence Tulula.

The Drummond family, as a whole, have always been true and loyal to their country, both in times of peace and war, and among those who lost their lives in defence of their country during the civil war we would mention Warren S., son of Rev. Warren Drummond; J. Freeman, son of Ephraim Drummond, and Rowland Drummond; the two first named were killed in battle, and the last named died of disease in the army the first year of the war.

The Westmoreland Family

The tradition which has been handed down in the Westmoreland family is that three brothers of this name came from England to America between 1740 and 1750. Their names were John, Robert and Thomas. John settled in Pennsylvania, Robert in Virginia, and Thomas on Enoree River, in the neighborhood of Van-Patton's Shoals. All of these settlements were made before the Revolution. Thomas took his hatchet and marked out six hundred acres of land and obtained a grant from King George for the same, which is still retained in the family. His death was caused by the bite of a rattlesnake. He had two sons, Thomas and John.

Thomas was a soldier in the Revolutionary War, and when it ended he was twenty years of age. John was too young for the war.

Thomas Westmoreland had nine children, viz.: John, Thomas, Robert, Andrew, Jesse, Dennis, Sallie, Betsey and Polly.

John, the eldest son, married Dice Johnson, and had several children, two of whom, Jesse and Sanford, reside in Spartanburg County.

Robert, another brother, had one son, O. P. Westmoreland, who married Mollie Fowler, and lived on the original grant of land.

Andrew Westmoreland married Temperance Johnson. One of his sons, James R. Westmoreland, Esq., married Rebecca E. Peydon and lived with her fifty-three years, and had eight children: John A., who married Maggie Rush; James White, who married Juan Leonard; Thomas, who died; Nice Tempie, who married J. W. Martin; Margaret, who married Professor F. B. Woodruff; Mary Jane, who married Hon, H. H. Arnold; Lolee, who married J. Warren Snoddy; and Wm. W. B., who married Minnie Woodruff.

John A. and Maggie (Rush) Westmoreland have five children, viz.: James Ripley, Fred Stroble, Nannie Peydon, Goldie Lullen and Bettie Bob.

The families of Westmoreland, both in the counties of Greenville and Spartanburg, have always maintained a high standard of citizenship. They have been specially noted for intelligence, uprightness and honesty, and have always been true to the best interests of their country, both in times of peace and in war.

The Archer Family

The name "Archer" is English. It is stated that three brothers emigrated from England to America before the war of 1776. One was killed at the battle of Brandy wine. After the war, one settled in Virginia, and one in North Carolina, near the foothills of the Blue Ridge. From the latter descended William Archer, who was born near Try on Mountain. He was a consistent member of the Baptist Church, and a saddler by trade, as was also his father. He moved to Spartanburg about 1835. Was a member of the first temperance society organized in the place. After a few years he removed to "the new purchase" of Indian land in Georgia in 1840; reared nine children to mature age, all of whom remained in Georgia except one son, John Bankston Archer, who was born on South Pacolet at the old homestead, April 19th, 1822. His educational advantages were limited, having attended only one session of a nine months school. Learning the saddler's trade, he, at the age of nineteen, returned to Spartanburg from Georgia and hired to work at his trade with David W. Moore, for one year at sixty dollars and board. At the end of one year (having performed extra work enough to buy his clothes) Mr. Moore paid him the promised sixty dollars. His being a churchman and clerk thereof, gave all' his children a hymn-book. The first meeting day thereafter John swapped his book for a hat.

With only seventy-five dollars in his pocket he married Rachel Thomas of New Jersey, a lady of intelligence and exemplary piety. By this marriage the following children were born: Leonidas Archer, living in Arkansas; Mrs. Florence Mulligan, wife of A. B. Mulligan John C. Archer of Spartanburg; E. L. Archer, whom we will further notice; and Mrs. Julia Switzer, wife of James N. Switzer.

John B. Archer is still remembered by the people of Spartanburg as a man of decided force of character, industry, perseverance and strict integrity. He possessed a clear judgment of men and business measures. He was clean in life and language, and a total abstainer from alcoholic drinks.

He died suddenly at the place of his birth, December 4th, 1893, in the seventy-second year of his age, and is buried at Spartanburg, Having felt the disadvantages of lack of education, he spent freely of his money to benefit his children therewith. His son, Hon. Edgar L. Archer, is well known to the people of Spartanburg County, being at present State senator from said county. He was born in 1852 in the town of Spartanburg. He graduated in 1871, and taught school for a few years. In 1875 he joined the South Carolina Conference and did regular work for a few years, but owing to failing health he was compelled to give up circuit preaching. At present he is engaged in farming about three miles from the city of Spartanburg. He has served in the House of Representatives, and in 1895 he was elected State senator to fill out the unexpired term of Hon. Stanyearne Wilson, the latter elected to Congress, and was elected again (1896) to serve four years longer. He is an ardent advocate of the temperance cause, and as a public officer an advocate of economy in all the departments of county and State. He married Miss Sleigh of Oconee County, S.C., a lady of intelligence and refinement.

Tribute to the Memory of Colonel B. B. Foster by His Daughter, Mrs. Ben Kennedy

General Barham Bobo Foster, the son of Anthony Foster and Elizabeth Bobo, was born in Spartanburg County, at the "Cross Roads," February 22d, 1817. When quite a boy he took an active part in politics, being an ardent nullifier. He was elected captain of a company before he was eighteen years of age. In his twentieth year he married Mary Ann Perrin, daughter of Samuel Perrin and Eunice Chiles. His marriage, he was wont to say, was his salvation. Full of vim and spirit, he would have been wild, but his accomplished Christian wife was the guiding-star whose steady brilliance pointed him ever heavenward. Happy for him that he was wise to follow her gentle guidance. His lifelong friend, Rev. J. G. Landrum, often said that Colonel Foster's wife made a man of him. After his marriage he lived for several years near Cedar Springs. Thence he moved near Glenn Springs, where he resided until after the war. His home was ever noted for cordial hospitality, and was a favorite resort for the young. He was a wide-awake successful farmer. I remember he

Lt. Col. B. B. Foster

used the first guano ever seen in his community. His nearest neighbor and true friend used to chaff him for subsoiling, telling him that "God knew which side of the ground to put on top." His neighbors honored him with every office he ever sought. He was a magistrate for years, and he held every office in the State militia from a captaincy to a major-generalship. In my childish eyes there was no grander sight than my father mounted on his parade horse "Dinah," dressed in his brigadier-general's uniform, drilling his men. I do not remember when he was not a legislator. I do remember when he ceased to be one; when his high sense of Southern honor would not allow him to swallow the iron-clad oath of office, for truly he had "aided and abetted the rebellion" with all his strength and resources.

In his youth he studied medicine under Dr. Young in Spartanburg. This was his chosen profession, but when his father's health failed he went home and took charge of the farm without a murmur. As long as he lived people sent for him far and near in sickness. He was a noted nurse, with splendid judgment and untiring vigilance.

He was a strong advocate of States' rights, hence when the State seceded he signed the secession ordinance, and never faltered once from his allegiance to this constitutional right. The signers of the secession ordinance from Spartanburg district were J. G. Landrum, a devout Baptist preacher of wonderful ability; James H. Carlisle, the great educator and devout Christian; Barham Bobo Foster, equally devout in his Christianity and fidelity to State; Dr. B. F. Kilgore, famous for his love of his State and of his people and of his God; Simpson Bobo, whose name still lives as a great leader of Methodism in Piedmont Carolina; Rev. Wm. Curtis, a leading female educator of the South; these were the signers, and their names have been enrolled for all time to come as men who were faithful in all things, who were discreet, wise, just and honorable.

As soon as South Carolina seceded he at once raised and drilled a company. Shortly afterwards he was elected lieutenant-colonel of the Third South Carolina Volunteers, went to Virginia and stayed until his health failed. He was sent home a constitutional wreck the winter of 1861 and 1862, but he did everything in his power for the soldiers and their families. When, in the fortunes of war, his sons both fell he bore it with proud agony. First his baby boy, Anthony, fell at Maryland Heights, and then the eldest, his pride and joy, fell in the leaden hail of Fredericksburg; and later, when the fortunes of war took his slaves and his home, he went with fire in his eye and a firm step and toiled in a new sphere for his loved ones. His energy was wonderful.

In his boyhood he sought and found his Savior during a meeting at Cedar Spring, I think, conducted by Rev. J. G. Landrum. Many years after he joined the Cedar Spring Baptist Church, his mother's church, and was baptized by Rev. Richard Woodruff, "Uncle Dickey." Afterwards he moved his membership to the Philadelphia church near his home. He was a very zealous, liberal member of that church until he moved to Union county, when he joined Sulphur Springs church. He moved to Jonesville and was instrumental in building the Baptist church at that place. He was one of its first deacons, and devoted to the church. When he went to Union to live with his daughter, Mrs. I. G. McKissick, he joined that church. He was always sent to every association and union meeting.

Two years before his death he had a stroke of paralysis. In June, 1897, Colonel Foster suffered with another stroke of paralysis at the home of his daughter, Mrs. Benjamin Kennedy, while he was on a visit there. Everything, of course, was done for him, but on the ninth of June, just one year from the time that his son-in-law. Colonel I. G. McKissick, had died, he passed away. The next day he was buried at the old Forest graveyard, noted in the history of Union county as containing the remains of Kennedys, Gists, Brandons, Thomsons, Fosters, Notts, Clowneys, Moores, Means, and others of the old families of that section of the State. Rev. A. A. James, himself a gallant Confederate soldier, conducted the funeral ceremonies. It was a pathetic scene that forced itself upon those who were present in the twilight of the summer's evening. There were gathered around the bier of the old soldier relatives and friends, old slaves and those who were strangers. In the midst of the tall old oaks that formed an amphitheater the funeral party listened with awe and admiration to the beautiful tribute paid Colonel Foster by his old friend and neighbor. One sentence uttered by Mr. James is treasured by the descendants of Colonel Foster. Speaking of his worthy qualities, of his unfaltering faith in the cause for which he fought, of his Christian bearing, of his wonderful resignation in the face of trying ordeals, the preacher said: "The descendants of this grand old man ought to catch the inspiration of this moment. His greatest loyalty to the South and his faith in the hereafter was that he never murmured, but bore with marvelous fortitude the terrible blow that came to him when his two children gave up their lives for the cause for which he had fought and lost everything but honor. No greater page of honor did he ever wish or crave than that it should be known that he was a Confederate soldier, and that he gave his all to save his State." In the quiet of this country graveyard, undisturbed even by the music of a church or the voice of a preacher, save when the funeral rites are being said, Colonel Foster sleeps his last sleep by the side of his wife. Nearby is the grave of Major Benjamin Kennedy, his son-in-law, who preceded him to this churchyard two years before.

I love to think of my father best ministering to the sick and helping his poor neighbors. Mother used to say: "Your father will certainly be delivered in time of trouble, for the Bible says 'Blessed is he that considereth the poor, the Lord will deliver him in time of trouble.'" Dear, brave old father! He could not be a blank. I believe he would have preferred to be a blot, so averse was he to sloth.

Colonel Foster was survived by three daughters. The eldest was Mrs. I. G. McKissick, the next Mrs. Benjamin Kennedy, and the youngest Mrs. James Andrew Thomson.

LOUIS PERRIN FOSTER, eldest son of Barham Boba Foster and Mary Ann Perrin, was born at his grandfather Foster's in the old "brick hones" near Spartanburg Court-house, November 4th, 1837. He was prepared to enter the sophomore class of South Carolina College by Rev. C. S. Beard and Captain A. F. Edwards. Captain Edwards taught the Spartanburg Male Academy for a number of years. Perrin boarded at Simpson Bobo's and attended school. While in this school he attended a meeting conducted by Rev. Daniel Baker and was converted under a sermon preached from the text: "What shall it profit a man if he gain the whole world and lose his own soul."

He joined the Philadelphia Baptist Church and was baptized by Rev. M. C. Barnett. He was prominent in church work and taught a Bible class of eighteen young men, all of whom volunteered, and I think only six survived the war.

He took a firm stand in college, remaining there during the students' rebellion when so many were expelled. After his graduation in 1857 he taught a year at the New Prospect Academy, in Spartanburg County, where he made many friends. He studied law under Bobo Edwards & Carlisle, and was ready to be admitted to the bar when the war commenced. With characteristic energy and decision, he dropped every interest and volunteered at once. He was elected lieutenant in Captain Benjamin Kennedy's company, went to Columbia to camp of instruction, and thence to Virginia. At the reorganization he volunteered for the war, and at the death of Captain Landford was made captain of Co. K, Third Regiment, S.C.V. He made a brave, faithful and popular officer. Once in 1862 he came home on furlough with a terrible abscess on his right elbow. During his stay his only brother was killed, and though suffering with his arm he immediately returned to his command. Just three months later he fell while leading a charge at Fredericksburg. There never lived a truer man, and a braver never died for freedom. Everybody loved him. Mothers would exhort their sons to emulate his virtues. The mother of one of our most faithful pastors told him she wanted him to take Perrin Foster as his model.

Capt. L. Perrin Foster

Ah, it is worthwhile to have lived as he lived, and to have died and gone from honor to glory. His remains were brought home and interred in the family burying ground, where they rest unmarked by marble or stone, neglected for want of a few paltry dollars.

His funeral sermon, together with that of his soldier brother, "Toney" Foster, was preached by Rev. J. G. Landrum from the text, "I have fought a good fight and have kept the faith; from henceforth there is laid up for me a crown of life." Loving hands bore him to rest, and many tearful eyes wept for the neighbor and friend whom they loved to honor.

Colonel Foster's youngest son, James Anthony Foster, as already stated, was the other sacrifice offered from this family on the altar of the Lost Cause. He had scarcely reached the age required for admission into the army when he volunteered as a private in Capt. J. W. Carlisle's company, in the 13th Regiment, S.C.V. Later, through the efforts of his brother, Captain L. P. Foster, he was transferred to his company in the 3d Regiment, S.C.V. In the terrific battle at Maryland Heights on September 13th, 1862, this young hero fell on the front of the firing line. His remains were buried on the field, and afterwards they were transferred to Hollywood cemetery in Richmond.

It was related of him by a fellow soldier, John Hyatt, of Union county. South Carolina, that just as they were going into battle he saw Toney Foster divide his last hardtack cracker with a comrade. The next moment the charge was ordered, and the young boy offered -up willingly his life for the cause of the South.

There was something fatal about the number 13 in this family. Perrin Foster was killed on the 13th of December at Fredericksburg, and Toney Foster was killed on the 13th of September at Maryland Heights.

The South was then engaged in fighting against fate and a losing struggle, and the death of Anthony Foster is another illustration of the fact that the South was robbing its very cradle for defenders.

Hon. Gabriel Cannon - This distinguished son of the "Old Iron District" was born August 25th, 1806, near the present site of Clifton No. 2, Spartanburg County. He was a son of John Cannon. His mother was a Miss Moore. He was a grandson of Ellis Cannon, who, in the early settlement of Spartanburg district, came from Virginia to South Carolina.

Gabriel Cannon was educated above the average man of his day. He attended the Word Academy at Cedar Spring — a classical school where he studied Latin, Algebra, Geometry, etc. At that time this school was probably the best in Spartanburg district.

After completing his education, which was about 1826 or 1827, he began, business

Hon. Gabriel Cannon

at the old Cowpens Furnace Iron Foundry either as an office clerk or a business manager of some kind. His principal employers were William Clark, for whom he named a son, and Wilson Nesbitt, who was for a time a representative in Congress.

After remaining at the Cowpens Furnace for a few years he engaged successfully in the mercantile business at New Prospect, S.C. Later he, with Joseph Finger, began the business of cotton and grist-milling and merchandizing at Fingerville, S.C., and carried on a successful business until interrupted by the civil war. After the war Colonel Cannon disposed of his interest at Fingerville and removed to Spartanburg, where he remained until his death, which occurred December 21, 1893.

From 1842 to 1846, and from 1866 to 1870 Colonel Cannon was a representative from Spartanburg in the House of Representatives. From 1846 to 1862, and from 1876 to 1880 he represented the same county in the State Senate. During the administration of Governor R. F. W. Alston, he was the lieutenant-governor of South Carolina, having been elected by the General Assembly in joint session to this honorable position.

He derived his title "colonel" from the fact that he was promoted from the captaincy of a cavalry company on South Pacolet to a colonelcy of a cavalry regiment some years before the outbreak of the civil war.

Colonel Cannon was a man who was popular and commanded great influence among the people of his native county, being a man of excellent judgment in all matters pertaining to the public interest. He was a trusted leader and true to his constituents, and always standing squarely up to their rights

in the legislative halls.

He was the first president of the National Bank of Spartanburg, and was among the first directors of the Asheville and Spartanburg Railroad. He was a consistent member of the Methodist Church, and all through his life was strictly temperate, and a man of unimpeachable moral character.

Colonel Cannon married first Miss Nancy Collins, daughter of Joseph Collins (see Collins family), by which marriage he had four sons: William Clarke Cannon, merchant at Spartanburg; Ellis Butler Cannon, now deceased; Albert Cannon, a progressive farmer on Broad River, in Henderson county, N.C.; and Lewis Cass Cannon, of Spartanburg, S.C.

He married a second time to Miss Mary Caldwell, sister of Chancellor Caldwell of Newberry, S.C. No children.

JOHN FIELDER was born in Virginia between Lynchburg and the Natural Bridge, on May 11th, 1780, and died in Laurens County, S.C., April 11th, 1889, aged one hundred and nine years lacking one month.

His father dying when he was quite young, his mother removed to South Carolina and settled below Ott's Shoals on Tyger River, where she married a Lanham. Young John was thrown upon his own resources at an early age, and found employment amongst the surrounding farmers, working for six dollars per month and board. Amongst his employers was a Mr. Means, living near Switzer's Station, who treated him kindly, and paid him for a year's service in a horse, saddle and bridle, which horse he worked for thirty years.

John Fielder

In course of time he bought some land, and married Miss Mary Miller, with whom he settled his future homestead three miles northwest of the town of Moore, where he lived happily many years and acquired a handsome property. By this marriage he raised a family of nine children, four sons and five daughters. Shortly after his marriage he enlisted as a soldier and served during the war of 1812 in Captain Dawkins's company, for whom he named his oldest child, who was born during the war.

His first wife dying in 1844 he married a second time a Mrs. Charlotte Fulton of Laurens County, with whom he lived happily several years upon her place near Musgrove's Mills.

This second wife dying he married a third wife, a Miss Mary Anderson of Laurens county, who proved a helpmeet indeed, caring tenderly for him in his old age. There were no children by the second and third marriages. He, with his first and third wives, lies buried in Nazareth cemetery, where also rest the remains of all his sons.

Of his four sons all died in early manhood unmarried except Thomas F. James was a farmer, Newton a physician, and William a student. Thomas F. married Miss Nancy Anderson, a daughter of Enoree James Anderson, who died in 1865, leaving no children. He settled adjoining his father's homestead. In 1866 he married a second wife, Mrs. Elizabeth Byrd, *née* Craig, of Laurens county, by whom he had an only son, John P., who married Miss Hetty Lake of Newberry, S.C., in 1895, and has two children, viz.: Thomas Franklin and Wilton Ward, and resides at Mcore, being engaged in railroad, cotton business and farming operations.

Thomas F., son of John, like his father, was a soldier. He served the Southern Confederacy in Co. A, Holcombe Legion, and was captured with his entire regiment on April 1st, 1865, and confined in Point Lookout prison till the war ended a few weeks afterwards. He was a good soldier, a fine citizen, perfectly honest and upright in all his dealings, energetic in business, and faithful to his friends and country. He was born in 1830 and died in 1888. Of the five daughters of John Fielder, the eldest, Elizabeth Dawkins, married J. M. Nesbitt, both of whom lived and died at Nesbitt's mills on Tyger River. She left three sons and four daughters. The sons were Wm. A. (see sketch), S. Newton, and Thomas M., the latter two living near and owning the mills on Tyger River. S. Newton married Miss Iris Jackson and has three children, John, Annie and Carrie. Thomas M. married Miss Nannie Parks and has four children, Peal, Alfred, Louisa and William.

Of the four daughters, Carrie, eldest daughter, married S. E. Mason (see sketch), both now deceased. Addie, second daughter, married Amos Shands; they have two children, Lula and Jesse; Annie, third daughter, married Captain John W. Wofford (see sketch). Louise, fourth daughter, married Wm. Rogers; they have four daughters, Lizzie, May, Lillian and Lucia.

Caroline, the second daughter of John Fielder, married a Wofford and moved to Mississippi, where his descendants are numerous. Elvira, the third daughter, married A. Carouth Jackson, and had four sons and two daughters: John A., Storeville, S.C., unmarried; Manilla M., married James M. Reed, Abbeville; S.C., has one daughter, Lucia (Mrs. Rev. W. C. Ewart).

Thomas C., merchant, Iva, S.C., married Miss Leila Bsaty; has two children, Louis F., and Thomas C., Jr. Alice F. (now deceased), married J. H. Brooks, leaving one child, Alice Jackson. Samuel O., married first Miss Aseneth Clinkscales (who died leaving six children), and second to Miss Sallie Reid, by whom he has six children; and James L., fourth son and youngest child, married Miss Rosa Madge and has six children. The fourth daughter, Mary Ann, married Wm. Parks, and moved to Mississippi, and has no children. The fifth daughter, Addie, married Robert W. West of Greenville County, S.C., but they lived near the Fielder home, stead, where the widow still lives, Mr. West dying suddenly a few years since. She has only two children living, viz.: Lula, married to J. Laurence Berry, residing near her mother, and has three children, viz.: Fielder, Mary and Robert W.; and second one son, William J., unmarried.

John Fielder was a remarkable man, especially so in his longevity and the many difficulties he encountered in life, all of which he overcame. Commencing poor and friendless, and without education, nothing but inherent abilities enabled him to overcome. He laid foundations wide and broad and deep for his children, and though denied early advantages, as his means increased he gave his children fair education, which was denied him. His descendants to-day are amongst the honored of the country.

He joined the church, Nazareth Presbyterian, in middle life, became one of its first board of deacons, and continued till his removal to Laurens, S.C. A few years before death he connected himself again with Nazareth, saying that he desired to die a member of the church in which he had spent most of his life. He was one of the mainstays of the celebrated Poplar Springs School. He was a true man in all the relations of life, and did much for his country, church, family and friends.

JOHN CONRAD ZIMMERMAN - 1802-1875 - The subject of this sketch was born in St. Matthew's parish, Orangeburg county, September 26th, 1802. His ancestors emigrated from Germany in the early part of the eighteenth century, and were among the early pioneers of Orangeburg, who rendered material service in. building up and settling that county.

In 1825 Mr. Zimmerman was married to Miss Selina Wannamaker of Orangeburg, a granddaughter of Lieutenant Jacob Wannamaker of the continental army — a name prominent in the history of Orangeburg. Five children survive this union.

In 1830 Mr. Zimmerman, at the earnest solicitation of a relative who had come to Spartanburg in quest of health, was induced to sell his estate in St. Matthew's and remove to the up-country. He purchased a farm on the Fair Forest, a few miles from Glenn's Springs, and devoted his time to planting with such success, that he was

John C. Zimmerman

enabled every few years to add a tract of land to his possessions, until finally he became the largest land owner in the country.

In 1845, having become sole proprietor of Glenn's Springs, Mr. Zimmerman devoted much of his time to improving the property, which in his hands became what it has continued to be, the most popular and frequented watering-place in the State, perhaps in the South.

In 1856 Mr. Zimmerman associated himself with Mr. John Bomar and Mr. D. E. Converse in the purchase of what was then known as the Bivingsville factory. This factory was most successfully managed by Mr. Converse, and during the four years of the civil war the company distributed to the poor of the county thousands of dollars' worth of yarn and cloth. Immediately after the cessation of hostilities the erection of a new and larger mill was commenced, and under the name of Glendale the old Bivingsville factory became the pioneer and mother of all the large and flourishing cotton factories which are the pride and boast of Spartanburg.

In disposition Mr. Zimmerman was frank, genial and generous, ever ready to lend a helping hand to the poor and needy, and most gentle and considerate in his intercourse with all men. His modesty, his gentleness, his unvarying courtesy, his kindness of heart and word, made him not only respected, but, perhaps, the best-loved man in his county. He was a gentleman of unbounded hospitality, the door of his elegant mansion was ever open, and he delighted to have his friends around him.

He died as he had lived, a devoted member of the Episcopal Church, without fear and without reproach and in perfect charity with the world.

[1] Colonel William Austin was a soldier of the Revolution. C. S. Thompson, Haywood County, N.C., writes that he has seen his uniform and sword hanging by his bedside.

[2] In the year 1825 he revisited the battle-field of Cowpens, and in company with Mr. Robert Scruggs, pointed out the place where he had a personal encounter with a British officer, in which the latter was killed. In the year 1887 the writer, with T. G. Collins and T. D. Earle of Landrum, in passing through the battle-field were piloted to this spot by Mr. Scruggs, who was then ninety years of age.

Chapter Thirty-Four - Captain Benjamin Kilgore

Was a Revolutionary soldier who was among the early settlers of upper South Carolina, after the treaty of Governor Glenn with the Cherokee Indians in 1755. He had one son, James, who married Harriet Benson of Columbia, S.C., and had children as follows: Josiah Kilgore, who was a graduate of the South Carolina College; Jesse Kilgore, who moved to Kershaw county, S.C.; Dr. Benjamin Kilgore, who moved to North Mississippi; James Kilgore of Newberry, S.C.; Mary, wife of Colonel T. B. Brockman of Greenville, S.C., who became the mother of Mrs. Harriet Anderson, wife of Captain David Anderson; and Margaret and Malinda, both of whom married Barrys of Tyger River.

Josiah Kilgore was the father of Dr. B. F. Kilgore, a sketch of whom we present herein; May, the wife of John Stokes, Esq.; Harriet, wife of Dr. Melmoth Hunter, of Laurens County, S.C.; Dr. William Kilgore and Clayton Kilgore.

In the office of Secretary of State, Columbia, S.C., the following papers are on file, showing the public service rendered by Benjamin Kilgore during the Revolution. These papers were copied by Dr. B. F. Kilgore while a member of the House of Representatives, previous to 1860.

"State of South Carolina,
    To Benjamin Kilgore   Dr.

"1780, May 27th. To captain's pay from March 6th, 1779, to this day in Colonel Williams' Regiment, 96 District, having been on duty the whole of that time as horseman, 432 days @ 7F. 1512."

"September 27th. To ditto from May 27th, 1780, when I was made a prisoner of while on duty, as above, and sent to Charleston and there kept until I made my escape returned home. I took command of the regiment this day, all my superiors being killed, *i.e.,* 124 days at 7F,   434

Old currency F.   1496

Sterling   278

"This is to certify that the above services was actually done by Captain Benjamin Kilgore.

By me, Robert M. Craig, Lieutenant-Colonel."

"September 25th, 1785.

South Carolina, Laurens District.

"Personally appeared Benjamin Kilgore before me, W. Mitchison, a Justice of the Peace of said county, and made oath as the law directs that the above account is just and true, and that he never has received anything of the same, and subscribed before me September 25th, 1785

Wm. Mitchison,   N. P. Benj. Kilgore.

"Received full satisfaction of the within on an interest N. 14 x."

DR. BENJAMIN FRANKLIN KILGORE was a son of Josiah Kilgore, whose ancestors came from Ireland; these settled first in Pennsylvania, but subsequently moved south.

Dr. Kilgore was born in Greenville County, near the Spartanburg line, August 6th, 1820. He attended the schools of his neighborhood, and afterwards attended the high schools in the districts of both Greenville and Spartanburg.

In 1837 he read medicine with his preceptor. Dr. A. B. Crook of Greenville, and graduated in the South Carolina Medical College, at Charleston, in 1840. He then took a postgraduate course at Lexington, Ky., and began the practice of medicine in 1841 in Kershaw district.

In the fall of 1846 he returned to Greenville district and soon afterwards purchased a valuable farm on Enoree River, a few miles below Woodruff, to which place he moved February, 1847, and began to farm as well as to do an extensive practice of medicine.

Dr. B. F. Kilgore

This place he owned at the time of his death, which occurred February 20th, 1897. From the time of his removal to Spartanburg district, he became closely identified with the interests of the district, serving as commissioner of roads, and was elected twice (1854 and 1858) as a representative from

Spartanburg to the State legislature. In 1860 he was elected a delegate to the convention of South Carolina which declared the ordinance of secession.

At the beginning of the civil war he enlisted as a private in Co. K, 3d Regiment, S.C.V. Shortly after he was appointed assistant surgeon of the 13th Regiment, S.C.V. (of which Dr. L. C. Kennedy was surgeon, whose health failing resigned), and September 23d, 1862, was promoted to surgeon of the same regiment, a position which he held until 1865, when he was made a director in charge of a hospital. After his return from the army he did only a limited practice and removed to Woodruff, where, from paralysis he died on the date already referred to, and was buried in the new cemetery nearby.

While Dr. Kilgore was located in Kershaw district in 1841, he met Miss Fannie A. Massey of the Waxhaw neighborhood, in Lancaster district, whom he married, and who, with two sons and three daughters, survives him, the names of which are John Belton Kilgore, who married Lora Westmoreland; Samuel M. Kilgore, who married Lilly Hunter; Jane, who married W. W. Simpson; Annie Virginia, who married Professor A. M. Stallworth, and Miss Hattie, unmarried.

Dr. Kilgore was a progressive citizen and an earnest patriot, and was endowed with an exceptionally fine mind, and used his time and talent for any measure he thought was for the progress and advancement of his county and State. It was largely due to his untiring energy and zeal that the Augusta and Spartanburg Railroad was built. At first he met with many discouragements, but lived to see his cherished hope consummated.

As a farmer he was specially devoted to sheep-raising and had among his extensive flock the finest breeds of Southdowns and Broadtails.

Dr. Kilgore was a true patriot, honest in the expression of his opinions and bold in his denunciations of wrong. A devoted husband and kind father, he was unselfish in disposition, magnanimous and warm in nature, and true and loyal in his friendships. These excellent traits in his character made a strong impress on the community in which he lived.

Col. W. W. Harris

COLONEL WILLIAM WASHINGTON HARRIS. Among those of the citizens of Spartanburg who belonged to a past generation in her history, and whose early life embraced a career that was remarkable, there are none more deserving of our special notice than Colonel W. W. Harris, the subject of this sketch.

Of the early life and ancestry of Colonel Harris we can gather but little.

He was born about 1795, and doubtless received the very best education that could be afforded in his day and generation. As soon as he grew to manhood he took up the study of surveying, and the State of Tennessee being then a frontier country and an inviting-field for this business, he went thither, but how much work he did in this line we are not advised. It appears that not long after he went to Tennessee the war with Great Britain broke out. This is known as the war of 1812. He enlisted in the army under the leadership of General Andrew Jackson, and participated -in the expedition against the Creeks in Alabama in 1813. In the latter part of August of said year, Fort Minis, forty miles north of Mobile, was surprised by the savages, who appeased their thirst for blood with the murder of nearly four hundred people; they did not spare even a woman or child, and but very few of the men in the fort escaped.. The news of this dreadful massacre spread consternation throughout the country, and the governors of Tennessee, Georgia and Mississippi Territory made preparations at once for organizing expeditions to march against and invade the country of the Creeks. The Tennesseeans under General Jackson were the first to the rescue. Several battles ensued, in which the Indian towns were destroyed, many of them put to death, and the whole nation routed.

In this expedition Colonel Harris either enlisted as an officer or became such soon afterwards. It is not definitely known what rank he held, but it is likely that it was in this expedition that he obtained the title of *colonel,* for his position, as we will show further on, was of such prominence as to cause him to be personally known and remembered by General Jackson. He used to relate some interesting incidents in connection with his army life under Jackson. He was officer of the day one night when Jackson was expecting an attack, and he came across a youthful sentinel who had been stationed to guard a bridge, an important point. This sentinel did not challenge him, and he stepped softly up and found him asleep. To report him as sleeping at such a time and to such an officer as Jackson meant death to the sentinel. To wake him and reveal himself and then not report him would show a lack of discipline, and this idea could not be entertained. Circumstances favored him in this dilemma. The sentinel was sitting on the "stringer" of the bridge with his gun lying beside him, his back to the deep water below. So Colonel Harris just took hold of the man's foot and turned him backwards into the water. While the young man was swimming out Colonel Harris concealed himself and waited until he saw the astonished sentinel resume his watch, it is supposed, to sleep no more till he was relieved.

Colonel Harris came to Spartanburg district while yet a young man without means, but with indomitable pluck and ambition. He married a daughter of Rev. David Golightly, who was a gentleman of considerable means. Although not pleased with the match he gave his son-in-law a small piece of land, but did not otherwise supply him with the necessary housekeeping utensils. To his grandson, George H. Camp, Esq., he stated that he first lived in a cabin, and that his only cooking utensils were a small skillet and oven. He plowed with grapevine traces, and the first thing he did on the morning after his marriage was to cut a maul, and in relating this circumstance to his grandson, he said: "Son, I have been busy ever since." Being a practical surveyor he soon found employment that was remunerative. After several years he went to Spartanburg, built a house and continued the business of surveying, and by honest industry and a reasonable amount of economy he accumulated a vast amount of real estate that would sell at this writing (1900) for $150,000.

Many years ago Wm. C. Camp, Esq., son-in-law of Colonel Harris, visited General (Old Hickory) Jackson at his residence, called "The Hermitage," in Tennessee. When informed that Mr. Camp was a son-in-law of Colonel Harris, he was glad to see him and to hear from his old friend. He sent him, through Mr. Camp, as a present a polished hickory walking-cane with a silver head, bearing an appropriate inscription, which was highly prized by Colonel Harris. His army sword is still in possession of some of his grandchildren.

Colonel Harris was a man of great firmness and decision of character, and no citizen in Spartanburg was more highly esteemed as a gentleman than he was. He was a consistent member of the Baptist church at Spartanburg, and the lifelong friend of his pastor. Rev. John G. Landrum, under whose ministrations he attended for a quarter of a century or more.

Colonel Harris had eight children, as follows: Julia, who married Rev. Elijah Ray of Union district, S.C., father of Wm. H. Ray of Hendersonville, S.C.; Sabrina, who married Andrew Holtsonzer; Harriet, who married Hiram Mitchell; Adaline, who married W.C. Bennett; Cornelia, who married Adam S. Camp; David G., who married Emily Lyles; and Tabitha, who married Wm. C. Camp, Esq.

The sons-in-law above mentioned were gentlemen of the highest respectability, honor and integrity. Mr. Hiram Mitchell was for many years a prominent merchant in Spartanburg, and an influential member of the Baptist church in that town, and died a steadfast Christian. Dr. W. C. Bennett, a dentist of repute, was also a prominent member of the Baptist church at Spartanburg, where he resided most of his married life. He was a man of public spirit and took an interest in every enterprise looking to the internal development of his country.

David G. Harris, only son of Colonel Harris, was a man much like his father in business energy and perseverance. He lived near Golightly on Fair Forest, and was a successful farmer. He had children as follows: W. W. Harris, chief clerk constabulary force in Columbia, who married a Miss Nevins; J. West Harris, a farmer in Spartanburg, who married a daughter of Mr. Miles Gentry; E. G. Harris, Professor of Mathematics and Civil Engineering in a school at Rolla, Mo.; Julia, who married Wm. H. Ray; Laura, who married J. Gwinn Harris of Forest City, Ark.; Ella, who married L. K. Ford near Golightly; James G. Harris, who lost both eyes from an explosion in a well, who subsequently died of fever, and who married a Miss Lee, a relative of General Stephen D. Lee; and Mary, who married Mack C. Poole, a merchant at Cross Anchor.

DAVID COOK JUDD was born at Northampton, Mass., December 13th, 1809, being the youngest of six children born of his parents. "He was trained from infancy to habits of industry, sobriety and self-reliance, and his character was early formed upon the principles of stern integrity and morality. He sprang, too, from a pious ancestry, and grew up in the bosom of that church which has been made famous in our land by the pastorates of Edwards and Stodard and Spencer. Under these influences he early became a professor of religion, himself uniting with the church of his fathers."

He was educated in the common schools of his town; but when quite a youth he entered upon the mercantile pursuits to which he devoted his long life. His first position was that of a clerk in a mercantile house in Boston, but soon after he entered the store of his brother in Springfield, Mass., where he acquired the habits of system, accuracy and thoroughness which strikingly characterized him through life. After he had attained his maturity he removed to Columbus, Ohio, where he spent a few years. Thence he turned his eyes southward and migrated to what was then the little village of Spartanburg, where he settled and began the business of merchandizing in 1842, which business he steadily continued until within about six months of the time of his death. In 1847 or 1848 he entered into a partnership in said business with his brother-in-law, Mr. Joseph Foster, which comprised the well-known firm of Foster & Judd. Besides his regular business as a merchant, he also, in connection with it, conducted for many years prior to the civil war between the States, the Spartanburg Agency of the Bank of the State of South Carolina, and served also for six years after said war as president of the National Bank of Spartanburg, which office he resigned on account of failing health. In all his business career and dealings he was honest, upright and conscientious, and as such he was eminently successful. No business man in Spartanburg was more distinguished than he for his diligence, integrity and fidelity.

D. C. Judd

Soon after he came to Spartanburg he became a member of the Presbyterian church at that place, which church organization was only in the second year of its existence; performed an interested and active part in the erection of the church building; was ordained a ruling elder August 15th, 1845, and served as teacher, superintendent and librarian of the Sabbath-school, relinquishing the latter office only a few years before his death on account of the infirmities of advancing age.

He also served during his day upon the city council of Spartanburg, and in other positions of responsibility and trust besides those already mentioned, and in all he proved himself to be a man of eminent ability and uprightness.

Mr. Judd was twice married, first to Miss Catharine Foster, who died in 1858, and subsequently to Miss Eliza Attleton, who survives him.

Having lived a life of spotless integrity, Christian consistency and official fidelity, he died, ministered to by loving hands, at his home in Spartanburg, February 25th, 1882, in his seventy-third year. His remains were followed by a large concourse of people to the spot where for over thirty-five years he had been accustomed to worship God.

HON. WILLIAM KENEDY BLAKE - One of the best known and representative citizens of Spartanburg was William K. Blake. He was born in Fayetteville, N.C., February 11th, 1824, and died at his residence at Spartanburg, S.C., January 9th, 1898. He descended from one of the old colonial families that settled on Cape Fear River and from a noble Revolutionary ancestry. His grandfather, Isham Blake, was personally known to Lafayette, and was one of his body-guard at the surrender of Cornwallis at Yorktown, and in 1825, when this distinguished Frenchman vis-

Hon. Wm. K. Blake

ited the United States upon an invitation from Congress, he visited the town of Fayetteville, which was named in his honor. Great preparations were made for his reception. Military companies, civic societies, schools and the citizens of the town and county turned out to welcome the generous friend of America from a foreign shore. During the presentation of a beautiful silken flag to Lafayette, wrought by the skillful hands of the ladies of Fayetteville, a touching scene occurred. The old hero was told that an old comrade, Isham Blake, a fifer in the continental army, was present. His eyes beaming with joy he begged to see him. Soon a tall and venerable man appeared. He needed no introduction; they embraced, wept and fought anew the battles of Brandywine and Yorktown.

Wm. K. Blake, after attending the common schools of his town, not having the means of his own, sought the assistance of his friends, who promptly remitted to him from time to time till his graduation in 1846, which was returned with his first earnings out of college.

Mr. Blake attended Randolph Macon College, Virginia, two years and then entered the University of North Carolina in 1844 and graduated from said institution, as already stated, in 1846. He "began the study of law and remained in Fayetteville until after his marriage in 1848 to Miss Ella Hawley, when he moved to Texas, where he had a brother living and where he intended practicing law. A residence of six months being required, however, before license could be obtained, he decided to open a school, which, in the meanwhile, would give him an opportunity to familiarize himself with the pleadings and practice of the courts of Texas.

Shortly after, he entered upon the practice of law, but his wife was taken sick, and not being able to secure the necessary medical treatment, he removed to Nashville, Tenn., and accepted a position in the High School in that city. A year later the cholera epidemic visited the city and he was one of its victims; he barely escaped with his life. Upon his partial recovery he returned to his native State, and as soon as his health permitted accepted a position in the Female College at Ansonville, and from the latter place he moved to Greensboro, where, in 1854, he was elected to a professorship. Here he was associated with Dr. Deems, who was then president of the college, and later was in charge of a large church in New York City, and who remained a personal friend.

In 1857 he was elected president of the Female Seminary at Fayetteville, his native town, and spent two years pleasantly there until he resigned to accept the presidency of the Female College at Spartanburg. Soon after he arrived in Spartanburg his wife died. She had been an invalid for many years.

He continued in charge of the Female College at Spartanburg until some time during the year 1863, when it suspended on account of the war.

In 1861 he married Miss Marina Gregg Jones of Edgefield, S.C., who had been a pupil in his school, and whose influence as a consecrated Christian for a third of a century is felt and appreciated by the people of Spartanburg.

When the war closed Mr. Blake began the mercantile business in Spartanburg. He was successful and remained in this business until failing health forced him to retire and transfer his store to others.

In 1868 he was elected chairman of the board of county commissioners for Spartanburg County, which position he held for four years, discharging the duties of the office with faithfulness and fidelity to the people. About this time he was elected and served for two years as chairman of the county Democratic Executive Committee, which was at a time when the State was at her greatest peril from Radical misrule and tyranny; and until the State was redeemed from said domination, which was in 1876, he was always foremost in the political campaigns of his county, contending for honesty of government and Anglo-Saxon supremacy.

Mr. Blake was never, however, a politician in the strict sense, of the word, but in 1880 the people called him to serve one term in the legislature. He was an excellent representative and attended to all the duties before him.

In 1875 he became secretary and treasurer of the Spartanburg and Asheville Railroad, which position he held for two years, discharging the duties of the office under the most trying circumstances with the same indomitable energy and perseverance which always characterized him. Lack of funds to prosecute the further work of the road for a time, caused him to retire from this office.

Having received his first degrees in Freemasonry while residing in Ansonville, N.C., Mr. Blake became an earnest and most enthusiastic member of this order. He had attained next to the highest degree in Masonry, and upon this being offered him he declined in favor of a man in Charleston, who was on his death-bed, only one Mason in the State being granted this degree. He was for one or two years, beginning with about 1870, the Grand Master of the Grand Lodge A. F. M. of South Carolina. No one ever occupied this chair with more eminence and ability than Mr. Blake. In the conferring of degrees, and especially the Eastern Star, he had no superior.

Mr. Blake was a loyal Methodist, a Christian gentleman and an honest advocate for the cause of temperance. He was at the time of his death, and had been for a number of years, one of the trustees of the Wofford College. He succeeded Mr. Bobo as superintendent of the Methodist Sunday-school at Spartanburg, and for several years he gave it his best thought and effort. For a long time he was a member of the "Legal Conference," and was treasurer and general manager for that body, and attended all of its meetings but the last, which met during his last illness.

It may be truly said of Mr. Blake that he was a good all-round man. For an impromptu speech on Fourth of July, Sunday-school, political, educational, Masonic, or any other live issue, he scarcely had an equal in the State of South Carolina. He was eloquent in the selection of language, musical in voice, and graceful in gesture. Born without means, with no security to obtain the necessary funds to procure an education except upon a pledge of honor, reared and trained by a pious parentage, which, by the blessings of God, established for him a character for industry, honesty and good habits, William Kennedy Blake lived a life and has left an example behind him worthy of imitation by the generations that come after him.

Joseph Foster

JOSEPH FOSTER was born at Canterbury, N.H., November 7, 1804. Having received a common school education in his native State, he was trained in early life to habits of industry and self-reliance. When about twenty-one years of age came to South Carolina, located at Greenville, and taught school for a year in connection with his brother Abiel Foster. The next year, 1827, he went to Union district and located near Fair Forest church; continued teaching and farming for some years.

On the 27th of December, 1831, he was married to Miss Minerva Margery Means. He was a member of the Fair Forest church (Presbyterian), and was elected elder in this church about 1835. The duties of this office he faithfully discharged until his removal to Spartanburg Court-house in August, 1847.

He identified himself with the church there (which was in its infancy), soon after was made elder, and held the office as long as he lived. After his removal to Spartanburg he went into the mercantile business in partnership with his brother-in-law, Mr. D. C. Judd. This business connection, known as the firm of Foster & Judd, continued until his death, January 31, 1877. He was gifted with rare business talents and a pleasant address, which enabled him to succeed in his enterprises.

He was an energetic, progressive man, temperate in his habits, always bright and cheerful in the home circle. His ancestors on his father's side were English, he was also through his grandmother, Mary Rogers Foster, in the direct line of descent from Rev. John Rogers, who was burned at Smithfield, the first martyr in Queen Mary's reign. His grandfather, Hon. Abiel Foster, was a member to Congress fourteen years under the confederation and the constitution; was a friend of General Washington, was chosen delegate to Congress under the confederation, February 18, 1783. Attended July 29, 1783. Was present when General Washington resigned his commission as Commander-in-Chief of the American Army, December 23d, 1783. This event is commemorated in an oil-painting hanging in the rotunda of the capitol at Washington. In this painting the Hon. Abiel Foster occupies a conspicuous position in the foreground.

Joseph Foster's children are Susan E., married Samuel C. Means; Alfred H., married Henrietta V. Brandon of Union — their children are Isabel, Mary Emma and Louise. Isabella J., married Robert H. Chapman of Asheville, N.C., died October 10th, 1866, leaving two sons, James A. Chapman, lawyer, Robert H. F. Chapman, merchant. S. Laura, married E. C. McLaughlin; J. Adolphus, married Sallie G. Farrar of Union county, and died November 15th, 1886. His descendants are all living in Spartanburg and Union counties.

CAPTAIN ALFRED HARRISON FOSTER, eldest son of Joseph and M. M. Foster, was born in Union county, S.C., in 1835. Being instructed by his father and others he received a good education, and after he grew up to manhood, spent several years as salesman in the store of Foster & Judd at Spartanburg, S.C.

For several years prior to the outbreak of the civil war Captain Foster was a member of the Morgan Rifles at Spartanburg (named in honor of Daniel Morgan, the

Capt. A. H. Foster

hero of Cowpens), a splendidly uniformed, equipped and drilled company under the command of Captain G. W. H. Legg, which formed a part of the old 36th Regiment, S.C. M. The State failing to receive this organization as a rifle company to form a part of a new regiment to be made up from the districts of York, Union and Spartanburg, the services of the Spartan Rifles, a new organization in the town of Spartanburg, having been already accepted by the State authorities before a general call was made for volunteer troops from the 36th Regiment, the Morgan Rifles divided on the day of said call (January, 1861) at the annual parade ground (Bomar's Old Field), about one-half offering their services on the ground, while the remaining part waited until the organization should be received and mustered in as a rifle company. [1] That part of said company which volunteered on the occasion referred to, recruited at once and organized under the name of *Morgan Light Infantry*. With this organization Captain Foster volunteered as a private. Captain Legg, of the Morgan Rifles, was elected captain of this new organization, which drilled every two weeks at Spartanburg until called into active service.

Under the organization of the 5th Regiment, S.C.V., from companies in the counties referred to Major Micah Jenkins, of York, was elected colonel; Captain G. W. H. Legg, of Spartanburg, was elected lieutenant-colonel, and Captain W. T. Thomson (Johnson Rifles), of Union, was elected major. This left a vacancy for the captaincy in the Morgan Light Infantry, and to this position Mr. John M. Benson was elected.

The company left Spartanburg for Charleston April 13th, 1861, the day of the fall of Sumter, and reached Sullivan's Island about one week later, where it remained encamped for six weeks. In the organization of the 5th Regiment, which at this time consisted of twelve companies, the Morgan Light Infantry was known as Company I. During the period that the company was encamped on Sullivan's Island much time was spent in drilling, and Captain Foster, the second sergeant of the company, had committed to his charge a number of young recruits called the "Awkward Squad," to which the writer, yet in his teens, belonged, and here was manifested his excellent qualifications as a drill-master.

Up to about the 25th of May, 1861, the 5th Regiment only formed a part of the State volunteer organization. To enter the service of the Confederate States a new enlistment and reorganization became necessary, which was done for the period of twelve months. The reputation which Captain Foster had already made for himself as a competent drill officer pointed him out as the most suitable man to lead the Morgan Light Infantry through the Virginia campaigns, where it was destined to go, and he was accordingly elected its captain, which position he held to the end of the war. His promotion, however, to this responsible position was done with due respect to Captain Benson, who was elected first lieutenant of the company, and at the end of his twelve months' enlistment was promoted to a higher rank in another service. The other officers elected were James S. Ballenger second lieutenant, and Robert A. Snoddy third lieutenant.

Upon the reorganization of the 5th Regiment, S.C.V., for the Confederate service, the Morgan Light Infantry, under Captain Foster, was known as Company F, and as such participated in the first battle of Manassas, and the subsequent service of the regiment for the period of enlistment.

At the reorganization in 1862, for three years or the war, part of the 5th Regiment, with other reenlisted companies, formed the new regiment known as the Palmetto Sharpshooters, of which Micah Jenkins was made colonel, and Captain Foster's company, with such new recruits as were added, became Company D in said regiment.

Captain Foster was in all the engagements of this gallant regiment except Williamsburg, Va., and Dandridge, Tenn. His personal record was part of that of the Sharpshooters, who were never driven from a position, and never failed to drive the enemy when they charged, with one or two exceptions. He took part in battles of First Manassas, Seven Pines, Mechanicsville, Gaines Mill, Fraser's Farm, Rappahannock Station, Thoroughfare Gap, Second Manassas, Ox Hill, Boonsboro, Sharpsburg, Fredericksburg, the Suffolk and Blackwater campaign, the Chattanooga and Knoxville campaign under Longstreet, including the fights at Campbells Station, Knoxville and Beans Station, Wilderness, Spottsylvania Court-house, Hanover Junction, Cold Harbor, Bermuda Hundred, Petersburg, Fort Harrison, New Market Heights, Darbytown Road, Williamsburg Road, and at the evacuation of Petersburg brought up the rear, and commanded the regiment during the frequent skirmishes on the road to Appomattox, and in all these engagements he was slightly wounded twice. At the surrender the regiment was in good discipline and would have made as good a company, numbers considered, as it ever did.   It surrendered more men than any other regiment in the army. Of Captain Foster's company, which was composed of the best material the country afforded, the total number enrolled from its last organization (1862) was about 134. Of this number 37 were killed and died of wounds received on battle-fields; 21 were wounded, and 20 died of disease, making a total of 78. At the surrender at Appomattox the company numbered between 10 and 25. Captain Foster left Appomattox April 13th, 1865, just four years to a day after he left home for the war.

In 1868 he established his business as a merchant in Union, S.C., which he has successfully conducted for thirty years. He is deeply interested in every enterprise looking to the upbuilding of his country, having assisted with his influence and financially in organizing and promoting cotton manufacturing in Spartanburg and Union counties, and especially is he interested in the welfare of his comrades, being at present the commander of Camp Giles, U. C. V., which meets in his city.

A truer patriot, a braver soldier or a more devoted son of Carolina never went forth to battle for his country than Alfred Harrison Foster, and what we say of him personally may be also truly said of his heroic band of followers through four long years of a bloody war.

The Choice Family

The Choices are of Welsh descent. The first to land in this country came with the early English settlers to Virginia and engaged in the cultivation of tobacco.

The founder of the South Carolina family, William Choice, was a patriot soldier in the Revolutionary war, and soon after the surrender of Cornwallis he settled on Reedy River, in the lower part of Greenville county. He was one of the three commissioners to locate Greenville Court-house at the falls of Reedy River. He lived to be eighty-nine years old and drew a military pension from the government for many years. He was the father of William Choice, who attained eminent success at the bar of Greenville city, his contemporaries being Judges O'Neall, Earle, Dawkins, Hon. B. F. Perry and others; also of Josiah Choice, who was killed at his home, near Paris Mountain, just at the close of the civil war, while defending his stock from a lawless raid of Federal cavalry.

His youngest son, Jefferson, having married a daughter of Jesse Cleveland, moved to Spartanburg to practice law, forming the firm of Thomson & Choice. Served one term as intendant of the town of Spartanburg. He died in 1860 much lamented.

CAPTAIN WILLIAM CHOICE, SR., son of Jefferson Choice, Esq., was born in Spartanburg. He attended the University at Georgetown, D.C., and received a good education. At the outbreak of the civil war he enlisted and was made a sergeant in the Spartan Rifles (Captain Joseph Walker). He served four years in the war, rising to the captaincy of Co. K, 5th Regi-

Capt. Wm. Choice

ment, S.C.V., which formed a part of Longstreet's corps, and took part in many of the great battles in Virginia with conspicuous gallantry, as has been stated to the writer by his comrades in arms. He is a quiet and upright citizen, and resides in the city of Spartanburg, never having aspired to public life. His son, William

Choice, Jr., a young man just grown, served through the late Spanish-American war as a private in the United States Marine Corps. He was on duty aboard the artillery cruiser Yosemite, which did service in the West India waters. While blockading the port of San Juan, Porto Rico, the Yosemite, while there alone, was attacked by four Spanish gunboats. The battle raged for five hours with most tremendous cannonading, when the Spanish boats retired, being badly hurt. One of them, the Antoine Lope, was beached and destroyed. After ten months service, the war being over, he was honorably discharged.

[1] The remaining membership of the old Morgan Rifles recruited, reorganized and volunteered in the Confederate service the month of November following tinder the leadership of Captain John Earle Bomar, and was known as Company C, in the Holcombe Legion.

269

Chapter Thirty-Five - Professor David Duncan

This eminent educator was born in the county of Donegal, Ireland, in 1790, and was graduated from Glasgow University at eighteen years of age, after which he spent four years in the English navy. He was at St. Petersburg at the time Napoleon burned Moscow. He came to America in 1817 and landed in Norfolk, Va., and from that time until his death he devoted his attention to educational work. From 1817 to 1835, he was the principal of the Norfolk Academy, and from the latter date until 1854 he was professor of ancient languages in the Randolph-Macon College, and from 1854 to 1881, in which year he died, he was professor of ancient languages in the Wofford College at Spartanburg, being among the first of the faculty of that institution.

Bishop W. W. Duncan, D.D.

He was twice married. His first wife was Miss Ann Shirley, who only lived one year after her marriage, leaving no children. His second marriage was to Miss Alice A. Peimont. She was reared in Norfolk, and was the daughter of Thomas and Alice (Robinson) Peimont. The latter was a niece of speaker John Robinson of the Virginia house of burgesses, of which Patrick Henry was a member, and it was during this time that he made his celebrated speech, in which among other things he said: "Tarquin and Caesar had each his Brutus. Charles I. his Cromwell, and George III. —" and when the speaker and terrified loyalists shouted "Treason! Treason!" finished the sentence — "and George III., may profit by their example. If that be treason, make the most of it." The Robinson family was of English descent and the Peimont of French.

By the marriage between Professor David Duncan and Alice A. Peimont seven children were born, viz.: Mary Elizabeth, who married Lucien H. Eomax; William Wallace, a sketch of whom we present in this volume; James Armstrong, Alice Amanda; David Robinson, who will receive further notice; Thomas C. and D'Arcy Paul. Only three of the above are living, viz.: David R., William W., and D'Arcy P.

James Armstrong Duncan became a doctor of divinity, and was one of the most distinguished and eloquent Methodist divines in the country. At the time of his death he was president of Randolph-Macon College, Va. Thomas Carey Duncan was killed in battle, in the seven days fight in front of Richmond, a brave and gallant soldier, being a member of Co. K., Palmetto Sharpshooters. D'Arcy P. Duncan is a prominent citizen in the State, being at present clerk of the railroad commissioners, and resides at Sumter, S.C.

BISHOP WILLIAM WALLACE DUNCAN. This distinguished divine of the Methodist Episcopal Church, South, now a resident of the city of Spartanburg, S.C., is the son of Professor David Duncan, a sketch of whom we present herein. He was born at Randolph-Macon College, Mecklenburg county, Va., December 20th, 1839, his father being at the time a professor in said college, but resigning the same in 1854 to accept the chair of Greek and Latin in the Wofford College at Spartanburg, The son, the subject of this sketch, came with him. He entered the freshman class the year of his father's removal, graduating four years afterwards.

Soon after his graduation he returned to his native State where he entered the ministry. He was admitted to the Virginia Conference in 1859. "He served as chaplain in the army during the war, both in Virginia and in South Carolina; and in the ten years that followed he did a Methodist preacher's work in the pulpit and on the pastorate, on circuits and stations ranging from the peaks of O'Her on the Blue Ridge to the surf-beaten shores of the Chesapeake.'" Among the stations in Virginia which he served during this period were Leesville, Danville, Norfolk and Petersburg, While stationed at the last mentioned place he was called to the professorship) of Mental and Moral Philosophy in Wofford College, which position he accepted and served with conspicuous success until he was elected bishop by the General Conference in 1886. In connection with the Wofford professorship he served as the representative of the college, soliciting contributions and delivering masterly educational addresses, which were well received everywhere, and which are still bearing fruit and will for generations to come.

The selection of Bishop Duncan by the Conference gave great satisfaction, and he has now for about fourteen years, with great faithfulness and fidelity, served his church and the Master's cause, visiting every part of the continent over which the jurisdiction of his church extends, and is warmly welcomed everywhere.

In the chair he is the master of assemblies, and wields the gavel gracefully but firmly. He is a man of business and the work of the Conference runs along smoothly and with dispatch under his efficient guidance.

In 1861 Bishop Duncan was married to Miss Medora, daughter of Hon. Ben Rice of Union, S.C., and they are the happy parents of three children: Colonel T. C. Duncan of Union, Mrs. Warren Du Pre, and Mrs. A. G. Rembert of Spartanburg.

In many respects Bishop Duncan is a remarkable man: "As a preacher he is practical and powerful. He despises the tricks of oratory, but ever has the eloquence of thought. He strives to correct the evil in the hearts and lives of his hearers rather than please them with rhetorical productions...He is a man of deep convictions, and has the courage necessary to fearlessly express them." He "makes no loud professions of spiritual attainments, but illustrates by a life of continual and arduous labors the highest type of Christian consecration." His labors are not only such as to meet the praises of men, but will receive the approbation of the Divine Master, whom he faithfully serves.

JESSE CLEVELAND. The Clevelands, it is said, were an ancient family deriving their name from a tract of country in North Riding of Yorkshire, England, still called Cleveland. In history there appear the names of two Alexander Clevelands. The junior of this name was the father of John Cleveland of Prince William County, Va., who was the father of several sons, among whom we would mention the names of Benjamin, John and Robert. The first mentioned, Colonel Benjamin Cleveland, lives in history as one of the heroes of King Mountain, a sketch of whom we have presented in another volume. [1]

The second son referred to, John Cleveland, was a Baptist minister of good standing, influence and ability.

The third mentioned, Robert Cleveland, was a captain in his brother's regiment at the battle of King's Mountain. Among his children he had two sons, viz.: Jeremiah and Jesse. The former resided in Greenville, S.C., and left behind him numerous descendants. The latter, Jesse Cleveland, the subject of this sketch, emigrated from Wilkes County, N.C., in 1810, and settled in Spartanburg. In the beginning and growth of said town no one was more identified with its business interests than Jesse Cleveland. He began and continued for many years the business of merchandizing, and was in truth the merchant of the town. Purchasing his goods in Charleston, Baltimore, Augusta and other places, and bringing them overland in wagons to Spartanburg, he had an extensive trade and business, and was noted not only for his superior business judgment, but fair and honorable dealing.

He married Mary Blassingame, and had children as follows: Mrs. Emily Choice, John B. Cleveland, Sr., Wm. B, Cleveland, Mrs. Elizabeth Bivings, Dr. Robert E. Cleveland, and Mrs. Mary H. Cleveland, the last named

Dr. Robert E. Cleveland

the only one surviving who resides at Greenville, S.C.

272

DR. ROBERT EASLEY CLEVELAND, son of Jesse Cleveland, was born in Spartanburg, S.C., January 6th, 1822. Receiving a good education, he read medicine and was graduated from the Charleston Medical College in 1843. Immediately he began practice in his native county, which was extensive, reaching into North Carolina, and his work was remunerative. "To his knowledge as a physician he brought the aid of common sense; always conservative in his views, he was never carried away by any new theories in his profession. His cardinal belief was in nature, and to assist her was his chief object...His treatment was especially successful in typhoid cases." As a surgeon he was conservative in the use of the knife.

Dr. Cleveland retired from the practice of medicine in 1870. After that time he gave his attention to extensive private business. He took great interest in the growth and prosperity of his native town and county.

He was particularly interested in railroad development, and forwarded in every way the building and success of the Spartanburg and Asheville and Air Line roads.

Dr. Cleveland, though not a graduate of any literary institution, his education having been confined to the high schools then common in the State, was a man of extensive reading and information, was social in his nature, hospitable in his home, and his store of anecdotes and conversational qualities caused his society to be much sought after.

Rev. John D. McCollough

In 1844 he married Miss Elizabeth, eldest daughter of John Bomar, Jr., who was one of the early and successful manufacturers of cotton in Spartanburg district. By this marriage two children survive, Dr. Jesse F. and Hon. John B. Cleveland, well known and popular citizens in Spartanburg County.

REV. JOHN D. MCCOLLOUGH. The first Episcopal clergyman resident in Spartanburg County was Rev, John D. McCollough. Air. McCollough was from Society Hill, on the Pee Dee, a planter of land inherited from an ancestor, one of the old Welsh colonists.

Having determined to enter the sacred ministry, he sold his property and removed to Columbia in 1847. He was elected principal of the Glenn's Spring Academy and removed to that place in January, 1848. Among his pupils of that year who still survive are William Means, Dr. J. N. Moore and Dr. Wm. F. Smith. There were no Episcopalians at Glenn's Spring and no Sunday services. There were, however, several members of the Church at Spartanburg, and to furnish these with the worship of their Church and to know the Lord's Day, Mr. McCollough was made a deacon with license to preach, and divided the Sundays between these two points.

273

The following information in quotation marks are extracts from a sermon preached in Spartanburg in 1897, by Mr. McCollough, which was published in the *Spartan:*

"There were then two clergymen of the Episcopal Church in the upper part of South Carolina, at Pendleton and Greenville, where congregations were organized by Episcopalians from the 'Low Country.'" A few services had been held in Spartanburg district by clergymen traveling in the summer. These were by the "Rev. C. C. Pinckey, who reports that in 1840 he spent a Sunday at Glenn's Spring and one at Limestone Springs, preaching on both occasions to very respectable congregations."

In 1841 Rev. R. H. Shindler, a deacon, was sent for the summer "to Limestone Springs, Glenn's Spring and Spartanburg Court-house." He reports "divine services twenty times at the places designated."... "Baptized two whites and three colored children. There is but one family in full communion with the church."

This family was that of Major L. H. Kennedy, residing near Cedar Spring. One of the children baptized was Mary Hamilton Legg, who was also the first married in the church of the Advent, and the first buried from its portals. The others are unknown. In 1843 Rev. C. P. Elliot was in Spartanburg district four months. He reports fifteen Sundays... "A single family who reside in the vicinity in Spartanburg" were the only Episcopalians in the district. This was the family of Major Kennedy. Mr. Elliot organized a congregation and reports the following names of vestrymen: Colonel H. H. Thomson, Charles Wear, G. W. H. Legg, L. H. Kennedy, Dr. L. C.Kennedy, A. S. Camp and W. L. Rowland. An application was made the next year to be received into the union with the Church in South Carolina, but was rejected on account of incompleteness and insufficiency of the organization.

In 1844 Rev. Mr. Phillips was in Spartanburg district. He reports: "I held service and preached in the Methodist house of worship of the village...on five Sundays. On one administered the Lord's Supper to three persons of our own and about twenty of the Methodist communion. An individual has offered to give us a lot for the church...The congregation consists...nominally of no more than six families and about the same number of communicants." He preached also at Glenn's Spring, Cedar Spring and Limestone Springs.

In 1845 Rev. R. D. Shindler reports "services at Spartanburg Court-house, and near there five." In 1847 Rev. M. H. Lance says: "I officiated twice at Spartanburg on Sunday to a large and respectful congregation in the Presbyterian church, kindly tendered, and administered the Lord's Supper to a respectable number of devout communicants...On the following day I baptized two children of our little flock." In the same year, 1847, Rev. L. C. Johnson says: "At the Court-house there are eleven communicants." These were the Kennedys, Irwins, J. M. Elford, Esq., and Major James E. Henry. Mr. Elford alone survives, a sketch of whom we present in another part of this work.

"In this missionary district, embracing eleven counties, there were in 1848 three well-organized congregations, viz.: at Pendleton, Greenville and

Abbeville, composed chiefly of colonists from the lower part of the State. Four more congregations organized were what we now call missions, and very feeble ones at that, viz.: at Landsford, Chester county, Laurens, Newberry and Spartanburg.

"In 1848 the aggregate number of white communicants reported was 115; probably 25 were omitted, say 140. In 1899 there are 11 clergy, 20 church buildings (six in Spartanburg district); 17 churches and organized missions.

"We are still a feeble folk, but the ratio of increase is not discouraging. In the whole United States during this period it has been fourfold; in this district, fivefold. Increase of communicants in the United States fivefold."

Mr. McCollough, made a deacon in 1848, divided the Sundays between Spartanburg, and Glenn's Spring. His first sermon "was in Spartanburg, July 2d, 1848, in what was then known as the Female Academy, now the residence of Captain Petty. This and the old brick building, near the old Spartanburg and Union depot, then the Male Academy, furnished places of worship for us until the 13th of September, 1851. On that day the first service was held in the little chapel, afterwards removed to Wellford. On the next day, Sunday the 14th, Bishop Gadsden made his first visit, and confirmed fourteen persons. This chapel continued to be our place of worship, until 1854, when we removed to the chapel of "St. John's School," and occupied it until 1857, when I removed to Winnsboro." Meantime a lot for the church, where it now stands, had been set off by Major J. E. Henry, and the corner-stone of church was laid in 1849. But the contractor for the brick church having left the State after only laying the foundation, and Major Henry dying before the deed was executed, matters were left *in statu quo* and the congregation gathered elsewhere. Mr. McCollough removed to Spartanburg in 1851, and opened a school in a small wooden building on the main street. "The school was well attended, and he procured the assistance of J. H. (afterwards Judge) Hudson, while the building of St. John's School was being erected. This was occupied in 1852, and was so filled with boys as to induce the enlargement of the building on a scale which was never entirely completed.

"In 1848 there were eleven communicants in Spartanburg, but when I was ordained, July 28th, 1850, they had been reduced by death and removal to five. One of these, Major J. M. Elford, referred to. From 1848 to 1857, there had been baptized 37 — 11 adults and 26 children; confirmed 22; married 9; buried 6... During these years I visited Laurens, Newberry, Yorkville, Anderson, and Pendleton while it was vacant...In 1851 regular services were held at Limestone Springs...In 1855 regular services were held at Union, and the corner-stone of the beautiful church there was laid May 1st of that year. There were two communicants in the district when I first visited it."

The corner-stone of the Episcopal church in Spartanburg was laid by Bishop C. E. Gadsden July 23d, 1850, and an address delivered by A. H. Cornish. Work on the building was suspended owing to complications mentioned until about 1860. It was finished under difficulties during "the war," and was consecrated to the worship of Almighty God.

The present number of communicants in said church, in round numbers, has been reported (January, 1900) to the writer as one hundred and fifty. It may be truly said that its present flourishing condition is due largely to the indefatigable work, in the Lord's vineyard in the early years of its existence, of Rev. John D. McCollough, whose name not only deserved to be preserved and perpetuated in the pages of the history of his church, but also in the annals of the history of Spartanburg as an educator and an humble minister of the gospel.

REV. ALBERT ALLISON JAMES was born in Yorkville, S.C., July 26th, 1824. He was educated mainly at Ebenezer Academy under the instruction of Rev. P. E. Bishop, and while yet a pupil united with the Presbyterian Church under the ministry of Rev. Ferdinand Jacobs in 1843. "He entered the Junior Class of Davidson College in 1846 and graduated two years later...Leaving college he entered the Theological Seminary at Columbia, S.C., in 1848, and graduated from that institution in 1851. He was licensed by the Bethel Presbytery the same year. His first charge was Fair Forest church in connection with the Spartanburg church, now in Enoree Presbytery, and he was installed pastor of Fair Forest in November, 1851, but continued to supply the Spartanburg church for three and a half years. Giving up the Spartanburg church, he supplied Salem church in Union district in connection with his Fair Forest pastorate for five years." Later he organized the Grindal Shoals church, which he supplied in connection with Fair Forest pastorate.

Rev. A. A. James

"When the war came on Mr. James was elected chaplain of the 18th South Carolina Volunteers, and served with this regiment throughout the war. When the war closed he returned to the same section of country from which he had gone, and taking up his work at Fair Forest he began to serve other contiguous churches. He was pastor of Alt. Calvary for sixteen years. Daring the period since the war he organized the Glenn's Spring, Pacolet, Jonesville, Trough Shoals and Enoree churches, and has supplied them all in connection with his work with the mother church."

Mr. James commands the love and esteem of the people of all churches. He is now in the forty-ninth year of his pastorate and in the seventy-sixth year of his age, but is still strong and active and "carries on a wonderful work of ministering to six churches widely separated from each other...He was for twenty years a director of Davidson College, and for eleven years a director of Columbia Seminary. He has been a member of four General Assemblies," and he was elected moderator of the meeting of the Synod of South Carolina which met at Lancaster, S.C., in 1888.

In 1853 Mr. James married Miss Sarah M., daughter of T. B, Collins, one of the first elders of Spartanburg church, which "union still exists, and is a happy one. Mrs. James is still spared to bless and help the labors of her husband."

Mr. James has done a great work in the ministry. Under the light of his preaching many souls have been converted and many afflicted hearts comforted. He has visited many sick-beds and ministered comfort and consolation in the dying hours. He has performed the marriage ceremony to about two hundred and thirty couples, and, as already stated, is universally popular with the entire people, and it is to be hoped that there are many bright years before him in the discharge of the great work in the Master's cause yet unfinished.

COLONEL THOMAS STOBO FARROW. Colonel T. Stobo Farrow was born in Laurens, S.C., in 1832, was educated at the South Carolina College, and settled in Spartanburg, and commenced the study of law in 1853, and soon after became editor and proprietor of the Spartanburg *Express,* which paper he edited for three or four years. He was three times elected by the Legislature of South Carolina to the office of Commissioner in Equity for Spartanburg district, and served as such three full terms.

Lieut.-Col. T. Stobo Farrow

At the outbreak of the civil war between the States he enlisted for the service in the Spartan Rifles and was elected a second lieutenant in the same, which office he resigned to accept the position of major on the staff of General A. C. Garlington in the South Carolina Army. When the State troops were transferred to the Confederate army he raised a company (Forest Rifles) and entered service, holding successively the positions of captain, major and lieutenant-colonel of the 13th Regt., S.C.V., and was wounded in the Second Manassas battle. Soon after the war he removed to Atlanta, Ga., where he practiced law for four years, but returned to his native State, and was one of the proprietors and editor of the Spartanburg *Herald,* established in 1875. This he conducted for eight years, which did much to redeem the misrule and corruption of a dominant political party at the time.

He was a member of the State Democratic Executive Committee that called the straight-out convention that nominated Wade Hampton in 1876, and served as a member of same committee during these exciting campaigns.

When the Democrats got control of the State Senate in 1877, he was elected clerk of the Senate to fill the unexpired term of Josephus Woodruff, and was reelected in 1882 for the same position for four successive terms, which office he resigned in 1885 to accept the position of Chief of Division in the office of Auditor for the Post-office Department in Washington during Cleveland's first administration, which office he resigned after four years' service.

In 1893, soon after Cleveland's second inauguration he was appointed Auditor for the War Department, which office he resigned after four years' service, returning to his home in Gaffney, S.C., to resume the practice of law.

Colonel Farrow has always taken interest in the development of railroad enterprises. The writer served with him as a member of the Cowpens Centennial Committee, which supervised the erection of the monument of Daniel Morgan on the public square at Spartanburg, S.C., in 1881. He is a prominent member of the Presbyterian Church.

In 1854 Colonel Farrow married Miss Laura A., daughter of Hon. James Edward Henry of Spartanburg, who died in 1858, leaving no children. Afterwards, in 1861, he married Miss Jeannie Bedon of Walterboro, S.C., who died in 1892, leaving four children: Jennie B., Julia D., Patillo, Hyder B., all of whom are living except Hyder B. Farrow, who died in 1898 at twenty-one years of age, just as he was entering upon a prosperous business career.

Recently (in 1900) Colonel Farrow was united in marriage with Mrs. E. A. Ellerbee of Gaffney, S.C., formerly Miss Ellenor Adalae LaCostae of Cheraw, S.C. He is still in the full vigor of health, and it is hoped that there are yet many years of happiness and usefulness before him.

JOSEPH MARSH ELFORD, was born in the city of Charleston, S.C., on the 21st day of January, 1822. He was the seventh son of James Maud Elford, the inventor and publisher of the Marine Signal Telegraph in nautical and marine education.

J. M. Elford, Esq.

Joseph was left an orphan at eight years of age, and was taken charge of by elder brothers and placed in the boarding-school of E. S. Courteney of Charleston, where he remained until about ten years of age, and was then carried away and placed in the care of Spencer Bobo of Cross Keys, Union county, and was by him sent to an old field school and remained there one year, and was thence removed to the wilds of the far West, in Panola county. Miss., a county then inhabited mostly with Indians, and there remained assisting on the farm and in farm work for about six years, when, health failing and becoming dissatisfied, he returned to Greenville, S.C., and entered as a clerk in the mercantile firm of McBee & Irwin; from thence he removed to Spartanburg in 1847, and assisted as co-partner in the firm of McBee & Bomar, where he remained until 1848, when he married the stepdaughter of one of the firm. Miss Elizabeth Blassingame,

278

daughter of John and Sarah Blassingame, and then purchased all of the interests of the concern and continued the same for four years or more, when he was made a magistrate and trial justice by the appointment of the governor, and served as such officer for over forty years.

In 1854 he entered the office of Dean & Trimmier, attorneys, as their assistant in office work, pursuing the study of law until 1855, when he was admitted to practice in the law and equity courts. He practiced his profession for nearly thirty years, when he retired and entered into the business of real estate and general insurance, in which he is yet employed, and, although now seventy-nine years of age, is daily in his office from 9 A.M. to 6 P.M., and is employed in clerical and other duties.

Mr. Elford claims no real title to the major only from serving as county or home commissary during the period of the civil war between the States. Thrice he attempted to become a volunteer soldier and to join some company in the army, but the strong petitions sent into headquarters from the widows and wives of soldiers, as well as home-staying citizens, to attend on them and assist in their home comforts and living, prevented and kept him at home as their assistant, and he now has letters and papers innumerable stored away in old trunks and boxes of compliments and satisfaction in the discharge of his duties.

Major Elford never had any aspiration for any public office. Repeatedly in his younger days was he announced by his friends as a candidate for the Legislature, but always entered up with thanks his disinclination to serve as such in the next paper issued. In his long line of citizenship he has served in the public capacity as chairman of the Board of Commissioners, in which position he was placed by choice of the Democratic county convention, and not at his desire or solicitation, and yet in all city and home affairs he has taken an active interest, and has served as city clerk and treasurer for upwards of forty years.

After the close of the civil war he became the trusted agent for all the old pensioners in the county, receiving only a small per cent, of their pensions for his services. He proved himself to be their faithful friend and counselor, performing his duty to their entire satisfaction. From the time that he accepted this agency all of them departed before the expiration of ten years. Some of them left their wives to his care, and he drew and arranged the obtainment of their pensions.

The following soldiers of the war of 1812 in Spartanburg County in obtaining their pensions from the government were represented by Mr. Elford, viz.: James C. Ballenger, first drawing March, 1872, and continued to death. Arthur Crocker, first drawing September 4th, 1871; died December, 1873. Lewis Camp, first drawing March 27th, 1872; afterwards he left the State and died in Georgia. Jesse Casey, near Hobby's, first drawing December, 1872; died December 1st, 1876. Daniel Epps, near Walnut Grove, first drawing May 1st, 1872; died August, 1872. John Fielder, formerly in Spartanburg County, first drawing October 7th, 1872; died in Laurens County. James N.

Gaston, near Reidville, first drawing December, 1871; died 1876. W. W. Harris, Spartanburg City, first drawing December, 1871; died May, 1875. Wm, Johnson, near Holly Springs, first drawing June, 1871; died 1873. James K. Means, near Glenn's Spring, first drawing July, 1873; died 1875 Hezekiah Pollard, [2] near Mount Zion, first drawing December, 1871; died at home. Wm. Reynolds, near Cashville, first drawing March, 1872; died 1876. Benjamin Vinson, near White Plains, first drawing September 4th, 1871; died, 1876. Judson Wilson, near Reidville, first drawing December 21st, 1871; died 1876. Robert West, near Glenn's Spring, first drawing March 28th, 1872; died March 25th, 1873. Isham Wilson, near Reidville, first drawing December 22d, 1871; died September 27th, 1876. John Vehorn, near Campobello, first drawing May 17th, 1872; died January 26th, 1876. John Wingo, near Mount Zion, first drawing December 4th, 1871; died at home. Coleman Wingo, near Mount Zion, first drawing April 9th, 1872; died at home. John Wilkins, near White Plains; first drawing October, 1871; died August, 1872. Isaac Young, near Poor's Ford, first drawing April, 1872; died November 15th, 1873.

Major Elford is now ripening into a good old age of seventy-nine years, but, blessed with health and abundant will-power, is active and young, to all outward appearances, as many a one of only three score and ten. But of all his rejoicings, he seems to rejoice more over the fact that, for fifty years or more, he has been elected annually without an intermission as one of the vestry officers of his church.

Major Elford has been prominent in the societies of the Odd Fellows and Free Masons, and in his younger years was a lieutenant in Spartanburg Volunteer Company, and, as such, took command of his company in the burial services of James Seay, who, as a soldier of the Revolution, was buried in the honors of war.

DR. WILLIAM THOMAS RUSSELL - In our humble efforts to preserve the memories of the dead none are more worthy of special notice in this volume than Dr. Wm. T. Russell, who was born in the State of Delaware, June 17th, 1827, and died at his home in the city of Spartanburg, February 4th, 1899, in the seventy-second year of his age.

Dr. W. M. Russell

Dr. Russell was of English and Scotch-Irish parentage, with sturdy Presbyterian convictions. His boyhood was spent on the farm at the village school, until the age of fifteen, when he was sent to a boarding-school or academy at Newark, Del., where he remained two years, and then entered Delaware College, in the same city, graduating in 1847. It was while a student at this college that he made a public profession of religion.

Entering the University of Pennsylvania at Philadelphia as a medical student, he graduated with the degree of Doctor of Medicine in 1850. The same year he began the practice of his profession at Canandaigua, N.Y., where he remained three years.

In 1853 he entered the Baltimore College of Dental Surgery, where he won the first prize for efficiency in dentistry.

He came to Spartanburg in 1854 and commenced the practice of medicine in connection with dentistry, and as a professional and finished gentleman he soon gained a popular reputation among the people, which he maintained to an eminent degree throughout the remaining years of his life. After coming to Spartanburg he married Miss Mary E. Stevens, a sister of Brigadier-General Clement H. Stevens, also of Bishop P. F. Stevens, who was known as the gallant commander of the Holcombe Legion in the war between the States. She, with two sons and four daughters, survives him.

Dr. Russell entered the Confederate service and was made surgeon of the Holcombe Legion, and served faithfully until the end of the war. By his unremitting kindness and attention to the sick, wounded and dying his comrades manifested their appreciation of the same by presenting him with a fine horse, which was done in camp with appropriate ceremony.

He was elected a ruling elder of the Presbyterian Church in 1857, and filled this office until his death.

Being especially interested in education he was for many years chairman of the board of trustees of the city schools.

Dr. Russell was positive in his convictions and aggressive in his undertakings. When he believed he was right it was difficult to convince him to the contrary. He was honest and progressive in his ideas, not only in medicine but in all matters of public interest. Only a short time prior to his death he advocated to the writer the idea of cleaning out all the streams in the county at the expense of the convict system, which he said would not only advance the farming interest but would prove a good hygienic measure.

As a physician and a humble professor of the Christian religion, he often ministered to troubled minds as well as diseased bodies, and his words of comfort and consolation carried solace to many a stricken home. This fact was peculiarly manifested by the large concourse who attended the funeral ceremonies, many of whom had received benefits and kindness from him, and who wished to emphasize their regard for him by paying this last honor to his memory. He was buried with masonic honors at Oak wood Cemetery, Spartanburg, S.C.

Professor WILLIAM WALKER, A. S. H., was born in Union county, S.C., May 6th, 1809, on Tyger River and near the village of Cross Keys in the same county. He was of Welsh descent, his father emigrating from Wales in the eighteenth century. His mother was a Miss Jackson, granddaughter of Ralph Jackson, Esq., who was elected by the State Legislature a justice of the quorum in Union district, S.C., only a few years after the close of the Revolution. It is said that she was a relative of General *Stonewall* Jackson, with whom

Mr. Walker during the civil war became quite familiar. During his service as hospital nurse he visited the general quite frequently, from whom he learned his mother's kinship to the illustrious general.

When about eighteen years of age the parents of Mr. Walker, who were in straitened circumstances, migrated to Spartanburg district and settled in the neighborhood of Cedar Spring. The scholastic education of the son, the subject of this sketch, was of an elementary kind. He made good use of the advantages afforded him and in course of time "gratified a large ambition which he had worthily imbibed to advance the psalmody of his church.

He joined the Baptist Church at a very early age, and amid the ebullitions of his early Christian piety and religious fervor he conceived the idea 'Praise the Lord' on 'stringed instruments,' the 'psaltery and harp,' as well as with the human voice, were not only requisites, but grand concomitants of religious worship.

Prof. Wm. Walker, A. S. H.

"To perfect the vocal modes of praise became the leading ambition of his long, laborious and useful life. Determined, *at once* he resorted to pen and paper. From the deep minstrels of his own bosom he gathered and arranged into meter and melody a wonderful book suitably adapted to the praise and glory of God."

He soon published a musical work entitled "The Southern Harmony." This popular book comprised the shaped notes or that peculiar style of musical notation which contradistinguishes the same from the more current literature of the present age.

Notwithstanding some depreciation by the press he adhered to his original system, and his reputation for attainments in his science soon spread all through the South and Southwest. "Everywhere his popularity as a music teacher went and his work received a most popular indorsement."

To distinguish him from others of the same name he was known as Wm. Walker, A. S. H, (author Southern Harmony).

Says a writer in *The Musical Million*: "Scarcely a hamlet, scarcely a church in the wooded coverts of those several sections, have not been made to reverberate the praises of God in accordance with the metrical spirit of that system he originated. 'The Southern Harmony' and his name, the name of the distinguished author, are as familiar as household duties in the habitations of the South."

Mr. Walker, not content with his first publication, determined to prepare and publish a more elaborate and thoroughly revised musical work, which he did under the title of the "Christian Harmony.'"

This book "has met with a like popular currency, and the two conjointly have given him a most enviable reputation as author, vocalist and teacher. Everywhere within the limitations of the South and West he organized 'singing schools,' as they were popularly denominated, and in each prepared, qualified and commissioned *in persona* many of the brightest of his pupils as instructors in the department of music."

He was author and co-publisher with the Miller Publishing House of Philadelphia, Pa., in publishing his musical works, and realized a large sum from the sale of his books throughout the country.

Mr. Walker was devoted to the service of a religious and pious life from early youth, and steadfastly held to it during his sojourn here on earth. His faith in his great Redeemer was of an intensely strong and abiding nature, and no misfortunes in life, of which he had many, ever caused him to despair or falter in the course he had chosen to guide him through the vicissitudes of life. He possessed in an eminent degree a happy disposition, an elastic feeling that all would be well in the end, and would never suffer his buoyancy of mind and heart to yield to any gloomy foreboding whatever might befall him. He quoted his great Psalmist: "That the righteous would never be forsaken nor his seed begging bread." He was possessed of a mind of a literary turn, and had a large and valuable library, and having been engaged for some years in the introduction and sale of books in the town of Spartanburg, he became possessed of many rare and valuable books of general interest.

He was a man of quite liberal views, and was ever ready with his means and influence to advance the cause of any enterprise which seemed to be a public benefit.

At the age of about twenty-four years Mr. Walker married Miss Amy Golightly and settled near Spartanburg. "His marriage was a happy one, their tastes being congenial and their dispositions naturally equable and uniform."

By this marriage ten children were born, five sons and five daughters, nine of whom survived him. Four sons are still living, Joseph D. Walker living in Arkansas, Absalom and Miles T. Walker residing in Texas, the latter being a Baptist minister. Franklin B. Walker, the youngest son, is a resident of Elberton, Ga. The daughters are Mrs. J. B. Davis, of Greenville, S.C.; Mrs. Emma Logan, of Forest City, N.C., and Mrs. Lou Lynch and Mrs. Flora Justice, of Rutherfordton, N.C. Miss Mary Walker, his third daughter, died in Spartanburg some years after the death of her father, which took place September 24th, 1875, She was laid to rest beside her father in Magnolia Cemetery, Spartanburg, S.C. His wife died in 1897 or '98 at the home of her youngest daughter, Mrs. Justice, in Rutherfordton, N.C. It is said that Mr. Walker died, as it were, "with melodies on his tongue for the goodness and tender mercies of God." [3]

DR. JOHN CHRISTIAN OELAND, son of John and Mrs. Catharine Louisa (Faber) Oeland, was born November 8th, 1829, "ear Glenn's Spring, Spartanburg District, S.C.

The father, John Oeland, was born November 6th, 1771, "in Denmark, Jutland State, Town Baebu. He emigrated to Charleston, S.C., date unknown, and engaged in the mercantile business successfully," and subsequently removed to his home near Glenn's Spring, February 8th, 1843. His first wife was Ann, third daughter of Mr. J. Hodge, married May 10th, 1798. No children. The second marriage was to Miss Faber, already mentioned, June 5th, 1826. By this marriage were born two sons and a daughter.

One of the sons was Professor Peter J. Oeland, a graduate of South Carolina College, who for many years was a successful school-teacher in Spartanburg County. The daughter. Miss Ann, became the wife of Dr. J, J. Vernon, a sketch of whom appears at another place in this volume. The other son is the subject of this sketch.

Dr. J. C. Oeland, living near Glenn's Spring, was instructed by Mr. Isham and Mr. Clough Beard, as well as at the Academy at Spartanburg, and prepared for the South Carolina College, which he entered in 1846 and graduated in 1849. In 1850 he began the study of medicine with Dr. J. J. Vernon as his preceptor, and in the fall of the same year entered the South Carolina Medical College at Charleston, where in two years he took the degree of M.D. He purchased a plantation on the waters of the North Tyger about two miles northeast of Wellford. Here he engaged in a successful practice extending for many miles around him. After practicing several years, however, his health failed; and being possessed of ample means he gradually gave up professional duties.

Dr. Oeland, being naturally endowed with the gift of ingenuity, devoted much of his time to the bent of his inclination — the study of chemistry, metallurgy and mechanical science. During his college days his interest in these studies gave him the appointment of "assistant" to the professor of these branches, and afforded him opportunities for practice and manipulation, of which he was quick to avail himself. His room was a fairly equipped laboratory, where he experimented more or less to the gratification of his fellow-students. Dr. Oeland, after entering on his professional work, availed himself of the appliances of the day and prosecuted the investigation and analysis of substances and waters brought to his notice.

Dr. John C. Oeland

During his life as a student in Charleston he was moved to know something of dentures manufactured from the gold base, and often made his way to the office of Dr. J. B. Patrick, where he had object-lessons and free instruction. He made several successful sets of teeth, refining and rolling the gold in his laboratory.

The writer in the earlier years of his life lived only about three miles from Dr. Oeland and saw much of him, and was impressed with his advanced and progressive ideas in everything pertaining to his profession, farm, garden and orchard. He was an up-to-date man in all that pertained to a beautiful and well improved country home. He sought the most improved varieties of fruits, grapes and melons. He was the first man in his neighborhood to introduce Peruvian guano in the cultivation of wheat. His apiary, to the uninitiated, was not only a matter of wonder and curiosity, but to his earnest and zealous mind it became a noble study, and as such he pursued it, bringing to the service the most improved hives and modern appliances in the culture.

Dr. John C. Oeland whilst in college had an attack of measles followed by pneumonia, and subsequently phthisis pulmonalis. He died August 7th, 1862, in the thirty-third year of his age. He was a Christian gentleman, a kind neighbor, a true friend, and a good physician.

October 23d, 1851, Dr. Oeland married Miss Margaret Snoddy, who still survives him. They had five children, viz.: Dr. John C. Oeland, well-known citizen and dentist in Spartanburg, standing at the head of his profession; James Snoddy Oeland, died in infancy; Isaac Raymond Oeland, Esq., attorney at law. New York City; Mrs. Mary Ellen Hammond, of Wellford, S.C.; and Miss Lizzie Oeland, who resides with her mother in Spartanburg.

DR. WILLIAM POOLE COMPTON was born in the year 1818 near Glenn's, Spring, S.C., on a plantation subsequently owned by Joseph Montgomery, deceased. From this place his father with his family moved to Giles County, Tenn.,

Dr. W. P. Compton

in 1821, where William P. grew up to manhood, receiving the best education that the common schools of that State at the time afforded. Returning to his native district, Spartanburg, he, in 1839, began the study of medicine in the office of Dr. J. J. Vernon at Spartanburg, and graduated in the South Carolina Medical College at Charleston in the spring of 1842. He settled in the practice at New Prospect, S.C., laboring on the North and South Pacolets.

In 1849 he went to the gold regions of California in company with Alexander Copeland, J. Madison Jackson, Watson Robbs, William Dodd and Calvin Foster. They traveled by an overland route, and were eleven months on the road before they reached the gold region. They remained there for about three years and were successful in their business operations, and most of the party returned home, together with Dr. Compton, richly rewarded for their labors.

After his return from California Dr. Compton married Miss Louisa Jackson, of South Pacolet, an accomplished lady, who died in 1871 or '72 leaving four sons and a daughter, all of whom are now dead.

At the commencement of the war between the States Dr. Compton organized a company composed of the young men on the Pacolets, of which he was made captain, and joined the 13th Regiment, S.C.V. After two years in the field he returned home on account of failing health, where his services were in constant demand as a physician.

On account of his personal worth and standing as a citizen he was twice elected to the Legislature of South Carolina, first in 1872 and again in 1876. He was a member of the famous "Wallace House," and was a member of the House of Representatives at the time of his death, which occurred on the 30th day of May, 1878.

During the year 1876 Dr. Compton married a second time to Miss Lizzie C. Landrum, a most estimable lady and second living daughter of Rev. J. G. Landrum, by which marriage a son (J. G. Landrum Compton) and a daughter were born.

Dr. Compton was an eminent physician and a man of sterling and solid worth, of a superior and well-balanced mind. He was a consistent member of the Baptist church at New Prospect, and also a member of the Masonic lodge at the same place, having served in the chair as Worshipful Master.

His death was deeply deplored, having a large field of practice at the time. For more than a quarter of a century he had served many households faithfully, and some in their most trying hours of affliction.

DR. THOMAS JOHN COMPTON eldest son of Dr. W. P. and Louisa Compton, was born at his father's old homestead on South Pacolet, Spartanburg County, S.C., November 23d, 1857, and died at the same place, September 30th, 1890, being thirty-three years of age.

He received his literary education mainly at New Prospect Academy under Professor John G. Clinkscales, and at Gowensville Seminary under Rev. T. J. Earle. After this he went West and spent several years, but learning of his father's death he returned home, and soon after began the study of medicine. He attended a course of five months in the Jefferson Medical College at Philadelphia, and two courses for the same length of time at the Medical College at New Orleans, and graduated there in the spring of 1883.

He located for practice at Pacolet Mills (Trough Shoals) and remained there for one or two years, and later for a few months at Landrum, S.C. But pulmonary disease had taken a deep root on his system, and he was compelled to give up practice. After a lingering illness for a few months he passed away.

Having received a finished medical education, he had already, at the time of his death, won a good reputation as a physician, and had he lived and retained his health he would doubtless have distinguished himself in the profession.

DR. LIONEL CHALMERS KENNEDY was born June 17th, 1816, in Charleston, S.C. He was the second son of Mr. Lionel Henry Kennedy, a lawyer by profession. He was a grandson of Jarves Henry Stephens, a man of mark in the Revolution under General Francis Marion. His father, in consequence of failing health, relinquished his profession and purchased a farm near Cedar Spring, to which he moved in 1836. Here he resided until his death, January 17th, 1875 being in the fifty-ninth year of his age.

Dr. Kennedy received his literary education mainly at the "South Carolina School," Meeting street, Charleston, read medicine in the office of Dr. B, F. Simmons in said city, and graduated in medicine from the Medical College at Charleston in 1834. In 1837 he came to Spartanburg and entered into a co-partnership with Dr. J. J. Boyd. They had a broad scope of practice extending into all parts of the county.

In April, 1842, Dr. Kennedy married Miss Helen F. Stephens, sister of Mrs. Wm. T. Russell, and daughter of C. W. and Sarah F. Stephens, of Pendleton, S.C.

Dr. L. C. Kennedy

During the civil war between the States he was surgeon of the 13th Regiment, S.C.V., and endured the hardships of camp life with manly zeal and courage until his health failed, when he resigned and returned home.

After the war he continued in practice to the time of his death. No physician in Spartanburg County ever attained greater eminence as such than Dr. Kennedy, He was thoroughly conversant with the literature of practice, both in medicine and surgery, and in his profession he was earnest, sympathetic and kind. In the social circle he was always charming. There was a magnetism about him which always attracted old and young. His influence was felt in every circle in which he moved, and this influence was always for good.

Rev. R. H. Reid

REV. ROBERT HARDEN REID. In an address delivered before the Reidville Female College, June 20th, 1882, by Governor B. F. Perry, the latter stated that, at the commencement of the South Carolina College in 1846, he was seated on the platform of the chapel with Colonel Wade Hampton, Governor Alston, Judge Whitner and other trustees of the college, listening to the addresses of the graduates, when one of them, a tall, slender youth, mounted the rostrum to deliver his valedictory. The first words he uttered with a trembling voice were characterized with so much earnestness and sincerity of tone that the attention of all were attracted to his eloquent and appropriate address, and it was then predicted for him a brilliant career at the bar and in politics. It was soon apparent, however, that he did not care for popular honors or distinction, but had chosen rather to exert his talents, eloquence and learning in the gospel ministry, where he thought his ability and usefulness would be productive of greater good to his fellow men. This man was Rev. R. H. Reid, the subject of this sketch.

He was the son of Andrew Reid, who was an elder of the Good Hope (Presbyterian) church for nearly a half century. He was born in Anderson county, S.C., near Moffettsville, July 17th, 1821, and is of Scotch-Irish descent.

He was prepared for college by Professor Westly Leverett, a famous teacher in his day, and he graduated from the South Carolina College, as already stated, in 1846. After this he took a regular course in the Theological Seminary at Columbia, S.C., and was licensed to preach by the Presbytery of South Carolina while in the middle class, that he might serve as chaplain of the Barhamville Collegiate Institute (near Columbia) during his last year in the seminary, which was his first ministerial work.

His first call was from the Presbyterian church at Anderson, S.C., which he accepted, and after passing a time in fasting and prayer, was ordained and installed in 1850.

In November, 1851, he was married to Miss Mary Julia, third daughter of Dr. William Anderson of Orrville, S.C., who has made for him a good wife and a hospitable home. She is distinguished for her Sunday school work, never having, for more than thirty years been absent from her post unless providentially hindered.

In the spring of 1852 Mr. Reid had two calls for his ministerial services, one from Liberty Springs and one from Nazareth, and after prayerful consideration he accepted the latter and moved to Spartanburg district, January, 1853. In the same year he was installed as pastor of Nazareth church, which office he held for forty years. After passing "his three score and ten" he tendered his resignation in consequence of diseases from which he had suffered for nearly a quarter of a century. Having grown into the affections of his congregation by a long and laborious work among them, his resignation was reluctantly accepted.

At the time of his installation as pastor of Nazareth church there were but four other Presbyterian churches in Spartanburg district, viz.: Antioch, North Pacolet, Mt. Calvary and First Church at Spartanburg. Since then quite a number have been organized in Spartanburg County, including Wellford, Center Point and Reidville, the material for which was largely made up of the original membership of Nazareth church. Mr. Reid was for several years the only resident minister of his denomination in Spartanburg district.

His coming to Nazareth greatly strengthened the membership and usefulness of that church. Preaching, which had been had only twice a month, was now changed to a service every Sunday, and an annual collection for Home and Foreign Missions and Bible Society was changed from an annual to a quarterly, and later on to monthly, and finally every Sabbath.

In his New Year's sermon in 1857 Mr. Reid brought before his congregation the subject of education. They took it up for consideration in a business meeting the following week, which resulted in receiving a large number of subscriptions for the building of an institution of learning. A building committee was appointed, a board of trustees elected, a site was chosen, and in October of the same year the corner-stone of the Reidville Female College (named in honor of Mr. Reid) and Male High School was laid. He is the founder of these schools and the first and only president of the Board of Trustees. These schools, now in their forty-first annual session, are in a prosperous and promising condition.

Mr. Reid first inaugurated the movement which led to the Enoree Presbytery and selected the name which was adopted. He presided over the first Democratic convention held in Spartanburg County after the close of the civil war, and served for four years as the first county school commissioner, laying off the school districts and establishing the public schools. He is public-spirited, taking interest in everything that has concerned the welfare of the county, while his whole life has been spent in the advancement of the cause of religion and education.

He still resides at Reidville, having in a measure recovered from diseases which afflicted him for a long time. Being now in his seventy-ninth year, he is thankful for all his opportunities of getting good and of having done a great and noble work.

By his marriage, referred to, he has three children: Rev. B. Palmer Reid, residing at Pendleton, S.C.; J. Whitner Reid, residing at Reidville; and Mrs. Ella Smith, wife of Rev. Robert P. Smith.

WILLIAM CARNEY CAMP, ESQ. was born near Warm Springs, N.C., in the year

Wm. C. Camp, Esq.

1815, and died February 15th, 1900, having reached the advanced age of eighty-five years. He was a son of Stephen A. and Annie (Alexander) Camp. His father was for many years a resident of Rutherford County, N.C., and was a citizen of prominence and influence in that County. His grandfather was Elias Alexander, who was born in 1749 and died in 1818. He emigrated from Maryland to North Carolina before the Revolution. His wife's maiden name was Nancy Agnes McCall.

The Alexanders were staunch Whigs and valiant soldiers during the Revolution, and five of this name were signers of the Mecklenburg Declaration of Independence, some of whom were uncles of the subject of this sketch.

The grandfather of Wm. C. Camp on his paternal side was Thomas A. Camp, who had twenty-four children by two wives.

Wm. C. Camp came to the present county of Spartanburg about the year 1835 or '36, and commenced the carpenter's trade under his kinsman, Adam S. Camp, but possessing a mind of more than ordinary intelligence he began the study of surveying, which he mastered in course of time, and enjoyed the reputation of being among the best in this line of his chosen profession. When in the prime of life he possessed great powers of physical endurance, was a good woodsman and has surveyed more acres of land and has been the means of settling more disputed lines among neighbors than any one who has ever surveyed in Spartanburg County. He has often been assigned by the courts to make surveys of lands in litigation, and the result of his work and reports thereon have seldom been overturned by the verdicts or decrees that followed.

He served for many years as a magistrate or trial justice, and was for several years a member of the Board of county commissioners for Spartanburg County, having been elected by the people to that responsible position. He resided for the last thirty-three years of his life near the town of Campton, which was named for him.

Soon after his removal to Spartanburg district, Mr. Camp married Miss Tabitha, youngest daughter of Colonel W. W. Harris of Spartanburg, Among the surviving children by this marriage are George H. Camp, Esq., Inman, S.C.; Mrs. Hattie Dean, wife of Dr. George R. Dean, Spartanburg, S.C.; Wm. W. Camp, Campobello, S.C.; C. Frank Camp, conductor, Asheville and Spartanburg Railroad; Mrs. Lizzie Monk, wife of R. B. Monk, Campton, S.C.; Stephen E. Camp, Kansas City, Mo.; and Thomas A. Camp, Spartanburg, S.C.

Wm. C. Camp was for many years a consistent member of the Baptist Church, and always occupied before the people of his county a position of influence and popularity. The excellent traits of his character, however, may be summed up in the following tribute to him from the pen of Dr. Carlisle, of Wofford College:

"Soon after the college opened a stranger came to my study one day and introduced himself as William Camp, a surveyor. He very clearly and briefly stated the object of his visit. His school life had been very short, covering only a very few months. He finds some things in his practical work as a surveyor that trouble him. Especially there is a 'fifty-seven and three tenths (57.3),' which he often has occasion to use. By using it he can get good results. But where does this mysterious number come from? How does it have such useful meaning in it? He had asked older surveyors questions like these, but had received no satisfactory answers. One had said to him: 'Billy, that's none of your business where it comes from. Use it as I tell you, and go on with your business.' But the squire was not a man to rest in an answer like that. It was striking to see how clearly his quick, practical mind seized explanations. As if by intuition he seemed to anticipate mathematical laws and truths, such as he had never learned from books. I soon felt that I was dealing with a man of rare abilities in some directions. This conviction was strengthened in frequent interviews through many years. What he might have become with full training in early life will never be known, As it was he showed strong qualities which fully met the expectations raised by a careful study of his fine head and face. These were strongly marked. Intelligence, sincerity, wit, good sense, and positive character were plainly written there, as all these traits were surely displayed in his long life. He was genial, full of life, a good talker, ready with an apt illustration or striking anecdote at every turn in conversation. He had rare insight into character, relieved by a disposition to be gentle rather than severe, and quick to see the playful, amusing features of life and conduct. There was no dullness or languor in company where he had the right of way. His business, during the active years of his life, threw him into free associations with the dwellers in several counties. Few men had more human beings to meet them pleasantly and familiarly. He was a welcome visitor in many a country home. And he was always ready to return the kindness at his own hospitable fireside.

Lately a younger generation has been touched to see the weight of years pressing down the manly form of the venerable 'squire.' But his kindly qualities of mind and heart remain. May the wintry frosts of prolonged life gather slowly around him. May it be granted to our old friend to have a gentle decline into the deepening shadows of age, and then a peaceful transition to 'the rest that remaineth.'   James H. Carlisle.

October 18th, 1899."

[Note. — The foregoing tribute to Wm. C. Camp by Dr. Carlisle was written a few months before his death.]

COLONEL OLIVER EVANS EDWARDS. In searching among the list of departed heroes of a "Lost Cause" in Spartanburg district, the memory of no one is dearer in the hearts of his surviving countrymen than Oliver Evans Edwards, who was born in the southwestern portion of said district, November 9th, 1819. He was the eldest son of the marriage between Zachary Edwards and Nancy Bobo, the latter a native of Spartanburg district. When about

Col. U. E. Edwards

ten or twelve years old his father emigrated to Cass County, Ga., where he grew up to manhood.

Reared under the guardianship of a pious parentage, he joined the Baptist church at Pettits Creek, Ga., in the year 1831, and later transferred his membership to the Baptist church in the town of Spartanburg, where he continued an active, zealous and devoted member to the day of his death. He was also one of its officers, and it was during his time that the present commodious brick structure of the First Baptist church on Church street was erected, through his liberality and business management.

Reaching the age of manhood he returned to his native State, and for one scholastic year he boarded at the house of General B. B. Foster and attended the flourishing school of Rev. Clough Beard at Glenn's Spring.

After this (about 1848 or '49) he selected the law as a profession and commenced its study under the legal tuition of Simpson Bobo, Esq., and by close application he was soon admitted and taken by his distinguished predecessor into partnership, which not only proved profitable but endured during his lifetime. As a lawyer he was prompt, decisive and indefatigable, always looking to the interest of his client.

In 1850 he was elected colonel of the 36th Regiment, S.C.M., which his father had commanded many years before. Prior to his promotion to office he was captain for several years of a volunteer company at Spartanburg.

In 1854 Colonel Edwards was chosen to the office of brigadier-general of the 9th Brigade, S.C.M., which position he held for a few years. In these offices he exhibited the tastes and talents that afterwards proved themselves on the stern arena of the battle-field.

General Edwards was elected to the House of Representatives from Spartanburg district; first in 1856, and also in '58 and '60. In his second canvass he received the largest popular vote, at that time, ever cast for any one candidate for that office by the people of Spartanburg. As a member of the Legislature he was active, useful and influential; being chairman of the military Committee during the last two terms of his service in that body. His labors in that capacity were arduous in consequence of the approaching revolution into which the country was drifting, making it necessary to remodel the militia system of the State. His duties were performed with fidelity to his country and honor to himself; though the overshadowing events of the times obscured and obliterated much of the work. It was while he was yet a member of the Legislature the latter called a convention which enacted the famous ordinance of secession; and, also, while in attendance upon the sessions of the House and absent from home on business, that the 5th Regiment, S.C.V., was organized under the command of Colonel Micah Jenkins, who led the regiment, after a few weeks' service on Sullivans Island, S.C., to Virginia, which was early in June, 1861, and soon after this Colonel Edwards joined him as a volunteer. The writer was with him in the part this regiment performed on that ever memorable day, July 21st, 1861, the date of the first battle of Manasses, which was the first great battle of the war, and the first test of the heroism, valor and patriotism that ever afterwards characterized the Southern soldier on many hard-fought battle-fields.

Remaining for a few weeks in Virginia and observing the gathering war cloud, he returned to South Carolina and organized the 13th Regiment,

S.C.V., of which he was elected colonel in the fall of 1861, and from that time until the glorious but terrible morning of "his last battle" he gave himself a true soldier to the cause which he had so ardently espoused; first on the coast of South Carolina and afterwards in Virginia. His regiment, which he could trust implicitly when the test of courage came, never faltered under his leadership.

Colonel Edwards died of a mortal wound received at Chancellorsville, Va., on the morning after Jackson's famous flank march on Hooker's right and rear. Previous to this he had been slightly wounded at the second battle of Manassas.

General McGowen had been taken wounded from the field, and the condition of the brigade was critical when Colonel Edwards took command. But he soon brought it to efficient action again and inspired the men by his own ingenious bearing till the fatal missile found its distinguished mark.

In Griffith's "Life of John G. Landrum," page 89, the author, who was captain of a company in McGowen's Brigade, refers to Colonel Edwards in the following complimentary words:

"He (Edwards) was known and loved and honored by the whole people of his county, and no truer, nobler, braver man fell in all the great civil war than this warmhearted Christian hero. The writer, [4] though not a member of his regiment, saw him receive his death-wound at Chancellorsville. McGowen's Brigade had just driven the enemy from a line of breastworks and were holding them against a furious charge for their recapture. McGowen had been wounded, and Edwards, as senior colonel, had assumed command of the brigade. He was walking dauntlessly on top of the breastworks a conspicuous mark for the enemy's bullets, one of which did not long shun the mark."

An officer who shared the casualties of Chancellorsville, and who was near him when he was wounded, being then under his command said: *"He just loved to fight,"* Said another: "It is known that on one occasion when the contest was ended and the mastery won, reviewing the sad work of passion, folly and sin, his heart was moved within him and he retired to a secret place and wept."

On the 23d of January, 1851, Colonel Edwards was married to Miss R. Jane Gary, daughter of Dr. Charles and Mrs. Mary Gary of Laurens district, S.C. She survives him as the present wife of Dr. J. J. Boyd of Spartanburg. It was with her that Colonel Edwards spent the happier moments of his unusually eventful life, and who was, throughout their entire married life, a constant and devoted companion.

After Colonel Edwards had been wounded at Chancellorsville. May 3d, 1863, he lived until the 21st of June following, and during this time he was tenderly waited upon by liis devoted wife. In the effort to bring him back to his home in Spartanburg, it was apparent that his vitality was growing weaker, and he was carefully lifted from the train at Goldsboro, N.C., and carried to the house of a friend, where he expired in a few days in the presence of his wife and others who had constantly .and tenderly waited about his bedside during his last hours of suffering.

Like a Christian he lived, like a Christian he died. He was wounded on Sunday morning, and after seven weeks of painful suffering he passed on Sunday morning to the Sabbath of rest in heaven. His immortal spirit, like that of Stonewall Jackson, who received his mortal wound on the same field, "crossed over the river to rest under the shade of the trees."

COLONEL JOSEPH WALKER.

In the great war between the States between three and four thousand men were enlisted in the service from Spartanburg district, and of this number only about three rose to the rank of colonel in the regular volunteer service of the Confederate States, viz.: O. E. Edwards, Benjamin T. Brockman and Joseph Walker, the latter the subject of this sketch.

Colonel Walker was born on Fair Forest Creek within two miles of the city of Spartanburg. He is a son of Jacob A. and Susan (Cannon) Walker, both natives of Spartanburg County, born respectively in 1811 and '14.

Col. Joseph Walker

The father was a son of Colonel John Walker, a native of Virginia, and the mother the daughter of John Cannon (sister of Hon. Gabriel Cannon), also a native of Virginia. They were married in 1833 and had four children, two sons and two daughters, of whom Colonel Walker was the eldest. The mother of this family died in 1850 and subsequently the father married Miss Adaline Patterson, who bore him five children, four sons and one daughter. Of these all are living except one son.

Colonel Walker was reared on his father's plantation, receiving a good common school education. In 1853 he secured a position as clerk in the store of John B. Cleveland, Sr., and remained with him for three years, during which time he received a good business education. From 1856 to 1860 he did business on his own account, availing himself of the means he had accumulated while a clerk. In 1860 he was united in marriage with Miss Susan E., daughter of Alexander Wingo, who was once sheriff of Spartanburg district. Mrs. Walker died in April, 1900.

A few months before the outbreak of the civil war the Spartan Rifles was organized at Spartanburg, composed as it was of the very best material which could be brought together in that town and surrounding country. To the command of this gallant company, numbering at first nearly one hundred men, Joseph Walker was elected captain; the lieutenants of the same being John H. Evins, T. Stobo Farrow, [5] and Dr. C. E. Fleming.

Upon the organization of the 5th Regiment, S.C.V. (Colonel Micah Jenkins), the Spartan Rifles formed a part of the same, being known as Company K. Colonel Walker commanded this company for one year, which was the term for which the company had enlisted. In April, 1862, upon the reorganization of the South Carolina troops, in Virginia, he was elected lieutenant-colonel of the Palmetto Sharpshooters, composed of twelve companies, and upon the promotion of Colonel Jenkins to a brigadier-generalship, he was promoted to the colonelcy of the regiment and served as such until the end of the war.

It would occupy considerable space in this volume to recount the distinguished service rendered the Southern cause by Colonel Walker at the head of the Palmetto Sharpshooters. When the record of that regiment is properly written and recorded in the pages of history, it will disclose his military career also. He participated in nearly all the battles in which Lee's army was engaged, and also in the Chattanooga and Knoxville campaigns under Longstreet, in all of which he proved himself to be a brave and loyal soldier and an able and efficient officer.

In referring to the battles of South Mountain and Sharpsburg, A. L. Walsh, in the Chester *Reporter,* says: "It was my privilege to be with him (Colonel Walker) as courier through that campaign, though he had two extra couriers detailed from cavalry, from South Mountain till we reached Shepherdstown. I never served under a more courteous, brave, and generous officer than Colonel Joseph Walker of Spartanburg, and but for the termination when it did, he would have been a brigadier-general." [6]

Colonel Walker and his regiment surrendered with Lee at Appomattox, and on his return to Spartanburg he engaged in business as a merchant until 1875; then was in the cotton and fertilizer trade until 1889, when he took part in the organization of the Merchants and Farmers Bank, and has since served as president of the same.

For ten years or more after the war he was the mayor of the city of Spartanburg, during which it commenced a new era of progress, which it still continues. He is a director in the Pacolet, Whitney, Beaumont and Prodnco Mills, and holds the same office in the Iron District, Fire Insurance, Converse College, Spartanburg Herald, Fidelity Loan and Trust, People's Building and Loan, and Columbia Phosphate companies, all this showing him to be a progressive business man, fully alive to the best interests of his county and State.

Colonel Walker was elected by the people of Spartanburg and the soldiers in the army from said county eligible to vote a representative to the State Legislature from 1864 to '66, and whatever service he rendered in that body was in the winter season when the armies were inactive and in winter quarters.

By his marriage in 1860 to Miss Wingo, he has two daughters living: Alice May, wife of J. Boyce Lee, merchant in Spartanburg; and Susan J., wife of L. Guy Harris, a manufacturer at Fairmount, S.C.

Colonel Walker was the first commander of Camp Joseph Walker, named in his honor. His only full brother, Felix Walker, was killed in the civil war at the battle of Seven Pines. A gallant young man, let his memory be preserved along with other heroes that perished in that great struggle for Southern liberty.

[1] See "Colonial and Revolutionary History of Upper South Carolina," p. 224.
[2] Hezekiah Pollard during the Civil War lost an only son, Willis, father of Boyce Pollard, who, on the coast of South Carolina, gave up his life in defense of his country.
[3] That part of the foregoing sketch of Mr. Walker, A.S.H., under quotation marks is extracted from a beautiful tribute to his memory by Judge T. O. P. Vernon, which was published in the "Musical Million," Singing Glen, Virginia, January, 1876.
[4] Captain Harrison P. Griffith, Limestone College, Gaffney, S.C.
[5] Lieutenant Farrow resigned soon after the organization of this company. Henry H. Thomson was elected to fill the vacancy occasioned by the same. He served until the battle of Sharpsburg, Md., where he was wounded and lost a leg.
[6] Colonel Walker informs the writer that Mr. Walsh had as many as two horses shot from under him while he was serving him as courier.

Chapter Thirty-Six - Hon. John Hamilton Evins

Son of Colonel Sam'l N. Evins, was born on the Tygers July 18th, 1830. He descended from distinguished ancestry. His grandfather, Alexander Evins, served under Mad Anthony Wayne and was wounded severely at the storming of Stony Point. He was one of the founders of Nazareth (Presbyterian) church, and was a ruling elder. His remains repose in the cemetery near-by.

The mother of our sketch was a daughter of General Thomas Moore, who fought in the battle of Cowpens against the British when a boy of only sixteen years. In later years he became prominent in the politics of the State and was a member of Congress from 1801 to '13, and from 1815 to '17. During the interval between these two periods in Congress he was in the field of the war of 1812 as a brigadier-general, commanding troops on the seacoast of South Carolina.

In early life John H. Evins received not only good educational advantages, but received what was better, the precept and example of parents who were distinguished for high-toned principles, broad views, liberal hospitality and earnest Christian character. He received his higher education at the South Carolina College, graduating from that institution in the class of 1853.

Selecting the law as his chosen profession, he was in course of time admitted to practice in the courts of South Carolina, after which he was associated in practice with that distinguished jurist, Hon. Thomas N. Dawkins, afterward one of the judges of the circuit courts of South Carolina, and with Jefferson Choice, Esq., an able and experienced lawyer at Spartanburg.

At the outbreak of hostilities between the States he was a lieutenant in one of the first companies (Spartan Rifles) raised in Spartanburg, and was gallant at the first battle of Manassas and other engagements of the war. At the battle of Seven Pines in 1862 he was so severely wounded in the left arm that amputation was proposed. He, however, sternly opposed this, and through the skill and attention of his brother, who was a surgeon in the army, his arm was saved. Upon his partial recovery, being permanently disabled from further ;active duties in the field, he continued in the performance of light military duty with the rank of colonel, until his election to the State Legislature in 1864, where he served two years.

Hon. J. H. Evins

At the close of the war Colonel Evins reopened his law office in Spartanburg, associating himself in the practice, after a time, with Major John Earle Bomar,. under the name of Evins & Bomar, and later Evins. Bomar & Simpson, with whom he devoted himself closely and successfully to his profession until 1876, when he was called to a higher sphere of usefulness.

In 1876 he was tendered the nomination for Congress from his district, and was elected to the forty-fifth Congress, and served continuously as the Representative of the Fourth Congressional district of South Carolina until his death, which took place October 20th, 1884.

In the memorial addresses delivered in Congress on the life and character of Hon. John H. Evins, January 20th and 21st, 1885, Congressman Dibble said: "In the death of Mr. Evins we have lost one with a character for honesty so high that slander could not reach it, a merit so modest that envy never assailed it, a public spirit so uniform that suspicion of self-interest never impugned it, a Christian consistency so unassuming that it escaped the sneers of the scoffer."

Mr. Hardeman of Georgia said: "Born on Southern soil and under sunny skies he imbibed in his nature their genial attributes as evidenced by the gentleness of his manner, the warmth of his nature and the purity of his life. Devoted to the South, his whole being was fired with an ardent love for the welfare of his people, the honor of his section and the glory of his State."

General Hampton, among other things, said: "The example left by such a life and the lessons taught by it ear of higher value to the world than all the

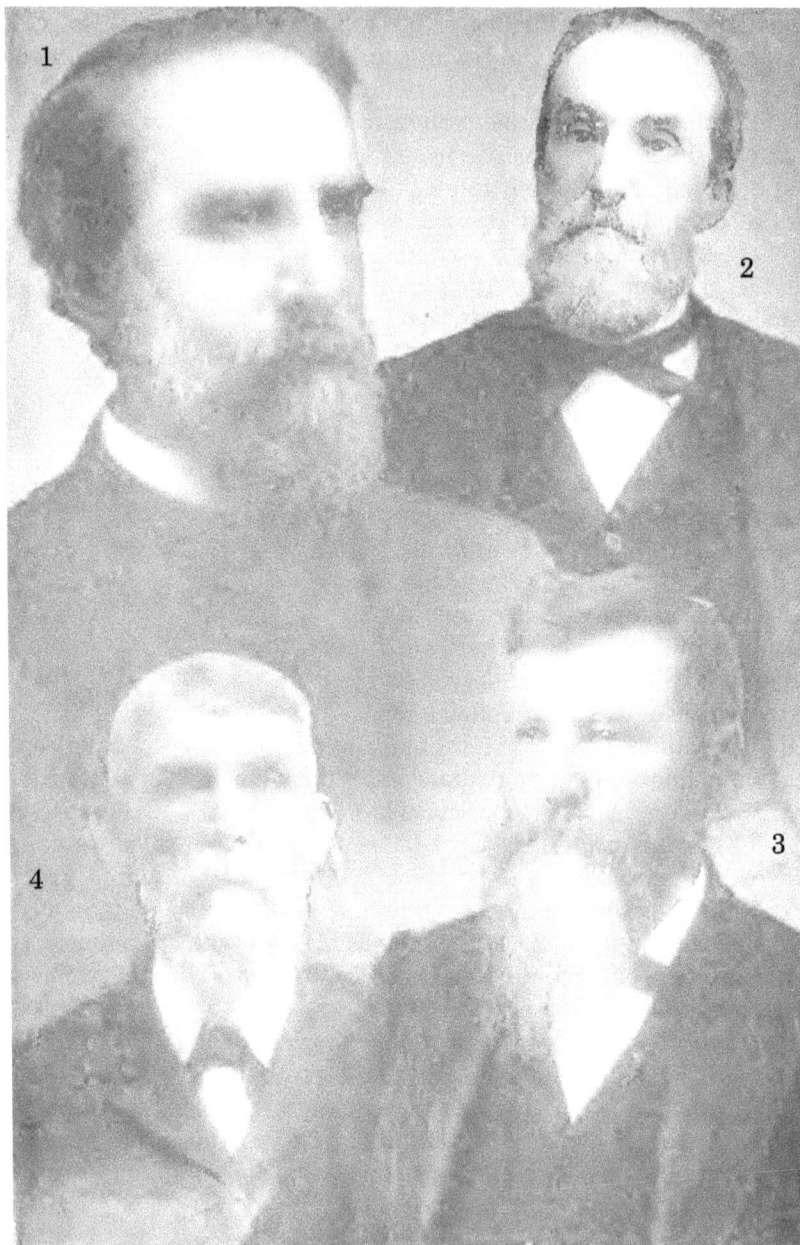

1 Major D. R. Duncan   2 Capt. J. W. Carlisle
3 Lieut. A. S. Douglass   4 Lieut. Chas. Petty
Surviving Officers Co. "C," 13 S.C.V.

prizes that ambition, wealth and power can win. These latter may for a time sway mankind, but in the balance, held by the hand of the Great Judge at the last day, they will weigh but as a feather against integrity, virtue and piety."

In early life Colonel Evins made a public profession of religion, joining Nazareth, the church of his fathers. In later years he transferred his membership to the Presbyterian church at Spartanburg, of which he was an elder, and also the superintendent of the Sabbath-school from 1868 until he entered Congress in 1877. "An unswerving fidelity to religion, his genuine and practical loyalty to his own church, and his eminent purity of life ever shone out brightly in all the circumstances in which he was placed."

In 1865 he married Miss Hattie D., daughter of Jefferson Choice, Esq., by whom he had eight children, viz.: Mary Elizabeth, Jefferson Choice, Samuel Nesbitt, Florence Moore, Margaret Emily, John Hamilton, Andrew Cleveland and Cleveland.

MAJOR DAVID ROBINSON DUNCAN, son of Professor David Duncan, and one of the leading members of the Spartanburg bar, was born at Randolph Macon College, Mecklenburg County, Va., September 27, 1836. He received his early education at Randolph-Macon College, at which his father was a professor and from which he himself graduated in June, 1855. He at once came to Spartanburg, whither his father had removed in 1854, and here, for one year, taught the Odd Fellows' High School as its first teacher. At the same time he devoted his leisure hours to the study of law, and at the age of twenty-one was admitted to the bar. He at once took up the practice of his profession in Spartanburg, where he has ever since practiced with the exception of four years during the civil war. In August 1861, he entered the service of the Confederate army as first lieutenant of Co. C, 13th Regiment, S.C.V. Upon the organization of the regiment he was made captain of his company, and was thus the junior captain of his regiment. He served in this capacity till the spring of 1864, when he was promoted to the rank of major. He was a brave soldier and a faithful conscientious officer. He was in the battles before Richmond, at Sharpsburg, Fredericksburg, Second Manassas, Cold Harbor, Chancellorsville, Gettysburg, Wilderness, Spottsylvania Courthouse, Second Cold Harbor and the engagements about Petersburg, he being in McGowan's brigade. Hill's division, and Jackson's corps.

At the close of the war he resumed his law practice. In 1865 he was elected a member of the lower house of the State legislature, and was reelected in 1870, and in 1872 was elected a member of the State Senate, serving in that body four years. In August, 1875, he was elected president of the Spartanburg and Asheville Railroad Company, and served as such four years, during which time the road was completed. This was the first railway built across the Blue Ridge in South Carolina.

In 1880 Major Duncan was elected solicitor of the seventh judicial circuit, and served eight years, being reelected for a second term in 1884. He is assistant division counsel of the Southern Railway Company. His law practice has been general in character, and he is recognized as one of the ablest practitioners in the State. Whether viewed from a civil, military or legal standpoint, he holds an enviable position, and one that does him great honor.

Major Duncan was married July 9th, 1856, to Miss Virginia, daughter of William and Martha Nelson, formerly of Alecklenburg county, Va. Mrs. Duncan is a descendant of Governor Thomas Nelson, of Virginia, who was one of the signers of the Declaration of Independence. The marriage of Major Duncan has resulted in the birth of four children, whose respective names are Mary Elizabeth, now the wife of John D. Garlington, of Laurens county; Martha Nelson, now the wife of John E. Wannamaker, of St. Matthews, Orangeburg county; William Nelson, a resident of Spartanburg County, and Carrie Virginia, whose home is with her parents.

Major Duncan and wife are members of the Methodist Episcopal Church, and in politics he is a Democrat of the true stamp and in the best sense of the word. He is a Royal Arch Mason, and Eminent Commander of Spartanburg Commandery of Knights Templar and a Knight of Pythias. He is one of the directors of the Spartan Mills Company, located at Spartanburg, S.C.

CAPTAIN JOHN WILSON CARLISLE (See picture grouped with Duncan, Petty and Douglass.) was born in Fairfield County, S.C., May 14th, 1827, entered the South Carolina College at Columbia, S.C., October, 1846, and graduated December, 1849.

He taught school for several years, and while teaching at Lancaster Courthouse, S.C., he read law with Minor Clinton of the Lancaster bar, who kindly gave him the benefit of his law library. He was admitted to the bar in 1854, and removed to Spartanburg in 1855 and began the practice of law.

February 5th, 1856, he married Louisa, daughter of Hon. Simpson Bobo, and became one of the firm of Bobo, Edwards & Carlisle.

In the summer of 1861 he assisted in raising a company which was organized at Spartanburg called the Forest Rifles. T. Stobo Farrow was elected captain, David R. Duncan first lieutenant, John W. Carlisle second lieutenant, and Alexander S. Douglass junior second lieutenant. This company, known as Co. C, entered into the organization of the 13th Regt., S.C.V. (Colonel O. E. Edwards), which belonged to Gregg's brigade, Hill's division and Jackson's corps, Army of Northern Virginia. Upon the organization of the 13th Regiment Captain Farrow was made major, Lieutenant Duncan was promoted captain, and Lieutenant Carlisle was promoted first lieutenant of Co. C. During the progress of the war Captain Duncan became major of the 13th Regiment, and Lieutenant Carlisle was promoted captain of his company, which position he held until the end of the war, surrendering the same at Appomattox, April 10th, 1865, with some twenty guns. All the commissioned officers of this company surrendered and are still living.

There was no company during the great civil war that rendered more gallant service or endured greater sacrifices than Co. C, 13th S.C. Regiment. From the company roll which we publish in this volume, it will be seen that, first and last, the number of men enrolled was 122. Of this number 26 were either killed outright or died of wounds received on field of battle, 35 were wounded and a number died of diseases. Captain Carlisle, during the great contest for Southern independence, proved himself to be an efficient and gallant officer, and his men were devoted to him.

Returning home after the close of the civil war Captain Carlisle resumed the practice of law. He was a member of the Constitutional Convention of South Carolina in 1865, and has served two terms in the State Legislature. He is still in good health and is practicing law with his son, Howard Bobo Carlisle.

HON. ALEXANDER SIMONTON DOUGLASS, son of Alexander and Janet (Simonton) Douglass, was born in Fairfield district, S.C., December 25th, 1833. His grandparents, Alexander and Grace Douglass, emigrated from the county Antrim, Ireland, to South Carolina about 1790, and settled in Fairfield district. His maternal grandfather, John Simonton, when about seventeen years old, came from Pennsylvania to South Carolina in 1779 in search of his brother Robert, who was enlisted in the Southern army. Not meeting his brother, he joined the command of Captain John McClure and was in the battle of Houck's defeat July 12th, 1780, and other engagements.

John Simonton married Margaret Strong, daughter of Charles and Janet Strong, whose maiden name was Janet Gaston, and who was the Mrs. Strong referred to in Mrs. Ellet's "Women of the Revolution," and in Howe's "History of the Presbyterian Church in South Carolina."

Alexander S. Douglass, after receiving his preparatory education in the neighborhood schools, entered the sophomore class in Erskine College at Due West, S.C., in 1850, from which he graduated in 1853 in a class of thirteen members. Dr. Grier, the president, informed the class that the faculty could not distinguish between the scholarship of four members who stood highest in the class. Mr. Douglass was the youngest of the four named by him.

After studying law under ex-Governor B. F. Perry, in Greenville, S.C., for about ten months, Mr. Douglass entered the University of Virginia at Charlottesville, in October, 1854, and took a full law course under professors of distinguished ability. Returning home from Virginia he read law in the office of Hon. R. B. Bozleton, at Winnsboro, S.C., for a few months, and was admitted to practice law in court of appeals in Columbia in December of the same year. He located in Spartanburg in January, 1856, and in December of the same year was admitted to practice in the court of equity in South Carolina by the equity court of appeals.

In January, 1857, Hon. John H. Evins and himself became the proprietors and editors of the Spartanburg *Express,* and continued together with that paper until Mr. Evins formed a law partnership with Jefferson Choice, Esq., in 1859, when he purchased his interest and became sole proprietor and editor. The paper was ably edited and gained popular favor from year to year, and no paper in the up-country did more in influencing the thoughts and sentiments of the people, being as it was, sound in Democratic principles.

In April, 1860, Mr. Douglass was a delegate from Spartanburg to the State Democratic Convention, which met in Columbia and appointed delegates to represent South Carolina in the National Democratic Convention, which met in Charleston, S.C., in the spring of the same year to nominate candidates for president and vice-president of the United States. What followed after the meeting of this convention is well known to every reader of our political history.

In August, 1861, Air. Douglass became a member of Co. C, 13th Regiment, S.C.V., and was elected junior second lieutenant at its organization. The company left Spartanburg on the 27th day of August, 1861, for Lightwood Knot Springs, near Columbia, where the 13th Regiment was organized and mustered into Confederate service, with O. E. Edwards, colonel; P. E. Calhoun, lieutenant-colonel, and T. Stobo Farrow (the first captain of Co. C), major. Then D. R. Duncan became, by promotion, captain; J. W. Carlisle, first lieutenant; A. S. Douglass, senior second lieutenant, and Charles Petty was elected junior second lieutenant.

In October, 1861, the 13th Regiment left Lightwood Knot Springs for the coast, and were distributed at different points, to watch the movements of the enemy. After the capture of Hilton Head and Bay Point by the Federal fleet, the companies of this regiment reunited at Coosawhatchie, and changing encampments from place to place — to Old Pocotaligo, Combahee Ferry, and Green Pond — it was finally consolidated (April, 1862) into a brigade consisting of the 12th, 13th and 14th S.C. Regiments, commanded by General Maxcy Gregg. Soon after, this brigade was ordered to Virginia, where it rendered distinguished service.

Lieutenant Douglass was with his regiment during the Seven Days around Richmond, and was engaged in battles of Gaines Mill and Cold Harbor, but soon after this was taken sick with fever, and was sent back to camp by the regimental surgeon. He recovered in a short while, and rejoined his regiment below Richmond opposite Harrison's Landing. He was with the army in its advance up the Rappahannock river, and was with General Jackson in his great movement to Manassas Junction in the rear of General Pope's army, and was in the second battle of Manassas.

After this, having had fever for several days, he was unable to accompany the army further; was sent back, and got a furlough; went home, and was unable to return for duty until October, when he joined his command at Bunker Hill, near Winchester, Va. He was in the battles of Fredericksburg, Chancellorsville, Gettysburg, Falling Waters, Mine Run, Wilderness, Spottsylvania C. H., Jericho Ford, Second Cold Harbor, Riddle's Shop, attack at Petersburg in front of line. Deep Bottom, Fussell's Mill, in which last engagement he was wounded, and in consequence of which he was absent from the army until October of the same year, when he returned to his command, after which he was in all the battles and marches in which his regiment was engaged, including the march to Jarrett's Station on the Weldon Railroad, in December, 1864, to meet movement of Federals; battles of

Gravelly Run, and Sunderland Station, April 2d, 1865 (the day that the Confederate lines were broken around Petersburg); and After this his command was constantly exposed to shells and Minie balls, and was about to go into an engagement at Appomattox, C. H., on April 9th, 1865, when it was recalled and it was announced that General Lee was about to surrender the army. General Custer of the Federal army passed in front of the old 13th Regiment with a white flag as it was going into the engagement.

Lieutenant Douglass witnessed that memorable scene which is too deeply impressed upon the memory of all who witnessed it ever to be forgotten, when General Lee returned from his interview with General Grant, and his soldiers gathered around him in many ranks deep — some climbing trees the better to hear and see — and in sorrow and in tears heard from his lips the sad result.

At the battle of Gettysburg Lieutenant Douglass had command of the ambulance corps of his brigade, which was composed of two men (selected for their faithfulness in the discharge of duty) from each company in each regiment, whose duty it was to march in rear of their respective commands in every battle and carry off the wounded as they fell to the ambulance, which carried them to the field hospital. He mentions an incident which took place at Gettysburg, which illustrates the bravery and character of the men who composed the ambulance corps: On the 2d of July, 1863, a Federal soldier was lying wounded in the hot sun, some distance in front of the Confederate lines, and was crying piteously to be removed. The brigade was lying behind some temporary breastworks made of fence-rails piled up in front of the men, and as soon as a soldier rose to an upright position he became the target of the Federal sharpshooters. Lieutenant Douglass got four men to volunteer to go with him and carry off this wounded Federal soldier to the Federal hospital at the Lutheran Seminary, which was within the Confederate lines. They were the target of the Federal sharpshooters until the four men got the wounded Federal on the litter, when, seeing the mission of mercy of Lieutenant Douglass and his men to their wounded comrade, they ceased firing at them. Two of these four men were from Spartanburg — Isham Kirby of Co. C, and A. Willis of Co. I, 13th Regiment, S.C.V. The other two were David Suber of Co. D, from Newberry, and Dick Taylor of Co. K, from Lexington — all members of the 13th Regiment.

In January, 1866, Mr. Douglass commenced the practice of law in Winnsboro, S.C., where he has resided ever since, and has been engaged in the active practice of his profession. He was a member of the State Legislature from Fairfield county during the sessions of 1882-83.

In November, 1860, he married Miss Mary E. Byers, daughter of James M. Byers of Union District, and by this marriage has two sons living, one of whom, W. D. Douglass, is associated with him in the practice of law. The other, J. B. Douglass, is a merchant in Gainesville,. Florida. His first wife died in 1867.

He subsequently married Miss Sallie M. McCants, daughter of James B. McCants of Winnsboro, who was his law partner until his death in 1880, and by this marriage he has three children living — two daughters and a son.

He is now an elder in the Presbyterian Church at Winnsboro, and has been the superintendent of its Sunday-school since 1860. He is yet in the vigor of health, and it is hoped that many long years of usefulness are yet before him.

HON. CHARLES PETTY (See picture grouped with Duncan, Carlisle and Douglas.) was born January 15th, 1835, near Gaffney, S.C. He was raised on his father's farm, and began his education in the "old field schools" of his neighborhood. He graduated at Wofford College in the class of 1857. Was teaching in the Spartanburg Female College when the civil war came on. He volunteered in Co. C, 13th Regiment, S.C.V., which rendered distinguished service during the war, and suffered heavy casualties. Mr. Petty was a lieutenant in this company during the entire war, and surrendered with General Lee's army at Appomattox.

After the war he engaged in farming, and teaching occasionally. In 1879 he became proprietor and editor of the *Carolina Spartan* (established in 1844 or '45), which position he now holds., and as such he has always advocated such measures as he believed to be for the best interests of his country. Mr. Petty (or Captain Petty, as he is now called) was, while a resident of Union county, chosen to represent said county in the Provisional Legislature of 1865-66, and was elected from Spartanburg County to the State Legislature in 1876, being a member of the famous "Wallace House."

In 1859 he married Miss Julia Davis of Wilkinsville, Union county, S.C. They have five children: Mrs. J. T. Calvert, Paul Petty, Mrs. Eva Petty Shearn (N.Y.), Mr. S.C. H. Henry, and Miss Agnes Petty.

DR. CHARLES EDWARD FLEMING son of James David and Sara Boatwright Fleming, was born in Columbia, S.C., August 29th, 1835, Graduated in the South Carolina College in 1855, with the degrees of A.B. and AM. In March, 1858, he graduated from the Medical Department of the University of Pennsylvania, and began practice in Spartanburg in 1859, which he continued until the outbreak of the civil war. He responded to the first call for volunteers by the governor of the State, and in the spring of '61 be-

Dr. C. E. Fleming

came second lieutenant of Co. K (Spartan Rifles), 5th Regiment, S.C.V., which was among the first companies to leave Spartanburg for the service. He served with this company for one year, when he was appointed surgeon of the 22d Regiment, S.C.V., which position he held until the surrender at Appomattox. At the close of the war he resumed the practice for a few months in Spartanburg, but subsequently gave up his profession and went to Philadelphia, where he took a full course in the Business College of Bryant & Stratton. Graduating there, he returned to Spartanburg and engaged in the business of hardware and in buying and selling cotton, in 1866, and for the following twenty-eight years was fully identified with the business enterprises of the growing city and county.

After dealing largely for years in cotton and fertilizers, he, being a member of the firm of Walker, Fleming & Montgomery, decided, with the firm, to build a cotton mill, and in 1881 purchased the fine water-power at Trough Shoals on Pacolet river. Armed with suitable letters of introduction, he went North and secured large sums of money, which, since that time, has led to the building of other extensive cotton mills in Spartanburg city and county.

After the dissolution of the firm, a few years later, Dr. Fleming was instrumental in building the Whitney Cotton Mills, and was interested in the building of Tucapau Mills at the time of his death, having organized and being president and treasurer of both.

Dr. Fleming was president of Pacolet Manufacturing Company, director of Merchants and Farmers Bank, Spartanburg, trustee and treasurer of the Kennedy Library, president of the first board of trustees of the graded school system of the city, trustee of the Converse College, and had filled every office given to laymen in his church. His death occurred June 23d, 1894. The following is an extract from the Spartanburg *Herald,* of date June 24th:

"Dr. Fleming was a man whose life and character was that of a typical South Carolina gentleman: the soul of honor — high in all his words, deeds and thoughts, but tender and sympathetic as a woman. In all the relations of life he was the exemplar of exalted manhood, beloved by all who knew him...Broad and liberal in all matters of a public nature, his advice and counsel was respected...It seldom happens that truth will allow so much to be said of a man; but his was a life worthy of emulation."

Dr. Fleming was married in 1862 to Lizzie, daughter of Hon. H. J. Dean of Spartanburg. He left four daughters and a son: St. Lawrence, Sara, Mabel, Edwin and Gladys.

COLONEL BENJAMIN T. BROCKMAN. In recording the names and gallant deeds of the heroes of Spartanburg there are none more deserving of special mention in the annals of our country's history than Colonel Benjamin T. Brockman, the subject of this notice.

He was a native of Greenville district, S.C., being the son of Hon. Thomas P.

Col. Benjamin T. Brockman

Brockman, a prominent and estimable citizen of that district, who, for some years before the beginning of the civil war, represented the same in the Senate of South Carolina. On his maternal side he is the great-grandson of Benjamin Kilgore, a distinguished captain in the Revolution, mentioned elsewhere in this volume.

Colonel Brockman was born December 11th, 1831, and received as he grew up a first-class education. Some time in the fifties he removed to Spartanburg district, purchased lands and began the business of merchandizing on the old Bancombs road about two miles southwest of Reidville.

At the outbreak of the civil war Colonel Brockman was elected captain of Co. B, 13th Regiment, S.C.V., and by gradual promotion become the colonel of said regiment. Having lost his life in defence of a "Lost Cause," it is due to his memory to state that no man stood closer to the people of his district than he did. He was a man of great benevolence and broad charity, contributing liberally of his means to relieve distress and suffering humanity wherever found. He was no respecter of persons, and would do as much for the poor of his surrounding country as he would do for the rich. He was everybody's friend and everybody was his friend. His public spirit was evident from the manner in which he built up his community. He was never married. Was promoted to the colonelcy of the 13th Regiment in May, 1863, succeeding the brave and fearless Colonel O. E. Edwards, who received his mortal wound at Chancellorsville, Va., on the third day of the same month.

No braver or more daring spirit ever led troops in battle than Colonel Brockman. He is vividly remembered by his comrades on the 12th of May, 1864, when he led that bloody charge near Spottsylvania Court-house, known to all veterans of that battle as the "Bloody Bend." Here he received what proved to be his death-wound. He was carried to a hospital in Richmond, Va., where he had an arm amputated. [1] He lived one month. He was expected home when the sad news came that gangrene had set in and his brilliant career was ended. His remains were deposited in Hollywood Cemetery in Richmond, where they still rest,

CAPTAIN JESSE K, BROCKMAN - Colonel Brockman was succeeded as captain of Co. B., 13th Regiment, by his only brother, Captain Jesse K, Brockman, born April 23d, 1839, who fell in the same battle (Spottsylvania) as Colonel Brockman, He was carried after several days from the field of battle to a field hospital, where he lingered for one week. He was buried by a noted spring near the battle-field, where he now sleeps.

Colonel Brockman and Captain Brockman "volunteered in the summer of 1861 (their commissions bearing date of August) and were made respectively captain and first lieutenant of the company which they had been active in getting up for service, which in compliment to the name was known as the 'Brockman Guards,' ...The fall of these young patriots was a heart-sickening blow, not only to the seven sisters and numerous other relatives, but also to the whole community. The wound of Captain Jesse K. Brockman was from the first reported mortal, and his young wife, leaving at home her two little boys, the elder scarcely out of arms, the younger a babe, made all possible haste to reach him. His wound was too severe to admit of his removal, and our troops having fallen back, he was left in the hands of the enemy at Spottsylvania. Before he was taken to the hospital he is said to have lain three days weltering in his blood on the battle-field, with no attention whatever except a little water which had been placed within his reach by the hand of some humane stranger.

"One friend was with him in his last days to witness his Christian resignation to his fate, and to bear his dying message to his despairing wife and helpless little sons. He was the youngest of a large family, and was from childhood the pet and darling of the household. His sensibilities were delicate and tender, his sympathies strong, his friendships ardent and sincere. He possessed much firmness and stability of character, and his patriotism was pure and unsullied. He forsook the smiles of a bride to encounter the perils and hardships of war. After nearly three years of sacrifice, toil and danger, and after passing through many terrible battles, he received his fatal stroke while waving his hat and cheering his men on to the deadly conflict. He expired May 28th, 1864, aged 25 years and 35 days."

Captain Jesse K. Brockman

Captain Brockman married January 10th, 1861, Miss Kittie Bryson, who still survives him. The two sons referred to are still living, viz.: Thomas P. Brockman, who married Ada Haynes of Spartanburg city, and now lives at Pacolet Mills with an interesting family, and Jesse K. Brockman, who married Jennie. Barry, daughter of Captain C. A. Barry, deceased, of Spartanburg County; now resides in Birmingham, Ala., with his wife and three children, viz.: Mary, Virginia and Jesse. He is at the head of a large and prosperous land abstract company, and ranks high as a business man, and is an elder in the Presbyterian church at Birmingham. He was raised and educated from his fourteenth year by Colonel T. J. Moore of Moore, S.C., whose wife is a near kinswoman.

CAPTAIN BENJAMIN KENNEDY was born November 21st, 1821, about four miles east of Union, S.C. He descended from distinguished Revolutionary ancestry. His grandfather, William Kennedy, Esq., emigrated from Virginia and settled in Union county some years before the Revolution. He married a Miss Brandon, a sister of General Thomas Brandon of Revolutionary fauie. In Howe's "History of the Presbyterian Church in South Carolina" we find the following: "William Kennedy was active in the war as a soldier, and subsequently filled various places of honor and trust. He was a member of the Legislature as long as he would consent to serve." He was for a long time county judge; was an elder in Brown's Creek (afterwards Union) Presbyterian Church. He reared eleven children, the youngest of whom was Benjamin, who married Lucie Gilbert of Abbeville, S.C. Lucie Gilbert was of French Huguenot descent. Her father, Pierre Gilbert, and mother, Elizabeth Bienaime, came to South Carolina in 1764 with a colony of Huguenots who left their native land on account of religious persecution. They came to this country under the leadership of Rev. Jean Souri Gilbert, an uncle of Pierre Gilbert. This colony settled in Abbeville County at a place on Little River which they called New Bordeaux.

Capt. Ben. Kennedy

After the death of Rev. Jean Souri Gilbert, Pierre Gilbert was the acknowledged leader of the colony, in both religious and political affairs.

Benjamin Kennedy and Lucie Gilbert were married about the year 1818. One son, John Louis, was born to them. But it was not long before the home was saddened by the death of the father. After the father's death another son came to cheer the widowed mother. He was named Benjamin for his father. Mrs. Kennedy lived to be an old woman, but she never married again. She devoted her life to the rearing and training of her two boys, and in a few years after her husband's death she removed to the vicinity of the present town of Jonesville, S.C., where she and her sons remained during their lives.

Young Benjamin, the subject of our sketch, was fond of his books and made rapid progress in Greek, Latin and mathematics, under such teachers as Rev. Jas. H, Saye and Abiel Foster.

The two brothers (John and Benjamin) did business together until after the civil war. They built a merchant mill on Fair Forest known as Kennedy's Mill, which received a good custom.

Benjamin Kennedy, before the war, was a major in the State militia, which office he held for several years.

At the opening of the civil war he volunteered, and went out as captain of Co. K, 3d Regiment, S.C.V.

At the end of twelve months, the term for which he volunteered, he resigned his commission and returned home for a short time. He then revolunteered, and was placed in the 3d Regiment, S.C. Reserves, under Colonel Wilson. Here he was acting adjutant for several months. He afterwards went to Florida with the 18th S.C. Regiment, and from that State to Virginia with the same regiment. He was in the trenches at Petersburg during the time of the explosion of the mine (1864), and narrowly escaped losing his life.

Before the fall of Petersburg Captain Kennedy was transferred to the cavalry in Johnston's army, because he was fortunate in possessing a horse.

He was present at the surrender of General Johnston's army in North Carolina. He then left immediately for his home.

After the war, Captain Kennedy married Miss Eunice Foster, daughter of Colonel B. B. Foster. He spent the remainder of his life on his farm, near Jonesville, S.C., where he died June 7th, 1894, aged seventy-two years. He left a wife and seven children to mourn the loss of a noble husband and father.

Captain Kennedy was a member and elder of the Fair Forest Presbyterian Church until shortly after the war, when he joined the Sulphur Spring Baptist Church, of which he was a consistent member and deacon at the time of his death.

He was a pure, virtuous and upright man all his days. "A good name is rather to be chosen than riches."

JOHN A. LEE. Among the present resident population of the city of Spartanburg, there are none who have been longer identified with the business and material prosperity of said city than John A. Lee, or *Major Lee,* as he is familiarly known and called by the people. He won the title of major from the fact that during the civil war he was commissioned and appointed by authority of the government of the Confederate

Major John A. Lee

States agent for the purchase of commissary supplies. He was born in 1824 near Pacolet, S.C., was raised on his father's farm, and received a good education in the common schools of his neighborhood.

Beginning business in Spartanburg in 1847, he is at present the eldest merchant in that city. He was at first associated with B. F. Bates in the mercantile business, the firm being known as Lee & Bates, which copartnership only lasted two years. He then did business for himself in the same line until 1853, when the firm name became Lee & Twitty, succeeded in 1855 by Lee & Briggs. After the war the same house reopened, and from 1867 to 1871 was known as J. A. Lee & Co. From then until 1883, when he took his son, Mr. Boyce Lee, into partnership with him, he was alone in business and succeeded in placing his mercantile house as the leading one in the city.

The present firm of J. A. Lee & Son ranks among the foremost in the city of Spartanburg, carrying a stock of merchandise not much short of $50,000, which consists of foreign, domestic and other first-class goods, together with a full line of groceries in a separate compartment of the extensive mercantile establishment, the trade of which extends through Spartanburg, Union and Laurens counties in South Carolina, and also in Polk, Rutherford and

Cleveland counties in North Carolina.

In all his business relations, at home and abroad, no one stands higher in the estimation of the people as a gentleman and business man than John A. Lee. He and his son have deservedly gained their present position as the most solid business men of the county, the father especially having won his reputation by industry, good management and economy — having started life, figuratively speaking, on nothing at all; and that he is a high-toned merchant lies in the fact that during his fifty-three years of business life he has not compromised a single debt.

Major Lee has not only been a successful business man, proving himself to be at all times high-minded and honorable, but he has always been liberal and public-spirited. From 1850 to 1865 he was postmaster at Spartanburg, which embraced the entire period of the civil war, and is familiarly known to the survivors of that period as the "War Postmaster." He is a consistent member of the Methodist Church and a generous supporter to all its benevolent objects.

He has been married three times: First to Miss Rosanna Briggs, by whom he has two children, viz.: Mr. J. Boyce Lee and Mrs. D. E. Hydrick.

Second, to Miss Lizzie Anderson, daughter of Rev. J. Monroe Anderson, who was a professor in Davidson College, N.C.

His third marriage was to Corrie, daughter of Mason G. Anderson. (See Anderson family.)

GEORGE COFIELD was born in Union county, S.C., February 16th, 1834. He is the second child in order of birth of nine children of Thomas K. and Anna (Caldwell) Cofield, the latter a native of Newberry county, born February 17th, 1811, being the daughter of Joseph Caldwell, and who married August 20th, 1831. His father, Thomas K. Cofield, born February 17th, 1811, a farmer, was the only child of Edward Cofield, a native of Virginia.

Geo. Cofield, Esq, President National Bank, Spartanburg, S.C.

George Cofield was reared on his father's farm where he was born, receiving his early education in the common schools of his neighborhood. In 1855 entered the Wofford College, from which he graduated in 1858. He was engaged in school-teaching one year before his graduation and taught three years afterwards.

In the spring of 1862 he enlisted in the service of the Confederate States, being a member of the Holcombe Legion, where he served until the latter part of 1863, holding the rank of second lieutenant. Returning home he remained a year, when in the autumn of 1864 he reentered the service in the Holcombe Legion, where he remained until the close of the war.

Returning to Spartanburg after this he engaged in merchandizing until 1870, when he went into the banking business. He was made assistant cashier of the Spartanburg branch of the Citizens Savings Bank of South Carolina. Upon the organization of the National Bank of Spartanburg, July, 1871, he was made its cashier, which position he held until 1885, when, upon the death of Mr. D. C Judd, he was made president, which position he still holds. In 1887, upon the organization of the Spartanburg Fidelity Loan and Trust Company he was made president, which position he still retains. For the past twenty-six years he has been secretary, treasurer and manager of various building and loan associations in Spartanburg, having wound up several during that time, while others are still in successful operation. He is one of the principal originators and president of the Iron District Fire Insurance Company organized in 1890 with a capital of $100,000. For many years he has been superintendent of the fire insurance company at Spartanburg, and is at present a stockholder in the Spartan mills and the Converse College Company.

In 1859 Mr. Cofield was married to Miss Mary C., daughter of David W. Moore, a well-known and popular citizen who resided in Spartanburg. By this marriage ten children were born, only three sons and three daughters of whom are now living. Their names are James, Clemintina, George, Margaret, Ruth and Robert.

Mr. and Mrs. Cofield are members of the Methodist Church. Mr. Cofield has filled several positions of responsibility in his church relationship, being at present a member of the board of stewards and of the board of trustees of the church. In the organization of the South Carolina Conference he was made a member of the legal conference and is also a member of the board of trustees of Wofford College at Spartanburg.

Mr. Cofield is in every sense a progressive and public-spirited citizen. While he has been closely identified with various financial operations, he has not held these for selfish gain, but in the broad sense of a public spirit. In the various institutions and industries which have gone to make up the material growth and prosperity of the city of Spartanburg, Mr. Cofield has always taken a leading part and her citizens have been benefited thereby.

GENERAL HUGH LEGARE FARLEY, son of Wm. ly. and Phebe M. (Downs) Farley, was born in Laurens, S.C., June 15th, 1844. He received his early education

Captain Hugh L. Farley

at Laurens Academy and afterwards attended the King's Mountain Institute, and was a cadet in that institution when the war broke out. At the age of sixteen he enlisted as a private in Co. G, 3d Regiment, S.C.V., and soon after enlistment was made a sergeant of his company, and at the expiration of twelve months' service he was promoted to orderly sergeant of his company, having in the meantime acted as its drill officer. Just before the battle of Fredericksburg he was elected ensign of his company. Beginning with the battle of Gettysburg, he served as adjutant of his regiment, and continued to serve as such until just before the battle of Chickamauga, at which time he was ordered to report to General J. B. Kershaw of McLaw's division, and through the memorable battle that followed he served as staff-officer to General Kershaw, and was sent to Richmond in company with two noncommissioned officers to represent Longstreet's corps to bear the official report of the battle of Chickamauga, and also to convey to the seat of government the colors captured of the enemy in that battle. In this battle he performed brave and gallant service, for which he was recommended for promotion.

Returning from Richmond he rejoined his regiment then before Chattanooga, serving through the winter campaign in East Tennessee, and was wounded before Knoxville.

After the battle of Knoxville he marched with his command to Gordonsville, Va., and was engaged in the battle of the Wilderness, where he was shot through the face. Recovering after a time, he took part in the engagement at Cold Harbor, and remained with his regiment until Grant invested Richmond and Petersburg. Then, under the recommendation which had been tendered him for promotion, he was transferred to the cavalry division of the Army of Northern Virginia, and was assigned the duty of drilling and organizing the dismounted cavalry of that branch of the army. In this service he acted as adjutant-general of the dismounted corps, remaining there until Sherman reached Savannah, at which time he was ordered to Columbia, S.C., on detached service. On the evacuation of Columbia, General Farley organized a company of scouts and marched in rear of Sherman's army, harassing his outposts, and served in this capacity until the end of the war, reporting in the meantime to General Johnston.

At the close of the war General Farley returned to his home at Laurens, S.C., and was the same winter (1865) chosen reading clerk of the House of Representatives of his native State.

In 1870 he took an active part in the disturbance of that year, which ended in the famous riot at Laurens, caused by the resistance of the people to Radical rule. Though not engaged in the riot, he was arrested, charged with participation therein, and was kept in confinement for two weeks, but was never brought to trial. He then moved to Spartanburg, where he engaged in the service of the Spartanburg, Union and Columbia Railroad for four years. After this he assumed the editorial management of the *Carolina Spartan* for four years, conducting that paper with marked ability, which embraced the period of the campaign of 1876, and during this time he was a spirited writer and an active canvasser in the campaign of that year.

In 1880 he was admitted to the practice of law and opened a law office at Spartanburg. In 1882 he was nominated in a primary election by the people of Spartanburg County for the Legislature, and was elected and served during the sessions of 1882-3.

In 1890 the farmer's movement swept the State and General Farley, as the candidate of that movement, was triumphantly elected adjutant and inspector-general, which office he held for four years. He was subsequently assigned to the work of making up the rolls of Confederate soldiers of South Carolina, but did not live to perfect that important work.

General Farley was a fearless man, a brave soldier and a genuine scion of the old Virginia stock from which he descended.

He was never married. His brothers and sisters were: Emma, wife of R. W. Boyd, attorney at law, Darlington, S.C., now deceased; Mary, wife of General R. P. Todd, Laurens, S.C., now deceased; Wm. Downs Farley, independent scout of General J. E. B. Stuart, killed at Brandy Station, who has made a name in history; Colonel H. S. Farley, an ex-Confederate soldier and professor of military tactics and mathematics at Sing-Sing Military Institute, N.Y., where he has been for many years; and L. E. Farley, a well-known and popular citizen of Spartanburg, who was a representative in the State Legislature from 1890 to '94. Both of the sisters referred to were educated before the civil war at Limestone Springs, under the Drs. Curtis, graduated and received gold medals.

COLONEL GEORGE WASHINGTON HAMILTON LEGG was born in Spartanburg County on the 26th of November, 1814. He was the son of Fortunatus Legg, Esq., a citizen of prominence in his day. The son, after he grew up to manhood, engaged for a time in the mercantile business. He selected the law, however, as a profession, and after studying one or two years was admitted to practice in the courts of his State.

Col. G. W. H. Legg

On the 22d of June, 1840, he married to Miss Clementine S. Kennedy, daughter of Lionel Henry Kennedy of Charleston, S.C., a learned lawyer of that city, who was the grandson of the celebrated Dr. Lionel Chalmers, a nephew of the Duke of Argyle of Scotland. His wife was Miss Mary Ann Jane Stephens, the daughter of J. Henry Stephens, an Englishman born in London, whose mother was a Miss Walpole, relative of Sir Robert Walpole, and whose father was Captain John Stephens of the British navy.

George W. H. Legg from the time he grew up to manhood occupied a position of prominence before the people of Spartanburg. Back in the forties he was postmaster in the town, and during his administration occurred an exciting incident, which possibly never happened in the experience of any other post-office official in the State.

A noted abolitionist from the North appeared in Spartanburg district and other places and made some incendiary publications which were against the peace and dignity of the State. It was believed that his purpose was to incite an insurrection among the negroes, and he was accordingly arrested and imprisoned in the jail at Spartanburg, where he was held for a time. He was having an extensive correspondence in and out of the State with persons believed to be in full sympathy and cooperation with his movements, and his mail was addressed to the post-office at Spartanburg.

A public meeting of the citizens of Spartanburg, both of the town and country, was called, and a vigilance committee was appointed, who demanded of Postmaster Legg the possession of the undelivered letters addressed to the individual referred to. This he refused to give, as his instructions from the government were to not *"deliver letters in his possession to any but those to whom they are directed or upon order."*

A warrant for his arrest was accordingly issued (August, 1849), which was a purely technical proceeding to which he readily submitted, referring the matter, however, to the postmaster-general of the United States. As this was a conflict between the State and Federal authorities the matter was referred to the attorney-general of the United States. It is needless to say that after a thorough investigation of the facts and the law bearing upon the same. Postmaster Legg was fully sustained for having carried out in good faith what he understood to be his official duty.

Colonel Legg was also for a number of years the intendant of the town of Spartanburg, and as such welcomed, in April, 1856, in behalf of the town, the Washington Light Infantry of Charleston, on the occasion of their visit to the battle-field of Cowpens.

He was public-spirited in every sense of the word, and took a lively interest in everything looking to the upbuilding of his town and country. Especially was he active and interested in the Spartanburg and Union Railroad, and upon its completion to Spartanburg in 1859 he was depot agent at the latter place until the outbreak of the civil war between the States.

Colonel Legg, although having received no military education or training, was nevertheless an accomplished and graceful commander of military organizations. He was first elected captain over the old Spartanburg Volunteers, and after this was elected major of the lower battalion, 36th Regiment, S.C. M., which office he held for several years. He was subsequently elected the first captain of the Morgan Rifles of Spartanburg, a handsomely uniformed and equipped company, which he commanded for about four years, until within a few months before the outbreak of the civil war, when he was elected colonel of the 36th Regiment, S.C. M. Under his call as commander of this regiment the first companies volunteered for the Confederate service. Over one of these companies, Morgan Light Infantry, Colonel Legg was elected captain, but upon the organization of the 5th Regiment, S.C.V., for active service, he was elected lieutenant-colonel, which position he held until the expiration of his term of service. Being well advanced in years, and afflicted with rheumatism, he was forced to retire from the service.

After the close of the war and up to, possibly, the time of his death, which took place on the 15th of May, 1880, he served as one of the trial justices for Spartanburg County. Having read law and been admitted to practice in earlier life, he was made a referee of some knotty court cases, and it is said his legal opinions were well thought of, and in special cases his views were sought by older lawyers.

As a public servant, whether in a civil or military capacity. Colonel Legg was faithful, honest and trustworthy. He was possessed of a kind heart and a magnanimous nature, which every one with whom he was associated felt and appreciated.

By his marriage with Miss Kennedy he had seven children, four of whom are living, occupying important positions. Among the latter we would mention Dr. George Legg of Greenville, and Professor Claude L. Legg, president of the Bennett School, a very large public institution in Charleston, S.C. Professor Legg is the youngest son, with whom the surviving widow resides.

[1] The writer has before him what possibly is the last letter ever written by Colonel Brockman. It is addressed to his sister, Mrs. Dr. Harris, of Rutherfordton, N.C., and reads as follows: "Richmond, May 24th, '64.   Dear Sister Mary: — I have been unfortunate in losing my left arm in the battle of the 12th of May, the bloodiest fight of the war. Jesse was wounded, I expect dangerously, and fell into the hands of the enemy. Poor fellow, the only brother I had is now, perhaps, cold in death, but we have to submit to these things. He was, as I am informed, acting with distinguished valor when he was shot... Excuse short note. My respects to the Doctor and a kiss to Edgar. Truly your brother, B. T. Brockman."

Chapter Thirty-Seven - Captain Harrison P. Griffith

Was born in Laurens County in 1837. He is of South Carolina descent, the paternal line extending through Stephen, his father, and Benjamin, his grandfather, to Ezekiel Griffith, his great-grandfather, who was a native of Wales and a soldier of the Revolution. His mother, Martha Woodruff, was a daughter of Thomas Woodruff,, the first settler of the town of Woodruff, who married Mary Patillo, daughter of Dr. Richard Harrison, a soldier of the Revolution and one of the first county court judges for Spartanburg, whose name is mentioned elsewhere.

Captain Griffith was reared on his father's farm in Laurens County, and educated at the Furman University. "In August, 186t, he enlisted in Co. E, 14th S.C. Regiment, brigade of General Maxey Gregg, was elected first lieutenant at the organization, and in the fall of 1862 was promoted to captain. His first battle was at Port Royal on the coast, and then going to Virginia he took part in the great combats of Gaines' Mill, Frazier's Farm and Malvern Hill; fought through the Maryland campaign and the famous battles of Fredericksburg, Chancellorsville and Gettysburg, in the latter battle receiving a wound in the leg. At the battle of the Wilderness, May, 1864, he was shot through both feet and disabled for further duty on the field. After his recovery he attempted to report for light duty, but the war came to an end before he could reach the field."

After the close of the civil war he engaged in farming for a few years, and in 1872 he established a school at Woodruff, called the Bethel High

Captain Harrison P. Griffith

School, which he conducted successfully for eight years. He was then made first president of the Cooper Limestone Institute, now Limestone College, which position he held for fifteen years.

Under the head of our Education Review, we have already noticed him in connection with this institution.

Since retiring from the office of president, he occupies the chair of English and Latin in what is now Limestone College.

Professor Griffith is a frequent contributor to current literature. In 1883 he published a volume, "Life of John G. Landrum," which was well received. More recently he has published in pamphlet form a thrilling account of his recollections of the battle of Chancellorsville and of Jackson's famous flank movement, which is the best this writer has ever met with.

In 1897 he was elected colonel of the Cherokee Regiment United Confederate Veterans, an honor

R. B. Monk

which was worthily bestowed. Captain (or Colonel as we now prefer to call him) Griffith is still in the full vigor of health and strength, and we trust there are still awaiting him many years of usefulness and prosperity.

ROBISON BISHOP MONK. Among the representative agriculturists and progressive business men of Spartanburg County, there are none worthy of more prominence than R. B. Monk, the subject of this sketch, who, by honest industry and perseverance, has accumulated a handsome competency for himself and family, thus proving what may be accomplished in this day and generation by conducting the business of the farm in a systematic and methodical manner.

He is a son of Thomas O. and Jane (McElreath) Monk, and was born in Spartanburg County, October 27th, 1833. He was reared to appreciate what it is to make an honest dollar by the sweat of his brow, and was educated in the schools of his neighborhood. He married first Miss Fannie Clifton, by whom he had one child, a daughter, who subsequently became the wife of Mr. James Geddes, a merchant at Spartanburg. Mr. Geddes and his wife are both dead. Three children survive them. He married a second time to Miss Lizzie, second daughter of William C. Camp, Esq., by whom he has a son — Robbie.

It may be said of Mr. Monk that his success as a farmer has been largely due to his excellent judgment and close attention to business. He would prove a success where others would fail.

In early life he embraced the Christian religion and became a member of the Presbyterian Church, but for reasons satisfactory to himself he subsequently joined the Baptist Church, of which he is a prominent member and deacon. He has been a regular attendant as a delegate upon the associations to which his church belonged for thirty-five years or more, and has often been a member of the State and Southern Baptist conventions and other religious bodies. He calculates first and last that he has spent as much time in these religious bodies as would make two and a half months.

Before the outbreak of the civil war between the States he was a captain of a militia company in Greenville district, S.C., and at the beginning of said war in 1861 he enlisted in Co. B, 22d Regiment, S.C.V., and continued with said regiment, participating in all the battles in which it was engaged until 1863, when, on account of a severe illness of typhoid fever, he was retired from the service.

Since the war he has lived the life of a quiet and industrious citizen. Although giving close attention to his private business, he is nevertheless liberal, benevolent and public-spirited in all matters looking to the upbuilding of his county and State. He is especially interested in the spread of a liberal education among the rising generations of his country, and is one of the trustees of Limestone College, Gaffney, S.C., which is one of the leading educational institutions of the South. To this honorable position he was selected with reference to his eminent fitness and business management.

WILSON HENRY MOORE, son of Peter and Rosa (Wood) Moore, was born June 13, 1835, in the immediate neighborhood where he now resides, which is near Arlington Mills in the present county of Spartanburg. He was educated in the Zoar Academy, taught at different periods by Lew Cocorel, Thomas W. Wingo, Wm. K. Dickson, Zera Green and others.

Public interest centers in Mr. Moore largely owing to the fact that he is one of the survivors of the terrible mine explosion near Petersburg, Va., July 30th, 1864.

In January, 1862, he volunteered in Co. B, 22d Regiment, S.C.V., commanded respectively by captains John Wheeler, Payton Ballenger, Robert G. Fleming, W. Alex Benson and George B. Lake, and was in the service all the time until he became a victim of the mine explosion. Besides Captain George B. Lake, Lieutenant W. K. Lake, and one private (Ransom Lee), Wilson Moore and Bee Keller, who was temporarily absent at the time of the explosion, were the only persons left in Co. B, 22d S.C. Regiment, to tell the horrors of the crater. Thirty-two men in this company were buried for eternity.

Wilson Henry Moore

It is known to every reader of the history of the civil war that the explosion of the mine near Petersburg was the result of an effort on the part of the Federal army to break through the Confederate lines near that place, and the horrors resulting therefrom can never be accurately described on the pages of American history. A Federal officer who was an eye-witness states: "It was a magnificent spectacle, and as the mass of earth went into the air, carrying with it men, guns, carriages and timbers, and spreading out like an immense cloud as it reached its altitude, so close were the Union lines that the mass appeared as if it would descend immediately upon the troops waiting to make the charge...Little did those men anticipate what they would see upon arriving there: an enormous hole in the ground about 30 feet deep, 60 feet wide and 170 feet long, filled with dust, great blocks of clay, guns, broken carriages, projecting timbers and men buried in various ways — some up to their necks, others to their waists, and some with only their feet and legs protruding from the earth."

Just a few hours before the springing of the mine at Petersburg Wilson H. Moore had just come off guard duty. Finding his comrades all lying lengthwise of the ditch for the convenience of room, he lay down crosswise of the same. He thinks that it was this position which saved his life, that he was thrown upward by the effect of the explosion. Being asleep at the time he was thrown upward, his first consciousness was the falling of clods of dirt upon his head; this caused him to throw up his hands, which were discovered protruding above the earth when the cloud of dust had passed off. Bee Keller, who was absent when the mine was sprung as stated, returning, found him in this position, and attempted to rescue him, when he was arrested by the enemy who had already entered the crater. He (Keller), with Captain Lake and Lieutenant Lake, who had been dug out alive, was carried to the rear and sent to prison. One of the legs of Wilson H. Moore, who was also dug out by the troops of the enemy, being fractured, he could not be removed. He says but for the protection of three white Federal soldiers, he would have been clubbed to death by the negro soldiers as they entered the crater. All day long from the hour of the explosion until 9 o'clock at night he lay in the earth with his limb fractured and undressed, without a drop of water and only with shirt and drawers on, having undressed before he laid down to repose with his comrades. The officers and litter-bearers of his own regiment having all been killed in the explosion, there was no one whose special duty it was to look after him after the crater had been recaptured by the Confederates. His sufferings were almost intolerable, and through a kind providence his life was miraculously saved.

Bee Keller, whom we have stated escaped this terrible explosion, was never permitted to return to his home. He died in prison a few months afterward. Lieutenant W. J. Lake, one of the officers already referred to, lived until the past year (1899), when he, too, "crossed over the river" to rejoin the spirits of his brave companions who had gone before him. Only two survivors, members of this company of brave heroes, are now living, Wilson H. Moore, the subject of this sketch, and Captain Geo. B. Lake. (See sketch.)

After the close of the civil war Wilson H. Moore returned home to pursue the life of an honest and industrious farmer, which character he has always maintained, commanding the respect and esteem of his neighbors.

October 20th, 1855, he married Martha Jane, daughter of Joseph Smith near Holly Springs, by whom he has children, viz.: Josiah Pinckney, Jesse Oliver, Laura Abbe and Wm. Henry.

Dr. M. O. Rowland

DR. MARCUS OBADIAH ROWLAND was born June 4th, 1836, in Spartanburg County, S.C. His ancestors were of Revolutionary stock. He is a son of H. J. and L. VV. (Trimmier) Rowland. His paternal grandfather was George Rowland and his maternal grandfather was Obadiah Trimmier, from whom he derives his middle name, who was among the first county court judges for Spirtanburg. He obtained a good education in the common schools of his neighborhood; studied medicine with Dr. L. C. Kennedy at Spartanburg, and graduated at the Medical College of South Carolina at Charleston in 1859, and began the practice at his father's old homestead place, near Boiling Spring, S.C., where he now resides.

In April, 1861, he entered the service as a member of the Lawson Fork Volunteers (Captain Rial B. Seay); was elected surgeon of said company, but after a time was discharged by a petition to return home and practice medicine, which he did for awhile; but being yet young in years, and there being an increasing demand for soldiers in the army, he revolunteered and entered the cavalry arm of the service, where he remained until the end of the war. Returning home he resumed the practice of medicine in connection with his farming operations. He was elected and served as a representative in the State Legislature from his native county from 1890 to '96, and was a member of the Constitutional Convention of South Carolina which met in 1865.

During the present year (1899) Dr. Rowland was appointed by the governor as one of the Board of Directors of the S.C. Penitentiary to fill the unexpired term of Cunningham resigned. A better selection to fill this important office could not have been made among the citizens of Spartanburg County or anywhere else. Dr. Rowland, outside of the fact that he has always stood well as a physician, is a progressive citizen and farmer; a man of sound judgment and conservative ideas; a popular and safe adviser among his neighbors and people, and a useful citizen and an obliging neighbor. He is a prominent member of the Masonic fraternity and has been Worshipful Master of New Prospect Lodge for a number of years. He is still in his years of activity and usefulness. He has never married.

LIEUT. WM. A. NESBITT, son of Jas. Madison and Elizabeth Dawkins (Fielder) Nesbitt, was born June 14th, 1840, and was killed at the Second Battle of Manassas, August 30th, 1862.

He was reared with industrious habits and educated in the best schools of his neighborhood, and when he had about reached the full years of his maturity he vol-

Lieut. W. A. Nesbitt

unteered in the service of his country. He first joined the Blackstock Company (K), Third Regiment, S.C.V., and passed safely through the battles of Bull Run (Blackburn's Ford) and First Manassas; subsequently joined Company H, Hagood's 1st South Carolina Regiment (Captain J. C. Winsmith), of which he was elected first lieutenant, which office he held at the time of his death. In the great battle in which he was numbered among the killed he acted with distinguished bravery. His colonel said that "Young Nesbitt acted with such signal gallantry that the sharpshooters of the enemy seemed to single him out as the victim of their wrath."

Lieutenant Nesbitt was pure in morals and was possessed of a pleasing disposition. Young, manly, industrious and temperate, he promised to be the comfort and roof-tree of his widowed mother and fatherless sisters.

His father's death preceded his a little more than a year, which took place October 3d, 1861, caused from illness which he contracted at Richmond, Va., while attending his son, who was prostrated with typhoid fever. He was a ruling elder in the Mount Calvary (Presbyterian) Church, and in a quiet, unostentatious manner discharged the various duties of his station in life. In this capacity "he was pious, faithful and self-denying; as a citizen, exemplary, benevolent and charitable; as a master, judicious, humane and kind. An affectionate husband and father, he left behind him a devoted wife, who survived him many years, and seven children to mourn his loss."

DR. GEORGE R. DEAN, a prominent member of the medical profession in the city of Spartanburg, S.C., was born January 25th, 1844, in Anderson county, S.C. His father, a Baptist minister, descended from Charles Dean, one of two brothers who landed at Alexandria, Va., in 1670, and settled near Mt. Vernon. His mother was descended from the Broyles (Scotch-Irish), a prominent family in Anderson county. His education was of the common school until 1860, when he entered Furman University at Greenville, S.C. In 1861 he went to the Citadel at Charleston, S.C., where he, with that gallant corps, fought the battles up and down the coast with other Confederate soldiers; and when the days of danger were over, he and his fellow comrades were recalled to the institution, and thus pursued their studies while the soldiers were passing weary hours in the camps. He was graduated from the Citadel after the

Dr. Geo. R. Dean

war as captain of Co. A, the highest office to which a cadet could attain, and stood second in a class of thirty-six.

After the war he taught school at Belton, S.C., and read medicine at the same time. He entered the South Carolina Medical College at Charleston in the fall of 1866, and graduated in the Jefferson Medical College, Philadelphia, in the spring of 1868.

Soon after this he married Miss Hattie, eldest daughter of Wm. C. Camp, Esq., of Spartanburg County, and two years afterwards removed to Spartanburg County, where he began the practice of medicine near Campton in connection with farming, proving successful in both. He was the pioneer of redeeming the old fields in his section thought to be worthless, and, as a result, cotton soon; became a large business in that portion of the county (Campton) where it was only grown a few years before in small quantities.

In 1886 Dr. Dean was elected and served as a representative in the State legislature from Spartanburg County, but having no special inclination to politics he declined reelection. In 1889 he moved to Spartanburg, where he has practiced his profession ever since. He is now president of the Southern Railway Surgeons' Association, member of the State Board of Health, and member of other medical associations. He is among the first in his profession, is a progressive and public-spirited citizen and a deacon of the first Baptist church at Spartanburg.

CAPTAIN JOHN HAYNE BLASSINGAME was born at Pendleton, S.C., in 1831. His father was John Blassingame and his mother was a Miss Sloan, sister of the late Colonel John T. Sloan of Columbia, for many years clerk of House of Representatives. His paternal grandfather. General John Blass-ingame, served in the war of 1812. When quite a boy the parents of Captain Blassingame removed to Alabama, where they lived for several years, during which time the father died. After this the family returned to South Carolina, when Mrs. Blass-ingame married John Bomar, Jr., one of the proprietors of Bivingsville (now Glendale) cotton factory.

At the age of twenty-three Captain Blassingame went West, and during the bloody riots in Kansas, when General Albert Sidney Johnston of U.S.A. was ordered to that State to quell the disturbances, he joined his forces and was promoted for bravery.

Capt. John H. Blassingame

After the riots were over he went farther west and settled in the Rockies, where he passed an eventful life full of interesting incidents.

When South Carolina seceded in December, 1860, and called for her sons to volunteer in her defence, he felt that he owed his allegiance to his mother State and immediately returned home to defend her rights. He rode all the way from Pike's Peak, a distance of 2,000 miles, on horseback, and upon his arrival in his native State he enlisted in Co. K (Spartan Rifles), 5th Regiment, S.C.V. He went to Charleston and afterwards to Virginia, where he served faithfully, rising from a private to the position of captain of his company, which subsequently formed a part of the Palmetto Sharpshooters.

While fighting bravely in one of the battles in Virginia he was dangerously wounded, but recovered after careful treatment. After recovery he returned to the army, where he served with distinguished gallantry until the end of the war.

Returning home after the war he was elected sheriff of his native county, but under the reconstruction measures of Congress, having served as captain in the Confederate army, he resigned before the end of his term.

After the reconstruction days had passed he was elected county treasurer by a large majority. This was in 1877, and two years later he was reelected and the following year was chosen sheriff. After serving one term assheriff he retired from public life.

322

"On August 16th, 1896, while guarding the house of a relative and neighbor during the temporary absence of the occupants he was shot down in cold blood by a colored burglar, who narrowly escaped being lynched."

As a gentleman, soldier and public citizen. Captain Blassingame was true and devoted to the best interests of his country; he was an exalted type of the gentleman of the old school, and was beloved and honored by all.

HON. STEPHEN ELLIOTT MASON was born in Spartanburg County, December 29th, 1835, and died at his home at Cavins in his sixty-first year.

Being the mainstay of a widowed mother his education was limited. He attended for awhile the high school at Woodruff taught by Elijah Davis, Esq.. but by dint of perseverance, gathering a little here and there at mature manhood, his education was far superior to many who had better facilities. While a young man the civil war broke out. Living at the time in Louisiana and engaged in farming, he at once entered the service in a Louisiana battalion in Starke's Brigade, doing valiant service for his country. His comrades testify that he was a gallant, faithful soldier, always ready to do his duty, however hard or dangerous.

After the war was over he returned to his native county and continued the avocation of a farmer on the old homestead. He was wide-awake, progressive and successful in his farming operations. The people of Spartanburg County, appreciating his worth as a citizen, elected him county commissioner (from 1876 to 1880 inclusive), and in 1884 he was elected a representative in the State Legislature.

He was a courteous and cheerful companion, given to hospitality, a just and honorable man, and a consistent member of the Presbyterian Church. At the

Hon. S. E Mason

time of his death he was a faithful, earnest teacher in the Baptist church (Unity) near where he lived. He was a prominent Mason in the Cavins Lodge; was one of the originators and officers of the Woodruff Agricultural Fair.

In every relation of life, as a man, as a citizen, host or neighbor, Mason or teacher, in the conduct of a private citizen, in the service of his State and county, in war and in peace, in all of the vicissitudes of life, his influence was always exerted for the elevation and betterment of his fellow man. As an evidence of all this, after his death, in consideration of his worth and service, the Baptist Sunday-school, the Masonic lodge and the session of his church, of which he was an elder, passed heartfelt, appropriate resolutions and entered them upon their minutes.

He married Miss Carrie, eldest daughter of Jas. Madison Nesbitt. Three children survive this marriage.

Mrs. Mason survived her husband two years. She was a lady of the highest type of Christian character. Her gentle and unassuming nature, her conscious rectitude of purpose and her zealous advocacy of all good causes made her a favored one in her community. Her "works do follow her."

HON. EBER SYLVESTER ALLEN was born September 4th, 1827. He was a son of Caleb Allen, a highly respected citizen, who left a good record behind him for devoted piety, honest indus-

Hon. E. S. Allen

try and a true Southern public spirit and patriotism. His mother's maiden name was Elizabeth Woodruff, a woman of sterling worth and filial duty, who was a daughter of Joseph Woodruff, the first settler in the present flourishing town of Woodruff, S.C., and from whom it derived its name. His only brother was Woodard Allen, a prominent, pious and influential citizen, who resided near Cedar Spring, S.C., whose wife was a Miss Wells, daughter of Jehu Wells, who still survives as a lady of the highest respectability and consistent Christian character and example. He had three sisters who arrived at the age of womanhood, viz.: Amanda, who married Wm. Todd; Louisa V., who married Dr. Wright, and Sarah H., who married Dr. M. W. Drummond. All these, now deceased, were ladies of sterling worth and refinement.

Eber S. Allen was educated in the best schools of his day, and was a man of more than ordinary intelligence and force of character, being well-informed on all the current topics of the day. When a young man he was elected captain of a militia company, and subsequently became colonel of the 45th Regiment, S.C. M. When the civil war between the States broke out he was among the first to enlist. He went as a private in the company of Captain F. M. Tucker, 18th Regiment, S.C.V., and was soon promoted to the position of quartermaster-sergeant of said regiment, and served in this capacity until the surrender at Appomattox, Like many others of that period he returned home much disheartened and broken down financially; but being gifted by nature with push and energy he soon accumulated a comfortable living for himself and family.

During the exciting political period of 1876 in South Carolina, when men of solid worth were needed to represent the people in the legislative halls. Colonel E. S. Allen was nominated and elected by the people of Spartanburg County a representative in the State Legislature, and was a member of the historic "Wallace House." He was elected a second time in 1880. He was also elected a director in the State Penitentiary, which position he held for eight years. In the various public positions which he held, both civil and military, he was always a trustworthy servant of the people

He was a consistent and influential member of the Baptist Church for nearly forty years; was treasurer of the old Tyger River (afterwards Spartanburg) Association for a number of years. He was also for a considerable time treasurer of Bethel Church at Woodruff, S.C., of which he was a member, and was also the teacher of the young men's Bible class for more than a quarter of a century, with great and lasting results.

In 1858 he married Miss Mollie A., second daughter of Harrison Drummond, by which marriage he had two daughters, both of whom preceded him to the grave. One daughter (Mrs. Sullivan) left four children, two sons and two daughters.

Colonel Allen died some time early in the nineties, a Christian strong in faith with no fears of death. His widow survives him as a resident of his old homestead near Woodruff, S.C.

CAPTAIN DAVID ADAM SWITZER was born in Orangeburg County, S.C., July 28th, 1831. He is a son of Frederick and Rosa (Brandenburg) Switzer, who removed from Orangeburg County to Spartanburg district about 1835 and settled on South Tyger River, near present Switzer Station, on the same estate now occupied by his family.

The name of his paternal grandfather was Frederick Switzer, who was a soldier of the Revolution. He emigrated from Germany to Orangeburg district about twelve months before the Revolution. His

Captain D. A. Switzer

first landing in America was in Charleston. He was a farmer by occupation, and died and was buried in Orangeburg County.

Some interesting incidents in connection with his soldier life during the Revolution are related by his descendants.

The maternal grandfather of Captain D. A. Switzer was John Brandenburg, who was a Revolutionary soldier, and as such his life was also eventful and replete with interest.

He was a merchant after the Revolution, and it is stated that he was a very ingenious man. Both of the grandfathers referred to suffered many hardships and dangers during the Revolution and were in several battles and skirmishes in that great struggle for American, liberty.

Referring again to Frederick Switzer, the father of Captain D. A. Switzer, he was twice married, first to Katy Brandenburg. By this marriage one son was born: John R. Switzer of Laurens county, S.C., who at this writing (1900) is about ninety years of age. By the second marriage to a Miss Brandenburg, sister or cousin of the first wife, he had children as follows: Frederick, who married Julia, daughter of Rev. Warren Drummond, both living in Arkansas, where they reared a highly respectable family and own large possessions; David A., the subject of this sketch; Mary, who married Harvey Drummond, a highly respected citizen and son of Rev. Warren Drummond. Both Harvey Drummond and his wife are now dead, but they reared a family of high respectability and social position. The next child in order was Luther Switzer, who died while reading medicine with Dr. L. C. Kennedy at Spartanburg. He was never married.

Henry, another son, was a resident of the State of Arkansas at the outbreak of the civil war. He volunteered and entered the Confederate service as captain of a company in a regiment organized in his State, as did also his brother Frederick, This regiment belonged to Holmes's division and did gallant service in the capture of Fort Helena on the Mississippi River. He was subsequently captured, and was kept for a time in close confinement where he contracted disease and died. He was a promising and gallant young man and was never married. One daughter, Barbary, of Frederick Switzer married Sanford Mahaffey of Laurens County, S.C. She died about fifteen months after her marriage.

James, the youngest son of Frederick, lives at the old homestead of his father. He is a progressive farmer and married Julia, daughter of John B. Archer of Spartanburg. They have six sons, viz.: James, John, Edgar, Paul, Wells and Carroll, all with him.

Captain David A. Switzer, the subject of our sketch, was educated mainly at Slabtown, S.C., under John L. Kennedy, an able instructor in his day and time. Before the civil war he was commissioned as captain of the Concord Beat company, which paraded near his present residence (Switzer, S.C.), and as such served with efficiency for eight years. This company formed a part of the old 36th Regiment, S.C.M. During the period that he commanded this company it was a part of his duty to preserve the peace and keep good order in his beat by the appointment of patrols, which duty he performed to the entire satisfaction of all.

At the beginning of the civil war Captain Switzer volunteered for the Confederate service, but being seriously afflicted with rheumatism he was rejected. He soon after went to Hot Springs, Ark., to restore his health, and after remaining there for a time returned home and volunteered a second time, but was again rejected by a board of examining surgeons. While at home he rendered valuable service to his country in providing for the poor and needy, and especially for the wives of the soldiers in his section who were in the army.

Since the war he has remained on his farm attending strictly to his private business, but is broad- and liberal-minded, and is a consistent member of the Baptist church. He has never aspired to politics or public office, but has always been classed as a progressive and industrious farmer and a useful citizen.

In the latter part of the seventies he married Miss Katy Mahaffey of Laurens County. By this marriage four children were born, viz.: Rosa, who married Dr. J. B. Stepp, one child, Katy G.; Willie, who died in childhood; Minnie, who married Ralph Jorden, one child, Catharine; and David A., youngest child, twenty-one years, unmarried.

COLONEL FLAVIUS JEFFERSON POOLE was born in Lexington County, S.C., October 19th, 1834. His grandfather, William Poole, was born in Westmoreland county, Va., and in early manhood moved to Lexington county, where he reared a family of two boys and three girls. The eldest of the sons was Aaron Poole, the father of the subject of this sketch, who married a daughter of George Crim of Lexington County. Of the five children that resulted from this marriage only Colonel Poole and one sister (Mrs. Carrie Jackson of Spartanburg) survive.

Both the grandparents of Colonel Poole were Revolutionary soldiers. When he was a lad his father died, but his mother married again and removed to Spartanburg County, where he was reared, living on a farm near Reidville and re-

Col. F. J. Poole

ceiving a limited education at the Reidville High School, which he attended for three sessions, paying his tuition and board out of the limited funds which he had accumulated before entering.

Professor Davis, who was then his instructor, was very anxious that he should continue at school, and learning that he was not in a position financially to pay board and tuition, proposed to instruct him free of tuition as long as he could continue in school. For this token of kindness and interest taken in him he has always had a loving remembrance of Professor Davis.

One day while realizing the awkwardness of his position — being without a job and without means with which to create one — he received a message from a kind friend asking him to call at his home, that he would like to see him, with which request he complied at once. This kind friend was none other than Colonel B. T. Brockman, who was then merchandizing about two miles from Reidville. A short time after this he learned that he had been recommended to Colonel Brockman by his good friend Wm. W. Calvert, with whom he had boarded while at school, and also with whom he had lived before. To this day Mr. and Mrs. Calvert are as dear to him as father and mother.

Colonel Brockman offered him a position in his store, which he accepted and went to work at once. This was in the year 1858.

Here he remained until the breaking out of the war between the States, when a company was raised in that community for the Confederate service.

This was called the "Brockman Guards" and became subsequently Co. B, 13th Regiment, S.C.V., of which F. J. Poole became second sergeant, and which was organized near Reidville, S.C., being composed of the very best material in that community.

Soon after the seven days' battle around Richmond Sergeant Poole was elected junior second lieutenant of his company vice T. A. Baswell resigned, and upon the death of Captain Jesse R. Brockman from wounds received in battle, he was promoted to the captaincy of his company, his commission dating from the 12th of May, 1864.

Captain Poole was wounded three times. First at Chancellorsville, which disabled him for three or four months; second, Jericho Ford; and third, at Jones's Farm, near Petersburg, He also suffered during the war from a severe attack of typhoid fever.

Company B, 13th S.C. Regiment, which Captain Poole had the honor of commanding, succeeding the gallant Brockman, slain in battle, had enlisted from first to last about 150 men. Of this number about 28 were killed and died from wounds received on battlefield. About 31 died of disease, and about 36 were wounded in battle and survived. At present about 38 or 40 members are living.

From Appomattox, after the surrender of General Lee, Captain Poole marched on foot to his home in Spartanburg. He was seventeen days on the road, having to lie over two or three days on account of the painfulness of the wound received at Chancellorsville.

After returning home in May, 1865, he began teaching, which he continued through the following year — 1866. In 1881 he removed to Piedmont, S.C., where he has since been employed in a mercantile firm.

Colonel Poole derives his present title of colonel from the fact that on the 5th of May, 1899, as commander of Camp Crittenden, No. 707, U. C. V., Piedmont, S.C., he was unanimously elected colonel by the camps of Greenville County, S.C., vice Colonel James A. Hoyt, resigned, which position he at present holds.

Capt. Andrew K. Smith

On the 18th June, 1863, Colonel Poole was married to Miss Mary E. Johnson, eldest daughter of Rev. Washington Johnson, a Baptist minister. Six children have been born unto them — two boys and four girls.

CAPT. ANDREW KENDRE SMITH. The subject of this sketch was the second son of Rev. Bornette Smith, a pioneer Methodist minister, who, with his father Charles Smith, a soldier of the Revolution,, emigrated to South Carolina soon after the close of the Revolutionary War.

Andrew was born May 15th, 1823, and was killed on the field of the second battle of Manassas, August 29th, 1862, being in the thirty-seventh year of his age. His early education was equal to that of many boys of his day and generation, but being the son of a pious parentage, he not only received good moral training, but having descended from Revolutionary stock, he inherited by inspiration, as it were, the principles fostered and maintained by a patriotic ancestry; and when the time came for South Carolina to call upon her sons, in her time of greatest peril, to defend her proud name and sovereignty, Andrew K. Smith was among the first to volunteer. He left Pacolet, S.C., for Charleston, April 15th, 1861, two days after the fall of Sumter, as first lieutenant in the company of Captain John J. Brown, which formed a part of the 5th Regiment, S.C.V., which was among the first volunteers from Spartanburg. He remained on Sullivan's Island until June of the same year, when he returned home with fever. Recovering from his sickness, he organized a company in September following, which was known as Company I, 13th Regiment, S.C.V., which went to the coast, but in April following enlisted for the war and went to Virginia, where it did valiant service.

On the second day of the second battle of Manassas Captain Smith was pierced through the temple by a Minie ball, and thus he gave up his life a sacrifice for the country he so dearly loved. He left a devoted wife, Mrs. Manerva Littlejohn Smith, and five little children to mourn the loss of husband and father. But like hundreds, nay thousands, of noble mothers that so illuminate those dark days in

Major John J. Brown

our country's history, Mrs. Smith was equal to the duties devolving upon her; and now, after a third of a century, we find her and her five children — two sons and three daughters — still living. The oldest son, H. C. Smith, is a merchant of Sherman, Texas. The other son is Dr. S. B. Smith, of Naples, Texas. The daughters are Mrs. G. W. Whitman, F. C. Haynes and N. G. Littlejohn.

No bosom ever carried a truer heart, no spirit was ever animated more with love of home and country's welfare than his; and in summing up its illustrious martyrs Spartanburg County may well be proud to enroll among her fallen heroes the name of Andrew K. Smith.

MAJOR JOHN JONES BROWN was born near Pacolet, S.C., October 2d, 1833. His educational advantages were limited, but he was raised by a highly respectable parentage.

In 1857 when the trouble arose between the States as to whether Kansas, on her admission into the Union, should be a slave or non-slaveholding State, he volunteered in a company from Union, S.C., went to Kansas and staid about a year, undergoing many hardships, but returned home in safety and resumed his work on his farm, where he remained until the outbreak of the war between the States. He was a strong secessionist, and in a few months after South Carolina passed the ordinance dissolving her relations with the Federal Union, he raised a company and volunteered in the service of his native State. His company formed a part of the 5th Regiment, S.C.V., the first service of which was on Sullivan's Island during the latter part of April and month of May, 1861.

Upon a call of the company which had enlisted in the State service to reenlist for the Confederate service, it refused, and was consequently disbanded. This was a matter of disappointment and mortification to Captain Brown. His company refusing to go to Virginia, he enlisted as a private in the company of Captain Wm. M. Foster's company, from Cowpens, which formed a part of the 9th Regiment S.C.V. (Colonel Blanding), and went to Virginia, where he served out his twelve months' enlistment.

When he joined Captain Foster's company at Pacolet depot, where the company took the cars for Virginia, fifteen of his original company on Sullivan's Island went with him, making, with himself, sixteen. Only four of this number ever returned to their homes at Pacolet, the other twelve having been killed or having died of disease, Captain Brown and two of his brothers being three of the four, all bearing wounds received in battle. Franklin Harvey was the other one of the four that returned.

In the spring of 1862, upon the reorganization of the army in Virginia, he, with Captain John Martin, raised a company and joined the regiment of Palmetto Sharp-shooters under Colonel Micah Jenkins. Martin was made captain and J. J. Brown first lieutenant.

Captain Brown was wounded slightly in the foot at Seven Pines, Va., and in the seven days' battle around Richmond he was wounded in the ankle. In this battle Captain Martin was wounded so badly that he died. J. J. Brown was then made captain of the company, but on account of the severity of the wound in his ankle received at White Oak Swamp was unable to take command of the same. Consequently he resigned, but remained with his regiment as sutler until the end of the war.

Returning home he resumed the business of farming in connection with merchandizing. Upon the location of the town of Gaffney, S.C., on the Air Line (now Southern Railroad), he removed there with his family, where he continued the business of merchandizing until' his death, which took place November 25th, 1886.

In November, 1864, he married Elizabeth Agnes,, daughter of Gen. B.F. Bates, a congenial and devoted companion, who survived him a few years. By this marriage ten children were born, nine of whom are living, viz.: Jane, who married J.N. Cudd, merchant at Spartanburg; Carrie, who married W.C. Carpenter, of Carroll & Carpenter, merchants, Gaffney, S.C.; Landrum, who married Mary Wilson, of Charlotte, N.C.; William F., who married Beona, daughter of Captain Moses Wood, of Gaffney, S.C.; Thomas, Mary S., Annie W., Paul and Idelle.

Major John J. Brown was an upright and progressive business man, a pure patriot and Christian, being at the time of his death an acceptable member of the Baptist Church. At the time of his death he was a trustee in the Cooper Limestone Institute, and the revival of this institution, known in former times as Limestone Springs Female High School, was largely due to his un- tiring energy and liberality.

CAPTAIN JACOB QUICKLE CARPENTER. This distinguished soldier of two wars was born in Lincolnton, N.C., about the year 1827. Upon the declara- tion of war against Mexico by the United States in 1846, being then only in his nineteenth year, he volunteered and went to Mexico as a member of a North Carolina regiment, and remained in the service for several years, re- turning home after peace was declared.

It is said of young Carpenter that in "a bloody and almost savage en- gagement that took place between the city of Vera Cruz and Mexico, a United States battery "had been left on a bridge that was commanded by Mexican artillery. That battery had to be taken, and into the smoke and carnage" young Carpenter "flung himself, the echo of his dauntless words reaching down these years, 'battery or a soldier's grave.' The deed was glorious, and thrice glori- ous was the victory!"

Capt. J. Q. Carpenter

Soon after the close of the Mexican war he settled in Spartanburg County, and began merchandizing at Grassy Pond, which business "he continued at said place with success until the outbreak of the war between the States.

At its beginning a company was organized embracing for the most part the territory of the Spartanburg portion of the present county of Cherokee. This company was composed of the very best young men that this section afforded. Its first captain was J. O. Carpenter, the subject of this sketch. The company organized with the 5th Regiment, S.C.V., and was known as Com- pany G of said regiment. It served in Virginia for the most part during the first year of the war, and participated in all the active campaigns and marches of that year. At the expiration of his term of twelve months' enlistment, and upon the reorganization of the armies of the Confederacy in 1862, 'Captain Carpenter was again elected captain of a newly-organized company, known as Company M, Palmetto Sharpshooters, but was permitted to serve only a few weeks. While gallantly leading his men into action he was killed at the battle of Seven Pines, May 31st o£ said year.

Thus fell a valiant son of Carolina, possessed with nerve and vigor to battle for his country's rights, heart within and foes without.

In 1850 Captain Carpenter married Miss Allie G. Clarke, daughter of Wm. G. Clarke, of Spartanburg district, by whom he had four children, viz.: Alice, who married I. C. Surratt; Sarah, who married J. I. Smith; Wm. C. Carpenter, of the firm of Carroll & Carpenter,. Gaffney, S.C.; and Jones Keith Carpenter, who married a Miss Bullock.

These "children were too young ever to recall the season when father enveloped them with strong, loving arms, and sadly do they realize how deprived they have been of lessons of wisdom and that flood of impulse and interest that can only flow from a father's heart. All honor to the mother who, with grand endurance, held the key of the souls of her precious immortals and stamped their character with father's image."

LIEUTENANT BENSON B. CHAPMAN, son of William and Elvira (White) Chapman, was born near New Prospect, S.C., January 25th, 1844. His father was married twice. First to a daughter of Major John Graves McClure, who was a valiant soldier of the Revolution, and second to a granddaughter of Daniel White (father of Henry White, Esq.), who also served in the Revolution.

The subject of this sketch was raised on his father's farm and received his academic education at New Prospect. For several years just preceding the civil war, he was employed as clerk in the general merchandise store of Mr. Aaron Cannon on South Pacolet River.

Lieut. B. Chapman

When the State called for troops he volunteered as a private in the Pacolet Volunteers (Captain W. P. Compton), which subsequently became Co. F, 13th Regiment, S.C.V., and for meritorious service in Jackson's corps of Lee's army he was promoted to a lieutenancv. He participated in that thrilling flank movement of Jackson's corps to the rear of Hooker's army at Chancellorsville, Va., May 2d, 1863, and early on Sunday morning of May 3d, when his regiment was advancing on the Federal batteries, his left leg was severed by a cannon ball.

After the war he finished his education at Wofford College. After that he taught a few years. Was elected school commissioner for Spartanburg in 1876, which position he has held to the present year (1900), with the exception of four years.

In 1886 Mr. Chapman united in marriage with Miss Montie M. Clemont, who died in 1892, leaving one son, Malcolm Malcolm, now twelve years of age.

In 1894 Mr. Chapman was fortunate in recovering the beautiful silk flag which had been presented to the Pacolet Volunteers by the ladies of the Pacolets, North and South. Upon the adoption of a battle-flag by the Confederacy this flag was not used, and during the war was placed for safe keeping in the court-house at Spartanburg. When the Federal cavalry raided that town early in 1865 a soldier by the name of Cahalan carried off the banner to Patterson, N.J., and presented it to his sister, Miss Cahalan, who, in 1894, made inquiries through the press for representatives of the Pacolet Volunteers. Mr. Chapman noticed the inquiry and answered it, and recovered the banner in October, 1894, by paying $5 for it, and has it now in his possession.

LIEUTENANT WILLIAM M. CHAPMAN, JR., the only brother and two years the senior of B. B. Chapman, was reared on his father's farm under the same conditions as his brother. He received an academic education at New Prospect.

At the breaking out of the civil war he was employed as a clerk in the general merchandise store of Dr. W. P. Compton, where the Pacolet Volunteers first organized in 1861, in which company he enlisted, and by his faithfulness to all his duties as a soldier and his gallant service on the field of battle in the corps of Stonewall Jackson, he was promoted to a lieutenancy, and remained true and faithful in the discharge of his duties as a soldier throughout the entire war of four years.

On Sunday morning, April 2d, 1865, but five days before the surrender of Lee at Appomattox, on the Southside Railway, near Petersburg, when McGowen's brigade made its last stand, there was an individual tragedy that caused grim soldiers, long inured to hardships and horrible tragedies of war, to shudder. The Federals were making an onslaught on the Confederate line in overwhelming numbers in front and also by flank. The commanding officer of the 13th Regiment gave the order to change front by companies to check the onslaught pressing from several directions. Lieutenant Chapman drew his sword to execute his part of this maneuver. The shriek and crash of a shell from a Federal battery firing down the line on the flank, and a soldier is seen with outstretched arm grasping his sword standing erect and rigid for a brief moment with his head completely severed from his body. This was Lieutenant W. H. Chapman. Some of his faithful comrades, who were captured a few minutes later when the lines were completely broken, tenderly wrapped him in a blanket and buried him under an oak tree near the spot where he fell.

"No useless coffin enclosed his breast,
   Nor in sheet nor in shroud they wound him;
  But he lay like a soldier taking his rest,
    With his grey jacket around him."

LIEUTENANT RUFUS MARION CROCKER, son of Arthur and Lucinda Crocker, was born in Spartanburg County, February 1st, 1838.

At the very outbreak of the civil war he volunteered in the service of his country, and was elected junior second lieutenant in Co. I, 13th Regiment, S.C.V., commanded by Captain Andrew K. Smith.

Lieutenant Crocker was a brave and gallant officer. We have before us his war diary, which is a valuable document, and gives an interesting account of the movements of the 13th Regiment up to the time of the battle of second Manassas, where he was seriously wounded. He participated in Stonewall Jackson's famous march around Pope's right and rear, a detailed account of which, together with his personal sacrifices, we copy from his diary as follows:

"1862, August 25th, crossed the Rappahannock and marched towards Manassas; got there 27th and took possession; lay there that night and burnt the cars and provisions that we could not use nor take along. Next day, 28th, we marched to Centerville, and from there by the Stone Bridge; met the enemy at railroad

Lieut. R. M. Crocker

cut and fought that evening and lay on the battlefield and renewed the fight next morning and fought all day until about 3 o'clock in the evening. Captain Smith was killed soon after I was wounded in the left leg, breaking one bone. My regiment lost half their number. I lay in the woods until the 5th of September. I hired conveyance to Warrenton, Va., to a hospital, and was taken down with fever; lay there until the 20th, and went to Culpepper Court-house and stayed there two nights and went to Gordensville and lay there one night, and went to Richmond; 1st of October started for home; got home the 4th, and had a severe time with my leg. January 21st, 1863, went to Columbia and caught erysipelas. June went to Columbia. Again August went to Columbia. September 25th started back to my regiment."

Lieutenant Crocker continued to serve his country until the end of the war, when he returned to his home. He met bravely all the battles of this life until his death, which took place some years after the close of the civil war. He lived the life of an honest, industrious and progressive citizen; was a prominent member of the Masonic fraternity, and for thirty years a deacon of the Baptist Church, leading an exemplary Christian life. Soon after he grew up to manhood he married to Mrs. Isabel Besaner of Lincoln County, N.C., who survives. By this marriage several children were born, and among this number is Rev. Wm. E. Crocker, a Baptist minister, who is now a missionary in China, and who, though yet young in years, has a bright and promising future before him.

COLONEL WILLIAM P. BISHOP, familiarly known as "Captain Buck," was born August 25th, 1828, in the present county of Spartanburg, being the son of Barney Bishop, a highly respected citizen, who resided on the waters of Lawson's Fork.

Colonel Bishop descends from a Revolutionary ancestry. His great-grandfather and -mother came from Ireland in the early settlement of the western portion of the Carolina s, and made settlement at or near Lincolnton, N.C. Two of their sons, Edward and William (the latter being the grandfather of the subject of our sketch), removed to the territory afterwards embraced in Spartanburg County, and settled on Standingstone Creek, five miles west of Spartanburg, where they lived and died, after raising

Col. Wm. P. Bishop

large families. Edward settled on what was afterwards known as the Mabry Place, near New Pisgah Church, and William settled on the opposite side of said creek. They were both Revolutionary soldiers.

At the outbreak of the war with Mexico, in 1847, his brother Simpson Bishop enlisted and went to Mexico. After the war, while en route home, he died at Mobile Ala., of wounds and disease contracted in the service, and was buried in that city.

Several years before the outbreak of the civil war between the States Colonel Bishop was elected and commissioned captain of the Lawson Fork Volunteers (Red Legs), and from this position he was promoted, by election, to major of the Upper Battalion, 36th Regiment, S.C. M., and after a few years he was elected to the colonelcy of his regiment. This last promotion, however, was after the ordinance of secession was passed by South Carolina, but before hostilities broke out. On the 24th day of December, 1861, he assembled the 36th Regiment at its usual place of rendezvous (Bomar's old field) pursuant to orders from the governor, and urgently called for volunteers for the defense of the State. On this occasion four companies volunteered defense, of one of which Colonel Bishop was elected captain, which entered service January, 1862. Colonel (or Captain, as he was now called) Bishop remained in command of his company for over a year, and until after it had been transferred to Virginia and had been into Maryland and back to Virginia, when he resigned and came home, where he remained during the severe winter months, when he returned to the front in Virginia. He was wounded twice at the siege of Petersburg: first slightly, the second time it was thought mortally, being shot through his right arm and through the body with a large Minie ball. At the hospital in Richmond he recovered sufficiently to be brought home. He was on his way to the front the third time when he received news of Lee's surrender.

In early life Colonel Bishop connected himself with the Baptist Church, and was made a deacon in the same some years afterwards; and to the present day has led a consistent and exemplary Christian life, is an upright citizen, a good neighbor, a kind husband and an affectionate father. He is to be classed amongst the leading progressive and successful farmers in his native county. On the 10th of November, 1847, Colonel Bishop married Miss Polly Brannon, a most estimable and lovable woman, who is also a descendant of Revolutionary ancestry. Her grandfather, Reuben Seay, was wounded at the siege of Yorktown. Fifteen children were born to Colonel Bishop and his wife — nine daughters and six sons.

CAPTAIN GEORGE BLOCKER LAKE was born in Edgefield County, S.C., January, 1841. His father, Dr. John Lake, was an eminent physician and zealous Christian. His mother excelled in literary attainments.

At the beginning of the civil war he enlisted in Company C, 1st South Carolina (Gregg's) Regiment, and was at Fort Sumter when the first gun of the war was fired. At the end of six months, the time for which it enlisted, young Lake reenlisted for the Confederate service in the ad Regiment, S.C.V., of which he was made sergeant-major. In the organization of this regiment one company (B) was composed of volunteers from Spartanburg, which was commanded respectively by Captains John Wheeler, Peyton Ballinger, Adolphus J. Foster, Robert G. Fleming and W. Alexander Benson.

Capt. Geo. B. Lake

Some time toward the end of the war, in the scarcity of officers, young Lake was created a lieutenant in this company, and upon the death of Captain Benson, caused by the explosion of a shell at Petersburg in 1864, he was promoted to the captaincy of the company.

Not long after this occurred one of the most noted events of the war — the mine explosion near Petersburg. Captain Lake and his company were immediately over what now forms the crater. When the mine, charged with 8,000 pounds of powder, was fired Captain Lake and thirty-one of his thirty-four men present were killed. He, with Lieutenant W. J. Lake and Wilson Moore (see sketch), was dug up and rescued by the Federals after two hours. He was then sent to Fort Delaware, where he was kept until the end of the war.

Captain Lake, in his account of this terrible explosion, says:

"My command was in the rear line of works, and we were asleep. I knew i nothing of what had happened until most of the dirt had been taken off of us. Before I was taken out, however, I came to consciousness, and talked to Lieutenant Lake by my side. When I found that nearly all my men had been killed and the remaining few with myself were prisoners, it was gloomy indeed. We were kept in the crater for a considerable time exposed to shells from our own batteries. These shells made terrible havoc with the Federal troops who had charged through the break, but after being driven back stopped in the crater for protection.

"I was in some of the hardest fought battles of the Confederate war, was for two weeks in Fort Sumter, where all the Federal iron-clads would steam up to within 800 or 1,000 yards of the fort, and they and the land batteries on Morris Island would hurl shell and shot by the ton, but I have never seen anything to equal the horror of the crater."

After the war was over Captain Lake returned to his home in Edgefield, and his valued service in that county since the war can be better appreciated by the perusal of the following letter, which the writer received from General M. C. Butter, of which the following is a correct copy:

"Kellogg Building,
"Washington, D.C., October 4, 1899.
"*Dr. J. B. O. Landrum, Campobello, S.C.*

"My Dear Sir: — I want to add a word to the sketch I understand you are preparing of my old friend Captain Geo. B. Lake of Edgefield. I presume you have a pretty full history of his services in the Confederate army, where his conspicuous gallantry attracted a great deal of attention, and received the encomiums of his superior officers.

"After the cessation of hostilities he returned to his home in Edgefield County, and, with the rest of us, took the responsibilities of citizenship in the trying days of reconstruction. He bore his share of those responsibilities with courage and patriotism, and never faltered in the line of his duty to his State any more than he did in his career as a soldier. In the exciting times of 1874 he organized. a rifle company at Edgefield, and was always on hand on occasions of excitement and peril at the head of his company. The fact that Captain Lake was at the head of a military company in that community gave confidence and assurance of public order among abiding people, and was notice to the lawless that if they disturbed the peace they did so at their own peril. They knew that Lake, although an unassuming citizen, would shoot to kill if an occasion should make it necessary.

"In brief, throughout the entire reconstruction period and since Lake has been true to his colors. He never struck them before radical reconstruction or in later days before sham "reform" or hypocritical demagogism. Poverty could not cow him, nor could bluster or threats intimidate him.

Very truly yours,
M. C. Butler."

Captain Lake and his family are now residents of Lexington, Ky. While he remained in the State, however, he was a member of the S.C. Division, U.C.V., with the rank of lieutenant-colonel.

His son Rev. John Lake is an able minister of the gospel of the Baptist faith.

LIEUTENANT WM. J. LAKE, whom we have already noticed in connection with the sketch of Captain Geo. B. Lake as one of the survivors of the mine explosion at Petersburg, was a native of Newberry, S.C., and was born about the year 1832. He volunteered in the service of his country when about twenty-eight years of age, and was elected first lieutenant of Co. D, 13th Regiment, S.C.V., afterwards joining Co. C, 23d Regiment, S.C.V., where he remained until he was elected lieutenant in Co. B, 22d Regiment, S.C.V. He remained with this company until he was wounded in the crater disaster at Petersburg in July, 1864. [1] He was then so disabled that he was compelled to retire, and bore till his death the

Lieut. W. J. Lake

suffering consequent upon the fracture of the hip caused by the mine disaster and sciatica superinduced by the same. Out of thirtysix men there were only five of his men that survived this disaster, only two of whom are now living: Captain George B. Lake and Wilson H. Moore. (See sketches.)

Lieutenant Lake was rescued from the crater at Petersburg after several hours of intense suffering, having been completely covered up by timbers and earth. Who can imagine the agony he must have suffered in such a living grave with a broken hip?

His death took place January 27th, 1899, in Miami, Florida, where he had gone in quest of a more agreeable climate. His remains were brought back to his native State and buried in her sacred soil, Rosemount Cemetery, Newberry. This was eminently proper, from the fact of his having served her so faithfully and gallantly and having suffered more for her sake than rarely ever falls to the lot of a soldier.

Among his surviving children are Forest Lake of Florida, Thos. D. Lake of Laurens, S.C., and Mrs. John P. Fielder of Moore, S.C.

No man in South Carolina stood higher in the estimation of his fellow citizens than William J. Lake. He was an honest and upright citizen, a consistent Christian and a member of the Methodist Church. He was well-read and well-informed on all matters pertaining to the public interest. "He was of gentle manners, kind and affable, and especially affectionate in his family. He died as he lived, true to his State, a noble Confederate to the last, and, above all, had his life embellished with the Christian virtues and graces."

CAPTAIN JAMES FOWLER SLOAN was born in Laurens County, S.C., August, 1819, being at this writing (August, 1900) eighty-one years of age. His educational advantages were limited, but he was an apt student and by the time he had reached the age of manhood he had acquired a good, practical education, and by dint of hard study mastered the theory of the system of surveying and learned the use of instruments from John Epton, Esq. Captain Sloan came to Spartanburg County in 1843 and settled near Rich Hill, where he now resides. Some time after this he was elected captain of a militia company which formed a part of the 37th Regiment, S.C. M., in which capacity and that of adjutant of said regiment he served until the outbreak of the civil war between the States.

Capt. J. F. Sloan

Upon the approach of hostilities between the States he was elected second lieutenant of the Batesville Volunteers (Captain John J. Brown), which company volunteered as *minute men,* and upon receiving the news of the bombardment of Fort Sumter, entered the service upon a notice of two days. After six weeks' service on Sullivan's Island, S.C., the company disbanded and went home.

When, however, in 1861, the Confederate government had called for troops. Captain Sloan raised a company of 80 odd men, which eventually reached 115, and was elected its captain, which was known as Co. B, Holcombe Legion. [2]

In 1862 when the army was reorganized in Virginia this company revolunteered, reelecting Captain Sloan as its commander. For being the best drilled and disciplined company in the Holcombe Legion, it received the first distribution of Enfield Rifles, which the survivors carried to the end of the war.

Captain Sloan, on account of ill health, and by the advice and certificate of his regimental surgeon, resigned and returned home.

After his resignation Lieutenant Alfred B. Bryant became (January, 1863) captain of the company, who served until March 25th, 1865, when he was killed near Fort Steadman, Va. He was succeeded on the same date by Lieutenant E. Henry Bates, who was promoted captain by General W. H. Wallace.

As soon, however, as he had recovered, he reentered the service, and became adjutant of Major Joel Ballinger's Battalion of State (S.C.) Reserves, which formed a part of Blanchard's brigade, and which performed during the last days of the Confederacy distinguished and fatiguing service, confronting: the army of General Sherman, marching four or five hundred miles, and being among the last to yield in that great struggle for Southern liberty. In this famous march Captain Sloan performed his part of it in a pair of wooden-bottomed shoes.

Captain Sloan has always lived the life of a farmer. He has never aspired to politics or public life, except that he held for sixteen years or more the ofhce of a civil magistrate. He has always been an honest and upright citizen and a staunch Democrat. He is a consistent member of the Presbyterian Church, and is held in high esteem by all whose pleasure it is to know him.

CAPTAIN THOMAS BOOKER MARTIN was born near the town of Fair Forest, S.C. (which is near his present home), May 25th, 1833. His father was John P. Martin, who, with a twin brother Thomas, was brought from Virginia to Spartanburg district, S.C., by their grandmother High (wife of Wm. High, the ancestor of all the families of this name in Spartanburg County), their mother having died while they were infants.

Capt. Thos. B. Martin

The mother of Captain T. B. Martin was a daughter of Edward Bomar, and being a woman of great piety made early religious impressions on the mind of her son.

Thomas B. Martin was raised on his father's farm, and attended the schools of his neighborhood. As he grew up to manhood, he learned the cabinet trade under his father and George Brem; he also learned housepainting, which he followed until some time after the civil war. He has always farmed and run public cottonginning and saw-milling.

In October, 1854, he married Miss N. A. Finch, daughter of John S. Finch. They have raised nine children, three boys and six girls. Soon after their marriage Captain Martin and his wife joined the Oak Grove (Baptist) church. All their children are members of the church of the same denomination. Captain Martin has been a deacon in his church for upwards of thirty years.

In 1861 Captain Martin volunteered in the service of his country, and was made orderly sergeant of Captain W. P. Bishop's company, which joined the Holcombe Legion under Colonel P. F. Stephens. This regiment remained about Adams Run, S.C., until August of the same year, when it was ordered to Virginia, and immediately entered into almost daily fighting until the second Manassas battle came off. Here the brother of Captain Martin, J. W. Martin, was mortally wounded and died in a few days afterwards.

Captain Martin having been detained at Adams Run, S.C., on account of typhoid fever did not return to his command until its return from the Maryland campaign. After this the commissioned officers of his company resigned, and a new election was ordered, which resulted in the election of Thomas B. Martain captain.

In 1863 the Legion was ordered to the Western armyr then under the command of General Joseph E. Johnston. Meeting General Grant's army at Big Black River, General Johnston's army fell back to Jackson, Miss., where it was besieged for seven days and nights under a continual fire, suffering terribly from exposure, lack of rations and water. The army was safely conducted out in night time. The command returned to Georgia and remained there for a time and then was again ordered to Virginia, reaching Weldon, N.C., May 7th, 1864, from which place companies were sent out along the railroad leading to Petersburg to guard railroad bridges, a portion of companies I and K of the Holcombe Legion being sent to Stony Creek Station, Va., under the command of Major Zeigler to guard the bridge there. They had not been there long before their force and number were betrayed, and they were surrounded and captured by a large force of Federals, Captain Martin being among the number captured.

Captain Martin has published a graphic account of his life in a Northern prison (see *Spartan* files, March 22d, 1893). After his capture at Stoney Creek Station he, with the other captured prisoners, was marched nearly all night to City Point on the James River. Here, after being guarded for a time by negro troops, the prisoners were packed in a steamboat and conveyed to Fortress Monroe, where they were landed and securely locked up for one night. From Fortress Monroe they were conveyed to Point Lookout, where they were searched. Captain Martin, being near the middle of the line, managed to conceal a gold watch and pistol by sitting flat on the ground and burying the same in a hole made therein until the searcher passed. The officers and privates were separated by a plaiik fence and were ordered not to communicate with each other. It was nevertheless done by writing on paper, tying to a rock, and at night when the back of the nearest guard was turned the written communication would be thrown over the fence. In this way the prisoners would get fresh news from home and the army by the arrival of new prisoners. After five or six weeks at Point Lookout Captain Martin and other officers were sent to Fort Delaware. He was again searched, but saved his gold watch by fastening the chain to his drawers' button.

The latter part of July or early in August of the same year five hundred officers, including Captain Martin, were drawn and sent to Charleston, S.C. They were packed almost to suffocation in an old sea-going vessel called the Crescent. The poor prisoners, suffering from seasickness and vomiting, could scarcely find room to stand or lie. The weather was very hot, and they could scarcely get any fresh air, as there was only one opening or hatchway to the lower deck. The supply of water gave out on the way, and afterwards evaporated seawater was furnished sparingly. The prisoners were so eager for it that they would fill their canteens with it while it was yet hot, and those who had strings or could procure strips of cloth, would tie the same around the necks of their canteens and throw them out through pigeon-holes to float along the water and cool. As the men were famishing for water it was hardly ever allowed to get cooler than blood-heat.

After days and nights, which seemed weeks to the prisoners, they were landed on Morris Island, S.C., and marched to a stockade fort between Batteries Gregg and Wagner. Here in small army tents they were fed on cooked rations. Their evening meal consisted of a scrap of bacon and a pint of mush made of spoiled corn-meal, which was himpy, sour and wormy. One evening Captain Martin counted in the portion of mush set apart to him 365 worms, some of them being woolly, and fourteen bugs. He says that he could have counted more, but thought he could not afford to lose more of one meal, upon which, no doubt in his perishing condition, his life depended. He ravenously devoured the balance. The supply of water was from holes made in the sand on the island, which was salty and unpalatable.

After about six weeks' imprisonment in the stockade fort, in which some of the prisoners died, the remaining ones were conveyed to Fort Pulaski - an old, battered, deserted, leaky fort at the mouth of the Savannah River - there to winter, perish and freeze, as many did. The weather was cold, which increased their suffering. Colonel Brown, in charge of the Federal garrison and guard at that place, informed the prisoners that he had orders not to give them a bite of meat for forty days, which order was nearly carried out. The citizens had abandoned the island, and the cats which had been left by them would go about the fort at night in search of something to eat. Occasionally one would venture in, and the door would be closed upon it immediately, and then a scramble for the cat would follow. Soon he would be captured and killed and dressed and in the pot or fryingpan to be devoured by the mess that caught him. The prisoners on another island reported that their only chance for meat was dogs, and they ate several of them. A small amount of fuel was allowed for cooking purposes only, and as they did but little of that they received but little warmth. Many of the prisoners were at all times prostrated with colds, pneumonia, and every disease which exposure and confinement subjected them to. Captain Martin was prostrated for days and nights with pleurisy, resting on a bunk of plank made with only two blankets.

After spending a part of the winter at this place he and the other prisoners were sent back to Fort Delaware. His health was so bad at that time that he does not remember leaving, nor anything of the voyage. His most intimate friends failed to recognize him on his arrival at that prison. In course of time, however, he regained his health and strength, and, becoming more reconciled to his surroundings, went to work making jewelry, such as finger-rings, breast-pins, watch chains, charms, etc., from sticks of gutta-percha purchased from Yankee sutlers. He was kept in prison until July 16th, 1865. After a circuitous journey of some weeks, *via* New York City, he landed safely home, in the embrace of loved ones who had mourned him as dead, six months having elapsed since he had last been heard from.

HON. JOHN A. HENNEMAN was born in Kranach, Bavaria, Germany, on February 3d, 1835. His father having died he turned his eyes to America as the country of his future habitation. He had a cousin, Balser Weber, residing in Center County. Pa., and the young lad first betook himself thither to his relative. This was in 1854, when he was only nineteen years of age. Later he located in Norfolk, Va., in the late fifties, working at the jeweler's bench, his chosen occupation. Here he met, for the first time. Miss Louisa Rate, an estimable English lady, who was destined to become his future wife. Determining to start out in business for himself, he heard through a commercial traveler of a possible opening at Spartanburg, S.C., to which place he went in 1859. Being pleased with the town and what appeared to be its future out-

Hon. John A. Henneman

look, he returned to Norfolk for his wife, to whom he was married in the Granby Street Methodist church, in that city, September, 1860, and henceforth, as residents of Spartanburg, their lives were identified with town, county and State.

It was but a few months, however, after their marriage and location in Spartanburg when the civil war between the States broke out. Although not a naturalized citizen, Mr. Heuneman volunteered his services to the Confederate goverument at the beginning of active hostilities. He was elected and commissioned as second lieutenant in Co. E, Holcombe Legion (Colonel P. F. Stevens), commanded first by Captain Wm. P. Roebuck, and later by Captain Andrew B. Woodruff. As an officer of this organization, he was always found in the thickest of the fights in which his regiment was engaged. At the second Manassas battle his arm was shot to pieces, which necessitated his retirement for a time. He was sent to the hospital at the University of Virginia, Charlottesville — a circumstance in which his son. Professor J. B. Henneman, became interested as a student there years later.

Upon his partial recovery from his wound, his arm being yet too frail for infantry service, he resigned his commission as lieutenant in the Holcombe Legion and enlisted in the cavalry branch of the service, where he remained until the end of the war. In one of the campaigns on the coast of South Carolina he was a second time dangerously wounded. It is recorded of him that he was a gallant soldier, noted for his courage and observance of army discipline.

"After the hard years of fighting and hardship he was among the golden-hearted band of ragged men who, with a courage no less dauntless and a fortitude no less enduring than they evinced on the battle-field, returned to their impoverished and ruined homes manfully to take up the burdens of defeat and oppression and create a new South from the ashes of the old one. He entered the jewelry business, in which he was an expert, and by years of strict attention and honest toil, made his house one of the leading firms of the up-country. His efforts were not without their reward; for he had won, in addition to his good name, an independent fortune, which made itself manifest in the unexampled prosperity of the city."

Mr. Henneman was a man of unusual brain-power and strength of mind and will, and as such, made a strong impression on all those with whom he came in contact.

In 1889 he was nominated by a number of his fellow citizens for mayor of Spartanburg city, and notwithstanding the fact that he made the race against one of the most popular men who ever held that office in that city, he was elected by a handsome majority. It was whilst attempting nobly to fulfill the duty enjoined upon him by the high office which he filled, that he met his untimely death. Walking the streets of his city his attention was called to a wife-beater — a negro brakeman. Commanding the peace and calling for a policeman, he was shot in the back and killed by the assassin, who was tried, convicted and suffered the penalty of death on the scaffold.

At one time while he was mayor of Spartanburg, Mr. Henneman exposed himself to great personal danger in the conscientious discharge of his duty, which proved again his sterling qualities of bravery and regard for the law. An infuriated mob, stirred to frenzy by crimes of atrocity, dragged a loaded cannon into the street in front of the jail for the purpose, by open violence, of battering down and taking the life of a prisoner incarcerated therein. By cool and fearless forethought Mayor Henneman walked into their midst, commanded the peace and mounting the cannon spiked it with a 20-penny nail, thus rendering it harmless.

His election as mayor was the beginning of the modern development of Spartanburg, giving the town an honest and progressive administration. Everywhere, during the same, was shown that equity, judgment and careful thought which portrayed unusual executive ability. In the midst of a bitter campaign he guaranteed to a noted politician in South Carolina an orderly hearing in Spartanburg.

In other walks of life Mr. Henneman won distinction. He was a member of the Masonic fraternity, and as such, was well known throughout the State. He was for a number of years the Worshipful Master of the Spartan Lodge, and was also a member of the Knights of Honor and other orders, in all of which he was highly esteemed.

By his marriage with Miss Louisa Rate he had children as follows: Rutledge, who has been in the jewelry business in South Carolina, New York and Virginia; John Bell, Professor of English Literature at the University of

Tennessee, Knoxville; George, who volunteered for the Cuban war and was captain of a company in the 10th Volunteers; Martha, who is at present in New York City; and Louise, wife of Dr. L. J. Blake.

HON. ARCH B. CALVERT, present mayor of Spartanburg, son of W. W. and Martha (Leonard) Calvert of Reidsville, S.C., was born May 31st, 1857. He attended the Male Academy at Reidville, and entered Wofford College October, 1876, and graduated in June, 1880. He read law in the office of Evins & Bomar at Spartanburg, and was admitted to practice in 1881.

From 1882 to '84 he served as a trial justice in the city of Spartanburg. He was elected mayor in October, 1893, and is now serving his fourth term. He has also served as United States Commissioner since 1884.

Hon. Arch B. Calvert

The present growth and prosperity of the city of Spartanburg is largely due to the splendid business management and executive ability of Mayor Calvert. He is the right man in the right place and takes a pride in every modern improvement looking to the future greatness and importance of the city over which he has the honor to preside, and which is soon destined to be one of the chief inland cities of the southeast.

Dr. J. T. Calvert (dentist), at Spartanburg, is the only brother of Mayor Calvert. He has two sisters, Mrs. O. P. Morgan, Spartanburg, and Mrs. Spencer, wife of A. M. Spencer, president of Clinton Presbyterian College.

JOSEPH SIMPSON AMOS was born September 3d, 1849, in Cherokee Creek, near Gaffney, S.C. His father, Charles Amos, born June 1, 1790, descended from Revolutionary ancestry, who emigrated from Virginia to South Carolina and made settlement on Thickety Creek, Cherokee county, obtaining title to a large body of land. He served as a soldier of the war of 1812. After this he did business for Michael Gaffney, at Gaffney's old field (now Gaffney City), for several years, and built the first mercantile house in that place. After this he was employed as manager for the Cowpens Iron Furnace Company, which business he con-

Joseph Simpson Amos

345

tinued for twenty-five years. He was married twice. First to a daughter of Rev. Joshua Richards, a Revolutionary soldier. By this marriage he had five sons, viz.: Franklin, Ross, Benjamin F., Rufus and James, who were gallant soldiers in the Confederate army. Franklin, the eldest, was a soldier in the Mexican war and served as commissary agent for the Confederate army. Ross was killed at the battle of Seven Pines. Benjamin F., member of the 5th S.C. Regiment, died in the service. Rufus, of a Georgia regiment, promoted to captain, was also killed at the battle of Seven Pines, and James, member of Captain Cleary's company, 13th Regiment, S.C.V., was killed at mine explosion at Petersburg (1864).

Charles Amos married a second time to Mary McElreath, whose ancestors were among the original settlers of Scotch-Irish on the Tygers. By this marriage two sons and several daughters were born. The sons referred to are Charles M. and Joseph S. Amos. The former was a gallant soldier in the Confederate army and was severely wounded. The latter, when only fifteen years of age, enlisted in Captain Cleary's company and was drilled for the army, but the war ended before he was called into active service.

The war thus ending adversely to the South, he, like thousands of others, found himself with nothing to depend upon but his honest industry and perseverance; and his remarkable success as a business man should serve as an incentive and inspiration to the rising generations of our country, not only to imitate, but to emulate the pluck, energy, judgment and management which he has displayed as a successful business man.

Mr. Amos at present resides in the city of Spartanburg, and was for four years a member of the city council at a time when a new era dawned upon her business prosperity. As a member of the street committee he rendered valuable service in straightening the streets and in beautifying the city, which service he rendered without remuneration. As a progressive citizen of Spartanburg, he is fully alive to every interest that concerns her welfare.

Mr. Amos is a member of the Baptist Church and a generous supporter to all of its objects.   In 1876 he married Miss Mary Gramling, a congenial companion. They have eight children, viz.: Ella, Sallie, Fannie, Joseph, Grace, Charles, Frank and John Edwin.

[1] For the particulars of this mine explosion and the casualties sustained by Co. B, 22d South Carolina Regiment, the reader is referred to the sketches of Captain Geo. B. Lake and Wilson H. Moore.

[2] The Legion was named in honor of Mrs. Governor F. W. Pickens, whose maiden name was Lucy Holcombe.

Chapter Thirty-Eight - Rev. J. S. Burnett

Was born in Knox County, Tenn., in 1821, and died at Asheville, N.C., at the age of seventy-three years. He received a fair education, but did not enjoy in early life the advantages which wealth affords. His first work was on the farm, and his next service was a clerkship in a mercantile house; but neither agriculture nor commerce were destined to elevate his life service, but a nobler and higher calling, that of the ministry, lay before him. He joined the Holstein Conference of the M. E. Church, South, and removed to Asheville, N.C., and was the first pastor to minister to the Methodist congregation at that place, and soon won the hearts of his little flock and the friendship and admiration of every one who knew him, of whatever denomination.

Rev. J. S. Burnett

He was married four times. First, to Miss Eliza Alexander, daughter of Colonel Mitchell Alexander, of Buncombe County, N.C. She died in 1860. His second marriage was to Mrs. Woodfin, of Asheville, N.C. His third marriage was to Miss Tucker, of Statesville, N.C., and his fourth wife was Miss Susie Spain.

Soon after the close of the civil war between the States Mr. Burnett took up his residence at Spartanburg, where he remained for several years, but subsequently returned to Asheville, where he resided the remainder of his life.

Mr. Burnett was truly a good and self-made man, upright and conscientious in the discharge of his duty in directing souls to Christ, and did a great and noble work in his vineyard. He possessed a heart overflowing wdth kindness and love for every man, and a nature that attracted to it and influenced for good every one with whom it came in contact. He occupied the best appointments in the conference, in Asheville for the most part, but for a while at Knoxville, Tenn.

Wilber E. Burnett, Cashier National Bank, Spartanburg, S.C.

Mr. Burnett had six children by his first marriage, of whom two are now living: W. B. Burnett, a prominent lawyer of Athens, Ga., and W. E. Burnett, of Spartanburg, S.C.

WILBER E. BURNETT, whom we have already noticed as the son of Rev. J. S. Burnett, was born at Alexanders on the French Broad River, in 1854. He came to Spartanburg when quite a small boy, and graduated at Wofford College. Soon after this he entered the National Bank of Spartanburg as bookkeeper, and is now cashier of the same bank. He is also treasurer of the Fidelity Loan and Trust Company; was originator of the Spartan Mills and was elected its first president, and also had the offer of the presidency of several other cotton mills. He is a director and one of the originators of Converse College and president of Wofford College Alumnæ Association, and has been a generous contributor to Converse and Wofford Colleges.

Mr. Burnett is in every sense a progressive and upright citizen, being fully alive to every business enterprise looking to the upbuilding of his city and county; and being yet young and active, he is destined to perform a still greater work than that which he has already accomplished.

He married Miss Gertrude Du Pre, youngest daughter of Dr. Warren Du Pre of Spartanburg.

HON. STANYEARNE WILSON, present representative in the National Congress from the 4th (S.C.) Congressional District, was born at Yorkville, S.C., January 10th, 1859.

His father was W. B. Wilson of York County, who was a lawyer of eminent ability, a graceful and eloquent speaker and stood at the head of the York bar.

The maiden name of the mother of the subject of this sketch was Arrah Minerva Lowry of Yorkville. She was descended from the Lowry family of York county and the Miller families of Cleveland and Rutherford counties. North Carolina, of whom several were engaged in the battles of King's Mountain and in western North Carolina. One of them was Susan Twitty, the seventeen year old heroine mentioned in Draper's King's Mountain, in the fight at her stepfather's house (Colonel Graham).

The name of the grandfather of Stanyearne Wilson was Wm. Stanyearne Wilson, whose mother's maiden name was Anna Eliza Blackburn, daughter of Professor George Blackburn of South Carolina College, who came from Ireland. He was one of the commissioners who established, in 1815, the boundary line between North and South Carolina.

Mr. Wilson, the subject of this sketch, at thirteen years of age, entered the King's Mountain Military School, where, at the age of sixteen, he graduated at the head of his class, winning a scholarship to the Washington and Lee University, Lexington, Va., and being offered a cadetship to West Point. He went to the university and completed his course there at the age of nineteen. He then returned home and studied law under his father, and was ad-

Hon. Stanyearne Wilson

mitted to the bar by special act of the Legislature, by reason of being under twenty-one years of age. He practiced law one year at Yorkville and then moved to Spartanburg, where he has since lived, devoting himself chiefly to his practice.

In 1884 he was elected to the State Legislature from Spartanburg County, and again in 1890. In 1892 he was elected from the same county to the State Senate, and to Congress in 1894-96 and 98. Amongst measures which he secured while in the State Legislature was the passage of the eleven hour labor law (prohibiting cotton factories from working women and children longer than eleven hours a day) and the general railroad law of the State, which constitutes a large part of the present Revised Statutes of the State.

Mr. Wilson was elected to the Constitutional Convention in 1895. In that body he served as chairman of the judiciary committee and of the steering committee.

In Congress he has been kept very busy in looking after the special interests of his district, participating in the debates and in general legislation. He has secured the establishment of sixty odd post-offices, several free delivery mail routes, a free delivery for Spartanburg city; has secured an appropriation for $250,000 with which the Congaree River will be opened for navigation as far as Columbia, thus bringing ships and cheap water rates to the center of the State. He has always been active in securing relief for our people in the departments and in Congress too numerous to mention in detail. He possesses not only good stumping abilities, but gifts in oratorical powers and eloquence. Being yet only in middle life he is destined to add additional reputation to his name along this line.

Mr. Wilson has been eminently successful at law; he is generous in disposition, and has contributed liberally of his means to assist friends in distress and to assist those in special need of help.

In 1887 he married Miss Lula Burrus, of Virginia, who died the following year. He married again in 1896 to Miss Hattie Hazard of Georgetown, S.C. both very beautiful women.

It may be interesting to the reader to know the names of the members to Congress from the district in which Spartanburg has always formed a part. From examination into the records we find in the Pinckneyville congressional district, composed of Spartanburg, Union, York and Chester, and the subsequent changes that were made in the formation of congressional districts, the representatives to the different congresses from time to time to have been as follows:

First, 2d, 3d, 4th and 5th, William Smith; 6th, Abraham Nott; 7th, 8th, 9th, 10th, 11th and 12th, Thomas Moore; 13th, Samuel Farrow; 14th, Thomas Moore; 15th and 16th, Wilson Nesbitt; 17, 18th and 19th, Joseph Gist; 20th, 21st and 22d, Wm. T. Nuckolls; 23d, Wm. K. Clowney; 24th, James Rogers; 25th, WmK. Clowney; 36th and 27th, James A. Black; 30th, 31st and 32d, Daniel Wallace; [1] 33d, 34th and 35th, James L. Orr; 36th and 37th, John D. Ashmore; 38th and 39th, no senators or representatives, James Farrow in the Confederate Congress four years; 40th, James H. Goss; 41st, 42d, 43d, 44th and 45th, A. S. Wallace; 46th, 47th, and 48th, John H. Evins; Colonel Evins dying during the 48th, General John Bratton was elected to complete his term; 49th, 50th and 51st, Wm. H. Perry; 52d and 53d, George W. Shell; 54th, 55th and 56th, Stanyearne Wilson, present incumbent.

COLONEL THEODORE GILLARD TRIMMIER, father of Thomas R. Trimmier, present clerk of court, Spartanburg, is numbered among the distinguished heroes that offered up their lives in defense of their country in the great civil war between the' States. He was the son of William [2] and Margaret Trimmier, and was born in the town of Spartanburg, S.C., April 11th, 1825. He was educated in the best schools of his town, though when quite a young man he went to Anderson County, where he engaged in the mercantile business for several years. While here he was married to Mary Letitia, daughter of Dr. Mathew Thomson, who resides with her son at Spartanburg.

In 1853 he returned to Spartanburg and engaged in the same business there until his removal to Alabama, which was in 1858.

Col. Theodore G. Trimmier

Before the outbreak of the civil war he served as a member of the brigade staff of General O. E. Edwards, 9th Brigade, S.C.M.

When the civil war began he responded to his country's call and was elected captain of a company known as the Sipsey Guards. This company was a part of the 41st Alabama Regiment. After a few months' service he was promoted to the rank of major of said regiment, and shortly after the battle of Murfreesboro, in which he took part, he was made lieutenant colonel of the same regiment. He was ordered to Virginia under Longstreet in 1864, when the 41st Alabama Regiment was thrown into Tracey's Brigade of Alabama. He took part in many of the important battles in Virginia in 1864 and '65. He was wounded at Hatcher's Run in the last fighting near Petersburg, while in command of the brigade. He was removed to Petersburg and lived some days after the amputation of his limb.

The colonel of the 41st Alabama Regiment at that time was the present Judge Stansell, of Eutaw, Ala., who pays the following tribute to the memory of Colonel Trimmier: "Theodore Trimmier entered the army of the Confederates States in 1862, at Tuscaloosa, Ala., as captain of Co. A, of the 41st Regiment of Alabama Volunteers.

"In July, 1863, he was promoted to the office of major of said regiment, and in June, 1864, to that of lieutenantcolonel of said regiment.

"He was with the regiment in all its various engagements with the enemy, forty or fifty in all, including the great battles of Murfreesboro, Jackson, Miss., Chickamauga. Bean's Station, Drury's Bluff, on James River, Va., and in the battle of White Oaks Road, southwest of Petersburg, on the 31st of March, 1865, where he was mortally wounded and died in a few days there-after.

"Throughout all this time of arduous service Colonel Trimmier was respected and honored by his officers and men, and no braver or more courageous soldier ever carried a sword."

CAPTAIN FRANCIS MARION TRIMMIER, a native of the "Old Iron District," and noted for the distinguished service rendered his country during the civil war between the States, was born July 7th, 1837. He was educated in the common schools of his town and afterwards learned the printer's trade in the office of the *Carolina Spartan*.

At the outbreak of the civil war he volunteered and was elected a lieutenant in Co. I, 13th Regiment, S.C.V. Upon the death of Captain A. K. Smith (see sketch) he rose to the captaincy of said company, which position he held until the end of the war. He was wounded three times: once by contusion, near Petersburg; once in the face just under the eye, from which he lost sight in that eye some years before his death, and once he was shot in both legs just below the knees.

Capt. F. M. Trimmier

After the close of the war he returned to Spartanburg, rented the *Carolina Spartan* office and began the publicatioti of that paper, and in a few years bought the paper out and ran it successfully by himself until he disposed of it, which was about 1878.

In 1868 he was elected clerk of the court of Spartanburg County; was again elected in 1872, '76, '80 and '84, and served until his death, which took place August 17th, 1888. His service in this capacity covered a period of almost twenty years.

Captain Trimmier, possessing rare business sagacity, had accumulated at the time of his death a handsome fortune. He possessed great popularity and influence among the people, and no man in Spartanburg did more than he for his friends. Without display he did many acts of disinterested benevolence, which were of almost hourly occurrence. He was surely a generous, a true, a patriotic and an honest man, whose memory deserves to be transmitted and perpetuated by the coming generations.

In the old cemetery at Spartanburg there stands a beautiful monument at the head of the graves of several members of the Trimmier family, and among others the subject of this sketch, and underneath his name are inscribed the words: "He that giveth to the poor lendeth to the Lord."

MAURICE AUGUSTUS MOORE. Dr. Maurice Augustus Moore was born August 10th, 1795, in York district (then Pinckney, S.C.). He was youngest son of Alexander Moore, at one time high sheriff of Camden county. They were known as the Drogheda Moores. The first of the family who came to this country, Sir Nathaniel Moore, Governor of Carolina under the Crown, 1705, was from the town Drogheda, Ireland, where the head of the family still retains the title of Marquis of Drogheda.

He studied medicine with Dr. Wm. Harris of Wadesboro, N.C., and completed his medical studies at the University of Pennsylvania, and located in 1823 in Yorkville in copartnership with his brother. Dr. William Moore, who was already doing a large practice in that vicinity.

Dr. Maurice A. Moore

In 1824 he married Miss Adeline Allison, who died in two years, leaving no children. After this he spent a year in Cuba, but returned to his home in Yorkville, S.C., and resumed the practice of his profession.

In 1833 he married Sophonista, eldest daughter of Judge Abraham Nott. He then removed to Union county and engaged in agricultural pursuits. In 1838 he became interested in the valuable medicinal properties of Glenn's Spring, and was the president of a joint stock company looking to the development of this property (see sketch of Glenn's Spring).

In 1841 he was elected cashier to the Bank of South Carolina at Columbia, where he went to reside. His health failing, however, under the confinement of bank work he resigned this position and returned in 1843 to Glenn's Spring where he lived the remainder of his life, his death taking place August 31st, 1871. For a few years he practiced at the Spring principally on invalids who came to the Spring, but subsequently withdrew from practice and became interested in the management of his plantation and systematic reading.

In 1860 he prepared and published in pamphlet form the "Life of Edward Lacy," a distinguished officer under Sumter during the Revolution. Later he contributed to the *Yorkville Enquirer* "Reminiscences of York," which were full of graphic anecdote and character sketches.

Dr. Moore was possessed of a fine physique, being six feet two inches in stature and weighing 225 pounds. He was well-proportioned, his face was handsome, his carriage was graceful and his manners were courtly. Both he and his wife were brilliant conversationalists, and all classes of society were made welcome at their home. The kindness and sympathy of Dr. Moore to the sick people around Glenn's Spring was unbounded, and his memory is cherished and his kindness is gratefully remembered by many who are yet living.

He had only three children, viz.: Maurice Augustus, deceased; Dr. J. Nott Moore, and Mrs. Celina E. Means, relict of Dr. T. S. Means.

DR. JAMES NOTT MOORE, son of Dr. Maurice A. Moore, was born in Union county, S.C., in 1837. He was educated at Union College and began the study of medicine at New Orleans in 1856, and was graduated from the South Carolina Medical College at Charleston in 1859, and continued his studies in Paris until called home by the approaching hostilities between the States. "Reaching his native State, he promptly tendered his services, and was appointed assistant surgeon of the first regiment of infantry, with which he served on the coast until 1862. He left the medical service for the line and was elected first lieutenant of Co. H, Haygood's Regiment, and was later promoted captain. After a long and gallant service, which terminated in

Dr. J. Nott Moore

the surrender of the Confederate armies, he began the practice of medicine at Union, and thence moved in 1880 to Spartanburg."

Dr. Moore is yet practicing at Spartanburg and stands high among the practitioners of his native county and State, having always met with remarkable success. He is a prominent member of the State and county associations, and has held the vice-presidency of the former.

In 1866 he married Miss Lucy Herndon, granddaughter of Colonel Herndon of Revolutionary fame.

DR. T. SUMTER MEANS, the youngest son of James Kelsoe and Margaret Clowney Means, was born in Union district, April 1st, 1833. His parents were of Scotch-Irish and Irish stock and his maternal grandfather of notable exploit in the Revolutionary war. Dr. Means graduated in medicine in the University of Pennsylvania in 1858, and directly afterward was elected one of the resident physicians of

Blockley Hospital, the richly endowed charitable institution of Philadelphia. He remained for two years, resigned his position and came home. Soon afterward located in Florida for the practice of his profession.

At the beginning of the Confederate war he enlisted in the Prairie Guards, a local volunteer company, as a private. In a few months, on the resignation of the first lieutenant, he was elected to that office. In a sortie on Santa Rosa Island, near Pensacola, he distinguished himself for cool courage and the ability to meet an emergency. In the reorganization of the company he was elected captain; was wounded at Shiloh and taken prisoner.

In 1864 he received an invitation for full surgeon, and changed from the line to the medical department of the army. He was brigade surgeon from then until the surrender after the battle at Bentonville, N.C.

He practiced medicine at Glenn Springs, Spartanburg County, for a few years after the war. In 1872 he removed to Spartanburg, where he soon became one of the leading physicians, and remained in the pursuit of his profession until his last illness.

He was for many years senior warden of the Episcopal Church, a trustee of the Kennedy Library, and at one time president of the county medical association.

Dr. T. S. Means

In 1863 he married Celina E. Moore, the only daughter of Dr. Maurice Moore, of Glenn Springs, a lady of intelligence and literary culture who survives him.

Dr. Means was a man of fine physique, remarkably handsome, a cheerful and sympathetic nature. He died after an illness of several months, June 19th, 1900, leaving many friends and no enemies.

S. BRYSON EZELL, third son of Rev. John S. and Mahala (Thomas) Ezell was born near Limestone Springs, February 8th, 1847. The father of the subject of our sketch, born January 29th, 1825, has been for a half century or more an earnest, able and humble minister of the gospel of the Baptist faith, who has always resided in Spartanburg County, and who has done a great work in the Master's cause. The brothers, Rev. Landrum C. and Rev. Humphrey K. Ezell, the former a resident of Spartanburg County, and the latter a resident of Fairfield county, are also acceptable, energetic, humble and popular ministers of the gospel of the same faith and order, doing a good work in the Master's vineyard.

S. B. Ezell

Bryson attended the old-field schools of his neighborhood and engaged in promiscuous work on his father's farm. In the latter he manifested much interest. He was diligent as a student and stood well in his classes.

At the beginning of his teens the civil war broke out. One older brother had died in infancy, the other one volunteered, as did the father also later on in the struggle, leaving the responsibilities of the farm and family somewhat npon his young shoulders. Still later, when in the straits of the Southern Confederacy, he went into the service, leaving home in July, 1864, and joining Co. D, 2d Battalion, S.C.V. His company being without tents or blankets except what had been carried by the boys from their homes, was much exposed to a very rainy season. As a result of this nearly all members contracted chills, and among this number was young Ezell, who was among the last to succumb. He left camps and went to the hospital and did not regain his health until after the surrender.

In February, 1866, he entered New Prospect Academy, where he remained five months, and then taught at Allgood Seminary the balance of the year. In 1868 he was appointed deputy sheriff of Spartanburg County under John Dewberry, sheriff, in which capacity he served four years. In the fall of 1872 he entered Wofford College, from which he was graduated in June, 1875. On August 11th, 1875, he was married to Miss Laura Maxwell of Spartanburg. In 1876 he entered the mercantile business at Spartanburg, which he has continued with success for more than twenty years.

Mr. Ezell is a director in the Central National Bank, the Spartanburg Savings Bank and Home Building and Loan Association of Spartanburg,

In 1867 he joined the Baptist church at Macedonia, and was baptized by Rev. Wade Hill. Upon removal to Spartanburg in 1868, transferred his membership to the First Baptist church there, where it remains. He is usually one of the delegates from his church to the association and attends quite frequently the Baptist State Conventions. Was clerk of the church for a number of years, and is at present a deacon and the superintendent of the Sunday-school, having held, with the exception of two years, the last position continuously since 1876. He takes a great interest in Sunday-school work, and has served as secretary, executive committeeman and president of both the county and State Sunday-school Conventions, has attended several of the International and one of the World's Sabbath-school Conventions, and is at present vice-president, for South Carolina, in the International Convention. Was one of the first superintendents to use the blackboard in the general exercises, in the school; gave at Inman, S.C., the first exhibition of modern Sunday-school work attempted in the county, and organized and taught in his school the first class in the State, completing a normal course and receiving diplomas of graduation. His efforts have assisted in giving permanency to the "normal class" and other advanced ideas in Sunday-school work in South Carolina.

Mr. Ezell is also identified with the educational interests of his section. Is a member of the board of trustees of Limestone College, and has served as both president and member of the board of trustees of "Connie Maxwell Orphanage." He is in every sense of the word progressive, liberal and public-spirited, is apparently in the full vigor of health, and it is to be hoped that a long and continued life of usefulness is yet before him.

REV. JOHN GILL LANDRUM was born in Rutherford County, Tenn., October 22d, 1810, and was the second child and oldest son of Rev. Merriman and Delilah (Jackson) Landrum. His parents were both born and raised near Cross Keys in Union county, S.C., from whence they moved to Tennessee in 1806. Of his father, who was a son of Reuben and Mary (Ray) Landrum, it is recorded, that as a husband and parent he was affectionate; as a citizen, upright and honest; as a politician, patriotic and a Jeffersonian Republican, and as a minister of the gospel he was universally

Rev. John G. Landrum

esteemed. His mother was the only daughter of Ralph Jackson, Esq., a highly respected citizen of Union district, who was numbered among the staunch Whigs during the Revolution, and soon after its close was appointed by the Legislature a justice of the quorum. While she received such education in books as the neighborhood afforded, she imbibed what was better — early lessons of piety and filial duty, and grew to be a woman of great dignity and moral power.

John Gill Landrum, named in honor of the great Bible commentator, was a frail and delicate child who seemed destined to an early grave, and for some time after he attained the age of manhood did not weigh more than eighty-five pounds. His parents considering him too weakly for any employment requiring physical exertion, thought it wise to give him whatever educational advantages it might be in their power to bestow, and at the age of five years he was started to school. His brother Kimbro Landrum, of Texas, says: "He was always at the head of his class, was the pride and life of his father and was loved by all his schoolmates.

It is further stated of him that so eager was he for knowledge, that even at an early age he manifested an interest in topics that were considered altogether too grave for a child. When about the age of eight or ten years, he was frequently sent on errands to Nashville, and would while there visit the legislative halls during the sessions of the Legislature and took a lively interest in its proceedings. During these visits he often saw David Crockett and Andrew Jackson, and on one occasion (1825) he saw Jackson and LaFayette ride together through the streets of Nashville. He witnessed the public reception that was given the latter during his last visit to this country.

The schools in the immediate neighborhood were inadequate to meet his now rapidly unfolding mind, and it became necessary to send him to a school of higher grade. Consequently he was sent to the boarding-school of Travis Nash, a few miles distant, who taught principally a grammar school. He attended this school probably two years, and at the closing examination carried off the first honors of his class. Among his school fellows was M. P. Gentry, who was afterward a member of the United States Congress, and the Whig candidate for governor of Tennessee against Andrew Johnson in 1854. Dr. Harden Scales and Dr. Webb, both distinguished men of Tennessee, were also students in Travis Nash's grammar school. After his course in this school, at the invita-tion of Newton Cannon, who was surveyor-general and afterwards became governor of Tennessee, and at whose house his father and mother had lived during the first year of their life in Tennessee, he entered the private school of a gentleman whose name was Montgomery, who was a professor of mathematics, or, as he was then called, *a graduate in numbers*. John had not been here long when by the sad and unexpected death of his father, he was called home and his school days seemed to be brought to a sudden close. Being the eldest son of the family the care of the widowed mother and younger brothers and sisters devolved upon him, but he proved himself equal to the demand of this new and trying position. He remained with his mother upward of fifteen months, superintending the affairs of the farm and other responsible duties. With the exception of three months in the Latin school of Randolph Alexander he had no further opportunity of attending school in his native State. Being yet young and slender it was decided that he should visit his relatives in South Carolina; many, including his grandmother, were living in Union district.

Before young Landrum had been in Union very long it was decided that he should remain a year and attend the school of John Bostick, an educated Englishman, who was pronounced by his pupil "a capital English teacher," adding further: "With him I completed what was then considered a good English education." He lived this year (1829) with his great-uncle, Rev. Thomas Ray, a pious, consecrated Baptist preacher, who bestowed upon him more than paternal affection.

It was while attending the school of John Bostick that John G. Landrum was licensed to preach the gospeL by the Baptist Church at Padgett's Creek, having made a public profession of religion before leaving his native State, and uniting with Mt. Pleasant (Missionary Baptist) church, of which his father was pastor at the time of his death. He had impressions to preach the gospel before leaving his native State, and it is stated that his first attempt in the pulpit produced "the profoundest impression on the church and congregation." He was still of a frail and tender body, and was called "the boy preacher," being only nineteen years of age.

After leaving school Landrum was employed to teach by Mr. David Boyce of Union county. This was in the year 1830. He was still a diligent student, devoting most of his spare time to reading and study.

On January the 15th, 1831, he was ordained in the gospel ministry by the Padgett's Creek Church, having received this solemn commission when he was but a little over twenty years of age. He had not been in the ministry long when a new field of labor opened up to him which was destined to be the scene of his life-work.

On the 13th of June, 1830, Rev. Thomas Bomar, a good man and excellent preacher, who had long been the pastor of Mount Zion, Bethlehem and New Prospect churches in Spartanburg District, fell dead at the house of John S. Rowland, by which death the said churches were without a pastor. A committee was appointed by Mount Zion Church, consisting of Dr. John W. Lewis and Edward Bomar, which resulted in the selection of Rev. John G. Landrum, who at once occupied the field made vacant by the lamented Bomar.

It would consume too much time and space in the brief narrative of John G. Landrum to give an extended review of his ministerial work, embracing a period of a half century, in connection with the churches already mentioned, First Baptist church at Spartanburg and churches in Greenville and Spartanburg counties and Newberry Court-house, by monthly appointment for a few years.

He was called to the supply of New Prospect church in 1832, and, excepting an absence of nine months in the army during the civil war between the States, preached to it without intermission for a period numbering exactly fifty years. This church was constituted in 1820 with only twenty-seven members. For the first twelve years of its history it met in a little inconvenient log-house, and had been during this time supplied with preaching by Revs. Thomas Howard, Thomas Bomar and William Harman.

Says Landrum's biographer: "There was little to encourage the youthful preacher when he first took charge of New Prospect. The membership had dwindled to seventeen. The uncouth, incommodious log-hut, called a meeting-house, stood in the midst of a community abounding in almost every kind of vice. The stillhouse, the grog-shop, those emissaries of Satan, were busy day and night, while horse-racing, Sabbath-breaking and their kindred vices were shedding baleful influences far and near. But under his ministry the little church began to revive; the neighborhood began to feel its influence; society began to improve, slowly at first and almost imperceptibly, but as the years came and went one stronghold after another was gained. Men began to talk of the great changes that had taken placeand to congratulate each other upon the success of their church and the progress of their community in intelligence and morality. Forests were cleared and houses beautified; schools were established and children educated; intelligence and thrift rapidly took the place of ignorance and indolence, and the community ere long became known far and wide as one of the most progressive civil and enlightened in the land. An elegant new house of worship soon took the place of the log-hut, and in 1873 the church embraced a membership of 457."

It is stated that about this time a committee was appointed by the church to look up the facts connected with its history, and it was ascertained that during Landrum's pastorate as many as fifteen hundred had been gathered into the church.

Says his biographer further: "We have long wondered at the almost marvelous growth of New Prospect Church, and the almost marvelous development of the country around it, and as we have done so, we have admired and loved more and more the great, good man who was the head and center of it all; and we have thought that if his life and work had been confined strictly to this church alone, and that if his name had never been heard beyond the limits of the New Prospect neighborhood, we could find even there enough of the fruits of his life and labors to justify us in pronouncing him one of the great men of the age."

Bethlehem church, six miles southwest of Spartanburg city, to which Landrum was called, was constituted in 1800. [3] When the Tyger River (Baptist) Association was organized in 1833, this church numbered 252 members. P'irst and last he was the pastor of Bethlehem thirty-six years, not continuously however, and during the intervening time of his pastorate of said church he supplied the pulpit at Bethel and other places.

When Landrum accepted the call of Mount Zion the church was only three or four years old. There were about twenty-five members that entered into the organization. At the constitution of the Tyger River Association, August 31, 1833, the church reported a membership of 125, showing a rapid increase of numbers during the first two years of his pastorate. The church is located on a high ridge near the historic Blackstock road, eight miles west of Spartanburg city. A new and elegant brick structure is now being erected near the site of the old building. The land, some six or eight acres in number, was donated by John Chapman, Sr.

During the fifty years of Landrum's ministry, he supplied the pulpit of Mount Zion church for about forty years. During an intervening space of about ten years between his first and second pastorate here the church was ably supplied by Rev. Micajah C. Barnett.

In our review of the progress of religion in Spartanburg County during the nineteenth century we have referred to the revival meetings in the towns of Spartanburg, Brushy Creek and other places, beginning as early as 1832, in which Landrum took an active part.

It was not until February 23d, 1839, that the Baptist church at Spartanburg was constituted and put into regular working order, with an organization of eleven males and fourteen females. Major John Earle Bomar, in a letter some time after the death of Landrum, wrote as follows: "Rev. J. G. Landrum had been preaching at Spartanburg occasionally, and a part of the time statedly, since 1830, '31 or '32. I remember to have seen among my father's old papers a subscription bearing date of one of these years, the object being to raise money to pay Landrum to preach at regular times. The old church building [4] was erected about the time the church was organized. About the same time there was no house of worship of any denomination in the town of Spartanburg, and preaching was held in the court-house and sometimes at private residences. On more than one occasion within my inemory it was held at my father's house, principally, I suppose, on account of -my grandmother, Mrs. Rebecca Earle, [5] who was at that time the only Baptist living in Spartanburg, if not the only professor of religion there, and was very old and cripple, being unable to leave the house."

At the first meeting of the Spartanburg church after its organization. Rev. John G. Landrum was chosen its pastor to preach every second Sunday and Saturday before. In October of the same year the church imited with the Tyger River Association, and in the same month forty-two members were added to the church by baptism, and others by letter. The revival went on, and in sixteen months the membership increased from twentyfive to one hundred.

In the *Spartan* files April 17th, 1856, an article is published headed "Historic Views of Spartanburg; or Facts and Memories of Eighty Years," by Derment. Says this writer: "In the days of 'Auld lang syne' there were none of the external evidences of general morality as afforded by churches and church edifices. To 1836 there was no such a thing as a church or stated preaching. The 'pure word' was administered from the bench of the judge to the citizens *en masse*. There were no outward temples consecrated to God, and of course, no marked sectarian divisions. While each had his individual system of religious faith and all enjoyed his religious predilections, their separate proclivities in that regard were never permitted to excite between them, discord or envyings. Of course there were professors of religion among them who had their respective memberships in different churches in the country. These men were respected, beloved. They were not suspected of being hollow-hearted hypocrites or unworthy members because their practices were not in accordance with the exalted standard of piety which the vain mocker in the plentitude of his own self-righteousness sets up in the formation of his judgment.

"Down to 1836 there were no church edifices. There were sermons delivered immethodically by different ministers of different denominations. In the latter part of the year 1835 incipient steps were taken by the members of the Baptist Church for the erection of a building for their worship. Almost simultaneously the adherents of the Methodist form of worship inaugurated a similar enterprise. The former, however, are entitled to the honor of priority. On the completion of these several churches pastors were installed or selected.

"Rev. J. G. Landrum was chosen by the Baptist church, and has ever since held that responsible position to the entire satisfaction of his church. How he has sustained himself with such eminent success has been remarkable, and embodies a high compliment to his purity, fidelity and geniality of nature. Then his flock numbered about twenty — not more. Now it is a little short, if any, of two hundred. What a vast increase! To-day that little church, the development of a germ planted in 1836, has grown in strength until it exerts a great moral power."

In October, 1857, Landrum was elected to preach two Sundays to the Baptist church at Spartanburg, the first and third Sundays, and on every Tuesday night and Saturday before the first Sunday in each month. To perform all this work now on his hands in Spartanburg,. Major John Earle Bomar stated: "he rode from his home, a distance of eight miles, through sunshine and rain, heat and cold, and very rarely missed an appointment."

Says his biographer further: "In the meantime, Spartanburg had grown to be a town of considerable proportions, and other denominations had entered the field in force. Wofford College was established within its limits with an able faculty, under the auspices of the Methodist denomination, and Landrum saw that the surrounding circumstances called for renewed efforts and increased vigilance if he would keep pace with the tide of progress and meet the demands of the times. He seemed to rise in power and resources as the tide rolled on, and upheld the purity of his faith and the dignity of his church with the same earnestness and convincing power with which he had at first stirred the depths of wickedness and shaken the foundations of unbelief. He was now in the prime and vigor of manhood, and his mind had reached the full maturity of its powers."

A period of nearly thirty years transpired during the ministrations of Landrum at Spartanburg. He resigned in 1865, "much to the regret," says Major Bomar, "of the church and congregation."

In 1854 Landrum was called to supply the pulpit of Bethel church (Woodruff, S.C.), organized as early as 1787, and, says his biographer: "When John G. Landrum assumed pastoral charge of the church in 1854 the congregation was perhaps the largest that assembled in any place in the county, and in intelligence and refinement it would have compared favorably with any congregation in the State. The present large and commodious house of worship had been completed, and...it was capable of seating a larger audience than any other church building within our knowledge. Yet on the second Sunday in every month it was crowded to its utmost capacity, and the preacher who stood in the pulpit was made aware of the fact that he stood face to face with the intelligence, wealth, chivalry and beauty of the land, and also with the enemy of souls moving in high life and imparting to his wiles the gloss of respectability and refinement.

"For six years Landrum met this vast audience monthly and held it and swayed it as perhaps no other man at that time could have done. He was now in the prime of life and his preaching powers had probably reached their climax. During his connection with the church one hundred and seven members were added by baptism and the church was greatly revived and strengthened."

Referring to his manner of preaching and style of delivery, his biographer further states: "Mr. Landrum was never a revivalist in the popular sense of the term. His preaching was of the character to make men think and act rather than to excite temporary emotions. Yet he certainly baptized a greater number of persons than any man that has ever lived in Spartanburg County...It is safe to conclude that the whole number must have amounted to more than six thousand.

"His manner of treating a subject in the pulpit was somewhat similar to that of Dr. Thomas Chalmers. He had but few points in a discourse, but these were strong ones, around which his mind seemed to move as if on hinges. No man ever imderstood better how to repeat an idea in ever varying forms of expression, each one of which advanced in regular climax toward the point of culmination until it was completely driven home to the hearts and understanding of his hearers.

"Mr. Landrum's manner of delivery was peculiarly his own. Some of his gestures would appear awkward, when judged by set rules of gesticulation, and many of his figures, as well as his modulation and emphasis, might fail to meet the abstract requirements of school-books, but from the moment he began the interest of his hearers in the subject presented increased, and as he proceeded and the eye kindled from the glowing fires within, they forgot to apply rules, and every tone and every movement of his body seemed in perfect keeping with the grand and mighty thoughts struggling for utterance."

In the year 1831 the Broad River (Baptist) Association met with Buck Creek Church in the present county of Spartanburg. From a historical sketch of said Association, prepared in the year 1875 by Rev. M. C. Barnett, we quote the following paragraph:

"The name of John G. Landrum now appears for the first time as a member of this Association. He was at this time quite a young man, [6] but possessing such gifts and qualifications as a minister, that the Association was proud of him almost to excess. He was appointed (per. haps imprudently) to preach on the Sabbath, in place of old and experienced ministers, which did not so well comport with the scriptural injunction in reference to the younger being subject to the elder. However, he did not, as I have been told, disappoint the anxious anticipations of his brethren. He always possessed the power of making great efforts. Some men fail when there is the greatest anxiety for their best performance. This is said by Alexander Campbell to have been a weakness of Andrew Broadus of Virginia, that most distinguished minister of the gospel. Landrum never disappointed the expectations of his friends on extraordinary occasions. I heard him preach at an association not fourteen years ago, on the 'Holiness of God.' His thoughts were sublime, and when he supported his position by a quotation from Isaiah's version: 'Holy, holy, holy is the Lord of hosts; the whole earth is full of his glory,' his voice echoed over the hills as musical as the 'sound of a dulcimer sweet'; while it fell upon the listening thousands in most overpowering eloquence, making it another one of his efforts that met the anticipations of his brethren.

"He has now been in the ministry between forty and fifty years. Of course his sermons are more profound, doctrinal and methodical than they were in his younger days, but whether they are more interesting to the common listener is doubtful."

Associated with Hon. Simpson Bobo, Major H. J. Dean, Dr. R. M. Young, Major John Stroble and others, John G. Landrum was among the first advocates in the temperance cause in Spartanburg district; but as we have referred to this in another part of this work, we forbear further comment under the heading of the subject of this sketch. [7]

Under the head of our review of the progress of education in Spartanburg County during the 19th century, at another place in this volume, we have noticed John G. Landrum in the capacity of school-teacher, and of his success in the Mount Zion Academy for a period of ten years or more, and it is unnecessary to reproduce that which has already been stated relating thereto.

John G. Landrum being possessed of an active and inquiring mind was a great searcher for the truth. He was well educated for a specific purpose. He kept himself posted on all the leading topics of the day. His library was full of choice books in almost every department of literature. He was fond of Grecian and Roman history, and was one of the best posted men in his State on the history of the Revolution.

From Griffith's narrative we quote the following paragraph: "In 1856 the first monument was erected on Cowpens Battle Ground, in the eastern part of Spartanburg County, by the Washington Light Infantry, a famous military company of Charleston, South Carolina. The company marched through the country with their baggage train and camp equipage and pitched their camp on the far-famed field. There was a vast concourse of people to witness the erection, and the ceremonies of dedication were of the most imposing kind. Rev. John G. Landrum had previously been selected as one of the orators of the day on account of his having been recommended to the company as being a man thoroughly conversant with the country's history. We have often heard the speech made on this occasion complimented as one replete with information, pathos and power."

Mr. Landrum took a deep interest in the general course of education, and particularly so in the country in which he lived. Says his biographer: "In 1857 the Baptists of South Carolina were called upon to raise one hundred thousand dollars as their quota of the half million with which it was proposed to endow the Southern Baptist Theological Seminary at Greenville, S.C. Landrum entered warmly and heartily into this movement, talked and worked for it both privately and publicly, and by his efforts and personal influence contributed in no small measure to its success. He was during several of these years vice-president of the State Baptist Convention, Judge O'Neall being president."

In our review of the progress of education in Spartanburg County we have noticed John G. Landrum's connection with the Cooper Limestone Institute (now Limestone College), and of his work in securing for the Spartanburg Baptist Association the title for this property from Hon. Peter Cooper of New York. He was also one of the trustees of the Johnson Female University, Anderson, S.C., and served on the Board of Trustees of Furman University, Greenville, S.C., for a period of fifteen or twenty years.

For about ten years before the civil war Mr. Landrum served as treasurer of the board of commissioners of the poor of Spartanburg district with but a trifling emolument, and performed the duties pertaining to the position with cheerfulness and exactness and, as far as we have ever heard, to the entire satisfaction of the public.

In a political way he served his country but very little, but he never neglected his duties as a citizen. He always took the warmest interest in public affairs, and scrutinized closely the political problems of the day. He was an ardent admirer of Calhoun, and agreed with him in the doctrine of State Sovereignty, and believed that the Government had no right to meddle with our State institutions. In 1851, by the united voice of the people of Spartanburg district, he represented them, with five others, in the State Convention, which met in Columbia the following year, which thought the time had not yet come for the State to secede from the Union.

Mr. Landrum was also a member of the State Convention of 1860 which passed the ordinance of secession. The result of the poll of the vote placed him at the head of the ticket. The convention was largely composed of religious men and quiet citizens of known integrity, who had never figured in politics; and the outpfrowth of its action — the bloodshed and disaster which followed — did not reflect upon the patriotism, tarnish the honor, nor impugn the motives of the men who confronted the impending issue which had been agitated before the American people for a half century or more.

Within a few months after the outbreak of the civil war between the States the 13th Regiment, S.C.V. was organized under the command of Colonel O. E. Edwards. Upon the organization of the same, Rev. John G. Landrum was duly appointed and commissioned by the Confederate authorities at Richmond, Va., its chaplain. He remained encamped with said regiment on the coast of South Carolina and in Virginia for the period of nearly one year, preaching and laboring almost incessantly among the soldiers of his regiment and in the hospitals, when, by reason of advanced age, his health began to decline, and at the urgent solicitation of many friends, he returned to his churches at home.

While acting as chaplain of the 13th Regiment, Mr. Landrum was duly appointed colporteur of the Sunday school and Colportage Board of the Baptist State Convention of South Carolina. In his field of labors he was assigned not only to his regiment, but among all others of the brave men in Virginia to whom God in his providence might give him access.

After fifty-two years a preacher of righteousness, and nearly seventy-two years in the battle of life, John G. Landrum died at his home at Landrum, S.C. (a town named in his honor), January 19th, 1882. His remains were interred at Mount Zion church, in the presence of a large concourse of friends. His life and services were commented upon favorably by the county and religious press, and appropriate resolutions were passed to his memory. A suitable monument was erected over his grave in August, 1884, by the contributions of his admiring friends of the last four churches which he served, viz.: Mount Zion, Bethlehem, New Prospect and Wolf Creek, together with his family, being the last honor paid to his memory. For a more extended account of his life and public service the reader is referred to the book, "The Life and Times of Rev. John G. Landrum," by Professor H. P. Griffith, published in 1885. This contains much interesting matter which we have been unable to notice in this sketch, including the memorial sermon on his death, delivered at Mount Zion, April 29th, 1882, by Rev. James C. Furman, D.D., and the address of Rev. R. H. Reed, pastor of Nazareth (Presbyterian) church, delivered at Mount Zion, January 21st, 1882, the day of his interment. The latter in his remarks stated that "John G. Landrum was no ordinary man. As a citizen he was public-spirited and liberal; always throwing his influence on the side of education and all railroad enterprises, and in everything looking to the welfare of his country."

Mr. Landrum was married twice: first to Elizabeth, daughter of John and Margaret Montgomery, and second, to Nancy M., daughter of Theron and Hannah Earle. By the first marriage he had seven children, viz.: Margaret Jane, died of burns in childhood; Mary Amarylis, wife of James S. Ballinger, now deceased; Franklin Vernon, residing in Chicota, Texas; John Belton O'Neall, author of this work; Elizabeth Cleveland, deceased, relict of Dr. W. P. Compton; Richard Furman, deceased; and Chevis Montgomery, residing at Greenville, S.C. By the second marriage there were three children, viz.: Earle, Harriet and Nancy Carolina. The two first died in childhood. The last named is the wife of Rev. E. E. Bomar, D.D., Richmond, Va.

Glenn's Spring

Mills, in his "Statistics," published in 1828, in giving the resources of Spartanburg, says: "Another spring, called the Sulphur Spring (from its supposed combination with this mineral), is found on the south side of Fair Forest Creek, eleven and a half miles from Spartanburg...In the latter part of the eighteenth century the spot was known as a 'deer lick.' Cattle were continually straggling from their pastures to the swamp around the 'lick.' A small boy who was sent to drive the cows home...fell into the ill-smelling mud of the quagmire. The boy bad a cutaneous eruption...In a few days...the eruption had disappeared; the mud had cured him...From this time for a number of years the place was a resort much sought by the people of the country around for mud baths. In 1800 there was a long dry spell; many springs

Hotel of Glenn's Spring Company

were dried up, and much inconvenience was experienced by the settlers...The drouth revealed on the edge of the quagmire an unsuspected spring, and a family living near were glad to avail themselves of this new water supply...On using soap in the water the curdling at once gave the suggestion that this spring was mineral,...the swamp was ditched off, and the 'Powder Spring,' as it was called, came to be known as possessing curative properties.

"The original grant of land on which the spring was found comprised a thousand acres. An old Baptist minister owned it at the beginning of the nineteenth century, and was thought to have made a fine sale when he got $300 for it.

"In 1815-16 Mr. James Means built a two-storied frame house near the spring; the water had so much reputation in the upper counties of the State that a demand was made for a boarding-house in the vicinity.

"On account of increased demands upon Mr. Means for accommodation by such people, which he did not like to refuse, he divided the tract of land in two, and sold the 500 acres on which the spring was situated to Mr. John B. Glenn for $800...Mr. Glenn enlarged his house and opened an inn for the entertainment of visitors and travelers. From this time the spring took his name, and for seventy-five years the spring has been known as Glenn's Spring.

"In 1835 Glenn's Spring had grown to such importance that fifteen gentlemen formed themselves into a stock company to buy the property of Mr. Glenn, determined to build and equip a hotel of sufficient size and convenience to meet the public demand. The charter was obtained in 1837, the name of the corporation being 'The Glenn's Spring Company,' Dr. Maurice A. Moore, president.

"Mr. Glenn was paid $15,000 for the property. In 1838 the hotel was formally opened. From then until the civil war it was frequented by many distinguished Southern gentlemen and others of less renown...The therapeutic value of the water is acknowledged by physicians throughout the United States. Its tonic properties in cases of nervous prostration are something marvelous, and for dyspepsia, anemia, diseases of the kidneys and liver, is not excelled perhaps by any mineral water known in the Materia Medica."

In 1877 the property was purchased by Dr. John W. Simpson and his son J. Wister Simpson, Esq. Dr. Simpson dying a few years later willed his interest to his two sons, J. W. and W. D. Simpson, both of whom are now dead. Under their wills the property went to their children, and is now known as The Glenn's Spring Company.

[1] During the last term of Daniel Wallace in Congress the Pinckneyville congressional district was changed and Greenville, Anderson, Pickens, Spartanburg ajid Union were thrown together, the same constituting the 5th Congressional District. James L. Orr was the first representative of this newly-formed district, who was also made Speaker of the House of Representatives at Washington.

[2] In Mr. Kennedy's famous novel, "Horse-Shoe Robinson," the colonel referred to is Obadiah Trimmier, father of William, who was the father of Colonel T. G. Trimmier. The absent lady referred to was Lucy TrimmierJ wife of Obadiah. She was a Stribling. Her grandfather was a Watson. The violin boy was William Trimmier mentioned herein; the boy thrown from the horse was Thomas, brother of William. The two small boys mentioned were Obadiah Watson and Marcus Tullias, sons of Obadiah and Lucy Trimmier, who were living on Toxaway. "Horse-Shoe Robinson" lived on Chauga, in Pickens County, S.C.

Four Trimmiers first came from France — two brothers, Obadiah and John, or Jack as he was called, and two sisters, Nancy and Elizabeth, neither of whom ever married.

Lucy Stribling came from Scotland at the age of twelve years. John Trimmier married a Ross, of South Carolina. They both died, leaving one son, Obadiah, who was raised by his grandfather Ross, partaking of the sports of his grandfather, who was a wealthy man; he was called Devil Obe, to distinguish him from the better Obe. He left two sons, Jim and Cam, by his first wife. He afterwards married a Gibson, and left one son, Obadiah, who lives in Jasper, Marian county, Tenn.

[3] See Griffith's Life of Landrum, "History of Bethlehem Church." Appendix, p. 287.

[4] This stood near the site of the present new jail building at Spartanburg.

[5] This is the lady already referred to at another place in this volume as the wife of Colonel John Wood, who was murdered by the Tories under "Bloody Bill Cunningham," November, 1781. She married a second time to Colonel John Earle, grandfather of Major John Earle Bomar.

[6] He was just twenty-one years old.

[7] For an account of the first temperance movement in Spartanburg County the reader is referred to Griffith's "Life of J. G. Landrum," p. 70-78.

Chapter Thirty-Nine - List of Senators and Representatives from Spartanburg County in the State Legislature from 1886 to 1900 Inclusive

The first representation from Spartanburg County after its organization in 1785 was not a representation from said county (afterwards called district) proper, but was from the Upper or Spartan district, which was laid out according to the act of the Provisional Congress of South Carolina, February, 1776. (See map "Colonial and Revolutionary History of Upper South Carolina," page 43.) Said election district comprised all the territory of the original county of Spartanburg and nearly all the territory of the original county of Union, and the electors in said district voted together in the selection of a senator and four representatives, to which, under the law, they were entitled. It appears that in the selection of four representatives, by common consent, two were selected from the lower (or Union) side and two from the upper (or Spartanburg) side of the district. This arrangement of voting continued in force until the State Constitution went into effect, which was ratified in June, 1790, and remained in force until after the close of the civil war between the States, when another constitution was enacted in 1868 by virtue of the Reconstruction Act of the Congress of the United States. The old constitution, as adopted, gave to Spartanburg proper one senator and two representatives. It made no provision for any reapportionment of representation. In obedience to this demand the constitution was amended in 1808, and under this amendment the representatives were apportioned among the several counties (or districts) of the State according to the number of white inhabitants and the amount of taxes paid in each district, one representative to be allowed for every sixty-second part of the whole taxes raised by the Legislature. Under the apportionment of 1809, the district of Spartanburg gained two members in the House, making four in all, and by another apportionment in 1830 an another member was gained, making five in all. This apportionment remained until the adoption of the Constitution of 1868, when the number of representatives was again reduced to four. Another apportionment, however, in 1892, increased the number of representatives to six, but in 1896, by reason of the formation of Cherokee county, which comprises a portion of the original county of Spartanburg, the number was reduced to five representatives, which at present remains.

The following is a list of senators and representatives from Upper or Spartan district and Spartanburg County proper in accordance with the foregoing statement. Those marked thus (*) were representatives from the Union section of the Upper or Spartan district from 1776 to '90 inclusive:

Upper or Spartan District

Senators — 1786-88, John Collins; 1788-90, William Smith.

Representatives — 1786-88, Thomas Brandon,* Samuel Mcjunkin, John Henderson and William Kennedy*; 1788-90, William Kennedy,* Thomas Brandon,* John Henderson and James Jorden.

Spartanburg County (or District)

Senators — 1790-1800, William Smith; 1800-02, James Jorden*; [1] 1802-08, Henry Wells; 1808-12, Isham Foster; 1812-16, William Smith; 1816-18, Obediah Trimmier; 1818-26, Isaac Smith; 1826-34, John Dodd; 1834-38, Thomas Poole; 1838-46, John Crawford; 1846-62, Gabriel Cannon; 1862-65, Joel W. Miller; 1865-68, John Winsmith, elected under Provisional Government of South Carolina after close of civil war; 1868-72, Joel Foster; 1872-76, David R. Duncan, 187680, Gabriel Cannon; 1880-84, Thomas J. Moore; 1884-86, E. H. Bobo; [2] 1886-88, John W. Wofford; 1888-92, R. M. Smith; 1892-96, Stanyearne Wilson; 1896-1900, E. L. Archer.

Representatives — 1790-92, John Henderson and James Jorden; 1792-94 — Obediah Trimmier and Henry Wells; 1794-96, Henry Wells and Robert

Goodloe; 1796-98, Thomas Moore and William Wells; 1798-1800, Thomas Moore and William Wells; 1800-02, B. Shumate and Isham Henderson; 1802-04; William Lancaster and Andrew B. Moore; 1804-06, Nathan Lipscomb and William Lancaster; 1806-08, Andrew B. Moore and William Lancaster; 1808-10, Andrew B. Moore, Daniel McKie and W. Nesbitt; 1810-12, A. B. Moore, John Means, Wilson Nesbitt and Daniel McKie; 1812-14, John Means, Wilson Nesbitt, Obediah Trimmier ami Daniel McKie; 1814-16, John Henderson, John Means, Wm. Reid and Samuel Farrow; 1816-18, John Dodd, James Hammett, William Reid and Samuel Farrow; 1818-20, William Reid, Samuel. White, Eber Smith and Samuel Farrow; 1820-22, John Dodd, John T. Earle, William Reid and Eber Smith; 1822-24, John Dodd, Daniel McKie, William Reid and John W. Lewis; 1826-28, James Crook, John Stroble, J. Bsannon and William Reid; 1828-30, John W. Lewis, William Poole, James Crook and Isaac Smith; 1830-32, John W. Lewis, Memory N. Chapman, Philip Bruton, John W. Smith and John Crawford; 1832-34, Thomas Poole, M. N. Chapman, J. E. Henry, John Crawford and Theron Earle; 1834-36, John Crawford, H. H. Thomson, Theron Earle, S. L. Westmoreland and Andrew Barry; 1836-38, John Crawford, H. H. Thomson, Andrew Barry, James H. Hoy and Samuel N. Evins; 1838-40, Wm. R. Poole, James H. Hoy, H. H. Thomson, S. N. Evins and John W. Hunt; 1840-42, J. E. Henry, H. H. Thomson, W. R. Poole, John R. Richards and John W. Hunt; 1842-44, Gabriel Cannon, Tench C. Carson, J. E. Henry, Thomas Littlejohn and J. Pinckney Miller; 1844-46, G. Cannon, B, B. Foster, E. P. Smith, J. E. Henry and Thomas Littlejohn; 1846-48, B. B. Foster, J. E. Henry, J. P. Miller, Samuel Otterson and.E. P. Smith; 1848-50, B. B. Foster, Robert W. Foster, J. E. Henry, E. P. Smith and J. P. Miller; 1850-52, E. C. Leitner, J. WTucker, T. W. Waters, E. P. Smith and H. J. Dean; 1852-54, J. VV. Tucker, E. C. Leitner, H. J. Dean, J. Winsmith and B. F. Bates; 1854-56, B. F. Kilgore, J. V. Trimmier, J. W. Miller, J. W. Tucker and A. G. Cambell; 1856-58, J. W. Miller, O. E. Edwards, J. Winsmith, James Farrow and O. P. Earle; 1858-60, O. E. Edwards, B. F. Kilgore, J. W. Miller, W. M. Foster and J. Farrow; 1860-62, O. E. Edwards, W. M. Foster, James Farrow, B. F. Bates and J. Winsmith; 1862-64, John H. Evins, Simpson Bobo, G. W. H. Legg, W. U. Foster and John W. Webber; 1864-65, John H. Evins, H. H. Thomson, Jr., James H. Carlisle, B. B. Foster and Joseph Walker; 1865-68, J. W. Carlisle, A. B. Woodruff, D. R. Duncan, G. Cannon and Alexander Copeland; [3] 1868-70, C. C. Turner, R. M. Smith, Javan Bryant and Samuel Littlejohn; 1870-72, R. M. Smith, J. B. Lyles, J. L. Wofford and D. R. Duncan; 1872-74, G. Cannon, T. J. Moore, A. B. Woodruff and W. P. Compton; 1874-76, John Eaiie Bomar, Gabriel Cannon, A. B. Woodruff and R. M. Smith; 1876-78, E. S. Allen, J. W. Wofford, Charles Petty and W. P. Compton; 1878-80, John Dewberry, John C. Anderson, John B. Cleveland and J. Y. Carlisle; 188082, E. S. Allen, J. W. Wofford, W. K. Blake and J. E. Black; 1882-84, E. H. Bobo, J. A. Corry, H. L. Farley and J. B. O. Eandrum; 1884-86, S. E. Mason, J. S. R. Thomson, Stanyearne Wilson and R. M. Smith; 1886-88, W. G. Austell, George R. Dean, S. J. Simpson and E. L. Archer; 1888-90, H. H. Arnold, W. G. Austell, W. G. Britton and S. T. D. Lancaster; 1890-92, Geo. B. Dean, Stanyearne Wilson, R. C. Sarratt and M. O. Rowland; 1892-94, L. E. Farley, M. O. Rowland, M. P. Patton, W. M. Foster, J. A. P. Lancaster and C. A. Barry; 1894-96, D. M. Miles, R. A. Lancaster, C. A. Barry, M. O. Rowland, C. P. Brown and R. E. Thompson; 1896-98, R. A. Lancaster, A. B. Layton, T. E. Johnson, W. G. Austell, D. M. Miles and C. A. Barry; [4] 1898-1900, D. E. Hydrick, C. P. Saunders, Robert J. Gantt, A. H. Dean and F. C. West.

[1] James Jorden died in 1802.
[2] Mr. Bobo was killed by accident in 1885. J. W. Woflford was elected to fill his unexpired term.
[3] This delegation was elected within a few months after close of civil war (1865) under the auspices of the provisional government of South Carolina.
[4] In this delegation Miles and Barry resigned, and to fill their unexpired terms D. E. Hydrick and F. C. West were elected.

Voting Precincts and Managers

The following extracts from the laws of South Carolina and Acts and Resolutions of said State relating to Spartanburg district show the following voting precincts and managers from 1806 to 1816 inclusive, and also appointments made of justices of the quorum and peace from December, 1805, to December, 1816, inclusive.

1806. [1] Court-house — *Managers:* Isham Foster, Samuel Miller and Richard Thomson.

Isaac Crow's — *Managers:* Willis Williford, Mathew Patton and John Brewton, Esq.

Wm. Abbott's — *Managers:* John Lipscomb, Esq., James Turner and John Turner.

1808. Court-house — *Managers:* Samuel Miller, Richard Thomson and John Bomar.

Isaac Crow's — *Managers:* Mathew Patton, Willis Williford and John Brewton.

Wm. Abbott's — *Managers:* John Lipscomb, John Turner and James Turner.

1810. Court-house — *Managers:* Samuel IMiller, Richard Thomson and Thomas Bowman.

Isaac Crow's — *Managers:* Mathew Patton, Willis Williford and John Brewton, Esq.

Joshua Richards's — *Managers:* John Lipscomb, Jos. Collins and Smith Lipscomb.

Gault's Store — *Managers:* Theron Earle, James Camp and James Young.

Green Pond — *Managers:* Tyre Glenn, James Hammett and Wm. Kippen.

1812. Court-house — *Managers:* Wm. R. Smith, Robert Benson and Thomas Bomar.

Isaac Crow's — *Managers:* John Means, Willis Williford and Burrel Bobo, Esq.

Joshua Richards's — *Managers:* Michael Gaffney, Smith Lipscomb and John Lipscomb.

Gault's Store — *Managers:* Theron Earle, James Camp and James Young.

Green Pond — *Managers:* Tyre Glenn, James Hammett and James Ford.

1814. Court-house — *Managers:* Wm. R. Smith, Andrew Barry and Thomas Poole,

Isaac Crow's — *Managers:* Willis Williford, Burrel Bobo and William Farrow.

Joshua Richards's — *Managers:* John Lipscomb, Smith Lipscomb and Michael Gaffney.

Gault's Store — *Managers:* Theron Earle, James Camp and James Young.

Green Pond — Managers: Tyre Glenn, James Hammett and James Ford.

John Tolleson's Store — *Managers:* Wm. Reid, James McCarter and John Gossett.

James Meadows's Store — *Managers:* James Ham, Jr., Hardy Williford and Lewis Parham.

1816. Court-house — *Managers:* Wm. R. Smith, Andrew Barry and Thomas Poole.

Isaac Crow's — *Managers:* Wm. Posey, Burwell Bobo and Wm. Farrow.

Joshua Richardson's — *Managers:* John Lipscomb, Smith Lipscomb and Micheal Gaffney.

Gault's Store — *Managers:* Theron Earle, James Camp and James Young.

Green Pond — *Managers:* —Tyre Glenn, James Hammett and James Ford.

John Tolleson's Store — Managers: Sam'l Whitby, James McCarter and John Gossett.

James Meadows's — *Managers:* James Hamm, Jr., Lewis Parham and John Grist, Sr.

Peter C. McMakin's — *Managers:* John Roddy, John Montgomery and William Perrin.

[1] It will be noticed that during the year 1806 provision was made for only three voting precincts in Spartanburg district as shown above. In the laying out of the Upper or Spartan district by the Provincial Congress of South Carolina, which met in November, 1775, only one voting precinct was provided, which was at a meeting-house near Joseph Kelsey's. The Upper or Spartan district embraced all of the territory of the original county of Spartanburg, and nearly all the territory of the original county of Union. See "Colonial and Revolutionary History of South Carolina." Copy of record, p. 42, and map, P43.

Justices of the Quorum and Peace

1805. *Justice of the Quorum:* Drury McDaniel.
Justices of the Peace: John Collins and John Dean.

1806. *Justices of the Quorum:* William Smith, John Lipscomb, William Lancaster, D. J. Puckett, James Gault, Burwell Bobo and Daniel Wilbanks.

Justices of the Peace: Wm. Lipscomb, James Lucas Bird, Aaron Casey, Samuel Lancaster, John Hunter, James Drury Anderson, John Ricknian, Samuel Morrow and John Walker.

1807. *Justices of the Quorum:* Wm. Smith, John Lipscomb, Wm. Lancaster, D. J. Puckett, James Gault, Burrell Bobo and Daniel Wilbanks.

Justices of the Peace: Wm. Simpson, James Lucas Bird, Aaron Casey, Samuel Lancaster, John Hunter Jones, Denney Anderson, John Rickman, Samuel Morrow and John Walker.

1808. *Justices of the Peace:* John Brewton, Daniel White, Daniel McKie, James Pord, Tyre Glenn and Andrew Ferguson.

1809. *Justices of the Quorum:* Drury McDaniel, Micheal Miller and Samuel Morrow.

Justices of the Peace: John Collins, John Dean, Henry Turner, Leonard Adcock, Wm. Nesbitt, John Rodd, and William Reid.

1810. *Justices of the Quorum:* John Lipscomb, Burrel Bobo, John Gossett and Wilson Nesbitt.

Justices of the Peace: John Hunter Jones, John Walker, Joshua Richards, Thomas Poole and Manly Ford.

1811. *Justices of the Quorum:* Daniel White and Joshua Richards.

Justices of the Peace: Wm. Kelso, Moses Casey, John Chapman, James Hammett, Samuel Woodruff and John Cook.

1812. *Justices of the Peace:* John Brewton, Andrew Ferguson, Joseph Camp and David Moore.

1813. *Justices of the Quorum:* Drury McDaniel, Micheal Miller and Samuel Morrow.

Justices of the Peace: John Collins, John Deah, Henry Turner, Leonard Adcock, Wm. Reid and Samuel Archibald.

1814, *Justices of the Quorum:* John Lipscomb, Burwell Bobo, Henry Turner and Samuel Archibald,

Justices of the Peace: John Hunter Jones, Thomas Poole, Edward Ballenger, Wm, Underwood and James Hamm, Jr.

1815, *Justices of the Quorum:* Daniel White, James Young, John Chapman and Wm, Reid,

Justices of the Peace: Wm, Kelso, James Hammett, Moses Casey, Samuel Woodruff, Ezekiel Dobbins, Ephriam Lewis, John Montgomery and Caleb James.

1816, *Justices of the Quorum:* John Brewton, John Collins, Thomas Wood and Fortunatus H. Legg.

Justices of the Peace: James Whitten, Eaton Walker, Robert Leggon, Joseph Camp, David Moore, Benjamin Wofford, Berry Hinds, Wm. Hendricks and David Lewis.

1814, *Commissioners of Free Schools:* Samuel Morrow, Burrel Bobo, John Crawford, Sam'l Woodruff, Wm. Reid, Joshua Richards, Samuel Archibald and Herbert Hawkins.

1816. *Coroner:* Fortunatus H. Legg.

First Census

Department of the Interior,
Census Office,
Washington, March 28, 1892.

Sir: — I hand you herewith a list containing the names of heads of families as shown by the original census returns of the first census, taken under the direction of the LTnited States Marshal, by Daniel Wright, Assistant to the Marshal, and returned by him on April 15, 1791. The population at that time was reported at 8,800. The charge for this list is $6.00.

Very respectfully,
J. H. Wardle, Acting Chief Clerk.

Dr. J. B. O. Landrum. Landrum, Spartan County., S.C. One inclosure.

Ann Wilkey, Chiles Connel, Isham Hannssen, Geo. Parkeson, John Bovvland, Sam Willkins, Henry Ayers, Naham Ward, John Bagwell, Dickson Grant, John Tinch, John Hammett, William Jeffress, Maryan Oats, James Ward, Reuben Mathes, James Ross, Robert Belsher, Job Sosberry, Thos. Hose, Jr., Thos. Foster, Robert Foster, Mary Walker, Thos. Hois, Sr., William Hois, Littleton Bagwell, Sarah Holcomb, Richard Harrison, James Kern, Peter Elder, John Smith, Robert Head, Mary Fortuneberry, Ephraim Elder, Isham Bobbite, Sam Ward, Wm. Ward, David Golightly, John Golightly, James Nesbitt, Ezekiel Farmer, Joseph Thomson, Margaret Muckelhaney, James Varner, Robert Goodlet, Willy Brown, Wm. Floyd, Taraes Jordan, John Letch, Michael Miller, Mary Willburn, Wm. Fields, John Smith, Wm. Gordin, John Stone, Comford Hide, Samuel Snoddy, John Snoddy, John Collins, Robert Miller, Samuel Brise, Randal Thomson, Wm. Moore, David Jones, John McKelroy, John McKelroy, Sr., Samuel Nesbit, John Willson, John Runnold, William Biter, John Gastin, James Hughes, William Runnold, William Dunnian, Thos. Radey, Isham Mathis, John Dunnan, Mathew Patton, Wm. Heman, Robert McMillian, Wm. McWilliams, Joseph Gillmoore, John McMillian, John Jackson, John Bigham, James Gilmoore, Jesse Davis, John McNight, Zophard French, John Young, Wm. Branham, George West,Wm, West, Isaac Anderson, James Hudggens, Joseph Blackwood, Hugh Thomson, Jas. McDowel, John McClure, Jane McClure, Henry Story, John Piper, John Jennins. Jeremiah Garner, Isaac Young, Sampson Bethel, Wm. Garret, John Cantrell. John Vance, Andrew Ray, Edward Stublefield, Edward WilHams, Wni. Shad, Alhn Anderson, John Lauthins, James Turner, John Casiah, Drury Carath, Chas. Jermon, John Stone, Mary Crow, Moses Casy, John Conch, Benj. Roads, Geo. Grizzle, Stephen Huff, Ansel Dollar, Wm. Casy, Benj. Stone, Elizabeth Waldrup, James

Couch, Benj. Couch, Edward Linch, John Cannon, Joseph Stone, Isaac Linch, Michael Waldrup, Wm. Stone, Jesse Shornberton, John Grizzle, Robert Watson, Aaron Casy, John Rainwaters, Sharich Waldrup, Robert Rainwaters, Chris. Roads, Reuben Dollar, John Carsey, John Stone, Sr., Ambres Dollar. Richard Friar, Wm. Waldrup, Joseph Couch, James Carsey, Landan Farrow, Samuel Farrow, Isaac Hendrix, Wm. Hendrix, Joseph Fowler, -Wra. Tippens, Chas. Melane, John Mullins, Henry Coon, Thos. Heyden, David Childress, Isaac Hembey, Wm. Humphris, Jonathan Dildine, Nathanel Hembey, David Childress, David Childress, Jr., Aaron Arnold, Daniel Rogers, Aaron Baneum, William Reaves, Oliver Mehaffcy, Christian Driver, John Westmoreland, Eli Kitchens, Thos. Cowden, Thos. Westmoreland, Joseph Massey, John Cantrill, John Cole, Michael Wood, Edward Garrot, Henry Wood, Hannah Ray, Robert Wood, John Redman, Thos. Lengley, Wm. Willson, Archibald Morrison, Timothy Garney, Thos. Childress, Thomas Crumpton, Abraham Moore, Daniel Grant, William Evit, Joshua Beddenton, John Smith, Wm. Bradshaw, James Crowder, Samuel Sharbitt, Joel Smith, Samuel Lancaster, Elijah Kidwill, Britton Williford, Augusta Cumpes. Aaron Lancaster. Nathaniel Woodton, James Ham, Samuel Smith, Zepho Smith, Thos. Spann, Richard Berden, Joseph Power, Cap Zadveford, John Wells, Edward Arnold, Elizabeth Spurgeon, Hannah Kitchen, Joel Dean, John Hambey, Henry Cole. Morgin Darnold, Dennev Anderson, Isaac Hambey, Delilah Hudgens, Barnet Damsey. Elijah Hen'drix, Thomas Ham, William Hendrix, John Childes, Ann Hembey, John Floyd. John Hambey, Francis Jeff. Joseph Hughes, John Pennenton, John Tate, Pentiol Ward, James Lindsey, James Wm. Lindsey, Noah Westmoreland, Wm. Massey, Franky Pearson, Margret Pearson, James Childress, Sarah Patton, John Durham, Thos. Stone, Wm. Moore, Philip Johnson, Mary Lockard, Robert Harper, Samuel Murrow, Thos. Mayberry, John Worper, Joshua Smith, James Lee, Thos. Thornton, John Hewit, John Will, James Smith, Nathaniel Davis, David Grayhams, John Beard, Aaron Pinston, Joseph Pinston, Emanuel Mullinax, Drury Hemery, Bucknier Smith, John Gibs, Wm. Wadkins, Joseph Davis, John Rease, Daniel Walker, Elisha McAbee, William Pool, Joseph Lively, Robert Armer, Daniel Foselin, James Roberson, Samuel Turner, William Garrot, Richard Turner, Elizebeth Pearse, George Lampkins, Wm. Crocker, James Wyott, George Lampkins, Jr., Reuben Laurens, Charles McAbee, Elisha Grihams, Soloman Abbit, Edward Heavin, Vinson Wiott, Mason Cambell, Wm. Turner Thompson, Watson Dudley, Henry McCray, Jonathan Low, Wm. Pool, Thomas Hughes, Elish Smith, William Walker, Jessey Cannon, Wm. Thompson, John Harris, Ellis Cannon, Authur Crocker, Wm. Hardgroves, Josiah Tenner, David Davis, James Clark, Samuel Dunneway, Robert Dunneway, Wm. Sanders, Boston Bert, Chas. Littlejohn, Jr., David Allin, John Humphris, David Humphris, Joseph Turner, Henry Pattit, John Stoveall, Wm. Williams, Joshua Pattit, John Heyden, Thos. Jones, James Tarril, Charles Hermit, Anms Dewberry, Jahn Henry, Hugh Heartgrove, James Peterson, John Ladin,John Wood, Molicks Jones, Abraham Bise, Wm. Bise, Wm. Lipscomb, Ezekial Howard, Chas. Barnet, Stephen Little, Geo. Riner, Nase Griffith, Henry Viot, Jas. Viot, Mathew Gulkney. Frederic Gillberry, Joseph Price, David Jones, Jonathan Bise, Amus Moore, Joseph Austill, Robert Story, Gibly Goodu'ian, James Simmons, Greffin Carter, David Jones, Wm. Thomson, Nathaniel Hemmet, David Henry, Henry Jones, James Brown, John Brown, Peter Patterson, Temponey Saffold, John Sheppey, Rich Christionton, Isam Saffold, Jonathan Haris, Samuel Sheppey, Margeret Johnson, Thos. Cole, Wm. Brock, John Trimmer, Ezsea Capsham, Moses Proctor, Vardy Magbey, Nathan Gabron, Wm. Bullock, James Oliver, Daniel McClaren, Thos. Haris, Joseph Rain, Joseph Champion, Jethro Sheal, Ausburn Wst, Wm. Ramley, Abraham Hamley, Thos. Rease, Rowlin, Jinnins, Elizabeth Jennins, Ephrain Hill, Susannah Jennins, Rebecca Sullivan, Joel Emry, Sarah Price, Nathaniel Burton, John Barnet, Alexander Elder, Thomas Hennah, James Farris, William Elder, Benjamin Spencer, William Stallians, Thomas Rogers, Robert Rogers, William Stephenson, Moses Pervins, Dr. Andrew Thomson, David Trail, Philip Martin, Obediah Trimmer, David Cooper, James Wood. Wm. Headen, Elijah Melton, Chas. Littlejohn, Richard Dix. James Penning, Nichodemus Thomson, Obediah Oliven, Thos. Norton, Thos. Gillenwaters, John Surrat, Allin Surrat, John Bise, Jesse Davison, Daniel Amus, Mary Walker, Rebecca Arnold, James Byrar, John Arnold, Nathaniel Robertson, Andrew Hopkins, John Dill, Stephen Reney, Benjamin Arnold, Redrick Arnold. Samuel Surrat. Joseph Dill, Wm. Bias, George Walker, Wm. Willson, George Taylor, Nathan Lankford, Wm. Hickman, Mary Brothers,. Thos. Kitchens, Wm. Davidson, Benjamin Bonner, Samuel Surrat, Dany Bonner, Joseph Hooper, John Raps, Joseph Dill, Wm. Tattes,' Charles Easter, John Turner, Zechariah Blacwill, John Dillback, Barbara Dillback, Samuel Turner, William Turner, Wm. Cooper, Jane Cooper, John Cooper, Jesse Temple, Isaac Cloud, John McClaren, Thos. Philips, Jesse Tatte, Wm. Taylor, Jenot Bise, Lewis Stanley, Wm. Bostick, Matt Colwell, Curtis Colwell, John Lefever, Calls Ballard, Wm. Mcgaurd, Andrew Macasson, Frank Clark, Gidian Brown, Edward Goode, Leanard Adcock, Hensey Turner, Reuben Worner, John Wootton, James Hane, Daniel Stillwell, George Martain, John Kirklin, Wm. Abbit, Aaron Templeton, Wm. King, Susannah Wiott, Archibald Harris, Mathew Obet, William Murrey, Marah Murrey, John Lackey, David Murrow, Robert Elder, Jeremiah Willson, John Elder, Samuel Kifcart, Thomson Chomney, Thos. Forristor, Meshach Wootton, James Seages, James Hewit, John Forrister, Samuel Heghman, John Heghman, Matthew Mullinax, John Williams, John Mullinax, Chas. Sages, Wm. Brishers, Jacob Isom, Owin Forrester, Thos. Cook, Jacob Fowler, Chas. Burton, Tobias Bright, James Cavender, Benj. Parke, Barzel Trail, Haman Elder, Samuel Elder, William Maderws, Walter Burwell, Wm. Sherley, Benjamin Meeans, Samuel Murrow, Thos. Sherley, Ezek. Sulivan, Caleb Lengram, Gedian Herrelson, Samuel Jentry, Matt Couch, Mark Powel, Benj. Couch, Wm. Blacksteks, John Strowd, Benj. Hooker, Spencer Bobo, Henry Huff, Jacob Cassey, John Heard, William Stone, Boardwine Waters, Thos. Farrow, John Couch, Sr., Adam Garwirl, Edward Hooker, William Timmons, David Neal, John Grizzle, James Head, John Story, Josiah Thornton, Arthur Hutchens, David

Brown, Robert White, Arthur Simpson, George McCarter, Wm. Simpson, Joseph Wade, Robert Serling, Henry Emry, James Crumpton, George Story, Joseph Kelsey, John White, Henry Story, Thomas Fenley, Sam Archibald, George Story, Richard Chesney, Thomas Kenneley, Gabriel Kob, Joseph Marlow, Jeremiah Wofford, Zechariah Grace, George Grace, Margret Young, Catren Cross, Joseph Wofford, David McKerley, Isaak Gentry, Geo. Devine, John Robuck, Thomas Young, Jennet Berry, Samuel Bell, Thomas Clerk, Wm. Childers, Wm. Beard, John Johnston, Thomas McRoro, Amus Britt, Burwell Pace, Robert Page, Samuel Woodrough, Geo. Burton, Enoch Bruton, Allen Jentry, Jonas Burton, James Delong, Nathan Chiles, Jeremiah Moore, James Bruton, Ambrose Hamons, Robert Hamons, James Suthenton, John Sims, Obediah Wingo, Agus Trayler, James Lawrence, Ephraim Drummer, Joel Trayler, Wm. Trayler, Robert West, John Chiles, Wm. Turner, Rowlin Johnson, Claburn Johnson, Wm. Johnson, Thomas Foster, Sam Timmons, Manley, Ford, Ann White, Henry Walding, Edmond Bishop, James Matthes. John Wood, Elizabeth Bishop, Henry Wells, Brodrick Mason, Thos. Tinfly, John James, Rowland Cornelus, David Cook, Joel Hurt, Randal Brown, Henry Cannon, Isaiah Waldrup, Wm. Smith, Thos. Salmon, Travis Reece, John Pacy, Benjamin Piper, Thos. Reece, Jeremiah Salmon, Thos. Williamson, Arthur Crocker, Jr., David Millhanks, Wm. Hammit, Benjamin Vaughn, Isham Foster, Wm. Benson, Wm. Wood, Stephen Miller, John Tath, Wm. Foster, Nathaniel Stokes, Mourning Hutchusson, Wm. Foster, Jr., Alexander Walker, John Walker, John Bishop, David Goodlet, Henry Turner, Darby Turner, Henry Chiles, Nathan Bishop, David Drummon, John P'oster, John Foster, Sr., Peter Lewis, George Lewis, Moses Timmons, Vinson Tap, Robert Connel, Wm. Bishop, Jesse Trayler, Henry Turner, Robert Wood, Abner Timmons, George Bishop, Geo. Miller, James Lawrence, Sr., Sillab Hutchusson, Jeston Chiles, Abraham Biarcayr, Richard Biarcayr, Thos. Doeg, Alex. Evins, Philip Johnson, Moses Biter, Sam Nealy, Sam Steward, William Anderson, John Miller, William Gaston, Thos. Paden, Wm. P. Davis, James Miller, Martin Oats, John Jeffeth, Rosey Trayler, Richard Cox, William Ford, Thomas Moore, James Crooks, Sam Colley, David Anderson, John Williams, Thos. Mathes, Jason Moore, Benjamin Huker, Chas. Moore, John Wittemoore, John Ford, Sr., Jesse Spenser, James McHenry, James McMahan, Francis Ward, Daniel Barnett, Daniel Stephen, Daniel Brag, David Drummers, James McKue, James Barnet, Josiah Colbeson, Amey Golightly, Samuel Colberson, Reuben White, James Mays, Thomas Golightly, Stephen Cruse, James Susk, James Barnet, John King, Jane West, Breton George, Hugh Gorley, Charles Smith, Moris Foster, Nathan Seal, Henry Foster, Thomas Gardian, Benjamin Carnelus, Wm. Aldridge, John Gibbs, Wm. Suddath, John White, John Smith, Peter Smith, James Smith, Jr., George Love, James Smith, Wm. Smith, Thos. Brown, Thos. Williams, Robert Lee, Solomon Croker, Nicholas Aldridge, John Brown, Joel Thomas, Thos. Smith, Rachel Lewes, John Pace, Joshua Edwards, John Penny, Moriah Nobles, Williamuth Burns, Jacob Penington, Edward Steward, Tames Clarke, Benjamin Jones, Robert Mecroro, David Hicks, Daniel Walden, Alexander McCarty, Thos. Hoge, Daniel, Evens, Navel Wayland, Elizebeth Smith, William Crane, John McKerley, David McClenhehan, James Rannels, Benjamin McMahakin, Alexander Wakefield, Sam Stags, Charles Gilly, Thomas Collins, Joel Gunter, Joseph Nesbitt, Thos. Jones, Shadrich Plommer, John Muckelheney, Wm. Ford, Anthony Person, Alexander Kellyr, Alexander Rodey, Alexander Ray, John McCumsey, Barman Shummitt, Rheuben Newman, John Layton, Obediah Grant, Thos. Todd, Wm. Earnest, Susannah Hembey, Mathew McRoro, Tener Hambey, Sarah King, Margret Densmore, Lucy Spellers, Sarah Barnet, Esther Cox, Simon Pack, Ruth McKerley, Reason Halon, Jonathan Sinyard, Jesse Span, David Bruton, Elizebeth Jackson, Melinton Smith, Joseph Hains, John Thonton, John Spels, John Medford, Joseph Carvines, Elizebeth McKerley, Christopher Stone, John Cavan, Rich Haris, James Sinyard, Philip Huff, Thomas Huckabee, James Oge, Wm. Lane, Isom Shote, Charles Pearson, Charles Brag, Benjamin Howard, William Level, Joseph Barnet, Jesse Rakestraw, Chas. James, Daniel Finch, Thos. Beshews, Jesse Austin, Micajah Barnet, John Leemaster, Edward Barnet, James Wofford, Wm. Smith, Mason Morys, John Sham, James Hewit, Thomas Betterton, John Huckebee, Dudley Read, John Grissit, Thomas Prewit, Wm. Prewit, John Grissit, Sr., Joseph Power, John Burden, John Avit, Elizebeth Smith, Sarah O'Shiells, Moses Prewit, Snoden Prewit, James Baddenton, John O'Shiells, James Bannit, John Cook, John Varnel, John Wafford, Charles Trail, William Prewit, William Swenney, Andrew Barry, Thomas Moore, Richard Barry, Andrew Cowin, James Cowin, Ariss Brown, Isaac Winfree. William Powers, Frances Powers, Drury McDaniel William McDaniel, Michael Brown Roberts, Daniel Allin, Matthew Landers, William Allen, Daniel Allen, Jr., Joseph Allen, John Deyoung, Mathew Alleckzander, William Burd, James Alexander, Henry Turner, Robert Harper, John Brooks, John Saterfield, John McGuire, Margery Flammon, James Alexander, Wm. Readmond, Thos. Neal, Joshua Gassnell, Abraham Belue, David Benson, Joal Callaham, John Moore, Thos. Divine, John Gowin, Thos. Jackson, Hannah Wm. West, George McDole, Wm. McDole, Wm. Tober, Andrew Kelsey, John Childris, Wm. Reaves, Wm. Reaves, St., Mossley Owins, James Saterfield, Wm. Saterfield, Samuel Fowler, David Mosley, Thos. Goodcher, John Salley, Richard Gibs, Richard Sanders, John Sintus, James Sintus, Aaron Weatherbee, Balis Earle, John Earle, Wm. Anderson, Ephraim Reece, Robert Simson, Richard Callin, James Taylerwhite, John Vaughn, Benjamin Clarke, Ellis Johnston, Wm. Robs, Frances Dods, Henry Jimisson, John Smith, James Willson, James Armus, Archibald Brooks, David Davis, Wm. Simmons, Wm. Fialds, John Staton, William Rannold, Ezkiel Ponder, John Brown, John Cooper, Robert Jimmison, Jr., David Davis, James Powel, John Edwards, Jesse Rains, Patty Craine, Thos. Brooks, Henry Morgan, Stephen Philips, Elisha Thomson, James Bright, Robert Nisbitt, John Jermer, John Pesmey, Thomas Wells, Thomas Underwood, Ransom Tinsley, Jesse Connel, George Connel, Zechariah Robertson, John Gray, Elizabeth Lett, Benjamin Vaughn, Barzil Lee, Joseph Robertson, Bettlaham Reason, Arthur Crocker, John Fath, William Roberts, Wells Griffith, William Mitchell, Absalom Lancaster, Robert Mc Dowel, Charles McNight, Thomas Barnet, Daniel Bennet, John Anders, Sandel Harty, Abraham Anders, Daniel Cornwell, Ephraim Lewis, William Alexander. John Johnson, John Lewis, Alexander Stevenson, James Millingin, Robert Millinson, James Burnit, Thos. Kimbell, James Rise, Hugh Stephenson, Wm. Liles, John Kelley, John Nesbit, Geo. Robuck, Benj. Wofiford, Samuel Thomson, Burwell Thomson, Phenix Vaughn, John Cain, Francis Fielder, Lucy Thomson, Benj. Busy, Wni. Moore, John Woodrough, Wm. Lindsey, Wm. Cope, Nathaniel Woodrough, Enuch Floyd, Wm. Spear, John White, Ebenazer Floyd, Wm. Cassilberry, Henry Huff, Ihon Speer, Nathaniel Gentry, Andrew Andrix, James Beard, Geo. Newman, John Cassilberry, Thos. Young, Edmond Claton, Samuel Gentry, Paul Cassilberry, Richard Chesney, John Biag, Richard Young, Stephen Willson, Patty Young, Frances Claton, Amus Scritchfield, Flennon Smith, Lasey Meabee, Matt Sparks, Samuel Sparks, John Lucray, George Kenit, Luck Lucray, Eliazer Lemaster, Isaack Brown, Wm. Briant, Robert Baker, James Pool, David Pullum, Thomas Barnet, Michael McGaffey, John Peterson, John Gofoit, Josiah Sparks, John Leemaster, Joseph Queen, Reuben Leemaster, Ralph Leemaster, George Pool, Mathew McBee, Richard Willis, Anthony Crocker, John Tollerson, James Robertson, James Gassit, Nemiah Norton, Bazil Scott, Jariel Barnet, John Burk, Richland Lee, Reuben Brand, Truelove Sparks, Ranson Clififin, Enos Land, John Barnet, Elijah Lanthins, Thos. Gore, Luke Brawnin, George Gibbert, Jeremiah Jibes, Edmond Ward, Thos. Henderson, West Harris, John Cole, Mathis Vance, Aaron Youngblood, Andrew Ray, Abraham Cantrel, James Madcap, Wm. Allford, Drurey Sergus, Neal Johnson, Joseph Warren, Thos. Stuman, James Sanders, Benj. Cantrel, Simuan Justice, John Nelson, Richard Henry, James Cantrel, Thos. Gorden, Wm. Morris, John Morris, Richard Morris, Watson Forrester, Joseph Morris, Thomas Gilbert, Samuel Gilbert, William Gordin, Garvis Gilbert, Daniel Gilbert, Abner Warnock, Molley Hooper, James Hooper, George Bushop, Samuel Woodrough, Nicholas Halley, Alexander Elixander, James Anderson, John Chromney, Michel French, Benj. Carley, Peter Pinyon, Elijah Kelley, John Thornton, Tames Crow, John Crow, Isaac Crow, Diany Clark, James Crow, Luke Thornton, Isaak Crow, Sr., Solomon Littlefield, James Browmen, Wm. Haris, Auston Claton, Jeremiah Claton, John Erwin, Henry Carley, Jonathan Floyd, Thomas Woodrough, Dennis Lindsey, William Parker, Sail Reason, Zechariah Caroole, John Crow, Wm. Smith, James Taylor, Henry Ernist, Elizabeth McFall, Robert Harison, Wm! Carley, John King, Benj. Peck, Seth Lewis, James Millingin, John Barnett, Leonard Carden, Frances Bellinger, John West, John Mason, John Burnett, Charles Witt, Robert Kimbell, Wm. McDowel, Benjamin Bradshaw, Wm. Boston, Edmond Clammons, Benjamin Clark, George Dooers, George McDowel, Wm. McDowel, Edmond Fowler, Daniel White, Spenser White, Wm. Veanible, John Anderson, Wm. Kelley, David McDowel, Wm. Anderson, Henry Young, John Carrel, James Gilmoore, Henry Woody, Thos. McNight, Alexander Heman, David Lewis, Alexander Coplin, Joseph Veanneble, Wm. Wood, Wm. McMillian, Wm. McNight, Robert Sims, John Floyd, John Hembey, John

Allin, Thomas Hightower, Frances Fowler, James Sandford, John Tackit, Jean McClerkin, Wm. Crow, John King, Elenezar Marss, Nancy Britton, Charles Witton, John Witton, John Young, Ephriam Parmely, Chiles Parmely, Joseph Woodrough, Nathaniel Woodrough, Sr., Henry Marideth, Samson Bobs, Thos. Mills, Wm. Wilder, Peter Brooks, Thos. Beinwaters, Spencer Bobo, Burwell Bobo, Jesse Casy, Edward Stone, Mary Nathons, John Ferrow, Isaac Couch, Rosiannah Ferrow, James Claton, Christopher Roades, Mary Couch, Mary Ledford.

List of Names of Soldiers from Spartanburg County who were Enlisted in the Confederate States including those Enlisted in the South Carolina State Militia, State Reserves and Cadet Corps During the Years 1861-'65 Inclusive.

1st Regiment, S.C.V.— Col. Gregg.

Company A. — Privates: M. Blackwood, John Blalock, P. B. Brannon, J. D. Cantrel, L. Duncan, J. A. Foster, J. P. Gardner, John Harper wounded May 12, 1864, died on way home, June 8, 1864, John Permenter, George Rutland killed at battle of Wilderness, W. B. Stone and W. A. Harper.

1st Regiment of Regulars, Col. Dunevant.

Company A. —Privates: J. M. Seay, James Stack, Samuel Sullivan, H. Tucker, David Rollins, John W. W. Sparks.
Company C. — Privates: C. C. Bishop, W. D. Brown, R. Burnett, E. 1. Edgnes, John Garrison, I. D. Hill, T. Howerton.
Company D. — Private: G. J. Eagana.
Company E. — Private: W. I. Collicot.
Company F. — Private: Theadore Linder,
Company G. — Private: B. Hammett.
Company H. — Private: B. O. Sparke.
Company I. — Privates: Alex. Ray, T. W. Ray, I. N. O'Couchran, W. Demsey, Thos. B. Foster and John Fallen.
1st Regiment of Infantry. Col. Johnson Hagood. Regimental Commissary, Capt. S.C. Means.
Company D. — Privates: Beverly Bush, James Lemaster, Jas. E. Smith and John Seay.
Company H. — Captain: J. Christopher Winsmith wounded twice in battle, was promoted major under consolidation act.
1st Lieutenants: Wm. A Nesbitt (see sketch), killed at Second Manassas; J. Nott Moore (see sketch), promoted from 2d lieutenant, was made captain under consolidation act.
2d Lieutenants: Glenn Bearden promoted from 1st sergeant, was made 1st lieutenant under consolidation act; James A. Johnson promoted from sergeant, resigned, W. W. D. Lanford promoted from sergeant, dropped by examining board, and Jas. E. Vise resigned.

Sergeants: Ewell Teague killed at 2d Manassas, Mike Patton transferred to C. S. Navy, W. A. Wofford, JaS.C. Skinner wounded at Wilderness, Henry Yarbrough, Sr., and Crook Nicholls was made sergeant of color guard.

Corporals: Isaac M. Bearden killed at 2d Manassas, Silas Shands killed at 2d Manassas, Herbert Spillers, and A. Prater killed at Wilderness.

Privates: John C. Bearden, O. P. Bearden, Wm. Bellott, Robert Bogan, Richard Cole, E. Y. Cunningham detached as an artificer by order of General Joe E. Johnson, N. B. Davis, Eber Fowler died at hospital, Simpson Fowler died in. hospital, John Fowler died in hospital. Elias Fowler, Robert Farmer, Ansel Gregory died in hospital, Willis Ginings, Edwin Harrison wounded in battle and disabled, Elias Harrison, Arch Harrison, Wm. H. Harrison, J. Allen Hines, Jas. Hughs, John Johnson, Thad Kendrick, Javos Kimbrell, Frank Lancaster died, Zachary Lancaster, Mike Lee, M. B. Middleton promoted captain Company I, 1st Regiment, S.C.V., Samuel McAbee, Geo. Moore died in hospital, Wm. Norton, F. M. O'Daniel killed at Wilderness, P. H. Otts, Geo. Poole, W. H. Posey wounded at Sharpsburg, disabled, Wiley Rhodes died in hospital, Coley Rhodes, Jas. E. Ramage, Anderson Simpson, John Spillers, Geo. Simmons, Jas. M. Smith, Erwin Stephens, Mills Sumner, J. B. Sumner, W. H. Taylor killed at Petersburg, Enoch Thomas, James Taylor died, Robert Taylor, John Taylor, Wm. Taylor, Theodore J. West killed at 2d Manassas, Edgar West, Elijah West died in hospital, Jeptha White and Henry Yarbrough, Jr.

2d Regiment S.C.V. — Col. J. B. Kershaw, Asst Surgeon: Henry J. Nott.

3d Regiment, S.C.V.— Col. Jas. H Williams, Lt. Col. B. B. Foster (see sketch).

Company A. — Privates: John M. Bright, Jas. E. Ham, A. Jennings, R. Jennings, A. McAbee, WilHs E. Rowley killed at Bentonville, McAbee, McAbee, John

Nolen and John S. Wilbanks.

Company B. — Privates: A. W. Bailey, David Brown, John A. Brown, Wm. Johnson wounded at Sharpsburg and Averysboro, foot amputated, Samuel J. Robinson killed at Fredericksburg.

Company D. — Captains: Thos. B. Ferguson promoted major and F. N. Walker wounded around Richmond.

1st Lieutenants: W. S. Bobo (Union County), C. P. Abernathy killed at Sharpsburg and J. P. Moore.

2d Lieutenants: N. P. Floyd, P. John Ray killed at Savage Station, Wade Allen wounded and died at Fort Delaware, F. M. Gorden wounded at Cedar Hill, Hiram Bobo.

Sergeants: Levi Campbell, Allen Garland died at Richmond, Chance M. Floyd, Hosea Ray, Robert L. Ray killed at Chickamauga, H. W. Duckett and Monroe M. Davis.

Corporals: J. D. C. Abernathy killed at Savage Station, T. C. Hill killed at Malvern Hill, Geo. M. Dillard, John W. Ferguson wounded at Savage Station, Chancellorsville and Spottsylvania, Robert C. Wilburn killed at Deep Bottom.

Privates: R. L. Allen wounded at Gettysburg, Jeremiah P. Pool killed at Bentonville, T. C. Burdine, John Burnett, Hosea Browning wounded at Savage Station, Chancellorsville and Spottsylvania, John Carson, Henry P. Cathcart wounded at Malvern Hill, Fredericksburg and Gettysburg, Jesse Cooper killed at Malvern Hill, W. T. Dodd, T. M. Cooper, Henry T. Ferguson, A. F. Floyd, J. M. Floyd killed at Rapidan, Warren Farmer wounded at Chancellorsville and Spottsylvania, Eliphas Ferguson, Young P. Franklin wounded at Cedar Hill, A. T. Farrow, Mark Finger wounded at Wilderness, Isaac Graham, J. F. Graham wounded at Savage Station, J. W. Gentry wounded at Sharpsburg, Edward Gentry wounded at Savage Station. Philip Huckabee, B. M. Hill wounded at Averysboro, N.C. P. W. Hollis, C. B. Hernbree wounded at Wilderness, — — Andrews killed at Maryland Heights, Drury Jackson, Dellard Jackson wounded at Savage Station, Asbury Graham wounded at Averysboro, Wm. Kelly, Marion Kelly, Thos. Lamb, Robert Lamb wounded at Savage Station, W. E. Lynch, Archibald Lynch, John Lynch killed at Knoxville, B. S. Lynch wounded at Bentonville, R. C. Murphy killed at Cedar Hill, John D. Myers wounded at Savage Station, A. E. McCravy, R. S. McCravy, Samuel McCravy killed at Savage Station, Peter Murray, Stephen Nix killed at Savage Station, Wm. Millen wounded at Spottsylvania Court House, Robert Ramsey, Perry Ramsey, Wm. Mullins, E. A. Pruit wounded at Spottsylvania Court House, Charlie Pope, Robert Poole, Casper Smith, Wm. Smith, Madison Stephens wounded at Savage Station, J. F. Stephens, Anthony Shands wounded around Richmond, Franklin Shands, T. B. Stone wounded at Chancellorsville, A. H. Stearns killed at Gettysburg, Samuel Shands killed at Bentonville, John Pruit, J. W. Sexton, James L. Tinsley, wounded at Wilderness and Fredericksburg, A. R. Tinsley wounded at Savage Station, J. P. Tinsley, W. B. Taylor wounded at Savage Station, Andrew Vamer, M. S. Varner, J. W. Varner, James Vaughn wounded at Gettysburg, C. M. Williams wounded at Wilderness and Averysboro, J. D. Williams, Harrison Workman wounded around Richmond, Frank Wesson, Thomas Woolbanks wounded around Richmond, John Woolbanks, Pink Lynch, Thos. Ray killed at Chickamauga and Robert Poole wounded at Manassas.

Company G. (called "the Briers.") — Privates: Wm. Cheek, Wm. Chesney, J. N. Chesney died in 1862, at Manchester, Va., N. Chesney, R. J. Chesney died 1862, at White Sulpher Springs, Va., George Chesney, James Craig died at Lynchburg, 1862, Eber Jones missing, J. A. Hobby mortally wounded at Fredericksburg, Patillo Landford mortally wounded at Fredericksburg, E. L. Landford, John Owens, Enoch Stone, B. H. Wofford and John Vonedore.

Company K. — Captains: Ben Kennedy (see sketch), Seaborn M. Lanford killed at Savage Station, L. Perrin Foster (see sketch) killed at Fredericksburg, Wm. H. Young killed at Gettysburg, Jos. Henry Cunningham killed at Chickamauga, John P. Roebuck wounded at Knoxville and Chickamauga, taken prisoner at Knoxville and remained in prison to the close of the war.

1st Lieutenants: John Y. Wofford discharged at Yorktown, Va., reeinlisted in 13th Regiment, S.C.V.,died at Jorden Springs, Va., while an officer in 13th

Regiment, S.C.V., John W. Wofford (see sketch) wounded at Savage Station, Chickamauga and Fredericksburg, surrendered in command of company at Greensboro, N.C.

2d Lieutenants: Wm. Bearden killed at Gettysburg, R. M. Smith discharged at Yorktown, A. Baxter Layton wounded at Sharpsburg, Wm. R. Thomas killed at Gettysburg.

Sergeants: David S. Bray surrendered at Greensboro, Wm. B. Wofford wounded at Fredericksburg and died of same at Richmond, Alexander Thomas wounded at Sharpsburg and Wilderness, surrendered at Greensboro, C. P. Varner wounded at Savage Station, Maryland Heights, Cedar Creek, Va., and Chickamauga, John N. McArthur surrendered at Greensboro, John L. Gentry killed at Savage Station.

Corporals: Jas. E. Vise discharged, Wm. A. Nesbitt (see sketch) discharged, reenlisted, was killed at 2d Manassas while an officer in 18th Regiment, S.C.V., Wm. A. Smith killed at Savage Station, Adolphus T. Davis died at Centerville, Va., Gamaliel W. James killed at Malvern Hill, F. Marion Lanford killed at Gettysburg, Nathan H. Pettitt killed at Chickamauga while color guard, W. H. Lancaster killed at Gettysburg, Jos. R. Rountree wounded and died of same, Albert S. Smith wounded at Sharpsburg and Gettysburg, surrendered at Greensboro, and Thos. H. West surrendered at Greensboro.

Privates: John B. C. Bass, surrendered at Greensboro, G. W. Bass surrendered at Greensboro, B. S. Beason surrendered at Greensboro, Burwell Beason surrendered at Greensboro, J. W. Bishop killed at Maryland Heights, J. W. N. Beard transferred to cavalry, J. C. Beard died at Glenn's Springs, S.C., I. Ira Bearden wounded at Sharpsburg and Frederickburg, surrendered at Greensboro, David Brice died in Virginia, F. Chris. Burch died at Richmond, W. S. Bearden killed near Richmond, Glenn Bearden horor ably discharged, W. H. Barnett killed in battle near Petersburg, Nimrod Cook died at Florence, S.C., Henry W. Cunningham died in prison near Point Lookout, G. W. Chummy killed at Chickamauga. G. W. Chummy died of wounds near Fishers Hill, Va., R. A. Drummond died at Warrenton, Va., John H. Elmore surrendered at Greensboro, J. Anthony Foster (see sketch) killed at Maryland Heights, C. T. Gwinn wounded at Fredericksburg, surrendered at Greensboro, Doc Gwinn wounded at Bentonville, N.C., lost an arm, Mansel Gwinn, Jefferson Gwinn killed at Bentonville, T. P. Plarmon killed at Maryland Heights, James Harmon killed at Chickamauga, John Harmon wounded at Sharpsburg, honorably discharged, Wm. Harmon wounded in Virginia, surrendered at Greensboro, J. P. Havener wounded at Savage Siation, died of same at Richmond, Geo. T. Hyatt surrendered at Greensboro, Jas. Hyatt surrendered at Greensboro, Jos. H. Hamby died at Warrenton, Va., Levi Hill wounded at Fredericksburg and Chickamauga, transferred to 3d Regiment, S.C.,V., Jas. A. Johnson honorably discharged, Samuel W. T. Lanham wounded at Spottsylvania, surrendered at Greensboro, now a congressman from Texas, Wm. Lawrence killed at Fredericksburg, Wm. Linsey killed at Sharpsburg, John J. Marco wounded in Virginia, honorably discharged, Perry Mattox killed at Maryland

Heights, S. S. Mayes died of wounds in Virginia, surrendered at Greensboro, Wm. J. Mayes died of wounds at Richmond, T. W. Meaders died of disease in Virginia, T. S. Meadows, killed in Virginia, Wm. McAbee surrendered at Greensboro, Joel McAbee wounded at Wilderness, J. E. McDonald killed at Wilderness, Joseph McArthur wounded in Virginia, surrendered at Greensboro, John Owens killed at Chickamauga, John W. Pearson wounded at Spottsylvania, Thomas Petty, B. F. Pettitt, Harvey Pearson, John S. Rountree wounded at Savage Station, Jos. M. Riddle wounded at Chickamauga, T. Riddle died of disease in Virginia, Mathew Rogers killed at Maryland Heights, Joseph Rogers killed at Chickamauga, Elias Rogers wounded in Virginia, Willis Rogers wounded at Fishers Hill, surrendered at Greensboro, Green Rogers wounded at Fishers Hill, surrendered at Greensboro, Benj. F. Roebuck surrendered at Greensboro, Jesse J. Roebuck died of disease at Lynchburg, Wm. P. Roebuck, captain in Holcombe Legion for twelve months, time expired, reenlisted and was killed at Spottsylvania, Geo. Simmons killed at Deep Bottom, John L. Shackelford discharged, A. C. Strebling wounded at Fredericksburg, Samuel Strebling discharged, John Strebling surrendered at Greensboro, B. Anthony Shands wounded at Savage Station and Petersburg, surrendered at Greensboro, Samuel Shands killed at Averysboro, N.C., John Stallions discharged, B. M. Smith killed in Virginia, Simeon Smith killed in Virginia, Elijah F. Smith surrendered at Greensboro, Robert Smith died in Virginia, W. P. Smith died of disease in Virginia, W. T. Shurbutt died of disease at Richmond, Z. S. Shurbutt transferred, A. T. Shurbutt killed at Savage Station, John Slater wounded in Virginia, surrendered at Greensboro, G. H. Stoney died of disease at Richmond, D. G. Stoney died of disease in Virginia, Jas. S. Stoney wounded in Virginia severely, T. S. Thomas wounded at Spottsylvania, surrendred at Greensboro, L. P. Thomas killed at Geetysburg. Wm. Thomas surrendered at Greensboro, Mitchell Thomas wounded in Virginia, surrendered at Greensboro, J. Turner died of disease in Virginia, W. J. Vehorn severely wounded at Wilderness, Lewis Vaughn surrendered at Greensboro, Jos. Vaughn died of disease in Virginia, Roddy Varney surrendered at Greensboro, Robt. M. Williams wounded at Chickamauga, lost a leg, Benj. Wofford, Jr. surrendered at Greensboro, W. Thomas Wofford killed at Spottsylvania Court House, Henry Wofford killed at Spottsylvania Court House, Wm. A. Wofford, T. J. West, G. W. West killed at Cedar Creek, Va., Elihu M. West, Henry West killed near Richmond, Henry A. Wingo surrendered at Greensboro, Rufus B. White discharged in Virginia, S. P. Westmoreland wounded in Virginia, W. M. Wright killed at Maryland Heights, Richard Woodruff discharged, James Wyatt and T. H. Zimmerman discharged.

5th Regiment, S.C.V., Col. Micah Jenkins, Col. Asbury Coward.

Lt. Co. Geo. W. H. Legg. Major Wm. M. Foster. Quartermaster John D, Wright.

Company D. Privates: M. L. Bishop and W. Ross killed at Wilderness.

Company I. Captain: W. D. Camp wounded at Seven Pines.

1st Lieutenants: Lawson Turner resigned in 1862, joined Western army, C. P. Petty resigned, J. T. V. Legg resigned, Daniel Anthony wounded seven days around Richmond.

2d Lieutenants: J. P. Scruggs resigned, Hugh Moore resigned, W. J. Clowney. B. H. Wright wounded, remained with company until surrender, C. C. Turner captured at Wilderness May 4, 1864, confined in Fort Delaware until July 1, 1865, and L. J. Cooksey.

Sergeants: Geo. Epton. W. S. George severely wounded and honorably discharged, W. T. McArthur wounded and transferred to Sharpshooters, Stephen McDonald, W. M. Tate transferred to Palmetto Sharpshooters, W. L. Lipscomb wounded at Clays farm, transferred to 26th Regiment, S.C.V., G. B. Culp wounded at Frazier's Farm, J. B. Humphries disabled and discharged, Samuel Cole killed at Frazier's Farm, Jos. Price wounded at Seven Pines, Samuel S. Austell died at Frazier's Farm, W. D. D. Poole wounded at 2d Manassas and at Knoxville from which he soon after died.

Corporals: Davis Moore discharged, Elias T. Mitchell killed at Campbells Station, Tenn., W. B. Parris, A. N. Turner wounded and discharged, T. D. Tate, Jas W. Coyle and J. P. Camp killed at Chickamauga.

Privates: J. R. Alleson, John Allen, Willis Allen discharged, Wm. G. Austell wounded, had leg amputated, J. Bishop seriously wounded at 2d Manassas, Wm. H. Bridges transferred, C. D. Bridges transferred, Chas. Blanton wounded seven days around Richmond, Wm. Bryant killed at Chickamauga. Robt. S. Byars killed at Wilderness, Rowland Briant, Franklin Blanton died during the war, W. J. Briant, W. A. Briant, R. Brown killed at Seven Pines, T. B. Bullock wounded Seven Pines, C. R. F. Crounlans disabled and discharged, W. D. Cash transferred, John E. Cooper killed in Virginia, John Cash transferred, John Cole died at Centerville, Va., O. V. Cleary killed in Virginia, G. B. Cleary, John Cantrel wounded at Seven Pines, T. J. Cantrel wounded at Seven Pines, L. A. Cantrel wounded at Seven Pines, L. J. Cook wounded at seven days around Richmond, J. Pinckney Cole wounded seven days around Richmond, Joseph Cash died at Sweet Water, Tenn., John Cash transferred, W. D. Cash transferred, John B. Cash wounded at 2d Manassas. Aaron Duncan wounded 2d Manassas, B. F. Davis, Jesse Duncan killed at Wilderness, E. B. Durham killed at Wilderness, Thos. Dewberry killed at Wilderness, John Ellis wounded seven days around Richmond, Epton wounded Deep Bottom, died of same, Henry Ervin died at home. Dr. J. B. Goudelock transferred to hospital, Wm. M. Gibson wounded at Seven Pines, Pinckner Garner, Jeremiah Gidney. Joseph Garner. J. M. Goudelock, F. Harvey wounded at Seven Pines, Richard Huskey, Joseph Huskey, H. H. Humphries, Alfred Harris, Robert Harris, L. H. Hill, John M. James wounded at 2d Manassas, J. W. James wounded at 2d Manassas, John Jones, C. C. Jarrett, Ad Kennett wounded at Deep Bottom, Abner Kennett killed at Wills Valley, Tenn., James Keller killed at Wilderness, O. Krisby, Leonard, Leonard W. M. Leonard, J. M. Lipscomb, A. D. Lovelace wounded seven days around Richmond. Wm. Lowe, Jefferson McAbee,

Jas. McAbee killed in Virginia, 1864, Abner McAbee killed at Petersburg, 1864, Jas. Madison, J. E. Millwood discharged, John Morah, O. P. Morgan wounded. Seven Pines, A. M. McDonald, David McComson died in hospital from disease, D. J. McArthur wounded at Seven Pines, Peter Morgan killed or died of disease, G. C. Moore wounded, Thomas Martin wounded, George McKenney wounded at 2d Manassas, John Osmert, Wm. Parris, J. W. Porter killed at Wildereness, Wm. Porter, Toliver Philips wounded at Wilderness, P. P. Pearson wounded, Wm. Petty, W. M. Pearson killed in Virginia, Skip Price, T. D. Price, John Reynolds, J. M. Reynolds, John Ramsey, Calvin Ramsey, Newton Raines, B. F. Rice, Jos. Reynolds, Henry Rice killed at Seven Pines, Pinckney Seates, Wm. Seates, Aaron Self wounded at New Market Heights, Va.. J. W. Self wounded at Wilderness, J. E. Scruggs, R. D. Scruggs, Drury Scruggs, Drury Scruggs wounded at New Market, Va., S. D. Sanders wounded at Seven Pines and died, Ansel Sprouse, John Sprouse killed at Mitchells Station, Tenn., Henry League killed at Seven Pines, Christon Thorne killed at Wilderness, Jesse Threft died in Virginia, 1861, Allen Threft, J. M. Turner killed at New Market Heights, Va., N.C. Washburne killed at Wilderness, D. K. Willis died in Virginia, Calvin Willis killed seven days battles below Richmond, Wm. Wyatt died in hospital, Manchester, Va., Jos. Wright, John C. Willis died of disease, 1861, L. J. Wyatt killed at Wilderness, Edward Waters, John Wyatt, J. N. Ward, Joe Young killed at Seven Pines. This company, recorded among the rolls in Coumbia, S.C., as Company I., 5th Regiment, S.C.V., is a part of what was Company I., 6th Regiment, S.C.V., before the reorganization of the company at Yorktown, Va., in 1862. Captain Camp and at least three-fourths of the company had belonged to the 6th Regiment prior to the reorganization, at which time the company largely recruited from Company C, 9th Regiment, S.C.V., commanded by Captain Wm. M. Foster who at said reorganization was elected Major of the 5th Regiment. This accounts for the long list of commissioned and non-commissioned officers on the roll representing as it does officers of different companies and regiments finally merged into one.

Company K. — Captain: R. B. Seay died of apoplexy in Virginia (see sketch), Wm. Choice (see sketch) and Jos. H. McDowell (see sketch) wounded at Louden Heights.

1st Lieutenant: J. T. Brian.

2d Lieutenants: Marcus McDowell died of disease in Virginia, Frank M. Smyre wounded in Virginia, H. C. Alley (jr. 2d lieutenant), and Wm. J. McDowell wounded at Sharpsburg, arm amputated.

1st Sergeants: G. W. Moss killed at Sharpsburg, A. A. Brian wounded in Virginia, M. L. Gentry.

2d Sergeants: J. A. Dodd, A. H. Turner died of wounds at 2d Manassas, J. L. McCall wounded at Manchanicsville, Va., and J. L. Duncan wounded in Virginia.

Corporals: B. F. Hammett, J. M. Woody wounded in Virginia, W. J. Bush, R. M. Wingo, W. H. Hammett and S. J. Jackson.

Privates: J. H. Bishop, A. Bishop, Govan Bush, J. M. Bush, G. M. Bush, R. Brannon, W. H. Brannon, M. B. Burrell, N. Burnett wounded in Virginia, D. Burnett, J. M. Benson appointed captain provost marshal's office in Columbia, Elias Belcher, Jasper Cook. Alfred Cook, Calvin Cook, Wm. Cook, J. C. Clement, Wm. Clement, John L. Clement wounded at 2d Manassas, J. B. Carter, J. T. Camp wounded Frazier's Farm, W. C. Crittendon wounded in Virginia, H. Cothran died of disease in Virginia, M. B. Christopher, John Clements, David Cudd, John Cudd, Jackson Carter died of disease in Virginia, __ __ Cambell drummer boy, missing at Richmond, John Chapman, Alfred Cantrel, James Collins, L. D. Demsey, N. T. Demsey, Christopher Golightly killed at Sharpsburg, H. P. Goforth wounded near Richmond, M. S. Gentry, H. P. Gentry, W. H. Gentry, John Gowen, Wm. Henderson, B. Hines, Spencer Henderson, H. Henderson, Wiley Hammett, W. H. Hammett, J. T. Hammett, B. Hammett killed at Petersburg, 1864, Joe Hammett, H. Hughey, P. B. Hall, Wm. Hall killed at Petersburg, 1864, Jas Howerton, S. T. Jackson wounded at Petersburg, A. D. Jackson, R. L. Jackson, A. Junior wounded, L. Jackson wounded at Petersburg, W. S. Kirby, H. Liles, Abner Low, Giliam Mabry wounded four times in a charge against Fort Steadman, J. T. McDowell killed at Sharpsburg, H. A. McDowell, J. C. McDowell, Calvin McDowell wounded at 2d Manassas, M. V. McDowell killed at Wilderness, Robert McDowell, Jones McDowell wounded at Frazier's Farm, died of same at Richmond, 1862, T. C. McCall, Joe. McCarter wounded at Petersburg. J. C. Moss, J. F. Moss killed at Petersburg, John Mason, Matt McClure. Wm. B. Nolen, J. M. Nolen, Wm. R. Pollard wounded at 2d Manassas, D. M. Prince, S. S. Pehuff, Wm. Rollins wounded 2d Manassas, D. M. Prince, S. S. Pehuff, Wm. Rollins wounded near Richmond, M. Rollins, T. J. Rollins missing after Wilderness, W. P. Robbins died of disease near Richmond, W. S. Royston, J. E. Royston killed at Petersburg, 1864, L. N. Suthenland missing after battle of Lookout Mountain, J. N. Seay died in A'irginia, E. P. Shields died at Chattanooga, L. L. Smith, Wm. Sizemore wounded at Loudon, Tenn., James Snoddy, Alfred Smith, Alberry Solsbee, J. A. Thomas, T. J. Turner died of disease in Virginia, W. J. White. C. H. White died of disease in Virginia, J. C. Wall wounded near Richmond, Leland Wolf died of disease at Chattanooga, B. F. Williams, J. C. Wilkins, J. M. Wall, R. J. F. Wall, O. P. White died in Virginia. A. D. Wingo, Hamp White died in Virginia anfl Jackson Williams.

6th Regiment, S.C.V., Col. Jas. H. Rion.
Company C. — Privates: C. Blackwell, O. Evans, L. Linder, H. U. McCall, J. F. Robins and J. Russell.

2d Regiment, S.C.V., Col. Bacon.
Company F. — Privates: John Brown, Jeff Brown. Millege Brown, L. B. Bagwell, John C. Hall, Wm. P. Hammett wounded at Sharpsburg, Alartin Mathes, Morgan Mathes, Martin McKenney, Judson McGee.

9th Regiment, S.C.V., Col. J. D. Blanding.

Company — Captain W. M. Foster, promoted Major of 5th S.C. Regt.

Lieutenants: John M. Martin, Wm. H. Cantrel and J. Aliah Alartin.

Sergeants: L. J. Turner, John J. Brown, T. C. Brown, D. J. V. Alartin.

Corporals: Obediah Robbins, A. M. Scruggs, F. S. Turner and J. M. Turner.

Privates: Alfred Bumpers, Wiles Beter, Alfred Burke, Wm. J. Bush, E. R. Brown, W. R. Bryant, R. T. Brown, W. F. Cannon. W. S. Cantrel, Alfred Cantrel. W. J. Cole, feillard Cash. Alarville Cash, J. B. Cash, R. M. Cash, Wm. Cooley. J. G. Cudd, Alexander Crocker, Mayberry Croker, Simeon Couch, Jerome Dawson, T. J. Dewberry, Nathan Dyer. G. Al. Epping. John Easier, Judge Edwards, John Edgins, M. V. Elder, Landrum C. Ezell, Geo. W. Findley, Thomas Foster, A. J. Gee, Smith Harris, Ananias Horn, Franklin Harvey, Wm. Harvey, Chas. Knight. G. M. Kinnett. Jas. Linder. W. P Lovelace. A. D. Lovelace. Geo. McKinney, D. J. McArthur, T. W A. Martin, J. J. Mitchell, J. R. Mitchell, E. T. Mitchell. David Owens, Wm. Potter, J. C. Parris, H. E. Price. B. T. Price, W. J. Price. James Petty, W. L. D. Rollins, J. C. Robbs, W. H. Spencer, Anson Sprouse, Geo. W. Sprouse, John Sprouse, John P. Smith, B. O. Turner, J. C. Turner. W. P. Tenison. Lewis Waldrop, W. J. White. J. N. Ward, J. J. Watson and J. P. Young. Note: No casualties or other information in connection with this company are recorded in the office of the State Historian at Columbia.

13th Regiment, S.C.V.

Colonels: O. E. Edwards died of wounds received at Chancellorsville, Benj. T. Brockman wounded at 2d Manassas, died of wounds received at Spottsylvania.

Lieutenant Colonel: T. Stobo Farrow wounded at 2d Manassas.

Majors: Jos. L. Wofiord and D. R. Duncan.

Adjutant: John C. Anderson.

Chaplains: John G. Landrum and Wallace W. Duncan.

Surgeons: Lionell C. Kennedy and Benj. F. Kilgore.

Company A. — Captain: R. L. Bowden (see sketch) severely wounded at 2d Manassas.

Corporal: Robert W. Bobo promoted from ranks, wounded twice.

Company B. — Captains: Benj. T. Brockman (see sketch), Jesse K. Brockman (see sketch) wounded at Spottsylvania, died of same, Flavonius J. Poole (see sketch) wounded at Chancellorsville, Jericho Ford and Petersburg.

1st Lieutenants: James W. Bennett killed at Jones Farm in 1864, Samuel J. Greer, wovmded at 2d Manassas, Chancellorsville and Gaines' Mill,

2d Lieutenants: Jas. M. Littlefield resigned, Jas. A. Snoddy and Thos. Baswell.

1st Sergeant: Jas. D. Leonard wounded at Chancellorsville and 2d Manassas, Anthony P. Wakefield discharged on account of wound received at Cold Harbor.

2d Sergeant: W. R. Kendrick severely wounded at 2d Manassas, died of same, Elbert P. Johnson died of disease at Richmond, 1862, Jas. G. Leonard, J. F. Stokes killed 2d Manassas.

Corporals: 1st. Miles Floyd, Thos. N. Fowler, 2d. S. S. Dilliard died in 1862, 3d. W. D. Howe, 4th. W. L. Morgan.

Privates: Jas. M. Anderson, Perry Ashley died in Winder hospital, 1862, Wheeler W. Barker mortally wounded at Fussel's Mill, Newton L. Bennett, Alvin Burnett severely wounded at Gettysburg, Perry Burnett, W. Pinckney Burnett wounded, John N. Burnett wounded at Ox Hill near Germantown, Jas. D. Burnett wounded Five Forks, Jas. M. Boiter, Wm. Brock died in Columbia, 1861, John Brown wounded, died of same at Ox Hill, John A. Brown, J. Franklin Brown killed at Jericho Ford, Wm. B. Brown killed at Spottsylvania, Alexander Brown, Herington Brown wounded at 2d Manassas and Gettysburg, died at Elmira, N.Y., Austin W. Bailey wounded at Spottsylvania, Jos. M. Brannon wounded at Gettysburg, Jos. Bridwell wounded at Frazier's Farm, Manly F. Bright, Wm. A. Bright wounded at Fredericksburg, Robert Bright died of disease in Cokunbia, 1862, Adam Bright died of disease at Richmond, Thos. P. Beecham killed at Gettysburg, Simeon Baswell wounded at Spottsylvania, Albert T. Collins killed at Gettysburg, West Cole, Pinckney Cole, Wm. Cole died at Laurel Hill, D. Jackson Cole died of disease at Laurel Hill, 1862, Ellison G. Christopher died of disease at Richmond, Samuel J. Chamblen died of disease at Richmond, Enoch Cannon, J. M. DeYoung, Wm. A. Robbins, Thos. Davis, John W. Davis died at home in 1862, Jas. M. Davis killed at Gaines' Mill, 1862, Wm. P. Davis, L. C. Davis died at Hanover, Va., John T. Dillard wounded at 2d Manassas and Spottsylvania, Jos. P. Darby, John Elmore wounded at Wilderness, John C. Edge wounded at Gettysburg, Elias F. Floyd, Silas W. Floyd, Miles Floyd, Mark F'oote discharged, Wm. J. Green killed at Spottsylvania, Elleson J. Green died at Beuna Vista, S.C., Benj Greer wounded in battle, Jas. H. Gaston killed at 2d Manassas, Hugh B. Grisham died Winder hospital, 1862, Jacob Griffin, John M. Griffin died at home, Thos. M. Howe, Benj. F. Howe killed at Gaines' Mill, John J. Howe wounded at Spottsylvania, JaS.C. Howe, J. N. R. Hill, C. J. Hill, Wm. T. Hughes died in hospital, Amos Holmes killed at Chancellorsville, Alichael Hadden, Jas. H. Hadden, John C. Hadden died Chimborazo hospital, ToUiver R. Johnson, Simeon P. Johnson wounded at Deep Bottom, John J. Jorden died in Richmond, Prue B. James severely wounded 2d Manassas, J. Franklin James killed at Spottsylvania, Miles M. Knight wounded five times, Robert M. Kenrick wounded 2d Manassas, Isaac P. Long wounded at Chancellorsville and Jones' Farm, Pettus V. Liles, Leonard Morgan wounded 2d Manassas, John T. Mash, John D. McVay died in Richmond, 1862, Wm. McElreath wounded at Chancellorsville, Manly McElreath died at Coosawhatchie, Peter H. Moore died at Coosawhatchie, Robert M. Mahaffy, Jos. K. Mahaffy, Green L. Mahaffy died in hospital, Massey Mayfield mortally wounded at Fussel's Farm, July, 1864, died of same at Richmond, John D. Murray died of wounds at Crawfordsville, S.C., Wm. P. Pearson Alvin Powers died at Richmond, 1863, Riley D. Reynolds died at Columbia, S.C., Martin Reynolds wounded at Laurel Hill, 1862, Nimrod B. Boddy, Willis T. Ray wounded at Wilderness, 2d Manassas and Gettysburg, John W. Ray wounded at Spottsylvania, Erwin Roe died at Richmond, 1863, Linsey W. Ralph, Wm. Ralph wounded at Wilderness, John W. Smith died at Richmond. Nathaniel Smith died at Richmond. Thos J. Smith wounded at Petersburg-, Daniel Smith killed 2d Manassas, Thos. Staggs wounded at Sottsylvania, Thos. M. Staggs killed at Jericho Ford, Stephen Sizemero died at Richmond. 1862. Reuben Sizemore wounded at 2d Manassas and Sqottssylvaniia, John F. Shaw died at Lynchburg, John Sovvell, Benj. Tiqr|ens, Elliot O. Thomas died in Columbia, F. Landrum Tillotson wounded at Gettysdurg, Wm. Vaughn died of wounds at Richmond, Samuel L. Vaughn. John M. AVilliams, Jas. Williams wounded at 2d Manassas, Ellison S. Waddel wounded at Malvern Hill, Jas. D. Wakefield. Jas. M. Wakefield died at Laurel Hill, 1862, John Wilson killed at Gettysburg, John Wright killed at Gettysburg, Edward H. Willis killed at Petersburg, Perry Waters died at Laurel Hill and Manning A. Wilson wounded at Wilderness.

Company C. — Captains: T. Stobo Farrow elected major of 13th Regiment at organization, D. R. Duncan promoted from 1st lieutenant and John W. Carlisle promoted from 2d to 1st lieutenant.

1st Lieutenant: Alex. S. Douglas wounded at Fussels Mill.

2d Lieutenants: Chas. Petty promoted from sergeant to 2d lieutenant and Adam W. Ballenger promoted from ranks, wounded near Petersburg (see sketches of Farrow, Duncan, Carlisle, Duglass, Petty and Ballinger).

Sergeants: 1st. Jas. M. Powell, Wilford I. Harris wounded near Petersburg August 25, 1864; 2d Lemuel Moorman killed at Fussel's Mill, Amos R. Shands; 3d Thos. W. Wingo, D. Rush Hudson.

Corporals: Geo. W. Wingo, J. V. Sleigh severely wounded at Petersburg August, 1864, Jas. W. White wounded near Cold Harbor.

Privates: David T. Alley, Thos. J. Alley killed at Gaines Mill, Andrew J. Archer, Eber E. Bailey killed at Spottsylvania, 1864, Chas. S. Baker killed at Fussels Mill, 1864, Wm. B. Ballenger, Joseph Ballenger killed Frazers Farm, John W. Burnett, Howard Bobo killed at Fussels Mill, C. C. Bearden, John L. Booker died at Coosawhatchie, 1862, Wm. J. Boniar, H. vSpencer Bullman killed at Gettysburg, John M. Burnett wounded at Gettysburg, died of same in Pennsylvania. Matt Burnett, Wm. Byars, Wm. C. Cannon, Jas. B. Cannon, D. E. Converse, D. M. Coan wounded at Spottsylvania and 2d Manassas, Jas. M. Corley wounded at Frazier's Farm, Wm. L. Cauthren wounded at Chancellorsville and Reeves Station, John T.Cautherm,Jos. E. Cauthern, Jos. E. Cauthern, David A. Cauthern, Z. Cowan wounded near Richmond, James E. Davis (Union) wounded at Jones' Farm and died July, 1865, T. Jefferson Dillard, Felix L. Dillard died of disease at Richmond, 1862, Christian B. Foster wounded at Riddles Shop, Va., Thos. M. Fowler wounded at 2d Manassas, died January 15, 1863, Albert H. Finch, Edward P. Gaines killed near Frazier's P'arm, Jesse W. Gaines killed at Reams Station, George Gossett wounded at Gaines Mill, G. W. Gossett wounded at Zd Manassas, Jos. H. Griffin, Robert Genobles wounded at Noels Station, Hiram Genobles, Albert G. Harris, Jos. S. Harmon wounded at Spottsylvania, P. Alberry Harmon wounded at 2d Manassas, John F. Harmon killed 2d Manassas, Cotesworth P. Huggins wounded at Fussels Farm, Wm. G. High, Monroe High, Frank M. High wounded at Reames Station, J. Van Buren High wounded at Reames Station and Gettysburg, Frank A. Johnson, W4n. Johnson wounded at 2d Manassas, Ishani F. Kirby, W. Simpson Kirby, Henry Keast, Austin Lee, A. C. Lockman, Edward E. Leitner, John N. Lemaster, Jos. J. Lawrence wounded at Wilderness, Wilson Lawrence, Wm. Lawrence wounded at Riddles Shop, Elias J. W. Lowe, James M. Lowe, Ephrim A. B. Lockman, Samuel Land, Wm. Lowe, Hiram McAbee wounded at Fussels Mill and Gettysburg, Albert McAbee wounded at Fussels Mill and 2d Manassas, David McMillen wounded at Gettysburg, John J. Moore, Lemuel F. Mason wounded at 2d Manassas, Walter H. Mitchell, Robert J. Owens killed at Frazier's Mill, Frederick J. Parham killed at Gettysburg, John Pierce, Wm. L. Swatsell killed 2d Manassas, Marcus L. Sutherland, John W. Ship, Abram Summers killed accidentally at Coosawhatchie December 15, 1861, Robert Smith killed at 2d Manassas, Wm. C. Sexton killed at 2d Manassas, Marcus W. Sexton wounded near Frazier's Farm, David W. Styles, Wm. R. Tanner wounded at Sharpsburg, Alonzo Tanner, M. Thomas killed at 2d Manassas, Marion L. Thomas killed at 2d Manassas, Wm. A. Thompson wounded at Jones Farm and died of same at Richmond, 1864, Wm. W. Tinsley died of disease at Laurel Hill, 1862, Ransom W. Tinsley wounded at Cold Harbor, Eber Tinsley, Albert H. Twitchell, Marcus Turner, John D. Turner, John T. B. Turner killed at Spottsylvania, Alexander W. Walker, Andrew J. Wingo wounded at Fredericksburg, Robert Wingo wounded at Spottsylvania, J. Frank Wingo, Ransom Wingo wounded at Sutherland Station, Alberry Wingo, Wm. F. White, Geo. W. Wilkie, Jas. Williamson, Chas. W. Williamson, James Williams and Peter C. Wheeler killed at Gettysburg.

Company E. — Captains: Joseph W. Wofford advanced by promotion to major, John Dewberry advanced by promotion from 1st lieutenant, wounded at Gettysburg, lost an arm, was captured and held till the close of the war, O. Robbins advanced by promotion from ranks, 1st lieutenant W. T. Thorne wounded, lost an arm, discharged.

2d Lieutenants: John Y. Wofford died July, 1863, McK. Willis killed at Jones Farm, 1864, and W. J. Poole.

Sergeants: 1st J. W. Berry; 2d Geo. A. Setzler, 3d J. H. Turner, 4th David Parris.

Corporals: Isreal Willis died at Charlottsville, Robert Price died at Charleston, B. B. Martin, Hazel Parris and S. M. White wounded at 2d Manassas.

Privates: Mathew Burnett wounded 2d Manassas, Thomas Belcher, Robert Byers, Barney Belcher, Jovan Bryant, John Byers, M. D. Bryant, Rowland Bryant killed at Gettysburg, James Bryant, C. C. Bonham wounded at Gettysburg, died at Fort Delaware, Albany Cash wounded at Riddles Shop, Lee Cash died at Charleston, Lawson Cash died at Richmond, Arthur Cash, Green B. Cash wounded at 2d Manassas, S. M. Cash, C.C.Calvert wounded Fussels Mill, James Calvert, T. Childers wounded at 2d Manassas, J. P. Cudd, Rufus Clement wounded at Wilderness, C. M. Cantrell wounded at North Anna, Ransom

Cartee, John Cartee, Farrow Cole, John Cash wounded at Jones Farm, W. B. Cash, Cadle wounded at Chancellorsville, died of disease, Henry Davidson wounded at 2d Manassas, lost a leg. Hazel Davidson, James Davidson died in hospital, J. W. Elder died in Richmond, A. C. Elder, Zebean Ezell killed at Williamport, Va., Wm. Ezell killed at Spottsylvania, A. C. Ezell wounded at Petersburg August 25, 1864, Isaac Epton, Wm. Epton, Jas. Epton, Wm. Garrett, Zebean Gilbert died in hospital September 26, 1861, John Gossett, W. M. Gossett killed near Petersburg, Wm. Giles, John Head died in Richmond, Va., H. Horn, A. Henderson died in hospital, Javan Henderson wounded at Ox Hill, Wm. Henderson killed at Chancellorsville, Wm. Henderson No. 2, Louis Henderson died in hospital, Jackson Henderson, Wm. J. Hines wounded at Wilderness, J. L. B. Hines died at Richmond, Albert Hines, John Z. Johnson wounded at Wilderness, Green Johnson, Wm. Johnson wounded at Spottsylvania, died of wounds, David Johnson died in hospital, Jas. Johnson, Marion Johnson wounded at Fredericksburg, lost an arm. — Kimmel. Anthony Lewis, Uriah Mullins wounded 2d Manassas, Jas. H. Moseley, Wm. Moselev, J. H. McKelvey died in Richmond, J. A. McKelvey, Wm. McKintree, T. C. McKintree, J. O. Martin died in hospital, Haden Morris, Hiram Owens wounded at Ox Hill, James Owens, Jackson Oliver, C. C. Peck, Thos. Price wounded at Wilderness, Docter Potter, Peyton A. Potter killed at 2d Manassas, Abram Potter. Wm. Potter, E. Potter, J. M. Randall, Jackson Robbins died in hospital, S. F. Robbins died at Richmond, O. Robbins wounded at Frazier's Farm, M. S. Shields, J. K. Seay wounded at Gettysburg, John Spencer, J. P. Turner killed at 2d Manassas. Lee L. Turner died in Richmond, H. M. Turner, Zera Thomas. R. Q. White. Francis Willis, David Willis wounded at 2d Manassas. Thos. Willis. John O. Willis killed at Widerness. Wm. P. Willis, E. White, Jas. A. Waldrep. John Webb killed at Gettysburg, Louis Webb, Benj. W. Wells, J. Wakefield, Wm. Wooton.

Company F. — Captains: W. P. Compton (see sketch) resigned, and Alexander Copeland promoted from 1st sergeant, surrendered in command of company at Appomattox, April 9. 1865.

1st Lieutenants: Pleasant G. Page died August, 1862, B. B. Chapman (see sketch) promoted from ranks, wounded at Chancellorsville, lost a leg, and W.D.O. Shields promoted from 2d lieutenant, surrendered at Appomattox.

2d Lieutenants: J. M. Jackson resigned on account of ill health, died Nov. 15th. '66. W. H. Caldwell died January 1862, on coast of S.C. W. H. Chapman promoted from ranks, killed in battle a few days before surrendered at Appomattox, and J. C. Burton.

1st Sergeants: David Rudisail killed December 13, 1862, at Fredericksburg, John White died August, 1862, in Virginia, Edward Alverson surrendered at Appomattox.

Corporals: G. W. Reece, J. B. Page died August, 1862, Wm. E. Cook wounded at Gettesburg and Calvin Tinsley.

Privates: Green Atkins died Feburary 1862, Thos. Atkins, John L. Alverson, killed at Reddles Shop, Va., B. F. Alverson, Matt Alverson, B. F. Alverson. Sr.,

B. F. Alverson. Jr., W. C. Alverson, J. H. Andrews died May, 1862, in Virginia, Peter Andrews died August, 1862, in Virginia, Joseph Andrews died April, 1863, in Virginia, W. P. Barnett wounded at Ox Hill, Va., O. Barton died 1864, Elijah Bishop, Simpson Bishop, Isaac Bishop, Wm. Blackwood, Alexander Blackwood killed at 2d Manassas, Marcus Blackwood, C. B. Bowling wounded at Fredericksburg, W. M. Bowling killed at Fredericksburg, Wm. Brooks. Kobert Bullington, J. P. Bullington, Tench Bullington, Epu.lla Burns killed Sharpburg, J. A. Burns wounded at 2d Manassas, W. J. Burton, Govan Bush, John Bush, J. C. Caldwell, W. M. Cambell wounded and discharged, Jas. Cambell wounded at Spottsylvania, Jas. Clark, M. G. Clark, Farrer Cole, Thos. Cooper died in 1862, in Virginia, J. H. Daniel died in 1863. in Virginia, John Daniel, T. J. Davis, J. B. Dill, J. P. Dill, James Dunlap, Wm. A. Erwin killed at Fredericksburg, Elias Farmer died 1862, Edmond Feagans killed July, 1864, T. R. Fleming wounded at 2d Manassas, Wm. H. Foster, Wm. Forest, T. A. Forest killed in 1863, Jos. Forest killed at vSpottsylvania in 1864, John L. French, Va. Golightly killed in 1863. Thos. Golightly killed at Ox Hill, Va., J. E. Hall, J. H. Hall, H. B. Hall wounded at 2d Manassas, surrendered at Appomattox, T. J. Hall surrendered at Appomattox, George Hall killed at Chancellorsville, Adam Haas wounded at 2d Manassas. Wm. Henderson, Elias Henderson, Calvin Henderson. F. L. Hines, J. C. Jackson, Jackson Johnson wounded and discharged, lost an arm, Tandy (Kase) Kimbrel surrendered at Appomattox, John Kimbrel died in 1863, Wm. King killed at Fredersburg, Calvin Lancaster surrendered at Appomattox, Crawford Lancaster, Thomas Lively, Collins McCarter transferred to Holcombe Legion, C. R. McClure killed near Petersburg September 30, 1862, David McClure. John B. McClure surrendered at Appomattox. Charles McClure, Wm. McClure, Jones PL McDowell killed 1864, Jerome McDowell died, Wm. McGinnis, David McMillen died 1862, John W. McMillen wounded and discharged, J. M. Mills wounded at Petersburg, surrendered at Appomattox, Thos. Mills killed in Virginia, G. Morrow wounded at 2d Manassas, Johnson Newman died in 1864, B. F. Nicholls, Jos. Nichoils, J. W. O'Shields, J. A. Pearson killed, E. L. Pope, C. T. Pope wounded at Gettysburg, Thos. Rayan, Charles Rayan killed at Gettysburg, G. C. Reece died in 1862, John Roddy, Mat Roddy killed at Fredericksburg, Wilson Seay killed at Spottsylvania, Franklin Seay killed at Chancellorsville, David Sizemore died 1861, Jackson Staggs wounded at Ox Hill, surrendeded at Appomattox, Jonathan Staton, Wm. Staton, James Stone died in 1863, Eber Tinsley, Thomas Tinsley died in 1862, Wm. Townsend killed at Spotsylvania, James Turner wounded at 2d Manassas, surrendered at Appomattox, John Turner, Jeff Turner killed in battle, Elias Vehorn killed in battle in 1863, Thos. Vehorn died in 1862, Alonzo Wallace died in 1863, R. J. F. Wall discharged, joined 5th Regiment S.C.V., F. A. West surrendered at Appomattox, J. C. C. Wilkins, P. A. Wilson, Wm. C. White, T. C. Wofford killed below Richmond in 1863, W. P. Wofiford, John Wofford killed at Gettysburg, John Young wounded and discharged, lost an arm, James Young died in 1863.

Company I. — Captains: Andrew K. Smith (see sketch) killed at 2d Manassas, and Franklin M. Trimmier (see sketch).

1st Lieutenants: S. F. Smith and B. F. Neighbors.

2d Lieutenants: J. R. Poole, J. W. White resigned, joined 20th Regiment, S.C.V., died on coast of S.C., July 21, 1863, R. M. Crocker (see sketch) wounded at 2d Manassas.

Sergeants: 1st T. H. Waters, 2d Wm. Waters, 3d Isaac Macomson, 4th. B. F. Neighbors wounded at 2d Manassas, W. E. Lipscomb died of wounds at Chancellorsville.

Corporals: J. M. Barnett, W. F. Coggins and M. C. Barnett.

Privates: John Allen wounded at 2d Manassas, W. C. Allen wounded at 2d Manassas, Josiah W. Bagwell wounded 2d Manassas, Jas. Bagwell, Samuel Bagwell wounded severely at 2d Manassas, Simpson Bagwell killed at 2d Manassas, L. Ballenger, T. R. Barnett, W. H. Barnett, Pinckney Brice, Wm. Carlyle, W. M. Coggins died of wounded at Wilderness, J. L. Coggins died on coast of S.C. in 1863, A. C. Crocker wounded at 2d Manassas, W. W. Crocker, A. W. Currant, Elph Elder, Samuel Elder, Robert Elmore, J. M. Finch, T. A. Forrest, J. F. French, A. C. Gossett died at Winder hospital, E. M. Gossett, R. W. P. Gossett killed at 2d Manassas, I George mortally wounded at 2d Manassas, Drury Griffin, John Griffin, B. F. Hammett, W. T. Hammett, T. C. Harmon, S. Harmon, Fowler Hembree wounded at 2d Manassas, lost an arm, Robert Hembree, Russel Hembree, E. A. Henley, E. M. D. Henley died at Richmond September 19. 1863, Jas. Henley, Thos. Henderson, Giles Hewett, W. J. Hutchings, P. J. Jenkins, Peter Johnson, Andrew Kirby, F. A. Kirby died at Columbia, October 12, 1861, Henry Kirby, Jasper Kirby, L. C. Kirby, T. J. Kirby, W'm. Kirby, Thos. Lemaster, Lee Lender, Willis Linder, J. C. Lipscomb, John H. Lipscomb, Nathan Lipscomb, T. H. Lipscomb missing, supposed to have died, T. M. Littlejohn, J. H. Lowe, J. H. McAbee, Wm. Millwood, John Patterson, John Petrie, L. H. Petrie, wounded at Fredericksburg December 18, 1862, lost an arm, P. C. Petrie, W. B. Quinn. Barham Reaves, G. B. (or T. J.) Reaves killed at 2d Manassas, Morgan Reaves, T. J. Reaves died during the war, W. J. Reaves, D. M. Richards, N. Roddy, Simpson Sanders, Jeff Satterfield, Wilson Satterfield, Wilson Seay. J. H. Smith, P. L. Smith, Stewart Sparks, Wm. Sparks,, James Sprouse, Jas. Stone, Wm. Thomas, A. J. Thompson, Elijah Thompson, M. Thompson, Wm. T. Thompson wounded at 2d Manassas, W. R. Thompson, F. M. Turner, T. J. Turner, Abner Waters. Simpson Weather, T. R. Wilkie, A. W. Willis, H. J. Willis, Drury Wood, F. A. Zimmerman died and J. N. Zimmerman died.

Company G. — Private: Frank Moss.

14th Regiment. S.C.V., Col. J. N. Brown.

Company E. — Captain: Harrison P. Griffith (see sketch).

Lieutenant: Jesse Gwinn promoted from sergeant to heutenant, wounded at Gettysburg.

Privates: James Gwinn dangerously wounded at Gettysburg, J. B. Jones seriously wounded in battle, John Pearson killed at Spottsylvania, Lewis

Pearson, Charles Phillips killed in Wilderness campaign, Sanford Reynolds, James R. Waddel killed in battle, W. B. Waddle, W. R. Waddle, George Waddle killed in battle. S. V. Waddle, T. P. Waddle, John A. Westmoreland. J. W.Westmoreland, Bluford Westmoreland wounded at Wilderness from which he afterwards died. Monterey Westmoreland, Dr. W. Thomas Westmoreland killed at Petersburg.

15th Regiment, S.C.V., Col. W. D. DeSaussure.

Company B. — Lieutenant: Postel P. Yarborough.

Privates: Thos. Anderson, Caleb Canady, David Canady, Sr., David Canady, Jr., Erwin Hembree died at Richmond, Benj. Hollingsworth killed at 2d Manassas, Wm. P. Huckabee killed at Boonesboro. Jas. M. Huckabee, Philip Huckabee killed at Chancellorsville, John Huff died at Richmond, Wm. M. Huff, Thos. H. Hughes killed at 2d Manassas, Ephrim Hughes wounded at Wilderness, Jas. H. Kelly wounded at Chancellorsvile, David Lamb, Wm. M. Poole, Jas. Rook killed. Franklin Rook killed at Sharpsburg. H. Caldwell Stone wounded at 2d Manassas, Wm. M. Waldrep, B. E. West, Frederick Wilbanks, Thos. Wilbanks, John F. Wilbanks. Elijah H. Whitemire killed at 2d Manassas, Thos. H. Whitwire and Hiram Yarborough.

Company F. — 1st Lieutenant: Moses Wood (see sketch) promoted from ranks, wounded at Wilderness, in command of company at surrender at Greensboro.

Sergeants: Jas. A. Rowland killed at Boonesboro, Smith Lipscomb promoted from ranks for bravery, killed at Averysboro, Dexter Shippey wounded at Gettysburg, promoted from ranks, surrendered at Greensboro, W. D. Wilkins wounded at 2d Manassas and Gettysburg.

Privates: W. W. Goforth wounded at Wilderness, Thos. Griffin left sick at Winchester, Va., was never heard from, W. D. Kirby wounded at Gettysburg, discharged, Charles Littlejohn, Henry Littejohn wounded at Gettysburg, Charleston, Va., and Chickamauga, M. R. Littlejohn killed on skirmish line, James Island, Samuel Purkerson died at Winchester, Va., Nuckells Shippey wounded at Chancellorsville, killed at Chickamauga, R. S. Wilkins wounded at Chancellorsville, T. T. Wilkins died at home during the war, F. W. Ward.

Company I. — Private: John H. Love. 16th Regiment, S.C.V.

Company G. — Private: James Anderson.

18th Regiment, S.C. W, Cols. Gadberry and Wallace.

Company C. — Privates: John Briddle surrendered at Appomattox, Marion W. Kelly surrendered at Appomattox, Wm. H. Waldrep surrendered at Appomattox, Thos. Waldrep killed near Petersburg, Lewis Yarborough captured and discharged from prison.

Company E. — Captains: F. Marion Tucker (see sketch) killed at 2d Manasass, Miles H. Ferguson wounded at Clay's Farm.

1st Lieutenants: B. G. Lambright and H. D. Floyd wounded at Petersburg, lost an arm.

2d Lieutenants: Burwell C. Bobo killed at Clay's Farm, J. Madison Stone, J. M. Anderson killed at Petersburg in 1864, John M. Shackleford.

Sergeants: 1st Isaac Evans, John H. Montgomery promoted to regimental commissary, and J. Madison Strebling.

Corporals: B. W. Hill wounded at Petersburg, and Elihu Littlefield.

Privates: Eber S. Allen (see sketch) promoted to assistant regimental quartermaster, Geo. W. Bass, Stephen Bass, Asahel Beason, Sampson Beason, John Beason killed at Five Forks in 1865, Samuel Bell, Jas. F. Brown, Adau C. Bettes, David Barker, Chas. A. Barry. Wm. Bullington, Fred Bailey wounded at Cay's Farm, Thomas Brady, Levi Cambell, Wm. Cambell, Jesse A. Couch died in prison Elmira, N.Y., Tolliver R. Couch, Lecil Couch, John Chummey, D. Crocket Crow, Marion Casey, Wm. Casey, John Chesney, Thos. Chesney died of disease at Charleston, S.C., Miles Compton wounded at Clay's Farm. Jas. Cathcart wounded at Clay's Farm, W. Oscar Evins wounded at Clay's Farm, lost a leg, Allen O Epps wounded at Petersburg, John Farmer died of disease at Stanton, Va., W'. Riley Fowler, Cornelius Fowler, Wiley H. Felker. Thos. Hembree killed at Rappahannock, Frank Hembree died of disease at Petersburg in 1864, Baylis Hindman died of disease at Charleston, Neville Holcomb, Baylis Hill killed at Clay's Farm, John M. Harrelson, Samuel S. Johnson, Wm. M. Kelley, Pinckney H. Kelley killed at Petersburg, Thos. M. Kelley, Thos. J. Kelley, M. Oliver Knighton, John Knight, G. Pinckney Littlefields, Albert Littlefields died at Charleston, John C. Layton, Christopher C. Layton. Thos. C. Layton died at Balden, Fla., Silas G. Lanford, Elisha J. Linder, T. Monroe Miles killed at 2d Manassas, Jacob Maddox killed at Petersburg in 1864, Andrew C. Moore (see sketch) killed at 2d Manassas, Thos. J. Moore (see sketch) discharged in 1862, joined Holcombe Legion, G. W. Martin, Robert Mayes died in Virginia, Isaaic W. Mayes, Wm. Neighbors, M. J. R. Neighbors killed at Petersburg in 1864, John New, John O'Shields, John D. Poole killed at 2d Manassas, Henry Patterson, Monroe O. Prewett, Edward M. Prewitt wounded at Appomttox in 1865, Virgil M. Rogers wounded at Petersburg, James S. Rhodes wounded at Petersburg. W. Simpson wounded at 2d Manassas, Jas. M. Rhodes, John F. Rhodes, J. M. Rhodes, Green D. Rook wounded at Petersburg in 1864, Samuel Sexton died at home, Zachraiah Spencer, Jonathan Shackelford, Pinckney Shackelford. Robert A. Sherbutt wounded at 2d Manassas, Madison A. Sherbutt wounded at Sharpsburg, Samuel Z. Sherbutt wounded at Sharpsburg, Benjamin C. Sherbutt, Carlisle W. Sherbutt died at Petersburg. James Stribling. John W. Stribling, James Spelts wounded at 2d Manassas. John Strange died at Charleston, Asa Smith, Grant Senn wounded at Rappahannock, Edward Smith, John Sexton, L. Madison Stone, Wm. Stone, Leander Stone wounded at Clay's Farm, Benj. Smith, James T. Taylor, Mordecai Taylor, Wm. Turner, Wm. M. Taylor died of disease at Charleston, John M. Terry died March, 1864, Robert Thomas, Thos. Varner killed at Petersburg in 1864, J. Frank Varner killed at Clay's Farm, John R. Wise wounded at Petersburg, John J. Williams wounded at Boonesboro, Adolphus Williams killed at Petersburg in 1864, Enoch C. Wofiford, J. T. Woodward, Eber Waters, H. S. Wyatt, T. M. Wilder killed at 2d Manassas, S. G. Woodward wounded at 2d Manassas, lost an arm, W. Frank West wounded at Clay's Farm in 1864, Frank C. Waters, Ransom Walker, John West, Lemaster West, Landon C. Waters, Wm. Whitmire, Sr., Wm. Whitmire, Jr., John Wilder, A. W. Watson and Robert Waldrep.

18th Regiment, S.C.V.

Company G. — Commanded by Captain Felix J. Walker and afterwards by Goodman Jeffries.

2d Lieutenants: Smith Lipscomb (see sketch) promoted from junior 2d lieutenant.

Privates: Alfred Briant died in prison at Elmira, N.Y., Lorenzo Huskey, Abe Kirby. Hiram Lipscomb wounded near Petersburg. Edward Lipscomb, Wm. R. Lipscomb, Wm. S. Lipscomb. John Lipscomb. Henry Littlejohn, Jackson Mullinax. Joseph Mullinax killed between Petersburg and Richmond, Washington Mullinax, Haas. Mullinax, J. Wright Mullinax, James Mullinax, James Mott, Thos. Messan, Jefferson Millwood, James Roundtree and Hosea Waters.

22d Regiment, S.C.V. — Cols. Joseph Abney and S. D. Goodlett, Surgeon: Dr. C. E. Fleming (see sketch).

Company B. — Captains: John S. Wheeler resigned, A. J. Foster promoted from 1st lieutenant, Robert G. Fleming severely wounded near Petersburg, May 20, 1864, and resigned or was discharged, W. Alexander Benson (see sketch) killed in the trenches in front of Petersburg and George B. Lake (see sketch) appointed after death of Benson, covered up by mine explosion at Petersburg.

1st Lieutenants: Peyton Ballenger (see sketch) commanded company for thirteen months, J. Smiley Wheeler killed at Jackson, Miss.

2d Lieutenants: Dillingham Ballenger died in Charleston, 1863, R. V. Hastings died in hospital Savannah, Ga., Wm. J. Lake (see sketch) covered up by mine explosion at Petersburg, hip fractured, dug out alive.

Sergeants: J. M. James wounded in Virginia, leg amputated, B. K. Vaughn, Alberry Ballenger discharged, R. M. Reese died of disease, I. S. Morgan killed by mine explosion at Petersburg, J. Ross Mason and J. M. McCue died during the war.

Corporals: R. J. Duncan and I. J. Mayfield died during the war.

Privates: J. Allen killed by mine explosion at Petersburg, J. Atkins, W. M. Atkins, J. B. Atkins, A. R. Ballenger transferred to Company D, Palmetto Sharpshooters, Josiah Barker wounded in 1862, killed by mine explosion at Petersburg, Thomas Barker killed by mine explosion at Petersburg, J. A. Barker, Jos. Barnett died in army, Wm. Barnett, Berry Bennett died in Charleston, West P.ennett died in Charleston (remains of Berry and West Bennett were brought home together), Jas. Brown killed at Boonsboro, Md., D. R. Brown killed during the war, Jos. Brown, John W. Bomar killed near Petersburg in 1864, E. Thos. Bomar killed by mine explosion at Petersburg,

Washington Bomar killed by mine explosion at Petersburg, L. S. Beshears died soon after enlistment, B. C. Burns died during the war, W. T. Cambell, Jasper Clayton killed by mine explosion at Petersburg. J. G. Clayton, Joel Cooley killed at Rappahannock by explosion of shell August 23, 1862, Lazareth Collins died during the war, Lorenzo D. Collins died of wounds in Virginia, P. F. Cooper died during the war, David Darby killed at Boonsboro, Md., September 14, 1862, James Darby killed by explosion of shell at Rappahannock August 23, 1862, A. B. Dobson died during the war, W. R. Dobson killed by mine explosion at Petersburg, J. Duncan killed by mine explosion at Petersburg, Joel Duncan killed by mine explosion at Petersburg, J. A. Duncan killed by mine explosion at Petersburg, W. J. Duncan killed by mine explosion at Petersburg, Moses Evins killed by mine explosion at Petersburg, D. Evins killed by mine explosion at Peterburg, Pink F. Floyd, Wm. Ford died during the war, Matthew A. Henson, Z. J. Haskins, Miles Haskins died during the war, Nathaniel S. Howe captured and died in prison. L. M. Hudson died in hospital in Virginia, Thos. W. Keller, Y. A. Keller died in prison ship, was thrown overboard, John Kendrick killed by explosion of mine, Petersburg, R. W. Kimbrel died soon after returning home from the army, Ramson Lee died during the war, A. Lister killed by mine explosion at Petersburg, J. P. Mason killed by mine explosion at Petersburg, G. W. Mason killed by mine explosion at Petersburg, M. A. McCue killed by mine explosion at Petersburg, W. A. McElreath wounded by explosion of shell on Rappahannock August 23, 1862, H. Wilson Moore (see sketch) covered up in crater by mine explosion at Petersburg, was dug out alive, Harris Owens killed by explosion of mine at Petersburg, J. Pollard, William Pollard wounded September II, 1862, Alexander Prewitt, Benjamin C. Brewitt lost in the war, J. Prewitt died during the war, W. W. Prewitt died during the war. J. M. Richards, killed by explosion of mine at Petersburg, Levi Richards killed by explosion of mine Petersburg, J. R. Smith, Wilson died at Charleston, M. A. Wison killed near Peterburg, R. C. Wood killed by explosion of mine at Petersburg, Benj. P. Wood and John Wheeler wounded at Secessionville, S.C. June 16, 1862.

Note. — For an account of the explosion of mine at Petersburg July 30, 1864, the reader is referred to the sketches published in this volume of Captain Geo. B. Lake, Lieutenant W. J. Lake and private Henry Wilson Moore.

Company C. — Captains: W. W. Hendrix, T. J. Wakefield promoted from ranks, resigned, E. J. Dean (see sketch) promoted from lieutenant, and Judson Wakefield promoted from ranks.

Lieutenants: T. E. Wood, D. M. Wood, Washington Johnson, J. M. Calvert, J. M. Thomas and E. J. Calvert killed at Boonsboro September 14, 1862.

Sergeants: J. P. McClemons, J. A. Monk, W. T. Glenn, Henry McHugh, W. Edge, J. P. Hollzelan wounded at Boonsboro, and J. T. Smith.

Corporals: J. P. Leonard, W. E. Wilson, W. W. Hughes, Jesse Hemp, J. D. Burnett and A. E. Childers.

Privates: John Biter, Peter Biter, Pinckney Biter, A. J. Bright, William J. Bright, J. L. Brockeman, Joseph Brown, Madison Burnett, James Calvert, A. C.

Childers, Thomas Childers, Richard Chapman, James Chapman, Isaac Coleman wounded at Boonsboro, Brazil Cox, Henry Cox, James Cox, Mills Dean (see sketch), William Dupree, Wm. Edge, W. T. Glenn, Jeremiah Green, Thos. Holtzclaw, W. P. Hamley wounded at Boonsboro, Jas. Henderson, J. C. Hughes wounded at Boonsboro, W. W. Hughes, T. F. Hendrix, W. P. Hendrix, J. F. Jones wounded at Boonsboro, W. N. Johnson, Anderson Johnson, Jas. L. Johnson, John Johnson. Howell Johnson, D. C. Leonard killed at Boonsboro, J. P. Leonard, Miles Lee, M. S. McElreath, J. H. McHugh, M. S. Monk, Henry Owens, T. A. Owens wounded at Boonsboro, Wm. Owens, J. M. Pearson. S. J. Pearson. W. J. Pearson, Jos. Pain. Jas. Rogers, John Rogers, S. V. Rogers, Zadok Rogers, Alfred Sisemore, Edward Sisemore, J. T. Siseniore, R. P. Sisemore, J. T. Smith, John M. Thomas, Penny Vaughn, Wiley Vaughn, Ellison Waddle, Alexander Wakefield, T. J. Wakefield, A. B. Waldrep, W. M. T. Waldrep, J. A. Waters, J. M. Waters. Zadok Wilson. P. P. Wood, J. W. Wood, J. P. Wood, R. M. Wood, Dr. T. E. Wood, O.V. Wood and M. A. Wood wounded at Boonsboro.

27th Regiment. S.C.V. — Col. Peter C. Guillard. Captain T. Y. Simmons.

Company B. — Privates: — Bowers killed at Walthal Junction, John Burnett. Wm. Belcher, John Edwards killed at Battery Wagner, John W. Edwards, John Floyd wounded at Weldon, N.C., Matthew Hollander, John Hollander. John C. Harris. Lee Kirby, John A'l. Kirby, John I.ittlcjohn. George Pittlejohn. Wm. Moss. John C. Mabry. Wm. McCreevy. Robert McDowell, John Phosphal, John Perry, Robert Perry, Lewis M. Palmer, Henry Page. Jas. M. Poole, John Pearson. Russel Quinn, Henry M. Seay, John Smith, C. C. Turner transferred to 5th Regiment, S.C.V., George W. Turner, Wm. Vaughn and Robert Wood.

27th Regiment, S.C.V.

Company G. — Captain: Henry Buist commanding.

Corporal: J. Golden.

Privates: W. Andrews captured at Petersburg June 24, 1864, and made prisoner of war, J. Burgess died of disease in hospital, Robert Burket, T. C. Burroughs, W. J. Cambell. J. McD. Cambell, J. Duckett killed accidentely in camp, E. Dunn, F. Grice captured at Petersburg June 24, 1864, and made prisoner of war. T. D. Gevin. W. P. Gevin, J. Gevin captured on Weldon R. R. and died in prison, W. Hays, B. W. Hill, F. James, W. I. McMaken, G. W. Moore died in hospital, E. W. Mooie captured and made prisoner of war, J. O'Sheilds, G. Powers, S. T. Riddle captured and made prisoner of war, Wm. Riddle captured and made prisoner of war, A. M. Rodgers captured and made prisoner of war, L. P. Rodgers captured and made prisoner of war, Wm. Smith, F. J. Smith, W. B. Smith, J. F. Smith, W. A. Stone, E. Thomas captured on Weldon R. R. and made prisoner of war, E. C. Tribble, J. E. Vise, T. J. Woodward captured at Petersburg and died a prisoner of war, H. P. Woodward, R. Wyatt captured and made a prisoner of war, and A. Zeikil captured and made a prisoner of war.

Company K. — Captain: Wm. Clarkson.

1st Lieutenants: J. G. Harris and A. D. Smith.

2d Lieutenants: A. D. Simmons and R. B. Seay.

Sergeants: M. McSweeney, Prater S. Montgomery died at close of war from disease contracted in camps, J. A. Collins, T. H. Turner H. L. Lotzen, Warren D. Chapman wounded near Drury's Bluff on James river and died a few days afterwards, W. P. Bishop and Wm. L. Perry.

Privates: Wm. Anderson, R. C. Allen, G. W. Bates, H. Bishop, C. Blackwood, G. H. Bridges, D. W. Bragg, J. T. Brannon, G. L. Bearden, E. Cantrel, T. B. Cantrel, R. H. Cantrel, T. H. Cannon, J. T. Carlton, M. S. Carlton, J. H. Castleberry, J. J. Crosby, J. B. Conlin, T. L. Cooksey, M. B. Chapman, H. M. Davidson, Wm. DeYound, D. J. Dewberry, J. Dupree, W. P. Edwards, W. D. Eskin, M. D. Ford, J. Floyd, H. Fowler, J. J. Foster, H. Gentry, T. B. Grififin, N. Griffin, J. P. Goforth, T. B. Hames, F. Harnes, J. Harvey, A. M. Hawley, M. Henderson, T. M. Hendricks, Wm. Heller, M. Hullender, T. Humphries, W. R. Horton, L. Kirby, J. M. Kirby, L. C. Kirby, James Kay, George Lucas, Posar Lewis, W. H. Linsey, H. Linstedt, B. Maul, J. M. C. Mayfield, D. T. McElreath, J. McElreath, W. G. McDowell, S. McCarter, J. C. C. Page, W. B. Parris, A. J. Perry, Sr., J. T. Pearson, A. P. Pearson, G. L. Pearson, E. V. Poole, L. Poole, J. A. Powers, A. R. Quinn, L. C. Quinn, W. Ray, J. D. Rodgers, J. R. Robinson, A. Smith, J. P. Smith, J. J. Spell, H. H. Turner, Wm. Turner, B. O. Turner, A. J. Timmons, W. S. Vaughn, E. Williams and W. Wilson.

Colored: March, musician, William, cook. Manly, cook, Jeffry, cook.

1st Regiment of Rifles. Col. J. L. Orr, commander.

Wm. H. Green, Oscar L. Linsey, Simeon B. Pearson wounded at Fredericksburg and died soon thereafter, and Samuel P. Wodruff.

Hampton Legion. John H. Bowen commanding.

Company K. — Privates: Lorenzo Christopher surrendered at Appomatox, — Duncan surrendered at Appomattox, Tom Cooper surrendered at Appomattox, Sanford Martin wounded at Dandridge, Miss., John McCrary and Arthur Rodgers killed at Seven Pines.

Palmetto Sharpshooters. Col. Joseph Walker (see sketch).

Ordinance Sergeant: Thomas Miller.

Company D. — Captain: Alfred H. Foster (see sketch) wounded at Frazier's Farm, surrendered at Appomattox.

1st Lieutenants: Robert A. Snoddy died of wounds at Cambell Station, Tenn., and James S. Bellenger (see sketch) promoted from 2d lieutenant, surrendered at Appomattox.

2d Lieutenant: Richard D. Ballenger (see sketch) died of wounds at Wilderness, Va., May 6, 1864.

Sergeants: Warren S. Drummond died of wounds at Cambell Station, Tenn., November 30, 1863, Legrande (Moss) C. Zimmerman surrendered at Appomattox, wounded near Petersburg, Franklin V. Landrum wounded severlv in battles around Richmond and Spotsylvania and slightly at 2d Manassas, surrendered at Appomattox, Alfred J. Tolleson transferred to Holcombe Legion, died during the war, Wm. H. H. Richardson wounded at Frazier's Farm and Atlee's Farm, surrendered at Appomattox, George Steading killed at Atlee's Farm, November 7, 1864, and Moses Foster surrendered at Appomattox.

Corporals: Paschel Hawkins, A. Jackson Nesbit wounded at 2d Manassas, Geo. W. Howell died of wounds 2d Manassas September 2, 1862, John J. F'oster killed at Seven Pines, Wm. S. Beacham died of disease December 19, 1861, Thos. Lee regimental color guard, died of disease at Charlottsville, Va., September 16, 1861, Wm. M. Foster wounded at Wilderness, John R. Pollard died of wounds at Cambells Station, Tenn., November 19, 1863.

Privates: Wm. H. Ballenger wounded at Seven Pines and Franklin, Tenn., Albert R. Ballenger wounded at Frazier's Farm, surrendered at Appomattox, Oscar P. Ballenger wounded at Wilderness, C. C. Bishop died of disease at Weldon, N.C., June 18, 1863, W. C. Bishop, T. W. Booker died of wounds at Cambell Station, Tenn., November 17, 1863, Thos. P. Booker surrendered at Appomattox, died soon afterwards of disease contracted in army, Richard Burnett killed at 2d Manassas, Jas. B. Burnett killed at Sharpsburg, Jos. Burnett, Granville Burnett (all four named brothers) surrendered at Appomattox, T. A. Bomar, Calvin Bright surrendered at Appomattox, Wm. J. Bright, H. H. Brown surrendered at Appomattox, David S. Burns killed at Petersburg, W. W. Chamblin died at Bristol, Tenn., 1864, John E. Cox surrendered at Appomattox, Levi Clanton transferred to Hplcombe Legion, Enoch Couch died at Richmond in 1862, A. C. Cunningham wounded in battles around Richmond, died of same eighteen years afterwards, Bradley Dalton surrendered at Appomattox, G. M. Davis wounded at Fredericksburg, Nathan Demsey, John R. Dickson surrendered at Appomattox, Robert Davis killed at Frazier's Farm, D. E. Finger died at Warren Springs, Va., John A. Foster killed at Frazier's Farm, Jos. H. Foster wounded at Seven Pines, shot through the head, remarkable recovery, reentered service and was killed at Carsville, Va., May, 1863, Wm. A. Foster died of wounds at Boonsboro September 14, 1862, A. J. Foster died in prison, J. M. Foster, Thos. J. Foster killed at Frazier's Farm, Abel A. Foster surrendered at Appomattox, Luther L. Foster surrendered at Appomattox, Wm. M. Glenn wounded at Gaines Mill, surrendered at Appomattox. Z. Dow Golightly killed at Williamsburg, Va., Jacob Golightly died in Atlanta, 1863, Jackson L. Green wounded at Frazier's Farm, Hampton A. Green killed at Atlee's Farm, B. H. Greer, VVm. D. Gaston surrendered at Appomattox, A. L. Gaston surrendered at Appomattox, Wm. M. Goin, Mitchell Goin, N. G. Goin discharged. Jas. A. Gregory wounded at Gains Mill. J. L. Hawkins. J. W. Hawkins surrendere at Apptomattox, Robert B. Howell wounded at Seven Pines and seige of Petersburg, John P. Howell killed at Cambell Station, Tenn., Richard A. Howell killed at Carville, Va., J. C. Hammett. W. K. Hutchinson missing in Maryland in 1862, supposed to have died of measles, Joseph F. Howerton surrendered at Appomattox, Robert Haynes died April, 1863, Daniel Johnson died at home 1863, G. B. James, Washington C. Knight surrendered at Appomattox, John L. Kemp died October 1, 1861, A. Keasler surrendered at Apptomattox. Thos. P. Lankford died of wounds at Fort Harrison, Ira Linsey, J. B. O. Landrum was a member of this company the first year of the war, 1861, when it was Company F. 5th Regiment, S.C.V., was honorably discharged and soon afterwards commissioned by Gov. Pickens as a lieutenant in State malitia, but in April, 1862, reentered the Confederate army and served to the end of the war as a member of Company E, 2d Regiment, S.C.V., Cavalry, P. Orr Miller, Jos. McVay died July 30, 1861. J. Joice McAbee killed in battle, David Moore killed at 2d Manassas, A. W. Moore wounded at Spotsylvania, J. G. Muller, R. R. McDowell died August, 1861, Jas. J. McDowell died August, 1861, Jesse M. Morgan died at home February 23, 1862, Martin Mathis, Alex. J. Nesbitt wounded at 2d Manassas, killed at Fort Harrison, Jas. R. Nesbitt surrendered at Appomattox, Wilson Nesbitt killed at Frazier's Farm, J. E. P. L. Nicholls wounded at 2d Manassas, Thos. W. Richardson (see sketch) wounded at Seven Pines, Benj. F. Richardson died March, 1863, J. G. Rogers, A. J. Surratt surrendered at Appomattox, John Surratt surrendered at Appomattox, Wm. Smith killed at Gaines Mill, Martin W. Smith kill at Seven Pines March 31, 1862, John M. Smith, Adolph Schappaul surrendered at Appomattox, Julius A. Settlemyer, Robert C. Shands, Wm. Settle killed at Sharpsburg, September 17, 1862, John L. Settle surrendered at Appomattox, Geo. F. Settle wounded and discharged, Jas. A. Snoddy surrendered at Appomattox, P. A. Stone, J. C. Sexton surrendered at Appomattox, Wm. M. Timmons surrendered at Appomattox, Henry Tucker, Thos. J.Tinsley, killed in battle, Jesse G. Tinsley killed in battle, Thos. Tinsley killed at Frazier's Farm, S. W. Turbyfield, R. J. Winn died at Richmond in 1861, J. R. Wood killed at Gaines Mill, N. Jefferson Woody transferred to 5th S.C. Regiment, W. Dudley Moody wounded at 2d Manassas, killed near Petersburg July 12, 1864, John C. Williams surrendered at Appomattox, Perry Workman killed near Petersburg, Va., July 15, 1864, Memory C. Wingo wounded at Frazier's Farm, seriously, and 2d Manassas, Samuel C. Wrightson wounded 2d Manassas, surrendered at Appomattox, A. B. Waldrep, W. A. Wood surrendered at Appomattox, T. H, Wofford surrendered at Appomattox, and H. H. Workman killed in seige of Petersburg.

Company H. — Captains: John M. Martin wounded at Frazier's Farm died of wounds, John J. Brown (see sketch) wounded at Frazier's Farm, discharged, Robert L. Poole killed at Seven Pines, and Jas. P. Mdbre promoted from ranks.

1st Lieutenants: J. D. V. Martin killed at 2d Manassas, and C. P. Brown promoted from sergeant.

2d Lieutenants: A. M. Sruggs and — Brawley.

Sergeants: T. C. Brown wounded at Frazier's Farm, S.C. Ezell wounded at Frazier's Farm and Spotsylvania, Geo. W. Kennett killed at Gainsville, Ga., W. P. Cooley wounded, J. W. Jolly, J. W. Quinn wounded.

Corporals: J. Benson Martin surrendered at Appomattox, J. Willis Martin surrendered at Appomattox, B. F. Davis wounded, J. W. Dawson (from York county), M. L. Martin and J. J. Watson.

Privates: C. M. Amos wounded at Frazier's Farm and Wilderness severely, surrendered at Appomattox, C. W. Brown wounded in Tennessee, Alfred Burke surrendered at Appomattox, Mathew Burke, wounded at Wilderness, John E. Black surrendered at Appomattox, W. L. Brown, Nathan Byars, Jason Blackwell, Tench Blackwell, A. W. Cash, A. J. Cantrel, A. M. Cash, Marville Cash, Smith Cash, T. G. Cash, Alexander Crooker, A. G. Calvert surrendered at Appomattox, E. M. Calvert, J. Turner Cantrel, A. C. Cooley killed at Gaines Mill, W. H. Cudd, John Crooker killed at Gaines Mill, M. Cooper wounded, Richard Champion killed at Frazier's Farm, John E. Cooley, J. N. Davis wounded at 2d Manassas, J. C. Davidson wounded at Knoxville, Tenn., J. M. Elliott, J. C. Eloyed wounded at Reames Station. C. J. Fowler, A. J. Gee died, W. H. Gentry, Simpson Humphries died at Martinsburg, Va., C. Humphries, J. Knott Jolly died of wounds near Richmond. Lee Linder wounded at Spottsylvania, N. L. Lovelace killed at Wilderness, F. M. Lamb, J. M. Martin wounded at Manassas, surrendered at Appomattox, Ross Massey, Wm, Massey wounded, Wm. Mosley died, Hugh Moore surrendered at Appomattox, W. F. McKelvey killed near Richmond, Wm. Owens killed at Dandredge, Henry Petitt killed at Frazier's Farm, James Parris killed at Frazier's Farm, Jos. Pritchard. Tolliver Phillips, J. F. Quinn, W. L. D. Rollins, J. S. Russell, B. F. Reaves, W. E. Rodgers wounded at Wilderness, Jas. Robbins, J. P. Scates, John Stephens, Henry Spencer killed at Williamsburg, Va., D. R. Willis, D. G. Whitlock (from Union county), H. M. Waters, J. M. West (from Union county), Rufus Willis and Jolin Wilkins died.

Company K. — Captains: John H. Evins (see sketch) wounded at Seven Pines, disabled and resigned, and John H. Blassingame wounded at Frazier's Farm and in charge on Fort Harrison.

1st Lieutenants: Henry H. Thomson wounded in thigh at Sharpsburg, limb amputated, John W. White died of wounds at Charlottsville, Va., and John T. Walker wounded at Frazier's Farm and at Fort Harrison.

2d Lieutenants: Robert P. Miller killed at Cambells Station, Tenn., Hiram H. Mitchell wounded seriously at 2d Manassas, James P. LockAvood wounded at Spotsylvania, and Wm. D. Anderson killed at Cambells Station.

Sergeants: Thos. C. Duncan killed at Frazier's Farm, Green B. Culp wounded at Gaines Mill, Horace A. McSwain killed at 2d Manassas, Wm. T. Miller wounded at Seven Pines, J. S. R. Thomson promoted in the enrolling service, Feilden Walden wounded at 2d Manassas, Petersburg and Fort Harrison, Henry F. McDowell wounded at Gaines Mill, and Pat L. N. Henry wounded at Frazier's Farm, was made lieutenant in the regular service, Wm. F. McArthur wounded at Williamsburg, Va.

Corporals: Jos. T. Holt killed at Frazier's Farm, Jas. J. Palmer (from Chester county) killed at 2d Manassas, Jas. A. Moore killed at Seven Pines.

Privates: Frank L. Anderson (see sketch), Hamilton Abbott killed at Frazier's Farm, Robert R. Abbott mortally wounded at Frazier's Farm, died at Manchester Hospital, James H. Allen died at home while on furlough. Tench J. Bullington wounded at Seven Pines and John B. Bethune discharged, received appointment to citadel, Jas. M. Bivings surrendered at Appomatox, J. Martin Bowen, Thos. B. Bright died in hands of enemy, Albert Brown killed at Frazier's Farm, Marsh S. Bryson killed at Seven Pines, Jesse H. Bullington surrendered at Appomattox, Geo. B. Bullock wounded at Frazier's Farm, disabled and discharged, Geo. J. Bullman wounded at Seven Pines, Wm. K. Bullman, Govan Bush killed at Petersburg, Andrew Bowie died in camp July 22, 1863, Geo. H. Camp wounded at Sharpsburg, disabled, L. M. Cannon, Nahum Cannon woiuided at 2d Manassas, Theodore L. Capers killed at 2d Manassas, Richard T. Crittendon wounded at Gaines Mill, died of disease in hospital, J. Cunningham died at Farmville, Va., John Dupreist wounded at Frazier's Farm, discharged, John Diirant killed on Darbytown road. Andrew S. Dnrant died in camp, Jas. B. Earnhart wounded at Gaines Mill, discharged, Asa M. Foster killed at Frazier's Farm, Richard Foster wounded at Frazier's Farm, lost an arm, Elias Gentry wounded at Seven Pines, Wm. M. Gibson wounded at Frazier's Farm, John Gibson, Daniel E. Gilchrist. Wm. H. Gray (from Union county) wounded at Seven Pines, Leitner Hall, Wm. D. Hammett died in enemy's hands, Arthur Harris wounded at Sharpsburg, Asbury Hammett, Andrew J. Hause wounded at Gaines Mill and disabled from further service, J. Caldwell Hawkins wounded at Seven Pines died in Hospital, R. E. Haynes, John W. Haynes, W. Simpson Haynes killed at Seven Pines, Thos. J. Hayes, Jos. F. Haynes wounded at Knoxville, Jas. D. Hensley wounded at Seven Pines, Peter A. Holt wounded, John C. Holt wounded 2d Manassas, died of same in hospital, Joel A. Horton died in hospital, Elisha W. R. Hughston killed at Seven Pines, Geo. R. Hughston killed at Seven Pines, Thomas F. Hughston wounded at Seven Pines, left in hands of enemy, Thos. M. Hughston, Wm. Hughston, Wm. P. Hughston, Wm. L. Johnson captured day before surrender at Appomattox, G. Allen Kirkland wounded at 2d Manassas, P. Govan Kirby, Maynard C. Layton wounded at Frazier's Farm, died at Chattanooga, David M. Lancaster wounded on Darbytown road, Va., Wm. McFarland died of disease in hospital, Wm. E. Maulden, Alfred M. McDonald wounded at 2d Manassas, Andrew H. Miller died in hospital, Samuel W. Miller killed at Frazier's Farm, Jos. Mims (from Colleton county), Eldridge T. McSwain captured at Seven Pines, Jas. C. Neil citadel cadet, was attached temporarily to company before 2d Manassas battle, Robert D. Owens died in enemy's hospital in Tennessee, W. Smith Patterson killed at Fort Harrison, las. A. Purgason, Jos. Petty died in hospital, Wm. S. Richardson mortally wounded at Frazier's Farm, died there in field hospital, Geo. F. Round discharged for disability, Whiteford A. Smith killed at 2d Manassas, Thos. C. Scott wounded at Lockout Mountain, Tenn., Charles Summons wounded at Seven Pines, Thos. G. Smith wounded mortally at Seven Pines, died there in field hospital, Jas. E. Solsbee wounded at Frazier's Farm, Calvin Stephens wounded at Frazier's Farm, Whiteford Smith wounded at 2d Manassas, Henry C. Stephenson wounded in thigh at Gaines Mill, leg amputated, Robert E. Tuck wounded at Frazier's Farm, Wm. A. Walden wounded at 2d Manassas and at Seven Pines, Absolem Walker wounded on Darbytown road, disabled and discharged, Felix Walker died of wounds at Manchester hospital, John E. Walker wounded at 2d Manassas and Petersburg, R. W. Watson killed at 2d Manassas, Rufus B. White wounded at Frazier's Farm, died in hospital, Andrew J. Williams, J. Aleck Williams, J. A. Williams, John B. Williamson wounded at Seven Pines, Monroe W. Wyatt, John Zimmerman killed at Frazier's Farm.

List of those who were not left as members of Company K, after reenlistment at close of first year's service: Joseph Walker captain, promoted to colonel P. S. S., John H. Evins 1st lieutenant, promoted to captain Company K, P. S. S., C. E. Fleming 2d lieutenant, promoted to C. S. surgeon, H. H. Thomson 2d lieutenant, promoted to 1st lieutenant, R. E. L. Ewart 1st sergeant, died in hospital, Alexander Bulleton died in hospital, Ibra Cannon discharged for disability, Andrew M. Evins wounded at 1st Manassas, died at home, M. M. Gossett discharged for disability, Hartwell A. McCravy, L. Nolen wounded at 2d Manassas, Samuel Land, Emory Watson, N. F. Walker discharged to take charge of State Institute for Deaf, Dumb and Blind, Cedar Spring.

Company M. — Captains: J. Q. Carpenter (see sketch) killed at Seven Pines, and Frederick G. Latham wounded at Frazier's Farm and 2d Manassas.

1st Lieutenant: Robert F. Montgomery wounded at Frazier's Farm.

2d Lieutenants: Samuel S. Ross served fourteen months when company was part of 5th Regiment, was honorably discharged, Luther Bonner killed at Frazier's Farm, John J. Camp, John Goforth and W. S. Alexander.

Sergeants: Jonas Harris wounded on Darbytown road, Seven Pines and Wilderness, Wm. Camp wounded at 2d Manassas, killed at Appomattox April 9, 1865, Ben. F. Bonner wounded at Seven Pines, George Bonner wounded at Petersburg.

Corporals: A. C. Robbs wounded at Wills Valley, Frazier's Farm and Sharpsburg, and John Vassey wounded at Wills Valley and Darbytown road.

Privates: Wm. Bridges wounded and disabled at Gaines Mill. Pinckney Bonner killed at Seven Pines, Wm. Black killed at Sharpsburg, D. B. Collins died at Richmond in 1863, M. C. Collins killed at Seven Pines, Obey Clary died at Franklin, Va., June, 1863, Enoch Cannon, Sr., Enoch Cannon, Jr., Jos. Coyle wounded at Gaines Mill, Lemuel Cobb wounded at Gaines Alill, Davis Whitman killed at Seven Pines, James Harrison killed at Wilderness, Rice Harris killed at Seven Pines, Wm. James wounded at Frazier's Farm, Dick Jolly wounded and disabled at Gaines Mill, discharged, Peter Morgan woimded at 2d Manassas, Arthur Morgan, Alfred Pritchard wounded at GainesMill, Hugh Ray discharged on account of disability, Benj. B. Scott, W. D. Scruggs wounded at Seven Pines, F. C. Surratt died of wounds in prison, W. A. Surratt transferred to calvery and killed, James Tate, John Surratt discharged by reason of being over age, Camellus Surratt, Jonas Vassey and Pink Goforth.

Holcombe Legion. Col. P. F. Stephens commander. Adjutant: Edwin H. Bobo. Surgeon: Wm. T. Russel (see sketch).

Company A. — Captains: Wm. Jas. Smith (see sketch) resigned in 1862, Thos. C. Brady died, Adolphus U. Brown promoted from ranks to sergeant then to captain.

1st Lieutenants: S. Crawford Miller, promoted from 1st sergeant.

2d Lieutenants: Joseph Copeland, Jesse Pinson killed at Petersburg November 5, 1864, James J. Foster killed at Hatchers Run.

Sergeants: John N. Miller, Thos. B. McMillen, killed at 2d Manassas, James E. Mason, Nathan Petitt, Enoch B. Floyd, John A. Gentry.

Corporals: Willis L. Brewton killed at 2d Manassas, David M. Trail wounded at Hatchers Run March 29, 1865, Simpson Thomas killed at Hatchers Run 1865, Henry J. Turner killed at 2d Manassas, W. Theadore Brown and Gillison R. James.

Privates: Frank L. Anderson (see sketch), Alexander Bridges, Thos. B. Birch killed at Rappahannock in 1862, Chas. A. Barry (see sketch), Nicholas Bridges, Robert J. Bullington died at Adams Run, Calvin L. Brewton wounded at Manassas, John Bogan, Samuel M. Caldwell, Wiesbury Dillard, Oliver Evans wounded at Manassas, Thos. Erwin, John F. Floyd killed at 2d Manassas, George W. Finch, Thomas A. Finch, Miles A. Finch died at Orangeburg, John P. Finch died in prison at Point Lookout. Thos. N. Fielder, Pat C. Gentry died of wounds at Harrisburg, Va., November 1, 1862, Thos. P. Hamm killed at Kingston, N.C. in 1862, Bird Hembree, Geo. W. Hill, Calvin Hill, James Hill, Henry Hill died of wounds at Kingston, N.C. December 14, 1862, Jerry Hill killed at 2d Marassa, Alfred Hill died of wounds at Hatchers Run March 29, 1865, Chambers Hembree died of wounds at Petersburg March 25, 1865, W. Pinckney Hoy, Thos. Hill, Wm. Hatchett died at Stoney Creek, Va., David W. Johnson, John L. Johnson, Elias R. Johnson, E. C. James, Jos. H. King killed at 2d Manassas, Chambers Linder wounded and captured at Petersburg November 25, 1865, Alvin C. McCraw, Isaac S. Miller wounded at Rappahannock August 23, 1862, Wm. H. Miller died of wounds at Sharpsburg, Edward B. Miller, Elijah McMillen, W. Frank Meadows, Thomas M. Meadows, wounded at Petersburg, November 9, 1864, Jesse Mathis, Thomas J. Moore (see sketch) promoted to regimental color ensign, captured at Five Forks, William Moore, Henry F. Mason killed at Manassas, Chric C. Morrow wounded at 2d Manassas died of same, Drayton O'Sheilds, Eber Pinson, James Pritchard, M. Turner Philips, D. R. Quinn died of wounds at Jackson, Miss., Drury J. Reynolds, Fowler W. Reynolds, David Ramsey, I. W. Satterfield accidently shot and died at Adams Hun, S.C., Ignatius Sanders wounded at Edisto Expedition January 24, 1862, Alfred Scruggs, Lewis Scruggs wounded at Petersburg March 5, 1864, Calvin Scruggs, Tellotson A. Scruggs, John D. Switzer died of wounds at Hatchers Run, Edniond Smith died of disease at Adams Run, James Smith died in prison at Point Lookout, Elihu P. Smith, Samuel F. Strange, Wm. Strange killed at 2d Manassas, Enoch Stephens wounded at 2d Manassas, Elias Spencer, Geo. W. Thomas killed at Petersburg October 27, 1864, while leading his comrades in a charge crying to them to follow him (see Spartan files, November 10, 1864), J. Newton Thomas, Geo. P. Trail died in prison at Point Lookout, W. Elliott Turner died at Winchester, Va., September 13, 1862, Isaac N. Varner killed at 2d Manassas, Simeon N. West wounded at 2d Manassas, David West, Benj. W. Walker killed at Jackson. Miss., July 14, 1863, Drury D. Webber, Rufus S. Willis, Smith Willis, wounded at Petersburg, Dec. 27th, 1864, Thos. Williams wounded at 2d Manassas, Wm. Wilhams, Wm. J. Wood killed at Warrenton, Va., September 1, 1862, and Robert Y. Williams died in prison at Point Lookout.

Company B. — Captains: Jas. F. Sloan (see sketch) resigned November, 1862, on account of ill health, Alfred B. Bryant promoted to captain January, 1863, killed near Fort Steadman March 25, 1865, and E. Henry Bates promoted to captain by General Wallace March 25, 1865.

1st Lieutenant: John G. Brown wounded at 2d Manassas.

Sergeants: Turtless L. Bryant wounded at Pittsburg, Va., John Lee, Lecil Lee, Green B. Crocker wounded at Petersburg December 8, 1864, Felix R. Mulligan wounded at Rappahannock December 8, 1864.

Corporals: Elijah S. V. Bryant wounded at Pittsburg,. Va., Calvin Littlejohn wounded at Rappahannock August 23, 1862, Larkins S. Lee, J. Boylin Bryant died of fever at home, A. T. Crocker, C. V. Hammett died, and Geo. V. Brown wounded at Pittsburg, Va., March 29, 1865.

Privates: John Allen, Wm. N. Brown company commissary, Wm. Brown, Columbus Bryant, David Bryant died' of fever in Mississippi, Harcanus Bryant wounded in battle, died in hospital at Columbia, Wm. Compton (from Laurens county), Spira Cash, Jas. L. Crocker killed at Kingston,. N.C., Dec. 14, 1862, Jas. H. Croker wounded at Malvern Hill April 6, 1862, Matteson Crocker, Henry C. Crocker, Thos. Crocker, John Dillard, Samuel Elden died at Adams Run, S.C., John Elder, Hillard Elder, Joshua D. Fenley killed at Petersburg November 12, 1864, Gaston Fleming wounded at 2d Manassas, died at Warrenton, Va., September 30, 1862, Ganum Fleming killed at 2d Manassas, Tillman Fleming died of fever in Virginia, Newton Fleming, John A. Gore, Jerry L. Gore, Wm. G. Gossett, Thos. Gossett wounded at 2d Manassas, Samuel Gossett, John W. C. Gossett, Jos. Harvey, Jr., killed at Rappahannock August 23, 1862, J. Caswell Harvey, Morgan Harvey killed at 2d Manassas, Jos. Harvey, Sr., John Harvey, Wade Harmon wounded at 2d Manassas, Coleman Hammett, Richard D. Hammett wounded at Jarretts' Station March 29, 1865, arm amputated at shoulder, Wm. Hawkins, James Hope, Columbus Harvey, Alfred Jennings, Elihu Jennings, Wm. E. Jett wounded at Rappahannock August 23, 1862, C. C. Kelmett wounded at Jarretts' Station March 29, 1864, W. E. M. Kirby wounded at Petersburg October 27, 1864, Sylvester Kirby wounded at Rappahannock August 23, 1862, R. B. M. Kirby wounded at 2d Manassas, Ransom L. Kirby, Monroe Kirby, Jas. M. Kirby wounded in battle, R. B. M. Kirby, Jr., died of disease in Virginia, Wm. Lands died at: Richmond, Richard Lands died of wounds at Richmond, Eliphas Lee, Thomas S. Lipscomb killed at 2d Manassas. Jas. Low died in prison at Point Lookout, Richard Lee, Sr., entered the service at sixty years of age, R. W. Lee, Wm. M. Lee, James Lee, Mathew C. Lee, John M. Lee, John P. Lee, Richard Millwood, Jas.

Millwood wounded at 2d Manassas, Hosea D. Mathis wounded at 2d Manassas, John Mathis, Gabriel Moore wounded at 2d Manassas, Frank McBee, Willis McBee wounded at Goldsboro, N.C., Jas. Owens, G. W. S. Poole died of measles at Adam Run, S.C., Levi Pearce wounded by accident, Asbury Petty died at Adams Run, Elijah Petty, Wm. Quinn, Josephus Quinn, Barham Reeves, Wm. L. Rush, Austin Rakestraw, Wm. A. Reed, Timothy S. Sloan, Seth M. Sloan wounded at Charlottsville and 2d Manassas, died of wounds, David H. Sloan wounded at 2d Manassas, Calvin Sprouse died in Virginia, Holman Thompson, Jas. J. Thompson died Adams Run, S.C., Wm. K. Thompson, John Thornton, Oliver K. Vandiver died at Petersburg, Va., H. K. Vandiver, Elisha Williams wounded at James Isand, S.C., Thomas Weathers, Alberry Weathers, George W. Wood, W. Lipscomb Wood, Samuel Zimmerman sent home on sick furlough and died, Berryman Jackson, free colored man, team driver, Jillson Bates, colored man, officers cook.

Company C. — Captains: John Earle Bomar (see sketch) honorably discharged on account of ill health, Jos. M. Bost wounded at Sapony church June 14, 1864, and died at Stoney Creek, Va., June 1, 1864, Jas. A. Tolleson wounded at South Mountain, died in Columbia, S.C.

1st Lieutenants: Wm. H. Trimmier promoted at Adams Run.

2d Lieutenants: Michael E. Miller died soon after the war, Wiley H. Bagwell wounded at Petersburg November 5, 1864, and died in hospital there, Geo. Cofield, John M. Daniel wounded at Rappahannock August 23, 1862, and D. Pinckney Gilbert.

Color Sergeant: John 11. Windle killed at Rappahantnock August 23, 1862.

Sergeants: Jas. G. Harris killed at 2d Manassas, T. W, Wyatt, J. Belton Tolleson wounded at 2d Manassas, died in hospital at Warrenton, Va., C. L. Bosse wounded at 2d Manassas and Petersburg, and Jas. T. Brown. Corporals, John V. Martin wounded at 2d Manassas and died in Field Hospital, J. Arthur Clark wounded at Saponey church, Va., T. M. Tuck wounded at 2d Manassas and died a prisoner at Boonsboro, September 14th, 1862. Privates, Jos. A. Adley, Samuel Austin wounded at Petersburg, November 5, 1864, A. Jackson Abbott wounded at Petersbug, November 25, 1865, Benj. W. Bagwell died at Adams Run in 1862, Marion Bagwell. Edward Brackett, Augustus G. Brannon wounded at Petersburg October 27, 1864, Alexander Brown,. John Brown wounded at Kingston, N.C., December 14, 1862, Reuben Brannon, Byas Bright, Moses Bell, Richard Bishop, Pink Bishop, Westley W. Burns, Wm. Belcher wounded at Sapony Church, July 14, 1864. and at Sapony Church June 29, 1864, Columbus Brannon, Geo. W. Bates, David Brewton, John Burnett wounded at Petersburg, November 7, 1864, lost a foot, Perry Burnett killed at Kinston, N.C., Edward Belcher, Eber Bearden, Charles Bridges, Jas. J. Caldwell, Wm. N. Caldwell, Geo. H. Camp, wounded 2d Manassas, Napoleon B. Camp, Wm. A. Chapman wounded at Edisto Island, 1862, Richard Cole, Jas. W. Caldwell wounded at Jackson, Miss., J. Bomar Caldwell wounded in Virginia in 1865, Thos. B. Caldwell wounded at Notaway Bridge May 8, 1864, Pink Cole wounded at Kinston, N.C., December 14,

1862, John M. Carson, Henry Dodd, Austin Demsey, John W. Dye wounded at Kinston, N.C., and at Jarretts Station, Samuel S. Davis, Isham H. Daniel, Benj. Freeman died in service,. John W. Garrett, John Gulledge died at Adams Run, S.C., W. Frank Gwinn drummer, killed near Florence, S.C., by railway accident, John S. Grififin died at Richmond, Jos. Gossett killed at Rappahannock August 23, 1862, John W. Godfrey wounded at Kinston, N.C., captured at Petersburgand died at Point Lookout, Alberry T. Hammett, John Harvey, Drayton Hawkins, Preston G. Kirby, David M. Lancaster, Aaron G. W. Land, Jas. Low, Abner Low, John W. Low, Henry Low, J. Miles Lee, John D. Lewis, John P. Martin, Wm. G. Moore, Wm. R. Miller wounded at South Mountani September 14, 1862, and died in Union prison, John D. McCullough wounded and died a prisoner, Walter H. Mitchell. John B. Mullins, John Merrell, Robert Miles, Hyram Nelson, John W. Nelson, John W. Owens wounded at 26. Manassas and Petersburg, John H. F. Poole died at Adams Run, S.C., Ira G. Petty died of wounds at Rappahannock, H. C. Pettitt wounded at Rappahannock, August 23, 1862, John Patterson died of disease, S. S. Painter, J. Wash Quinn, Pinckney A. Ramsaur wounded at 2d Manassas, A. A. Surratt, H. H. Smith died at Adams Run, S.C., in 1862, James M. Seay wounded at 2d Manassas and Petersburg in 1864, W. H. Sullivan died at Mt. Pleasant, S.C., in 1862, R. L. Sprouse killed at Sapony Chruch, June 29, 1864, R. M. Seay wounded at 2d Manassas, Henry A. Smith, Edward Stephenson, E. Stephens died in service, Jas. R. P. Tinsley served through the war, Richard Tillotson captured in Virginia, released at Point Lookout, J. J. Tillotson captured in Virginia, released at Point Lookout, Bomar Trollinger served through the war, Richard H. Tuck killed at Petersburg November 5, 1864, T. M. Tuck wounded at 2d Manassas, captured at South Mountain and reported dead, Jackson Tuck, E. W. Turner, Alfred J. Tolleson wounded at Petersburg November 7, 1864, and died at Richmond, J. Wm. Tolleson wounded at Petersburg, Jesse Vinson captured at Fisher's Run and never heard from, W. J. Wooton wounded at 2d Manassas, T. Westley Wyatt, John Wyatt, John P. Willis wounded at Sapony Church, June 20, 1864, Lacey Weathers wounded and disabled at 2d Manassas, Marcus Wingo wounded at 2d Manassas and disabled, discharged, John Williams, Benj. F. West, Wm. H. Walker and J. W. Vanderver wounded at Petersburg November 5, 1864.

Company E. — Privates: Alfred Allen, Berry Baughcum, Jas. E. Bobo wounded at Petersburg, Jonas E. Bragg, John F. Bragg, Willis M. Bragg, W. Pinckney Bragg, Elias Carlton died at Petersburg, Elijah Carlton died at home. John Carlton killed at 2d Manassas, Benj. F. Cooper, Wm. D. Cooper wounded at Stoney Creek, Va., John Franklin Cooper died in Maryland, Willis C. Carwell, C. Pinckney Carwell wounded at Petersburg, Jonas Edwards died at Adams Run, Perry Edwards, Young A. Fowler, Lewis H. Gwinn died at Adams Run, Jesse Godfrey wounded at Boonsboro September 14, 1862, Wm. Godfrey wounded at Kinston, N.C., December 14, 1862, Bardie Grubbs, J. Hewett, Robert Hewett, Erwin Hewett, O. Perry Hand (from Laurens county). Wash Johnson, Jos. J. Johnson killed at Petersburg, Abner Jennings, David

King, Thos. Kenedy, L. Meridith Lanford, E. Frank Lanford, Wm. J. Lanford killed at 2d Manassas, J. Merril Lanford killed at Kinston, N.C., Wm. L. Lanford, Asbury Lanford died in hospital, Presley Loving died at Goldsboro, N.C., Wm. Marier, Thos. J. Marier, Elijah Marier, Jas. H. Morgan wounded at 2d Manassas, Jerry Morgan, Alfred M. Page died at Richmond, Willis D. Page died at Adams Run, Jas. C. Page, P. A. Pearson wounded at 2d Manassas, died in field hospital, John C. Pearson killed at 2d Manassas, Drayton Riddle, Thos. W. Ray, Jerry H. Roebuck killed at 2d Manassas, Jackson R. Roberts, Seabern R. Roberts, Anderson Simpson died in Alabama, Samuel N. Simpson, Jack D. Stephens died at home, Wallace Thompson wounded at Stoney Creek, J. M. Thomas, Rev. Richard Woodruff, Jeff J. Waddell wounded at 2d Manassas, died at Warrenton, Va., William R. Waddell, wounded at Jarretts Station, Noel Waddell, John L. Wright killed in Maryland, Jesse G. Westmoreland wounded at Rappahannock August 23, 1862, Phihp Waddell, S. P. Westmoreland, John D. W. Woodruff, Jas. D. Young, Isaac Roebuck, Isaac Knight and John D. Woodruff wounded at Stoney Creek.

Company I. — Captains: Wm. P. Bishop (see sketch) resigned November, 1862, afterwards joined Charleston BattaUon, and Thos. B. Martin (see sketch) wounded at Kinston, N.C., December 14, 1862, promoted from sergeant in 1863, captured at Stoney Creek in 1864.

1st Lieutenant: Jno. Bankston Davis resigned May, 1862, and joined Colonel Talcott's regiment of engineers.

2d Lieutenants: Andrew P. Bishop resigned May, 1862, and joined 5th Regiment, S.C.V., Marcus B. Chapman resigned April, 1862, and joined Charleston Battalion, Benj. M. High promoted from sergeant, resigned in 1862, Jas. G. Mabry promoted from ranks, resigned in 1863, Collins McCarter promoted from ranks, was in command of company at surrender at Appomattox, Cicero B. Tillotson promoted from ranks, captured at Stoney Creek, and Middleton Ray discharged at Winchester, 1862.

Sergeants: John W. Wingo, Thos. J. Eubanks wounded at 2d Manassas and died at Warrenton, Va., and Ellis T. Jackson wounded at 2d Manassas.

Corporals: Jos. W. Westmoreland died in camp in 1863, Thos. J. Gowen died in prison Elmira, N.Y., D. I. Wingo wounded at 2d Manassas, and Thos. G. Robbins died in prison Elmira, N.Y.

Privates: Cornelius Bush, Geo. W. Bishop captured at Stoney Creek, Va., exchanged, died at home, Jabez Ballenger, Henry M. Ballenger died at home, Wm. Y. Ballenger captured at Five Forks, Va., Jas. I. Bulliman captured at Five Forks, Va., died in prison at Elmira N.Y., Samuel Burns disabled and discharged, Jas. M. Camp captured at Stoney Creek, died in prison at Elmira, N.Y., Ben Gambell, Martin M. Casey, Tench Childers, Andrew B. Cole captured at Stoney Creek, died in prison at Elmira, N.Y., Elijah Cole M. Casey, Tench Childers, Andrew B. Cole captured at Stoney Creek, died in prison at Elmira, N.Y., Elijah Cole died in hospital in Virginia, Mathew Cole killed at Kinston, N.C., Henry Cudd died at home in 1862, John I. Durham, George Durham wounded at Petersburg: in 1864. Isaac Eubanks captured at Stoney Creek, exchanged, died at Spartanburg, Wm. Eubanks captured at Five Forks, Benj. Freeman died in hospital in Virginia. James Gowen died in prison at Ehmira, N.Y., Martin V. Gowan wounded at 2d Manassas, leg amputated, Jos. Harvey wounded at Goldsboro, N.C., Alexander Henderson, Ramson Henderson wounded at Edisto Island, S.C., April, 1862, died in Savannah, David F. Jackson captured at Stoney Creek, Va., died at Elmira, N.Y., Jefferson I. Lawrence wounded at 2d Manassas, died at home, Jasper Lively captured at Stony Creek, died in prison at Elmira, N.Y., James Lawrence, Eliphes Lee, Jas. P. Mahaffey, John I. Manovs. Tames McCarter wounded at Stoney Creek, Va., captured and exchanged, Jos. M. McCarley, McGuinnis R. Spencer wounded at 2d Manassas, Dado Miller, Andrew J. Mangrum died in Mississippi in 1863, Wm. Neighbors died at Adams Run in 1862, Benj. F. Nicholls, John H. NichoUs, Ishmeal Oliver wounded at 2d Manassas, Miller Owens died in hospital, Bailus Painter captured at Stony Creek, died in prison at Elmira, N.Y., Thos. Sheilds, Hannon Smith wounded at 2d Manassas, John Smith wounded at 2d Manassas, Joshua R. Lapp, Wm. Thompson captured at Stoney Creek, Jas. A. Tupper captured at Stoney Creek, died in prison at Elmira, N.Y., Joseph B. Turner died in hospital, Randolph Turner, George Tice, Joseph West captured at Stoney Creek, died at Elmira, N.Y., William S. West, James P. West, James G. Westmoreland, John C. Westmoreland wounded at Sharpsburg, died in hospital, Lorenzo D. Westmoreland captured and died in prison, Louis S. Westmoreland died at home, Thos. C. Williams, James Weatherwood wounded at Kinston, S.C., died at Moseley's Hall, December 17, 1863, Richard West captured at Stoney Creek, died in prison at Elmira, N.Y., J. G. Robbins wounded at 2d Manassas, and W. P. Willis wounded at Petersburg November 5, 1864. 1st Regiment of Calvary, S.C.V., Col. John L. Black commanding.

Company B. — Captain: Niles Nesbitt promoted to major in 1864.

1st Lieutenants: Leake and B. N. Young. Sergeant: L. S. Crow.

Corporals: Thos. Fowler and Seabern Drummond.

Privates: Mat Alexander, Isaac H. Brewton, John Bass, W. H. Barnett wounded at Gettysburg, Jos. C. Barnett, J. Nesbitt Brown, Pinckney Crow died in 1864, Robert C. Crow wounded at Boonsboro, Elias Cathcart, Jas. H. Cathcart died in hospital in 1862, John Cathcart, Robert C. Cathcart wounded on John's Island, S.C., J. Mat Chapman, W. R. B. Caldwell, Austin Y. Desheilds, Wm. D. Dickey, Ira L. Drummond wounded at Smithfield, N.C., Wm. R. Henderson died of wounds at Summerville, S.C., D. Leander Gray, J. A. Henneman, Leonard Hill, J. Alexander Jackson captured at Gettysburg, died in prison at Point Lookout, Robert Jackson captured at Gettysburg, died there in field hospital, D. P. Layton killed at Culpepper, Va., J. C. Layton, J. Oliver Layton died of wounds at Adams Run, S.C., Oscar L. Linsey, Thos. C. Littletields, P. B. Miller died at home, C. P. Miles, W. Otts, Perry Pearson, Frank Parkam died at Adams Run, S.C., W. B. Page, John T. Pool, W. H. Posey, Hampton Posey, Lewis Pool, Wm. H. Ray, J. M. Rampley, M. O. Rowland, W. J. Tillotson wounded at Smithfield, N.C., John W. Ward, T. J. M. Ward, John Wells killed at

411

Boonsboro, W. M. Wingo, S. Pink Woodruff, John Woodrufif, killed at Upper-ville, Va., P. B. Woodrufif, Wm. Woodruflf, W. D. Wilkins, C. D. Wilkins, J. C. Woods, A. P. Willis killed at Brandy Station, and Thos. Young.

Company E. — Henry L. Culler died of wounds at Gettysburg.

Company K. — M. O. Rowland surrendered at Raleigh.

2d Regiment of S.C.V., Calvery. Colonels M. C. Butler and T. J. Lipscomb.

Company A. — Dallas Chamberlin died in camp in 1865, J. S. Drnmmond and Ligon.

Company E. — Captains: Alvin H. Dean (see sketch) resigned in 1862, af-terwards elected lieutenant, and Geo. B. Dean (see sketch) promoted from 1st lieutenant.

1st Lieutenants: Wm. H. Coan died at home, and Crawford S. Thompson wounded at Brandy Station.

2d Lieutenant: John G. Wham.

1st Sergeants: Abraham Greenleaf, Benj. Wallace wounded at Brandy Sta-tion, and James Pearson.

Sergeants: Edward J. Zimmerman, Andrew J. Caldwell, Henry J. Fleming, Edward L. Miller and James Wham.

Corporals: Thadeus T. Westmoreland, John F. Kelso, Lewis L. Wingo and Jesse Brown killed at Brandy Station.

Privates: Madison Alexander, Francis Allen, McQueen J. Allen, Wm. Allen, Marion Bagwell, Jesse Beacham, Williams Bobo died at Adams Run, S.C., Da-vid Brewton, J. Frank Brockman, John Brockman, Samuel Brown, John (Jake) Burns. Wm. Burns, Noah Cannon, Tas. Casey, James Chapman, Jas. Z. Coan, Jos. Collins, John (Dr) Dickson died at Charleston in 1864, Carrol Dill, Berry Duncan, Joseph Farrow, Patello W. Farrow, J. Landrum Finch, I. H. Fleming, Neil Floyd, Amsey W. Gaston, Jonathan Gentry, H. H. Gramling, Alfred Harris, Isaac Johnson, James Kelso, J. B. O. Landrum, Woodson Loftis, Perry Mason, M. M. McElreath, Richard T. McElreath, James Moore, John Moore, A. Jackson Morgan, Jacob M. Morgan, John H. Morgan, Robert I. Morgan, Thos. W. Mor-gan, Wm. L. Morgan, Isaac J. Nesbitt, Marion (Mace) Pearson, Wm. Robinson, Edward Rush, Bud Smith, S. Frank Smith, Richard P. Snoddy, Sidney W. Tur-byfield, Thos. Timmons, Abernathy Waldrep, John M. VValdrep, H. Verias Westmoreland wounded at Upperville, Va., Berry Wilson, A. Jackson Wingo, J. Simpson Wingo, T. Calvin Wingo, Thos. W. Wingo wounded at Brandy Sta-tion August 1, 1863, John Younger and James Younger.

Besides the roll as given above, there were enrolled in this company eighteen members from Greenville county, twelve members from Laurens county and one member from N.C. The casualties of the company are rec-orded only in a few instances, such as come within the recollection of the writer, who was a member of the same from April, 1862, to the end of the war, having served the first year of the war as a member of Company F, 5th Regiment, S.C.V.

Company F. — (Noah) Floyd, W. R. Gaston and Robert M. Smith wounded at John's Island, S.C., in 1864, arm amputated. 5th Regiment, S.C.V., Calvery. Col. Zimmerman Davis.

Company K. — Sergeants: Wm. J. Means. Thos. Blassingame captured at Stoney Creek in 1864, Jas. Fortenberry, Jos. M. Foster and John A. Pool.

6th Regiment, S.C.V., Calvery. Hugh K. Aiken commanding. Major: Thos. B. Ferguson promoted from captain. Company E.

Company A. — Privates: Hampton Beasley and Thomas Feilder.

Company C. — Sergeant Garvin D. Shands and private John H. Cunningham killed at Gravel Run.

Company E. — Privates: Zachariah Allen. Elbert Anderson, Hiram Bobo, Calvin Bomar, Henry (Toad) Ferguson, James Greer, Randolph Page, Geo. H. Shands, Eliphas C. Smith, Elihu Smith and Elihu Smith (son of Asa).

Company H. — Captain: J. J. McGuire.

Sergeant: E. B. Gaston wounded at Trevillion Station.

Privates: J. H. Bonham, R. Eber Brewton, J. Bullington, M. Collins died in Virginia, P. Collins died at Adams Run, S.C., W. S. Collins, D. H. Elder, Kenard Foster, W. Henderson, L. T. Jackson, J. McCarter, J. M. McFarland, W. L. Parker, A. L. Reagan, J. Ravan, J. M. Rudersail, Alexander Rudersail died in prison at Elmira, N.Y., E. Turner, John Turner, W. M. Walden, D. P. West, Wm. West and W. S. West.

7th Regiment, S.C.V., Calvery. Commanded by Col I. G. McKissick, who was afterwards promoted to Lieu. -Col. of said Regiment.

Company C. — Private: James J. Camp. Company F. — Private: John Carson. 1st Regiment of Artillery. Captain A. S. Gillard.

Company K. — Privates: John Blackwell, James L. Ezell, Elias Johnson (company clerk), and Andrew B. Martin.

Gist Guard Artillery, S.C.V.
Captain: Edward Chichester.
Sergeant: Wm. A. Hill.
Privates: John Bailey, Elijah Bellings, — Brock, Mark D. Bryant, Wm. S. Bearden. Aaron Casey, David Casey drowned off Sullivans Island, JoS.C. Casey, J. Penn Casey wounded at Battery Wagner, S.C., Wm. Casey, Marion Casey, John W. Davis wounded at Fort Sumter, Isaac Evins, Benj. F. Hill, John Howard, Albert Littlefields, Frank Littlefields, J. M. Littlefields, Thos. J. Lipscombe, Giles Poole, Robert Poole, John Stallings, Thos. Stallings, Samuel Stripling, James Stripling, Thos. Stripling, Jos. L. Wofford, Frank Woftord, Wm. Hembree, Thomas Vaughn wounded at Fort Sumter, Wilson Vaughn, Elehu West, Westley West.

McBeth's Light Artillery.
Captain: Robert Boyce.
Corporal: Solomon Anderson.
Bugler: Jos. W. Bennett.

Privates: Wm. Beason, Benj. Bennett, John T. Crow, Spencer B. Crow, Wm. Crow, James Crow, — Crow, — Crow, John Davis, Wm. Davis, John Hayes wounded at 2d Manassas, Robert D. Lanford, Hosea Lanford, John Littleford, John McCrady, W. A. McCrady wounded at Sharpesburg, H. Coleman Poole, Giles Poole, Alexander Shaff, Eliphas M. Smith, Isaac C. Tinsley and Richard C. Thomson.

Spartanburg Rangers (called Spartan Rangers).

This cavalry company was composed almost entirely of boys seventeen years of age, they equipped themselves and formed a part of the State Reserves which were called out in 1864. They were in a great many engagements and rendered gallant service.

Captain: Wm. T. Wilkins (see sketch).

1st Lieutenant: Cleveland Bivings.

2d Lieutenants: Jas. McDowell and Edward Means (from Union).

Sergeants: Edward Bivings, Thos. A. Irwin and Anderson Chamblin.

Corporals: Jesse F. Cleveland, Jake Ross and Edward Mimms (from Colleton).

Privates: James Bomar, Duncan Brooks (from Greenville), Thos. J. Burnett, Peter Camp, FieldenCantrel, Wm. B. Cleveland (Greenville), Barney F. Cleveland (Greenville), K. Davis, John Demsey, John Dodd, James Dobbins, Charles Drayton, Daniel Fairchilds, Wm. Finch, John Foster, Logan Gaffney, John Greer, Sam. Greer, Sam. Hendricks, Jackson Hendricks, C. Holden, L. Hunt, T. Earle Johnson, John P. Leonard, N. J. Leonard, Miles Mason, David McDowell, T. Moore. — Odel, James Odam, Charles Petty, Columbus Petty, Earle Smith, Jackson Smith, J. D. Smith, Guilford Smith, Jeferson Solsbee, Charles Sheilds, Ike Smith, Augustus Wilkins, Wm. Willis, P. D. Willis, E. J. Willis, T. J. Wood and Albert Walker.

4th Regiment, S.C. Reserves.

Company I. — Captain: T. E. Wood. Lieutenants. P. T. Beacham, Jas. H. Anderson and John Thompson.

Sergeants: T. M. Leonard and W. D. Branderson.

Privates: D. A. Dupree, Robert Alexander, Clarence Lockwood, George Logan, Herman Renaker, Lewis M. Leonard, Wm. Henderson, Duncan Cameron, Wade Barker, W. D. Reynolds, Taylor Jones and Hilliard Hendrix.

5th Regiment, S.C.V., State Troops. Col. J. H. Williams commanding.

Ordinance Sergeant: A. W. T. Simmons.

Company E. — Captain: Oliver H. Moss.

Lieutenants: 1st. T. P. Gaston, 2d. D. M. Brice and Jr., 2d Wm. C. Miller.

Sergeants: Jeptha Turner, W. C. Burton, W. T. Wyatt and A. J. Pearson.

Corporals: J. W. S. Bomar, Pat P'arrow. M. M. Smith and W. N. Pearson.

Privates: J. M. Alexander, Jas. Arnold, Westley Burris, D. Bailey, Henderson Bitter, D. T. Burton, Thos. Barker, G. H. Bragg, A. Burthcome, W. C. Bennett, Javan Barnett, J. D. Burnett, P. B. Beecham, C. M. Calvert, Z. Clanton, W. W.

Calvert, Andrew Coan, Andrew Duncan, G. E. Be Bard, John Evins, Andrew Elmore, J. M. Elford, J. B. Edwards, L. H. Fleming, J. R. Frey, Jos. Finley, A. D. Gregory, Wm. Garrett, W. D. Howe, Pleasant Hawkins, Geo. Hamlin, A. J. Hors, Hines Halt, Wiley Hendrix, E. B. Hendrix, J. E. Lynch, Elias Lowe, C. M. Leonard, Aaron Land, Lacy McAbee, Jos. McElreath, Abner McElreath, W. J. McElreath, J. P. McClimmons, G. Mason, R. Martin, J. E. Moore, John McFarland, John Maxwell, W. A. Mayfield, L. R. Pearson, Anthony Pearson, W. Rogers, J. E. Robertson, John Robertson, Sebron Roberts, W. P. Ray, Daniel Rogers, E. Runelds,. Jas. Steadman, Wm. Smith, J. H. Snow, R. Sizemore, Mat Toney, D. I. Twitty, J. H. Vandike, M. B. West, Newton Ward, Zed Wilson and A. W. Wood.

Company F. — Captain: S. M. Snoddy (see sketch).

Lieutenants: 1st. T. P. Gaston, 2d. D. M. Brice and Jr. 2d. Wm. C. Miller.

Company G. — Captain: Joel Ballenger, afterwards promoted to Major of 1st S.C. Battalion of State Reserves.

Lieutenants: 1st. B. H. Wright, 2d. J. C. Hams and Jr. 2d. James Tinsley.

Company H. — Captain: J. W. Bobo.

Lieutenants: R. W. Bobo (Union county), Daniel McLaughlin and Wm. Layton.

Rolls of companies F, G and H, 5th Regiment of S.C. State Troops are not recorded in ofitice of State Historian at Columbia, S.C.

1st Battalion of State Troops. Major Joel Ballenger commanding.

Company A. — Captain: Daniel H. Smith (see sketch).

Lieutenants: 1st W. P. Scott, 2d Noah Wolf and Jr., 2d M. J. Scott.

Sergeants: T. W. Davis, R. H. Dodd, J. E. Carter and W. P. Smith.

Corporals: W. T. Thomas, Isaac Foster, H. C. Beard and A. P. Clement.

Privates: Alfred Aiken, B. S. Beason, B. D. Beason, John F. Bagwell, R. N. Brown, J. L. Barnett, J. B. Barnett, Rufus Brannon, B. F. Bates, Harrison Cannon, Thos. W. Cooper, W. C. Crow, A. J. Cudd, R. C. Cudd, D. B. Cash, W. Columbus Collins, Jesse Couch, Perry Couch, C. M. Cudd, T. W. Cooper, Wm. Cunningham, S. B. Ezell (see sketch), E. Y. Ferguson, John Freeman, J. Freeman, E. G. Finch ___ at Cosawhatchie, "Doc" Gwin lost an arm, Geo. Gwin, John Green, W. M. Hembree, W. H. Horton, Lewis Hankie, White Hammett, J. L. Hammett, W. H. Hembree, W. H. Horton, C. Jones, Jas. Kimbell, J. S. Kimbell, J. D. Kirby, Jerry Lee, Simpson Lanford, J. P. Leonard, Lee Little, J.W. Littlejohn, Wyatt, Lipscomb, Jerry Lee, Dave McDowell, A. J. McElreath, Jesse Mattox, Hamp Meddows, Jas. Northey, Jeff Northey, J. W. Noland, Simeon Pearson, Jeff Pearson, Sydney Potter, T. M. Pearson, Jasper Philips,. Pink Petty, Littleberry B. Quinn, Dolph Quinn, Hobby Rogers died at Combehee, Page Rollins, T. S. Reid, L. S. Reed died in camp, Thomson Robbs, Samuel Shands, "Doc" Shands, A. D. Shands, S. Shands. killed at Averysboro, N.C., R. O. Shuttlesworth, T. W. Stribling, LeviSmith, Perry Smith Lun Smith, Hilliard Smith, SimeonSmith, J. U. Surratt, D. G. Story, T. W. Stribling, Wm. H. Tapp, Wm. Turner, John Turner, D. F. L. Turner, Wm. Turner, John Varner, R. P. Van Patton, Benj. Wofford, Hiram White, F. J. West, W. M. Webster, A. J. Wood, Jos. Waddel, Eli Wall, Wm. Watson, W. C. Webster, Frank J. West, Hiram White, H. A. Wingo, Benj. Wofford, A. N. Wood and Daniel Yarborough.

Battalion of State Cadets.

Captain Hugh S. Thompson commanding.

Company A. — Lieutenant: Geo. R. Dean (see sketch). Privates: D. P. Duncan and C. L. Fike.

Company B. — Private: L. C. Cannon.

Arsenal Cadets. Lieutenant J. B. Patrick commanding.

Companys A and B. — Privates: B. F. Bates, Mills Dean: (see sketch), F. W. Johnstone and Geo. Sistrink.

www.ingramcontent.com/pod-product-compliance
Lightning Source LLC
Chambersburg PA
CBHW021210090426
42740CB00006B/182